Mongolia

Michael Kohn

D1420059

Contents

Destination Mongolia

Mongolia occupies a special place in the minds of many dreamers. The vast landscapes, nomadic horseman and the evocative legends of the Mongol horde have enticed wayfarers here for the past 800 years.

Soon after famed dinosaur hunter Roy Chapman Andrews visited in the 1920s, Mongolia's doors were all but slammed shut for most of the 20th century. But the fall of communism, a vigorous new democracy and a healthy free-market economy has paved the way for intrepid travellers to follow in Andrews' footsteps.

Many visitors come for Naadam, the two-day summer sports festival that brings Ulaanbaatar to a standstill. But the real adventure begins where the pavement ends: on Mongolia's immense plains and sprawling massifs, which support millions of domesticated and wild animals. While camels cross the sun-scorched Gobi, fleet-footed gazelle bound through the eastern grasslands and giant mountain sheep skip across the Khangai ridge tops.

Nomads still roam the grasslands. Packing their belongings onto sturdy camels three or four times a year, they go where the grass is greenest, and hunker down for the long and brutal winter. Hospitality is a way of life, and a night in a nomad's felt ger (yurt) is a highlight for any traveller. The cultural experience is complemented by burgeoning ecotourism and adventure opportunities. Mountain biking, kayaking and mountaineering are a few options, not to mention world-class fishing and the granddaddy of all adventures – a horse trek across spectacular alpine scenery.

Mongolia, the 'Land of Blue Sky', is a remarkable country of spectacular light and traditional culture. It is an invigorating and exhilarating place to visit, and remains one of the last unspoiled travel destinations in Asia.

GRAHAM TAYLOR

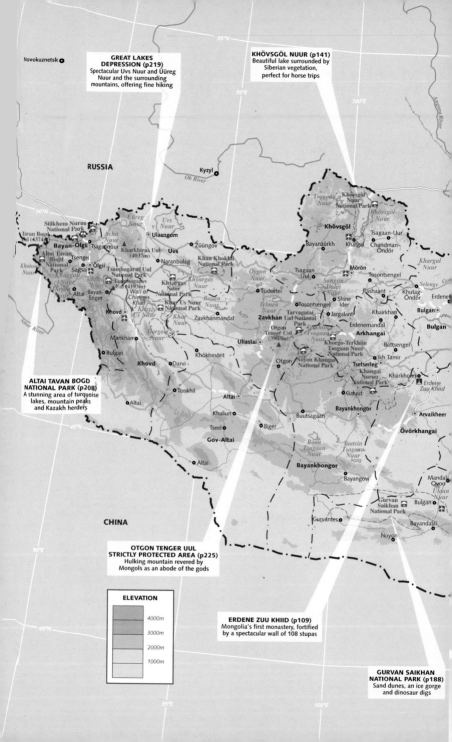

GREAT LAKES DEPRESSION (p219)
Spectacular Uvs Nuur and Üüreg Nuur and the surrounding mountains, offering fine hiking

KHÖVSGÖL NUUR (p141)
Beautiful lake surrounded by Siberian vegetation, perfect for horse trips

Novokuznetsk

RUSSIA

Kyzyl

Ob River

Siilkhem Nuruu National Park
Tavan Bogd Uul (4374)
Bayan-Ölgii
Tsengel
Tsagaanuur
Ychit Nuur
Ulaangom
Üüreg Nuur
Uvs Nuur
Züüngov

Altai Tavan Bogd National Park
Sagsai
Ölgii
Tsambagarav Uul National Park
Tsagaan Uul
Kharkhiraa Uul (4037m)
Naranbulag
Uvs
Khan Khokhii National Park

Khoton Nuur
Khurgan Nuur
Wall of Chinggis Khaan
Tolbo Nuur
Tolbo
Bayan-Enger
Khyargas Nuur National Park
Khyargas Nuur

Oygon Nuur
Tsagaan Uul
Sangiin Dalai Nuur

Khövsgöl National Park
Khövsgöl Nuur
Khövsgöl
Bayanzürkh
Khatgal
Tsagaan-Uur
Chandman-Öndör
Khargal Nuur

Bayan-Ölgii

Tavan Bogd Uul (4193m)

Khovd
Khan Us Nuur National Park
Bayan Nuur
Tüdevtei

Möron
Tosontsengel
Selenge River
Erdenet

Mankhan
Bulgan
Dörgön Nuur
Khar Nuur
Zavkhanmandal
Zavkhan
Telmen Nuur
Tosontsengel
Shine Ider
Jargalant
Rashaant
Khutag-Öndör
Bulgan

Khovd
Darvi
Khökhmörit
Uliastai
Otgon Tenger Uul (3905m)
Tsagaan Nuur
Khorgo-Terkhiin Tsagaan Nuur National Park
Tarvagatai Uul National Park
Erdenemandal
Battsengel
Ikh Tamir
Arkhangai
Bulgan

Tonkhil
Otgon
Noyon Khangai National Park
Khangai Nuruu National Park
Tsetserleg
Kharkhorin
Erdene Zuu Khiid

Altai
Khaliun
Altai
Biger
Gov-Altai

Galuut
Bayankhongor
Arvaikheer
Övörkhangai

CHINA

Tseel
Altai

Buutsagaan
Böön Tsagaan Nuur
Taatsiin Tsagaan Nuur
Bayankhongor

Bayangovi
Mandal-Ovoo
Ulaan Nuur
Bulgan
Bayandalai

OTGON TENGER UUL STRICTLY PROTECTED AREA (p225)
Hulking mountain revered by Mongols as an abode of the gods

Gurvan Saikhan National Park
Gurvantes
Noyon

ELEVATION
4000m
3000m
2000m
1000m

ERDENE ZUU KHIID (p109)
Mongolia's first monastery, fortified by a spectacular wall of 108 stupas

ALTAI TAVAN BOGD NATIONAL PARK (p208)
A stunning area of turquoise lakes, mountain peaks and Kazakh herders

GURVAN SAIKHAN NATIONAL PARK (p188)
Sand dunes, an ice gorge and dinosaur digs

AMARBAYASGALANT KHIID (p129)
Remote monastery that is an architectural gem

GORKHI-TERELJ NATIONAL PARK (p99)
Accessible park with good ger camps; great for horse riding and hiking

KHENTII (p152)
Lush forested region and home turf of Chinggis Khaan

DARIGANGA (p168)
Vast steppeland of extinct volcanoes, herds of gazelle, sand dunes and golden grassland

ULAANBAATAR (p50)
Museums, monasteries and the focus of the country-wide Nadaam Festival

0   400 km
0   250 miles

RUSSIA

CHINA

Lake Baikal

Irkutsk

Ulan Ude

Chatanga

Borzya

Erdeentsav
(Chuluunkhoroot)

Sükhbaatar
Dulaankhaan
Eröö
Darkhan   Bugant
Bayangol   Selenge
Züünkharaa
Batsumber
Gorkhi-
Terelj
National Park
Lun
ULAANBAATAR   Terelj
Khustain   Nalaikh
National Park
Züunmöd
Töv
Amarbayasgalant
Khiid

Bayan Uul
Onon-Balj
National Park
Dadal
Wall of Chinggis

Batshireet
Binder

Khentii
Bayan-Ovoo

Khalkhgol

Bulgan
Choibalsan
Dornod
Sümber

Buir
Nuur

Mörön   Öndörkhaan
Matad

Delgerkhaan
Mönkhkhan
Sükhbaatar
Uulbayan   Baruun-Urt

Buren
Delgerkhaan   Bayantsaggan
Gov-Sümber
Govi-
Ugtal   Choir   Ikhkhet
Delgertsgot
Erdenedalai   Airag   Delgerekh
Mandalgov   Bayanjargalan   Altanshiree
Gurvan
Saikhan
Dundgov   Ondorshil
Khuld   Saikhandulaan   Sainshand
Züünbayan
Erdene
Mandakh
Manlai   Zamyn-Üüd
Érliàn (Ereen)

Asgat
Erdenetsagaan
Shiliin Bogd
Uul (1778m)
Bayandelger
Ongon   Dariganga

Sükhbaatar

Dalanzadgad
Ömnögov
Khanbogd
Bayan-Ovoo   Khatanbulag

Huhot

Baotou
Yellow River

BEIJING

Yinchuan

Mix up vast landscapes of empty deserts, snow-capped mountains, dramatic gorges and sparkling lakes. Liberally sprinkle in the centuries-old felt homes of the nomad and a cry of an eagle. Add Buddhist temples, fascinating ruins, abundant bird and animal life, and legendary hospitality. Then garnish with the omnipresence of the greatest warrior of them all, Chinggis Khaan. Mongolia's highlight abound. The following photos show some our favourites. Just as good are **Gorkhi-Terelj National Park** (p99), **Terkhiin Tsagaan Nuur** (p119), **Üüreg Nuur** (p220), **Otgon Tenger Uul** (p225) and many more.

BRADLEY MAYHEW

Visit one of Mongolia's architectural wonders, Amarbayasgalant Khiid (p129)

Photograph the magnificent *takhi* (p103), Mongolia's wild horse

MICHAEL KOHN

Chill out beside the icy blue waters of Khövsgöl Nuur (p141) or go hiking, kayaking or horse riding

GRAHAM TAYLOR

FELICITY VOLK

Catch a morning ceremony at Mongolia's oldest monastery, Erdene Zuu Khiid (p109)

Cheer on the wrestlers at the Naadam Festival (p83), held annually in July

GRAHAM TAYLOR

Slide down the dunes at mighty Khongoryn Els (p191)

JUSTIN JEFFREY

8

KEREN SU

Soak in the towering statue of Avalokitesvara at Gandantegchinlen Khiid
(p63)

BRADLEY MAYHEW

Clamber to the bottom of Yolyn Am
(p190), a dramatic ice-covered gorge

Be invited into a ger (yurt) camp in Altai Tavan Bogd National Park (p208)

BRADLEY MAYHEW

Getting Started

Mongolia offers plenty of scope for off-beat, adventurous and simply fascinating travels. While there are plenty of tourist attractions that are worth visiting, Mongolia is not the sort of place where travellers need a rigid sightseeing schedule or day-to-day route that must be followed to a T.

An eight-day horseback trip through the mountains outside of Ulaan-baatar, done independently or with a group, can be just as rewarding as a driving tour to the country's best-known attractions, if not more so. What makes the journey unique is Mongolia's unbounded hospitality and nomadic culture; a visit to a herder's ger is often the best part of any trip to Mongolia and something that can be done without mounting a major expedition.

See Climate Charts (p236) for more information.

Organising a trip is surprisingly easy, and you'll make some headway by connecting with tour operators and hotel owners ahead of time. Russian Cyrillic is widely used and not too difficult to pick up, making street signs relatively easy to read. In Ulaanbaatar, an English speaker is never too far away. Trips can be made to suit all budgets, though backpackers should expect to pay slightly more than they would in south Asia; jeep-hire costs can add up. Vehicle breakdowns, petrol shortages, extreme weather and shocking roads present their own challenges. But the country is also stunning, safe and relatively healthy; with a bit of resolve and patience, any amount of travel is possible.

WHEN TO GO

Mongolia has an extreme continental climate; it is so far inland that no sea moderates its climate. Only in summer does cloud cover shield the sky. Humidity is usually zilch and sunshine is intense. With over 260 sunny days a year, Mongolia is justifiably known as the 'Land of Blue Sky'.

The main travel season is from May to early October, though Ulaanbaatar can be visited any time of year if you can tolerate the cold. From

---

DON'T LEAVE HOME WITHOUT...

- Checking the latest visa situation (p246). Most nationalities are given a 30-day tourist visa that can be extended for 60 days with a per-day charge of US$2. US citizens can stay visa free for 90 days. All visitors must register (p247) if staying longer than 30 days.

- Packing some camping gear. Tents, sleeping bags and other equipment are available in Mongolia, but you'll save money by bringing your own.

- Buying necessary photo equipment and film. Slide film is expensive in Ulaanbaatar and not available in the countryside.

- Taking out travel insurance (p270). Mongolia is a safe country, but accidents do happen, and an emergency evacuation is very expensive.

- Stocking up on English-language travel literature and books.

- Bringing necessary medicine (p272).

- Buying wind and sun protection.

- Studying your phrasebook. You'll find that LP's *Mongolian Phrasebook* is worth its weight in gold.

mid-October to mid-May, sudden snowstorms and extreme cold can ground flights, block roads and cause the transport system to break down completely.

The best time to see the Gobi is September and October. May isn't bad, though there can be wind storms during this time, and the weather can be unpredictable. Gobi summer temperatures hit 40°C but winter winds often send the mercury plummeting to -30°C or lower.

Mongolians, especially nomads, consider March and April the worst months. After the long winter, livestock will already be thin, and a lack of rain means many will die, causing financial and psychological hardship. Staying with a nomad family at this time is not recommended if the spring is a harsh one.

June and September are both very pleasant times to visit. Early July gives you the best weather for the northern part of the country. The rainy season, from late July through August, cools things down and the turn the countryside to green, but will also turn jeep trails into muck. Rains in the north also bring biting flies and mosquitoes.

July is the time to see the Naadam Festival (p83). Unfortunately, this is the peak tourist season, when Ulaanbaatar's inadequate accommodation and creaky transport is stretched to breaking point.

Weather patterns at any time can change rapidly. One minute you're walking around in a T-shirt and sandals, the next you need an overcoat and boots, then it's back to T-shirts. Temperature differences have been known to range over 37°C in one day. This is especially the case during autumn and spring.

Ulaanbaatar is possibly the coldest capital city in the world. Temperatures generally start to drop below 0°C in October, sink to -30°C in January and February and remain below freezing until April. You can expect some horrific dust storms during spring (March to May). June brings the heat. July to September is pleasant, but it can still suddenly turn cold, and unfortunately, most of the city's rain falls in this period. Summer daylight lasts until 10pm.

HOW MUCH?

Local newspaper
T300

Guanz (canteen) lunch
T1200

Internet per hour
T800

Taxi from the airport to Sükhbaatar Square
T5000

Best seat at the Naadam opening
US$12

LONELY PLANET INDEX

Litre of petrol
T560-650

Litre of bottled water
T500

Can of Chinggis beer
T900

Souvenir T-shirt
T10,000

Shashlik (kebabs)
T1500

COSTS & MONEY

Within Mongolia, travellers on organised tours spend around US$100 per day (more for extra luxuries). Independent travellers can see the same sights and stay in mid-range accommodation for around US$80 per day. If you share the cost of a private jeep or minivan and camp rather than stay in more expensive ger camps, you can bring this down to about US$25 to US$40 per day. If you are hitching and using public transport around the countryside, allow about US$10 to US$15 per day for this.

Accommodation and food will cost at least US$10 per day in Ulaanbaatar, but allow up to US$20 per day for half-decent accommodation, some tastier, Western-style meals and trips to the theatre and museums.

TRAVEL LITERATURE

Lost Country: Mongolia Revealed, by Jasper Becker, is the strongest piece of contemporary travel writing about Mongolia. Insightful, witty and a darn good piece of investigative journalism, this book details what occurred in Mongolia during the darkest years of communism.

Wild East, by Jill Lawless, is a tightly written, very funny account of the author's experience in Mongolia, during which she spent two years editing the *UB Post*. This lightning-fast book serves as a good armchair read before visiting Mongolia.

TOP TENS

Must-Read Books
One of the best ways to prepare for a journey to the steppes is to immerse yourself in some books on Mongolia. Here are our favourites:

- *The Lost Country,* by Jasper Becker (opposite)
- *Genghis Khan: Life, Death and Resurrection,* by John Man (p19)
- *Twentieth Century Mongolia,* by B Baabar (p18)
- *Travels in Tartary and Thibet,* by Abbé Huc
- *Wild East,* by Jill Lawless (opposite)

- *Dragon Hunter,* by Charles Gallenkamp
- *On the Trail of Ancient Man,* by Roy Chapman Andrews (p37)
- *Among the Mongols,* by James Gilmour
- *The Modern History of Mongolia,* by Charles Bawden (p18)
- *The Last Disco in Outer Mongolia,* by Nick Middleton (p12)

Survival Phrases
While bouncing around in your jeep or entering a nomad's ger, bear in mind these key phrases:

- Hold the dog! *Nokhoi khorio!*
- Is there any petrol? *Bezin bain uu?*
- *Exactly* what time are we going to leave? (ask while jabbing at your watch, and emphasis the word *'Yag'*, or the answer will invariably be 'now') *Yag, kheden tsagt yavakh ve?*
- Does your hotel have heating? *Ene zochid buudald halaaguur bain uu?*
- Are your sheep fattening up nicely? *Mal sureg targan tavtai uu?*

- Not too much, please (food, tea, vodka). *Dunduur.* Or, *jaakhan, jaakhan.*
- Is there any food available (said when entering a rural restaurant)? *Belen khool bain uu?*
- I would like to ride a calm (nonagressive) horse. *Bi nomkhon mori unmaar baina.*
- In which direction is ___ town? *___ sum ail zugt baina ve?*
- Please write down your address and I will send your photo later. *Ta nadad hayagaa bichij ogno uu. Bi tand zurag ilgeene.*

Road-Trip Delights
There are certain essential factors that make every road trip complete:

- Hot-water bathhouses
- Paved roads
- Drivers named Bold or Dorj
- Spare parts found by the roadside
- Yak cream with fresh blueberries on Russian bread

- Yogurt delivered by passing nomads
- Getting a lift
- Ability to sing at least one song in English and Mongolian
- Stomach for blowtorched marmot
- Mars bars

Lost In Mongolia, by Colin Angus, describes the first descent of the Russian river, the Yenisey, completed by the author and three friends in 2001. While only half of the book actually takes place in Mongolia (the other half is in Russia), it stands as a thrilling account of exploration in one of the more remote parts of the country.

In the Empire of Genghis Khan, by Stanley Stewart, is a mildly entertaining and brutally honest introduction to Mongolia by an Englishman who travelled 1000 miles by horseback across Central Asia and Mongolia.

Edge of Blue Heaven, by Benedict Allen, chronicles a horse trek to western Mongolia, followed by a solo camel trek across the Gobi. Of all the books listed here, this one has the best photographs.

The Last Disco in Outer Mongolia, by Nick Middleton, is an easy-to-read, but dated journal of his limited travels in the late 1980s. While sometimes inaccurate, it's a humorous read with historical insight.

Eagle Dreams: Searching for Legends in Wild Mongolia, by Stephen J Bodio, describes remote and enchanting Bayan-Ölgii aimag. It gives a good account of Kazakh contemporary life and the 'eagle hunters'.

INTERNET RESOURCES

Lonely Planet (www.lonelyplanet.com) Includes info on Mongolia with links to other websites, and the Thorn Tree, which is a travellers' forum with up-to-date tips on getting in and around Mongolia.

Mongolia National Tourism Centre (www.mongoliatourism.gov.mn) Includes lists of hotels, ger camps and travel agencies.

Mongolia Online (www.mol.mn) Has an arts calendar and covers news, currency-exchange rates, and weather in Ulaanbaatar.

Mongolia Today (www.mongoliatoday.com) A colourful online magazine covering all aspects of Mongolian culture.

Mongolia WWW Virtual Library (www.indiana.edu/~mongsoc) An excellent resource with lots of links.

UN in Mongolia (www.un-mongolia.mn) This website has lots of information, especially on the UN's Eastern Steppe Diversity project; check out the cultural magazine *Ger*.

Itineraries

CLASSIC ROUTE

THE BIG LOOP Three Weeks / Ulaanbaatar to the Gobi & the North, & back

This loop takes in a swath of geographic diversity and top attractions.

From Ulaanbaatar, head south to the eerie rock formations of **Baga Gazrin Chuluu** (p177) and the ruined castle at **Süm Khökh Burd** (p177). Perhaps visit **Eej Khad** (p98) en route, but you'll need to do some off-road navigation. From Süm Khökh Burd, travel southwest to the ruins of **Ongiin Khiid** (p178), a desert monastery on a pretty river. From here head south.

At least two days are needed to explore the dinosaur quarry at **Bayanzag** (p188), the spectacular ice canyon at **Yolyn Am** (p190) and the massive sand dunes at **Khongoryn Els** (p191). More days are required for a camel trek.

From the dunes, set off on the long jeep ride north to **Erdene Zuu Khiid** (p109), the country's oldest monastery. Head west to **Tsetserleg** (p115), a good place to break the journey, before proceeding to **Terkhiin Tsagaan Nuur** (p119) for two days of fishing, swimming, hiking or horse riding.

If time is running short, retreat to Ulaanbaatar via **Ögii Nuur** (p117). Otherwise, an additional five to seven days are needed for a trip north to spectacular **Khövsgöl Nuur** (p141). On the route back to Ulaanbaatar from here visit remote **Amarbayasgalant Khiid** (p129), an architectural gem.

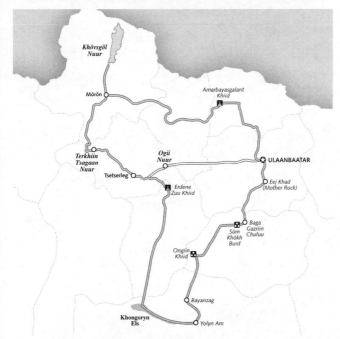

This loop includes some of Mongolia's best historical and natural sights, giving you both the Gobi and forested north. You'll need three weeks if you want to include some horse or camel trekking and fishing. Although seemingly on 'main routes', this is still a rough, remote and unpredictable journey.

ROADS LESS TRAVELLED

WESTERN MONGOLIA   Three Weeks / Khovd to Uliastai

The western aimags (provinces) offer adventurous travelling and exploration. Adrenaline junkies, can break out a mountain bike, kayak or mountaineering gear.

Start with a flight to Khovd, from where you can hire a jeep and driver for a bird-watching expedition at **Khar Us Nuur National Park** (p215). Looping back through Khovd city, continue northwest to the beautiful pastures and valley around **Tsambagarav Uul** (p215) and **Tsast Uul** (p207). You could easily spend a couple of days here before moving on to **Ölgii** (p203), a great place to recharge your batteries. Heading west from here, plan on spending three days at **Altai Tavan Bogd National Park** (p208). With more days, you could complete a good horse trek around **Khurgan Nuur** and **Khoton Nuur** (p208). With proper equipment, permits and some logistic support, it's even possible to scale Mongolia's highest peak, the 4374m Tavan Bogd Uul.

From Ölgii, the main road winds northeast to Ulaangom, passing **Üüreg Nuur** (p220) en route. At least three more days are needed to explore the **Kharkhiraa valley** (p220) and **Khyargas Nuur** (p221). With your own jeep, the road-less-travelled plunges east to Uliastai. But you'll save time by flying back to Ulaanbaatar. Alternatively, with a bit of planning, it's possible to fly to Kazakhstan or drive to Russia, using Ölgii as a jumping-off point.

Western Mongolia is a long way from the tour buses and crowds of central Mongolia. Although increasingly popular, it is still easy for explorers to hike in pristine valleys and camp by isolated lakes. This is also the most ethnically mixed region, with a significant population of Kazakhs.

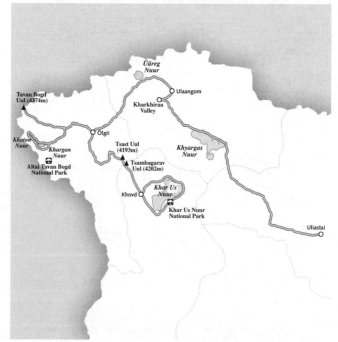

TAILORED TRIPS

CAMPING IT UP

Camping allows you to take advantage of Mongolia's awesome, unfenced landscapes, and is a good alternative to pricey ger camps. There are even beautiful camping areas close to Ulaanbaatar, around the **Gorkhi-Terelj National Park** (p99) and the **Bogdkhan Uul Strictly Protected Area** (p94).

Taking a jeep west from Ulaanbaatar to Tsetserleg offers plenty of scope for camping at many nature reserves, including **Khustain National Park** (p103), where you can spot the rare *takhi* horse in the wild, and pristine **Naiman Nuur** (p107), with its eight shimmering lakes.

The two best camping areas in Mongolia are **Terkhiin Tsagaan Nuur** (p119) and **Khövsgöl Nuur** (p141), both filled with fish and lined with hiking areas. For something more remote, try the lake-studded **Darkhad Depression** (p148), where Dukha reindeer herders live in tepees.

With its glaciers, rushing rivers and deserts, western Mongolia offers more extreme forms of camping. The best options are around **Tsast Uul** (p207) and **Altai Tavan Bogd National Park** (p208).

Travellers heading east can find good spots in the Dariganga region, especially **Shiliin Bogd** (p170), where you'll get great sunrises and sunsets. In the forests of Khentii, are **Balden Baraivan Khiid** (p156), where volunteers are rebuilding a monastery, and **Dadal** (p157), Chinggis Khaan's old stomping grounds.

THE BUDDHIST HERITAGE

After viewing Ulaanbaatar's two exquisite monasteries, Gandan or **Gandantegchinlen** (p63) and **Choijin Lama** (p64), take a short trip south near Zuunmod to see **Manzushir Khiid** (p94), a monastery on a forested flank of Bogdkhan Uul. Add to the pilgrimage by travelling there on foot over the mountain from Ulaanbaatar, a seven-hour hike.

Heading west from Ulaanbaatar, travel on a decent road to **Övgön Khiid** (p113), located at the foot of the pretty Khogno Khan Uul. From here you are just a couple of hours from Mongolia's oldest monastery, **Erdene Zuu Khiid** (p109). The huge walls that surround the complex were built from the ruins of Karakorum, Chinggis Khaan's 13th-century capital.

From Erdene Zuu, swing southwest to the lovely mountainside hermitage of **Tövkhön Khiid** (p108), where the famed Buddhist artist Zanabazar had a workshop and retreat. The best way to reach the small monastery is by a short horseback ride.

Returning on the same road, proceed to the town of Tsetserleg and the **Zayain Gegeenii Süm** (p115), now converted into one of the nicest museums in the country. Heading back east, top off the temple-run with the jewel in this class, **Amarbayasgalant Khiid** (p129).

The Author

MICHAEL KOHN

Michael's peregrinations across Mongolia began in late 1997 when he was employed to work as the English editor for the *Mongol Messenger* in Ulaanbaatar. His three-year stint with the paper included freelance work with the Associated Press and BBC, a gig as a talk-show host on Mongol radio, a starring role in a Mongolian film, and a short run as a local TV news broadcaster. His travels led him across all 21 aimags, sometimes by bicycle or in the back of a truck with sheep and other times in helicopters or Hum-Vees with politicians and diplomats. Michael's articles on Mongolian culture, politics and history have appeared in the *New York Times*, the *Baltimore Sun*, the *Far Eastern Economic Review* and the *San Francisco Chronicle*. His previous work with LP includes Central Asia and Tibet.

My Favourite Trip

Intent on experiencing the Mongolian winter to its fullest, I set off by plane from Ulaanbaatar to mystical Bayan-Ölgii, knowing full well this was also the time to witness the Kazakh 'eagle-hunters' in action. By hired jeep from Ölgii city I continued west in -20°C temperatures to Altai Tavan Bogd National Park (p208), where I came to know half a dozen local men who proudly showed me their eagles. They invited me for the hunt and set me up with a horse to follow them as they scoured the valleys and ravines for prey. By night we ate communal dinners of boiled sheep parts, and huddled around the stove to fend off the cold. Ten days and an equal number of numb toes later, I finally witnessed a kill – two golden eagles swooping down

from the sky to converge on an unfortunate fox. Trotting back to the hunters' home, I felt the true spirit of Central Asia still alive, just as Marco Polo and countless other romantics had witnessed it over the centuries.

Snapshot

The fact that Mongolia's liberal and conservative (former-communist) parties entered into a power-sharing agreement in the wake of dead-even elections in 2004 says much about how far the country's democracy movement has progressed since 1990. Free and fair elections, unheard of in neighbouring Central Asian states, have become the norm here; a fact that has made Mongolia a darling among international lenders and the donor community. This willingness to cooperate, with each other and with the international community, has marked Mongolia as an up-and-coming Asian state with potential for rapid modernisation.

Democracy has shown itself in parliamentary elections since 1996, with voters overturning the ruling party three times in succession. The most recent polls stripped the former-communist MPRP of its overwhelming control and created a 'grand coalition government' that includes ministers from both sides and a prime-ministership that will be swapped after two years.

Mongolia's reversal of fortune is evident on the streets of downtown Ulaanbaatar, where Korean taxis, Land Cruisers and Hum-Vees have all but erased the Russian Lada, and where fashion boutiques and elegant restaurants have made 'dollar shops' a distant memory. It is here that a burgeoning middle class is forging Mongolia's future, utilising the growing mining and tourism sectors.

The present, however, still has its share of rough edges. Only half of Mongolians have access to clean drinking water and one-third still lives under the poverty line. Infrastructure is rudimentary and important economic sectors such as livestock husbandry have proven susceptible to uncontrollable forces – some 11 million head of livestock were killed between 1999 and 2002 in the wake of bad winter storms.

The ongoing changes have also brought out many contradictions in Mongolian society. You may, for instance, witness scenes such as a nomadic herder with a mobile phone, an Internet café next to a barely operational telephone transfer centre, a Mormon church beside a Buddhist meditation centre, and a woman in risqué clothing assisting her grandparents down the street who are dressed in *dels* (traditional coats).

But rapid change comes at a cost. The urban and rural poor grumble about ongoing corruption, and the environment suffers from new legislation that favours mining and business. Also disturbing are suggestions by prominent politician N Enkhbayar that Mongolia attempt an agricultural revolution, thus spelling the end of the nomadic life.

With big brother Russia now out of the picture, and a frosty relationship with China, Mongolia has turned to countries such as Japan, Korea, Germany, the USA and the UK for assistance in redevelopment. Mongolia, a willing participant in Western-style economic shock therapy and political reform, has, for better or worse, flung itself into the globalised world. Despite obvious challenges ahead there is hope that Mongolia can be a model for other developing countries. Its efforts to meet international expectations were recently rewarded with admission to the 'Millennium Challenge Account', George W Bush's multibillion-dollar foreign-aid program designed to spur growth in low-income countries that display democracy and good governance.

FAST FACTS

Population: 2.45 million (2003)

GDP: US$1840 per capita, ranking Mongolia 175 out of 200 countries

Leading 2004 exports: copper, wool, gold, cashmere, leather

Gold output: increased 75% during 2004

Literacy rate: 98%

Voter turnout: often over 80%

Inflation: about 6%

Horse-to-person ratio: 13 to 1

Urban unemployment: 30%; rural unemployment: 12%

Average life expectancy: 64 years

History

The Mongolians, or Mongols as they were previously known, recorded their history for centuries in oral epics sung by bards, until writing was introduced nearly 800 years ago. Because of their substantial – and mostly unhappy – contact with neighbouring countries, much also has been written about them. Chinese dynastic histories stretching back 5000 years tell of the Mongols and their predecessors, describing them as ravenous barbarians greedy for Chinese produce and likening them to wolves. Though much of Mongolia's written history is rooted in Chinese history, the details given here present a more objective point of view.

Charles Bawden's *The Modern History of Mongolia* is recognised as the authoritative work on Mongol history. A good, contemporary follow-up is B Baabar's *Twentieth Century Mongolia*.

IN THE BEGINNING

Little is known about Mongolia's earliest inhabitants, but archaeological digs have uncovered human remains in the Gobi and other regions that date back nearly 500,000 years. Some of their stone tools can be seen in Ulaanbaatar's National Museum of Mongolian History (p61). It is thought that early inhabitants of the region were among America's first settlers, crossing Siberia and the Bering Strait in pursuit of game during the last ice age. Certainly superficial similarities such as facial features, the tepees of the Dukha and the spirit worship of shamanism point to a link with Native Americans.

Early Chinese manuscripts refer to 'Turkic-speaking peoples' living in what we now call Mongolia as early as the 4th or 5th century BC. The Chinese – who had numerous military clashes with these nomadic tribes – referred to them as the Xiongnu or 'The State Holding the Bows Beyond the Great Wall'. Some Xiongnu tribes moved west, and their descendants, the Huns, united under Attila and terrorised Central Europe in the last days of the Roman Empire.

THE MONGOLS

The Black Rose (1950), directed by Henry Hathaway, stars Orson Welles, Tyrone Power and Herbert Lom as Saxon warriors off to meet the great Mongolian leaders. It's one of Hollywood's many attempts at recreating the Mongol Empire.

The name 'Mongol' was first recorded by the Chinese during the Tang dynasty (AD 618–907). At that time, Mongolia was dominated by the Uighurs, a Turkic people who built several cities. The Uighurs followed the teachings of a Persian saint, Mani, who was much influenced by Christianity. An inscription found in the ruins of their city, Khar Balgas (p118), tells how Manichaeism transformed 'this country of barbarous customs, full of the fumes of blood, into a land where people live on vegetables; from a land of killing to a land where good deeds are fostered'.

The Uighur's lasting legacy in Mongolia is the downward flowing script – *The Secret History of the Mongols* epic and all subsequent Mongolian texts were written in this script until Stalin intervened in the 1940s. The ever-changing forces of Central Asia eventually saw the end of the Uighurs and later control by the Kitan and Jurchen peoples.

Chinggis Khaan

Until the end of the 12th century, the Mongols were little more than a loose confederation of rival clans. Until a Mongol named Temujin was

TIMELINE

200 BC	AD 840
Xiongnu Mongolian empire reaches the Yellow River	The Kyrghz defeat the ruling Uighurs

CHINGGIS KHAAN

Chinggis was born in 1162 (some say 1155 or, more likely, 1167) and named Temujin (Ironsmith) after a Tatar chief his father had just killed. Legend says that Temujin was born with a clot of blood the size of a knucklebone in his fist, auguring great bloodshed. His ruthlessness became obvious when, as a teenager, he killed his half-brother Bekter in cold blood for stealing one of his fish.

When his father was poisoned by the Tatars in 1171, the nine-year-old outcast was plunged into years of struggle as he strove to keep himself and his family alive. Revenge became Chinggis' obsession.

Temujin eventually married his long-betrothed wife, Bortei of the Konggirait tribe. In 1189 he was proclaimed Chinggis Khaan (Oceanic King), and the khaan of the Borjigan Mongols, when eight princes swore allegiance to him.

Within 15 years he had destroyed the Tatar, Taichuut and Naiman tribes. Like George W Bush, his 'you're either with us or you are against us' philosophy dictated his next target. Eventually, his confederation of Mongol tribes, led by his brilliant generals Subedai and Jebe, would create the largest land empire that the world had ever seen.

Little is known about the man himself. We know that he was afraid of dogs and a great believer in spirits and shamans. One of most influential people in the Mongol empire was Chinggis' shaman Kököchu, also known as Töv Tengri, who eventually tried to install a rival to Chinggis, until the khaan ordered the shaman's back broken during a staged wrestling bout.

Towards the end of his life Chinggis summoned the 71-year-old Chinese Taoist and alchemist Chang Chun to his camp in the Hindu Kush to demand the elixir of immortality. The potion obviously failed and Chinggis eventually passed away in August 1227, near Yinchuan, in modern China's Gansu province.

born in 1162. At the age of 20, Temujin emerged from a power struggle to become the leader of the Borjigin Mongol clan, and later managed to unite most of the Mongol tribes. He was given the honorary name of Chinggis (Genghis) Khaan, meaning 'oceanic (or universal) king', and in 1206 he declared the formation of the Mongol empire, with himself as supreme leader.

Chinggis Khaan set up his capital in Karakorum (p109), in present-day Kharkhorin, and launched his cavalry against China and Russia. In 1209 he headed south to defeat the Tangut (Western Xia) empire on the Yellow River and then harassed the Jin dynasty of China, themselves 'barbarian' nomads known as the Jurchen.

Chinggis Khaan then turned westwards to conquer his last rivals, the Karakhitai, an offshoot of the Naiman tribe. He was about to return to finish off China when news arrived that a group of Mongol merchants in Central Asia had been killed and several ambassadors had been roughed up by the forces of the Khorezmshah. It was to be a strategic mistake as Chinggis turned his fury westward.

In 1219 the Mongols took Otrar in modern-day Kazakhstan, poured molten silver into the eyes of the Khorezmshah commander Inalchuk and went on to destroy the great Central Asian cities of Samarkand, Bukhara, Merv, Balkh, Herat and Ghazni. Finally after six years of bloody campaigning, Chinggis Khaan returned to Mongolia in 1225. By the time of his death two years later, the Mongol empire extended from Beijing to the Caspian Sea.

Recent books on Chinggis Khaan paint the man as a courageous leader and just lawgiver, attempting to reverse centuries of bad press. The two best are *Genghis Khan: Life, Death and Resurrection*, by John Man, and *Genghis Khan and the Making of the Modern World*, by Jack Weatherford.

1206	1235
Chinggis Khaan proclaims himself ruler of the Mongol empire	Ögedei Khaan, Chinggis' third and favourite son, completes construction of Karakorum

The Great Khaans

With the death of Chinggis Khaan the empire was divided between his sons. Chaghatai (Tsagaadai) inherited the lands of Central Asia, Hülegü formed the Il-Khanate in Persia and Tolui took Central Mongolia. Batu, Chinggis' grandson, went on to establish the Golden Horde in central Eurasia, with its capital at Serai.

In 1229 power passed into the hands of Chinggis' favourite son, Ögedei, who continued the military conquest. His generals swept through the Volga region and the Russian cities of Rostov, Yaroslavyl and Novgorod, sacking Kiev in 1240. The Mongols pushed into Poland and Lithuania, burned Krakow and swung south into Hungary and Bohemia, poised to inflict more carnage as the rest of Europe prayed in their cathedrals for a miracle.

Then in 1241 the Mongols suddenly stopped, turned around and headed back to Mongolia. Both Chaghatai and Ögedei Khaan had died, and Mongol custom dictated that all noble descendants of Chinggis had to return to Mongolia to democratically elect a new leader. Europe was saved. A brief power struggle ensued until Möngke (Monkh) Khaan claimed the throne.

After the death of Ögedei Khaan, his Christian widow Toregene Khataan ruled the Empire for five years. She was later put to death by Möngke Khaan as part of a rival family plot.

THE MONGOL WAR MACHINE

Thanks to the Mongols, the 13th century was to be exceeded in cruelty and bloodshed only by the 20th century. Chroniclers reported horrific massacres of 1.6 million people at Herat, 1.7 million at Nishapur and 800,000 at Baghdad. Up to 30% of the population of Central Asia was massacred in an unprecedented catastrophe that decimated irrigation and agriculture for generations.

Mongol military technique was honed in epic hunting expeditions. Forces were organised decimally into *tümen* (10,000 soldiers), *zuun* (100 soldiers) and *arvan* (10 soldiers). Members of hostile tribes were separated and spread throughout different tümen. Chinggis Khaan was protected by a *keshig*, or imperial guard of 10,000 soldiers. There simply was no such thing as a civilian population in Mongolia.

The Mongols were the masters of psychological warfare. Cities that surrendered to the Mongols without a fight were spared, while those that resisted were utterly obliterated, so as to induce the surrender of the next city. Yet rarely was torture used; killing was businesslike, with soldiers given strict quotas on the number of civilians to kill. Chinggis perfected the techniques of feigned flight, mobility, hostage taking, surprise attack and human shields. He also developed a large intelligence network of spies and traders who sent information along an efficient communications system. Contrary to popular misconceptions, diplomacy was chosen over warfare whenever possible.

At the root of their dominance was the Mongol's horsemanship. Each Mongol soldier took five horses on campaign and could ride for weeks, allegedly surviving only on mare's milk and horse's blood. Technology was also on their side. Their compound bows of bone, sinew and wood had a range of 250m, twice as long as the European longbow, and they could shoot forward or backwards while riding. They completed their arsenal with mangonels (giant catapults used to hurl stones), and explosives given to them by the Chinese. Ironically, it was firearm technology that later kept the nomads at a continual disadvantage.

Ultimately it was easier for the Mongols to conquer than to hold on to power. For as a Chinese general once told Kublai Khan, the empire that is conquered on horseback cannot be governed on horseback.

1279	1368
Kublai Khaan, Chinggis Khaan's grandson, completes the conquest of China	The Mongols are driven out of China

The Mongol conquest continued as Hülegü, son of Chinggis, swept through Iran and destroyed Baghdad, killing the caliph in traditional Mongol fashion by rolling him in a carpet and trampling him to death with horses, thus avoiding the spillage of any royal blood.

In 1259 the Mongols were poised to take Egypt when they suddenly stopped, turned around and headed back to Mongolia yet again – Möngke Khaan had died (of dysentery). His brother Kublai (Khublai) was elected khaan mid-campaign in southern China.

Kublai (Khublai) Khaan (c 1216–94) completed the subjugation of China, effectively ending the Song dynasty (960–1279), and became emperor of China's Yuan dynasty (1271–1368). He established his winter capital in Khanbalik (City of the Khan), known then in Chinese as Dadu (Great Capital) – today's Beijing. In Khanbalik, in 1274, he met and hired a young Marco Polo. Kublai's summer camp was north at Shangdu, later immortalised as Xanadu by the opium-inspired poet Samuel Coleridge.

Kublai soon realised that the Mongol empire had reached the limits of its expansion. In 1260 the Mongols lost a major battle to the Egyptian Mamluks. Two attempts to invade Japan (in 1274 and 1281) ended in failure; the second was thwarted when a typhoon claimed the lives of 140,000 Mongol troops, the largest fleet of its time ever assembled.

Instead of looking for more wars to fight, Kublai concentrated his efforts on keeping the vast empire together. It was during this period of wealth and extravagance that Marco Polo and other travellers ventured into the empire and described it in their journals to an amazed Europe.

The grandeur of the Mongol empire in China lasted over a century. After Kublai Khaan died in 1294, the Mongols became increasingly dependent on, and influenced by, the people they ruled. They were deeply resented as an elite, privileged class exempt from taxation, and the empire became ridden with factions vying for power. By the mid-14th century, Mongol rule began to disintegrate, until they were expelled from Beijing by the first emperor of the Ming dynasty (1368–1644), Zhu Yuanzhang.

THE MONGOL LEGACY

The Mongols left a mixed legacy. Though demonised by foreign historians, Chinggis Khaan nonetheless managed to introduce a written script for the Mongolian language, instituted a tradition of religious tolerance and initiated the first major direct contact between East and West, in what later became known as the Pax Mongolica. He is attributed with the introduction of the Yasaq, or Mongolian legal code, which influenced Mongol government for centuries. Mongolian rule was an artistic high point for many of the khaans' domains, and Chinggis brought craftsmen back into Mongolia to create a Mongolian artistic renaissance.

There was, however, a darker legacy. The Mongols introduced the Black Death to Europe in 1347, and its war machine destroyed great cultures of the Middle East and Central Asia, many of which were never to recover.

THE DECLINE

The collapse of the Yuan dynasty caused over 60,000 Mongols to return to Mongolia. Their unity dissolved and they resumed their traditional lifestyle of frequent clan warfare. A major civil war was fought from 1400

Khublai Khan: His Life and Times, by Morris Rossabi, paints a picture of the man who entertained Marco Polo, conquered the Song dynasty and bridged the gap between Europe and Asia.

The Mongols, by Jeremiah Curtin, has a foreword written by Theodore Roosevelt and is one of the best full accounts of the Mongol conquests.

http://baatar.freeyellow .com/index.html is a good general website containing culture, history, good links and curious detail, such as translations of letters written by Mongol warlords to the leaders of Europe.

to 1454 between two main groups, the Khalkh in the east and the Oyrat (Oirad) in the west. A long period of stagnation and decline followed.

A revival of sorts occurred under Altan Khaan (1507–83), who united the Khalkh, defeated the Oirad and brought most of Mongolia under his control. The war with the Ming dynasty of China was renewed in an attempt to recapture the lost empire of the Yuan dynasty, but this proved fruitless. Altan signed a peace treaty with China in 1571 and turned his troops southwest against Tibet.

At the height of his power, Altan was seduced by Buddhism – strangely enough, the religion of Tibet, with whom they were at war. Altan became a devout believer and Buddhism became the religion of the Mongol nobility for 200 years, as well as the state religion. The monks tried desperately to reunite the quarrelling clans, but Mongolia's tendency to fragment persisted and the nation sunk into medieval stagnation.

After the death of Altan Khaan, Mongolia reverted to a collection of tiny tribal domains. Meanwhile, the Manchus (whose predecessors were the Jurchen), ancient enemies of the Mongols, established the Qing dynasty (1644–1911). Despite their military prowess, the Manchus at first made no aggressive moves against Mongolia; they did not need to as the Mongols were doing a great job of defeating themselves. The Zungar Mongols of the west (who ruled Bukhara, Kashgar and Turfan) were locked into a fierce military struggle with the Khalkh Mongols of the east.

The Zungar seemed to be gaining the upper hand, and it was at this time that the Khalkh made what was probably a fatal mistake – they invited the Manchu Qing emperor, Kangxi, to send troops to fight their Zungar enemy. Like most Mongols, the Zungar warriors were highly skilled horseback archers. However, the Manchus possessed new technology in the form of muskets and cannons, which the Mongols couldn't combat. In 1691 Khalkh Mongolia submitted to Manchu rule and by 1732 the Zungar had been resoundingly defeated.

REVOLUTIONS

In 1911 China's last dynasty, the Qing, crumbled. Mongol princes, long dissatisfied with the brutal Manchu occupation that had befallen their country, declared independence from China. A theocratic government was established under Mongolia's religious pontiff, the eighth Jebtzun Damba (Living Buddha), who was declared the Bogd Khaan (Holy King). In May 1915, the Treaty of Kyakhta – which granted Mongolia limited autonomy – was signed by Mongolia, China and Russia.

The Russian Revolution of October 1917 came as a great shock to Mongolia's aristocracy. Taking advantage of Russia's weakness, a Chinese warlord sent his troops into Mongolia in 1919 and occupied the capital. In February 1921, retreating White Russian (anticommunist) troops entered Mongolia and expelled the Chinese. At first the Bogd Khaan seemed to welcome the Russians as saviours of his regime, but it soon became apparent that the Russians were just another ruthless army of occupation.

Mongolian nationalists believed their best hope for military assistance was to ask the Bolsheviks for help. The White Russians, however, disappeared from the scene when their leader, Baron von Ungern-Sternberg, was captured, tried and shot. In July 1921 Damdin Sükhbaatar,

William of Rubruck, who paid a visit to Karakorum in 1253, is thought to have passed on the secret of gunpowder to Roger Bacon upon his return from the Orient.

The Devil's Horsemen, by James Chambers, is an interesting summary of the Mongol invasion of Eastern Europe and discusses the Mongol role as a 'superpower'.

The Conqueror (1956), directed by Dick Powell, sees John Wayne exchange his ten-gallon hat and rifle for brass-studded armour and bow and arrow. An unintentionally funny movie.

1732	1911
Zungar Mongols routed by Manchurian China, bringing Outer Mongolia under Manchu rule.	Independence from China

THE MAD BARON

One of Mongolian history's most unusual characters was Baron Roman Nikolaus Fyodirovich von Ungern-Sternberg, a renegade White Russian officer who believed he was the reincarnation of Chinggis Khaan, destined to restore the Mongol warlord's previous empire. Contemporaries paint a fine picture of Baron von Ungern-Sternberg, later known as the Mad Baron, describing him as haunted-looking, with a psychotic stare that fixed on people 'like those of an animal in a cave'. He spoke with a high-pitched voice and his bulging forehead bore a huge sword scar, which pulsed with red veins whenever he grew agitated. As a finishing touch, one of his eyes was slightly higher than the other.

The Bolshevik victory in Russia forced the Baron east, and he slowly accumulated a desperate army of renegade mercenaries. He enforced discipline with a reign of terror, roasting deserters alive, baking defiant prisoners in ovens and throwing his rivals in locomotive boilers. He was a deep believer in soothsayers and also a fervent Buddhist, convinced that he was doing his victims a favour by packing them off to the next life sooner rather than later.

With an army of 6000 troops (and the tacit backing of the Japanese), the Baron crossed the Mongolian border in the summer of 1920 with the aim of establishing a Pan-Mongol empire. By October his forces attacked Urga, but were driven back four times before finally taking the city. He freed the Bogd Khaan (who had been imprisoned by the Chinese) to general joy, but this turned to horror as the next three days saw an orgy of looting, burning and killing. In May 1921 the Baron declared himself the Emperor of Russia.

After only a few months, the Bolshevik advance forced the Baron to abandon Urga in a futile attempt to defend Mongolia's northern border. Out on the steppes, his own followers tried to kill him, shooting him in his tent, but he managed to escape. A group of Mongolian herders later found him dying in the grass, tortured by biting ants. He was eventually taken by the Bolsheviks, deported to Novosibirsk and shot on 15 September 1921, presumed mad. He was defiant to the end. Dr Ferdinand Ossendowski, a Polish refugee living in Mongolia in the early 1920s, offers an excellent account of the Mad Baron in his book *Beasts, Men and Gods*. For a more contemporary account, read Jasper Becker's book, *The Lost Country*.

the leader of the Mongolian army, marched uncontested into Urga (as Ulaanbaatar was then known), along side Bolshevik supporters. The People's Government of Mongolia was declared and the Bogd Khaan was retained as a ceremonial figurehead with no real power. Led by a motley cast of seven revolutionaries, including Sükhbaatar, the newly formed Mongolian People's Party (the first political party in the country's history, and the only one for the next 69 years) took the reins of power.

SOVIET CONTROL

On 26 November 1924, the Mongolian People's Republic (MPR) was declared and Mongolia became the world's second communist country. The Mongolian People's Party was renamed the Mongolian People's Revolutionary Party (MPRP). Soviet and Mongolian communists worked secretly to eliminate all noncommunist contenders for power.

After Lenin's death in Russia in 1924, Mongolian communism remained independent of Moscow until Lenin's successor, Stalin, gained absolute power in the late 1920s. Then the purges began in Mongolia. MPRP leaders were disposed of until Stalin finally found his stooge in one Khorloogiin Choibalsan.

1921	1924
Chinese and White Russian invaders defeated; Mongolian independence proclaimed	Bogd Khaan (Holy King) dies; the Mongolian People's Republic declared by the communists

A joint Mongolian and Russian military force defeated the Japanese in a three-month battle in eastern Mongolia in 1939. Japan, forced to re-think its strategy, decided to turn its military south instead.

Following Stalin's lead, Choibalsan seized from aristocrats their land and herds, which were then redistributed to common nomads. Herders were forced to join cooperatives and private business was banned. The destruction of private enterprise without sufficient time to build up a working state sector had the same result in Mongolia as it did in the Soviet Union: famine. Choibalsan's policy against religion was just as ruthless – in 1937 some 27,000 people were executed or never seen again (3% of Mongolia's population at that time), of whom 17,000 were monks.

Choibalsan died in January 1952 and was replaced by Yumjaagiin Tsedenbal – no liberal, but not a mass murderer. From that time until the mid-1960s, Mongolia enjoyed, in relative terms, a period of peace. With the Sino-Soviet split in the early 1960s, the Mongolians chose the lesser of two evils and sided with the Soviet Union. Chinese aid to Mongolia ceased; the Mongolian government expelled thousands of ethnic Chinese and all trade with China came to a halt.

Throughout the 1970s, Soviet influence gathered strength. Young Mongolians were sent to the USSR for technical training, and Tsedenbal's wife, an uneducated Russian peasant named Filatova, saw to it that Russian culture – food, music, opera and dance – replaced Mongolian traditions.

Despite opposition from the USA and Taiwan, Mongolia became a member of the UN in 1961.

Mongolia's march in Soviet footsteps continued right up to *perestroika* (economic, political and social restructuring) when Tsedenbal's successor Jambiin Batmöngke initiated a series of striking reforms in 1986. Decentralisation meant that enterprises were given more freedom to operate without central officials making all the decisions. Government departments were reorganised and high-ranking officials were reshuffled.

The unravelling of the Soviet Union resulted in decolonisation by default. In March 1990, in sub-zero temperatures, large pro-democracy protests erupted in the square in front of the parliament building in Ulaanbaatar and hunger strikes were held.

Things happened quickly: Batmöngke lost power; new political parties with a bewildering variety of names sprang up; and hunger strikes and protests continued. In March the Politburo resigned, and in May 1990 the constitution was amended to permit multiparty elections in July of the same year.

DEMOCRACY TAKES HOLD

In 1995 the *Washington Post* selected Chinggis Khaan as its 'Man of the Millennium'.

Ironically, the communists won the elections, taking 85% of the seats in the Great Khural. Although Ulaanbaatar residents gave much support to the opposition parties, rural areas voted overwhelmingly for the communists. The MPRP, now calling itself 'ex-communist', announced it would share power with several young democrats – some were even given ministries. Freedom of speech, religion and assembly were all granted. The era of totalitarianism had ended.

The MPRP held sway until 1996 when the Mongolian Democratic Coalition trounced the ruling MPRP, unexpectedly ending 75 years of unbroken communist rule. But the inexperienced Democrats did not have an easy time of government. Between 1996 and 2000 the country went through four prime ministers, one resigning and two others losing a vote of no-confidence.

1937	1990
Choibalsan's Buddhist purge leaves 700 monasteries destroyed and 27,000 monks and civilians dead.	Pro-democracy protests held; communists win multiparty elections

Corruption reared its ugly head several times. The plug was pulled on the MonMacau Casino one month before its planned opening in the basement of the Chinggis Hotel, and three democratic members of parliament were jailed in 1999 for accepting bribes in return for the casino tender.

In the July 2000 general election the Democrats paid the price for political squabbling and economic hardships. The ex-communist MPRP won 72 out of 76 seats and their leader Nambaryn Enkhbayar was sworn in as prime minister. Little changed economically, but many voters saw Enkhbayar's reign as something of a throwback to the authoritarian past; it didn't help that President Natsagiin Bagabandi was also an MPRP man, giving the party a monopoly on government.

Fed up with the one-party state, the fickle Mongolian voters brought the Democrats back in July 2004. The surprise result saw the Democrats taking 34 seats to the MPRP's 37. Four other seats were won by smaller parties and independents and, at the time of research, one seat was undecided. Because neither party could muster the 39 seats needed to form a government, the MPRP and the Democrats were forced into an unlikely four-year alliance, leaving the country without an opposition.

Bizarrely, Israel, with its history of national unity governments, has coached Mongolian politicians in the delicate art of compromise. In August 2004, after lengthy consultations, 41-year-old Tsakhiagiin Elbegdorj, a former military journalist, was selected as prime minister. According to the power-sharing agreement, he will be replaced by a member of the MPRP in 2006.

Recent DNA testing on Y-chromosomes proves that more than 16 million men across Central Asia share a common ancestor who lived in the 13th century. Because of his widespread conquests – of both kingdoms and women – Chinggis Khaan is widely believed to be this forebear.

1996	2004
Democratic election victory ends 75 years of MPRP rule	Democrats and MPRP forced into 'national unity government' after hung election

The Culture

THE NATIONAL PSYCHE

Mongolians call themselves Asian by ethnicity but Western by culture. As abstract as that might sound, your first encounters with Mongolians might knock back a few preconceptions. It could be the European influence in which that their Russian masters immersed them throughout the 20th century, or perhaps the long hours they now spend glued to CNN and MTV. But the Mongolian likeness to Western thinking – and the distance it has put between itself and the rest of Asia – probably owes more to its nomadic past and its environment than it does to any external influences.

The freedom to move about with their herds, the timelessness of the land and the delicate relationship with the earth and its resources have all had a profound effect on the Mongolian character. These persuasions have made Mongolians humble, adaptable, unfettered by stringent protocol, good humoured and uncannily stoic; causing visitors to wonder if these are the same people that for centuries were vilified in the West as the 'scourge of God'.

The *soyombo* is the national symbol of Mongolia and signifies freedom and independence. Its components symbolise many other characteristics. Legend attributes the *soyombo* to Zanabazar, the Living Buddha.

The great emptiness of their landscape has seemingly kindled a strong curiosity of outsiders. But, more significantly, it has also made hospitality a matter of sheer necessity rather than a chore or social obligation. Hospitality is something that is, quite simply, crucial to survival. In effect, every home on the steppes serves as a hotel, restaurant, pub, repair shop and information centre. This hospitality extends readily to strangers and it is usually given without fanfare or excitement; foreigners are often perplexed by the casual welcoming they receive at even the most remote of gers.

The Mongolian ger plays a vital role in shaping both the Mongolian character and family life. Its small confines compels families to interact with one another, to share everything and to work together, tightening relationships between relatives. It promotes patience, makes inhibitions fade away and prevents privacy. It also hardens the sensibilities; ger dwellers must fetch their own water and fuel, difficult tasks especially in the dead of winter.

The weather and the seasons also play a significant role in shaping the Mongolian character. Spring in particular is a crucial time for Mongolians. Because the country's rainy season comes towards the end of summer, spring is dry, dusty, windy and unforgiving. This is the time when the weaker animals die and, it is said, when people die. Spring is a time of despair. Despite the severe temperatures, it is actually during winter that Mongolians feel most comfortable. After a difficult summer filled with chores and tending to livestock, winter is a time of relaxation.

Modern Mongolia, Reclaiming Ghengis Khan, edited by Paula Sabloff, is a pictorial account of recent developments in Mongolia. Written with a sometimes controversial edge, it discusses the economy, ger etiquette, social issues and Chinggis Khaan's principles, and suggests these are the foundations of modern Mongolia.

Lastly, modern politics, economics and external forces all play a small role in filling out the Mongolian psyche. When communism and Russian influence arrived during the 20th century, Mongolians became imbued with a desire for education and literacy, something that was once thought to be fit only for the monastic class. For many years communism influenced the way Mongolians viewed the inner workings of the United States and Western Europe; that is, with suspicion. But where democratic principles failed to make inroads, it was popular youth 'capitalist' culture (in the form of smuggled blue jeans, magazines, posters and pirated Beatles cassettes) that stirred young Mongolians to look toward the west. By the mid-1980s, the MPRP had given up trying to control this 'underground' youth movement and could do little when it appeared openly in urban areas.

Post-1990, this curiosity welcomed globalisation, and only a handful of old hardliners protested when the rest of the country was busy opening up strip clubs, paparazzi newspapers and tattoo parlours. A rekindled interest in the past also brought about the celebrity status of Chinggis Khaan. In Ulaanbaatar, and even in many parts of the countryside, the modern world has found a place alongside the traditional.

RESPONSIBLE CULTURAL TOURISM

The lack of responsibility among independent travellers has caused tourist authorities to think twice about their 'open-door policy'. Some officials are even considering the 'Bhutan model' of limiting tourism to the top-end market. In order to keep Mongolia open to all budgets, be mindful of several factors and unwritten rules that will keep everyone happy.

- Hospitality is an old custom on the steppes; visitors are invited in without question on arrival at a distant ger. While you should enjoy Mongolia's unique hospitality, please do not take advantage of it. We continue to hear reports about travellers who rely on nomads for their accommodation and meals, without paying (in money or kind). If you spend a night, leave a minimum of T5000 or a useful gift such as rice, children's books in Mongolian or AA- or D-size batteries.
- Mongolians are not keen on bargaining and don't play the 'bargaining game'. When haggling for a hotel room or jeep, never expect to get the price you demand.
- Don't pay to take a photo of someone, nor photograph someone if they don't want you to. If you agree to send someone a photograph, please follow through on this.

When visiting a ger, note the following customs and habits. See also p48 for some hints when eating as a guest.

- Say hello *(sain bai-na uu)* when you arrive (but repeating it again when you see the same person is considered strange to Mongolians).
- Avoid walking in front of an older person; or turning your back to the altar or religious objects (except when leaving).
- Leave weapons outside.
- If someone offers you their snuff bottle, accept it with your right hand. If you don't take the snuff, at least sniff the top part of the bottle.
- Try to keep ger visits to less than two hours to avoid interrupting the family's work.

Bear in mind the following superstitions and religious habits.

- When offered some vodka, dip your ring finger of your right hand into the glass, and lightly flick a drop (not too much – vodka is also sacred!) once towards the sky, once in the air 'to the wind' and once to the ground. If you don't want any vodka, go through the customs anyway, put the same finger to your forehead, say thanks, and return the glass to the table.
- Don't point a knife in any way at anyone; pass a knife handle first; and use the knife to cut towards you, not away.
- Don't point your feet at the hearth, at the altar or at another person. Sleep with your feet pointing towards the door.
- If you have stepped on anyone, or kicked their feet, immediately shake their hand.
- Don't stand on, or lean over, the threshold.
- Don't lean against a support column.
- Don't touch another person's hat.

LIFESTYLE

Women of Mongolia, by Martha Avery, contains a string of interviews that enable local women to speak about the changes and challenges affecting both nomadic and urban women.

About half of all Mongolians live in a ger, the one-room round felt tent traditionally used by nomads. The other half live in Russian-style apartment blocks. Only since the late 1990s have Mongolians started constructing more elaborate Western-style homes; most of these are upgraded dachas found outside of Ulaanbaatar.

Apartments are rabbit-hole affairs, usually two or three rooms, with Russian furnishings and large carpets hanging from the walls. Gers are often equipped with traditional furnishings painted bright orange with fanciful designs. Set out in like manner, gers have three beds around the perimeter, a chest covered with Buddhist relics at the back wall and a low table upon which food is set. Everything revolves around a central hearth, with the women's side to the right and the men's to the left. The head of the household sits at the northern end of the ger with his most honoured guest to his right. The area near the door is the place of lowest rank and the domain of children.

Mongolian women occupy a valued role in the household and are often in charge of daily affairs. Economic hardship over the past 15 years has forced women to shoulder heavier workloads to supplement the family income, but few hold positions of power; company directors and politicians, however ceremonial, are usually men. Economic problems have also broken up homes and prevented marriage. To combat this, the government has promised stimulation packages to support newlyweds and newborns.

State of Dogs (1998), directed by Peter Brosens and Dorjkhandyn Turmunkh, is an avante-garde portrayal of Mongolia through the eyes of a dead mongrel before its rebirth as a human. It's a stirring idea and well made, but a tad slow.

The government, however, does little to recognise the rights of gay and lesbian couples. Homosexuality is a taboo subject in Mongolia (although it is legal) and it is only since the mid 1990s that a small gay community has emerged in Ulaanbaatar.

One-third of Mongolians live below the poverty line, which means they earn less than US$30 per month. But unlike other impoverished countries, this does not necessarily mean that people are going hungry. You'll find most people in Mongolia live in a healthy, robust state even if they have been out of work for months or even years. The reason behind this is the strong family network. One family member with a decent job has the responsibility to support his or her family and distribute his wealth among siblings.

THE CULT OF THE GREAT KHAAN

Contrary to popular belief, Chinggis Khaan (known as Genghis Khan in the West) is alive and well. His ubiquitous face adorns money and postage stamps as well as bottles of Chinggis Khaan vodka. Ulaanbaatar's most famous hotel, rock band and brewery are named after him. Despite his reputation abroad, an understandable, renewed nationalism has resulted in reverence for the Great Khaan, history's best-known Mongolian.

Chinggis has suffered from over 800 years of bad press in the West. The Muslim historian Rashid-al-din summed up the Western perception of the man when he 'quoted' Chinggis, saying that the single greatest pleasure in his life was 'to cut my enemy to pieces, drive them before me, seize their possessions, witness the tears of those who are dear to them and to embrace their wives and daughters'.

To Mongolians, though, Chinggis Khaan embodies strength, unity, and law and order. He introduced a written script in the Mongolian language and preached religious tolerance. Chinggis is the young king who united the warring clans and gave Mongolians a sense of direction. This is what post-communist Mongolia looks for today – a leader in the mould of Chinggis who can rise above confusion and uncertainty.

THE MONGOLIAN NAME GAME

Mongolians have been on a first name basis for as long as anyone can remember. Flipping through a phone book reveals a bevy of Bats, bunches of Bolds, a bundle of Baatars and cascading columns of Dorj. Realising that last names could be of use (in registering taxpayers and the prevention of inbreeding), in the late 1990s the government ordered every Mongolian to start using their clan name. The problem was that the communist government had forbidden the names since the 1920s, in an effort to suppress loyalties based on lineage that might supersede the state, and most people had forgotten their clan.

The identity crisis has caused a boom in amateur genealogy, as families have gone back to their villages to retrace their roots and learn their name. Not surprisingly, some 20% of the population claims to be a 'Borjigan', the clan name of Chinggis Khaan. Authorities encourage creativity, and people who can't re-trace their name are making them up – after their profession, their hobby, their favourite mountain or a nickname. Mongolia's lone spaceman, Gurragchaa, named his family 'Cosmos'. Another clan name up for grabs is 'Family of Seven Drunks', which hasn't had many takers.

Relatives working abroad also send home money – approximately 100,000 Mongolians live and work abroad, about 8% of the workforce. In downtown Ulaanbaatar, an average salary is US$100 per month and steadily climbing.

POPULATION

Half the population of Mongolia live permanently in urban areas and around 25% are truly nomadic. Another 25% are semi-nomadic, living in villages in the winter and grazing their animals on the steppes during the rest of the year. With population growth at an all-time low (it has fallen from 2.4% to 1.4% over the past 15 years), the government is planning subsidies for newborns and newlywed couples.

The economic collapse of the early 1990s forced many Mongolians back onto the steppes to eke out an existence as livestock breeders. But since the late 1990s there has been a major shift back to urban areas, especially Ulaanbaatar, which is bursting at the seams. With the exception of a handful of places benefiting by either mining or tourism, rural areas languish in neglect.

The harsh winters of 1999 to 2002, in particular, forced many nomads, whose herds had been wiped out, to move to the city. Since 1999, Ulaanbaatar's population has increased by around 30,000 people every year and will breach the one million mark by 2008, if not sooner.

The great majority (about 86%) of Mongolians are Khalkh Mongolians (*khalkh* means 'shield'). Clan or tribal divisions are not a significant social or political issue in modern Mongolia. The other sizable ethnic group, the Kazakhs, make up about 6% (110,000) of the population and live in western Mongolia, mainly in Bayan-Ölgii aimag.

The remaining 8% of the population are ethnic minority groups. These groups are located along the border areas and in the far west, and their numbers range from some 47,500 ethnic Buriats who live along the northern border to just 200 Dukha, the reindeer people of northern Khövsgöl aimag.

Before 1990 Russians constituted about 1.5% of Mongolia's population, though very few remain. The Russians were more tolerated than liked, but most Mongolians still have better things to say about the Russians than the Chinese, who are generally regarded with suspicion.

Wild East (2000), directed by Michael Haslund-Christensen, is the story of two young city traders doing what it takes to earn a living though the worst winter in living memory. It's both humbling and courageous.

Mongolia has the world's lowest population density at just 1.4 persons per sq km.

More Mongolians live outside Mongolia than in it. Around 3.5 million Mongolians live in China and nearly a million live in Russia. Descendents of Mongolian armies can still be found in Afghanistan and on the shores of the Caspian Sea.

SPORT

Mongolian sports – wrestling, horse racing and archery – are an extension of the military training used for centuries by Mongolian clans.

Wrestling is still the national pastime. The Mongolian version is similar to wrestling found elsewhere, except there are no weight divisions, so the biggest wrestlers (and they are big!) are often the best. Out on the steppes matches can go on for hours, but a time limit was recently implemented for the national Naadam (after a recent final round dragged on for four hours). Wrestlers now have 30 minutes to dump their opponent before a referee moves the match into something akin to 'penalty kicks' (the leading wrestler gets better position from the get go). The match will end only when the first wrestler falls, or when anything other than the soles of the feet or open palms touch the ground.

The biggest wrestling tournament is the national Naadam which has 512 contestants and is held in Ulaanbaatar, 11–12 July. Other tournaments are held throughout the year at the Wrestling Palace (p82).

Mongolia's second-biggest sport is horse racing. Jockeys – traditionally children between the ages of five and 12 years – race their horses over open countryside rather than around a track. Courses can be either 15km or 30km and are both exhausting and dangerous – every year jockeys tumble from their mounts and horses collapse and die from exhaustion at the finish line.

Winning horses are called *tümnii ekh,* or 'leader of 10,000'. Riders and spectators rush to comb the sweat off the best horses with a scraper traditionally made from a pelican's beak. The five winning riders must drink some special *airag* (fermented mare's milk), which is then often sprinkled on the riders' heads and on the horses' backsides. During the Naadam Festival, a song of empathy is also sung to the two-year-old horse that comes in last.

The last of the 'three manly sports' *(Eriin Gurvan Naadam)* is archery, which is actually performed by men and women alike. Archers use a bent composite bow made of layered horn, bark and wood. Usually arrows are made from willow and the feathers are from vultures and other birds of prey. After each shot, judges who stand near the target emit a short cry called *uukhai,* and raise their hands in the air to indicate the quality of the shot. The website www.atarn.org has several articles on Mongolian archery.

According to legend, the sport of polo began when Chinggis Khaan's troops batted the severed heads of their enemies across the steppes. Whether true or not, polo has recently been 're-born' in Mongolia with the help of foreign polo players. It hasn't quite caught fire yet, but there may be an exhibition in summer. Likewise, matches of polo on camelback are organised for some Gobi Naadams.

Basketball and other Western-style sports are increasing in popularity. There is now a professional basketball league in Ulaanbaatar and even at the most remote gers you'll find a backboard and hoop propped up on the steppe. Mongolia's best player, the 2.1m tall Sharavjampts, had a stint with Harlem Globetrotters and is now back in Ulaanbaatar where he has launched his own Globetrotter-style show team.

A Mongolian legend states, one Amazonian-type female entered a wrestling competition and thrashed her male competitors. In order to prevent such an embarrassing episode from happening again, the wrestling jacket was redesigned with an open chest, forcing women to sit on the sidelines.

RELIGION

Around 80% of Mongolians claim to be Buddhist of the Mahayana variety as practiced in Tibet. Some 5%, mainly Kazakhs living in the western Bayan-Ölgii aimeg (province), follow Islam. Approximately 5% claim to be Christians, Mongolia's fastest-growing religion, and around 10% are atheist (the creed of the former communist state). In the northern aim-ags of Khentii, Selenge, Bulgan and Khövsgöl, the Buddhism practiced is mixed with elements of shamanism. Freedom of religion has only opened up again since the fall of communism in 1990 and there is grow-ing competition between Buddhism and Christianity in both the city and rural areas.

Buddhism

The Mongols had limited contact with organised religion before their great empire of the 13th century. It was Kublai Khaan who first found himself with a court in which all philosophies of his empire were repre-sented, but it was a Tibetan Buddhist, Phagpa, who wielded the greatest influence on the Khaan.

It took centuries before Buddhism really took hold. In 1578 Altan Khaan, a descendant of Chinggis Khaan, met the Tibetan leader Sonam Gyatso, was converted, and subsequently bestowed on Sonam Gyatso the title Dalai Lama (*dalai* means 'ocean' in Mongolian). Sonam Gyatso was named as the third Dalai Lama and his two predecessors were named posthumously.

In 1924 when Bogd Khaan – the eighth Jebtzun Damba (reincarnated spiritual leader of Mongolia) – died, the communist government pre-vented a successor from being found. The years of repression to follow culminated in the spring of 1937 when the government dispatched its army to destroy religion in one fell swoop. Within a few months nearly all of Mongolia's 700 monasteries had been destroyed and some 17,000 monks arrested and never seen again.

It wasn't until the democracy movement took hold in 1990 that free-dom of religion was restored. Some ex-Communist Party officials have even become lamas and more than 160 monasteries have reopened, although some of them are little more than a part-time altar in a ger.

Two to three generations of Mongolians grew up without Buddhism. Most people no longer understand the Buddhist rituals or their mean-ings and the monasteries suffer from a chronic lack of trained Buddhist lamas, a problem that is currently being addressed by visiting theological teachers from Tibet, India and the West.

Islam

In Mongolia today, there is a significant minority of Sunni Muslims, most of them ethnic Kazakhs, who live primarily in Bayan-Ölgii. These Kazakhs have connections with Islamic groups in Turkey and several have been on a hajj to Mecca.

Christianity

Nestorian Christianity was part of the Mongol empire long before the Western missionaries arrived. These days, with poverty, unemployment, alcoholism, domestic violence and confusion in abundance, Christian missionaries, often from obscure fundamentalist sects, have been keenly seeking converts.

Mongolian authorities are wary of these missionaries, who sometimes come to the country under the pretext of teaching English. In Ulaanbaa-tar, there are now more than 50 non-Buddhist places of worship. Mor-mons, the most recognisable, have built modern churches in Ulaanbaatar, Nalaikh, Choibalsan, Erdenet and other cities. The Catholics, also here in large numbers, have constructed an enormous church on the eastern side of Ulaanbaatar.

Religions of Mongolia, by Walther Heissig, provides an in-depth look at the Buddhist and Shamanist faiths as they developed in Mongolia.

In 1903, when the British invaded Tibet, the 13th Dalai Lama fled to Mongolia and spent three years living in Urga's (Ulaan Baatar) Gandan Monastery.

The online magazine www.mongoliatoday.com has several interesting articles on Mongolian culture, religion, society and ethnography.

Shamanism

Whether shamanism is actually a religion is open to debate (there is no divine being or book of teachings), but it is a form of mysticism practiced by some Mongolians in the north, including the Dukha, Darkhad, Uriankhai and Buriats. It was the dominant belief system of Chinggis Khaan and the Mongol hordes but has now been pushed to the cultural fringes.

IMPORTANT FIGURES & SYMBOLS OF TIBETAN BUDDHISM

This is a brief guide to some of the deities of the Tibetan Buddhist pantheon. It is neither exhaustive nor scholarly, but it may help you to recognise a few of the statues you encounter in Mongolia. Sanskrit names are provided as these are most recognisable in the West; Mongolian names are in brackets.

The Characters

Sakyamuni The Historical Buddha was born in Lumbini in the 5th century BC in what is now southern Nepal. He attained enlightenment under a *bo* (pipal) tree and his teachings set in motion the Buddhist faith. Buddha is recognised by 32 marks on his body, including a dot between the eyes and a bump on the top of his blue hair. His right hand touches the earth in the witness *mudra*, or hand movement, and the left hand holds a begging bowl.

Maitreya (Maidar) The Future Buddha, Maitreya is passing the life of a Bodhisattva and will return to earth in human form 4000 years after the disappearance of Sakyamuni Buddha to take his place as the next earthly Buddha. He is normally seated with his hands by his chest in the mudra of 'turning the Wheel of Law'.

Avalokitesvara (Janraisig) The Glorious Gentle One, he is the Bodhisattva of Compassion and is either pictured with 11 heads and 1000 pairs of arms *(chogdanjandan janraisig)*, or in a white, four-armed manifestation *(chagsh janraisig)*. The Dalai Lama is considered an incarnation of Avalokitesvara.

Tara The Saviour, Tara has 21 different manifestations. She symbolises purity and fertility and is believed to be able to fulfil wishes. Statues of Tara usually represent Green Tara *(Nogoon Dar Ekh)*, who is associated with night, or White Tara *(Tsagaan Dar Ekh)*, who is associated with day. White Tara is the female companion of Avalokitesvara.

Four Guardian Kings Comprising Virupaksa (red; holding a snake), Dhitarastra (white; holding a lute), Virudhaka (blue; holding a sword) and Vaishravona (yellow; sitting on a snow lion), the kings are mostly seen guarding monastery entrances.

The Symbols & Objects

Prayer Wheel These are filled with up to a mile of prayers and are turned manually by pilgrims to gain merit. Wheels can be the size of a fist or the size of a small building, and are powered by hand, water and wind.

Wheel of Life It symbolises the earthly cycle of death and rebirth, held by Yama, the god of the Dead. The six sections of the circle are the six realms of rebirth ruled over by gods, titans, hungry ghosts, hell, animals and humans. Around this are the 12 experiences of earthly existence.

Stupas (suvrag) They were originally built to house the cremated relics of the historical Sakyamuni Buddha and as such have become a powerful symbol of Buddhism. Later stupas also became reliquaries for lamas and holy men.

Shamanism is based around the shaman – called a *bo* if a male, or *udgan* if a female – who has special medical and religious powers. If a shaman's powers are inherited, it is known as *udmyn*, or if the powers become apparent after a sudden period of sickness and apparitions it is known as *zlain*.

One of a shaman's main functions is to cure any sickness caused by the soul straying, and to accompany the soul of a dead person to the other world. Shamans act as intermediaries between the human and spirit worlds, and communicate with spirits during trances, which can last up to six hours.

Shamanism, which survived communism in large part because there were no books or buildings to destroy, has coexisted and intermixed with Buddhism in Mongolia and other parts of inner Asia for centuries. Pockets of shamanism are flourishing, particularly in the Khövsgöl and Dornod aimags, and among the Khoton people of Uvs.

Ovoos, the large piles of rocks found on mountain passes, are repositories of offerings for local spirits. Upon arriving at an *ovoo*, walk around it clockwise three times, toss an offering onto the pile (another rock should suffice) and make a wish.

ARTS

From prehistoric oral epics to the latest movie from MongolKino film studios in Ulaanbaatar, the many arts of Mongolia convey the flavour of nomadic life and the spirit of the land. Influenced by Tibet, China and Russia, Mongolia has nonetheless developed unique forms of music, dance, costume, painting, sculpture, drama, film, handicrafts, carpets and textiles.

There are several art and music festivals every year, one of the biggest being the **Roaring Hoofs Music Festival** (www.roaringhoofs.de). In late October you could check out the Altan Namar (Golden Autumn) festival, usually held at the circus.

For more information on the arts in Mongolia, contact the **Arts Council** (☎ 011-319 015; www.artscouncil.mn) in Ulaanbaatar.

Literature & Poetry

The heroic epics of the Mongols were all first committed to writing over 750 years ago. Later, Mongolia developed an enormous amount of Buddhist literature. Surprisingly, the National Library of Mongolia in Ulaanbaatar holds the world's largest single collection of Buddhist sutras.

Only recently have scholars translated into English the most important text of all – *Mongol-un nigucha tobchiyan (The Secret History of the Mongols)*. The text was lost for centuries until a Chinese copy was discovered in 1866 by the implausibly named Archimandrite Palladius, a Russian scholar-diplomat then resident in Beijing. Intriguing structural comparisons have been made between the *The Secret History of the Mongols* and the Bible, prompting theories that the Mongolian author was strongly influenced by the teachings of Nestorian Christianity.

The website www
.ulaanbaatar.net/culture
.shtml has links to the
National Art Gallery.

While fiction has never enjoyed much popularity, Mongolians have always been fond of poetry. Dashdorjiin Natsagdorj (1906–37) is Mongolia's best-known modern poet and playwright, and is regarded as the founder of Mongolian literature. His own writing included the dramatic nationalist poems *My Native Land* and *Star*, and his famous story, *Three Fateful Hills*, which was adapted into an opera that is still performed in Ulaanbaatar.

The most prolific poet to look out for is Danzan Ravjaa (1803–56), a monk from the Gobi desert known for his poems of wine and love. The best-known contemporary writer is O Dashbalbar, a nationalist, politician and xenophobe who died under mysterious circumstances in 2000.

Cinema

During communism, Mongolia had a vibrant film industry which was led by Moscow-trained directors who excelled at socialist realism. MongolKino's most famed directors, L Vangad and D Jigjid, directed many communist-era films including *Serelt* (Awakening), one of the all-time classics. This anti-Buddhist film described the life and times of a young Russian nurse sent to Mongolia to set up a hospital in a rural area. It starred Dorjpalam, the mother of Democratic leader Sanjaasurengiin Zorig. Other classic films that still bring a tear to the Mongol eye are *Tungalag Tamir* (directed by R Dorjpalam and Dolgorsuren) and *Sükhbaatar* (directed by I Heificth).

MongolKino fell on hard times when Soviet subsidies dried up after 1990. Directors and actors lost their jobs and Hollywood action films filled the void. After Richard Gere came to Mongolia with the Dalai Lama in 1995, the film *Pretty Woman* was watched almost religiously. The Mongolian film industry has only started to bounce back, buoyed by young film students that have gone to Western countries for training.

The biggest star of the new generation is Byambasuren Davaa, whose touching tale *The Weeping Camel* went from obscurity to award winner in 2004. Her next film, *Mongolian Dog*, is about a nomad family, their dog and reincarnation.

Mongolians are avid movie watchers. The best place to catch a film is the three-screen multiplex Tengis (p80), next to Liberty Square in Ulaanbaatar.

The Weeping Camel (2004), directed by D Byambasuren and Luigi Falomi, is a moving documentary about a camel that has rejected its offspring and how the family that owns them attempts to reconcile their differences.

Music
MODERN

Young Mongolians in Ulaanbaatar can now watch videos of Western music on cable TV, but they also enjoy listening to local groups, which sing in the Mongolian language but have definite Western influences. These include the dinosaurs of Mongolian rock, Kharanga; pop bands such as Chinggis Khaan; the sweet sounds of the popular female vocalists, Ariunna and Saraa; and the band Hurd, which mixes rock and ballads with Mongolia's national instrument, the *morin khuur* (horsehead fiddle). Recent years have seen a profusion of one-hit-wonder boy bands and hip hop acts; the latest big acts are Lumino and Tatar. Bands and singers perform live acts all the time, often at the UB Palace (p80), but on occasion at the Naadam stadium or some other outdoor venue. Most souvenir stores sell cassettes and compact discs of these and other Mongolian musicians.

Chinggis Blues (1999), directed by Roko and Adrian Belic, traces the inspirational journey of a blind American blues singer from San Francisco to Tuva to learn the secrets of *khöömii* (throat singing).

TRADITIONAL

Get an urbanised Mongolian into the countryside, and they will probably sing and tell you it is the beauty of the countryside that created the song on their lips. Mongolians sing to their animals: there are lullabies to coax sheep to suckle their lambs; songs to order a horse forward, make it stop or come closer; and croons to control a goat, to milk a cow or imitate a camel's cry.

Traditional music involves a wide range of instruments and uses for the human voice found almost nowhere else. Throat singing, or *khöömii*, found in Mongolia and neighbouring Tuva, is an eerie sound that involves the simultaneous production of multiple notes. See the boxed text (p216) for more details.

Another unique traditional singing style is *urtyn duu*. Sometimes referred to as 'long songs' because of the long trills, not because they are long songs (though some epics are up to 20,000 verses long), *urtyn-duu*

The website www .mongolart.mn has extensive information on dance, music, film, theatre and art. The site is supported by the Arts Council of Mongolia.

involves extraordinarily complicated, drawn-out vocal sounds, which relate traditional stories about love and the countryside. The late Norov-banzad is Mongolia's most famous long-song diva.

Several souvenir shops in Ulaanbaatar, including the State Department Store, sell recordings of traditional music. Anyone who takes a long-distance trip on public transport will hear impromptu Mongolian folk songs – normally when the transport breaks down.

Architecture

Constructing permanent buildings is contradictory to a nomadic society. Ulaanbaatar, largely a Soviet creation, is filled with Brezhnev-era apartment blocks and Stalinist government buildings. The only constructions that can be considered old are Buddhist temples, which were largely designed by Chinese and Tibetan architects between the 17th and 20th centuries. Traditional Mongolian architecture consists solely of the ger, a well-designed home for nomadic use.

Gers can be erected in about an hour and are easily packed up and moved. The circular shape and low roof are well suited to deflect wind. The door always faces south, also protection against the predominantly northern winds. The felt used to make the ger is traditionally made by the herders themselves, often in late summer, from the wool from their own flocks. At some ger camps, tourists sites and even the back of bank notes you might find gers set on giant wooden carts. Your guide may proudly explain that this was how the khaans moved around during the Imperial age, but recent findings have proven this to be a historical myth.

Painting & Sculpture

Much of Mongolian traditional art is religious in nature and is closely linked to Tibetan art. Traditional sculpture and scroll painting follows strict rules of subject, colour and proportion, leaving little room for personal expression. Tragically, most early examples of Mongolian art were destroyed during the communist regime. Gandan Monastery's master artist Purevbat has revived Buddhist art since the late 1990s, after receiving training from masters in India and Nepal.

Mongolian painting in the 20th century was dominated by socialist realism but has recently spread to embrace abstract styles. There is a vibrant modern-art scene in Ulaanbaatar. A couple of artists to look out for are M Erdenebayar and his abstract scenes of horses and S Saransatsralt whose conceptual paintings are occasionally provocative. Ancient beliefs and customs are often incorporated in the work of S Tugs-Oyun. More pieces can be found by following the links to Mongolian Masterpieces at www.khanbank.mn and clicking on community collections. In Ulaanbaatar you can see contemporary pieces at the Mongolian Artists' Exhibition Hall (p66) diagonally opposite the post office.

One of the most enduring images of communism was a socialist-realism painting of a young, wide-eyed Sükhbaatar meeting a lecturing Lenin. You may even see a copy of it in some offices. While many still assume the incident occurred, contemporary historians now disregard the story as mythical propaganda.

TRADITIONAL PAINTING & SCULPTURE

Mongolia's best-known painter was Balduugiyn Sharav (1869–1939). He spent his childhood in a monastery and later travelled all around the country. His most famous painting is *One Day in Mongolia*, which you can see in the Zanabazar Museum of Fine Arts (p61). It is *zurag* (painting), a classic work of Mongolian landscape storytelling, crowded with intricate sketches depicting just about every aspect of the Mongolian life, from felt-making to dung-collecting.

Zanabazar was a revered sculptor, politician, religious teacher, diplomat and Living Buddha. Many Mongolians refer to the time of Zanabazar's

The website www.uma.mn has links to virtually every member of Ulaanbaatar's artistic community.

life as Mongolia's Renaissance period. His most enduring legacy is the sensuous statues of the incarnation of compassion, the deity Tara. For more on the man, see p130.

Some of Zanabazar's bronze sculptures and paintings can be seen today in Ulaanbaatar's Gandan Khiid (p68), the Zanabazar Museum of Fine Arts (p61) and the Winter Palace of Bogd Khaan (p63).

SCROLL PAINTING

Religious scroll paintings *(thangka)* grace the inner sanctuaries and chanting halls of monasteries all over the country. They are tools of meditation, used by practitioners to visualise themselves developing the enlightened qualities of the deities depicted.

The website
www.mongols.com
has pages on art, music,
culture and religion.

Thangka cloth is traditionally made by stretching cotton on a frame and covering it with chalk, glue and *arkhi* (milk vodka). Colours are made from minerals mixed with yak-skin glue. Mongolian scroll paintings generally mirror the Tibetan variety, but you can notice distinctive regional features such as the introduction of camels, sheep and yaks in the background. Soviet-style scroll paintings were even produced at one stage, portraying the glorious working classes in *thangka*-style, as if they were religious figures.

Appliqué scroll paintings, made from Chinese silks, were popular at the turn of the 20th century. There are some fine examples in the Zanabazar Museum of Fine Arts (p61).

Environment

Mongolia is the sort of country that naturalists dream about. With the world's lowest population density, huge tracts of virgin landscape, minimal infrastructure, varied ecosystems and abundant wildlife, Mongolia is rightfully considered to hold the last bastion of unspoiled land in Asia. Mongolia's nomadic past, which did not require cities or infrastructure, along with Shamanic prohibitions against defiling the earth, have for centuries protected the country from overdevelopment.

Traditional beliefs, however, are always at odds with modern economics. The environmental situation started going downhill when the Soviets introduced mining, railways, factories and power plants, but compared with the disastrous environmental record evoked in China or neighbouring Central Asian countries such as Kazakhstan and Uzbekistan, Mongolia emerged from this period relatively unscathed. The new threat is capitalism. With no more subsidies coming from the USSR, Mongolia has spent the past 15 years looking for ways to earn revenue, and the easiest solution has been the sale of its resources. Consequently, its wildlife and landscape are now being degraded at an alarming rate, but there is hope among conservationists that ecotourism will provide a new direction for government fiscal policy.

Mongolia's Wild Heritage (1999), by Christopher Finch, was written in collaboration with the Mongolian Ministry of Nature & Environment. This outstanding book contains brief but relevant information on Mongolia's fragile ecology and contains excellent photos.

THE LAND

Mongolia is a huge and landlocked country. At 1,566,500 sq km in area, it's about three times the size of France, over twice the size of Texas, and almost as large as Queensland in Australia. Apart from the period of Mongol conquest under Chinggis Khaan and Kublai Khaan, Mongolia was until the 20th century about twice its present size. A large chunk of Siberia was once part of Mongolia, but it is now securely controlled by Russia, and Inner Mongolia is now firmly part of China.

The southern third of Mongolia is dominated by the Gobi Desert, which stretches into China. Only the southern sliver of the Gobi is 'Lawrence of Arabia–type desert' with cliffs and sand dunes. The rest is desert steppe and has sufficient grass to support scattered herds of sheep, goats and camels. There are also areas of desert steppe in low-lying parts of western Mongolia.

Much of the rest of Mongolia is covered by grasslands. Stretching over about 20% of the country, these steppes are home to vast numbers of gazelle, birdlife and livestock. The central, northern and western aimags (provinces), amounting to about 25% of Mongolia, are classed as mountain forest steppe. Home to gazelle and saiga antelope, they have relatively large numbers of people and livestock.

Mongolia is also one of the highest countries in the world, with an average elevation of 1580m. In the far west are Mongolia's highest mountains, the Mongol Altai Nuruu, which are permanently snow-capped. The highest peak, Tavan Bogd Uul (4374m), has a magnificent glacier towering over Mongolia, Russia and China. Between the peaks are stark but beautiful deserts where rain almost never falls.

The far northern areas of Khövsgöl and Khentii aimags are essentially the southern reaches of Siberia and are covered by larch and pine forests known by the Russian word *taiga*.

Near the centre of Mongolia is the Khangai Nuruu range, with its highest peak, Otgontenger Uul, reaching 3905m. On the northern slope

Roy Chapman Andrews wrote several excellent books on Mongolia's flora and fauna following his research expeditions across the country in the early 1920s. Look out for his classic titles *Across Mongolian Plains* and *On the Trail of Ancient Man*.

of these mountains is the source of the Selenge Gol, Mongolia's largest river, which flows northward into Lake Baikal in Siberia. While the Selenge Gol is the largest in terms of water volume, the longest river is the Kherlen Gol in eastern Mongolia.

Just to the northeast of Ulaanbaatar is the Khentii Nuruu, the highest mountain range in eastern Mongolia and by far the most accessible to hikers. It's a heavily forested region with meandering rivers and impressive peaks, the highest being Asralt Khairkhan Uul (2800m). The range provides a major watershed between the Arctic and Pacific oceans.

Mongolia has numerous saltwater and freshwater lakes, which are great for camping, bird-watching, hiking, swimming and fishing. The most popular is the magnificent Khövsgöl Nuur, the second-oldest lake in the world, which contains 65% of Mongolia's (and 2% of the world's) fresh water. The largest is the low-lying, saltwater lake Uvs Nuur.

Other geological and geographical features include caves (some with ancient rock paintings), dormant volcanoes, hot and cold mineral springs, the Orkhon Khürkhree (Orkhon Waterfall), the Great Lakes Depression in western Mongolia and the Darkhad Depression west of Khövsgöl Nuur.

Conservation Ink has produced two excellent information pages on Altai Tavan Bogd National Park and Khövsgöl Nuur National Park, complete with photos and brief introductions to these ecosystems. Both are available in PDF format; click on www.conservationink.org and follow the links.

WILDLIFE

In Mongolia, the distinction between the domestic and wild (or untamed) animal is often blurry. Wild and domesticated horses and camels mingle on the steppes with wild asses and herds of wild gazelles. In the mountains there are enormous, horned wild argali sheep and domesticated yaks along with wild moose, musk deer and roe deer. Reindeer herds are basically untamed, but strangely enough they can be ridden and are known to return to the same tent each night for a salt-lick.

Animals

Wildlife flourishes in Mongolia despite a number of impediments: an extreme climate, the nomadic fondness for hunting, the communist persecution of Buddhists who had set aside areas as animal sanctuaries, and a penniless government that lacks the political will to police nature-

THE GREAT ZUD

The winters of 1999–2000 to 2001–02 were the coldest and longest in living memory. They were classed as *zud*, a Mongolian word that can mean any condition that stops livestock getting to grass; in this case heavy snowfall and an impenetrable ice cover. Unusually early snowfalls compounded an earlier summer drought and rodent infestation, which left animals emaciated and pastures degraded before winter even hit. Other causes for the *zud* trace back 10 years; it was the move towards capitalism that promoted the boom in livestock that caused overgrazing, leaving pastures tired and depleted. After three seasons of bad winter the livestock population plummeted from 33 million to 24 million.

In the worst-hit areas of Dundgov, Bayankhongor, Arkhangai and Övörkhangai, herders lost between a quarter and half of their livestock (their only form of income, food, fuel, security – almost everything in fact). The disaster was equal to the great *zud* of 1944, when 7.5 million livestock were lost, but at that time herders had the safety net of the communist collective. During the recent freeze, only a handful of international agencies came to the aid of the herders.

Some analysts have suggested that the disaster was exacerbated by the inexperience of numerous new herders, who chose not to embark on the traditional month-long trek *(otor)*, which takes herders to other pastures in autumn. Tragically it was the poorest herders who were the most affected, just when they least needed it.

protection laws. Your chances of seeing some form of wildlife are good, though the closest you will realistically get to a snow leopard, argali sheep or moose is in a museum.

Despite the lack of water in the Gobi, some species (many of which are endangered) somehow survive. These include the wild camel *(khavt-gai)*, wild ass *(khulan)*, Gobi argali sheep *(argal)*, Gobi bear *(mazaalai)*, ibex *(yangir)* and black-tailed gazelle *(khar suult zeer)*. In the wide open steppe, you may see the rare saiga antelope, Mongolian gazelle, several species of jerboa rodent (endemic to Central Asia) and millions of furry marmots *(tarvag)* busy waking up after the last hibernation, or preparing for their next.

Further north in the forests live the wild boar, brown bear *(khuren baavgai)*, roe deer, wolf *(chono)*, reindeer *(tsaa buga)*, elk *(khaliun buga)*, musk deer and moose, as well as plenty of sable *(bulga)* and lynx *(shiluus)* whose furs, unfortunately, are in high demand. Most of the mountains are extremely remote, thus providing an ideal habitat for argali sheep, ibex, very rare snow leopards *(irbis)* and smaller mammals such as the fox, ermine and hare.

Mongolians consider wolf parts and organs to contain curative properties. The meat and lungs are good for respiratory ailments, the intestines aid in digestion, powdered wolf rectum can sooth the pain of haemorrhoids and hanging a wolf tongue around ones neck will cure gland and thyroid ailments.

BIRDS
Mongolia is home to 449 recorded species of bird. In the desert you may see the desert warbler, McQueen's bustard and saxaul sparrow, as well as sandgrouse, finches and the cinereous vulture *(tas)*.

On the steppes, you will certainly see the most charismatic bird in Mongolia – the demoiselle crane *(övögt togoruu)* – as well as the hoopoe *(övöölj)*, the odd falcon *(shonkhor)*, vulture *(yol)*, and golden and steppe eagles *(bürged)*. Other steppe species include the upland buzzard, black kite and some assorted owls and hawks *(sar)*. Some black kites will even swoop down and catch pieces of bread in midair if your throw the pieces high enough. These magnificent raptors, perched majestically on a rock by the side of the road, will rarely be disturbed by your jeep or the screams of your guide ('Look. Eagle!! Bird!! We stop?') but following the almost inaudible click of your lens cap, these birds will move and almost be in China before you have even thought about apertures.

The website wcs.org/sw-around_the_globe/Asia/mongolia has details on the Wildlife Conservation Society projects in eastern Mongolia, and its efforts to track the movements and habitat of the gazelle.

In the mountains, you may be lucky to spot species of ptarmigan, buntings, woodpecker, owl and the endemic Altai snowcock *(khoilog)*. The lakes of the west and north are visited by Dalmatian pelicans, hooded cranes, relict gulls and bar-headed geese.

Eastern Mongolia has the largest breeding population of cranes, including the hooded and Siberian varieties and the critically endangered white-naped crane, of which only 4500 remain in the wild.

FISH
Rivers such as the Selenge, Orkhon, Zavkhan, Balj, Onon and Egiin, as well as dozens of lakes, including Khövsgöl Nuur, hold 76 species of fish. They include trout, grayling *(khadran)*, roach, lenok *(eebge)*, Siberian sturgeon *(khilem)*, pike *(tsurkhai)*, perch *(algana)*, the endemic Altai osman and the enormous taimen, a Siberian relative of the salmon, which can grow up to 1.5m long and weigh 50kg.

American actress Julia Roberts stepped out of her usual star-studded element in 2000 and hosted a documentary on the horses and nomad culture of Mongolia. The programme was filmed by Tigress Productions (UK) and can be viewed at the Khustain Nuruu information centre (p104).

ENDANGERED SPECIES
According to conservationists, 28 species of mammals are endangered in Mongolia. The more commonly known species are the wild ass, wild camel, Gobi argali sheep, Gobi bear and ibex; others include otters, wolves, saiga antelopes and some species of jerboa. The red deer is also

---

THE FIVE SNOUTS

Mongolians define themselves as the 'people of five animals' *(tavan kosighu mal)*: horses, cattle (including yaks), sheep, goats and Bactrian camels. The odd one out is the reindeer, which is herded in small numbers by the Dukha or Tsaatan people *(tsaa* means 'reindeer') near the Siberian border. Chickens and pigs are rare in Mongolia. A rough ratio exists for the relative values of the five animals: a horse is worth five to seven sheep or seven to 10 goats. A camel is worth 1.5 horses.

The horse *(mor)* is the pride of Mongolia and there are few nomads, if any, who haven't learned to ride as soon as they can walk. Mongolian horses are shorter than those in other countries (don't call them ponies – Mongolians will be offended). They provide perfect transport, can endure harsh winters and, importantly, produce that much-loved Mongolian beverage: fermented mare's milk, or *airag*. Mongolians have over 300 different words to describe the country's two million horses, mostly relating to colouring.

Together, cows *(ükher)* and yaks *(sarlag)* number around 1.8 million, and are used for milk and meat (especially *borts*, which is dried and salted meat) and for their hides. Most yaks are actually a cross between a yak and cow, known as a *hainag* in Mongolian, as these supply more milk than thoroughbred yaks.

Fat-tailed sheep *(khon)* are easy to herd and provide wool for housing, felt, clothes, carpets and meat (the ubiquitous mutton) – every nomadic family wants to own at least a few sheep. Goats *(yamaa)* are popular for their meat and, especially, for cashmere wool. There are around 10.8 million sheep and 10.7 million goats in Mongolia.

Camels *(temee)* are used for long-distance (though slow) transport, and once crossed Mongolia in large caravans. They're valuable for their adaptability and their wool, and number about 257,000. White camels are particularly auspicious.

---

in dire straights; over the past 18 years its numbers have fallen from 130,000 to just 8000 and are falling. Brown bears have been also been hit hard by poachers – in October 2000, Vietnamese smugglers were caught trying to leave Mongolia with 80 brown bear gall bladders (each worth up to US$200).

There are 59 species of endangered birds, including many species of hawk, falcon, buzzard, crane and owl. Despite Mongolian belief that it's bad luck to kill a crane, the elegant white-naped crane is threatened with extinction due to habitat loss. German ornithologists have recently conducted surveys on the white-naped crane, of which there are just 5000 breeding pairs left in the wild. The best place to see them is in Dornod's Mongol Daguur Strictly Protected Area.

Every year the government allows up to 300 falcons to be captured and sold abroad; the major buyers are the royal families of Kuwait and the United Arab Emirates. On top of this, unknown numbers of other falcons (possibly in their hundreds) are illegally smuggled out of the country.

One good news story is the resurrection of the *takhi* wild horse. The *takhi* was actually extinct in the wild in the 1960s. It has been successfully reintroduced into three nature reserves after an extensive breeding program overseas. For more on the *takhi* see p103.

The *takhi* (wild horse) also goes by the name Przewalski's horse. It was named after Colonel Nikolai Przewalski, an officer in the Russian Imperial Army, who made the horses' existence known to Europe after an exploratory expedition to Central Asia in 1878.

In preserved areas of the mountains, about 1000 snow leopards remain. They are hunted for their pelts (which are also part of some shamanist and Buddhist traditional practises), as are the snow leopards' major source of food, the marmot. For details on the attempt to save the snow leopard see p198.

Every year the government sells licences to hunt 300 ibex and 40 argali sheep, which are both endangered species, netting the government over US$500,000.

Plants

Mongolia can be roughly divided into three zones: grassland and shrubland (55% of the country); forests, which only cover parts of the mountain forest steppe (8%); and desert vegetation (35%). Less than 1% of the country is used for human settlements and crop cultivation. Grasslands are used extensively for grazing and, despite the vast expanses, overgrazing is not uncommon.

Forests of Siberian larch (sometimes up to 45m high), Siberian and Scotch pine, and white and ground birch cover parts of northern Mongolia.

In the Gobi the saxaul shrub covers millions of hectares and is essential in anchoring the desert sands and preventing degradation and erosion. Saxaul takes a century to grow to around 4m in height, creating wood so dense that it sinks in water.

Khentii aimag and some other parts of central Mongolia are famous for the effusion of red, yellow and purple wildflowers, mainly rhododendrons and edelweiss. Extensive grazing is the major threat to Mongolia's flowers, trees and shrubs: over 200 species are endangered.

Mongolians collect various wild herbs and flowers for their medicinal properties. Yellow poppies are used to heal wounds, edelweiss adds vitamins to the blood, and feather grass will cure an upset stomach.

NATIONAL PARKS

The Ministry of Nature & Environment (MNE) and its Protected Areas Bureau (PAB) control the national park system with a tiny annual budget of around US$100,000. This is clearly not enough, but through substantial financial assistance and guidance from international governments and nongovernmental organisations, the animals, flora and environment in some parts of the country are being preserved. Unfortunately, in many protected areas the implementation of park regulations are weak, if not nonexistent.

The MNE classifies protected areas into four categories. In order of importance, they are:

National Parks Places of historical and educational interest; fishing and grazing by nomadic people is allowed and parts of the park are developed for ecotourism.

Natural & Historical Monuments Important places of historical and cultural interest; development is allowed within guidelines.

Natural Reserves Less important regions protecting rare species of flora and fauna, and archaeological sites; some development is allowed within certain guidelines.

Strictly Protected Areas Very fragile areas of great importance; hunting, logging and development is strictly prohibited and there is no established human influence.

The Academy of Natural Sciences web page has a section on Mongolia (www.acnatsci.org/research/mongolia/index .html) that has details on ecology projects near Khövsgöl Nuur National Park.

The 54 protected areas in Mongolia now constitute an impressive 13.5% of the country. The strictly protected areas of Bogdkhan Uul, Great Gobi and Uvs Nuur Basin are biosphere reserves included in Unesco's Man and Biosphere Project.

At the time of independence in 1990, some proposed that the *entire country* be turned into a national park, but the government settled on 30% (potentially creating the world's largest park system). This goal, however, has stalled since 2000 as a direct result of the MPRP-led government's failure to see more land placed under protection. The expansion of mining operations and the sale of mining rights have taken precedence.

The area around Bogdkhan Uul, near Ulaanbaatar, was protected from hunting and logging as early as the 12th century, and was officially designated as a national park in 1778.

Permits

To visit these parks – especially a strictly protected area, national parks and some national monuments – you will need a permit, either from the local PAB office, or from rangers at the entrances to the parks. The permits are little more than an entrance fee, but they are an important source of revenue for the maintenance of the parks.

Entrance fees are set at T3000 per foreigner and T300 per Mongolian (although guides and drivers are often excluded).

If you are not able to get a permit and are found in a park without one, the worst penalty you're likely to suffer is being asked to leave or pay a fine to the park ranger.

If you think you might need permits for conducting research in a park, it's best to contact the MNE's **Protected Areas Bureau** (PAB; ☎ 011-326 617; fax 011-328 620; Ministry of Nature & the Environment, Baga Toiruu 44, Ulaanbaatar). The ministry is just behind the Ulaanbaatar Hotel.

ENVIRONMENTAL ISSUES

Mongolia's natural environment remains in good shape compared with that of many Western countries. The country's small population and nomadic subsistence economy have been its environmental salvation.

However, it does have its share of problems. Communist production quotas put pressure on grasslands to yield more crops and support more livestock than was sustainable. The rise in the number of herders and livestock through the 1990s has wreaked havoc on the grasslands; some 70% of pastureland is degraded and around 80% of plant species near village centres have disappeared.

While browsing through Ulaanbaatar souvenir shops keep an eye out for two great ecology books: *Lake Khövsgöl National Park – A Visitor's Guide* (1997), published by Discovery Initiatives, and *The Gobi Gurvansaikhan National Park*, written by Bernd Steinhauer-Burkart.

Forest fires, nearly all of which are caused by careless human activity, are common during the windy spring season. The fires destroy huge tracts of forest and grassland, mainly in Khentii and Dornod aimags. In 1996 alone around 80,000 sq km of land was scorched, causing up to US$1.9 billion in damages.

Other threats to the land include mining (there are over 300 mines), which has polluted 28 river basins in eight aimags. The huge Oyu Tolgoi mine in Ömnögov will require the use of 360 litres of water *per second*, which environmentalists say might not be sustainable. China's insatiable appetite for minerals and gas is opening up new mines, but the bigger threat is China's hunt for the furs, meat and body parts of endangered animals. Chinese demand results in the killing each year of 2000 musk deer and well over 200,000 marmots.

RESPONSIBLE ECO-TOURISM

Mongolia's environment, flora and fauna are precious. Decades of Soviet exploitation, urban sprawl and development have greatly affected the ecology; Mongolia does not need tourism to exacerbate the problems. Please bear the following pointers in mind as you travel around the country. If camping and/or hiking, please note the boxed text on p230.

- In protected areas or areas of natural beauty try to keep to existing jeep tracks rather than pioneering new trails, which quickly degenerate into an eroded mess.

- Patronise travel companies and ger camps that you feel advance sustainable development, safe waste management, water conservation and fair employment practices.

- When on a jeep trip have a designated rubbish bag. Make an effort to carry out rubbish left by others.

- Don't buy goods made from endangered species.

- Do not engage in or encourage hunting. It is illegal in all parks and reserves.

- Don't spend all your money with one company (easily done on a tour) but spread your money through the economy. Support local services, guides and initiatives.

- When fishing, buy a permit and practice standard 'catch and release' policy. Use barbless hooks.

Urban sprawl, coupled with a demand for wood to build homes and to use as heating and cooking fuel, is slowly reducing the forests. This destruction of the forests has also lowered river levels, especially the Tuul Gol near Ulaanbaatar. In recent years the Tuul has actually gone dry in the spring months due to land mismanagement and improper water use.

Large-scale infrastructure projects are further cause for concern. The 18m-tall Dörgön hydropower station, currently being built on the Chon Khairkh Gol in Khovd, will submerge canyons and pastures. Conservationists are also concerned about the 'Millennium Rd', which is being built without the completion of environmental impact studies. Its completion is sure to increase mining and commerce inside fragile ecosystems. The eastern grasslands, one of the last great open spaces in Asia, will come under particular threat.

Air pollution is becoming a serious problem, especially in Ulaanbaatar. At the top of Zaisan Memorial in the capital, a depressing layer of dust and smoke from the city's three thermal power stations can be seen hovering over the city. This layer is often appalling in winter, when all homes are continuously burning fuel and the power stations are working overtime. Ulaanbaatar has also suffered from acid rain, and pollution is killing fish in the nearby Tuul Gol in central Mongolia.

The World Wide Fund for Nature website at www.wwf.mn has relevant news on the environment and topical information that affects the country. It also includes statistics, data and conservation threats.

Food & Drink

The culinary masters of Mongolia's barren steppes have always put more stock in survival than taste. Mongolian food is therefore a hearty, if somewhat bland, array of meat and dairy products. Out in the countryside, potatoes are often considered exotic, leavened bread a treat and spices a cause for concern.

The reasons for this stem from the constraints of a nomadic lifestyle. Nomads cannot reasonably transport an oven, and so are prevented from producing baked goods. Nor can nomads plant, tend to or harvest fruits, vegetables, spices or grains. Nomads can, however, eat the food that their livestock produces.

Mongolian food is seasonal. In the summer months, when animals can provide milk, dairy products become the staple food. Meat (and copious amounts of fat) takes over in winter, supplemented with flour in some form and potatoes or rice if these are available.

Flour and tea were only introduced into the Mongolian staples after the Mongols established trade links with China. The Chinese have been particularly influential in Inner Mongolia (now in China), where the mixing of cuisines resulted in 'Mongolian barbeque', a dish that is unheard of in Mongolia itself.

Menus have been expanding over the past decade, thanks to the government-sponsored 'Green Revolution', which allows urbanites to grow vegetables in small, private garden plots. The opening of markets has brought in packaged and processed food products, as well as international restaurants; the vast array of good foreign-owned restaurants in Ulaanbaatar comes as a pleasant surprise to visitors expecting a mostly muttonish diet.

Imperial Mongolian Cooking: Recipes from the Kingdoms of Ghengis Khan (2001), by Marc Cramer, describes a variety of recipes from Mongolia, China, Central Asia and other lands that were once part of the Mongol Empire. Many recipes are from the author's grandfather, who worked as a chef in Siberia.

STAPLES & SPECIALTIES

Almost any Mongolian dish can be created with meat, rice, flour and potatoes. Most meals consist of bread *(talkh)* in the towns and cities and *bortzig* (fried unleavened bread) in the gers, and the uncomplicated *shuulte khool* (literally, soup with food) – a meal involving hot broth, pasta slivers, boiled mutton and a few potato chunks.

Buuz (steamed mutton dumplings) and *khuushuur* (fried mutton pancakes) are two of the most popular menu options you'll find in restaurants. *Buuz*, similar to Chinese *baoza* or Tibetan *momo*, are steamed pasta shells filled with mutton and sometimes slivers of onion or garlic. Miniature *buuz*, known as *bansh*, are usually dunked in milk tea. *Khuushuur* are best if prepared in the form of small meat envelopes, but are less tasty if squashed into a pancake.

Traveller Dan Bennett describes his adventures dining with a Mongolian family, and the challenges of eating sheep's head, at www.fotuva.org/travel/potato.html.

Other dishes include *tsuivan*, lightly steamed flour slices with meat, and *khuurag* (fried food), which can be prepared with rice (*buudatei khuurag*) or vegetables (*nogotei khuurag*).

The classic Mongolian dinner staple is referred to simply as '*makh*', or meat, which consists of boiled bones, fat, indiscernible organs and the skull, all sent swimming in a plastic bucket. This is still the most common food in rural areas, but is eaten less frequently in the cities.

The other main highlight of Mongolian cuisine is *khorkhog*, made by placing hot stones from the fire into a pot or milk urn with chopped sheep, some water and sometimes vodka. The container is then sealed and left on an open fire. When eating this meal, it is customary to pass the hot, greasy rocks from hand to hand, as this is thought to be good for your health.

Dried meat *(borts)* is very popular among Mongolians, and many jeep drivers like to take it on long-distance trips to add to soups.

Mongolians don't concern themselves much with breakfast; a bowl of hot milk tea *(süütei tsai)* and some pieces of fried unleavened bread *(bortzig)* will usually suffice. Deserts are equally uncommon, although *süütei budaa*, made from rice, sugar and milk, is an occasional treat.

In summer, you can subsist as the Mongols do on dairy products, or white foods *(tsagaan idee)*: yogurt, milk, fresh cream, cheese and fermented milk drinks.

Milk *(süü)* may be cow, sheep or goat milk and the yogurt *(tarag)* is always delicious. *Khoormog* is yogurt made from camel's milk. When you visit a ger you will be offered some dairy snacks, such as dried milk curds *(aaruul)*, which are as hard as a rock and often about as tasty. You may also be served a very sharp soft, fermented cheese called *aarts*. *Tsötsgiin tos* is butter.

The well-researched www.9v.com/crystal /kerij-e/docs/cooking.htm includes historical notes on Mongolian cuisine, plus cooking techniques and recipes to dispel the myth that Mongolian menus stop at 'boiled mutton'.

DRINKS
Nonalcoholic Drinks

Mongolians are big tea drinkers and they will almost never start a meal until they've had a cup of tea first, as it aids digestion. However, Mongolian tea *(tsai* in Mongolian; *shay* in Kazakh) tends to be of the lowest quality. In fact, it's mostly 'tea waste', which is made up of stems and rejected leaves that are processed into a 'brick'.

A classic Mongolian drink is milk tea with salt *(süütei tsai)*. The taste varies by region; in Bayan-Ölgii you may even get a dollop of butter in your tea, similar to the stuff prepared in Tibet. If you can't get used to the salty tea, try asking for black tea *(khar tsai)*, which is like European tea, with sugar and no milk. (The word 'Lipton' is often understood and used in restaurants as an alternative to black tea.)

Scientists claim that drinking a few cups of *airag* (fermented mare's milk) on a consistent basis can improve health, clear the skin and sharpen the eyesight.

TRAVEL YOUR TASTEBUDS

One taste of fresh *öröm* (sometimes called *üürag*) and you'll soon find yourself scraping away at the bottom of the bowl. This rich, sweet tasting cream is made by warming fresh cow's milk in a pot and then letting it sit under a cover for one day. Yak milk (which contains twice as much fat as cow milk) will make an even sweeter cream. Another excellent treat, available in summer, is Mongolian blueberry jam. Most regions produce a sour version but the blueberries from around Khövsgöl Nuur are as sweet and tasty as you'll find anywhere.

We Dare You

Bodog is not for the faint of heart. This authentic 'Mongolian barbeque' first involves pulling the innards out of the neck of a goat or marmot. The carcass is then stuffed full of scalding rocks and the neck cinched up with wire. The bloated animal is then thrown upon a fire (or blowtorched) to burn the fur off the outside while the meat is cooked from within. Like most things involving a blowtorch, preparing *bodog* is true men's work. Furthering the adventure, it's worth noting that the bubonic plague, or Black Death as it was known to medieval Europe, can be passed by handling marmot skins. There is less of a chance of catching the disease between mid August and mid October.

Other regional delicacies include *kazy*, the salted horsemeat sausages prepared by Kazakhs in Bayan-Ölgii aimag. Gobi people occasionally eat camel meat; the cut might be a bit gamey as it is the older camels that are usually killed for their meat.

Alcoholic Drinks

Mongolians can drink you under the table if you challenge them. There is much social pressure to drink, especially on males – those who refuse to drink vodka *(arkhi)* are considered wimps. The Russians can be thanked for this attitude, which started in the 1970s.

Locally produced beer labels such as Chinggis and Khan Brau are growing in popularity as most young people consider it trendier to drink beer rather than go blind on the hard stuff preferred by their fathers and grandfathers. Korean beer companies, Hite and Cass, have opened up bottling factories in Ulaanbaatar and imported brews such as Heineken are also popular.

While it may not seem obvious at first, every countryside ger doubles as a tiny brewery or distillery. One corner of the ger usually contains a tall, thin jug with a plunger that is used for fermenting mare's milk, known as *airag* or *koumiss*, with an alcohol content of about 3%.

Although you aren't likely to get drunk from *airag* alone, many Mongolians distil it further to produce *shimiin arkhi*, which boosts the alcohol content to around 12%. Go easy on the *airag* from the start or your guts will pay for it later.

> Because of his failing health, the advisors of Ögedei Khaan (a son of Chinggis) suggested that he halve the number of cups of alcohol he drank per day. Ögedei readily agreed, then promptly ordered that his cups be doubled in size.

CELEBRATIONS

Tsagaan Sar, the Mongolian New Year, is a festival for a new beginning. Everything about the holiday is symbolic of happiness, joy and prosperity in the coming year, and it is food that represents many of these rites.

Mongolians are an optimistic lot – a full belly during Tsagaan Sar represents prosperity in the year ahead; *buuz* (mutton dumplings) in their thousands are therefore prepared and consumed during the holiday. Likewise, the central meal of the holiday must be the biggest sheep a family can afford to buy; pride is at stake in how much fat will appear on the table.

The *buuz* itself carries one of the most important symbols of the holiday – one dumpling will hide a special silver coin that represents wealth to the lucky individual who finds it (watch your teeth!).

During Tsagaan Sar, food even plays a role in the decoration, as the centrepiece is made from layers of large biscuits called *ul boov*. Young people stack three layers of biscuits, middle-aged folk five layers and grandparents seven layers. Littering the table are chocolates and boiled sweets, decorations and the sheep itself, representing wealth in the year ahead.

> Mongolia has about 175 distilleries and 27 breweries; drink with caution as some 11% of these places regularly fail health quality inspections.

WHERE TO EAT & DRINK

The most basic Mongolian eatery is the ubiquitous *guanz* (Гуанз), or canteen. *Guanz* are usually found in buildings, gers or even in train wagons, and can be found in most aimag towns, all over Ulaanbaatar and along major roads where there is some traffic. They usually offer soup, *süütei tsai* and either *buuz* or *khuushuur*.

In the countryside, the ger-*guanz* is a great way to see the interior of a ger and meet a family, without the lengthy stops and traditions expected with normal visits.

In the countryside most *guanz* seem to close for dinner (and often lunch as well). In reality, opening hours are often at the whim of staff. The city *guanz*, which is a good option for budget travellers or people in a hurry, will sometimes masquerade under more alluring names, including *tsainii gazar* (tea house). Some of the ones on main streets now stay open 24 hours, but the usual hours are 10am to 7pm.

> A chunk of salt inside your *buuz* during Tsagaan Sar means safety and protection. If too much flour is used when preparing the dumplings, and there are leftovers, it's a sign that the family will have enough clothing in the year ahead.

ULAANBAATAR'S TOP FIVE EATERIES

- **Silk Road Bar & Grill** (p78) European-style menu, with wonderful chicken shish kebabs.
- **Chin Van Khanddorjiin Örgöö** (p75) Lavish ger restaurant.
- **Millie's Café** (p76) Western snacks.
- **Ikh Khuraldai** (p76) Mongolian/German inspired menu.
- **Shashlyk stands** (p78) Shashlyk cooked by an Uzbek chef, opposite the Wrestling Palace or Mongolian Artists Exhibition Hall.

Most restaurants are too expensive for the average Mongolian and frequented only during special occasions. Mongolians don't mind blowing an entire week's salary on a good meal, so long as they are enjoying it with friends or family.

Restaurants, usually open 10am to 10pm daily, are nearly always more hygienic than the *guanz* and therefore a good choice for children and families. You will probably be assigned an overly attentive waiter or waitress who will polish your silverware to perfection and pour your drinks. In Ulaanbaatar, many restaurants – especially the good ones – will be busy and often full between about 1pm and 2pm. It pays to get a table before 12.30pm to beat the rush.

Menus are usually in Cyrillic but use the decoder on p49 and point to what you want. Listed menu items are often not available, *'baikhgui'* ('we don't have any') so you may need to make a few attempts.

Three words often understood by Mongolian waiters and cooks are 'beefsteak' (a large mutton mince patty, often topped with a fried egg), 'schnitzel' and 'goulash'. These are served with mashed potato, rice or pickled vegetables. There's often a long list of salads, of which cabbage and potato salads will be available. Bread or *mantuu*, a doughy steamed bread roll similar to the Chinese *mantou*, are normally available.

Quick Eats

The concept of the street café is new in Mongolia and many Mongolians feel awkward about eating on the pavement, where, they claim, car exhaust and dust can pollute their meal. Likewise, Mongolians don't eat while on the go, with the exception of ice cream.

Some Mongolians, however, have warmed to the idea of *shashlyk* (grilled meat kebabs). This delicious snack, served with bread and slices of onion and cucumber, is usually prepared by expat Uzbeks, but only in summer. While they may look very tempting, avoid the more itinerant-looking *shashlyk* sellers as their meat is often low grade or old.

VEGETARIANS & VEGANS

Mongolia is a difficult, but not impossible, place for vegetarians. If you don't eat meat, you can get by in Ulaanbaatar, but in the countryside you will need to take your own supplements and preferably a petrol stove. Vegetables other than potatoes, carrots and onions are rare, relatively expensive and usually pickled in jars, so the best way for vegetarians to get protein is from the wide range of dairy products. In aimag capitals you can patch together a meal by poking around the shops. In villages you should be able to track down instant noodles and hot water.

Vegans will either have to be completely self-sufficient, or be prepared to modify their lifestyle for a while.

William of Rubruck's description of 13th-century Mongolian cuisine is at http://depts.washington.edu/uwch/silkroad/culture/food/rubruck2.html. Based on his writings, it would seem the Mongol have been partial to a drink for the last 750 years.

HABITS & CUSTOMS

While traditions and customs do surround the dinner table, Mongolian meals are generally casual affairs and there is little need to be overly concerned about offending your hosts.

In a ger in the countryside, traditional meals such as boiled mutton do not require silverware or even plates; just trawl around the bucket of bones until a slab catches your fancy. Eat with your fingers and try to nibble off as much meat and fat as possible; Mongolians can pick a bone clean and consider leftovers to be wasteful. There'll be a buck knife to slice off larger chunks. A common rag will appear at the end of the meal for you to wipe off the grease (have a bandana ready if you are fussy about hygiene).

Most other meals in the rest of Mongolia are eaten with bowls, knives, forks and spoons. Chopsticks haven't been used in Mongolia since the early 20th century and few Mongolians can use them. Food is always passed with the right hand.

It is always polite to bring something to contribute to the meal; drinks are easiest, or in the countryside you could offer a bag of rice or sweets for desert. 'Bon Appetite' in Mongolian is *saikhan khool loorai*.

Meals are occasionally interrupted for a round of vodka. Before taking a swig, a short ritual is employed to honour the sky gods and the four directions. There is no one way of doing this, but it usually involves dipping the left ring finger into the vodka and flicking into the air four times before wiping your finger across your forehead.

It is not easy to convince a Mongolian that you don't want to drink alcohol. Rather than making excuses it is much easier to just go through the motions and put the cup to your lips, sipping as much as you can bear. Pass the cup back to your host and allow him to polish off what remains in the cup.

The woman of the household may offer you a variety of small food items. Try to taste everything you have been offered. An empty bowl is a sign to the host that you want more food. If you are full, just leave a little bit at the bottom of the bowl. If you are eating with Kazakhs, covering the bowl with your right hand means you are done.

> The tradition of dipping the ring finger into vodka began centuries ago; if the silver ring on the finger changed colour after being submerged it meant that the vodka was poisoned.

DOS AND DON'TS AT THE TABLE

Do

- Cut food towards your body, not away.
- Accept food and drink with your right hand; use the left *only* to support your right elbow if the food is heavy.
- Drink tea immediately after receiving it; don't put it on the table until you have tried some.
- Take at least a sip, or a nibble, of the delicacies offered even if they don't please you.
- Hold a cup by the bottom, and not by the top rim.
- Cover your mouth when you are using a toothpick.

Don't

- Point a knife at anyone. When passing the knife offer the handle.
- Get up in the middle of a meal and walk outside. Wait until everyone is finished.
- Don't cross your legs or stick your feet in front of you when eating. Keep them together if seated or folded under you if on the floor.

EAT YOUR WORDS

Mongolian language is a scrambled-up soup of lispy vowels and throaty constants. Get behind the cuisine scene by getting to know the language. For pronunciation guidelines, see p278.

Useful Phrases in Mongolian

I can't eat meat.
bi makh i-dej cha-dakh-gui — Би мах идэж чадахгүй.

Can I have a menu please?
bi khool-nii tses avch bo-lokh uu — Би хоолны цэс авч болох уу?

How much is it?
e-ne ya-mar ü-ne-tei ve — Энэ ямар үнэтэй вэ?

What food do you have today?
ö-nöö-dör ya-mar khool-toi ve — Өнөөдөр ямар хоолтой вэ?

When will the food be ready?
khool khe-zee be-len bo-lokh ve — Хоол хэзээ бэлэн болох вэ?

Food Glossary

shöl	шөл	soup
ban-shtai shöl	банштай шөл	dumpling soup
gu-ril-tai shöl	гурилтай шөл	handmade noodle soup
goi-mon-tai shöl	гоймонтай шөл	noodle soup
no-goon zuush	ногоон зууш	vegetable salad
bai-tsaa-ni zuush	байцаан зууш	cabbage salad
luu-van-giin zuush	луувангийн зууш	carrot salad
niis-lel zuush	нийслэл зууш	potato salad
khuu-rag	хуураг	fried food
khuu-shuur	хуушуур	fried meat pancake
buuz	бууз	steamed mutton dumplings
tsui-van	цуйван	fried slices of dough with meat
bif-shteks	бифштекс	patty
makh	мах	meat
kho-ni-ny makh	хонины мах	mutton
shni-tsel	шницель	schnitzel
khuur-ga	хуурга	fried meat and flour in sauce
khor-khog	хорхог	meat roasted from the inside with hot stones
shar-san ön-dög	шарсан өндөг	fried egg
talkh	талх	bread
shar-san ta-khia	шарсан тахиа	fried chicken
zai-das/so-sisk	зайдас/сосик	sausage
za-gas	загас	fish
bu-daa-tai	будаатай	with rice
no-goo-toi	ногоотой	with vegetables
tom-stei	төмстэй	with potato
tsö-tsgii	цөцгий	sour cream
tsai	цай	tea
ban-shtai tsai	банштай цай	dumplings in tea
süü-tei tsai	сүүтэй цай	Mongolian milk tea
ra-shaan us	рашаан ус	mineral water
shar ai-rag	шар айраг	beer
air-ag	айраг	fermented mare's milk

Ulaanbaatar
Улаанбаатар

In less than a decade, a shift towards capitalism has transformed Ulaanbaatar from a Soviet-styled backwater into a dizzying tangle of shops, cafés, billboards and traffic jams. First-time visitors are taken aback to see that the centre of the Mongol world is no longer the magical Buddhist outpost so described in antiquarian history books.

Although Tibetan caravans no longer line the streets and the Chinese quarter has all but vanished, the city is still spirited with a heady cross-section of society – crimson-robed monks rub shoulders with sombre-suited politicians and businesspeople, while teenagers toting mobile phones skip past bewildered nomads fresh off the steppes.

UB, as it has been affectionately labelled by foreigners, dwarfs any other Mongolian city in size and importance. Despite its sprawl, it's easy to escape to a public square, grassy park or beer patio. The Tuul Gol offers a cool respite to the south while the four holy mountains surrounding the city provides its backdrop.

A wander from the centre of UB inevitably leads into timeless ger suburbs, where mangy mongrels patrol the unpaved lanes and most residents still live in traditional circular felt tents. Of great contrast are the narrow lanes off Sükhbaatar Square that are undergoing a renaissance of ultra-progressive fashion shops and trendy cafés.

The city is a pleasant place to visit and to base yourself for trips around the country. It has interesting monasteries and museums and excellent cultural shows, so try to spend some time here before heading out to the glorious valleys, steppes or deserts of Mongolia.

HIGHLIGHTS

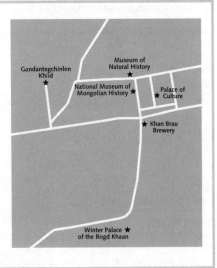

- Witness a mystical ceremony at **Gandantegchinlen Khiid** (p63), the country's largest monastery
- Check out the ominous dinosaur skeletons in the **Museum of Natural History** (p60)
- Take in a must-see performance of traditional dance, song, horse-head fiddle and contortionists at the **Palace of Culture** (p80)
- Wander the grounds of the beautifully preserved **Winter Palace of the Bogd Khaan** (p63)
- People-watch over a pint on the deck of the **Khan Brau** (p79)
- Weave through Mongolia's ancient past at the **National Museum of Mongolian History** (p61)

| TELEPHONE CODE: 011 | POPULATION: 870,000 | AREA: 1,368 SQ KM |

HISTORY

The first recorded capital city of the recent Mongolian empire was created in 1639. It was called Örgöö and was originally located at the monastery of Da Khuree, some 420km from Ulaanbaatar in Arkhangai aimag, or province. The monastery was the residence of five-year-old Zanabazar who, at the time, had been proclaimed the head of Buddhism in Mongolia. Because it consisted of felt tents, the 'city' was easily transported when the grass went dry. Some 25 movements were recorded along the Orkhon, Selenge and Tuul *gols* (rivers). Throughout such movement, the city was given some fairly unexciting official and unofficial names, including Khuree (Camp) in 1706.

In 1778 the capital was erected at its present location (GPS: N47° 55.056', E106° 55.007') and called the City of Felt. Later, the city became known as Ikh Khuree, or Great Camp, and was under the rule of the Bogd Gegeen, or Living Buddha.

In 1911 when Mongolia first proclaimed its independence from China, the city became the capital of Outer Mongolia and was renamed Niislel Khuree (Capital Camp). In 1918 it was invaded by the Chinese and three years later by the Russians.

Finally, in 1924 the city was renamed Ulaanbaatar (Red Hero) in honour of the communist triumph and declared the official capital of an 'independent' Mongolia (independent from China, not from the Soviet Union). The Khangard (Garuda), symbolising courage and honesty, was declared the city's official symbol. In 1933 Ulaanbaatar gained autonomy and separated from the surrounding Töv aimag.

From the 1930s, the Soviets built the city in typical Russian style: lots of ugly apartment blocks, large brightly coloured theatres and cavernous government buildings. Tragically, the Soviets also destroyed almost all of the monasteries and temples. Ulaanbaatar is still young, and unlike many Russian and European cities there is very little that is old or glorious about the place.

ORIENTATION

Most of the city spreads from east to west along the main road, Enkh Taivny Örgön Chölöö, also known as Peace Ave. At the centre is Sükhbaatar Square, often simply known as 'the Square', which is just north of

Peace Ave. Sprawling suburbia is limited by the four majestic mountains that surround the city: Bayanzurkh, Chingeltei, Songino Khairkhan and Bogdkhan. The river to the south, the Tuul Gol, also somewhat limits the growth of suburban expansion.

Around the Square are the Central Post Office (CPO) and the Palace of Culture, and a couple of blocks west of the Square is the State Department Store.

The city is divided into six major districts, but there's a multitude of subdistricts and microdistricts. Mongolians rarely use street names and numbers, so tracking down an address can be difficult. A typical address might be something like: Microdistrict 14, Building 3, Flat 27. The problems with this are numerous – you are unlikely to know which microdistrict it refers to, many buildings are not numbered or signed, and all street signs are in Mongolian Cyrillic. This is why most locals will give you an unofficial description, such as 'Door 67, building 33, last door of a white-and-red building, behind the Drama Theatre'. To find your way around Ulaanbaatar, a good map, phrasebook and sense of direction are vital.

The train station is southwest of the centre. Bus no 4 runs from here to Sükhbaatar Square. The airport is 18km southwest of the city; to get to Sükhbaatar Square take bus No 11 or 22.

Maps

There are several maps available of Ulaanbaatar; the best is the 1:10,000 *Ulaanbaatar City Map* (T5500), updated annually.

The best place to obtain maps of UB and Mongolia is the **Map Shop** (Map pp56-8; ⊙ 9am-1pm & 2-6pm Mon-Fri, 10am-4pm Sat) on Ikh Toiruu, near the Elba Electronics shop. You can also buy good topographic maps of Mongolia here. Maps can also be found in bookshops, the State Department Store and hotels.

INFORMATION
Bookshops

With the exception of Xanadu and Scrolls (see opposite) there are few places to buy English-language material in Mongolia; you could try poking around the newsstand on the ground floor (referred to as the 1st floor in Mongolia) of the **State Department Store** (Peace Ave 44) or at the bookshop on the 3rd floor. For pricey souvenirs or art books try the

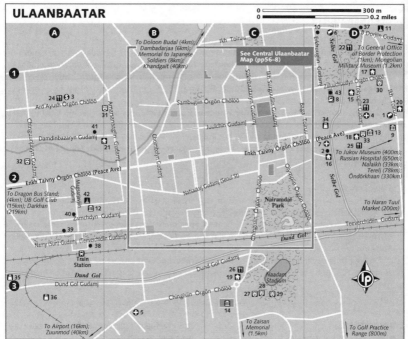

souvenir shops at the Bayangol Hotel, the Monastery-Museum of Choijin Lama, the Museum of Fine Arts and the Winter Palace of the Bogd Khaan. Battered Russian and Mongolian books end up at the bookstalls near Selbe bridge on Peace Ave.

Scrolls (Map pp56-8; ☎ 9915 0656; Juulchin Gudamj 22; ⊗ 11am-6pm) This used-book shop carries mostly French, German and English non-fiction titles. It usually

has a few Lonely Planet guidebooks and the odd Mongolia travelogue. Scrolls also does book swaps and buy-backs.
Xanadu (Map pp56-8; ☎ 319 748; www.xanadu.mn; Marco Polo Building; ⊗ 10am-7pm Mon-Fri) This is Mongolia's only real English-language bookstore, with a good selection of fiction and nonfiction. It also carries some Lonely Planet titles, Mongolia travelogues and the *International Herald Tribune* (T4500). Xanadu is located in the Marco Polo Plaza, west of the Monastery-Museum of Choijin Lama.

ULAANBAATAR

ULAANBAATAR IN...

Two Days

Start at **Gandantegchinlen (Gandan) Khiid** (p63) where you might be able to catch a morning ceremony. Walk back to town for lunch at **Modern Nomads** (p75) before an afternoon of two museums – the **Natural History** (p60) and **Mongolian History** (p61) – both close to Sükhbaatar Square. Dinner at **Silk Road Bar & Grill** (p78) is a must, topped off by a pint at the **Khan Brau** (p79).

On your second day, visit the **Winter Palace of Bogd Khan** (p63) before huffing it up to the **Zaisan Memorial** (p67) – a good workout before the calories you'll put at **Ikh Khuraldai** (p76). In the afternoon, pay a visit to the small but atmospheric **Monastery-Museum of Choijin Lama** (p64) before an evening of song and dance performance at the **Tumen Ekh Song and Dance Ensemble** (p80).

Four Days

Follow the two-day schedule above and on day three start at the **Naran Tuul market** (p84) for some hardcore shopping if you are off to the countryside. If the Naran Tuul is too daunting, the next best place to shop is the **State Department Store** (p84). Even for those weary of sightseeing, it's really worth checking out the **Victims of Political Persecution Memorial Museum** (p61).

On your final day hire a mountain bike from **Karakorum Expeditions** (p70) and go for a ride along the Tuul Gol. Then swap your cycling kit for dance gear and groove at **Muse** or **Medusa** (p80).

Emergency

It might take a few minutes to get hold of an English speaker for these numbers.
Emergency aid/ambulance (☎ 103)
Fire (☎ 101)
Police emergency (☎ 102)

Internet Access

Ulaanbaatar has dozens of clean and comfortable Internet cafés where you can surf the Web and access accounts. Hourly rates are reasonable at about T800; but double that price at hotel business centres. Connections are generally good. You can scan photos in many places for around T200.

icafé (Map pp56-8; ☎ 313 316; fax 320 616; Baga Toiruu west; per hr T600; 🕑 9am-10pm Mon-Fri, 11am-10pm Sat & Sun) You can also send and receive faxes here. It is located at the southern door of the National Information Technology Park.

Internet Centre (Map pp56-8; ☎ 312 512; Tserendorjiin Gudamj 65; per hr T700 weekdays, T600 weekends; 🕑 9am-1.30am) One of the largest Internet cafés with at least 20 computers.

Mouse House (Map pp56-8; ☎ 330 126; Baga Toiruu east; per hr T800; 🕑 9am-midnight) Located just south of the Ard Kino.

Za Internet Café (Map pp56-8; ☎ 320 801; Peace Ave 62; per hr T700; 🕑 24hr) Located 100m west of the State Department Store, at the time of writing this was the only 24-hour Internet café.

Laundry

Almost all of the hotels in Ulaanbaatar offer a laundry service for between T500 and T1500 per kilo, but they may not advertise it – so just ask. If you can be bothered, it's not difficult to do some laundry yourself – the markets and shops sell small packets of detergent and bleach. Laundromats aren't easy to find but there are a few around.

Metro Express (☎ 470 789, 9919 4234) has 10 branches scattered across the city, including one next to the Dalai Eej supermarket (Map pp56-8). A load of laundry costs T3200 and turn-around time is two hours.

Left Luggage

Most hotels and guesthouses can store luggage while you are off getting lost in the Gobi. There is usually no fee if you've stayed a few nights.

Libraries

The **National Library of Mongolia** (Map pp56-8; Chingisiin Örgön Chölöö) has a vast amount of English-language books and documents; the trouble is accessing it. Texts are kept in storage and you need to fill out a small slip of paper (*shefer*) to request the book you want. If you don't have a **library card** (T3000) you'll need to leave some ID for a deposit. Nearly all texts in English are of the Mongolia genre.

You might also try the **American Center for Mongolian Studies** (Map pp56-8; ☎ 314 055; www .mongoliacenter.org; Mongolian National University, Bldg 1, Room 205), which was planning to open a small library of books on Mongolia.

Media

Mongolia's media used to be little more than state-controlled propaganda vehicles, but liberalisation has certainly changed the atmosphere. Literally hundreds of newspapers have sprung up, with controversies and scandals forming popular topics. Ulaanbaatar's two English-language weekly newspapers, *Mongol Messenger* and the *UB Post*, are well worth picking up for local news and entertainment information.

Medical Services

While Ulaanbaatar may be a fairly healthy city, its hospitals are abysmal and best avoided. If you need medical attention your embassy should have a list of reputable hospitals and doctors. Pharmacies (Aptek; Аптек) are common in Ulaanbaatar, stocking Mongolian, Russian, Chinese and Korean medicine. Check expiry dates carefully.

Russian Hospital (☎ 458 140, 450 007; Peace Ave 131) Many Mongolians recommend this hospital in the 15th district.

Russian Hospital No 2 (Map p53; ☎ 450 129, 450 230; cnr Peace Ave & Tokyogiin Gudamj) This is the best Mongolian hospital in town, though its hardly the place you'd want to visit for a critical ailment. It's 200m west of the British embassy. Check-ups cost US$10 to US$20.

SOS Medica Mongolia Clinic (Map p53; ☎ 345 526; Gutal Cooperation Bldg, Chingisiin Örgön Chölöö; ☽ 9am-12.30pm & 2-6pm Mon-Fri) This clinic has a staff of Western doctors on call 24 hours (after hours call ☎ 9975 0967). Its services don't come cheap (examinations start from around US$120), but it's the best place to go in an emergency.

Yonsei Friendship Hospital (Map p53; ☎ 310 945; Peace Ave; ☽ 9am-4.30pm Mon-Fri) This South Korean–sponsored clinic is fairly reliable and reasonably priced. English-speaking doctors are sometimes on hand and the prices are very reasonable (less than T5000 for a check-up). The hospital is located close to the Selbe Gol bridge.

Getting dental work done in Mongolia is a precarious prospect. Because the quality

of service can change, contact SOS Medica (see above) for recommendations. The **Dental Group** (☎ 452 201) at the Russian Hospital is not a bad choice. Another option is the Mongolian-run **Dental Hospital** (Map pp56-8; ☎ 315 732; ☽ 9am-7pm Mon-Fri, 9am-5pm Sat & Sun) 200m northwest of the CPO.

Money

Banking is a snap in Ulaanbaatar and you won't have to go far to change cash or travellers cheques, or get a cash advance on your credit card. Many banks in central Ulaanbaatar even offer 24-hour services. The bigger hotels also offer exchange services for their guests.

Mongolians often change money at open markets such as the Container Market or Naran Tuul where private changers offer the best rates, but the crowds and confusion at these places aren't worth the risk for just a few extra tögrögs.

ATMs (accepting Visa cards only) are popping up in many places including the lobbies of the Ulaanbaatar, Bayangol and Chinggis Khaan hotels.

If you are relying on plastic, take out a fair bit of cash before heading into the bush as only a few rural banks can do a cash advance.

Both Golomt and Trade & Development Bank will allow you to receive money wired from abroad. It will cost the sender US$50 to wire any amount of money; there is no charge for receiving cash. For general information on money, see p242.

Ard Kino Exchange Office (Map pp56-8; 1st fl, Ard Kino cinema; ☽ 10am-8pm) It is safe, convenient and offers consistently good rates.

Golomt Bank (Map pp56-8; ☎ 330 436; ☽ 24hr) Around-the-clock banking services. Changing travellers cheques into tögrög carries a fee of 1.5%. You can get a cash advance with no commission on Visa or Mastercard. There are six branches around town, including Seoul St and just south of the corner of Juulchin Gudamj and Baga Toiruu.

Khan Bank (Map pp56-8; ☎ 456 154; cnr Sambuugiin Örgön Chölöö & Baga Toiruu; ☽ 24hr)

Mongol Post Bank (Map pp56-8; ☎ 310 103; Kholboochdiin Gudamj 4; ☽ 9am-1pm & 2-4pm Mon-Fri)

State Department Store (Map pp56-8; Peace Ave 44) Also has exchange booths.

Trade & Development Bank (T&D Bank; Map pp56-8; ☎ 327 095; ☽ 9am-4pm Mon-Fri) Travellers cheques are changed into tögrög with a 1% fee or into US dollars with a 2% fee. For foreigners, the place to do business is on the 2nd floor of the main branch on the corner of Juulchin Gudamj and Baga Toiruu. Here you also get a cash advance on your credit card; MasterCard carries a 4% commission, American Express and Visa are both commission-free. The bank will also replace lost Amex travellers cheques. A second branch is located on Peace Ave, opposite the Ulaanbaatar Hotel.

Permits

If you are travelling to border areas such as Altai Tavan Bogd National Park in Bayan-Ölgii, the **General Office of Border Protection** (☎ 452 599; Border Defence bldg; ☺ 9am-5pm Mon-Fri), in the east of the city, is the place to come for permits. Bring a passport and a map showing your route. In 2003 the price for the permit dropped from US$25 to T3000, though it could change right back. The office is in a grey building just west of the Military Museum.

Police

The police can be found on Sambuugiin Örgön Chölöö or on Negdsen Undestnii Gudamj but, as in the rest of the country, don't expect much assistance.

Post

Central Post Office (CPO; Töv Shuudangiin Salbar; Map pp56-8; ☎ 313 421; cnr Peace Ave & Sükhbaataryn Gudamj; ☺ 7.30am-9pm Mon-Fri, 9am-8pm Sat & Sun) Located on the southwest corner of Sükhbaatar Square. As you enter the main hall, the oversize-package desk is on the left and the Telecom office is to the right. The Postal Counter Hall is the place to post mail and check poste restante (counter No 1; letters are free but there's a T200 charge to pick up a package, and you'll need to show your passport). EMS express (priority) mail can also be sent from here. There is also a good range of postcards, small booklets about Mongolia in English and local newspapers for sale. Note that while open, most services are nonexistent on Sunday.

DHL (Map p53; ☎ 310 919; dhluln@magicnet.mn; Peace Ave 15-A; ☺ 9am-6pm Mon-Fri, 9am-1pm Sat) Near the Edelweiss Hotel.

FedEx (Map pp56-8; ☎ 320 591; Amaryn Gudamj 2; ☺ 9am-6pm Mon-Fri) Located in the Tuushin Hotel. A 500g letter to Australia is US$36; to the UK and USA it is US$45.

TNT (Map pp56-8; ☎ 311 655; tntmongolia@magicnet .mn; Bldg 44, off Seoul St; ☺ 8.30am-6.30pm Mon-Fri) Located in the yellow brick apartment building behind the State Circus.

UPS (Map pp56-8; ☎ 320 101; ups@mgl.mn; Baga Toiruu 5; ☺ 9am-6pm Mon-Fri) Located in the 'City Center' building opposite the Ard Kino.

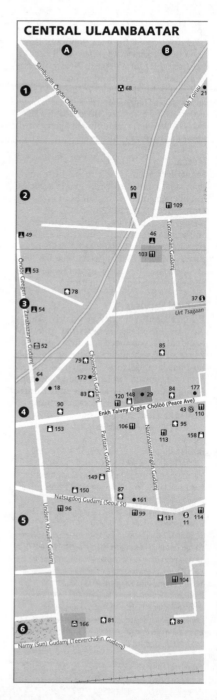

CENTRAL ULAANBAATAR

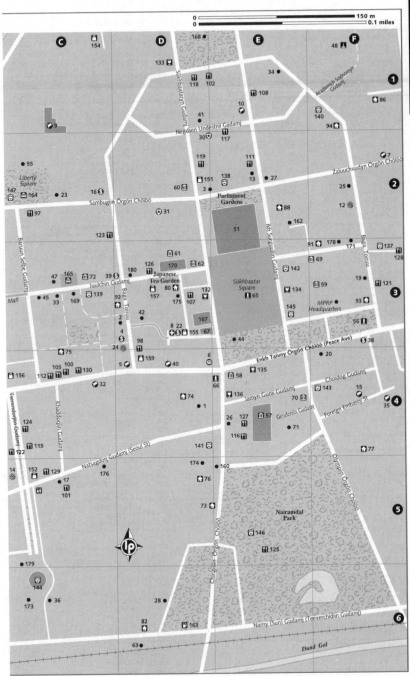

Telephone & Fax

For local calls, you can use the phone at your hotel, often for free. Other hotels, including those with business centres, and some of the street stalls with telephones charge T100 for a call to a landline (six digits) or T200 for a call to a mobile number (eight digits). You can also make local calls from the CPO or at any number of street-side peddlers whose entire business is selling phone calls on ubiquitous portable white phones.

Private, inexpensive international phone offices *(Olon Ulsiin Yariin)* are sometimes tucked into corners of shops, restaurants or computer-game centres. One is located at Peace Ave 62, next to the Za Internet Café (Map pp56–8). International phone calls from the CPO are more laborious and more expensive, but it's open all night.

Most middle to top-range hotels have a fax machine that can be used by guests for about T1500 to T2000 per page. The CPO offers a less user-friendly service, with cheaper rates. Hotels charge around T500 to receive a fax on your behalf. You can also send and receive faxes from icafé (p54).

Toilets

Public toilets can be found on Seoul St by the Natsagdorj Library and opposite California restaurant.

Tourist Information

The government agency, **Mongolian Tourism Board** (MTB; Map pp56–8; ☎ 318 493; fax 318 492; www.mongoliatourism.gov.mn), deals mostly in policy implementation. It is planning a tourist information centre on the 2nd floor of Urt Tsagaan pedestrian mall at the west end of Juulchin Gudamj. The centre is expected to have tour advisors, a hotel-booking desk, a travel agent and a ticket agent for theatre performances and events.

Otherwise, the staff at most of the backpacker guesthouses can answer tourist-related queries.

Travel Agencies

Staff at backpacker guesthouses can help with visa registration and get you a train ticket.

The Russian embassy usually refers travellers to **Legend Tour** (Map pp56–8; ☎ 315 158, 9984 2999; www.legendtour.ru; Seoul St, Sant Asar Trading Centre) for visa help. Some travellers have given some negative feedback about this operation, but it may be your only choice if you want that elusive Russian visa. Another place to try is **Erdeme Tour** (Map pp56–8; ☎ 9909 7197; Seoul St; ☒ 9am-6pm Mon-Fri & 9am-3pm Sat) in the Aeroflot building.

The following agencies are good for organising air tickets. For details of local agencies offering tours either within or outside of Ulaanbaatar, see p69.

Air Market (Map pp56–8; ☎ 366 060, 9927 9114; www.air-market.net; south of cnr Peace Ave & Chingisiin Örgön Chölöö)

Air Network (Map pp56–8; ☎ 322 222; fax 328 567; airnetwork@magicnet.mn; Baga Toiruu west; ☒ 9am-7pm Mon-Fri, 10am-3pm Sat & Sun)

Air Trans (Map pp56–8; ☎ 310 061, 313 131; airtrans@magicnet.mn; cnr Sükhbaataryn Gudamj & Sambuugiin Örgön Chölöö) Very reliable air-ticketing agency.

Silk Road Network (Map p53; ☎ 320 405; fax 330 405; silkroad@mongolnet.mn; Baga Toiruu 37b)

DANGERS & ANNOYANCES

Ulaanbaatar is a fairly carefree and easygoing city; treat it as you would a mid-sized European city, and be similarly conscious of the potential risks.

Theft

Pickpockets and bag slashers are a recent and growing problem, although theft is seldom violent against foreigners, just opportunistic. Our mailbags are full of letters written by travellers who have lost their wallet to sticky fingers and one guesthouse owner reported that 5% of his guests are picked in UB.

Crowded places are the trouble spots: getting onto a bus or held up in human traffic at the Naran Tuul market. The entrances to the CPO and State Department Store used to be notorious for theft but are now better patrolled by police. But watch out for pickpockets who sometimes masquerade as coin sellers.

Pickpockets often work in teams; two or three will block your path and push from the front while another dives a hand into your pockets. During winter, the pockets of bulging coats are popular targets.

At Gandantegchinlen Khiid, unsuspecting tourists, mesmerised by enchanting ceremonies, have been relieved of their money and passports. The same goes for foreigners engrossed in computer screens at Internet cafés. The best place to keep money is your front shirt pocket; leave other valuables in the safe in your hotel. It is even possible to get a temporary safe-deposit box at one of the 24-hour Golomt Banks.

If you do need to bring a credit card or a travellers cheque with you, keep it in a money belt and buried under your clothes. On public transport or in markets, carry your bag in front of you.

Violent Crime

Violent crime and muggings most often occur in the darkened alleys, courtyards and ger (traditional felt yurts) districts that lie off the well-lit boulevards. Avoid these areas. Foreigners should use an official taxi – as opposed to a private vehicle – for lifts around town late at night.

Be careful when leaving nightclubs in Ulaanbaatar, where alcohol and comparatively rich foreigners are a potentially vulnerable mixture. Try to leave in a group rather than alone.

Alcoholism

Alcoholism is becoming less of a problem these days as beer rapidly replaces vodka as the local beverage of choice. You'll still encounter drunks in and around Ulaanbaatar, especially around Naadam time, but they are usually more annoying than dangerous. Be sensible in bars and nightclubs; you're only asking for trouble if you flash around a lot of money or get into arguments about the virtues or otherwise of Chinggis Khaan or other issues of sensitivity.

Queues

It could be the warrior-like bloodlines from Chinggis Khaan, a penchant for wrestling or habits from the communist days where demand always exceeded supply, but Mongolians rarely queue – they bustle, huddle and scramble. You will often need to sharpen your elbows, learn some appropriately argumentative phrases in Mongolian, and plough headfirst through the throng. Being polite won't really help, nor will getting angry.

Other Annoyances

Virtually no stairways in the whole country have lights, so carrying a torch (flashlight) is a good idea, even during the day.

Electricity, heating and hot-water shortages and blackouts are common through-

out the year. Although official policies have relaxed considerably since the arrival of democracy, some of the old KGB-inspired thinking still occurs among the police.

Most offices have security guards in the lobby checking the ID cards of everyone who enters and leaves the buildings – it can sometimes be a nightmare getting past them.

The number of street children and beggars in Ulaanbaatar has noticeably decreased in recent years but there are still a few around. While it is better not to give anything as this just encourages them to stay on the street, handing out food and drinks is better than money.

SIGHTS

Most sights are located within a 15-minute walk from Sükhbaatar Square. The Winter Palace of the Bogd Khan and the Zaisan Memorial are a short bus ride south of the city. Gandantegchinlen Khiid is about 2km to the northwest.

Museums
MUSEUM OF NATURAL HISTORY

Sometimes called the State Central Museum, the **Museum of Natural History** (Байгалын Түүхийн Музей; Map pp56-8; ☎ 321 716; cnr Sükhbaataryn Gudamj & Sambuugiin Örgön Chölöö; adult/student T2000/1000, photos T5000, video T10,000, photos of dinosaur skeletons extra T5000; ☺ 10am-5.30pm, closed Mon & Tue mid-Sept–May) is worth a quick visit. It has exhibits featuring Mongolia's geography, flora and fauna, including the requisite section with stuffed and embalmed animals, birds and even fish. Geologists will like the geology section (especially the awesome **meteorites**).

More impressive, though, is the Palaeontology Hall and its array of complete **dinosaur skeletons**, including a 3m-tall, five-ton, flesh-eating tarbosaurus. For a bird's-eye view, clamber up the stairs outside the hall to a gallery on the 3rd floor.

The gallery next door to the hall is full of interesting knick-knacks such as petrified wood, dinosaur eggs and some huge leg bones, which look like something out of the Flintstones. Look out for the world-famous 'fighting dinosaurs', a velociraptor and protocerotops that were buried alive (probably when a sand dune collapsed on top of them) in the midst of mortal combat, some 80 million years ago. For more on

Mongolia's remarkable dinosaurs see the boxed text on p189.

There is also a **camel museum** on the 2nd floor.

The museum is old and rambling, with doors and corridors going all over the place, so trace your route using the map given out free with your ticket. The shop sells a pricey English guidebook to the museum (T4500).

ZANABAZAR MUSEUM OF FINE ARTS

The **Zanabazar Museum of Fine Arts** (Занабазарын Уран Зургийн Музей; Map pp56-8; ☎ 326 060; Juulchin Gudamj; adult/student T2500/400; ☼ 9am-5pm May-Sep, 10am-5pm Oct-Apr) has an excellent collection of paintings, carvings and sculptures, including many by the revered sculptor and artist Zanabazar. It also contains other rare, and sometimes old, religious exhibits such as scroll paintings (*thangka*) and Buddhist statues, representing the best display of its kind in Mongolia. A bonus is that most of the exhibit captions in the museum are in English.

At the top of the stairs is a glass folder with a detailed explanation of Zanabazar and his work. There are some fine examples of the sculptor's work including five Dhyani, or Contemplation, Buddhas (cast in 1683) and Tara in her 21 manifestations.

Also worth checking out are the wonderful *tsam* masks (worn by monks during religious ceremonies) and the intricate paintings, *One Day in Mongolia* and the *Airag Feast*, by renowned artist B Sharav. These depict almost every aspect of nomadic life. The ground floor has some copies of portraits of the great khaans (kings) and some 7th-century Turkic stone carvings.

Worthy of a visit in itself, the **Red Ger Art Gallery** (☎ 323 986) on the 1st floor showcases modern artwork by Mongolia's top contemporary painters. English-speaking guides are also available.

NATIONAL MUSEUM OF MONGOLIAN HISTORY

Still sometimes referred to by its previous name, the Revolutionary Museum, the **National Museum of Mongolian History** (Монголын Түүхийн Үндэсний Музей; Map pp56-8; ☎ 325 656; cnr Juulchin Gudamj & Sükhbaataryn Gudamj; admission T2500, photos T5000; ☼ 10am-4.30pm Tue-Sat) is well worth a visit.

The 1st floor has some interesting exhibits on petroglyphs, deer stones (stone sculptures of reindeer and other animals) and burial sites from the Hun and Uighur eras. The 2nd floor houses an outstanding collection of costumes, hats and jewellery, representing most of Mongolia's ethnic groups.

The 3rd floor is a must-see for fans of the Mongol horde. The collection includes real examples of 12th-century **Mongol armour**, and correspondence between Pope Innocent IV and Güyük Khaan. Written in Latin and Persian and dated 13 November 1246, it bears the khaan's seal. There is also a display of traditional Mongolian culture with, among other things, a furnished ger, traditional farming and domestic implements, saddles and musical instruments.

Also on display are Buddhist items, including the controversial **Ganlin Horn**, made from human thigh bones, and used by head monks to call and exorcise evil spirits. All the exhibits have English captions, except for the dull gallery of Soviet-era history.

VICTIMS OF POLITICAL PERSECUTION MEMORIAL MUSEUM

This little-known **museum** (Map pp56-8; ☎ 320 592; cnr Gendeniin Gudamj & Olympiin Örgön Chölöö; admission T2000, photography T5000, video T10,000; ☼ 9am-5pm) consists of a series of haunting displays chronicling the bloody communist purges of the 1930s – an aggressive campaign to eliminate 'counter-revolutionaries'. During the campaign, intellectuals were arrested and put on trial, sent to Siberian labour camps or shot. Mongolia lost top writers, scientists and thinkers.

The museum was inspired by the deeds of former prime minister P Genden, who was executed in Moscow by the KGB in 1937 for refusing Stalin's orders to carry out the purge. Stalin found a more willing puppet in Marshall Choibalsan, whose purge ended in the deaths of more than 28,000 Mongolians, mostly lamas. The house containing the museum once belonged to Genden and it was his daughter, Tserendulam, who converted it into a museum in 1996. The museum, undergoing renovations at the time of research, is located southwest of the Ministry of External Relations.

The large, white square building located just southwest of the museum, is called the **Wedding Palace** (Khurimiin Ordon; Map pp56-8). Built

ZORIG – THE FATHER OF MONGOLIAN DEMOCRACY

On 2 October 1998, 36-year-old Sanjaasurengiin Zorig, a leader revered as the father of Mongolian democracy, was stabbed 18 times by masked assailants in his apartment.

Zorig was a well-liked government minister and top candidate for the vacant position of prime minister. In 1990 he had taken a leading role in the pro-democracy demonstrations.

The killers have never been brought to justice, though his death is linked to a corrupt casino deal, which he helped to block. Everyone is under suspicion, from his fellow democrats to as far afield as the Macau mafia.

Zorig's murder came as a great shock to the Mongolian people, who lined the streets in their tens of thousands for the burial procession. A statue of Zorig was unveiled on his birthday, 20 April 1999, opposite the Central Post Office, honouring the mild-mannered, bespectacled man who helped bring democracy to Mongolia.

in 1976 by the Russians, it has since been used for over 150,000 wedding ceremonies, including the marital vows of a few foreigners.

OTHER MUSEUMS

The **Ulaanbaatar City Museum** (Map p53; ☎ 450 960; Peace Ave; admission T1000; 🕑 9am-6pm Mon-Fri) is the brown-roofed Russian-style building which is next to the Wrestling Palace. It has a few interesting black-and-white photographs of early Ulaanbaatar and an old map of the original ger settlement, though not much else.

The **Centre for Arts & Antiques** (Map pp56-8; ☎ 328 948; Juulchin Gudamj; admission T3000; 🕑 10am-5pm Tue-Sun) has rotating private collections of well-presented Mongolian art. It's located just west of Builder's Square.

The **Hunting Museum** (Map pp56-8; Öndör Gegeen Zanabazaryn Gudamj; admission T1000; 🕑 10am-5pm Mon-Fri, 10am-2pm Sat), on the 2nd floor of the 'Baigal Ordon' (Nature Palace) on the street leading to Gandan Khiid, shows off centuries-old trapping and hunting techniques that are used by both nomads and urban cowboys. It's usually locked so ask for the key from the ladies running the hotel downstairs.

The **Railway Museum** (Map p53; ☎ 944 493; Octoberyn Gudamj; admission free; 🕑 9am-noon & 1-4pm Mon-Fri) is great for kids and railway buffs. It is about 400m northeast of the station. Other train-spotting options include the old engines parked in front of the Jiguur Grand hotel.

The monstrous grey building of the **Mongolian Military Museum** (☎ 454 492; Lhagvasurengiin Gudamj 2; admission T1000; 🕑 10am-5pm), on the dusty the northeast edge of town, contains

two halls of war memorabilia dating from Chinggis Khaan–era weapons to cosmonaut Gurragchaa's space suit.

About 350m south of the Military Museum is the **GK Jukov Museum** (☎ 453 781; Peace Ave; admission T1000; 🕑 9am-4pm Mon-Fri), dedicated to the Khalkh Gol War (1939). Housed inside the former home of General Jukov, who led the Mongolian–Russian forces against the Japanese, it is located at the eastern end of Peace Ave.

The **Theatre Museum** (Map pp56-8; ☎ 326 820; Amaryn Gudamj; admission T1000; 🕑 10am-4pm Mon-Fri) is worthwhile if you're interested in the dramatic arts – the collection of puppets is wonderful. The museum is on the 3rd floor of the Palace of Culture (its entrance is on the northern side of building).

The **Museum of the General Intelligence Agency** (Map pp56-8; ☎ 264 281, 9979 5584; admission T1000; 🕑 10am-4pm Mon-Fri) is dedicated to the Mongolian version of the KGB and the spy game dating back to the Chinggis Khaan era. Secret-service recording devices and miniature pistols are some of the items on display, but the explanations are in Mongolian so it's worth bringing a translator. If it's locked, try ringing or ask at the front desk of the GIA headquarters on Juulchin Gudamj.

The **International Intellectual Museum**, (Map p53; ☎ 461 470; Peace Ave; admission T1000; 🕑 10am-6pm Mon-Sat), also known as the Mongolian Toy Museum, is in a pink building behind the unmissable round 'East Centre'. It has a collection of puzzles and games made by local artists. The friendly curator, Zandraa Tumen-Ulzii, has travelled the world to various games conferences and may cryptically say '10-minute, 10,000 dollars', indicating your reward for quickly solving one of his more difficult puzzles.

Monasteries & Temples

Around the start of the 19th century, over 100 temples *(süm)* and monasteries *(khiid)* served a population of only about 50,000 in Ulaanbaatar. Religious historians estimate that maybe over 50% of the population at the time were monks or nuns. During the Stalinist purges of the late 1930s, most of the city's temples and monasteries were destroyed. Several thousand monks and nuns were murdered, while many more fled or abandoned their Buddhist life. Only since the early 1990s have the people of Mongolia started to openly practice Buddhism again.

WINTER PALACE OF BOGD KHAAN

Built between 1893 and 1903, the **Winter Palace of the Bogd Khaan** (Богд Хааны Өвлийн Ордон; Map p53; ☎ 342 195; Chingisiin Örgön Chölöö; admission T2500, photography US$5, video US$10; ⏰ 9am-5.30pm summer, 9.30am-4.30pm Fri-Tue winter) is the place where Mongolia's eighth Living Buddha, and last king, Jebtzun Damba Hutagt VIII (often called the Bogd Khaan), lived for 20 years. For reasons that are unclear, the palace was spared destruction by the Russians and turned into a museum. The summer palace, on the banks of Tuul Gol, was completely destroyed.

There are six temples in the grounds. The white building to the right as you enter is the Winter Palace itself. It contains a collection of gifts received from foreign dignitaries, such as a pair of golden boots from a Russian tsar, a robe made from 80 unfortunate foxes and a ger lined with the skins of 150 snow leopards.

The Bogd Khaan's penchant for unusual wildlife explains the extraordinary array of stuffed animals in the Palace. Some of it had been part of his personal zoo – look out for the photo of the Bogd's elephant, purchased from Russia for 22,000 roubles.

The interior of the temples are often dark and the exhibits are behind glass, so you are unlikely to get any great photos. A torch is an advantage here. The exceptions are the excellent *thangka*, costumes and other items, which are upstairs in the Winter Palace and under good lighting. Mongolia's Declaration of Independence (from China) is among the exhibits.

The museum has also been a favourite among local thieves, who over a period of 10 years had been scalping the roof of its gold ornaments until a guard stopped them at gunpoint in 2001. You can pick up your own souvenirs legally in the excellent gift shop, the first building on the right as you enter.

The Winter Palace is a few kilometres south of the Square. It is a bit too far to walk, so take a taxi or catch bus No 7 or 19. A little **pamphlet** (T1000), available at the entrance, gives a very brief explanation of the temples in English, and includes a handy map showing the temple locations.

GANDANTEGCHINLEN (GANDAN) KHIID

The **Gandantegchinlen Khiid** (Гандантэгчинлэн Хийд; Map pp56-8; Öndör Gegeen Zanabazaryn Gudamj; admission free; ⏰ 9am-9pm), roughly meaning 'the great place of complete joy' is the largest monastery in Mongolia. It is one of Ulaanbaatar's most impressive sights.

Building was started in 1838 by the fourth Bogd Gegeen, but like most monasteries in Mongolia the purges of 1937 fell heavily on Gandan. When US vice-president Henry

---

THE BOGD KHAAN (1869–1924)

The eighth Jebtzun Damba (Lord of Refuge) is most commonly referred to as the Bogd Khaan (partly because his real name is over 14 syllables long). He was a colourful and controversial character. A practical joker, the Bogd Khaan's favourite gag was to shock his ministers with wires attached to the battery of his car. His love of exotic animals (he owned an elephant and various tropical birds) was matched only by his weakness for alcohol (he was sometimes drunk for days at a time).

Depending on which version of history you read, the Bogd Khaan was either a great visionary and nationalist, or possibly a sexual predator who had been blinded by syphilis. One of his wives was the former wife of a wrestler and was well known for her sexual exploits with her hairdresser.

Wallace asked to see a monastery during his visit to Mongolia in 1944, then prime minister Choibalsan guiltily scrambled to open this one to cover up the fact that he had recently laid waste to Mongolia's religious heritage. The *khiid* remained a 'show monastery' for other foreign visitors until 1990 when full religious ceremonies commenced. Today, over 500 monks belong to the monastery.

As you enter the main entrance from the south, a path leads towards the right to a courtyard containing two temples. The northeast building is **Ochidara Temple** (sometimes called Gandan Süm) where the most significant ceremonies are held. Following the *kora* (pilgrim) path clockwise around this building, the large statue behind glass is Tsongkhapa, the founder of the Gelugpa sect. The two-storey Didan-Lavran temple in the courtyard was home to the 13th Dalai Lama during his stay here in 1904.

At the end of the main path as you enter is the magnificent white **Migjid Janraisig Süm** (admission US$1; ☺ until 6pm), the monastery's main attraction. Lining the walls of the temple are hundreds of images of Ayush, the Buddha of longevity, which stare through the gloom to the magnificent Migjid Janraisig statue (see the boxed text, below).

To the east of the temple are four colleges of Buddhist philosophy, including the yellow building dedicated to Kalachakra, a wrathful Buddhist deity.

To the west of the temple is the **Öndör Gegeen Zanabazar Buddhist University**, established in 1970. It is closed to foreigners.

The souvenir shop, to the left as you enter the main southern gate of the monastery, sells nontouristy religious artefacts, including miniature copper bowls, incense

and scroll paintings, as well as items such as Mongolian felt hats.

You can take photos around the monastery, but not inside the temples. Try to be there for the captivating ceremonies – they usually start at around 10am, though you may be lucky and see one at another time. Most chapels are closed in the afternoon.

Pickpockets sometimes target the monastery, so take care, especially when among crowds.

MONASTERY-MUSEUM OF CHOIJIN LAMA

This **monastery-museum** (Чойжин Ламын Хийд-Музей; Map pp56–8; ☎ 324 788; admission T2200, photo T5500, video T11,000; ☺ 8am-10pm Jun-Oct, 10am-5pm Nov-May) is also known as the Museum of Religion. It was the home of Luvsan Haidav Choijin Lama ('Choijin' is an honorary title given to some monks), the state oracle and brother of the Bogd Khaan. The construction of the monastery commenced in 1904 and was completed four years later. It was closed in 1938 and probably would have been demolished but it was saved as a museum in 1942 to demonstrate the 'feudal' ways of the past. Although religious freedom in Mongolia recommenced in 1990, this monastery is no longer an active place of worship and will probably remain a museum.

There are five temples within the grounds. As you enter, the first temple you see is the **Maharaja Süm**. The **main temple** features statues of Sakyamuni (the historical Buddha), Choijin Lama and Baltung Choimba (the teacher of the Bogd Khaan), whose mummified remains are inside the statue. There are also some fine *thangka* and some of the best *tsam* masks in the country. The *gongkhang* (protector chapel) behind the main hall contains the oracle's throne and

---

MIGJID JANRAISIG STATUE

A 20m gold and bronze statue of Avalokitesvara (Janraisig), built by the Bogd Khaan in 1911, once stood in the main temple at Gandan Khiid. The magnificent statue was removed by the communists in 1937 and taken to Leningrad (St Petersburg). Its fate is still unknown; one theory is that it is still hidden in storage and another that it was melted down to make bullets.

In October 1996, after nearly five years of work, a new statue called Migjid Janraisig (which means 'The Lord Who Looks in Every Direction') was consecrated by the Dalai Lama. Located in the temple of the same name, the 26.5m-high, 20-ton statue is made from copper, gilded with gold donated from Nepal and Japan, and covered in gold brocade and over 500m of silk. The statue contains precious stones, 27 tonnes of medicinal herbs, 334 sutras, two million bundles of mantras and, in the base, an entire ger, plus furniture!

a magnificent statue of *yab-yum* (mystic sexual union).

The other temples are: **Zuu Süm**, dedicated to Sakyamuni; **Yadam Süm**, which contains wooden and bronze statues of various gods, some created by the famous Mongolian sculptor Zanabazar; and **Amgalan Süm**, containing a self-portrait of the great Zanabazar himself and a small stupa apparently brought to Ulaanbaatar by Zanabazar from Tibet.

The museum is two blocks south of the Square. A useful **booklet** (T1000) in English is available at the monastery entrance and some of the caretakers inside can give a brief English-language commentary. A concrete ger inside the grounds has a good selection of reasonably priced souvenirs, and probably the best range of books about Buddhism and Mongolia in Ulaanbaatar.

OTHER MONASTERIES & TEMPLES

Belonging to Gandan Khiid, **Gesar Süm** (Map pp56–8; ☎ 313 148; cnr Sambuugiin Örgön Chölöö & Ikh Toiruu west; admission free) is named after the mythical Tibetan king. The lovely temple is a fine example of Chinese-influenced architecture. It is a popular place for locals to request, and pay for, *puja* (a blessing ceremony).

Tasgany Ovoo (Map pp56–8), about 300m north of Gesar Süm, is worth a look if you haven't yet seen an *ovoo*, a sacred pyramid-shaped collection of stones. A 12m-high Buddhist monument is planned for the top of the hill, which is also known as Zaany Tolgoi, or Elephant's Head.

On the way to Gandan Khiid, the new **Lamrim Süm** (Stages of the Path Temple; Map pp56–8) has a small temple with statues of Tsongkhapa, the Tibetan Buddhist reformer, and Sakyamuni, the historical Buddha. Nearby, **Ikh Khuree Zurhain Datsan** (Map pp56–8) is a prayer-reading centre. For a small fee, monks can prognosticate your future or read prayers to make your wishes come true.

The **Bakula Rinpoche Süm** (Map pp56–8; ☎ 322 366; admission free), also known as the Pethub Stangey Choskhor Ling Khiid, was founded in 1999 by the late Indian ambassador, himself a reincarnate lama from Ladakh. The Rinpoche's ashes were interred inside a golden stupa inside the temple in July 2004. The monastery, used mainly as a cen-

tre for Buddhist teaching, also has a centre for Buddhist medicine.

Dashchoilon Khiid (Map pp56–8; ☎ 350 047; Academich Sodnomin Gudamj; admission free) was originally built at another location in 1890, but was destroyed in the late 1930s. The monastery was recently moved into three huge concrete gers that once formed part of the State Circus. Now the monastery is used by over 100 monks. You can get to there from a lane running off Baga Toiruu – look out for the orange and brown roof.

Otochmaaramba Khiid (Map p53; ☎ 458 489; admission free; ⏱ 9am-5.30pm) can be easily seen from the northeastern bend of Ikh Toiruu. Although not as interesting as the others, it's still worth a visit. The monastery is the location of the **Manba Datsan** traditional-medicine clinic and training centre, which re-opened in 1990.

In the northeast, **Dambadarjaa Khiid**, completed in 1765, was once home to 1200 monks. 'Dambadarjaa' means 'Propagation of Religion' in Tibetan, which is rather ironic considering that it was dismantled in 1937 and converted into a hospital. Only the ruins of a few of the 30 small temples have been restored, but it is worth a look. Less than 2km north of here is a new **memorial** dedicated to Japanese soldiers. The only way to get there is by taxi.

Art Galleries

As well as music, Mongolians love the visual arts, and there are a few galleries worth visiting. See the website www.ulaanbaatar.net/culture.shtml for more information.

MONGOLIAN NATIONAL MODERN ART GALLERY

Sometimes called the Fine Art Gallery, the **Mongolian National Modern Art Gallery** (Монголын Уран Зургийн Үзэсгэлэн; Map pp56–8; ☎ 313 191; admission T2000, photos T5000, videos T10,000; ⏱ 10am-6pm), contains a large and impressive display of modern and uniquely Mongolian paintings and sculptures. It has a mixture of depictions of nomadic life, people and landscapes, ranging from impressionistic to nationalistic. The artworks are always interesting, and are titled in English. The Soviet romantic paintings depicted in *thangka* style are especially interesting, but the most famous work is Tsevegjav Ochir's 1958 *The Fight of the Stallions*.

NINTH JEBTZUN DAMBA

When the eighth Jebtzun Damba, Bogd Khaan, died in 1924 the communist government refused to allow any future 'reincarnations', ensuring their control over Mongolian Buddhism. After restrictions against religion were lifted in Mongolia in 1990, the Dalai Lama proclaimed a ninth Jebtzun Damba as the new spiritual leader of Mongolian Buddhism.

The ninth Jebtzun Damba was born in Tibet in 1932, and was accepted as the ninth reincarnation at the age of four, but his identity was kept a secret from Stalin's thugs. He fled Tibet in 1960 and, in the early 1990s, he moved to Dharamsala, in northwest India, where he is close to the current Dalai Lama.

In 1999 the 67-year-old lama surprised everyone by turning up in Ulaanbaatar after casually applying for a tourist visa in Moscow. ('Occupation: Reincarnation of Tibetan deity Vajrapani'!) Mobbed by adoring crowds everywhere he went (it was his first ever visit to Mongolia), he was pressured to leave after he overstayed his visa and he finally returned to Dharamsala.

The entrance is in the courtyard of the Palace of Culture. The main gallery is on the 3rd floor, there are temporary exhibits on the 2nd floor and a shop on the 1st floor.

OTHER GALLERIES

If you want to see more Mongolian art, and maybe buy some, head into the **Mongolian Artists' Exhibition Hall** (Монголын Зураачдын Үзэсгэлэн Танхим; Map pp56-8; ☎ 327 474; cnr Peace Ave & Chingisiin Örgön Chölöö; admission free; ☼ 9am-6pm), on the 2nd floor of the white marble building diagonally opposite the CPO. This is a rotating collection of modern and often dramatic paintings, carvings, tapestries and sculptures. The displays often change and there's a good souvenir shop.

Even more interesting is a visit to the artist studios in the **Mongolian National Artists Union** (Уран Бүтээлчдийн Урлан; Map p53; www.uma .mn; cnr Erkhuugiin Gudamj & Ikh Toiruu; ☼ 9am-1pm & 2-6pm). The artists are welcoming and you can offer to buy their work on the spot. It's in a blue building with a bronze statue of a seated monk above the door. The **Arts Council of Mongolia** (Map pp56-8; reservations ☎ 319 015; www.artscouncil.mn) conducts tours here for US$25 per group of five.

Other Sights
SÜKHBAATAR SQUARE

In July 1921 in the centre of Ulaanbaatar, the 'hero of the revolution', Damdin Sükhbaatar, declared Mongolia's final independence from the Chinese. The Square (Сухбаатарын Талбай; Map pp56–8) now bears his name and features a statue of him astride his horse. The words he apparently proclaimed at the time are engraved on the bottom of the statue: 'If we, the whole people, unite in our common effort and common will, there will be nothing in the world that we cannot achieve, that we will not have learnt or failed to do.'

Sükhbaatar would have been very disappointed to learn that the Square was also where the first protests were held in 1990, which eventually led to the fall of communism in Mongolia. Today, the Square is occasionally used for rallies, ceremonies and even rock concerts, but is generally a serene place where only the photographers are doing anything. In 2003 the square got a make-over, with new blocks of granite, a lighting system donated by China and a plaque that lists the former names of the city – Örgöö, Nomiin Khuree, Ikh Khuree and Niislel Khuree.

As you face north from the statue, the large grey building before you is **Parliament House**, commonly known as Government House, which, like every ger, was built to face south. An inner courtyard of the building actually holds a large ceremonial ger used for hosting visiting dignitaries.

Directly in front of it is a **mausoleum**, built in 1921, which contains the remains of Sükhbaatar, and possibly Choibalsan.

To the northeast is the tall, modern **Palace of Culture**, a useful landmark containing the Mongolian National Modern Art Gallery and several other cultural institutions. At the southeast corner of the Square, the salmon-pinkish building is the **State Opera & Ballet Theatre**.

The **National Museum of Mongolian History** is the square, grey building west of Government House. The yellow-and-white building on the western side of the square is the Ulaanbaatar City Hall. Next door, the green Golomt Bank building and adjacent Bodicom Tower was built in 2002.

South of the Golomt Bank, the clay-red building is the **Mongolian Stock Exchange**, which was opened in 1992 in the former Children's Cinema. One corner is now partitioned off as an Internet café.

The small park opposite the Stock Exchange contains a **0-kilometer marker**, the point from which all distances in Mongolia are measured. For a blast from the past, walk east from the southeast corner of the Square to the **Lenin statue**. (For an even more dramatic bust of Lenin walk into the former **Lenin Museum**, on the north side of Liberty Square.)

NAIRAMDAL PARK

Also called the Children's Park, **Nairamdal Park** (Найрамдал Парк; Friendship Park; Map pp56-8) is a large swath of unkempt grass, scattered concrete statues and even a Mongolian-style Disneyland. It is quite photogenic on Sundays when hundreds of children descend upon it.

There are the usual children's rides, including a Ferris wheel (agonisingly slow, but with great views from the top) and, our favourite, the 'aerobicycle', a sort of tandem bike on a monorail track 3m high (watch out in winter when you'll become a target for snowball throwers!). A lake in the south of the park offers boat rides in summer and ice-skating in winter.

You can enter the park from south of the Monastery-Museum of Choijin Lama, or opposite the Bayangol Hotel.

ZAISAN MEMORIAL

The tall, thin landmark on top of the hill south of the city is the Zaisan Memorial (Зайсан Толгой). Built by the Russians to commemorate 'unknown soldiers and heroes' from various wars, it offers the best views of Ulaanbaatar and the surrounding hills. The views are better at night, however, when you can't see the ugly power stations and the layers of dust and pollution, but there's no public transport there after 10pm (when the sun sets in summer).

To get there, catch bus No 7 straight to the base of the staircase leading up to the memorial. This bus departs from the Bayangol Hotel or Ard Kino.

ACTIVITIES

For a swim, try the heated **indoor pool** (Map p53; ☎ 318 180; Zaluuchuudyn Örgön Chölöö; per hr T4000; ☺ 8am-8pm Wed-Sun, closed Jul & Aug) at the Zaluus Youth & Cultural Centre. There's also a private **gym** in the building next door that you can use for T3000 an hour.

The **UB Golf Club** (☎ 9979 9945, 9976 3377; one round US$20, caddy US$5, ball boy US$1) isn't quite Pebble Beach but it's really the only place to whack a ball around. The greenskeepers like to give the place a wild element and balls tend to get swallowed up even on the fairways – down marmot holes or in the high grass. Don't get lost here or you, too, could become a permanent fixture (we found a human skull on the seventh hole!). It's located 15km west of the city, about 3km before the Nairamdal Zulsan International Children's Centre. If you just want to practice your stroke, there is a **mini driving range** on the 6th floor of the Ulaanbaatar Hotel (Map pp56–8). At the time of writing a Korean company was building an outdoor **golf practice range** by Ikh Tenger, at the southern end of Olympiin Örgön Chölöö.

The **Mon-Kor bowling alley** (Map pp56-8; ☎ 312 243; Baga Toiruu 31; 10am-1pm per game T1150, 1-5pm T1750, 5pm-midnight T2300) has four lanes and modern facilities. It is opposite the Children's Creativity Centre. If you feel like a game of pool, there are dozens of billiards and pool halls around town.

Adrenaline junkies may want to spend an afternoon paragliding with a local aviation enthusiast, **Alex** (☎ 682 014, 9919 5965; per day US$30). The price includes transportation and a two-hour lesson. Note that spring is a dangerous time to paraglide in Mongolia because of the unpredictable winds. September is best for beginners. Alex also gives ultralight aircraft tours for US$100 per hour.

WALKING TOUR

On this walk through the city you can visit Ulaanbaatar's best monasteries and historical sites while staying within the downtown area. Some parts are fairly exposed to the summer sun so bring a hat and sunblock.

Start off from the bottom of Öndör Gegeen Zanabazaryn Gudamj, the wide, dusty

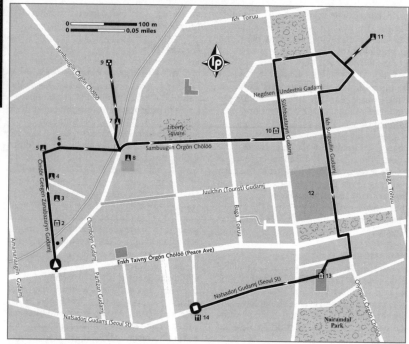

approach road to the Gandan Khiid. Heading up the right side of the road you'll pass a **Shaman Centre (1)**, the **Hunting Museum (2**; p62) and then two temples popular for prayer reading – the **Lamrin Süm (3**; p65) and the **Ikh Khuree Zurkhain Datsan (4**; p65).

No proper walking tour of Ulaanbaatar could miss the spiritual heart of the city, **Gandan Khiid (5**; p63), once called 'Baruun Khuree', the western camp. After strolling through the grounds of Gandan, exit via the east gate through the ger district that forms a traditional, protective circle around the temples. Outside the gate you may find **fortune tellers (6)** who make divinations using coins, sheep ankle bones and tarot cards. Further east down the path, at opposite ends of the large intersection, are the **Gesar Süm (7**; p65) and **Bakula Rinpoche Süm (8**; p65). Behind Gesar Sum you can take a short detour to the top of Tsagaan Tolgoi hill to check out **Tasgany Ovoo (9**; p65) and the good view of the city.

From Bakula Rinpoche's temple you'll have to huff it for about 20 minutes through town to Dashchoilon Khiid, on the far side

> **Start/Finish:** cnr Öndör Gegeen Zanabazaryn Gudamj & Peace Ave
> **Distance:** approx 3km
> **Duration:** around 1½ hours

of the Little Ring Rd (Baga Toiruu). En route you can break your journey at the **Museum of Natural History (10**; p60), home to a rich collection of fossils and dinosaur bones. **Dashchoilon Khiid (11**; p65), in old Khuree, formed a cornerstone of Zuun Khuree, the eastern camp, which at its height had even more temples than the Gandan area. Dashchoilon was spared the communist destruction because the large circular buildings were converted into the State Circus in 1940.

From Dashchoilon Khiid, continue south across **Sükhbaatar Square (12**; p66) and its statue of Sükhbaatar on his horse to the **Monastery-Museum of Choijin Lama (13**; p64). For an appropriate place to end this walk, continue down Seoul St for lunch at the **Chin Van Khanddorj ger restaurant (14**; p75).

COURSES
Language

The best places to ask around for 'exchange lessons' are the National University of Mongolia and the Institute of Foreign Languages in Ulaanbaatar, as well as the embassies and aid and development agencies. Also check out the English-language newspapers for any advertisements about language courses. Several language schools in Ulaanbaatar organise long- and short-term courses. You can also learn Mongolian from someone who wants to learn or practise your language (English, French, German and Japanese are particularly popular). Some recommended schools in Ulaanbaatar include:

Bridge Mongolian Language Center (Map p53; ☎ 367 149; www.bridge.url.mn/english; Room 205, Sunrise Center, Damdinbazaryn Gudamj) In the suburbs of the 4th district, this language centre is a cheaper option than Santis, and offers an intensive two-week survival course, as well as longer courses and individual tuition. Costs are US$3 per hour for a private lesson or US$2 per person for a group lesson.

International Language Center (Map pp56-8; ☎ 313 727; baesgyu@yahoo.com; Choimbolyn 6) Next to the Kharaa Hotel, this school has a Mongolian-language course for T2000 per hour.

Santis Language School (Map pp56-8; ☎ 318 313; fax 326 373; santis@magicnet.mn; 5th fl, Unen Newspaper Bldg, Amaryn Gudamj) Located just east of the Tuushin Hotel, Santis can arrange private Mongolian language tuition for US$5 per hour, and also offers 50-hour, six-week group courses for around US$4 per hour, though most of these start in September.

Buddhism

The **Federation for the Preservation of Mahayana Tradition** (FPMT; Map pp56-8; ☎ 9911 9765; fpmt-mongolia@magicnet.mn; Builder's Square, Juulchin Gudamj) is involved in the regeneration of Buddhist culture in Mongolia. The centre offers free lectures and courses on various aspects of Buddhist tradition and meditation. Lectures are given in English; look for the pink-tiled building west of the Mormon Church.

University Courses

The **National University of Mongolia** (NUM; Map pp56-8; ☎ 320 159; www.num.edu.mn; Ikh Surguuliin Gudamj 1, PO Box 46/337, 210646) is northeast of Sükhbaatar Square. The school offers specialised classes on Mongolian culture and language, and has a foreign-student department.

Flexible group and private Mongolian-language lessons are available at the **Institute of International Studies** (Map pp56-8; ☎ 329 860, 9918 5103; fax 329 450; dashpurev@magicnet.mn).

The **American Center for Mongolian Studies** (Map pp56-8; ☎ 314 055; www.mongoliacenter.org; National University of Mongolia, Bldg 1, Room 205) has a good website listing courses and can recommend study possibilities. At the time of writing it was preparing to open a small library on books about Mongolia.

ULAANBAATAR FOR CHILDREN

Nairamdal Park (p67) is the best place in the city to let your kids run around for a while. Supervise closely as not all the rides are up to Western standards. Kids will enjoy clambering up to the top of the **Zaisan Memorial** (p67) more than dawdling through the monasteries and museums, although the dinosaur exhibit at the **Natural History Museum** (p60) is sure to get their juices going. If your kids have their own roller skates, the pavement on **Sükhbaatar Square** (p66) is the best in town. One museum kids won't want to miss is the **Railway Museum** (p62) and perhaps the puzzle- and toy-stuffed **International Intellectual Museum** (p62).

TOURS
Tours Outside Ulaanbaatar

Of the hundred or more travel agencies offering tours that have sprung up around Ulaanbaatar in the past few years, the dozen or so listed below are recommended as being generally reliable.

Many agencies run their businesses from home and their offices are notoriously difficult to find. It is far better to communicate by fax, phone or, even better, by email. Ring in advance if you want to actually meet with someone.

Budget travellers often organise ad-hoc tours via their guesthouse or Chez Bernard Café (p78). If you do this try to meet the driver and guide before the trip and ensure that everyone knows the itinerary and exactly what is included. Khongor, Bolod's, Gana's and UB guesthouses (see p72) all run fairly standard trips that get consistently good reviews. Shop around and see who can off the most creative schedule at the best price. Bolod is known for his off-beat ideas, included visits to shamans and tank-driving excursions. Trips by car range

ULAANBAATAR

between US$25 to US$40 per person, all inclusive.

Active Adventures (☎ 321 276, 9917 7029; www.activemongolia.com) This reliable Scottish–German operation specialises in rugged hiking, rafting and horseback trips, plus fishing expeditions. Most of the trips are to Khövsgöl, Arkhangai and Khentii aimags. Contact Sylvia Hay.

Blue Sky Travel (Map p53; ☎ /fax 312 067, 9925 6673; www.travel2mongolia.mn; PO Box 181) Blue Sky offers a wide range of professionally run tours. The office is north of the international railway ticket office.

Gobiin Ogloo (Map pp56-8; ☎ 315 552; fax 323 394; www.gobinogloo.mn; Amaryn Gudamj 2; PO Box 1014) A German-speaking agency next to the Tuushin Hotel (the last entrance and up to the 5th floor).

Happy Camel (Map pp56-8; www.happycamel.com; Peace Ave 27) It operates out of Chez Bernard; see p78.

Juulchin (Map pp56-8; ☎ 328 428; fax 320 246; www.mongoljuulchin.mn; Bayangol Hotel, 5B, Chinggis Khaan Örgön Chölöö) This former government tourist agency, now privatised, offers a wide range of tours around the country, including rafting, bird-watching, fishing, skiing, hiking and jeep trips around the Gobi. Its office is at the back of Bayangol Hotel.

Karakorum Expeditions (Map pp56-8; ☎ 320 182, 9911 6729; fax 315 655; www.gomongolia.com; PO Box 542) The leader in bike and hiking tours in western Mongolia, it also combines trips to China. The company has a good philosophy: a big plus is that they run snow-leopard research trips and wildlife tours. The office is behind the State Circus in the Gangaryn Gurav building. Contact Graham Taylor.

Khövsgöl Lodge Company (Map pp56-8; ☎ 9911 5929; fax 310 852; klm@boojum.com; Room 16, Bldg 13, Sukhbaatar District) This experienced outfitter is part of the US-based Boojum Expeditions. It is in an apartment block behind the Drama Theatre, but you are better off calling first to get someone to meet you. Contact Bobo or Anya.

Nature Tours (Map pp56-8; ☎ 311 801; fax 311 979; www.naturetours.mn; Seoul St, Cho-Burt bldg 106). A reliable outfit, it runs the usual range of tours around the country. It also has ger camps in Terelj and Khogno Khan Uul.

Nomadic Expeditions (Map pp56-8; ☎ 313 396, 325 786; fax 320 311; www.threecamellodge.com; Peace Ave 76) This is the Mongolian office of the US-based travel company (see the boxed text, p257).

Nomadic Journeys (Map pp56-8; ☎ 328 737; fax 321 489; www.nomadicjourneys.com; Sükhbaataryn Gudamj 1) A Mongolian-Swedish joint venture concentrating on low-impact tourism. It runs fixed-departure yak, camel and horse treks and can also arrange rafting trips on the Tuul Gol. Its trip in Terelj is unique – you ride yaks (and horses) and carry your own portable ger by yak cart. Contact Jan Wigsten or Manduhai.

Nomads (Map pp56-8; ☎ /fax 328 146; www.nomadstours.com; Suite 8-9, 3rd fl, Peace & Friendship Bldg, Peace Ave, PO Box 1008) Offers a wide range of fixed departure tours, including popular horse treks in Khentii and through Terelj, visiting Gunjiin Süm. Nomads also offers fabulous jeep trips to more remote areas in the far west and camel treks in the Gobi.

Nomin Tours (Map pp56-8; ☎ 313 232; fax 314 242; www.nomintours.com; 3rd fl, State Department Store)

Samar Magic Tours (Map pp56-8; ☎ 311 051, 9928 2459; fax 327 503; www.samarmagictours.com; PO Box 329) Specialises in fishing and wildlife tours and eco-volunteer programs. It has a ger camp near Terelj and the office is in the entrance of the El Latino restaurant (see p77). Contact Spanish- and English-speaking Christo Camilo Gavilla Gomez.

Skyland Tour (Map pp56-8; ☎ fax 315 556; www.skylandtour.mn; Juulchin Gudamj 37-1) Trips are organised from a 'tourist information office' 200m north of the State Department Store.

SSS Travel (Map pp56-8; ☎ 328 410, 9915 5590; fax 311 915; www.ssstravel.mn; Sükhbaataryn Gudamj 1) Geared up for the backpacker set, it specialises in custom budget tours around the country. Country accommodation is often with local families rather than hotels. It sells ISIC cards for US$5 and also has an info booth at the airport arrivals hall.

Tours of Ulaanbaatar

It is not particularly easy to join an organised tour of Ulaanbaatar if you have arrived as an independent traveller. You can try to contact one of the companies offering tours listed above and see what they have available; however, seeing the sights of the capital can be easily done without joining an organised tour, especially if you have a taxi for the day. Although not really necessary, if you do hire a taxi, a guide-cum-interpreter, especially one who speaks your language if you're not confident in English, could be handy.

The **Arts Council of Mongolia** (Map pp56-8; ☎ 319 015; www.artscouncil.mn) sponsors two excellent specialised city tours twice a month or by appointment. 'Myths and Truths: the Socialist Legacy in Mongolia Tour' visits places associated with the communist era, and the 'Mongolian Buddhism Tour' explores Ulaanbaatar's Buddhist legacy beyond the main tourist attractions. Both tours provide lunch and excellent commentary. Prices vary depending on the size of your group, but count on paying about US$70 per person.

FESTIVALS & EVENTS

The biggest event in Ulaanbaatar is undoubtedly the **Naadam Festival**, held on 11 and 12 July. Some visitors may not find the festival itself terribly exciting, but the associated activities during the Naadam week and the general festive mood make it a great time to visit. For more information, see the boxed text on p83.

Around Naadam and other public holidays, special cultural events and shows are organised. It's worth reading the local English-language newspapers and asking a Mongolian friend, guide or hotel staff member to find out what may be on.

The **Khan Brau Challenge**, held on the first Saturday of June, is an 18km run/scramble/walk from the Zaisan Memorial to Manzushir Khiid. The T15,000 entry fee covers registration, food and beer at the end of the run and a ride back to UB. The course record is held by an Israeli who made it over in just two hours, though most people take four to six hours to complete the course.

The last week in October sees the **city's birthday**, now nearing 370 years. Events and concerts are usually put on at this time at the Palace of Culture or State Opera Theatre. See www.artscouncil.mn for details. At the end of July, on a date set by the lunar calendar, you can see **tsam mask dancing** at Dashchoilon Khiid.

SLEEPING

There is a fairly good range of places to stay in the capital city, but rarely is there anywhere that could be regarded as good value. During the week surrounding the Naadam Festival accommodation may be in short supply, and prices are often higher.

Budget

APARTMENTS

If you are planning to stay in Ulaanbaatar for a while or you are travelling in a small group, it's worth looking around for an apartment to rent. Most owners or landlords obviously prefer long-term rentals, particularly to resident expats, but if business is slow you may be able to arrange something with a short-term lease. A reasonable, furnished, two-bedroom apartment with a kitchen costs from US$200 to US$300 per month. Finding an apartment is usually a matter of asking around or checking over the classified sections of the local English-language papers. **Mongolian Properties** (Map pp56-8; ☎ 324 545; fax 313289; www.mongolianproperties.com; Seoul St 48/13) has apartments for rent on a long-term basis. Another agent to try is **CTB Real Estate** (realestate_ctb@hotmail.com).

You could also ask at the guesthouses, which sometimes rent out apartments for US$10 to US$20 per night for short-term stays. You must pay for the electricity and

---

GOING UNDERGROUND

One result of Mongolia's recent social upheaval and rising poverty has been the appearance of street children in Ulaanbaatar. Their numbers peaked in the mid-1990s at some 6000, but has since dropped into the hundreds. Many of these homeless children live in the city's underground sewers and heating pipes – the only places where the kids can survive in winter temperatures of -30° C.

Most of the children were abandoned by parents unable to care for them (unemployment is 35% in Ulaanbaatar), were sent from relatives in the countryside, or ran away from alcoholic fathers or parents (80% of street kids come from one-parent families). Many of the kids (especially boys) prefer the freedom of the streets in summer rather than the strict rules and classes of homeless shelters, but winters are brutal. Girls often end up in prostitution. Both sexes suffer from poor health, with high rates of malnutrition, syphilis, scabies and body lice.

Ulaanbaatar has around 20 shelters, many run by foreign nongovernmental organisations, with beds for around 500 children. Several aid agencies work with the children, including **Save the Children** (www.savethechildren.org), the National Centre for Children and the **Lotus Children's Centre** (www.lotuschild.org). The **Christina Noble Foundation** (www.cncf.org) operates a shelter on the edge of town and runs several education and health programs.

SSS Travel (Map pp56-8; ☎ 328 410; www.ssstravel.mn; Sükhbaataryn Gudamj 1) offers a day walk in Yarmag ger district that includes a visit to the Lotus Children's Centre. Part of the cost of the visit goes back to the centre as a donation.

phone. Water and heating is free thanks to the unmetered centralised hot-water system installed by the Russians.

GUESTHOUSES

Life in the city's guesthouses is much like sharing an apartment. Most guesthouses offer a hot shower and a kitchen. Almost all offer trips to nearby attractions, as well as visa extension and registration, laundry and the booking of train tickets. They are firmly aimed at backpackers and can be crowded and lacking in privacy over Naadam. If overbooked you may be shoved into an apartment with the owner's grandmother – there's always room for one more.

Bolod's Guesthouse (Map pp56-8; ☎ 9919 2407; www.bolodtours.com; Peace Ave 61, door 20, room 22; dm US$5; 💻) Clean and bright, high-ceilinged rooms, more spacious than at most other guesthouses, make this a good-value budget option. It has a cosy atmosphere and a central location. Bolod is a genuinely gracious host and provides good tours and visa support if you're stuck. Enter through the white-and-grey gate opposite the CPO.

Khongor Guest House (Map pp56-8; ☎ 316 415, 9925 2599; http://get.to/khongor; Peace Ave 15, apt 6; dm/s/d US$4/10/12; 💻) The experienced, English-speaking Toroo offers well-appointed accommodation in three separate buildings, each convenient and central. Each dorm bed comes with a light and safety box. The reliable management does an excellent job with logistics, trips and visa matters (check out the glowing guestbook on its website). In winter the guesthouse runs trips to the northern *taiga* where travellers join wolf hunters for a traditional hunt. The entrance of the Khongor is around the back of the third building west of the State Department Store. A sister guesthouse, the **Azusaya** (Map pp56-8; Peace Ave 15), is aimed specifically at Japanese travellers. It's one stairwell entrance past Khongor.

Gana's Guest House (Map pp56-8; ☎ /fax 367 343; www.ganasger.mn; Gandan Khiid ger district, House No 22; dm in room/ger US$3/5, d US$15; 💻) This is UB's oldest hangout for overlanders. Staying out in the suburbs, near the temples and in a ger, is a unique experience and the main reason to come here. It's also a great place to meet other travellers with a view to assembling a jeep-load of people. Facilities have improved somewhat and the shower

and toilet block function most of the time. All beds come with a free breakfast.

Mongolia Resorts Guesthouse (Map pp56-8; ☎ 322 490, 9909 1899; www.mongolianresorts.com; Civil Defence Building, 3rd & 4th fl, Seoul St 13; dm US$5, d with/without bathroom US$30/14) This is the only backpacker place in town that resembles an actual hotel, rather than an apartment-style place, which makes it a good option if you are travelling in a large group. There is a communal feel here; it's popular with British backpackers, and the American owner Lee Cashell is usually available to help with travel arrangements. It is about 50m east of Aeroflot.

Chinggis Backpackers (Map pp56-8; ☎ 317 207; www.mongolianbutterfly.com; off cnr Baruun Selbe & Peace Ave; dm US$10) Another apartment-style place, this one has very clean rooms although US$10 is a bit much to ask for a dorm bed. The owner is a butterfly collector and can organise 'butterfly and insect collection tours' among other off-beat ideas. The hostel has a prime location in a courtyard 100m east of the State Department Store. Don't confuse this place with **Chinggis Guesthouse** (Map pp56-8; ☎ 325 941; chingisguest@magicnet.mn; bldg 33, door 67; dm US$6, d US$12), another place that gets good reports from travellers. This one is located behind the National Drama Theatre.

UB Guesthouse (Map pp56-8; ☎ 311 037, 9119 9859; www.ubguest.com; bldg 41, south of cnr Baga Toiruu & Juulchin Gudamj; dm US$4, d US$12; 💻) Although this Korean-Mongolian joint venture gets good reviews, it can get pretty crowded here in peak season and the common room simply can't handle all those bodies. Still, the dorms are well appointed and the bathrooms very clean. The price includes breakfast, and hot water and tea bags. It's a great place to find other people to share a jeep. The guesthouse is located above the Golomt Bank on Baga Toiruu west. The entrance is around the back.

Serge's Guesthouse (Map pp56-8; ☎ 320 267, 9919 8204; sergetour@yahoo.com; Peace Ave 25, entrance 4, door 31; dm US$3.50-4, d US$6-10) Located next to the Naran Tuul building, this backpacker crash pad has a few rooms in two apartments.

Idre's Guest House (Map pp56-8; ☎ 316 749, 9916 6049; www.idretour.com; Teeverchidiin Gudamj, bldg 23, entrance 2, door 44, 3rd fl; dm US$3.50, d US$9; 💻) Similarly cheap and dishevelled, Idre's is tucked behind the old long-distance bus station. As you walk behind the station, turn right and

---

AUTHOR'S BUDGET CHOICE

Zaya Backpacker Hostel (Map pp56-8; ☎ 316 696, 9918 5013; www.magicnet.mn/~backpackza; Peace Ave 63; dm/s/d US$4/10/16; ⌨) This hidden gem of a guesthouse has clean, quiet, remodelled rooms with single, double and dorm space available. Zaya speaks English, Russian and Chinese and her assistance gets high marks from travellers. The place is often full so try to make a reservation online. The building is located inside a courtyard off Peace Ave, between Los Bandidos restaurant and Za Internet Café. It's the best guesthouse if you're looking for a bit of quiet and a reasonable amount of privacy.

---

look for the nine-storey apartment block. Idre has a ger at Zuunmod and can arrange horse-riding trips to the area.

HOTELS

Ulaanbaatar's budget hotels are not even half as good value as its guesthouses. Most are Soviet-era leftovers and are dark, deserted or noisy, with barely functioning facilities.

Mandukhai Hotel (Map pp56-8; ☎ 322 204; s/d/tr T8000/16,000/20,000, lux s/d T23,000/38,000) This Soviet-style hotel is looking pretty rundown these days, with unremarkable rooms and dodgy plumbing. The location is OK, just west of the State Department Store, hidden in apartment blocks about 100m north of Peace Ave – look for the hotel's yellow pagoda-style roof.

Negdelchin Hotel (Map p53; ☎ 453 230; fax 458 301; Peace Ave 16; s US$14, d with bathroom US$25, lux US$35) This small, scruffy hotel has a variety of rooms. It is located 50m west of the Wrestling Palace.

Railway Hotel (Map p53; ☎ 944 357; 2nd fl, train station; dm/d T5000/16,000) The rooms here have been renovated and are good enough if you are just changing trains and need a rest.

CAMPING

There are no official camping grounds in Ulaanbaatar but you'll find endless patches of grass to pitch a tent on Bogd Khan Uul to the south of the city. Try the valley behind the Zaisan Memorial. The main problem, of course, is what to do with all your stuff during the day; theft is a problem, so you're probably better off going to Gachuurt (p102) or Manzushir Khiid (p94).

Mid-Range

Places in this range are not particularly good value, but they normally include breakfast. Ask whether the arbitrary government tax of 15% is included or not.

Zaluuchuud Hotel (Map pp56-8; ☎ 324 594, fax 324 231; Baga Toiruu 43; s/d/ste US$30/60/90) Recently renovated, the Zaluuchuud has climbed into the mid-range category with spiffy rooms equipped with TV, fridge and hot-water pot. The singles are a bit cramped and the doubles are overpriced but you could try bargaining.

Hotel Örgöö (Map pp56-8; ☎ 313 772; fax 312 712; cnr Juulchin Gudamj & Jigjidjavanyn Gudamj; s/d US$25/40, ste US$50-60) This place has a perfect location immediately west of the State Parliament House, and at a pinch could be called cosy, but the rooms are unkempt and poor value in themselves. Keep an eye on your stuff as security is an issue here.

Marco Polo Hotel (Map pp56-8; ☎ 310 803; fax 311 273; s/d US$40/55) This friendly, clean place is a good option in this price range. The standard rooms with desk, fridge and TV include breakfast. Credit cards are accepted. The hotel is surrounded by apartment blocks and hard to find; approach it from Erkhuugiin Gudamj to the east.

Genex Hotel (Map pp56-8; ☎ 319 325; fax 323 827; www.generalimpex.mn; Choimbolyn Gudamj 10; s/d US$35/50, half-lux US$48/80, lux US$75/120) Located near Ikh Toiruu, this clean, modern hotel has nice half-lux rooms, but the standard rooms don't have an attached shower. Prices include breakfast and credit cards are accepted.

Kharaa Hotel (Map pp56-8; ☎ 313 733; Choimbolyn 6; d/half-lux/lux US$25/35/45) It's on the same street as the Genex, but closer to Peace Ave. The rooms here are clean but unexciting.

Flower Hotel (Map p53; ☎ 458 330; fax 455 652; www.flower-hotel.com; Zaluuchuudyn Örgön Chölöö; s/d US$44/77, half-lux US$71/93, lux US$93/132; ⌨ ⌨) Japanese investment has given this place a glossy finish. It's in a nice neighbourhood but is inconvenient to the Square. The standard rooms, with shared bathrooms, are overpriced.

Sarora Hotel (Map pp56-8; ☎ 327 831; Seoul St 12-6; s/d US$20/30, half-lux US$60/90, lux US$80/90) This Japanese-oriented place, with very pink rooms, is southwest of Merkuri market.

White House Hotel (Map p53; ☎ 367 837; fax 369 973; www.whitehousehotel.mn; Damdinbazaryn Gudamj; s/d/lux US$60/80/120) This is a decent choice, more for the facilities than its location (about a 25-minute walk from the Square). The hotel has a classy English bar plus French and Japanese restaurants. Breakfast is included. It's just off Amarsanaagiin Gudamj.

Anujin Hotel (Map p53; ☎ 451 039; fax 450 720; anujin@mongol.net; Peace Ave; s/d/lux US$50/65/80) An acceptable option in this range but, like the others, not worth the price. It's next to the British embassy.

Undruul Hotel (Map p53; ☎ 455 108; fax 455 016; www.discover.mn; Ikh Toiruu; s/d US$50/70) It's about 400m northeast of the Anujin Hotel, and of a similar standard.

Jiguur Grand (Map pp56-8; ☎ 322 939; fax 322 805; Teeverchidiin Gudamj 13; s/d US$40/50, half-lux US$70/90) The Jiguur has well-equipped rooms (albeit lacking in style); it's just west of the bridge.

Top End

All top-end places include breakfast, but often they also include service and government charges of between 10% and 20%. Major credit cards are accepted and reservations are advisable in the peak season, especially around Naadam Festival time. The following should have their own supply of hot water and electricity, which is a real bonus if normal supplies are cut off to the rest of the city. At the end of 2007 the Shangri-La chain plan to open a five-star hotel on Sükhbaatar Square.

Bayangol Hotel (Map pp56-8; ☎ 312 255; fax 326 880; www.bayangolhotel.mn; Chingisiin Örgön Chölöö 5; s/d US$70/90, lux US$130/160) Popular with upmarket organised tours, the Bayangol has a central spot just south of the National Drama Theatre. There is an imported-goods shop here and the Western-style Casablanca restaurant on the 1st floor is recommended even if you are not staying here.

Chinggis Khaan Hotel (Map p53; ☎ 313 380; fax 312 788; www.chinggis-hotel.com; Tokyogiin Gudamj 5; s/d US$79/102, lux US$113/136, ste US$170; P ⌨) This bizarre cubist pink-and-black hotel is meant to be the most luxurious in town, although some readers complain that the

standard rooms are small and stuffy. Facilities include a gym and a pool, both of which cost extra, plus a shopping centre, nightclub, Chinese restaurant and a rooftop patio bar that offers good views of the city. The hotel is on the eastern edge of downtown – you cannot possibly miss it.

Tuushin Hotel (Map pp56-8; ☎ 323 162; fax 325 903; www.ulaanbaatar.net/tuushinhotel; Amaryn Gudamj 2; s/d US$66/88, half-lux US$77/105, lux US$132/176; ⌨) This hotel has an excellent location close to the Palace of Culture. The rooms are spacious and the price is inclusive of tax and breakfast.

Continental Hotel (Map pp56-8; ☎ 323 829; fax 329 630; www.continentalhotel.ulaanbaatar.net; Olympiin Örgön Chölöö; s/d US$79/107, half-lux US$105/132, lux US$130/168; P ⌨ ☒) This new, White House–inspired hotel is a favourite with US business consultants. Aside from the buffet breakfast, it offers a gym, sauna and billiards.

Edelweiss Hotel (Map p53; ☎ 312 186; fax 325 252; www.edelweiss.mn; s/d US$70/90, half-lux US$90/120, lux US$140/180; P ⌨) Near many embassies, it has comfortable rooms with balconies (ask for a south-facing room). Facilities include restaurants, a pub, sauna and billiards.

Palace Hotel (Map p53; ☎ 343 565; fax 322 805; www .palace.mn; d US$69/83, half-lux US$89/109, lux US$109/129; ⌨) Recently renovated, this place has good rooms and all the mod-cons. It's close to the Winter Palace of the Bogd Khaan.

Puma Imperial (Map pp56-8; ☎ 313 043; fax 319 148; www.mongolianpumahotel.com; Amaryn Gudamj 1; s/tw/d US$63/100/105; ⌨) This new Mongolian-run hotel occupies a prime location just east of Government House and next to MIAT. The rooms are fine, but some can be small and stuffy so ask to look first before checking in. It also has a self-contained family room (US$110) and an Indian restaurant on the 1st floor that has a menu similar to Hazara restaurant (p76) but cheaper.

EATING

The two best roads for all kinds of restaurants and cafés is Baga Toiruu west or Peace Ave near the State Department Store.

Restaurants

Despite its history as the mutton capital of the world, Ulaanbaatar has surprisingly risen to the upper echelons of Asia's restaurant scene. The city is covered with locally owned bistros that attempt European

---

SPLURGE!

Ulaanbaatar Hotel (Map pp56-8; ☎ 320 620; fax 324 485; http://welcome.to/ubhotel; Baga Toiruu; s/d US$60-70/90, ste US$90/120, lux US$120/160; 🖳) Probably the most popular and convenient place in this range, the UB is located just east of the Square. It's one of the very few hotels that was built and flourished during the former communist days. It still retains a certain old-world feel with high ceilings, chandeliers, a marble staircase and a lavish ballroom. It makes for a wonderful retreat if you've just come in from a long, dusty haul across the Gobi. The hotel also has a sauna, billiards room, business centre, travel agency, coffee shop, two restaurants and a golf practice range.

---

cuisine such as 'chicken gordon blue' (sic). But peppered among the pretenders are a number of excellent restaurants (many of them foreign-run) that serve anything from a New York steak to Belgian waffles.

MONGOLIAN

If you want to try some Mongolian food – but are fussy about hygienic kitchens and want a menu in English – head for one of the middle or top-end hotel restaurants, or a ger restaurant (see following).

Modern Nomads (Map pp56-8; ☎ 318 744; Baga Toiruu north; dishes T2500-35000, BBQ T6500, 🕑 lunch & dinner) Billed as a 'healthy alternative to Mongolian meals', this place serves traditional Mongolian tea, *khuushuur* (fried mutton pancakes) and *buuz* (steamed meat dumplings). The all-you-can-eat BBQ allows you to choose your own meat and vegetable ingredients, which are then grilled up by a chef up while you wait. In fact, this is the same 'Mongolian BBQ' that you'll find around the corner from your flat in London or Sydney, but nowhere else in Mongolia. Waitresses will bring fried bread and pâté while you wait, a good thing since the service is slow. It's recommended as a one-off.

Zochin Buuz (Map pp56-8; 🕑 24hr) It serves up industrial-sized *buuz*, plus soups and *beefshteks ondogtei* (beefsteak with egg). Very popular with locals and expanding rapidly, there are at least 10 Zochin Buuz outlets across the city. One is opposite the Russian embassy and another is next to Ard Kino.

GER RESTAURANTS

Two ger restaurants cater for visitors on organised tours who want to taste good – as opposed to truly authentic – Mongolian food, together with a traditional cultural show featuring some excellent music. If you are travelling independently and want to

come along, give them a ring or visit them to find out when they have a show, and if they have a spare table.

Abtai Sain Khaani Örgöö (Map p53; ☎ 9988 8090, 9525 6670; meal US$10; 🕑 lunch & dinner) Mongolia's biggest ger, near the US embassy, is a 7.5m-high ger restaurant decked out with snow-leopard pelts and bear skins.

Chin Van Khanddorjiin Örgöö (Map pp56-8; ☎ 320 763; Seoul St; meal T8050; 🕑 breakfast, lunch & dinner) This incongruous ger restaurant is converted from an authentic 19th-century aristocrat's home, now smack in the middle of suburbia.

ASIAN

While there is no love lost with the southern neighbour, this hasn't stopped Mongolians from diving whole-heartedly into the Chinese culinary world. Dozens of new Chinese restaurants have been joined by a clutch of Korean and Japanese restaurants, some with expensive but worthwhile buffets.

The best place for Japanese is the restaurant **Fuji Sanshiro** (Map p53; Flower Hotel; Zaluuchuudyn Örgön Chölöö). A few other hotels have decent Asian restaurants, including a Japanese restaurant at the White House, a Chinese place at the Chinggis Khaan and the Singaporean-styled Casablanca restaurant at the Bayangol.

Arirang Pyongyang Restaurant (Map pp56-8; ☎ 328 990; cnr Seoul St & Undsen Khuuliin Gudamj; meals T5000, sushi platter T10,000; 🕑 lunch & dinner) Offers a mix of Japanese and Korean dishes. Sushi is half-price here on weekends but the real reason to come here is to see the 'Friendship Cultural Centre of North Korea'. The backroom exhibit is disappointingly small but still worth visiting if you have an interest in the hermit kingdom.

Big Camp Hot Pot (Map pp56-8; Da Khuree Khaluun Togoo; ☎ 317 172; Baga Toiruu west; dishes T1500-2000; 🕑 lunch & dinner) This grimy-looking Chinese restaurant is one of many in downtown UB. There is no English menu so bring Lonely Planet's *China* guide, if you have it. Try the *gongbao jiding* (chicken and peanuts) or *fanqie chaodan* (egg and tomatoes).

Chinggis Restaurant (Map pp56-8; ☎ 321 257; Baga Toiruu 31 north; buffet T9900, à-la-carte dishes T5000-7000; ☾ lunch & dinner) This Korean joint comes from the Chinggis Khaan school of interior design; the are walls loaded with animal skins, antique pots and tree bark. If you don't go for the buffet, try the house specialty *kalbitan* (beef-rib soup). Traditional Mongolian dancing and singing performances go from 7pm to 10pm.

Jin Hai (Map pp56-8; ☎ 9919 4488; cnr Ikh Toiruu & Sambuugiin Örgön Chölöö; ☾ lunch & dinner) This fine Chinese option offers buffet meals and is inside the concrete beast opposite the Gesar Süm.

Little Hong Kong (Map pp56-8; ☎ 310 186; cnr Peace Ave & Baruun Selbe; meal with drink T4500; ☾ lunch & dinner) This place gets mixed reviews, though it certainly has a wider menu than the other Chinese restaurants, including, obviously, Cantonese dishes. It's also a little pricier than other Chinese places but there's pleasant outdoor seating in summer.

Doner Land (Map p53; ☎ 360 361; Ard Ayush Örgön Chölöö; meal T2500; ☾ lunch & dinner) Located in the Moscow Complex in the 3rd/4th microdistrict, this no-fuss Turkish restaurant serves up excellent kebabs and doners with a side dish of rice and salad. Another Turkish place is located on the patio of the State Opera Theatre on Sükhbaatar Square (summer only).

Hazara (Map p53; ☎ 9919 5707, 9515 7604; Peace Ave 16; dishes T5000-6000; ☾ lunch & dinner) Hidden behind the Wrestling Palace this long-time favourite of expats serves North Indian fare from a specially built tandoori oven. It's an atmospheric place; each table is covered by colourful canopy. It's also a four-time winner of 'best dinner restaurant' in the *Mongol Messenger* annual reader's poll. If you were wondering, the name refers to a tribe of Afghans descended from 13th-century Mongol troops who never went home.

Taj Mahal (Map pp56-8; ☎ 311 009; Baga Toiruu 46; dishes T4000-5000, thalli T6000; ☾ lunch & dinner) More central and cheaper than Hazara, but with equally good food, the Taj Mahal is another good choice. Amiable owner Babu prepares a range of tandoori and North Indian dishes such as *murgh makhni* (butter chicken). The lunchtime *thalli* (set menu) gives you three curries, dhal, salad, rice, bread and desert. We liked the interior too – the papier-mâché elephant and reconstruction of the Taj Mahal façade adds a nice touch. It is reached through an archway behind the Central Sports Palace.

Bangkok Thai Restaurant (Map pp56-8; ☎ 325 588; cnr Peace Ave & Chingisiin Örgön Chölöö; dishes T3500-6000; ☾ lunch & dinner) This colourful Thai restaurant has chicken curries, deep-fried fish, fruit platters and views of the Square. It is in the 2nd floor of the Mongolian Artists' Hall.

City Coffee (Map pp56-8; ☎ 328 077; cnr Peace Ave & Chingisiin Örgön Chölöö; ☾ breakfast, lunch & dinner) On the 1st floor of the Mongolian Artists' Hall, it has some surprisingly good Chinese and Korean dishes.

Seoul Restaurant (Map pp56-8; ☎ 329 703; dishes T4000-10,000; ☾ lunch & dinner) In a building in Nairamdal Park is Mongolia's fanciest restaurant, the kind that plays host to presidents visiting from other countries (for proof, check out the picture board on the 1st floor). The main hall has a Korean buffet and band stage where nightly performances are held. There's also a *shabu-shabu* barbecue on the wood-panelled balcony.

X.O. (Map pp56-8; 1st fl, Seoul Restaurant; ☾ lunch & dinner) This Japanese restaurant has cosy floor-seating cabins and is done up like a little bamboo garden.

WESTERN

Millie's Café (Map pp56-8; ☎ 330 338; Marco Polo Bldg; ☾ breakfast, lunch & dinner Mon-Sat) This long-time expat favourite is *the* place for lunch. Get there early before it gets packed out with consultants, aid workers and journalists sipping excellent shakes and freshly squeezed orange juice. Also excellent here are the steak sandwiches, lasagne and lemon pie. It's a good place for a decadent breakfast of imported coffee and waffles. The restaurant is on the west side of the Monastery-Museum of Choijin Lama. It also has a small branch in the Ulaanbaatar Hotel for coffee and cakes.

Ikh Khuraldai (Map p53; ☎ 343 577; Chingisiin Örgön Chölöö; meal with drink T7500; ☾ lunch & dinner) Done up like the inside of a ger, with the silver tree of Karakorum poking up from the floor, this place has a fun, Mongolian feel embellished by an excellent German-inspired menu. It's a real meat-and-potatoes place – go for the 'Mongolian warrior battle platter'. It is next to the Palace Hotel.

Los Bandidos (Map pp56-8; ☎ 314 167, 9919 4618; dishes T4000; ☻ lunch & dinner) It is advertised as 'the only Mexican and Indian restaurant in Mongolia', a claim that we won't try to argue. Los Banditos is a disorienting mix of Mexico City (décor and cuisine) and Bombay (chef and music) but somehow it works, mainly due to the fine nachos, fajitas, enchiladas and vegetarian garbanzo beans. It's hidden between apartment blocks, just off Peace Ave, not far from the Peace & Friendship Building.

Marco Polo (Map pp56-8; ☎ 318 433; Seoul St 27; pizzas T2500-3500; ☻ lunch & dinner) This place gets our vote for the best pizza in town. The interior is dressed up like a bizarre Bavarian hunting lodge with lots of stuffed birds and heavy wood tables. There's a strip bar upstairs so try not to let the kiddies start wandering off.

UB Deli (Map pp56-8; ☎ 325 240; Seoul St 48; mains T3500-5000; ☻ breakfast, lunch & dinner) This newcomer puts up a stiff challenge for the title of top American-style restaurant. It gets crowded at lunchtime when hungry expats scarf down chicken Caesar salad, shepherd's pie, and hot and cold sandwiches, including Philly cheese, San Francisco Monte Christo and grilled reuben. The Alice Springs Chicken (T8000), a sandwich topped with cheese and tomato, is very tempting. It delivers for a small fee.

California (Map pp56-8; ☎ 319 031; Seoul St; meal with drink T9000; ☻ lunch & dinner) One of UB's most popular new restaurants, this place stands out for its burgers, steaks, salads and excellent wines, plus a few things you can't get anywhere else, such as a proper iced tea. Breakfasts (even the menu), are modelled after the American restaurant chain Denny's.

El Toro (Map pp56-8; ☎ 328 517; Lucky Center, Peace Ave; steaks T4500; ☻ lunch & dinner) Owned by firebrand politician L Gundalai, this rustic steakhouse is a carnivore's delight – the 650-gram T-bone steak will put a few hairs on your chest. It is stuck behind a building off Peace Ave.

Le Bistro Français (Map pp56-8; ☎ 320 022; Ikh Surguuliin Gudamj 2; meal with wine T10,000–15,000; ☻ breakfast, lunch & dinner) This simply decorated bistro with black-and-white Parisian scenes hanging on the walls, serves up pâté, quiche and snails in garlic butter for starters. The pork chops are a recommended main dish but the desserts are overpriced. Avoid it altogether if you're down to pinching tögrögs.

Sericon (Map pp56-8; ☎ 9911 7417; Juulchin Gudamj; gyros T4000, lamb kebab T4200; ☻ lunch & dinner Mon-Fri) This Greek restaurant is tucked into the east side of the Mongolian GIA building. The food is very good and you can buy the excellent contemporary leather art off the walls.

Planet Pizza (Map pp56-8; ☎ 319 394, 321 122; Tserendorjiin 66; ☻ breakfast, lunch & dinner) With the demise of Pizza Della Casa, this has taken over as the city's premier pizza-delivery joint. It has free delivery or you could eat in-house. Don't confuse it with the substandard 'Pizza King' a few doors down.

Pizza Della Casa (Map pp56-8; ☎ 324 114, 312 072; pizzas T2500-3500; ☻ breakfast, lunch & dinner) Once considered the one of the top restaurants in UB, we've noticed a sharp decline in quality lately. Still, its pizzas, pastas and calzone have maintained a certain following and are reasonably priced. There are two locations, one on Peace Ave near the Peace and Friendship Building, and a second on Baga Toiruu east, near the Ulaanbaatar hotel. It has free delivery for orders over T5000.

El Latino (Map pp56-8; ☎ 311 051; Peace Ave 3; dishes T2000-3500; ☻ lunch & dinner Mon-Sat) Owner Christo serves up Cuban dishes, complemented by Cuban music, cigars, espressos and cocktails. The dishes include omelettes, *huevos rancheros* (fried eggs on tortillas, with salsa), good salads, French toast with honey, and fried bananas. There are plans to build a second restaurant in Nairamdal Park.

Irish House Café (Map pp56-8; ☎ 318 786; Ikh Surguuliin 5; dishes T2000; ☻ lunch & dinner) This place, serving up steaks, pork roast and stroganoff, is a popular neighbourhood restaurant for a business lunch.

Apanas Ukrainian Restaurant (Map p53; ☎ 453 716; Tokyogiin Gudamj; dishes T2000-3000; ☻ lunch & dinner) Hanging grape trestles and paintings of peasant villages set the scene for this Ukrainian restaurant featuring borsch and sweet crepes. It is opposite the four-storey Mormon Church.

AUTHOR'S CHOICE

Silk Road Bar & Grill (Map pp56-8; ☎ 9191 4455; Jamiyan Guunii Gudamj; meal with drink T7500; ✾ lunch & dinner) This new restaurant has a short but sweet European-style menu, with wonderful chicken shish kebabs, barbecued lamb and pepper steaks, plus a good selection of soups or salads – try the zucchini soup. The eye-pleasing décor is all wrought iron and bas-relief scenes of the ancient Silk Road from China to Europe. Enkhee, the friendly owner and brainchild of Pizza Della Casa and Los Bandidos, sometimes has live music but one of the best reasons to visit is the view – a spectacular setting above the mystical Monastery-Museum of Choijin Lama, with views of Bogdkhan Uul.

Cafés

In summer, most restaurants disgorge deck chairs and tables to the pavements, forming an excellent café culture where you can sip a coffee or Coke and watch Ulaanbaatar go about its business.

Michele's French Bakery (Map pp56-8; ☎ 329 002; Tserendorjiin Gudamj; pastries T1800-2500, bread T500-1000; ✾ breakfast, lunch & dinner) This place has intimidating pastries that look almost too perfect too eat. The baguettes (T500) are always fresh and the apple strudels (T950) are particularly recommended; grab a few before leaving on countryside road. Nearby is the Japanese bakery **Sakura** (Map pp56-8; sandwiches T2300).

Chez Bernard (Map pp56-8; ☎ 324 622; Peace Ave 27; ✾ breakfast, lunch & dinner) The most popular backpacker hang-out in UB, this Belgian-owned café has European breakfast platters crammed with fruit, cheese, yogurt, eggs, bacon and toast. There's a good selection of bakery items, including strudels and waffles, and a noticeboard for organising trips to the countryside or swapping used books. The deck is the kind of place where you could while away a few hours with a book.

Sacher's Café (Map pp56-8; ☎ 324 734; Baga Toiruu west; ✾ breakfast, lunch & dinner) This place has filter coffee, German magazines and both indoor and outdoor seating. Feel free to blow your budget on the excellent Austrian-style cakes, pretzels and breads, including Chinggis Beer bread.

Modern Nomad's Coffee Shop (Map pp56-8; ☎ 311 879; Sükhbaataryn Gudamj 1; ✾ lunch & dinner) This place is well located to break up your tour of the museums. Hopefully, by the time your read this, the owners will have fixed the cappuccino machine. Even sans coffee, the sandwiches are fairly priced (try the excellent tuna melt). From 3pm to 6pm you'll get 'happy-hour' discount prices.

Mini Coffee (Map pp56-8; ☎ 327 836; Negdsen Undestnii Gudamj; ✾ breakfast, lunch & dinner) It's a neighbourhood café serving sandwiches, cold drinks, pasta and filling breakfasts.

Quick Eats

The colonel hasn't yet spread his wings on the steppe yet (though there are constant rumours of a Western chain coming), but a few locally owned places are worth visiting for a quick bite.

For something really quick and filling, order some *shashlyk* (meat kebabs), usually served with onions and cucumber, from any number of street Uzbek vendors (June to August only). The best ones are opposite the Wrestling Palace or outside the Mongolian Artists Exhibition Hall.

If you want a plate of greasy mutton and noodles (about T800) – or, better, some *buuz* or *khuushuur* for about T120 each – look out for the ubiquitous *guanz* (canteens). Be careful because some of the rougher places are not hygienic. Good places to try are Zochin Buuz (p75) and Khaan Buuz (Map pp56–8), opposite the State Department Store. There are also a few *guanz* close to Ard Kino on Baga Toiruu west.

Berlin (Map pp56-8; ☎ 328 505; cnr Baruun Selbe & Sambuugiin Örgön Chölöö; ✾ breakfast, lunch & dinner) An old stand-by, this cafeteria-style place has good-value burgers and spaghetti. Long lines form during lunch hour.

Indra (Map pp56-8; ☎ 323 769; Jigjidjavan 9; ✾ breakfast, lunch & dinner) Located just off the Square, this popular eatery, housed in a converted basketball court, serves hygienic pasta, ramen, salad and pizzas.

Self-Catering

You will soon get to know the main markets in Ulaanbaatar if you are either staying in an apartment with a kitchen, stocking up for a trip to the countryside, or happen to be a vegetarian. These days there are very few things you can't get in the city if you look hard enough, though you may have to visit several markets to track them down. Most markets are open from about 10am to 8pm daily, and are worth a visit, if only for the atmosphere, fresh bread and tasty ice cream.

Container Market (Map pp56-8; Bömbögör market; Ikh Toiruu west) This is the cheapest place for everyday food purchases. There is an organised indoor section and a chaotic outdoor area where everything is sold out of truck containers. It's just south of Bakula Rinpoche Süm.

Dalai Eej & Merkuri Markets (Map pp56-8; off Tserendoriin Gudamj) These are conveniently located next to each other, about 100m west of the State Circus. Merkuri (Мэркури) is sort of a flea market for food where you can bargain with individual vendors for all manner of imported goods, meat, cheese and vegetables, as well as luxuries like caviar and crab sticks. Dalai Eej (Далай Ээж) is a run-of-the-mill supermarket (but has a great selection of wines) and the adjacent Passage Market has household goods, as well as **Werner's Deli** (☎ 9515 1418; ☒ 11am-7pm Mon-Sat), which sells German sausages, cold cuts and sandwiches.

State Department Store (Map pp56-8; Peace Ave 44) The ground floor has a good selection of fruit, deli and imported goods such as corn flakes and cheese, though at slightly higher prices than elsewhere.

DRINKING

Vodka, Mongolia's drink of choice during the communist era, has been nudged aside by a boom in beer drinking and brewing. There are many good, clean and safe watering holes in the downtown area and while there is no bar district, they are still close enough to put together some semblance of a pub crawl. Many imported beers are available, but the brand of choice is the locally brewed Chinggis, which comes in green cans or on tap. Most of the places listed here open around noon and close when the last straggler leaves (though occasional crackdowns mean bars will shut by midnight). You can't buy *airag (koumiss)* in any bar, but a ger on Liberty Square usually sells the stuff in summer.

Budweiser Bar (Map pp56-8; ☎ 324 469; Sükhbaataryn Gudamj) On the west side of the square, this quiet pub is a good place for Czech beer and pub grub such as fried chicken or lamb.

Brau Haus (Map pp56-8; ☎ 314 195; Seoul St) This huge bar and restaurant combo is part of the Khan Brau group. It's got a flash, airy interior with a band stage and a more expensive upper tier. On Wednesday and Saturday nights it has a stock-exchange system whereupon the prices of beer falls to half price if no-one is buying, but rises again as more orders are put in.

Chinggis Club (Map pp56-8; ☎ 325 820; Sükhbaataryn Gudamj 10; large beer T1800) This very pleasant German-run pub brews its own Chinggis Beer (you can see the vats through a glass wall). There's also good German-inspired food and the beer mats are fine souvenirs!

Dave's Place (Map pp56-8; ☎ 9979 8185; mongol iadave@yahoo.com) This intimate bar on the patio of the Palace of Cultural is run by an Englishman named Dave who often joins his patrons for a pint. Thursday 'Quiz Night', starting at 9.30pm, has become somewhat of an institution, with the winners receiving a jar of cash and a free beer. It has live music on Friday. In cool weather the whole operation retreats to a speakeasy-style bar in the basement.

Greenland (Map pp56-8; Peace Ave; beer T1000-1800) This Oktoberfest-style tent, behind the Mongolian Artists' Exhibition Hall, serves up suds to stein-banging Mongolians and their foreign friends.

Khan Brau (Map pp56-8; ☎ 326 626; Chingisiin Örgön Chölöö) For Mongolians, this legendary bar is a place for the A-listers to be seen. You can rub shoulders with Mongolian celebrities while waiting (and waiting and waiting) for your meal and beer to arrive. The light *(shar)* beer will make you cringe but no-one seems to mind because the location, near the city's main intersection just south of the CPO, more than makes up for taste. The dark beer is a bit better. There is live music most nights, and the Mongolian owner of the place usually jams with his band, appropriately called 'Shar Airag' (Beer).

Tenth Floor Terrace (Map p53; 10th fl, Chinggis Khaan Hotel; ☒ noon-2am Jun-Aug, 8pm-2am Sep-May) It's one of the better hang-outs, popular with expats and Mongolians. In daytime, the sweeping views make it a good place to contemplate Soviet town planning and architecture.

ULAANBAATAR

ENTERTAINMENT

Culture vultures will want to check the weekly English-language *UB Post* or *Mongol Messenger* for events. The **Arts Council of Mongolia** (Map pp56-8; ☎ 319 015; www.artscouncil .mn) produces a monthly cultural events calendar, which covers most theatres, galleries and museums. You can pick up a brochure at hotel lobbies or the MIAT office. Theatres and galleries sometimes post English ads outside or you could just buy a ticket and hope for the best.

Nightclubs

Nick Middleton's book, *The Last Disco in Outer Mongolia*, written in the late 1980s, referred to what was Ulaanbaatar's only disco at the time – in the Bayangol Hotel. Now there are dozens of places to choose from although they go out of fashion pretty quickly (none from our last edition appear below), so you'll have to ask expats what's popular. Beer costs around T2000 in most places and don't be surprised to find the odd stripper or go-go dancer in residence.

Face Club (Map pp56-8; ☎ 313 961; Juulchin Gudamj; men/women T3000/1000 Sat-Thu, T5000/3000 Fri; ☺ 10pm-3am) The Face Club is a lively little place with a Tahitian theme. It has live bands and DJs.

Hollywood (Map p53; ☎ 9914 0203; Zaluus Youth & Cultural Centre, Zaluuchuudyn Örgön Chölöö; admission free; ☺ 7pm-4am) This is a popular nightclub decorated with movie posters and is more upmarket than most places.

Arirang Disco (Map p53; ☎ 329 032; admission free; ☺ 10pm-6am) is in the same building as Hollywood but draws a Cass-drinking student crowd. Cass is a cheap Korean beer.

Medusa (Map p53; ☎ 313 011; men/women T3000/ 2000 Sun-Thu, T5000/3000 Fri & Sat; ☺ 9pm-3.30am) In the Chinggis Khaan Hotel, this place was the flavour of the month when it opened in July 2004.

Muse (Map pp56-8; ☎ 312 601; Maral Tavern Bldg, Baga Toiruu; men/women T3000/2000; ☺ 9pm-3.30am) One of the top nightclubs for the yuppie crowd, it's located just north of the Zaluuchuud Hotel.

New Tornado (Map p53; Zaluuchuudyn Örgön Chölöö; Sansar district; admission free; ☺ 9pm-3am) This place is popular with young expats, travellers and English teachers that live in the neighbourhood. It's near the tunnel opposite the Flower Hotel.

River Sounds (Map pp56-8; ☎ 320 497; Olympiin Örgön Chölöö; admission T3000 Sun-Wed, T5000 Thu-Sat; ☺ 8pm-3am) UB's only dedicated live-music venue with jazz bands the norm, although it has the occasional indie rock band.

UB Palace (Map p53; ☎ 682 892; Chingunjaviin Gudamj; admission T2000; ☺ noon-4am) Housing four pubs, an enormous disco hall, billiards room and an Internet café, this monstrosity is a favourite late-night den of debauchery for the teen set. One reader warns that vomiting on the floor carries T3000 penalty.

Cinemas

Tengis (Map pp56-8; ☎ 313 105; www.tengis.mn; Liberty Square; regular show T2500, matinee T1500) Opened in 2004, this is Mongolia's first modern movie theatre. Three air-conditioned halls, comfortable seats (with cup holders!) and a modern projection system make this a very worthwhile experience. It usually has one or two Hollywood blockbusters (in English, subtitled with Mongolian) and a Korean or Mongolian film. The complex also has a fast-food joint, bakery and what is reputed to be UB's best espresso bar.

Od (Star) Kino (Map p53; ☎ 360 675; Amarasanaagiin Gudamj; T2000) It shows the odd film in English.

Theatre

TRADITIONAL MUSIC & DANCE

A performance of traditional music and dance will be one of the highlights of your visit to Mongolia and should not be missed. You'll see outstanding examples of the unique Mongolian throat-singing, known as *khöömi*; full-scale orchestral renditions of new and old Mongolian music; contortionists guaranteed to make your eyes water; traditional and modern dancing; and recitals featuring the unique horse-head violin, the *morin khuur*.

The State Folk Song and Dance Ensemble puts on performances for tourists throughout the summer in the **National Academic Drama Theatre** (Map pp56-8; ☎ 310 466; cnr Seoul St & Chingisiin Örgön Chölöö; admission T6000; ☺ 6pm). Shows are less frequently staged at the **Palace of Culture** (Map pp56-8; ☎ 321 444) on the northeast corner of Sükhbaatar Square.

Nightly performances of the **Tumen Ekh Song and Dance Ensemble** (Map pp56-8; ☎ 327 916, 327 379; State Youth & Children's Theatre, Nairamdal Park; admission T6000, photos T3000, videos T10,000; ☺ 6pm)

MORIN KHUUR

The instrument most identified with Mongolia is the horse-head fiddle, known as the *morin khuur*. It has two horse-hair strings, with the distinctive and decorative carving of a horse's head on the handle. According to legend, the instrument was created by a herdsman to sing his sorrow over his horse's death – the instrument was formed out of the ribs and mane of the horse.

Traditionally, the *morin khuur* often accompanies the unique long songs that regale the beauty of the countryside and relive tales of nomadic heroes. You can hear the *morin khuur* at ceremonies during the Naadam Festival in Ulaanbaatar, or at a performance of traditional music and dance.

---

are the most popular cultural show in town. You can buy CDs (T20,000) of the performance after the show. There is a café and gallery in the traditional-style hall.

OPERA & BALLET

State Opera & Ballet Theatre (Map pp56-8; ☎ 322 854, 9919 4570; admission T5000; ☯ closed August) Built by the Russians in 1932, this is the salmon-pinkish building on the southeast corner of Sükhbaatar Square. On Saturday and Sunday evenings throughout the year, and sometimes also on weekend afternoons in the summer, the theatre holds stirring opera (in Mongolian) and ballet shows.

One of the best local operas is *Three Fateful Hills* – sometimes known as the *Story of Three Lives* – by Mongolia's most famous poet and playwright, D Natsagdorj. The debut performance of *Chinggis Khaan*, by B Sharav, was shown in 2003. Another recommended opera is *Uran Khas*, written by J Chuluun. Other productions include an exhilarating (but long) rendition of *Carmen*, plus plenty of Puccini and Tchaikovsky.

A board outside the theatre lists the shows for the current month in English. Advance purchase is worthwhile for popular shows because tickets are numbered, so it's possible to score a good seat if you book early. If you are a little cheeky, you can have a look around inside the theatre during the day on weekdays (when there is no show in the evening).

DRAMA

National Academic Drama Theatre (Map pp56-8; ☎ 310 466, 9919 4570; cnr Seoul St & Chingisiin Örgön Chölöö; admission T5000; ☯ ticket sales 9am-6pm) During most of the year, this large, fire-engine-red theatre shows one of a dozen or so Mongolian-language productions. These productions are penned by, among others, William Shakespeare and Jean-Paul Sartre,

as well as various Mongolian playwrights. There are only between six and 10 performances every month – maybe a few more in summer. A list of upcoming shows is painted in Cyrillic on a board to the right as you look at the theatre. You can buy tickets in advance at the booking office, which is on the right-hand side of the theatre.

On the left-hand side of the theatre, as you approach it from the road, is a door that leads to a **puppet theatre** (☎ 320 795). Unfortunately, there are very few performances, but invariably something is organised during the week of the Naadam Festival.

Gay & Lesbian Venues

Although Ulaanbaatar has no dedicated gay or lesbian bar as such, the local gay community manages to rendezvous at one central location or another on a Friday night, usually by word of mouth. A recent meeting place was **City Life** (Map pp56-8; ☎ 9015 2576; Zaluuchuudyn Örgön Chölöö; ☯ noon-2am), located behind Government House.

Circus

State Circus (Map pp56-8; ☎ 320 795, 9918 1134, 9525 8788; admission T5000; ☯ closed August) Formed in 1940, the circus has been housed in the recognisable round building with the blue roof at the end of Tserendorjiin Gudamj since 1971.

There are some impressive acrobatics and juggling, and extraordinary contortionists, but watching a poodle do the lambada in a tutu was not a highlight. Performances are sporadic and it can be hard to find out exactly when a performance is on, so check the local media or with the Arts Council. Buy tickets at the salmon-coloured building, south of the circus building.

Performances usually start at about 5pm, and sometimes matinees are held in summer (but not in August). Try to get there

30 minutes before the show starts to find a good seat. Nobody warns you, but flash photography is strictly prohibited.

Sport

The annual Naadam Festival features wrestling, horse racing and archery; see opposite for more details. In the lead-up to Naadam, you should be able to catch some informal, but still competitive, wrestling at the Naadam Stadium. Another venue is at the stadium in the southern part of Nairamdal Park, with events on weekend afternoons. For wrestling at other times of the year check out the schedule at the **Wrestling Palace** (Map p53; ☎ 456 443; Peace Ave; admission T1000-5000), which is the long, unsigned, yellowish building north of the Ulaanbaatar Hotel. Wrestling and boxing are also held at the **Central Sports Palace** (Map pp56-8; Baga Toiruu) during the year.

Some of the local populace enjoy other sports, however. Fiery games of basketball are often held on summer evenings at the Central Sports Palace.

On weekends during the short summer (but not around the time of the Naadam Festival), the newly formed Mongolian Football League plays football (soccer) matches at a **football pitch** (Map p53) just south of the Naadam Stadium.

In winter, amateur hockey matches are played at a rink in the 3rd/4th microdistrict outdoor rinks. Khandgait (p102) is sometimes also the venue for ice motorcycle racing.

SHOPPING

The closest thing that Ulaanbaatar has to a shopping mall is the western half of Juulchin Gudamj, which is lined with some useful shops, including hairdressers and pharmacies.

Camping Gear & Tools

An open-air stall located at the southwestern corner of Peace Ave and Öndör Gegeen Zanabazaryn Gudamj sells low-grade, Chinese-made tents.

UB Outdoor Equipment Centre (Map pp56-8; ☎ 9917 7029, 321 276; info@activeadventures.com; Ikh Toiruu 6) Stocks German-made Vaude gear, maps and accessories, and will hire inflatable kayaks for do-it-yourself river expeditions (US$25 for one day, US$40 for two days). It

can be found at the Pro Shack tool shop (see below), and at the time of writing were getting ready to open a downtown shop.

Ayanchin Outfitters (Map pp56-8; ☎ 327 172; www .ayanchin.com; Seoul St 21) This place sells Western camping, fishing and hunting equipment, plus GPS units. But you'll pay through the nose for this stuff, sometimes up to 50% more than you would in your own country, so shop around first. It has a small outlet in the Sky Shopping Center (Map p53).

Pro Shack (Map pp56-8; ☎ 318 138; Ikh Toiruu 6; ⏰ 9am-6pm Mon-Fri, 10am-5pm Sat) It has Ulaanbaatar's best selection of tools and hardware. It's worth visiting if you need tools for a self-guided jeep or bike trip.

Toread (☎ 9918 0000; Teeverchidiin Gudamj; ⏰ 10am-8pm Mon-Sat, 10am-4pm Sun) It sells Chinese-brand (but acceptable quality) camping gear at reasonable prices.

Zagas Tour (Map pp56-8; ☎ 318 551; Baga Toiruu west & Peace Ave; ⏰ 9am-9pm Mon-Sat, 10am-7pm Sun) Has camping gear and fishing equipment. It's on the 3rd floor of the Flower Centre.

Shonkhor Saddles (Map pp56-8; ☎ 311 218, after hours Ganbold ☎ 9191 1190, Battor ☎ 9983 9060; bldg 39 1-1; ⏰ 9am-6pm Mon-Fri) This shop sells saddles and other horse paraphernalia, perfect if you are organising your own horse trek. It's behind the CPO.

Crafts & Souvenirs

Cheap, easy to take home and unique to Mongolia are the bright landscape paintings that you will see in all the souvenir shops. The ones for sale from the art students (who sometimes hang around the Square and CPO) are far better and cheaper (from T400 to T3000). Some days, students may pester you a dozen times in one afternoon; then you won't see one for days. Gandan Khiid and the State Department Store are also good places to buy these types of paintings.

The best contemporary artwork in the country is on sale in the **Red Ger Art Gallery** (Map pp56-8; ☎ 319 015) inside the Zanabazar Museum (p61).

If you are serious about your musical instruments try the **Egshiglen Magnai National Musical Instrument Shop** (Map pp56-8; ☎ 312 732; ⏰ 9am-6pm Mon-Sat), opposite the Museum of Natural History. *Morin khuur* (horse-head fiddles) range from T40,000 to T100,000, and there are also *yattag* (zithers) and two-stringed Chinese fiddles.

THE NAADAM FESTIVAL

The biggest event of the Mongolian year for foreigners and locals alike is the Naadam Festival held 11–12 July. Part family reunion, part fair and part nomad Olympics, Naadam (meaning 'holiday' or 'festival') has its roots in the nomad assemblies and hunting extravaganzas of the Mongol armies.

Small Naadams are held though out the country. The quality and number of sports and activities at countryside Naadams will be lower than the main Naadam in Ulaanbaatar, but you'll get better seats, witness genuine traditions, and even make up the numbers during a wrestling tournament! Watch out!

The Ulaanbaatar Naadam has all the trappings of a tourist holiday, with cheesy carnival events and souvenir salesmen outside the stadium. First-time visitors still consider it 'a must see', but others will scope out a countryside Naadam. These are not advertised and may take a day or two to reach so some planning it required. If you are already in the countryside, hunker down in a provincial capital or village centre and watch the events unfold.

Day one of the Ulaanbaatar Naadam starts at about 9am with a fantastic, colourful ceremony at Sükhbaatar Square (often missed by visitors).

The opening ceremony, which starts at about 11am at the Naadam Stadium, includes an impressive march of monks and athletes, plus song and dance routines. By comparison, almost nothing happens at the closing ceremony. The winning wrestler is awarded, the ceremonial yak banners are marched away, and everyone goes home. It is held at about 7pm on the second day, but the exact time depends on when the wrestling finishes.

Archery is held in an open **archery stadium** (Map p53) next to the main stadium but the horse racing is held about 28km west of the city on an open plain called Hui Doloon Khutag. The only way to get out here is by taxi (about T14,000 return). Your hotel or guesthouse can probably arrange a vehicle, or ask at **Chez Bernard** (Map pp56–8; Peace Ave 27).

A recent addition to the Naadam program is anklebone shooting. This entails flicking a sheep anklebone at a small target (also made from anklebones) about three metres away. The competition is held in an anklebone shooting covered area (Map p53) near the archery stadium.

Admission to the stadium (except for the two ceremonies), and to the archery and horse racing are free, but you'll definitely need a ticket for the opening ceremony and possibly the last round or two of the wrestling and closing ceremony. Ticket costs vary per section; the north side of the stadium (which is protected from the sun and rain by an overhang) is more expensive with tickets going for up to US$12. This section is also less crowded and everyone will get a seat. These tickets are distributed via the tour operators and hotels.

Alternatively, you can get a cheap seat for as little as T2000. There is no ticket window, but you can buy a ticket from scalpers who hang around the stadium or even from the police who man the gates. The original price will be printed on the ticket; you can expect to pay twice this for the service charge. Guesthouse owners normally help their guests buy tickets.

A cheap ticket will get you though a designated gate, but these sections are grossly oversold and there is no guarantee you'll get a seat. If you are a lucky seat holder you may soon find a granny or kid on your lap. The large bandstand on the west end of the stadium offers some shade.

To find out what is going on during the festival, look for the events program in the two English-language newspapers.

Also worth looking at is **Argasun** (Map pp56–8; ☎ 315 360; Partizan 48; ☯ 10am-6pm), a *morin-khuur* workshop near Aeroflot.

The major cashmere and wool factories are Goyo (Mongolian-American joint venture), Gobi Cashmere (government-owned) and Buyan (owned by the prominent politician Jargalsaikhan). Gobi Cashmere has several showrooms, including one on Peace Ave opposite the Russian Embassy and another, the **Gobi Original Cashmere House** (Map pp56–8) opposite Gesar Süm. The State Department Store has cashmere on the 2nd and 5th floors. Tserendorjiin Gudamj, between the State Circus and the State Department Store, is Mongolia's version of Fifth Avenue, with a dozen fashion shops; try **Moda Mongolia** (Map pp56–8; ☎ 232 925).

The art and souvenir shops in the hotels are naturally more expensive than they should be, but they do have a reasonable selection of paintings, cashmere products, books, postcards, stamps and music. Several shops are actually in gers mounted on carts, notably outside the Bayangol Hotel and National Museum of Mongolian History. The best place for kitsch – Chinggis Khan key chains, T-shirts and coffee mugs – is the 5th floor of the State Department Store and the shops in the Winter Palace or the Monastery-Museum of Choijin Lama. If you are shopping for antiques, don't forget to get a certificate for sale to show to the customs agents. Other shops to try are:

Tsagaan Alt Wool Shop (Map pp56-8; ☎ 318 591; Tserendorjiin Gudamj; ☻ 10am-6pm Mon-Fri, 10am-5pm Sat) This nonprofit store, which sends money directly back to the craftspeople, has all manner of wool products, including toys, clothes and artwork. It's Christian-run, in case you were wondering about those Jesus Christ felt tapestries.

Eternal Art Antique Shop (Map pp56-8; ☎ 369 704; Sükhbaataryn Gudamj 1) One of the premier antique shops in the city. Credit cards are accepted.

Antique & Art Gallery (Map pp56-8; ☎ 324 234; Peace Ave 19; ☻ 10am-8pm Mon-Fri, 10am-6pm Sat & Sun) There are three rooms of antiques, *thangkas* and *tsam* masks here.

Vessels of Honour (Map pp56-8; ☎ 330 269; Marco Polo Plaza; ☻ 9am-6pm Mon-Sat) Another Christian place that directly supports artists; this one has some interesting contemporary artwork.

Naran Tuul Market

This **market** (Наран Туул Зах; ☻ 9am-7pm Wed-Mon), east of the centre, is also known as the Black Market (Khar Zakh), but it's not the sort of place where you go to change money illegally and smuggle goods – though this certainly happens.

First established in the 1940s, and run by Chinese traders in different parts of the city, the market is now in the southeast corner of the city, on Teeverchidiin Gudamj, east of Ikh Toiruu. In summer up to 60,000 people a day squeeze into the market.

There's a T50 entrance fee. Once inside, there's an indoor area that contains a food market and few *guanz*. Prices are certainly lower than at the shops and markets in the city, but it's hardly worth the effort to come to this market just to save a few tögrög.

An undercover area has a decent selection of clothes, such as bags, leather boots

and fake North Face jackets. This is also one of the cheapest places to get traditional Mongolian clothes such as a *del* (T25,000), jacket (T20,000) and *loovuuz* (T3,500). Towards the back of the market you'll find saddles, riding tack and all the ingredients needed to build your own ger. The back area is also where you'll find antique and coin dealers, but they don't issue any official documentation (unlike the antique shops in town), making it illegal to export. New items, such as the snuff bottles (made in China anyway), can be purchased without worry.

The market is notorious for pickpockets and bag slashers so don't bring anything you don't want to lose. Don't carry anything on your back, and strap your money belt to your body. If you feel a group of men blocking your way from the front, chances are their friends are probing your pockets from behind. Some travellers have had rocks thrown at them for taking photos in the market.

A taxi to the market should cost about T1000 from the centre of town. Minibuses come here from Peace Ave (look for the sign 'Зах'). To walk from the square will take about 45 minutes. Try to avoid Saturday and Sunday afternoons, when the crowds can be horrendous.

Photography

Mon Nip Camera Shop (Map pp56-8; ☎ 315 838; Peace Ave 30; ☻ 10am-8pm) This place is an official Canon camera dealer. You can also get cameras on the 3rd floor of the State Department Store.

Tavan Bogd Photo Shop (Map pp56-8; ☎ 328 554; M-100 bldg, Juulchin Gudamj; ☻ 9am-8pm Mon-Fri, 10am-8pm Sat & Sun) A reliable place to buy and develop print film, northwest of Sukhbaatar Square.

Shopping Centres

Known as *ikh delguur* or 'big shop', the **State Department Store** (Их Дэлгүүр; Map pp56-8; ☎ 319 292; Peace Ave 44; ☻ 9am-10pm Mon-Sat, 10am-10pm Sun) is virtually a tourist attraction in itself, with the best products from around the city squeezed into one building.

Aside from a worthless information desk, the 1st floor has a supermarket, café, magazine stand, optometrists and silversmiths selling traditional cups and belt buckles.

The 2nd floor has outlets for clothing, cashmere and leather goods. The 3rd floor has electronics, a Mobicom shop, CDs, books, sports equipment, camping and fishing gear. Most visitors head straight for the 5th floor, which has one of the best collections of souvenirs in the country, including carvings, wall hangings of Chinggis Khaan, and a good, but expensive, range of antiques. If you're keen you can also be fully decked out in the traditional *del* (long robe), *loovuuz* (fox-fur hat) and *gutul* (boots). This floor also has the travel agency, Nomin Tours.

Foreign-exchange counters are found on the 1st, 2nd, 3rd and 5th floors with cash only changed. The store also sells phone and Internet cards. There are plans for a food court on the 7th floor, but this may just be a developer's pipe dream.

If you are based on the east side of town, the **Sky Shopping Centre** (Map p53; ☎ 319 090; ☻ 10.30am-9pm) may be more convenient than the State Department Store and offers similar goods and services. Stock up on clothing, food and household items here; it has a branch of the camping store Ayanchin Outfitters, plus traditional clothes, souvenirs and cashmere. It's behind the Chinggis Khaan Hotel.

GETTING THERE & AWAY
Air

At the time of research Mongolian Airlines (MIAT) was losing many of its domestic routes to the private airline, Aero Mongolia. As such, the information contained here may have changed. No matter how the situation and pending privatisation plays out, MIAT will probably hang on to its international routes. Note that domestic routes only allow you to check 10kg of luggage. You'll pay T1500 per kg over the limit. For details of international flights to UB, see p249.

The **MIAT airline head office** (Map pp56-8; international booking ☎ 322 144, 325 633, domestic booking ☎ 322 610, 322 686; fax 313 385; www.miat.com; ☻ 9am-8pm Mon-Fri Apr-Oct, 10am-5pm Sat, 9am-6pm Mon-Fri, 10am-3pm Sat Nov-Mar) is close to Sükhbaatar Square, hidden behind a building next to the Puma Imperial Hotel. The office may move in 2006 but the phone numbers should stay the same. There are plans to open a domestic ticket office at the airport, which means, in theory, you can make a last-minute booking over the phone and pick up the ticket at the airport. MIAT accepts credit cards for international and domestic flights. If paying cash, foreigners are supposed to use US dollars only. There is a convenient exchange office in the office.

Most staff have a smattering of English (certainly Russian and possibly German) so it is sometimes worth ringing them, but you are far more likely to get what you want if you visit their head office. Look out for special deals. In the summer of 2004 MIAT was offering return weekend tickets to Beijing for US$190.

Aero Mongolia (Map pp56-8; ☎ 9191 2903; www .aeromongolia.mn; reservation@aeromongolia.mn), which has operated since 2003, is reported to be a safe and reliable airline by travellers. Destinations to/from UB include Choibalsan, Khovd, Ulaangom, Mörön and Bankhongor. The temporary office is located in the lobby of Business Plaza, just south of the National Drama Theatre.

Blue Sky Aviation (Map pp56-8; ☎ 312 085; fax 322 857; www.bsamongolia.com) has one 9-seat Cessna 208 aeroplane. It can be chartered for any part of the country and is often hired out by tour groups and mining companies. It's available for medical evacuations.

Foreign airline offices include:

Aeroflot (Map pp56-8; ☎ 320 720; fax 323 321; www.aeroflot.mn; Seoul St 15; ☻ 9am-6pm Mon-Fri, 10am-3pm Sat) The English-speaking staff are helpful. Tickets can be reserved in advance, but must be paid three days before departure. US dollars and credit cards are accepted.

Air China (Map p53; ☎ 328 838, 452 598; fax 312 324; Ikh Toiruu Bldg 47; ☻ 9am-1pm & 2-5pm Mon-Fri, 9am-noon Sat) Located on the Big Ring Rd in the northeast of town.

Korean Air (Map p53; ☎ 326 643; fax 320 602; Chinggis Khaan Hotel, 2nd fl; ☻ 9am-5pm Mon-Fri) Payment with US dollars and tögrög.

United Airlines (Map pp56-8; ☎ 323 232; fax 311 794; ganaa@airtrans.mn; Sükhbaataryn Gudamj 1; ☻ 9am-6pm Mon-Fri, 10am-4pm Sat) Located within the Air Trans office, it's handy for booking flights out of Seoul and Beijing.

Bus, Minivan & Jeep

Minivans and buses heading for destinations in the north and west (but not east) leave from the Dragon (Luu) bus stand on Peace Ave, 7km west of Sükhbaatar Square. Minivans for all destinations use the Naran Tuul market. For the Gobi, the Mandalgov-bound minivans use the Dragon station while vans for Ömnögov usually use Naran Tuul.

Overall, the Dragon bus stand is better for the casual traveller (riders at Naran Tuul are often traders with lots of bulky luggage to deal with). Naran Tuul, however chaotic, has many more vehicles leaving throughout the day.

Local bus No 26, trolley-bus No 2 and some minivans (ask the tout) link Dragon bus stand with Sükhbaatar Square. No. 13 van goes to the Naran Tuul market.

Most departures from the bus stands are between 8am and 9am. If you're taking a long trip, get to the station by 7am to sort out what is going where. Almost all services are in Russian vans or jeeps. For local destinations you might find a Korean compact car or even a regular bus.

Both bus stands are essentially a bunch of vans sitting in a lot with their destinations posted in the dashboard (in Cyrillic). You might find a bus or two but these are becoming infrequent with the surge in minivans. Tell the drivers where you want to go and you'll be directed to the correct van. Some vehicles may be ready to go but others might not be leaving for another day. Dragon has a **ticket office** (☎ 634 902) but this only sells seats for the daily bus to Erdenet (T6000, noon departure).

Don't expect to leave straight away, even if the van is already bursting with people and cargo. There are no fixed schedules and the drivers depart when they see fit. Try to find out exactly what time the driver is leaving and if it's not going immediately you could ask the driver to save your seat and you can return later.

If you are new to Mongolia, can't speak the language and can't read Cyrillic, catching a bus or minivan may be a bit overwhelming at first. A Mongolian friend or guide would make finding your van and paying for a seat a lot easier. For more information try calling the minivan companies at ☎ 321 730, 634 902 or 9525 3146.

Dragon and Naran Tuul both serve towns in Töv aimag. For Nalaikh (T500) and Baganuur (T3000) use Naran Tuul. For Zuunmod (T700) and Eej Khad (T5000) use Dragon. These minivans go every hour or so.

Both stands also have jeeps and vans for hire at around T250 per kilometre. Budget

travellers could try to deal directly with a driver for a multiday trip, as you would do in the countryside, although it's usually safer to go through a trusted travel agent or guesthouse. Drivers from the stands probably won't have much experience in finding sites of interest for tourists, and any attempt to do so will probably get them lost.

The following is a list of prices for a seat in a minivan or jeep to selected locations at the time of research. Note that you'll also see vehicles to smaller villages. You'll find, for example, vehicles from Naran Tuul direct to Dadal (T20,000) in northern Khentii.

Destination	Cost
Altai	T25,000
Altanbulag	T8000
Arvaikheer	T10,000
Bayankhongor	T18,000
Bulgan	T10,000
Choibalsan	T18,000
Dalanzadgad	T17,000
Darkhan	T4000
Kharkhorin	T9000
Khovd	T35,000
Khujirt	T8000
Mandalgov	T11,000
Mörön	T20,000
Öndörkhaan	T10,000
Sükhbaatar	T15,000
Tsetserleg	T12,000
Ulaangom	T35,000
Uliastai	T25,000

Hitching

Hitching is a necessary form of transport in the countryside, but is less certain and more difficult to organise out of Ulaanbaatar. Most Mongolians get out of the capital city by bus, minibus, train or shared jeep/taxi, and then hitch a ride on a truck for further trips around the countryside, where there is far less public transport. Unless you can arrange a ride at a guesthouse, you should do the same.

Taxi

Taxis (shared or private) can only travel along paved roads, so they are only useful for trips around Töv aimag, to the towns along the main road to Russia (Darkhan, Erdenet and Sükhbaatar) and to the tourist site of Kharkhorin.

The cost of hiring a taxi to these places should be the same rate as for around Ulaanbaatar – currently T250 to T300 per kilometre. The taxi drivers may want more for waiting if you are, for example, visiting Manzushir Khiid, or because they may be returning with an empty vehicle if dropping you off somewhere remote. This is not unreasonable, but it *is* negotiable.

To avoid any argument about the final charge make sure that you and the driver have firstly agreed on the cost per kilometre, and have discussed any extra charges. Then write down the number shown on the odometer/speedometer before you start.

See the Ulaanbaatar map for locations of some taxi stands.

Train

The train station has an information office, a left-luggage office, a phone office, a hotel and a restaurant.

From Ulaanbaatar, daily trains travel to northern Mongolia and on to Russia, via Darkhan and Sükhbaatar, and southeast to China, via Choir, Sainshand and Zamyn-Üüd. There are also lines between Ulaanbaatar and the coal mining towns of Erdenet and Baganuur.

DOMESTIC

Tickets for domestic trains are available from a modern-looking building directly east of the Square outside the train station. Unfortunately, no-one inside speaks anything except Mongolian or Russian. Boards inside the office show departure times (in Cyrillic) and ticket prices for hard seats and soft seats. There's also a full timetable at the information desk on the station platform.

The **domestic railway ticket office** (Map p53; ☎ 94 137, 94 135; ⊙ 8am-12.30pm & 2.30-9pm) can book a ticket up to a month in advance for an extra T450, which is not a bad idea if you have definite plans and want a soft seat during peak times (mainly July to August). If you speak Mongolian, there is an **inquiries number** (☎ 94 194, 194).

INTERNATIONAL

Trains link Mongolia with its powerful neighbours, China and Russia. Getting a ticket in Ulaanbaatar isn't the ordeal it once was, but you should still plan ahead.

The yellow **International Railway Ticketing Office** (Map p53) is about 200m northwest of the train station. Inside the office, specific rooms sell tickets to Beijing, Irkutsk (Russia), Moscow, and Ereen and Hohhot (both in China). The easiest place to book a ticket is in the **foreigners booking office** (☎ 94133, inquiries ☎ 944 868; Room 212; ⊙ 8am-8pm Mon-Fri). It's upstairs and staff here speak some English. On weekends you can use the downstairs booking desk. You'll need your passport to buy a ticket. You can book the ticket by phone for a T4500 booking fee. If you cancel a ticket there is a minuscule T1000 charge.

You can book a ticket for international trains out of Ulaanbaatar up to one month in advance – but for the Moscow–Beijing or Beijing–Moscow trains you will have to scramble for a ticket on the day before departure (but ask the day before). For train times and details see p252 and p255. If you have troubles booking a berth, ask your guesthouse manager or hotel reception desk for assistance.

A taxi between Sükhbaatar Square and the train station costs about T900.

DOMESTIC TRAIN TIMETABLE

Destination	Train No	Frequency	Departure	Duration	Fare (hard/soft seat)
Choir	284	Mon, Wed, Fri, Sun	5.50pm	6 hrs	T2000/5300
Darkhan	211 (fast)	daily	3.50pm	5 hrs	T2100/5400
Darkhan	271	daily	10.30am	8 hrs	T2100/5400
Erdenet	273	daily	7.20pm	11 hrs	T2900/7200
Sainshand	286	daily	9.50am	10 hrs	T3200/7600
Sükhbaatar	263	daily	8.45pm	7¾ hrs	T2700/6700
Sükhbaatar	271	daily	10.30am	7¾ hrs	T2700/6700
Zamyn-Üüd	276	Tue, Fri, Sun	4.30pm	15½ hrs	T4100/9700
Zamyn-Üüd	34 (fast)	Mon, Wed, Fri	8.10pm	12 hrs	T4100/9700

GETTING AROUND
To/From the Airport

Buyant-Ukhaa International Airport is 18km southwest of the city. You can change money at a branch of the T&D Bank. There's also a post office and Internet access for T50 per minute. SSS Travel also operates a tourist booth when planes arrive.

From the city to the airport, bus No 11 (T200) stops at the Ard Kino on Baga Toiruu and opposite the Bayangol Hotel. On its way to the airport Bus No 22 stops near Liberty Square and Ikh Toiruu, near the Map Shop. Coming to the city from the airport, it turns right on Peace Ave and then left up the east end of Baga Toiruu. To find the bus stop near the airport, head out of the terminal, walk north for a few hundred metres and look for a group of locals mingling around a tin shelter.

If you have a lot of gear, or have just arrived in Mongolia, it's worth paying extra for a taxi. Make sure that you pay the standard rate, currently T250 to T300 per kilometre, which works out around US$5 one way to Sükhbaatar Square.

Bicycle

Mongolian drivers are downright dangerous so riding a bike around town can be hazardous to your health. There are no bike lanes and you should never expect to have right of way. Almost no-one rents bikes as well. Some tour operators may have bikes available, which would be more useful in the surrounding countryside than the city itself. Try asking Karakorum Expeditions (see p70), which rents mountain bikes for US$25 per day. Chinese-made bikes are sold at the Naran Tuul market or sometimes outside the State Department Store.

Bus & Minivans

Local public transport is reliable and departures are frequent, but buses can get crowded. Sometimes, you can count yourself extremely fortunate if you even see a seat, let alone sit on one. Conductors collect fares (currently T200 for a bus or T100 for a trolley-bus for any trip around Ulaanbaatar, including to the airport) and usually have change. Pickpockets and bag slashers occasionally ply their trade on crowded routes. Seal up all pockets, hold your bag on your chest and be careful when boarding.

Green minivans (T200) run along a similar route to the buses. Most will run the length of Peace Ave, often turning back at the Naran Tuul market or the train station. Van No. 13 goes to the Naran Tuul Market. The fixed routes posted in the windows are incomprehensible to most passengers. The best way to handle these vehicles is to tell the conductor where you're headed and wait for a positive response.

For short trips it's just as cheap to take a taxi, especially if there is more than one of you. Some of the useful buses and trolley-buses are listed below:

Destination	Bus No	Trolley-Bus No
Airport	11, 22	-
Dragon bus stand	2	26
Nalaikh	33	-
Naran Tuul market	32	-
Peace Ave (east)	1, 13, 20, 21, 23	2, 4, 5, 6
Peace Ave (west)	4, 21, 22, 23	2, 5, 26
Train station	6, 20	4
Winter Palace	3, 19	-
Yarmag	8	-
Zaisan Memorial	7	-

All destinations of trolley-buses and buses will be in Cyrillic; the route number is next to the destination sign on the front of the trolley-bus or bus. The route is often marked on the side of the bus.

Car

There is nowhere in the city to rent a car or motorbike, and it's unlikely there will be for some time. Even if this option becomes available we do not recommend driving your own car. A simple fender bender, whether or not it was your fault, can land you in jail with a steep fine to pay. It simply isn't worth it. The cheapest way to have your own wheels is to rent a taxi by the day. You'll be expected to pay the standard T250 per km, plus a daily rate if you are not doing many km.

Taxi

In Ulaanbaatar, there are official and unofficial taxis; in fact, just about every vehicle is a potential taxi. All charge a standard T250 per kilometre, though you'll need to check the current rate as this will increase regularly. Don't agree to a set daily price because you will always pay more than if you pay the standard rate per kilometre. Nowadays, all taxis and even some private cars have metres.

Taxi drivers are remarkably honest, and within the city you won't be overcharged too much or too often. Most reset the meter (or odometer) as soon as you get in. If they don't reset it, make a note of the reading so you know how many kilometres you've covered.

Getting a taxi is just a matter of standing by the side of a main street and holding your arm out in the street with your fingers down. Alternatively, you can find them at designated taxi stands opposite the Zanabazar Museum of Fine Arts, outside the train station, in Liberty Square and the State Department Store. After dark, women should generally avoid using a private car, and stick to an official taxi.

The most visible official taxi company is **City Taxi** (☎ 300 000), which runs a fleet of modern, yellow Hyundai Accents.

Central Mongolia

This is the Mongolian heartland; a classic landscape of rolling hills, steppe, occasional forests and several volcanoes. It's also the political heart of the country. A number of pre-Mongol civilizations had their capital in this region, and later it was Chinggis Khaan who moved the Mongol capital from eastern Mongolia to Karakorum.

The region also stands as Mongolia's religious power base. It was at the ruins of Karakorum that Abtai Khaan built Mongolia's first monastery *(khiid)*, Erdene Zuu. The great painter, sculptor and diplomat Zanabazar lived nearby.

Central Mongolia's aimags, Töv, Arkhangai and Övörkhangai, are the most visited areas in the countryside. They're near Ulaanbaatar, the roads and transport are far better here than in the rest of Mongolia, and there is plenty to see, including ancient monasteries, gorgeous lakes *(nuur)* and many national parks.

The rivers and trails of Gorkhi-Terelj National Park beckon the outdoor enthusiast. At Khustain National Park you can break out the binoculars and spot the reintroduced *takhi* horse. Alternatively, you can set out from Ulaanbaatar on foot, climb the holy Bogdkhan Uul to the south of the city, and camp out by Manzushir Khiid. Travelling by horse is another great way to get around the region. Travellers with more time on their hands can spend weeks exploring the ancient sites and remote areas of the mighty Khangai and its surrounding plains.

The people of central Mongolia, comprised mostly of the Khalkh majority, are accustomed to foreigners, and you can expect somewhat better services than in other parts of the country.

CENTRAL MONGOLIA

HIGHLIGHTS

- Trek between Ulaanbaatar and Manzushir Khiid, through beautiful and lush **Bogdkhan Uul Strictly Protected Area** (p94)

- Rock climb, raft or relax in the **Terelj area** (p99), where you can stay in a ger camp or get away from it all with a tent

- Focus your camera lens on the magnificent *takhi* horse at **Khustain National Park** (p103), where the wild horse roams free once again

- Explore **Erdene Zuu Khiid** (p109), the centre of Mongolian Buddhism, and the nearby remains of Karakorum

- Camp by the striking **Terkhiin Tsagaan Nuur** (p119), a volcanic lake offering great fishing and lovely sunsets

- POPULATION: 321,200
- AREA: 199,000 SQ KM

History

The 'animal art' and many deer stelae found in the valleys of Arkhangai aimag are evidence of tribal existence here around 1300 BC, but the region really came into its own in the 3rd century BC, when the nomadic Xiongnu set up a power base in the Orkhon valley. Various 'empires' rose and fell in the Xiongnu's wake, including the Ruan-Ruan, the Tujue and the Uighurs, who built their capital at Khar Balgas in AD 715. These Turkic-speaking peoples held sway over vast portions of Inner Asia and harassed the Chinese (whose attempts to defend the Great Wall were never really successful). They had their own alphabet and left several carved steles that describe their heroes and exploits. The most famous is the Kultegin Monument (p118), located relatively near to Khar Balgas.

Chinggis Khaan and his merry men were only the latest in a string of political and military powers to use the Orkhon valley as a base. Chinggis never spent much time here, using it mainly as a supply centre for his armies, but his son Ögedei built the walls around Karakorum (near present-day Kharkorin) in 1235, and invited emissaries from around the empire to visit his court.

Centuries after the fall of the Mongol empire, it was religion, rather than warriors, that put a spotlight back on central Mongolia. Erdene Zuu Khiid was built from the remains of Karakorum and, with Manchu and Tibetan influence, Buddhism pushed the native shaman faith to the fringe of society.

The first eight Bogd Gegeen Khaans ruled from central Mongolia, and built up the most important religious centres, including Urga (now Ulaanbaatar), which shifted location along the Tuul Gol (River) for more than 250 years, until settling at its present site in the mid-18th century.

Climate

The central aimags lie in a transitional zone, with southern portions nudging into the Gobi and northern areas covered in Siberian *taiga*, with steppe in between. Winter daytime temperatures of -30°C to -15°C are typical, lasting from late November to early February. March and April suffer from strong, dry winds and changeable weather. July and August are good times to travel as the wet weather finally turns the steppe into a photogenic shade of green. October will bring cool evenings and snow flurries before the onset of winter.

Getting There & Away

A good paved highway, running from Ulaanbaatar to Kharkhorin, is traversed by share jeeps, minivans and buses that depart daily from the Dragon and Naran Tuul bus stands.

If coming from western Mongolia, the route through Arkhangai is more interesting that the dull journey via Bayankhongor – the main access point is via the town of Tosontsengel in Zavkhan. If you are in Bayankhongor, the 210km road over the mountains affords some spectacular scenery. Hitchhikers might find a ride on a logging truck, but you'll save a lot of time by hiring your own vehicle.

Getting Around

Töv aimag has a network of good unpaved and paved roads, so you can easily use public transport to make day or overnight trips from the capital.

For the other aimags, share jeeps will travel from the nearest provincial centre to other destinations, but off the main paved road, traffic throughout these regions is light. In Övörkhangai, public transport will get you to Erdene Zuu Khiid, Khujirt and Arvaikheer, but if you want to get further afield to Tövkhön Khiid, Orkhon Khürkhree or Naiman Nuur, you'll need your own transport. In Arkhangai, the main road is one of the few routes in Mongolia where hitchhikers can easily get to a few places of interest, including Taikhar Chuluu and Terkhiin Tsagaan Nuur.

A jeep is fine for getting around, but travelling by horse grants the best access via the river valleys and into the mountains.

TÖV TӨB

pop 111,900 / area 81,000 sq km

Ulaanbaatar is an autonomous municipality; the aimag that surrounds it is called Töv, which means 'central'. Just an hour's drive from Ulaanbaatar are restored monasteries in beautiful valleys, and mountains with some wonderful hiking. A large portion of

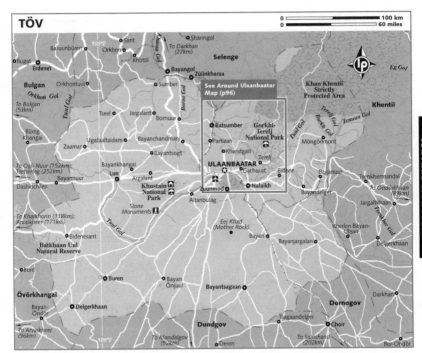

TÖV

0 ━━━━━━━ 100 km
0 ━━━━━━━ 60 miles

CENTRAL MONGOLIA

the aimag is made up of the Gorkhi-Terelj, Khan Khentii and Bogdkhan Uul national parks. The ethnic groups include the Khalkh, the Kazakhs and the Barga.

Töv may not be the most spectacular aimag in Mongolia, but it's an excellent place to start your exploration, or to see some of the countryside if your time is limited.

ZUUNMOD ЗУУНМОД
☎ 01272 / pop 17,000 / elev 1529m

Nestled in a valley 43km south of Ulaanbaatar, Zuunmod is a laid-back town and the capital of Töv aimag. If travelling independently, you may need to stay in Zuunmod to visit the nearby monastery, Manzushir Khiid, or hike in the nearby mountains. Otherwise there's little reason to linger.

There's an **Internet Café** (☎ 22044; per person T600; ☽ noon-9pm Mon-Fri) in the Telecom office. The post office is also here. The police station is in the south of town.

Sights
The chief attraction in Zuunmod is the **Central Province Museum** (☎ 23619; admission T1000;

☽ 9am-1pm & 2-6pm), opposite the southeast corner of the park – look for the sign in English. Like most aimag museums, it gives a good summary of the local geology, flora and fauna, and has a stuffed-animals section – the moose is gigantic. There are also some interesting black-and-white photos of Manzushir Khiid, including the once-regular *tsam* dances.

The nearby **Ethnography Museum** (☎ 22161; admission T1000; ☽ 9am-7pm) is often closed; just knock on the back window. Inside you'll find a shaman's costume, an antique ger and a ping pong table.

Not in the same league as Manzushir Khiid but worth a brief visit, **Dashichoinkhorlon Khiid** (Дашчойнхорлон Хийд) is a 500m walk directly east of the department store and across the creek. If you ask the monks, you can go inside the temple. Ceremonies start at around 11am on most days.

Sleeping & Eating
You can camp anywhere near town, although Manzushir Khiid is a better option than Zuunmod.

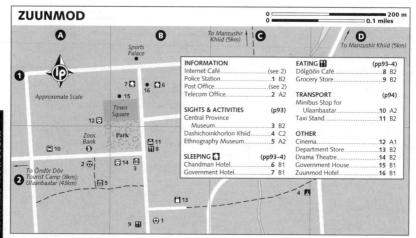

ZUUNMOD

0 ━━━━━━ 200 m
0 ━━━━━━ 0.1 miles

To Manzushir Khiid (5km)
To Manzushir Khiid (5km)

Sports Palace

Approximate Scale

Town Square

Park

Zoos Bank

To Öndör Döv Tourist Camp (8km); Ulaanbaatar (43km)

INFORMATION	
Internet Café...................(see 2)	
Police Station.....................1 B2	
Post Office........................(see 2)	
Telecom Office.....................2 A2	
SIGHTS & ACTIVITIES	**(p93)**
Central Province	
Museum.............................3 B2	
Dashichoinkhorlon Khiid..........4 C2	
Ethnography Museum...............5 A2	
SLEEPING	**(pp93–4)**
Chandman Hotel....................6 B1	
Government Hotel..................7 B1	

EATING	**(pp93–4)**
Dölgöön Café......................8 B2	
Grocery Store.....................9 B2	
TRANSPORT	**(p94)**
Minibus Stop for	
Ulaanbaatar.....................10 A2	
Taxi Stand.......................11 B2	
OTHER	
Cinema............................12 A1	
Department Store.................13 B2	
Drama Theatre....................14 B2	
Government House.................15 B1	
Zuunmod Hotel....................16 B1	

Government Hotel (☎ 22184; s/d T6500/13,000) The large and refurbished rooms are just about all that's on offer in Zuunmod. There's a bar and restaurant downstairs.

Across the street and behind the defunct Zuunmod Hotel, the smaller Chandman Hotel was being renovated when we visited.

Öndör Döv Tourist Camp (☎ 457 108; fax 455 016; www.discover.mn; per person US$40) Geared towards package-tour groups, this unspectacular and overpriced ger camp is about 8km south west of Zuunmod. Horse rental is also exorbitant at US$15 per hour.

There are a couple of fly-blown *guanz* on the main north–south street, where you might get some milky tea and *khuushuur* (fried mutton pancakes). The best of the lot is probably **Dölgöön Café** (☻ 9am-9pm Mon-Sat), on the eastern side of the central park. There's a grocery store opposite the police station.

Getting There & Away

Minivans run through the pretty countryside between Zuunmod and Ulaanbaatar (T700, one hour, hourly) between 7am and 8pm, from Ulaanbaatar's Dragon bus stand. The road is paved and in good condition. The bus stop in Zuunmod is just a short walk west of the main street.

A chartered taxi from Ulaanbaatar will cost between US$10 and US$13 one way. Taxis can be hired in Zuunmod from the taxi stand on the east side of the park. The fare should be the standard rate paid in Ulaanbaatar. Some drivers may want a waiting

fee for hanging around Manzushir Khiid if you are going up there. This is reasonable as you may be there for an hour or two.

BOGDKHAN UUL STRICTLY PROTECTED AREA БОГДХАН УУЛ

The mountain Bogdkhan Uul (2122m) was proclaimed a national park as far back as 1778. During the Soviet period the park's status was formalised and it was renamed after Choibalsan. It is now the Bogdkhan Uul Strictly Protected Area (42,651 hectares). The park is not yet part of Ulaanbaatar's urban sprawl, though plans have been laid to build a road over the mountain if and when a new airport is built. Also in the park is the holy peak of Tsetseegün Uul.

The main activities in the park are **hiking** and **horse riding**. For information on hiking to the main peak from Zaisan Memorial or Manzushir, or combining the two in an overnight hike from Manzushir to Ulaanbaatar (see opposite). For details on renting a horse, see p98.

Entrance to the park costs T3000.

Manzushir Khiid Манзушир Хийд

Only 5km on foot to the northeast of Zuunmod, and 46km from Ulaanbaatar, is this **monastery** (elev 1645m; GPS: N47° 45.520', E106° 59.675'; ☻ 9am-sunset). Established in 1733, Manzushir Khiid (pronounced 'Manshir') had over 20 temples and was once home to 350 monks. Tragically, it was reduced to rubble during the Stalinist purges of 1937.

The main temple has been restored and converted into a museum, but the other buildings in the area remain in ruins. The monastery and museum are not as impressive as those in Ulaanbaatar – it is the beautiful setting that makes a visit worthwhile.

Manzushir Khiid overlooks a beautiful valley of streams, and pine, birch and cedar trees, dotted with granite boulders. The monastery, and most of the area between it and Zuunmod, is part of the Bogdkhan Uul Strictly Protected Area, where the abundant wildlife includes elk, wolves and fox. In the 19th century, 2000 monks stood guard on the mountain against poachers – lawbreakers were hauled away in chains, beaten within an inch of their lives, and locked inside coffin-like jail cells.

As you enter from the main road from Zuunmod you'll be required to pay an admission fee of T5000 per person, which covers the T2000 museum entrance fee and the T3000 national park fee. You'll have to buy both tickets even if you don't plan on entering the museum.

From the gate it's a couple of kilometres to the main area, where there is a shop, a lacklustre museum, a restaurant and several gers offering accommodation. Look for the huge two-tonne **bronze cauldron**, which dates from 1726 and was designed to boil up 10 sheep at a time.

The remains of the monastery are about 800m uphill from the museum. The caretaker lives in the compound next door and will open up the main building for you. The **monastery museum** has exhibits on the layout of Manzushir and some photos that show what it looked like before Stalin's thugs turned it into rubble. The museum also has some fine Buddhist art and *tsam* masks, as well as several examples of the controversial **Ganlin Horn**, made from human thigh bones.

If you have time, it's worth climbing up the rocks behind the main temple, where there are some Buddhist **rock paintings**. The views from the top, are even more beautiful, and you'll find yourself in the midst of a lovely pine forest. You can continue from here all the way to Ulaanbaatar if you are equipped for an overnight trip (hang onto your national park ticket as a ranger may ask for it). See p96 for more details on this route.

Tsetseegün Uul Цэцээгүн Уул

Of the four holy mountains, easily the most magnificent is Tsetseegün. At 2256m, Tsetseegün is the highest point in the Bogdkhan Uul range, which dominates the skyline to the south of Ulaanbaatar. From the city, you can't get an idea of just how beautiful this area is, but once you're in the forest it has a whole different feel.

If you are **hiking** around this mountain, you need to pay the national park fee. You can do this at the gate to the Bogdkhan Uul Strictly Protected Area or at Manzushir Khiid.

There are numerous approaches to the summit, some easier than others; most go up one way and descend by another route. One popular option is to hike from Manzushir Khiid to Ulaanbaatar, either to the Zaisan Memorial (around a 10-hour walk) or the Observatory (six hours). You'll need to get an early start or camp overnight in the park.

The trip is only really sensible from the beginning of June to the end of September. During the rest of the year, no matter how pleasant the weather is in the morning, sudden thunderstorms and icy winds can come out of nowhere (although this happens occasionally in summer as well). It's important to take a compass and know how to use it, as it's easy to get lost in the forest. You'll need to make an early start and, as there is little or no water on top of the ridge, carry all the water you will need, plus extra food.

Some scrambling over fields of granite boulders is necessary, and the chance of

CENTRAL MONGOLIA

FOUR HOLY PEAKS

The four peaks surrounding Ulaanbaatar are considered holy. Tsetseegün, Chingeltei, Songino Khairkhan and Bayanzürkh Uuls (mountains) correspond, more or less, to the four points on the compass. The peaks are great for hiking, and they're popular for their forests of larch trees, grasslands and stunning bird and other animal life, including red deer, ibex and sable. The forest is the southernmost limit of the Siberian larch forests. There is no shortage of thunderstorms in summer, and there's heavy snow in winter, so be prepared.

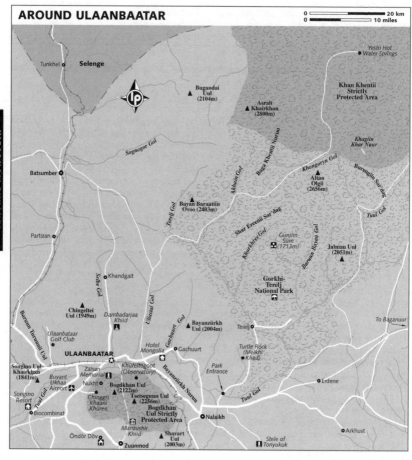

AROUND ULAANBAATAR

slipping and injuring yourself should not be taken lightly. It would be wise to inform a friend or guesthouse owner in Ulaanbaatar of your itinerary and the time of your expected return.

MANZUSHIR KHIID TO ULAANBAATAR ROUTE

This approach to Tsetseegün from the south side is the easiest route by far. As you face the monastery, cut over to your right (east) until you get to the stream. Just follow the stream until it nearly disappears and then head north. About three hours' walking should bring you out over a ridge into a broad boggy meadow, which you'll have to cross. If you've walked straight to the north, the twin rocky

outcrops of the summit should be right in front of you. When you start to see Ulaanbaatar in the distance, you're on the highest ridge and close to the two large *ovoo* (sacred pyramid-shaped collection of stones) on the **summit** (GPS: N47° 48.506′, E107° 00.165′). From the *ovoo* you can return to Manzushir or descend to Ulaanbaatar.

A second route from the monastery begins from the left (west) side of the temples, passing a stupa on the way up to the ridge. This is the route used by the Khan Brau challenge (see p71) and the way down to UB is marked with yellow tags. It's faster but you'll miss the *ovoo* on Tsetseegün.

The way down from Tsetseegün is harder to find; you'll just have to estimate from your visual reference of the city. The quickest way is to head due north, towards the observatory and down to the valley where you'll cross the train tracks. The road is close by and you can catch a taxi to UB for around T3000. A longer route takes you to the Zaisan memorial, on the southern fringe of the city. Be careful not to drop down too soon or you'll end up at Ikh Tenger, one valley short of Zaisan. Ikh Tenger is where the president lives with machine gun–wielding guards, who will be none too pleased if you drop by unannounced. If you see a flimsy barbed wire fence you are in Ikh Tenger; to get out, just continue west along the fence and over the next ridge.

ZAISAN ROUTE

It is more of an uphill battle if you start from the Zaisan Memorial. From the memorial, move past the huts and head up the valley for 100m or so, then cut into the forest to your left. It's a very steep slope until you get to the top of the first ridge (approximately a 30-minute walk). On top of the ridge, you should find a large *ovoo* and an obvious path. From here, the slope levels off and becomes an easy walk through a pleasant forest for the next two hours. If you follow the yellow tags set for the Khan Brau Challenge you'll follow the quickest route to Manzushir but will miss reaching Tsetseegün.

SHAVART ROUTE

Shavart Uul, which appropriately means 'Muddy Mountain', is a lesser peak of 2003m to the southeast of Tsetseegün. As you climb, you'll note seven large rocks on your left. This route takes five hours in each direction. Getting to the starting point requires a car or taxi.

OBSERVATORY ROUTE

This is the easiest route on the Ulaanbaatar side, mainly because you hit the fewest boulders. However, this route is also the least interesting. The walk takes about three hours in each direction.

The problem is that getting to the **Observatory** (Khureltogoot; ☎ 480 331, 480 292) is difficult. You could catch a bus for Nalaikh and get out at the toll gate, then walk the last 6km up the hill. Otherwise, you'll have to take a taxi.

Sleeping
WEST OF BOGDKHAN UUL

If you just want to do some walking and stay in a comfortable place outside of the city there are a few choices available to you.

Chinggis Khaani Khuree (☎ 311 783, 9916 1727; with/without meals US$30/10) Located at the western entrance to the park, this ger camp can justifiably claim to be 'different'. It goes the whole hog with the Chinggis Khaan theme: there's a museum with leftovers from the movie about the great man and it includes costumes, weapons, armour and ger carts. The restaurant has to be seen to be believed: each seat is an enormous throne, and they're set inside a huge ger with a bear-skin welcome mat and walls lined with the skins of 84 unfortunate snow leopards. The aeroplane engine on the grounds is from the plane that crashed in Khentii in 1971, killing Lin Biao, who attempted to assassinate Mao.

Nukht Hotel (☎ 310 241; d/half-lux T14,000/45,000, q ger T28,000) Sometimes called the Nukht EcoTourism Centre, this is in another agreeable area for hiking, only 10km from Ulaanbaatar. It caters almost exclusively for organised tours, though if you ask nicely, and business is quiet (and they are open), you might get a bed for the night. The turnoff for the road to Nukht is south from the main road to the airport; on the corner are the remains of the tiny stadium used for the Naadam Festival in the 1940s.

MANZUSHIR KHIID AREA

The area around the monastery is one of the best camping spots near Ulaanbaatar. You should get permission from the caretaker at the monastery if you are camping nearby, or just hike off into the woods.

Manzushir Ger Camp (☎ 01272-22535, 9930 9216; without food US$8; meals US$2) In a lovely spot amid trees about 200m northeast of the monastery's parking lot, this convenient ger camp is pretty basic but still represents good value. There's a restaurant in the grounds, but it may only be open if a tour group is staying there, so take some food. Horse rental here is US$5 per hour.

Ovooni Enger Ger Camp (☎ 9919 2982, 9515 0782; with/without meals T10,000/5000) Another good option, this camp is 800m off the road to Manzushir (look for the sign just after entering the park gate).

CENTRAL MONGOLIA

Getting There & Away

The most accessible entrances to the park are reached via Zaisan Memorial, the Observatory and Manzushir. There is another entrance from Chinggis Khaani Khuree.

The monastery is easy enough to visit in a day trip from Ulaanbaatar or Zuunmod (from where it's a 7km drive; taxi plus waiting time T3000). If you are walking from Zuunmod, you can either walk along the main northern road after visiting Dashichoinkhorlon Khiid, or you can save some time by walking directly north from Zuunmod, eventually joining up with the main road.

Trekking to Manzushir by horse is a good idea, but Zuunmod is not set up for tourists and it will require some effort to track one down. You could ask around the ger suburbs of the town, at Öndör Döv ger camp (14km west from Manzushir), or make inquiries from one of the guesthouses, such as Idre's (p72), in Ulaanbaatar. At Manzushir itself, wranglers from the nearby ger camps rent horses for US$5 per hour.

SONGINO KHAIRKHAN UUL
СОНГИНО ХАЙРХАН УУЛ

This small mountain to the west of Ulaanbaatar has the unusual name of 'onion mountain'. The mountain is close to the village of Biocombinat, about 5km west of the airport. From the village, cross the wooden bridge and follow the road as it veers left, past the **Songino Resort** (GPS: N47° 51.153', E106° 40.488'), towards the mountain itself. The road from the airport to Biocombinat is fairly busy and flagging down a taxi or bus shouldn't be problem. There are good **camping** and **fishing** spots along the river here, plus accommodation at **Songino Resort** (☎ 9015 9922; dm with 3 meals T7000) and nearby **Khairkhan ger camp** (☎ 9015 9922; 8-bed ger with meals T15,000).

EEJ KHAD (MOTHER ROCK) ЭЭЖ ХАД

Van loads of weekend pilgrims can be found venturing a rough 48km south of Zuunmod to the sacred rock known as **Mother Rock** (Eej Khad; GPS: N47° 18.699', E106° 58.583'). Mongolians often come here to seek solace and advice, and make offerings of vodka, milk and silk scarves called *khatag*. Pilgrims ask for three wishes to be granted, circle the rock three times and make three separate visits.

There are several sacred rocks nearby that are thought to generate good luck, including one called **Dog Rock**, which Mongolians rub their body against to cure ailments.

Minivans depart from the Dragon bus stand at Ulaanbaatar on weekend mornings (T2000, or T4000 return with a two-hour wait at Eej Khad). There are far fewer services on weekdays. It's also possible to stop here on your way to the Gobi, but be prepared for some off-roading as the jeep trails south of here will quickly peter out.

There is nowhere to stay near Eej Khad. You can camp, but stay well away from the crowds of pilgrims.

NALAIKH НАЛАЙХ

The poor village of Nalaikh, 35km southeast of the capital, is part of the Ulaanbaatar autonomous municipality because it once jointly supplied the capital city with its coal. Coal is now primarily supplied by Baganuur, as Nalaikh's mine closed down 15 years ago. However, small-scale private excavations (legal and illegal, and sometimes with child labour) continue in the mines. There's little reason to visit except to see a **Kazakh community**; in the 1950s many Kazakhs from Bayan-Ölgii were 'persuaded' to work in Nalaikh's mine.

To find Nalaikh's **mosque**, face the bright-blue town hall, turn 180° and walk about 25 minutes over a small hill. It's very basic and has a blue tin roof. Bus No 33, which stops

---

MOTHER ROCK

During communism, visiting Eej Khad (Mother Rock) was a political crime, though some people still went in secret. Sometime in the late 1970s the communists decided to do away with the 'feudal' site once and for all. Workers tried dynamite to blow it up, and a tractor to haul it away, both to no avail. The next day workers awoke to find their tractor burnt and destroyed. Soon after the incident the official that ordered Eej Khad's destruction died and his family members became ill. It is said that all the other members of the team suffered a string of bad luck. Most Mongolians can recite a similar tale of provocation and retribution at the holy rock.

outside the Yonsei Friendship Hospital in Ulaanbaatar, travels to Nalaikh twice hourly (T230, 45 minutes) during the day.

AROUND NALAIKH

Around 19km southeast of Nalaikh is an 8th-century Turkic **stele of Tonyukuk** (GPS: N47° 41.661', E107° 28.586'). The stele is covered in runic script and there are *balbal* (stone figures) and grave slabs nearby.

To get the stele you'll need to have your own transport. From Nalaikh, take the main highway towards Baganuur and travel for 16km until you see a sign that says 'Tonyukok'. Turn right onto this track and travel another 10km to reach the stele. Just past the site, a huge hanger contains a few relics found around the site; you could ask the local watchman to let you inside, though there is little to see.

TERELJ AREA ТЭРЭЛЖ

Terelj, about 55km northeast of Ulaanbaatar, is a deservedly popular destination. At 1600m, the area is cool and the alpine scenery is magnificent, and there are great opportunities for hiking, rock climbing, swimming (in icy cold water), rafting, horse riding and, for hard-core extreme-sports fanatics, skiing in the depths of winter.

Terelj was first developed for tourism in 1964 and 30 years later it became part of the **Gorkhi-Terelj National Park**. A few of the tourist developments here are hard on the eyes and ears; some ger camps have concrete car parks, ugly electricity poles, TV antennae and discos at night, and locals overcharge for goods and services. But you can easily get away from all this if you want.

In later summer, the mosquitoes at Terelj can be appalling – at times, the worst in the country – so make sure you have insect repellent with you.

There is a T3000 entry fee to the park for each person, which you'll have to pay at the park entrance, 6km from the main road. The collection of buildings by the gate was supposed to be visitor centre before funds for the project dried up.

The actual village of **Terelj** (GPS: N47° 59.193', E107° 27.834') is about 27km from the park entrance, at the end of a paved road. It has a nice location near the river but there's not much here apart from a few shops, a café and a ger camp.

Günjiin Süm Гүнжийн Сүм

Surrounded by magnificent forests, not far from the lovely river, the Baruun Bayan Gol, the temple was built in 1740 by Efu Dondovdorj to commemorate the death of his Manchurian wife, Amarlangui. Once part of a huge monastery containing about 70 sq metres of blue walls, five other temples and a tower, Günjiin Süm is one of the very few (if not the only) Manchurian-influenced temple in Mongolia to survive over the centuries. Only the main temple, and some of the walls of the monastery, remain.

Unlike most other monasteries in Mongolia, Günjiin was not destroyed during the Stalinist purges, but just fell into ruin from neglect, vandalism and theft. Although you wouldn't know it, extensive restoration has been carried out – which gives you some idea of how damaged it must have been.

The temple is not a must – there are many better and more accessible temples and monasteries in Ulaanbaatar and Töv – but more of an excuse for a great **overnight trek**, on horse or foot, or as part of a longer trip in the national park.

Günjiin (elev 1713m; GPS: N48° 11.010', E107° 33.377') is about 30km (as the crow flies) north of the main area where most of the ger camps are situated in Terelj. With a guide you can hike directly over the mountains, or take the easier but longer route along the Baruun Bayan Gol to get there. You can reach it in a day on horseback, while hikers should allow two days each way for the journey.

Khan Khentii Strictly Protected Area

To the northeast, Gorkhi-Terelj National Park joins onto the Khan Khentii Strictly Protected Area (also known as Khentii Nuruu), comprising over 1.2 million hectares of the Töv, Selenge and Khentii aimags. The Khan Khentii park is almost completely uninhabited by humans, but it is home to **endangered species** of moose, brown bear and weasel, to name but a few, and to over 250 species of **birds**.

You can hike in this park; see below for some suggestions. You can also get here on horseback.

Activities
HIKING
If you have good maps, a compass and some experience (or a proper guide), hiking in

the Terelj area is superb in summer, but be careful of the very fragile environment, and be aware of the mosquitoes and unpredictable weather. The fact that helicopters are sometimes used by travel agencies to start or finish treks in this area shows you how remote the terrain can be.

For more sedate **walks** around the Terelj ger camp area, just follow the main road and pick a side valley to stroll along at your leisure. From the main road, look out for two interesting rock formations: **Turtle Rock** (Melkhi Khad; GPS: N47° 54.509′, E107° 25.428′), in a side valley to the south of Terelj, which really looks like one at a certain angle, and the **Old Man Reading a Book**, on top of a hill.

Some suggested easier hikes are to Günjiin Süm or along the Terelj or Tuul *gols* towards Khentii Nuruu. This is a great area for wildflowers, particularly rhododendron and edelweiss. Places of interest on more difficult, longer treks in Khentii Nuruu include:

Altan-Ölgii Uul (2656m) The source of the Akhain Gol.
Baga Khentii Nuruu North of Akhain Gol.
Khagiin Khar Nuur A 20m-deep glacial lake, about 80km up the Tuul Gol from the ger camps at Terelj.
Yestii Hot Water Springs These springs reach up to 35°C, and are fed by the Yuroo and Estiin *gols*. Yestii is about 18km north of Khagiin Khar Nuur.

HORSE RIDING
Travelling on a horse is the perfect way to see a lot of the park, including Günjiin Süm and the side valleys of the Tuul Gol. To travel any long distances, you will need to have experience, or a guide, and to bring most of your own gear. Horses can be hired through any of the ger camps, but you'll pay high tourist prices. A mob of horse boys hang around Turtle Rock offering horse riding at US$5 per hour, or somewhere between US$12 and US$20 for the day. Alternatively, approach one of the Mongolian families who live around the park and hire one of their horses, though they may not be much cheaper.

RAFTING
Tuul Gol, which starts in the park and flows to Ulaanbaatar and beyond, is one of the best places in the country for rafting. The best section of the river starts a few kilometres north of Terelj village, and wraps around the park until it reaches Gachuurt, near Ulaanbaatar. Nomadic Journeys (see p70) runs rafting trips here for around US$45 per day.

SKIING
If you're unlucky enough to be in Mongolia during the -30°C winter, and can stand leaving your heated hotel, you might as well make the most of it and enjoy some outstanding cross-country skiing around Terelj. There are no set trails, so just take your own gear and ask the locals, or at any ger camps that are operating, for some good, safe areas to try.

Tours
Most foreign and local tour companies include a night or two in a tourist ger at Terelj in their tours. Several local agencies based in Ulaanbaatar, such as Terelj-Juulchin (see opposite), Nomadic Journeys and Nomads (see p70), run some of the more interesting trips around Terelj.

Sleeping
CAMPING
Although the area around Terelj and the national park would appear to be a good place to camp, it's not actively encouraged by park authorities for many reasons: the potential damage to the pristine environment; the genuine risk of forest fires from careless campers; and the fact that no money can be made from campers.

Unless you hike out into the hills it's best to get permission to camp, either from the nearest ger or, for a fee, a ger camp. Pitch your tent away from the main road, don't use wood fires and take all of your rubbish out.

GER CAMPS
During the peak season of July and August (and also at the more popular camps), it's not a bad idea to book ahead, although some places don't have phones. Outside of the normal tourist season (July to September), it's also a good idea to ring ahead to make sure the camp is open and serves food. A few places are open in winter, mostly for expats who want to ski.

Most ger camps cater mainly for organised tours and may not be so interested in independent travellers, but it is certainly worth asking anyway. If you are the only guests at a camp you may have to find staff to open up the restaurant, showers etc. The ger camps offer almost identical facilities and prices – about US$30, including three good Western meals, or US$15 without food.

Apart from the ger camps listed, many individual families rent out a spare ger, and/or hire horses, normally at cheaper rates than the ger camps. You'll have to ask around as none advertises.

Tsolmon (☎ 322 870, 9929 5732; 1 person US$30, 2 people each US$16, 4 people each US$12, 3 meals US$18 extra) About 13km along the main road from the park entrance, Tsolmon is in a beautiful secluded valley 3km east of the main road. It also has beds in a cabin for US$2 more than the gers.

Miraj (☎ 325 188, 9918 1502; with food US$30) Located 14km along the main road from the park entrance, Miraj is in a prime area for hiking. Horses cost US$5 per hour or US$10 per day. Hot showers are available.

Domogt Melkhi Khad (☎ 9913 7384; ger T15,000) This reasonably priced camp is easily found next to Turtle Rock. About 5km past the camp in a secluded valley is Gorkhi camp, which has similar prices; look for its sign.

Dinosaur Tourist Camp (☎ 9919 6552; per person US$10-15) Located 15.5km along the main road from the entrance, this place is easy to identify by the huge, concrete dinosaurs out the front. Even if you don't stay here it's still a good place to stop if you have kids.

San (☎ 312 146; with meals US$19, 2-bed ger without meals T10,000) This place has a variety of options, making it one of the cheaper places around. It's 18.5km along the main road. There's nice hiking nearby but no hot showers.

Terelj-Juulchin (☎ 460 613, in UB ☎ 312 000, 9919 4578; www.terelj-juulchin.url.mn; ger bed US$14, hotel bed US$18, hotel lux US$35) Terelj-Juulchin gives you the option of staying inside the two-storey hotel, with attached bathroom, or in one of the gers set up in what looks like a car park. There is a decent restaurant here with Chinggis Beer on tap (T2200). You could also inquire about a slightly cheaper room in the annex, which has cold-water showers. It's 25.5km from the park entrance.

UB2 (☎ 9977 4125, 9918 2242; ger bed T5750, s/d T11,500/20,700, lux T23,000/34,500) This large hotel complex and restaurant marks the end of the road, next to the village of Terelj.

Gurvan Tulga (☎ 9981 9784; without meals T5000) In Terelj village, this camp occupies an attractive location above the river, but gets crowded with Mongolian tourists.

Ecotourism Ger Camp (☎ 9973 4710; bergroo@ hotmail.com; with/without meals US$16/6) For an off-beat experience, you could wade across the Terelj Gol and hike to a pleasant ger camp run by a Dutchman named Bert. You'll need to get directions from the Terelj-Juulchin hotel (it's a 30-minute horse ride from here) or inquire about the place at Chez Bernard in UB.

Jalman Meadows (4-day package incl transfers to/ from UB per person US$165) Nomadic Journeys run this remote and low-impact ger camp in the upper Tuul Valley, which makes a good base if you are headed to Khagiin Khar Nuur, an eight-hour horse ride away.

On the eastern fringe of the park, 22km past the Terelj turn-off and just off the road to Baganuur, is **Chinggis Tourist Camp** (GPS: N47° 49.893′, E107° 31.339′; with/without meals US$30/15). Make inquiries at El Latino restaurant in UB (p77).

Getting There & Away

BICYCLE

A mountain bike would be an excellent way of getting around some of the Terelj area if you could stand the 70km of uphill riding to get there and cope with the traffic in Ulaanbaatar along the way. Karakorum Expeditions (p70) in Ulaanbaatar is the only outfit to rent bicycles (US$25 per day).

BUS

The road from Ulaanbaatar to Terelj, which goes through part of the national park, is in pretty good nick. A bus departs at 4.30pm from Durvun Zam (corner Peace Ave and Öndör Geegen Zanabazaryn Gudamj) and goes to the centre of the park, a few kilometres past the turn-off to Turtle Rock. The same bus comes back directly to UB. If this doesn't pan out you'll have to hitch.

HITCHING

Hitching *out* of Ulaanbaatar can be difficult because vehicles going to Terelj could leave from anywhere. The cheapest way to hitch to Terelj is to take a minivan for Baganuur or Nalaikh and get off at the turn-off to Terelj, where you are far more likely to get a lift.

Hitching *back* to Ulaanbaatar from along the main road through Terelj is not difficult, as almost every vehicle is returning to the capital.

TAXI

A taxi from Ulaanbaatar is easy to organise; jeeps aren't necessary because the road is

CENTRAL MONGOLIA

paved all the way. You should only pay the standard rate per kilometre, which works out at about US$25 one way, but the driver may understandably want more because his taxi may be empty for part of the return journey. You can also arrange with your taxi to pick you up later.

When there's enough demand shared taxis to Terelj sometimes leave from Naran Tuul jeep station in Ulaanbaatar. This is more likely on summer Sundays when locals make a day trip to the area.

GACHUURT ГАЧУУРТ

East of Ulaanbaatar, the village of Gachuurt is nothing special but the surrounding area is delightful. If you're tired of the comparative hustle and bustle of UB and crave some serenity and clean air, Gachuurt is definitely the place for you. You can hire horses from nearby gers, catch fish, and go rafting in the Tuul Gol (check out Khövsgöl Lodge Company or Nomadic Journeys in Ulaanbaatar, p70), hike in the nearby valleys, and camp anywhere you want. And all of this is only 21km from Ulaanbaatar.

Sleeping & Eating

There is no hotel or restaurant in the village itself, so bring your own food and tent if you want to stay nearby. About 2km before the village there are plenty of serene spots to pitch your tent – just look for somewhere nice from the window of your bus or taxi.

Ger camps come and go around Gachuurt and it's often a matter of asking the guesthouse owners in UB for suggestions. A small outfit called **Tavantes Undaga** (☎ 9919 1900, in English ☎ 9918 4280; T10,000) has ger accommodation and runs excellent half- or full-day horse trips. The camp is located 8km from the village towards Terelj, but its best to call first. Ask for Batsukh.

Hotel Mongolia (☎ 710 154; fax 325 861; www .hotel-mongolia.com; s/d US$80/120, ste US$180-250; meals T2500-3500) This is a ger camp that would impress even Khublai Khan. Owned by the Khan Brau beer and restaurant empire, Hotel Mongolia is the unmissable walled palace resembling ancient Karakorum, a few kilometres short of Gachuurt. Aristocratic, oriental-style rooms are either in cosy ger buildings, small 'temples' or the city walls themselves. The hotel includes a business centre, souvenir shops and a field

behind the walls where mini-Naadams are held according to tour-group bookings. The high season is 14 June to 22 August, after which prices drop by 20%. Even if you don't stay here, it's worth visiting for the kitsch ambience and excellent Asian-style restaurant, which serves a few delicacies such as horse stomach.

Getting There & Away

Buses pick up passengers every hour or so from the east end of Peace Ave, near the Jukov statue, a couple of kilometres east of the city centre, bound for Gachuurt. You can also easily get a taxi from Ulaanbaatar. The road continues past Gachuurt, up the Gachuurt Gol as far as Sansar, but public transport doesn't go this far.

CHINGELTEI UUL ЧИНГЭЛТЭЙ УУЛ

To the north of Ulaanbaatar, Chingeltei Uul (1949m) has some pretty forests near the top. You can reach the base of the mountain by bus No 3, 16 or, best of all, 18 from Sambugiin Gudamj, near Liberty Square in Ulaanbaatar. By taxi, you can go all the way up to a gate from where it's a 2km walk to the summit.

BAYANZÜRKH UUL БАЯНЗҮРХ УУЛ

This peak is in the Bayanzürkh Nuruu (Rich Heart Mountains), to the east of Ulaanbaatar. There's a little forest at the top and views from the summit (2004m) are good. You can reach the base of the mountains by taking the bus from UB to Nalaikh and getting off before the women's prison. Of the four holy mountains, this is the best for mountain biking.

KHANDGAIT ХАНДГАЙТ

About 40km north of Ulaanbaatar, **Khandgait** (GPS: N48° 07.066', E106° 54.296') is another lovely area of cow pastures, small mountains, pine forests and wildflowers, surrounding the small village of the same name. Like Terelj, there are plenty of opportunities for hiking, rock climbing, and, in winter, ice-skating and cross-country skiing (it's possible to rent skis and sleds here in winter). If you're lucky, you might see some ice motorcycling at this time too.

Khandgait is a cheaper and less touristy alternative to Terelj, but because of this Khandgait suffers from a lack of transport and good facilities. Khandgait is not part of a national park, so no permit is required.

The first half of the road between Ulaan-baatar and Khandgait is paved; the second half is reasonably rough. The road goes past Khandgait and continues north to smaller, lovelier and more secluded valleys. Halfway between UB and Khandgait are the Damba-darjaa Khiid (see p65) and Japanese soldiers memorial.

Sleeping

This is great countryside for camping. Just pick any site, preferably near a river, and enjoy; but be careful about wood fires and be sure to take your rubbish out. A ger camp located behind the Children's Camp was not open to the public at the time of research but might be worth asking about.

Getting There & Away
HITCHING

Hitching to Khandgait from UB will take a few rides to get out of the suburbs and you'll probably be expected to pay. A better option is to take bus No 16 out of town. It's easier to hitch a ride back to the city – just about every vehicle going along the main road at Khandgait is going to UB.

MINIBUS & TAXI

About once an hour in summer a minivan (T500) leaves from Doloon Budal, a jeep stop on the northern road out of Ulaan-baatar, several kilometres from downtown (reached by bus No 16).

A taxi (jeeps aren't necessary) from UB is easiest, but, naturally, more expensive at around US$25 return, plus waiting time. You can arrange for the taxi to pick you up later.

KHUSTAIN NATIONAL PARK
ХУСТАЙН НУРУУ

Also known as Khustain Nuruu (Birch Mountain Range), this park was established in 1993 and is about 100km southwest of Ulaanbaatar. The 50,620-hectare reserve protects Mongolia's wild horse, the *takhi*, and the reserve's steppe and forest-steppe environment. In addition to the *takhi*, there

TAKHI – THE REINTRODUCTION OF A SPECIES

The Mongolian wild horse is probably the most recognised and successful symbol of the preservation and protection of Mongolia's diverse and unique wildlife. The *takhi*, also known as Przewalski's horse (named after the Polish explorer who first 'discovered' the horse in 1878), used to roam the countryside in great herds.

They finally became extinct in the wild after poachers killed them for meat, and overgrazing and human encroachment reduced their fodder and breeding grounds. The last wild Mongolian *takhi* was spotted in the western Gobi in 1969.

At that time, only about a dozen *takhi* remained alive, living in zoos in Russia and Europe. Special breeding programs in Australia, Germany, Switzerland and the Netherlands have brought the numbers of *takhi* outside of Mongolia to about 1500. The entire global population of *takhi* are now descended from the bloodline of three stallions, so computerised records have been introduced to avoid inbreeding.

Between 1992 and 2004, with assistance from international environmental agencies, *takhi* were reintroduced into Mongolia at Khustain National Park, Takhiin Tal in Gov-Altai, and Khomiin Tal in Zavkhan. Today there are about 150 *takhi* in Khustain, 60 in Takhiin Tal and 12 in Khomiin Tal.

The *takhi* are the last remaining wild horse worldwide, the forerunner of the domestic horse, as depicted in cave paintings in France. They are not simply horses that have become feral, or wild, as found in the USA or Australia, but a genetically different species, boasting two extra chromosomes in their DNA make-up. The *takhi* are sandy coloured except for a dark dorsal stripe. The tail and legs are dark and the legs have zebra stripes. The skull and jaw is heavier than a horse's, there is no forelock and the mane is short and erect.

New arrivals are kept in enclosures for a year to help them adapt to a new climate. The laws of nature are allowed to run their course; an average of five foals are killed by wolves every year in Khustain. The park gets locals onside by hiring herders as rangers, offering cheap loans to others and offering employment at a cheese-making factory on the outskirts of the park.

For more info check out www.treemail.nl/takh.

are populations of maral (Asiatic red deer), steppe gazelle, deer, boar, manul wild cat, wolf and lynx. A visit to the park has become a popular overnight excursion from Ulaanbaatar in recent years.

Entry to the park is a one-off fee of US$5 (free for locals). It's worth spending at least one night in the park, as you are most likely to see *takhi* and other wildlife at dusk or dawn.

The park is run by the Khustain Nuruu National Park Trust, which is supported by the Dutch government and the Mongolian Association for the Conservation of Nature and the Environment (Macne).

Orientation & Information

The information centre at the entrance to Khustain National Park has a ger with displays on the park and the *takhi* horse, a small souvenir shop and videos that include a documentary on Mongolian horses featuring Julia Roberts. Ten kilometres south into the park's core area is the former park headquarters. Another 13km or so west is Moilt camp.

Sights & Activities

The park offers horse riding, hiking and jeep excursions in an effort to make the park self-financing. Several hiking routes have been established. One good **hike** takes you from the visitors centre to Moilt camp (22km) in about five hours.

A good horseback trek takes you to some Turkic **stone monuments** (GPS: N47° 33.201', E105° 50.991') located southwest of the park and then on to the Tuul Gol. Horse rental is US$10 per day. Contact the park for details.

With your own jeep you can drive to Moilt camp. Park regulations require you to take a **park guide** (1-2 hr US$5, 2-5 hr US$10, more than 5 hr US$15) and stick only to existing tracks. Wildlife watching is best at dusk and at dawn. The takhi could be in any number of places and park guides can direct your driver to the best spots.

The park runs a three-week volunteer program where you can help with research. See www.ecovolunteer.org for details.

Sleeping

Independent camping is not allowed inside the park so you have to camp outside the park boundary. The best place to go is the south side of the park by the Tuul Gol.

There is a small **ger camp** (with/without meals per person US$35/20) at the entrance to the park. Rooms are available in the main building for US$40 per person. There are also cabins at **Moilt camp** (incl 3 meals & entrance fee US$35).

To book accommodation in the park contact **Macne** (☎ 011-311 318, 9919 8619; www .hustai.mn; bldg 10, entrance 2, 1st fl) in Ulaanbaatar. It is about 250m southwest of the Bayangol Hotel.

Getting There & Away

To get to the park travel 100km west from Ulaanbaatar, along the road to Kharkhorin, where there is a signpost pointing you the 13km south to the park entrance. A Russian minivan departs on Friday from Khustain Nuruu at 4pm and returns from UB to the park at 7.30pm (from the Tsuki building next to the State Circus). On Sunday the van leaves the park at 3pm and returns from UB at 5.30pm (from Tsuki). The cost is US$10 one way.

ÖVÖRKHANGAI
ӨВӨРХАНГАЙ

pop 113,200 / area 63,000 sq km

Övörkhangai contains what is probably Mongolia's most popular attraction: the magnificent monastery, Erdene Zuu Khiid, built from the ruins of the ancient Mongol capital of Karakorum (now the modern town of Kharkhorin). Övörkhangai means 'south Khangai', a reference to the spectacular mountains of central Mongolia known as the Khangai Nuruu, which dominate the northwest part of Övörkhangai. The southern part of the aimag, past Arvaikheer, is uninteresting desert steppe. The main ethnic group is the Khalkh.

If travelling by rented jeep, it is easy to combine a visit to Kharkhorin with some other places that are clustered near the borders of Arkhangai, Bulgan and Töv aimags: Khogno Khan Uul, the sand dunes of Mongol Els, Batkhaan Uul Natural Reserve, Shankh Khiid, and the waterfall of Orkhon Khürkhree. The paved road, which reaches Kharkhorin and the aimag capital of Arvaikheer, is also a definite attraction – but the road to Orkhon Khürkhree is often atrocious.

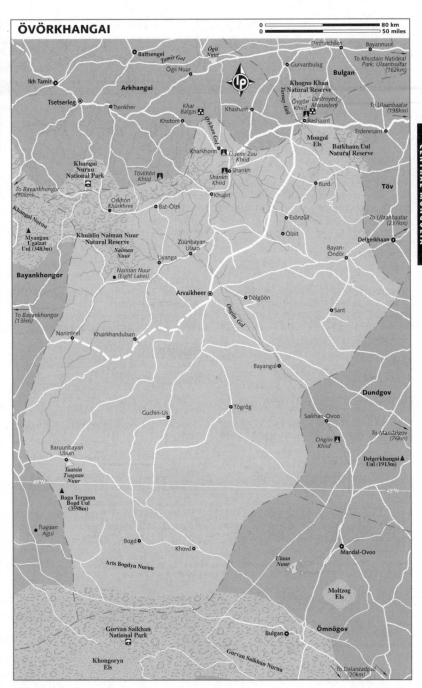

ÖVÖRKHANGAI

0 — 80 km
0 — 50 miles

Dashinchilen
Bayannuur
To Khustain National Park; Ulaanbaatar (162km)

Battsengel
Tamir Gol
Ögii Nuur
Ögii Nuur
Gurvanbulag
Bulgan

Ikh Tamir
Khogno Khan Natural Reserve

Arkhangai
Övgön Khiid
Destroyed Monastery
To Ulaanbaatar (198km)

Tsetserleg
Tsenkher
Khar Balgas
Khashaat
Rashaant
Erdenesant

Khotont
Mongol Els
Batkhaan Uul Natural Reserve

Orkhon Gol
Kharkhorin
Erdene Zuu Khiid
Shankh

Khangai Nuruu National Park
Tövkhön Khiid
Shankh Khiid
Burd
Töv

To Bayankhongor (90km)
Orkhon Khürkhree
Bat-Ölzii
Khujirt
Esönzüil
To Ulaanbaatar (237km)

Khangai Nuruu
Ölziit
Delgerkhaan

Myangan Ugalzat Uul (3483m)
Khuislin Naiman Nuur Natural Reserve
Naiman Nuur
Züünbayan-Ulaan
Bayan-Öndör

Bayankhongor
Uyanga
Naiman Nuur (Eight Lakes)
Arvaikheer
Dölgöön
Sant

To Bayankhongor (13km)
Ongiin Gol

Nariinteel
Khairkhandulaan
Bayangol
Dundgov

Guchin-Us
Tögrög
Saikhan-Ovoo
To Mandalgov (76km)

Baruunbayan Ulaan
Ongiin Khiid
Delgerkhangai Uul (1913m)

Taatsin Tsagaan Nuur

45°N
45°N

Baga Terguun Bogd Uul (3598m)

Tsagaan Agui
Bogd
Khovd
Ulaan Nuur
Mandal-Ovoo

Arts Bogdyn Nuruu
Moltzog Els

Gurvan Saikhan National Park
Bulgan
Ömnögov

Khongoryn Els
Gurvan Saikhan Nuruu
To Dalanzadgad (20km)

CENTRAL MONGOLIA

Fishers can catch lenok all along the Orkhon Gol; areas south of Kharkhorin should be best.

ARVAIKHEER АРВАЙХЭЭР
☎ 01322 / pop 22,900 / elev 1913m

A nondescript but friendly aimag capital, Arvaikheer is of little interest except as a place to eat and rest, refuel the jeep or arrange onward public transport. Arvaikheer has the requisite hotel, cinema, school and administrative building, and the monastery and museum are worth a look.

There is no need to go to Arvaikheer if you only want to visit Kharkhorin and northern Övörkhangai, as a paved road reaches Kharkhorin from Ulaanbaatar. The police station is southeast of the town square.

Information
Bathhouse (shower/sauna T800/3000; ☺ 9am-10pm Tue-Sun)
Internet Café (☎ 22193; per hr T600; ☺ 8.30am-12.30pm & 2-6pm Mon-Fri) In the Telecom office.
Khan Bank (☎ 22040; ☺ 9am-1pm & 2-4.30pm)
Telecom Office (☎ 24098; ☺ 24hr) The post office is also here.

Sights
GANDAN MUNTSAGLAN KHIID
This comparatively large monastery (Гандан Мунтсаглан Хийд), about 900m north of the town square, contains a fine collection of *thangka* (scroll paintings), including one depicting the original monastery, which

was destroyed in 1937. The current monastery was opened in 1991, and now has about 60 monks in residence. Visitors are welcome. To the left of the temple is a small shop selling religious items.

MUSEUMS
Since Övörkhangai lies partly in the forested Khangai region and the Gobi Desert, the **Aimag Museum** (☎ 22075; admission T1000, photos T3500; ☺ 9am-12.30pm & 2-6pm Mon-Fri) boasts a better-than-average selection of stuffed mountain and desert animals. There are also some fossils and arrows, local artwork and leftovers from Karakorum. Upstairs are intricate carvings.

Just around the corner is the **Zanabazar Memorial Museum** (admission & hours same as Aimag Museum), which has a collection of religious artwork connected to the master sculptor.

OTHER SIGHTS
On a hill northwest of town is a Russian 'friendship monument'. Walk further along the ridge and then drop down to the left where you can spot some **rock carvings**.

Sleeping
Like most aimag capitals, camping is a better option than the dreary hotels, but in Arvaikheer you'll have to walk a kilometre or so to find a quiet place to pitch your tent. It's best to head out to the area north of the monastery or drive 5km south to the Ongiin Gol.

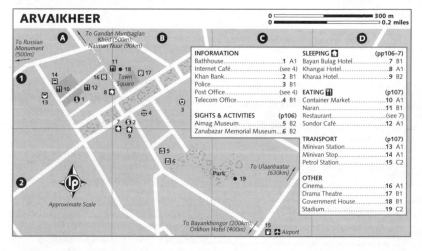

ARVAIKHEER

INFORMATION		SLEEPING 🏠	(pp106–7)
Bathhouse	1 A1	Bayan Bulag Hotel	7 B1
Internet Café	(see 4)	Khangai Hotel	8 A1
Khan Bank	2 B1	Kharaa Hotel	9 B2
Police	3 B1		
Post Office	(see 4)	EATING 🍴	(p107)
Telecom Office	4 B1	Container Market	10 A1
		Naran	11 B1
SIGHTS & ACTIVITIES	(p106)	Restaurant	(see 2)
Aimag Museum	5 B2	Sondor Café	12 A1
Zanabazar Memorial Museum	6 B2		
		TRANSPORT	(p107)
		Minivan Station	13 A1
		Minivan Stop	14 A1
		Petrol Station	15 C2
		OTHER	
		Cinema	16 A1
		Drama Theatre	17 A1
		Government House	18 B1
		Stadium	19 C2

Bayan Bulag Hotel (☎ 23374; dm T6000, half-lux/ lux per person T8000/10,000) It has five clean, carpeted rooms. The half-lux and lux rooms have good bathrooms with 24-hour hot water. The attached restaurant is one of the best places in town to eat.

Kharaa Hotel (☎ 23655, 23755; d US$15, half-lux/ lux US$20/25) This place has standard three-bed rooms with a shared bathroom. If the hotel isn't busy, solo travellers should be able to pay for just one bed; at other times you'll have to pay for at least two beds for privacy. Half-lux and lux rooms include bathroom and shower. Hot water comes on for a couple of hours in the morning and evening – check the times with reception. The place is clean and bright but overpriced so try for a discount.

Orkhon Hotel (☎ 22095; dm/lux T3500/10,000) Located out on the southern edge of town near the main road, this place is OK for budget travellers who can put up with dingy rooms.

Khangai Hotel (☎ 24444; dm/half-lux US$5/7, lux US$14-20) This place is central but the cheaper rooms are poor value. The dorms have very uncomfortable box-spring beds and neither toilet nor working tap. The half-lux is tattered but has a toilet. Better value are the tidier lux rooms, which have toilet and shower.

Eating & Shopping

Choices are limited but one good option is the Bayan Bulag Hotel. Otherwise there are plenty of *guanz* and tea houses *(tsainii gazar)* near the container market. The bustling daily market also has yogurt, *airag* (fermented mare's milk) after June and sheepskins, as well as the normal range of packaged foods.

Sondor Café (dishes T800-1000; ⏱ 8am-8pm) This popular *guanz,* masquerading as a café, is near the market. Locals also recommend the Naran restaurant behind the Government House.

Getting There & Away

You can travel quickly along the 430km paved road between Ulaanbaatar and Arvaikheer. (There are plenty of *guanz* along the way.) The paved road finishes just west of Arvaikheer; from there it is about another 200km along the usual rough road, with the occasional collapsed bridge, to the

next aimag capital of Bayankhongor. With a jeep, an experienced driver and lots of time you could venture south to Dalanzadgad, 377km away in Ömnögov aimag, either via Saikhan-Ovoo or (more adventurously) via Guchin Us, Khovd and Khongoryn Els.

AIR

MIAT is scheduled to fly between Ulaanbaatar and Arvaikheer every Tuesday and Saturday for US$60/106 one way/return, en route to/from Bayankhongor. The airport is less than 1km south of town.

HITCHING

The Ulaanbaatar–Arvaikheer road is one of the busiest in the country – at least one vehicle goes in both directions every minute. Hitching a ride on a truck or in a private car should be comparatively easy. Going further west along the main road to Bayankhongor won't be as easy, but it is possible. In Arvaikheer, trucks hang around the market, so try there or at the petrol station on the main road.

JEEP

If you want to hire a jeep to see the sights around northern Övörkhangai, it's better to catch a bus from Ulaanbaatar to Kharkhorin and hire a jeep there, rather than go to Arvaikheer. Shared and charter jeeps are rare in Arvaikheer, but you could try around the market. You can also hire a motorbike and sidecar for shorter trips.

MINIVANS

Minivans and smaller microbuses run along the paved road between Arvaikheer and Ulaanbaatar daily (T10,000, seven hours). Look for them just east of the market. At least one car a day will travel north to Khujirt (T3000, two hours); as usual, when the driver says departure time is 'now' that means around 4pm.

NAIMAN NUUR НАЙМАН НУУР

Worth visiting if you have a jeep is the area known as Naiman Nuur (Eight Lakes), which was created by volcanic eruptions centuries ago and is now part of the 11,500-hectare **Khuisiin Naiman Nuur Natural Reserve**. The **lakes** (GPS: N46° 21.232′, E101° 50.705′) are about 50km southwest of Orkhon Khürkhree, but the roads are often virtually impassable.

CENTRAL MONGOLIA

Companies such as Nomads and Nomadic Expeditions (p70) run tours here, including horse-riding trips.

KHUJIRT ХУЖИРТ

South of Erdene Zuu, Khujirt is a small, soporific town noted for its mineral hot springs and health resort. Most travellers pass through the town en route to the waterfall, Orkhon Khürkhree, but there are some interesting **grave sites** worth looking out for a couple of kilometres out of town on the road to Kharkhorin. Khujirt lures Mongolians with promises of health restoration at its Russian-style **spa resort**. The bathhouse includes hot and cold mineral baths (T1000) plus mud treatment (T2400). The authentic local experience also includes a series of vitamin injections and you'll see doctors walking around in white smocks and patients in their bathrobes and slippers, a surreal and somewhat creepy experience for foreign visitors.

The road between Kharkhorin and Khujirt (a bumpy 54km) is one of the best places in the country to see **falcons** and **hawks**, particularly the *sar* (moon) hawk. If you are ever likely to get a photo of one of these birds, this is the place.

Sleeping & Eating

Located next to the spa resort, **Khujirt Tur** (☎ 9971 5262; per person T10,000) is the best choice in the area. The shower block has piping hot-water showers and flush toilets.

All rooms in **Elma Hotel** (☎ 013259-21340, 9909 2321; tw/lux T10,000/16,000) come with a private bathroom but no hot water. It's in the spa resort compound.

The Khujirt Tur ger camp serves meals for T4000. A cheaper *guanz* is in back of the resort.

Getting There & Away

Buses (T7000) run every Monday, Wednesday and Friday from UB's Dragon bus stand. They return to Ulaanbaatar the following day, passing within 5km of Kharkhorin. Faster minivans also do the run occasionally for T10,000.

With the number of Mongolians using the Ulaanbaatar–Kharkhorin road to get to Khujirt in summer, it shouldn't be hard to hitch a ride between Kharkhorin and Khujirt.

AROUND KHUJIRT

Orkhon Khürkhree Орхон Хүрхрээ

Apart from the springs at Khujirt, the main attraction in the area is this **waterfall** (GPS:N46° 47.234', E101° 57.694'). It is situated in the historically significant Orkhon Valley, whose river flows an incredible 1120km to the north before it joins the mighty Selenge Gol. Also called Ulaan Tsutgalan (Улаан Цутгалан), the waterfall was formed by a unique combination of volcanic eruptions and earthquakes about 20,000 years ago. The falls are naturally most impressive after heavy rain.

Ironically, these rains will also make the 82km road from Khujirt almost impassable: the river floods, the road is prone to mud slides and bridges often collapse. You should always ask around Khujirt for information about the current state of the road before heading out here. Usually the drive takes three hours from Khujirt.

A little way downstream from Orkhon Khürkhree, you can climb down to the bottom of the **gorge**. The gorge itself is only 22m deep, but it is dotted with pine trees and is quite scenic from the bottom. Hardly anyone lives in the area, and the only sign of civilisation you'll see along the way are a few gers. There are **hot springs** about 29km from the falls, on the south side of the valley, and up a side canyon. You'll have to ask locals for directions.

There is a designated camping area by the falls, but it is always very cold at night, so be prepared.

If you haven't brought a tent, you can stay at the **Orkhon Old Government House** (bed in ger/house US$15/20) set on a gorgeous, secluded island. It is difficult to find: 500m before the bridge, turn left and drive parallel to the river (ie upstream) and ask for directions. Prices include all meals. The people running the place are friendly and they can arrange horses, which is probably the best way to see this region.

If you have a rod and reel, you could try catching your dinner. Good spots for catching lenok can be found downstream from the waterfall.

Tövkhön Khiid Төвхөн Хийд

High in the mountains marking the north side of the Orkhon Valley sits this recently rebuilt **monastery** (GPS: N47° 00.711', E102° 16.005'). Zanabazar founded the site in 1653 and lived, worked and meditated here for 30 years. Several **pilgrimage sites** have grown up around the temple and hermit's caves, including one that is said to be Zanaba-zar's boot imprint. The main temple closes following morning services (between 10am and 11am).

The temple is located in **Khangain Nuruu National Park** (admission T3000), just outside the aimag, and is best reached with your own vehicle. A good 4WD can drive the steep road up to the monastery in 20 minutes, but a better idea is to walk (one hour) up the hill through the forest. The route is obvious and in summer locals wait at the base of the hill offering horse rides (T1000) to the top. The monastery is around 50km from Bat-Ölzii village.

SHANKH KHIID ШАНХ ХИЙД

Shankh Khiid, once known as the West Monastery, and Erdene Zuu are the only monasteries in the region to have survived the 1937 purge. Shankh was renowned because of its connections with the great Zanabazar and is said to have once housed Chinggis Khaan's black military banner. At one time the monastery was home to more than 1500 monks. As elsewhere, the monastery was closed in 1937, temples were burnt and many monks were shipped off to Siberia.

The **monastery** (GPS: N47° 03.09', E102° 57.236'; admission T1000, photos T1000) is exactly halfway along the main road between Kharkhorin and Khujirt, in the village of Shankh. If you have your own transport, it's a good place to stop between both towns.

KHARKHORIN (KARAKORUM)
ХАРХОРИН (КАРАКОРУМ)

In 1220 Chinggis Khaan decided to move his capital from Khentii aimag to Kara-korum, 373km southwest of modern-day Ulaanbaatar. Permanent structures were only erected after Chinggis' death by his son Ögedei Khaan. Karakorum served as the political, cultural and economic capital of the Mongols for only 40 years, before Kublai Khaan moved it to Khanbalik, in what is now Beijing.

Following the move to Beijing, and the subsequent collapse of the Mongol empire, Karakorum was abandoned and then de-stroyed by vengeful Manchurian soldiers

in 1388. Whatever was left of Karakorum was used to help build Erdene Zuu Khiid in the 16th century, which itself was badly damaged during the Stalinist purges.

The Soviet-built town of Kharkhorin (and its gigantic flour factory) was built a couple of kilometres away from Erdene Zuu. Although there is little left to recall the ancient glory, the hidden history of Kara-korum and the restored temples at Erdene Zuu Khiid justifiably attract visitors.

There are some calling for a transfer of Mongolia's capital from Ulaanbaatar to Kharkhorin between 2020 and 2030, to echo the 800th anniversary of Chinggis' transfer of the Mongol capital from 1220 to 1236. Who knows, in 25 years the sleepy town of Kharkhorin may become Mongo-lia's version of Brasilia, Canberra or Astana (the capital of Kazakhstan).

Information

Kharkhorin has no information office, but the guides at Erdene Zuu can answer most tourist-related questions. At the time of re-search Kharkhorin was still without Inter-net access. The best place to check for the eventual Internet hook-up is the Telecom office, which is about 250m west of the con-tainer market; the post office is here too.

A container market (*khudaldaany töv*) in the centre of the town has most things you might need.

Bathhouse (per person T800; ☽ 10am-8pm) On the main road, next to the market.

Khan Bank (☎ 2124; ☽ 9am-5pm Mon-Fri) Can change US dollars, euros and travellers cheques.

Sights
ERDENE ZUU KHIID

Erdene Zuu (Эрдэнэ Зуу Хийд; Hundred Treas-ures) was the first Buddhist monastery in Mongolia. The monastery was started in 1586 by Abtai Khaan, but wasn't entirely finished until about 300 years later. It had between 60 and 100 temples, about 300 gers were set up inside the walls and, at its peak, up to 1000 monks were in residence.

Like Karakorum, the monastery was abandoned and then vandalised by invad-ing Manchurians. Attempts at restoration were made in about 1760 and again in 1808 under the direction of the famous archi-tect, Manzushir, but then came the Stalinist purges of the 1930s. All but three of the

CENTRAL MONGOLIA

THE ANCIENT CAPITAL

Hardly a single stone remains of ancient Karakorum, the Mongol capital, but an intriguing picture can be painted using contemporary accounts of visiting missionaries, ambassadors and travellers.

Situated at the crossroads of trade routes, the city was surrounded by walls with four gates. Each had its own market, selling grain in the east, goats in the west, oxen and wagons in the south and horses in the north.

The surrounding town of gers was an impressive sight, though the missionary William of Rubruck (1215–95) dismissed the city as no bigger than the suburb of Saint Denis in Paris. Giovanni de Piano Carpine (1180–1252), an envoy sent to the Mongols in 1245 by Pope Innocent IV, described the city vaguely as 'at the distance of a year's walk' from Rome. Marco Polo gave a brief description of the city, though he never made it there.

The Mongol khaans were famed for their religious tolerance and split their time equally between all the religions; hence 12 different religions co-existed within the town. Mosques, Buddhist monasteries and Nestorian Christian churches competed for the Mongol's souls. Even powerful figures such as Ögedei's wife and Khublai's mother were Nestorian Christians.

The centrepiece of the city was the Tumen Amgalan, or Palace of Worldly Peace, in the southwest corner of the city. This 2500-sq-metre complex, built in 1235, was the palace of Ögedei Khaan. The two-storey palace had a vast reception hall for receiving ambassadors, and its 64 pillars resembled the nave of a church. The walls were painted, the green-tiled floor had underfloor heating, and the Chinese-style roof was covered in green and red tiles. Whenever he was at court, the khaan sat on a panther skin atop a great throne, to which stairs ascended from one side and descended from the other.

A team of German archaeologists has recently uncovered the foundations of the palace, close to the stone turtle (see opposite). You can also see a model of the palace in the Museum of Mongolian History in Ulaanbaatar.

The most memorable aspect of the city was a fountain designed in 1253 by the French jeweller and sculptor Guillaume Bouchier (or Bouchee) of Paris, who had been captured by the Mongols in Hungary and brought back to embellish Karakorum. The fountain was in the shape of a huge silver tree, which simultaneously dispensed mare's milk from silver lion's heads, and wine, rice wine, bal (mead) and airag (fermented mare's milk) from four golden spouts shaped like snake heads. On top of the tree was an angel. On order a servant blew a pipe like a bugle that extended from the angel's mouth, giving the order for other servants to pump drinks out of the tree.

Mongolian noblemen lived in the north of town, near the Orkhon Gol. Rubruck disparagingly describes various pleasure domes and epic feasts (during one of which the Mongol guests guzzled 105 cartloads of alcohol). There were also quarters of craftsmen and traders, populated by a great mix of people brought back to Karakorum from all over Asia. So cosmopolitan was the city that both foreign and Mongol coins were legal tender.

temples in Erdene Zuu were destroyed and an unknown number of monks were either killed or shipped off to Siberia and never heard from again.

However, a surprising number of statues, tsam masks and thangkas were saved from the monastery at the time of the purges – possibly with the help of a few sympathetic military officers. The items were buried in nearby mountains, or stored in local homes (at great risk to the residents). Sadly the statues are still not safe: an Israeli security system was installed in the monastery halls in 2000 after several statues were stolen.

The monastery remained closed until 1965 when it was permitted to reopen as a museum, but not as a place of worship. It was only with the collapse of communism in 1990 that religious freedom was restored and the monastery became active again. Today, Erdene Zuu Khiid still retains much of its former glory, and is considered by many to be the most important monastery in the country, though no doubt it's a shadow of what it once was. Restoration of the monastery is one of Mongolia's top cultural projects, but little funding is made available from the government or international agencies.

Information
Entrance to the **monastery grounds** (🕑 9am-6pm summer, 10am-5pm winter) is free. If you want to see inside the temples, however, you'll have to go to the ticket desk and souvenir shop on your left as you enter the grounds from the south and buy a ticket for US$3, which includes a guided tour of the site. Permission to take photos in the temples is an additional US$5 and video is US$10.

The souvenir shop sells expensive souvenirs, as well as slide film (T8000). The monastery is an easy 2km walk from the centre of Kharkhorin.

Temples
The monastery is enclosed in an immense walled compound. Spaced evenly along each wall, about every 15m, are 108 stupas (108 is a sacred number to Buddhists). The three temples in the compound, which were not destroyed in the 1930s, are dedicated to the three stages of Buddha's life: childhood, adolescence and adulthood. See the boxed text on p32 for a brief description of some of the gods you will see in the monastery.

Dalai Lama Süm was built to commemorate the visit by Abtai Khaan's son, Altan, to the Dalai Lama in Tibet in 1675. The room is bare save for a statue of Zanabazar and some fine 17th-century *thangka* depicting the dalai lamas and various protector deities.

Inside the courtyard, **Baruun Zuu**, the temple to the west, built by Abtai Khaan and his son, is dedicated to the adult Buddha. Inside, on either side of Sakyamuni (the historical Buddha), are statues of Sanjaa (Dipamkara in Sanskrit), the past Buddha, to the left; and Maidar (Maitreya in Sanskrit), the future Buddha, to the right. Other items on display include some golden 'wheels of eternity', *naimin takhel* (the eight auspicious symbols), figurines from the 17th and 18th centuries, and *balin* (wheat dough cakes, decorated with coloured medallions of goat or mutton fat), made in 1965 and still well preserved. Look out for the inner circumambulation path leading off to the left, just by the entrance.

The main and central temple is called the **Zuu of Buddha**. The entrance is flanked by the gods Gonggor on the left and Bandal Lham (Palden Lhamo in Sanskrit) on the right. Inside, on either side of the statues of the child Buddha, are (to the right) Otoch Manal, the Medicine Buddha and (to the left) Holy Abida, the god of justice. The temple also contains statues of Niam and Dabaa, the sun and moon gods respectively, a few of the *tsam* masks that survived the purges, some carved, aggressive-looking guards from the 16th and 17th centuries, and some displays of the work of the revered sculptor and Buddhist, Zanabazar.

In the temple to the east, **Zuun Zuu**, there's a statue depicting the adolescent Buddha. The statue on the right is Tsongkhapa, who founded the Yellow Hat sect of Buddhism in Tibet. The figure on the left is Janraisig (Chenresig in Tibetan, Avalokitesvara in Sanskrit), the Bodhisattva of compassion.

As you walk north you will pass the **Golden Prayer Stupa**, built in 1799. The locked temple next to this is said to be the first temple built at Erdene Zuu.

The large, white temple at the far end is the Tibetan-style **Lavrin Süm**, where ceremonies are held every morning, usually starting at around 11am, though the times vary so ask at the office. Visitors are welcome, but photographs during ceremonies are not.

Other Sights
Apart from the main temples, there are several other interesting things to see. The **gravestones** of Abtai Khaan (1554–88) and his grandson Tüshet Khaan Gombodorj (the father of Zanabazar) stand in front of the Dalai Lama Süm and are inscribed in Mongol, Chinese, Tibetan and Arabic scripts. In the northeast of the monastery are the base stones of a gigantic ger (now called the **Square of Happiness and Prosperity**), set up in 1639 to commemorate Zanabazar's birthday. The ger was reported to be 15m high and 45m in diameter, with 35 concertina-style walls, and could seat 300 during the annual assemblies of the local khaans. At the time of research, Japanese aid money was going into a project to refill the lake that once stood near the giant ger.

TURTLE ROCKS
Outside the monastery walls are two 'turtle rocks'. Four of these sculptures once marked the boundaries of ancient Karakorum, acting as protectors of the city (turtles are considered symbols of eternity). The turtles originally had an inscribed stone stele mounted vertically on their back.

One is easy to find: just walk out of the northern gate of the monastery and follow the path northwest for about 300m. Often, an impromptu **souvenir market** is set up next to the turtle rock. You'll need a guide or directions to find the other turtle rock.

ANCIENT KARAKORUM

Just beyond the turtle, stretching for about a kilometre south and east, is the site of ancient Karakorum. The foundations of Karakorum's buildings are all underground and little has been excavated so you need to use a little imagination when contemplating the grandness of it all. The plain had been littered with bricks, ruined walls and pillars until the mid-16th century when everything was picked up and used to build the walls and temples of nearby Erdene Zuu.

Since 2000, German archaeologists have uncovered two small portions of Karakorum. One team is working on Ögedei Khaan's palace and the other has unearthed a section of Karakorum's central road further south. The researchers have found a surprising quantity of Buddhist relics in the palace; indicating that the building may have been turned into a temple after Khublai Khan moved the capital to Khanbalik (current-day Beijing).

PHALLIC ROCK

If you have some time, it is worth looking for the bizarre 'phallic rock', which points erotically to something interestingly called a 'vaginal slope'. It is surrounded by a stone fence, hidden up a small valley, and visible from the main road to Ulaanbaatar, about 1km from Kharkhorin. It's a 30- or 40-minute walk from Erdene Zuu Khiid. A giant penis, painted onto a sign by the road, 'points' you in the right direction.

Legend has it that the rock was placed here in an attempt to stop frisky monks, filled with lust by the shapely slope, from fraternising with the local women.

GREAT IMPERIAL MAP MONUMENT

This large new **monument** (admission T500), built in 2004, is located on a hill overlooking Kharkhorin to the southwest. The three sides show various empires based on the Orkhon Gol, including the Hunnu period (300–200 BC), the Turkic period (AD 600–800) and the Mongol period (13th century). There are good panoramic views from here.

Sleeping

CAMPING

It's very easy to find a perfect camping spot along the Orkhon Gol, only a kilometre or two from Kharkhorin. From the road heading west, turn left before the bridge and head a kilometre or so to a small island in the river, which is perfect for camping.

GER CAMPS

As most tourists in Mongolia eventually visit Kharkhorin, the town has seen an explosion in the number of ger camps. Prices below are per person without meals.

Tsingun Khuree (☎ 9918 1570; US$12) The closest ger to town is next to the Erdene Zuu parking lot. It has a good setup and a huge restaurant serving chicken (T4000), mutton schnitzel (T2700) and fruity ice cream (T800).

Karakorum (US$10-15) and **Ögödei** (US$10-15) Seven kilometres north of town past the airstrip, there are two large ger camps within 1km of each other. Both are fairly charm-free and cater almost exclusively to groups.

A bunch of five camps are in a lovely valley 3km west of town.

Bayankhangai (☎ 9913 7823; US$8) This camp is the first you come to in the valley. You get what you pay for: it's cheap but rather run-down.

Riverside (☎ 9975 3950; US$10) About 300m past Bayankhangai, towards the river, this decent camp has clean gers and hot showers. The hostess speaks English.

Ulaan Zagalmaa (☎ 9986 2825; US$15) and **Nomin** (US$15) There is little to differentiate Riverside from these two camps. The owners of each will try to price-match the other so try bargaining.

Anar (☎ 9919 8043; US$15, breakfast US$4, lunch US$7, dinner US$5) This place is bigger and more commercialised than the others in the valley; it's complete with Chinggis Khaan statues and ger gift shop. It has a great location in the southwest corner of the valley, with plenty of walking and horse-riding opportunities.

Khublai Khan (T10,000, meals T2500) Located on a hill to the southeast of town.

Möngön Möd (about US$15) and **Chandman** (about US$15) On the road to Shankh Khiid, both camps offer better-than-average services.

GUESTHOUSES & HOTELS

Monkhsuuri (☎ 9937 4488, 2031; per person incl breakfast & dinner US$5) This small homestay in located in the suburbs northwest of the market. There's a washbasin (the owner can boil up hot water) and basic pit toilet. Monkhsuuri works as a guide at Erdene Zuu and is most easily contacted there.

Crown Café (☎ 9924 2980; without meals T2000) Has gers and 'mini gers' in its backyard. It has a restaurant (see below).

Bayan Burd (Rich Steppe; ☎ 2315; per person T6000, lux T8000, shower/sauna T1000/1500) This clean and well-established hotel is 400m northeast of the market; look for the red sign.

Möngön Mod (SilverTree; ☎ 2777; d/tr T10,000/12,000) The building looks like it's about to collapse but the rooms inside aren't too bad. The hot-water shower is fairly reliable.

Zon Hotel (☎ 2520, 9926 9799; per person T3000) Next to the Möngön Möd, this rough-and-ready place has basic rooms with a washbasin and pit toilet.

Eating

All the ger camps serve meals or you can self-cater at the market. A few *guanz* line the main road between the market and the bank.

After a long journey from Ulaanbaatar, the European **Crown Café** (☎ 9924 2980; meals T1200-3000; ☺ 9am-midnight) comes as an excellent surprise. Stuff yourself silly with Hungarian goulash (T1100), fried chicken (T3000), tomato soup (T900) or hot French fries (T600). Look for the huge yellow sign on the main road.

Getting There & Away

Erdene Zuu and the nearby sights are a 2km walk from town; otherwise ask around for a lift (about T500).

AIR

MIAT has occasional flights in summer between Ulaanbaatar and Kharkhorin for US$53/92. The landing strip is 6km from Kharkhorin, so you can either walk or take a jeep, if available.

HITCHING

Hitching along the main road between Ulaanbaatar and Kharkhorin is fairly easy, but remember that a lot of vehicles will be carrying tourists, so they may not want to pick up a hitchhiker. Getting a lift between Arvaikheer and Kharkhorin is less likely, but if you're patient something will come along.

Hitchhiking between Kharkhorin and Khujirt shouldn't be too much of a hassle; many Mongolians take the Ulaanbaatar to Kharkhorin road to reach the popular spa town of Khujirt. In Kharkhorin, ask around the container market, or just stand by the road.

JEEP

A few jeeps are available for charter in Kharkhorin, but in the tourist season they may be hard to find. Ask around the jeep/truck station, or at the hotels.

The road from Kharkhorin to Khujirt (54km) is rough but scenic. The aimag capital, Arvaikheer, is 138km to the southeast. The 160km road between Kharkhorin and Tsetserleg is being rebuilt in places but remains fairly roughshod.

MINIVAN

Minivans run daily to Ulaanbaatar (T9000, eight hours) from the container market, leaving sometime after 8am, whenever they are full. As the road is all but sealed, this is one of the more bearable long-distance trips in the countryside.

A post office van runs every Wednesday and Friday afternoon to Khujirt (T1600) and Arvaikheer (T4700). Inquire at the post office for details.

EAST OF KHARKHORIN

There are several interesting places in the aimag between Kharkhorin and Khustain National Park (p103) en route to/from Ulaanbaatar.

Khogno Khan Uul Хөгнө Хан Уул

You can see this 1967m peak to the north of the main road. At the southern foot of the mountain are the ruins of **Övgön Khiid** (Өвгөн Хийд; GPS: N47° 25.561', E103° 41.686'; admission free), built in 1660 and destroyed (and the monks massacred) by the armies of Zungar Galdan Bochigtu, a rival of Zanabazar, in 1640. The monastery reopened in 1992 and there are a couple of monks from Ulaanbaatar. The head lama is a charming lady who professes soothsaying abilities.

The mountain is actually in Bulgan aimag but is most easily accessed from the Ulaanbaatar–Arvaikheer road.

The ruins of the earlier **destroyed monastery** (GPS: N47° 26.267', E103° 42.527') are a lovely

45-minute walk along a well-defined path up the valley to the right. The surroundings belong to the 46,900-hectare **Khogno Khan Natural Reserve** and you might spot ibex, wolves and many varieties of hawk. There are lots of **hiking** possibilities around here.

SLEEPING

Camping is excellent in the valley, though the only water comes from a hard-to-find well at the lower end of the valley. All of the following ger camps have horses for rent for about US$3 per hour.

Khiidiin Baaz (Monastery Ger Camp; with meals US$25) This well-built ger camp and wood lodge is a short walk from the temple. It is run by the monks at the Övgön Khiid.

Batkhan ger camp (bed & meals US$30) Not as good as Khiidiin Baaz, it's 1km from the monastery.

Nature Tour ger camp (with/without meals US$30/15) Located 4km southwest of Khiidiin Baaz.

Bayangobi ger camp (with meals US$40) Some travellers have stayed for about US$15 without meals, when the camp isn't busy. The camp can be reached by branching south for 6km off the main road, 3km west of the turn-off to Khogno Khan Uul.

GETTING THERE & AWAY

To get there from Kharkhorin by jeep turn north off the main road, 80km east of Kharkhorin. The road passes several ger camps until, after 8km, you reach Nature Tours ger camp, where you turn right for the remaining 4km or so to the monastery ruins. There is a short cut if you are coming from UB (turn right after the Bichigt Khad ger camp).

There is no public transport to the monastery but you can take a Kharkhorin, Khujirt or Arvaikheer-bound minivan from Ulaanbaatar, get off at the turn-off on the main road (T5000) and then hitch (or more likely walk) the remaining 12km.

Mongol Els Монгол Элс

As you approach the border of Övörkhangai from Ulaanbaatar, one surprising sight that livens up a fairly boring stretch of road are the sand dunes of Mongol Els. If you don't have the time to visit the Gobi (where there are not a lot sand dunes anyway), these are certainly worth wandering around.

Mongol Altai (GPS: N47° 20.320', E103° 41.196'; ☎ 9111 3559; with/without food US$20/15) is a ger camp that has a good location next to the sand dunes. It is 10km south of Övgön Khiid, not far off the main road.

Batkhaan Uul Батхаан Уул

The *sum* of Burd, in the northeast corner of Övörkhangai aimag, is host to some spectacular **birdlife**. Some of the area is part of the 22,000-hectare Batkhaan Uul Natural Reserve. The Mongol Els are also nearby.

The area is just south of the main road between Ulaanbaatar and Arvaikheer. With your own jeep, it is an easy day trip from Khujirt or Kharkhorin.

ARKHANGAI АРХАНГАЙ

pop 96,100 / area 55,000 sq km

Arkhangai has astounding scenery: several volcanoes and volcanic lakes, wide rivers full of fish (the best times for fishing are in August and September), extensive forests, and pastures where yak thrive. It also boasts the stunning lake, Terkhiin Tsagaan Nuur, ruins of ancient kingdoms and probably the nicest aimag capital in the country. The main ethnic groups are the Khalkh and the Oold.

Much of Arkhangai, which means 'north Khangai', is on the northern slope of the spectacular Khangai Nuruu mountain range. These are the second-highest mountains in Mongolia and are protected by the Khangai Nuruu, Noyon Khangai and Tarvagatain Nuruu national parks. The range is well-watered, so expect lovely forests, meadows and plenty of streams to quench your thirst, but it also floods, so expect muddy roads and even snowfalls in the summer.

Another drawback is that the aimag, particularly along the road between Tsetserleg and Ulaanbaatar, is notoriously bad for flies in summer – take repellent or you will regret it. If the flies make your life a misery, you can always indulge in *airag* (Arkhangai is renowned for the quality of its *airag*).

One jeep road runs in an east–west direction through the aimag between Ulaanbaatar and Tosontsengel in Zavkhan aimag via Tsetserleg; another from Kharkhorin joins at Tsenkher. The raised gravel road is in pretty good shape. From the roads in Arkhangai look out for small rock for-

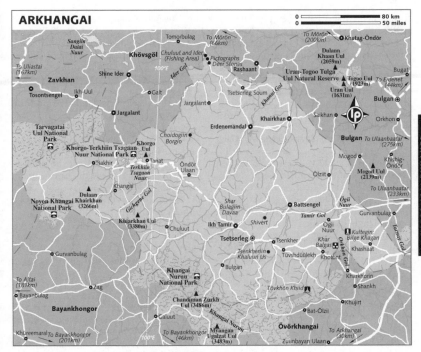

ARKHANGAI

mations. These are **ancient grave sites**, which may predate Chinggis Khaan.

TSETSERLEG ЦЭЦЭРЛЭГ
☎ 01332 / pop 17,800 / elev 1691m

Tsetserleg is the only aimag capital in Mongolia that could, at a pinch, be called beautiful (*tsetserleg* means 'garden'). The town is ringed by scenic mountains, the streets are tree-lined and a lovely little temple overlooks the town.

Tsetserleg is a good place to break up your journey if you are combining a visit to Kharkhorin and/or Khujirt with a trip to Terkhiin Tsagaan Nuur or Khövsgöl Nuur. There are some decent restaurants and hotels, hiking opportunities and good camping spots. Maybe it's the mountain air, but the people of Tsetserleg seem to be friendlier than in other aimag capitals.

There is nowhere else in the aimag with a similar selection.

Information
Internet Café (☎ 21110; ☽ 9am-1pm & 2-6pm Mon-Fri) In the Telecom office.

Post Bank (☎ 22673; ☽ 9am-1pm & 2-5pm) Changes cash, inside the Telecom office.
Strictly Protected Areas Office (fax 21223; khangainuruu@yahoo.com; ☽ 10am-5pm) It has information on Arkhangai's national parks and can give advice on tourist sites, fishing licences and park fees.
Telecom Office (☎ 21108; ☽ 24hr) The post office is also here.

Sights
The **Museum of Arkhangai Aimag** (☎ 22281; admission T2500, exterior photos T2000, interior photos T5000; ☽ 9am-6pm) is one of the best in the country. It's housed in the temple complex of **Zayain Gegeenii Süm**, which was first built in 1586 but expanded in 1679, when it housed five temples and up to 1000 monks. Miraculously, the monastery escaped the Stalinist purges because it was made into a museum.

The main hall concentrates on features of traditional Mongolian lifestyle, with exhibits of costumes, traditional tools, a ger, musical instruments, weaponry and saddles. The displays have some useful English captions. The second hall concentrates on religious icons. The other two rooms of the former main prayer hall are empty. The last hall focuses on local artwork.

Further up the hill there is a small **abandoned temple**. There's nothing to see, but the setting under the cliffs, overlooking the town, is spectacular. There is a trail to it from behind the museum. Behind the temple is a large, nearly vertical, rocky hill called Bulgan Uul, where there are some **Buddhist inscriptions**.

At street level the **Buyandelgerüülekh Khiid** (Буяндэлгэрүүлэх Хийд) is now the town's main functioning monastery. The temple has an atmospheric clutter of assorted religious artefacts, and religious services are held regularly, either in the main hall or in a ger next door.

In the north of town a trail leads to the pretty Gangin Gol, which offers great **hiking** potential. At the mouth of the valley is a ger camp and a pitiful **nature museum** of stuffed animals, which isn't worth the T1000 or T2000 the caretaker will demand.

Sleeping
CAMPING

The Gangin Gol has some great camping spots, though someone may come and collect a dubious 'fee' for camping in a 'nature reserve' (it's not). A few hundred metres past the ger camp is a grassy enclosure perfect for camping.

There are some nice spots a few kilometres south of town on the banks of the river.

GER CAMPS
Gurvan Bulgan (☎ 9973 4073; US$10, meals T2000) This ger camp has a nice location in the Gangin Valley, though it's a little disorganised. The camp has a water problem so don't expect a shower here.

Khavtgai Mod (☎ 9911 8262; without meals T10,000) On a hillside a couple of kilometres out of town to the west, it has a good location in the forest and valley views.

HOTELS
Naran Hotel (☎ 9933 2900, 9933 9006; s/d US$4/8, half-lux US$6, lux US$8-15) This new hotel is the best value in town. The rooms are spotless and the lux rooms have glorious bathrooms. The standard rooms use a shared bathroom down the hall.

Bulgan Hotel (☎ 22233; 4-bed dm T3000, half-lux T3500, lux T5000) This is the old Communist-era stalwart. The rooms are simple but pleas-

ant. The half-lux and the lux rooms are virtually identical, except that the 'lux' rooms are downstairs, which nets them better hot water. The dorms use a separate shower room, which has continuous hot water for T400 a go. Prices are per person.

Sasa Hotel (bed T3000) Around the corner from the Bulgan, it is similarly run-down but has larger rooms.

Sundur Hotel (☎ 22359, 9974 0100; s/d US$5/10, half-lux/lux US$10/15) This flashy hotel has a variety of singles and doubles. The cheapest rooms have only a toilet and no shower, but all others have nice bathrooms with hot water (at fixed times of the day only – check the times with reception). There is a good restaurant downstairs.

Zamchin Hotel (☎ 22274; d/lux US$9/10) It's another good choice. The Zamchin has spacious clean rooms but is away from the centre, on the western road out of town.

Eating
Cactus Bar (☺ 10am-10pm) This is a basic eatery that serves hot *khuushuur* by day and beer by night. It is opposite the Telecom office. Hours may be sporadic.

Fairfield (☎ 21026; ☺ 9am-6pm Mon-Sat) One of the most bizarre and welcome restaurants in Mongolia is run by an expat British couple (in Tsetserleg?!). The well-run café serves up pizza, lasagne, steak sandwiches, and beef in beer sauce, all for less than T1000 each. Finish this off with a mug of English tea, a warm cinnamon bun (T100) and an old copy of the *Economist* and you may well think you've just died and gone to heaven. (Our minivan bought up the entire week's supply of cinnamon buns.) This restaurant is worth rearranging your whole itinerary around if you are on a long trip!

Tsakhiur (☎ 22577; meals T900; ☺ 10am-10pm Sun-Fri) This upmarket restaurant (it has tablecloths) near the department store on the north end of town serves local favourites such as goulash and *puntutste khuurag* (clear or glass noodles).

Shopping
The **Art Shop** (☎ 22921; ☺ 10am-8pm) sells Mongolian *dels* (traditional cloaks) and jackets, plus locally produced art and artefacts. It's opposite the Telecom office.

Everyday goods are best bought at the department store on the north end of town.

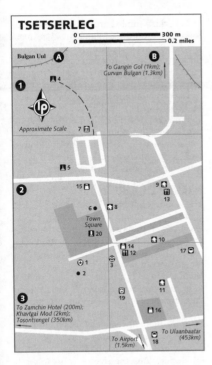

TSETSERLEG

CENTRAL MONGOLIA

The daily market *(khunsnii zakh)*, on the corner of the main road and the road to Ulaanbaatar, is pretty good and you can stock up on most supplies.

Getting There & Away

There are no flights to Tsetserleg, the only way here is by shared minivan or jeep.

HITCHING

All types of vehicles go to and from Tsetserleg and, generally, along the main road through Arkhangai. If you want to hitch, hang around the minivan/jeep stand and something will come along eventually. A useful sign, listing fixed fares for a ride in a truck to various destinations, is posted in the window of the ticket office.

MINIVAN & JEEP

Microbuses and minivans run between Tsetserleg and Ulaanbaatar (T11,000, nine hours). In Tsetseleg, try the minivans at the jeep stand opposite the market, though many vehicles will be headed for local destinations such as Ikh Tamir and Kharkhorin.

Jeeps (per km T250) hang around on the main highway, across from the south entrance of the market.

There are two routes between Tsetserleg and Ulaanbaatar – directly east via Ögii Nuur (453km) or along the longer but better road via Kharkhorin (493km).

Heading northwest, the road from Tsetserleg to Tosontsengel (350km) goes through some wonderful mountain and wildflower scenery, and is in reasonably good condition.

If you are travelling from Tsetserleg to Mörön (for Khövsgöl Nuur), the quickest route is due north via Erdenemandal. However, if you've come this far (and have a couple of days to spare) it's worth heading a bit further west through central Arkhangai to Terkiin Tsagaan Nuur, before heading north to Mörön via Galt.

ÖGII NUUR ӨГИЙ НУУР

On the road between Ulaanbaatar and Tsetserleg, near the border with Bulgan aimag, this **lake** (GPS: N47° 47.344', E102° 45.828') is a wonderful place for birdlife. Cranes and ducks, among other species, migrate to the area around late April. The lake is also renowned for its fishing (and the bugs by the shore!).

CENTRAL MONGOLIA

The lake and Khar Balgas ruins can only be reached from the direct road linking Tsetserleg with Ulaanbaatar. The lake makes a nice overnight stop. There are good camping spots or you can stay at the **Ögii Tourist Camp** (with/without meals US$28/13) run by Skyland Tour.

KHAR BALGAS ХАР БАЛГАС

The ruined citadel of Khar Balgas (Kara Balgasun in Turkic) is in Khotont *sum* on the banks of the Orkhon Gol. The city was founded in AD 751 as the capital of the Uighur khanate, which ruled Mongolia from 745 to 854.

There's not much to see except the outer walls (with gates in the north and south), a **Buddhist stupa** and the ruler's *kagan,* or **castle**, in the southwest corner. From the walls you can see the rows of stupas on either side of the walls and the remains of irrigated fields in the surrounding countryside. The city had an elaborate plumbing system, which brought water into the city from the nearby river.

The **ruins** (GPS: N47° 25.782', E102° 39.490') lie east of the road connecting Ögii Nuur and Khotont and aren't easy to get to. If you are travelling to/from the Kultegin Monument the best place to cross the river is 6km northeast of Khar Balgas; anywhere else it's bog city.

KULTEGIN MONUMENT КУЛТЭГИН ХӨШӨӨ

When Chinggis Khaan decided to move his capital to Karakorum, he was well aware that the region had already been the capital to successive nomad empires. About 20km northeast of Khar Balgas lies the remainder of yet another of these pre-Mongol empires, the Turkic *khaganate* (Pre-Mongol empire). All that's left of the *khaganate* is the 3m-high inscribed monument of Kultegin (684–731), the *khagan* (ruler) of the ancient empire. The **monument** (GPS: N47° 33.837', E102° 49.931') was raised in AD 732 and is inscribed in Runic and Chinese script. You can see a copy of the stele in the entrance of the National Museum of Mongolian History.

Just over 1km away is another **monument to Bilge Khagan** (683–734), younger brother of Kultegin. Ten years after the death of Bilge the Turkic *khaganate* was overrun by the Uighurs.

A Turkish funded archaeological expedition, based out of a huge hanger near the site, is working on making reproductions of the monuments. If you don't see the monuments where they should be ask the friendly caretaker to let you into the hanger.

The two monuments are 25km northwest of Khashaat in a region called Tsaidam, about 47km north of Kharkhorin, and are hard to find. Amateur historians who relish a challenge are best off packing a GPS into their jeep; otherwise ask at gers en route from either Khashaat or Ögii Nuur.

TAIKHAR CHULUU ТАЙХАР ЧУЛУУ

The nondescript town of **Ikh Tamir** is 22km along the main road west of Tsetserleg. The reason to stop here is to inspect the enormous Taikhar Chuluu rock formation. The rock is the subject of many local legends, the most common one being that a great *baatar*, or hero, crushed a huge serpent here by hurling the rock on top of it. Locals claim there are some ancient Tibetan inscriptions on the rock, though you'll be lucky to spot them through 30 years of Mongolian graffiti. There is even an **ovoo** at the top.

Taikhar Chuluu is about 2km north of Ikh Tamir along the river – you can see it from the main road. Locals recommend the three-hour **hike** to the large wooden ovoo at the top of the forested peak to the southwest of Ikh Tamir.

Sleeping

You could camp anywhere along the Khoid Tamir Gol.

Taikhar Ger Camp (☎ 9919 9969, 9911 1666; with/without meals US$30/10), next to the rock, has reasonable facilities but the US$20 charge for three Mongolian meals is exorbitant. The **Tungalug Tamir** (☎ 9981 0242; per person T4000) camp nearby has hot showers and is more geared to the backpacker set.

TAIKHAR CHULUU TO TERKHIIN TSAGANN NUUR

Chuluut Gorge & Zuun Salaa Mod

Cyclists might want to note that 89km from Ikh Tamir, and about 60km east of Tariat, is a kitsch *guanz* and hotel, decorated with various dead animal heads, where you can get basic food and accommodation.

About 30km east of Tariat is the dramatic **Chuluut gorge**, which makes a nice picnic stop. The **Chuluut Tur ger camp** (GPS: N48° 08.523', E100° 16.621'; ☎ 9919 3735; without meals T4000) has a good location above the gorge. Around 1km east of the camp, a few hundred metres from the road, is the sacred tree, **Zuun Salaa Mod**, draped in prayer scarves and debris.

There is also accommodation in Tariat (see p120).

Choidogiin Borgio Чойдогийн Боргио

To the northeast of **Tariat** village, Choidogiin Borgio, where the Chuluut and Ikh Jargalantiin *gols* converge, is a good **hiking**, **fishing** and **camping** area. Some companies run tours in the area but the place is difficult to reach by yourself, even with a jeep, as the roads are awful.

TERKHIIN TSAGAAN NUUR
ТЭРХИЙН ЦАГААН НУУР

Known in English as the Great White Lake, this freshwater lake (and the volcanic area around it) is certainly the highlight of Arkhangai, and one of the best in a country full of beautiful lakes. Surrounded by extinct and craterous volcanoes (part of the Tarvagatain Nuruu range), Terkhiin Tsagaan Nuur is not as forested or as large as Khövsgöl Nuur, but it is closer to Ulaanbaatar, relatively undeveloped and just about perfect for camping (though there are a few flies in summer). The lake, birdlife and mountains are now protected within the 77,267-hectare Khorgo-Terkhiin Tsagaan Nuur National Park. The national park fee of T3000 applies.

The lake, which was formed by lava flows from a volcanic eruption many millennia ago, is excellent for **swimming**, though a bit cold in the morning – try the late afternoon, after the sun has warmed it. Hidden along the shore are stretches of sandy beach, perfect for lounging with a book or fishing line.

The **fishing** is good, though you should get a permit for around T2000 per day. There are several park rangers who sell permits but they can be hard to find. Dramatic sunsets round off the day perfectly.

The park entrance is by the bridge.

One good excursion takes you to the top of **Khorgo Uul** volcano. A road leads 4km from **Tariat** (also known as Khorgo) village to the base of the volcano, from where it's a 10-minute walk up to the **cone** (GPS: N48° 10.921', E99° 51.543'). The volcano is in the park so you'll need to pay the park fee of T3000 if you haven't already.

Festivals

If you've got a taste for yak cream, or are keen on yak racing, plan a visit to Terkhiin Tsagaan Nuur in the second week of June, when **Tsolmon travel company** (☎ 011-322 870, 9929 5732) hosts its annual **Yak Festival** by the lake.

Sleeping & Eating
CAMPING

Except for a few annoying flies, Terkhiin Tsagaan Nuur is one of the best camping spots in Mongolia. There is good fishing, endless fresh water, and flat ground for pitching a tent. The western end of the lake, where it joins the Khoid Terkhiin Gol, is muddy. The best place to camp is the eastern part where there are some pine trees and lovely side valleys (in case the flies near the lake get too much). The lake is right on the main road, so just pick your camping spot anywhere around 8km west of Tariat. The area is cold year-round, and often windy, so a good sleeping bag is vital.

GER CAMPS

There are several camps built up along the shore of the lake, but they are all fairly spread out so it's not too crowded.

Khorgo I (GPS: N48° 12.246', E99° 50.834'; ☎ 011-322 870; with/without meals US$30/14) In a lovely location in the Zurkh Gol Khundii (Heart River Valley) by the northeast section of the lake, Khorgo I is run by the Tsolmon travel company in Ulaanbaatar. The camp has hot showers and there is excellent hiking nearby. To get there take the road north of Tariat into the park and take the branch to the right when you get near the volcano.

Tsagaan Nuur (GPS: N48° 10.621', E99° 48.691'; without meals US$10, meals T2500) This is the first camp on the lake. Horses are T3000 per hour. The owners also rent fishing rods.

Further around the lake you'll see some 'ger hotels' that charge T3000 per person. There is also a shop nearby selling soft drinks, confectionary and fishing equipment.

Maikhan Tolgoi (GPS: N48° 10.821', E99° 45.725'; ☎ 9911 9730, 9515 9333; without food US$10) At the time of writing this was the last cluster of gers on the northern part of the lake. (Although

CENTRAL MONGOLIA

the construction of more ger camps seems inevitable.) Maikhan Tolgoi has a good location on a headland.

HOTELS

Tariat village, about 6km east of the lake, is the only town in the area. Accommodation is basic, but you could ask around for Tunga, a local English teacher, who maintains a **guest ger** (US$3 including meals) in her yard. Tunga also organises horse trips and transport to the lake.

Taliin Mongol (☎ 300301, 9911 4554; r T3000-4500) This two-storey hotel in Tariat has a restaurant and several cramped, scruffy and depressing rooms. The toilet is outside.

Getting There & Away

There are occasional minivans to/from Ulaanbaatar and Tsetserleg. From anywhere else you are better off hitching.

From the lake to Tosontsengel (179km), the main road climbs over Solongotyn Davaa, a phenomenally beautiful area. You can see patches of permanent ice from the road. The road has been upgraded to an all-weather gravel road, but is still rough in patches.

NOYON KHANGAI НОЁН ХАНГАЙ

A few intrepid souls push on to Noyon Khangai, a remote camping and hiking area in the mountains southwest of Terkhiin Tsagaan Nuur. It's a very difficult place to reach, but may be worth the effort if the jeep road, which is either muddy or potholed, is passable. The mountainous region on the aimag border to the south is the 59,088-hectare Noyon Khangai National Park.

From Khangai, the capital of Khangai *sum*, you need to follow the river west (upstream) into the mountains.

BILL WASSMAN

Gers at Erdene Zuu Khiid (p109), Kharkhorin

GRAHAM TAYLOR

Monks perform an impromptu ritual, central
Mongolia (p90)

SCOTT DARSNEY

Migjid Janraisig Süm (p64), Ulaanbaatar

Musician at the Naadam
Festival (p83), Ulaanbaatar

GRAHAM TAYLOR

BRADLEY MAYHEW

Ger camp by Turtle Rock (p100),
Gorkhi-Terelj National Park

BRADLEY MAYHEW

Camels crossing the desert, the Gobi (p172)

BRADLEY MAYHEW

Eagle trained to hunt (p209), western
Mongolia

Bactrian camel (p180), the Gobi

GRAHAM TAYLOR

GRAHAM TAYLOR

Wrestlers at the Naadam Festival (p83), Ulaanbaatar

FELICITY VOLK

Opening parade of the Naadam Festival (p83), Ulaanbaatar

Archers competing at the Naadam Festival (p83), Ulaanbaatar

GRAHAM TAYLOR

BRADLEY MAYHEW

Preparing for a horse race at the Naadam Festival (p83), Ulaanbaatar

BILL WASSMAN

Young man in a café,
Ulaanbaatar (p50)

JERRY GALEA

Woman wearing a *del* (traditional coat), Baruun-Urt
(p166)

GRAHAM TAYLOR

Herders tending their flock, Arkhangai
(p114)

Nomad herder, northern Mongolia (p121)

SCOTT DARSNEY

Northern Mongolia

CONTENTS

Log cabins, pine forests and monstrous fish do not conform to the classic image of Mongolia's desolate steppes. But strung along its northern border are three aimags (provinces) of such lush and serene vegetation that one might confuse them for bits of Switzerland or the Rocky Mountains.

Selenge, Bulgan and Khövsgöl aimags have more in common with Siberia. Winters are long and cold, with snow staying on the ground until May. Summers bring wildflowers in profusion and the snowmelt fills up lakes and rivers, many of which flow north to Lake Baikal. The area teems with elk, reindeer and bear, and the rivers and lakes are brimming with fish. Beautiful Khövsgöl Nuur, the major feature of the region, pokes Siberia in the belly.

Although the majority of the people are Khalkh, here are also Buriats and Turkic-speaking peoples, including the Dukha, the reindeer herders. Shamanism has long been the faith of choice in the forests and, after decades of persecution, it is being revived and encouraged.

The fragile environment is crucial to the economy and this area is a major battleground between environmentalists, who want to expand the coverage of national parks, and business interests, that want to log the forests and explore for minerals. Although ecotourism is making inroads, the concept of sustainable development is still relatively unknown. Old hunters lament that wildlife is now more difficult to spot.

If you are travelling by train to or from Russia, you'll pass through Selenge. With a little time on your hands make a diversion and take in the wondrous Amarbayasgalant Khiid or do a horse trek by the shores of Khövsgöl Nuur. These are also top attractions for domestic tourists; you may come across a vanload or two of urban Mongols off to see the sights, stopping en route to taste the local *airag* (fermented mare's milk) or pick berries in the forests.

HIGHLIGHTS

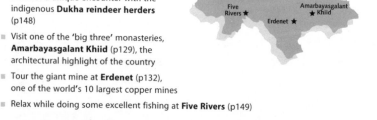

- Ride a horse into the mountains above **Khövsgöl Nuur** (p141), Mongolia's largest alpine lake
- Trek into the forests beyond Tsagaannuur for a unique encounter with the indigenous **Dukha reindeer herders** (p148)
- Visit one of the 'big three' monasteries, **Amarbayasgalant Khiid** (p129), the architectural highlight of the country
- Tour the giant mine at **Erdenet** (p132), one of the world's 10 largest copper mines
- Relax while doing some excellent fishing at **Five Rivers** (p149)

- POPULATION: 286,100
- AREA: 101,900 SQ KM

Climate

In the region around Khövsgöl aimag, the terrain is mainly *taiga* (subarctic coniferous) forest of Siberian larch and pine trees, where there's plenty of rain (often 600mm a year). Snowfall can exceed two metres in some regions during winter. After winter, the lakes and rivers remain frozen until May; travel can be hazardous at this time as trucks and jeeps can fall through the thin ice. July is warm and relatively dry, but this is also the time of the tourist crunch, leaving ger (traditional circular felt yurt) camps teeming.

Getting There & Away

Selenge aimag is accessible by paved road or rail from Ulaanbaatar. If your destination is Khövsgöl Nuur, the quickest way into the area is either on a flight from Ulaanbaatar to Mörön or by jeep via Bulgan. Main jeep tracks also run from Ulaangom and Tosontsengel in the west to Mörön, but tracks heading north from Tsetserleg in central Mongolia are more difficult to find. To travel between Selenge aimag and the east, you'll have to come back through Ulaanbaatar first, or go by horse.

Getting Around

Improvements to the roads to the Russian border and to Erdenet make life a lot easier in getting into the region. The fun starts as you travel further west, with the usual dirt roads and rocky terrain. Travellers who enjoy train travel can ride the rails as far as Erdenet and hire a vehicle from there. The horse is a popular form of transport in the mountains. While there is very little organised adventure travel, some tour companies offer mountain-biking trips in the region. A few crazies have even paddled kayaks down the Selenge Gol to Sükhbaatar city!

SELENGE СЭЛЭНГЭ

pop 101,800 / area 42,800 sq km

Selenge is the first – or last – aimag seen by train travellers shuttling between Ulaanbaatar and Russia. The main reasons to visit are the majestic, but remote, monastery

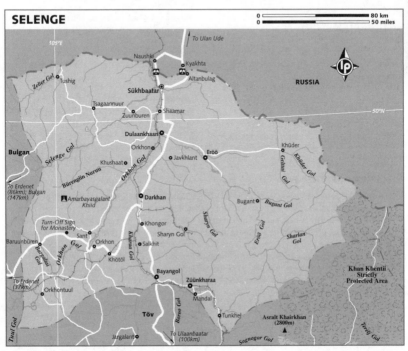

Amarbayasgalant Khiid and some beautiful scenery.

Ethnic groups in the aimag include Khalkh, Buriat, Dorvod, Oold and Russians. The Buriats, Russians and even Chinese live in wooden huts in villages hugging the train line and the main paved road that bisect the aimag. These people look after some of the 300,000 hectares of grains, fruits and vegetables.

Many others live in Darkhan, Mongolia's third-largest city. In the southeast, the open-pit coal mine at Sharyn Gol produces about two million tons of coal each year to provide electricity for the Erdenet mine in Bulgan aimag. But the biggest economic hope for Selenge lies in the Canadian-owned Boroo gold mine, which produces five tonnes of gold per year, netting US\$65 million.

The mighty Selenge Gol starts in the mountains of western Mongolia and flows into Lake Baikal in Siberia, draining nearly 300,000 sq km of land in both countries. The other great river, the Orkhon Gol, meets the Selenge near the aimag capital of Sükhbaatar.

SÜKHBAATAR СУХБААТАР

☎ 01362 / pop 20,300 / elev 626m

Near the junction of the Selenge and Orkhon *gols* (rivers), the capital of Selenge aimag was founded in the 1940s. Although it is Mongolia's chief border town, it is a quiet, pleasant place. There is little reason to stay, however, unless you want to break up the train journey to/from Russia, you prefer travelling on cheaper local trains, or you are smuggling goods.

Orientation & Information

Just north of the train station is the centre of town, where you'll find the main hotel, market and town square.

Private moneychangers appear at the station whenever a train arrives. If you are leaving Mongolia try to get rid of all your tögrög – they are worthless anywhere in Russia (including on the Trans-Mongolian Railway in Russia). The police station is to the south of town.

The daily market, behind the Selenge Hotel, is lively and friendly and, as a border town, well stocked.

Internet Café (per hr T520; ☺ 24hr) Adjacent to the Telecom office.

Telecom Office (☎ 22385; ☺ 24hr) The post office is also located here.

Trade & Development Bank (☎ 23120; ☺ 9am-4pm Mon-Fri) Changes travellers cheques, US dollars, euros and can give a cash advance on Visa and MasterCard. It is in the round orange building south of the station.

Zoos Bank (☺ till late Mon-Fri, also open Sat & Sun) If the T&D is closed try Zoos, near the town square.

Sleeping

CAMPING

Selenge aimag is particularly pleasant for camping. At Sükhbaatar, the best place to try is across the train line and among the fields, just west of town. Alternatively, there are great spots among the hills northeast of the market.

HOTELS

Kharaa Hotel (dm T5000, tr T21,000, half-lux T16,000, lux T25,000) Close to the main square, this hotel has remodelled, but unexciting rooms. Look for the 'hotel bar' sign.

SÜKHBAATAR, THE HERO

It won't take long before you wonder who Damdin Sükhbaatar is – a statue of the man astride a horse dominates the square named after him in Ulaanbaatar, his face is on many currency notes, and there is a provincial capital and aimag called Sükhbaatar.

Born in 1893, probably in what is now Ulaanbaatar, Sükh (meaning 'axe'), as he was originally named, joined the Mongolian army in 1911. He soon became famous for his horsemanship but was forced to leave the army because of insubordination. In 1917 he joined a resistance army, fought against the Chinese and picked up the added moniker of *baatar* (hero).

In early 1921, Sükhbaatar was appointed Commander-in-Chief of the Mongolian People's Revolutionary Army, which defeated the Chinese and, later, the White Russians. In July of that year, he declared Mongolia's independence from China at what is now known as Sükhbaatar Square.

He packed a lot in a short life – he was dead at 30. The exact cause of his death has never been known, and he did not live to see Mongolia proclaimed a republic.

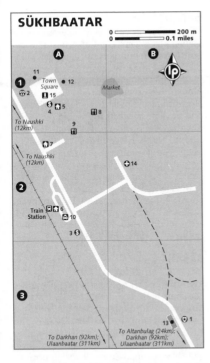

SÜKHBAATAR

could give you a lift to Ulaanbaatar – but definitely not across the Russian border.

TAXI
The road to Ulaanbaatar (311km) through Darkhan (92km) is well paved, so jeeps are not necessary. Because of the popularity and regularity of the train, there are relatively few shared vehicles to Ulaanbaatar, but many to Darkhan (T2500, two hours) and Altanbulag (T1000, 20 minutes). These vehicles depart from outside the train station.

TRAIN
International trains going to/from Moscow, Irkutsk or Beijing stop at Sükhbaatar for two or more hours while customs and immigration are completed. This usually takes place late at night or very early in the morning – not the best time to wander around Sükhbaatar. See p255 and p254 for more information about international trains.

Direct, local trains travel between Ulaanbaatar and Sükhbaatar (T2700/6700 for a hard/soft seat), with a stop at Darkhan. Train No 271 departs Ulaanbaatar at 10.30am daily, arriving at 7.56pm. The same train departs for Ulaanbaatar the next morning at 6.10am. Returning to UB, you could also opt for the No 263, departing Sükhbaatar at 9.45pm.

The **train station** (☎ 40124; ☷ 8am-noon, 3-5pm & 8-10pm) sells local tickets and also tickets for Ulan Ude (T14,300), Irkutsk (T26,800) and Moscow (T103,100), but you'll need a Russian visa.

Selenge Hotel (☎ 22555; dm/half-lux/lux T3000/8000/12,000) This old stand-by has dark, musty rooms with toilet but no running water. It's a yak's spit from the train station.

The station itself has a small **hotel** (s/d T5000/6000).

Eating
Rossiya Restaurant & Market (☎ 9136 0099; ☷ 10am-midnight) Rossiya serves basic Mongolian and Russian dishes. It's located close to the market.

Shin Shin Chinese Restaurant (☎ 9949 8956; ☷ 11am-10pm) To counterbalance the Rossiya, this Chinese place, closer to the road, serves decent meals in a dingy atmosphere.

Failing these two options, there's hot Mongolian goulash at the Selenge Hotel.

Getting There & Away
HITCHING
Because of the regular transport along the main road between Ulaanbaatar and Sükhbaatar, you'll get a lift pretty easily along this road. From Sükhbaatar, trucks, which congregate outside the grain elevators,

NORTHERN MONGOLIA

ALTANBULAG АЛТАНБУЛАГ

Just 24km east of Sükhbaatar is Altanbulag, a small, peaceful border town opposite the Russian city of Kyakhta. From the border you can easily see **Kyakhta Cathedral**. The Mongolian government recently decided to allocate 500 hectares at Altanbulag as a **Free Trade Zone** for the development of trade with Russia. Hopefully this will be more successful than the Free Trade Zone in Choir, in Dornogov aimag.

Both Kyakhta in Russia and Altanbulag are of some historical importance to Mongolians. In 1915 representatives from Russia, China and Mongolia met in Kyakhta to sign a treaty granting Mongolia limited autonomy. This was later revoked when China invaded again in 1919. At a meeting in Kyakhta in March 1921, the Mongolian People's Party was formed by Mongolian revolutionaries in exile, and the revolutionary hero Sükhbaatar was named Minister of War.

Altanbulag is worth a look if you have some spare time in Sükhbaatar. Minivans run between Sükhbaatar and Altanbulag at various times during the day, and also to Ulaanbaatar. There is no fixed schedule, so make local inquiries. Otherwise, you can charter a taxi.

Border regulations since 2004 permit foreigners to cross this border by vehicle. The border is open between 9am to 7pm. The border guards don't take kindly to strangers, so keep your distance unless you have a Russian visa.

DULAANKHAAN ДУЛААНХААН

Forty-seven kilometres south of Sükhbaatar, this tiny village is worth a stop if you have your own vehicle. Dulaankhaan is home to a **bow and arrow workshop**, one of only three in Mongolia. Bows and arrows are made from ibex and reindeer horn, bamboo and, even, fish guts. Only 30 to 40 sets are crafted every year because they take about four months to complete. Each set sells for about T180,000. In the village, look for the two-storey wood building, next to the red-and-blue monument. Ask for Boldbaatar.

The village is 6km west of the Sükhbaatar–Darkhan highway. Expect to pay about T15,000 for a taxi from Sükhbaatar. There is nowhere to stay in the village so carry on to Sükhbaatar or Darkhan, or camp nearby.

BUGANT БУГАНТ

Most of Selenge consists of fields and flood plains, but Bugant is an area of birch and pine forests, mountains and abundant wildlife. At one time, the town was known for its sawmill and nearby gold mine, but these industries are on their way out. The crystal-clear Eröö Gol flows through the town, and one possible **horseback trip** would be to follow the river upstream to its source in the Khentii Nuruu range. **Hiking** is a possibility, but if you go wandering through the forest during the hunting season, wear bright colours to avoid being mistaken for an elk.

Bugant is in Eröö *sum,* a remote area about 110km southeast of Dulaankhaan. Access is strictly by jeep or truck over a bad, often muddy, road. Shared jeeps run when full from Darkhan for T4000 per person.

DARKHAN ДАРХАН

☎ 01372 / pop 73,400

The epitome of socialist town planning, Darkhan grew up in the 1960s. It's now Mongolia's third-largest city, but a virtual ghost town compared to Ulaanbaatar. The city is not actually part of Selenge aimag, but an autonomous municipality, Darkhan-Uul. It was supposed to be the Pittsburgh of Mongolia, a northern industrial base, so authorities gave it a name that translates to 'blacksmith'. The end of communism closed many factories but the city limps on with its coal-mining pits at Sharyn Gol, a few tanneries and agricultural production. The Russians designed the city in their image but Darkhan's once-sizeable Russian community is all but gone for lack of opportunities.

It is not somewhere you would rush to see, but you may need to stay here while you arrange transport to Amarbayasgalant Khiid.

Orientation

Darkhan is spread out. The city is divided into an 'old' town near the train station and a 'new' town to the south. Near the central post office in the new town is Darkhan's pride and joy: a 16-storey building, for a long time Mongolia's tallest.

Information

Darkhan Internet Service (☎ 29128; per hr T600; ☼ 9am-10pm)

Golomt (☎ 23928; ☼ 9am-1pm & 2-5pm) It is 200m west of the taxi stand.

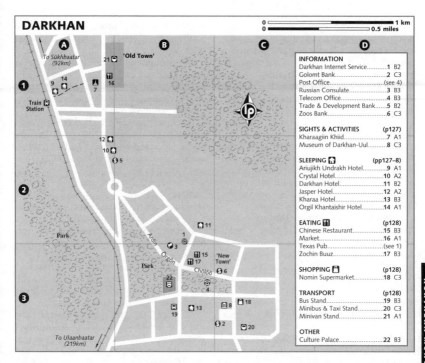

DARKHAN

Russian Consulate (☎ 23996) Offers no assistance to foreigners.

Telecom Office (☎ 23275; ☙ 24hr) The post office and an ATM machine are located here.

Trade & Development Bank (☎ 33713; ☙ 9am-3pm & 4-5.30pm Mon-Fri) Changes cash, travellers cheques and gives advances on Visa and MasterCard.

Zoos Bank (☎ 24173; ☙ 8am-10pm Mon-Fri) Opposite the Telecom office.

Sights

KHARAAGIIN KHIID

Probably the most interesting sight in Darkhan is Kharaagiin Khiid (Хараагийн Хийд). Housed in a pretty log cabin in the old town, this monastery has recently become very active. With a host of protector deities and a tree encased in blue *khatag* (silk scarves), it has the feel of a pilgrimage centre. Until 1989 the building served as an elementary school. As elsewhere, photography is forbidden inside unless special arrangements are made.

MUSEUM OF DARKHAN-UUL

This **museum** (admission T500; ☙ 9am-6pm), also named the Traditional Museum of Folk Art, contains a well-laid-out collection of archaeological findings, traditional clothing, religious artefacts and a few obligatory stuffed animals. The museum is upstairs in a building on the northern side of the shopping square, opposite the minibus and taxi stand.

Sleeping

CAMPING

Despite the size of Darkhan, it isn't hard to get away from the town and find a nearby secluded spot. Southwest of the train station are some empty fields – but get away from the drunks who hang around the station. The fields to the north of the Darkhan Hotel are also good.

HOTELS

Crystal Hotel (☎ 36966; s/d/lux T12,000/15,000/25,000) Stuck halfway between the new and old towns, this is probably the nicest place in town, with modern amenities and nice bathrooms.

Jasper Hotel (☎ 36478; s/d/tr T12,000/16,000/22,000, lux T35,000) It is an identical twin to the Crystal, next door.

Ariujikh Undrakh Hotel (☎ 35203; s/d T6000/ 10,000) Stay at this acceptable hotel if you are waiting for a train, or have just stumbled off one in the middle of the night. It has some provocative wall posters.

Orgil Khantaishir Hotel (☎ 35235; s/d T6000/ 10,000) It's similar (even with its wall posters) and next door to the Ariujikh Undrakh.

The station itself has a **hotel** (☎ 42263; r T5000, lux T6000) on the top floor.

Darkhan Hotel (☎ 20001; s/d T6000/10000, lux T12,000-16,000) This Soviet-era monster has standard and lux rooms, all with attached bathroom and hot water. Pay for your room when you register to avoid a possible increase in the check-out price.

Kharaa Hotel (☎ 20019; s/d T4300/8000, half-lux T13,000) The basic rooms here have a sink, toilet and hot water, but for a shower you'll need to upgrade to a half-lux. The entrance is through the Chinggis Beer Bar.

Eating

Most hotels listed above can scare up some food, and both the Ariujikh Undrakh and Orgil Khantaishir have 24-hour restaurants.

Zochin Buuz (☎ 9037 1033; ☺ 9am-11pm) Similar to its Ulaanbaatar namesake, this clean café serves up local favourites such as *buuz* and goulash.

Texas Pub (☎ 9939 9979; ☺ 10am-midnight) Roy Rogers could not have designed a better restaurant. This Texan-themed joint has an English-language menu with Hungarian goulash, steaks, salads and pasta plus Chinggis beer on tap.

Chinese Restaurant (☎ 9937 9496; ☺ noon-midnight) This unimaginatively named eatery has passable Chinese dishes including *niurousi chaofan* (fried rice with beef). It's at the end of an apartment block.

If you are self-catering, the best place to shop is the new Nomin supermarket. The market in the old town is well stocked and worth a quick look. There are lots of different sections and a few hard-to-find things such as vegetables and watermelons.

Getting There & Away

MINIVAN, TAXI & JEEP

Constant demand ensures that shared taxis (T5000) and minivans (T3500) regularly do the five-hour run to Ulaanbaatar. Vehicles depart from a bus stand just west of the Kharaa Hotel, where you can also get a seat

in a van to Erdenet (T4000, three hours). For Sükhbaatar (T2500, two hours), vans leave from outside the market in the new town.

Darkhan enjoys the privilege of having a paved road to Ulaanbaatar (219km), Sükhbaatar (92km) and Erdenet (180km). Many *guanz* (canteens or cheap restaurants) along the way sell *airag* and basic meals.

For Amarbayasgalant Khiid you'll have to hire your own jeep for T250 per kilometre at the bus stand near the Kharaa Hotel. A round-trip should cost around T40,000 but you'll need to bargain.

TRAIN

Darkhan is the only train junction in Mongolia: all northern trains to/from Ulaanbaatar, and all trains to/from Erdenet, stop here. If your time is short, and you want to see some scenery in comfort (ie in a soft seat), take the train between Darkhan and Ulaanbaatar: the train travels during the day, the trip is short and the scenery is mildly interesting in Töv aimag.

All hard-seat carriages to Ulaanbaatar and Erdenet are jam-packed, uncomfortable and dirty. It is definitely worth spending a few extra tögrög for a soft seat. The **domestic ticket office** (☎ 42301; ☺ 7.30-8.40am, 2.30-6.30pm & 10.30pm-3am) at Darkhan train station is at windows one and two. Window three is reserved for international tickets.

A daytime train (No 272) leaves Darkhan at 8.33am, arriving in Ulaanbaatar at about 4pm. An overnighter (No 264) departs Darkhan at 11.40pm, arriving at 6am. Other trains leave in the middle of the night. Tickets cost T2100/5400.

The daily five-hour trip between Darkhan and Erdenet (T1700/4200 for hard/ soft seat) goes through some lovely countryside, but you'll miss it as the train leaves Darkhan between midnight and 4am.

The daily Ulaanbaatar–Sükhbaatar train (No 271) leaves Darkhan for Sükhbaatar at 5.38pm (T1000/2300, two hours), or an ungodly 2.50am. See p255 and p254 for details about international trains that stop at Darkhan.

Getting Around

Darkhan is spread out, so you will probably have to take a taxi or two, or rent a motorcycle and sidecar (with driver) from the market. Taxis charge a reasonable T400 from the new town's shopping square and the old town's train station.

AMARBAYASGALANT KHIID
АМАРБАЯСГАЛАНТ ХИЙД

The star attraction of Selenge aimag, this monastery is considered to be one of the top three Buddhist institutions in Mongolia (along with Erdene Zuu in Kharkhorin and Gandan in Ulaanbaatar) and the country's most intact architectural complex. It is well worth visiting on the way to/from Khövsgöl Nuur, or other areas in northern or western Mongolia. Otherwise, you are better off incorporating the monastery into a three- or four-day countryside trip to take in the surrounding scenery.

Amarbayasgalant Khiid (GPS: N49° 28.648', E105° 05.122'; www.amarbayasgalant.org) was originally built between 1727 and 1737 by the Manchu emperor Yongzheng, and dedicated to the great Mongolian Buddhist and sculptor, Zanabazar (see the boxed text, p130), whose mummified body was moved here in 1779. The monastery is in the Manchu style, down to the inscriptions, symmetrical layout and imperial colour scheme.

The communists moseyed in around 1937, but 'only' destroyed 10 out of the 37 temples and statues, possibly because of sympathetic and procrastinating local military commanders. The monastery was extensively restored between 1975 and 1990 with the help of Unesco. These days about 70 monks live in the monastery, compared to over 2000 in 1936.

The temples in the monastery are normally closed, so you'll have to ask the monks to find the keys and open them up if you want to see any statues or *thangkas* (scroll paintings). There are around five temples open to tourists. To the west of the complex you'll find eight new stupas and a meditation centre.

The main hall has a life-size statue of **Rinpoche Gurdava**, a lama from Inner Mongolia who lived in Tibet and Nepal before returning to Mongolia in 1992 and raising much of the money for the temple's restoration. It's normally possible to climb up to the roof for fine **views** of the valley.

To help with the restoration work, foreigners are charged an entry fee of T3000, plus T5000 to take photos inside the temples. Ceremonies start at around 9am.

Some travellers have raved about the scenery of the mountain range, Bürengiin Nuruu, north of Amarbayasgalant.

Sleeping

The area surrounding Amarbayasgalant Khiid is an excellent camping spot, though water is scarce – you'll have to search hard for a camp site with any, or stock up before you head out.

Basic **Amarbayasgalant ger camp** (GPS: N49° 25.122', E105° 03.839'; ☎ 011-683 025, 9919 7886; with/without meals US$30/12) is about 10km south of the monastery; you'll pass it on the main road. It has showers, toilets and should now have electricity. The midges around this area can be appalling in late summer.

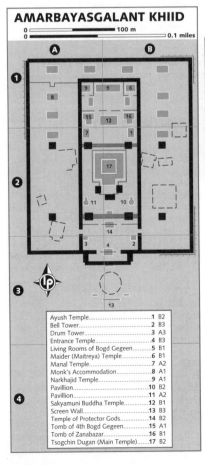

AMARBAYASGALANT KHIID

Ayush Temple	1	B2
Bell Tower	2	B3
Drum Tower	3	A3
Entrance Temple	4	B3
Living Rooms of Bogd Gegeen	5	B1
Maider (Maitreya) Temple	6	B1
Manal Temple	7	A2
Monk's Accommodation	8	A1
Narkhajid Temple	9	A1
Pavillion	10	B2
Pavillion	11	A2
Sakyamuni Buddha Temple	12	B1
Screen Wall	13	B3
Temple of Protector Gods	14	B2
Tomb of 4th Bogd Gegeen	15	A1
Tomb of Zanabazar	16	B1
Tsogchin Dugan (Main Temple)	17	B2

ZANABAZAR

Born in 1635, Zanabazar is one of Mongolia's most remarkable and versatile figures. At the tender age of three, he was deemed to be a possible *gegeen* (saint) so at the age of 14 he was sent to Tibet to study Buddhism under the Dalai Lama. A descendent of Chinggis Khaan, he was also proclaimed the reincarnation of the Jonangpa line of Tibetan Buddhism and became the first Bogd Gegeen (reincarnated Buddhist leader of Mongolia). He is also known in Mongolia as Öndür Gegeen.

While in Tibet, Zanabazar learnt the skills of bronze casting. He returned to kick-start a Mongolian artistic renaissance and become Mongolia's greatest sculptor. In his spare time he reputedly invented the *soyombo* (see p26), the national symbol of Mongolia, and reformed the Mongolian script. Zanabazar was also a political figure and his struggle with the Zungar (see p21) leader Galdan led to Mongolia's submission to the Manchus in 1691.

Zanabazar died in Beijing in 1723. His body was taken to Urga (modern Ulaanbaatar) and later entombed in a stupa in Amarbayasgalant Khiid. You will see many of Zanabazar's creations in monasteries and museums in Mongolia, and there is a fine collection of his art (particularly his Tara and Dhyani Buddha statues) in the Zanabazar Museum of Fine Arts in Ulaanbaatar. His sculptures of Tara are supposedly based on his 18-year-old lover. You can recognise images of Zanabazar by his bald, round head and the *dorje* (thunderbolt symbol) he holds in his right hand and the bell in his left hand.

Monastery Guesthouse (per person T3000) is made up of three buildings outside of the monastery grounds that can house up to 20 people.

Getting There & Away

HITCHING

Vehicles to the monastery are few and far between, though with a tent, enough food and water and some determination, you will probably get there. The cheapest and best way from Ulaanbaatar is to catch a train to Darkhan, take a shared jeep to Khötöl, hitch (which is easy) from there to the turn-off, then hitch another ride (much more difficult) to the monastery. The problem is finding the correct jeep track – compounded by the fact that jeeps all take different routes to the monastery.

When all is said and done you are better off visiting the monastery as part of a jeep or minivan trip to Khövsgöl, or chartering a jeep (about T40,000 return) from Darkhan.

JEEP

From Ulaanbaatar, travel north to the T-intersection for Erdenet (just short of Darkhan). Take the Erdenet road for 90km and then turn right onto a level dirt track; look for the blue sign (GPS: N49° 12.874', E104° 59.169') that says 'Amarbayasgalant 27km'. Ignore any other signs en route

(some travellers have been confused by an Amarbayasgalant sign posted after the bridge, 60km after the Darkhan turn-off). Altogether, the journey to/from UB takes seven to eight hours.

If you are coming from Erdenet, roads lead northeast from Baruunbüren. From the south, tracks branch off north from the Orkhon–Baruunbüren road. If your driver hasn't been there before you'll need to stop and ask for directions at gers en route.

BULGAN БУЛГАН

pop 62,800 / area 49,000 sq km

Bulgan aimag is a curious mixture: the south is dry grassland and the north is green and has enough forest to support a small timber industry; scattered in between are about 50,000 hectares of wheat and vegetable crops – Mongolia's agricultural heartland – and Erdenet, Mongolia's largest copper mine. The ethnic groups comprise Khalkh, Buriat and Russians.

A small mountain range, the Bürengiin Nuruu, bisects the aimag, and though it only reaches a maximum altitude of 2058m, it provides plenty of lush habitat for wild animals and livestock. Herbs, often used for medicinal purposes, are being cultivated in the region with some success. Elk are abundant in this region. Mongolia's largest river,

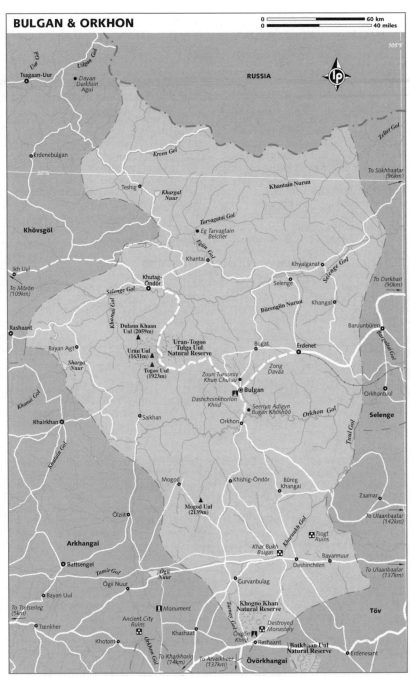

the Selenge Gol, crosses the aimag's north, and the Orkhon and Tuul rivers meander around the southern parts.

ERDENET ЭРДЭНЭТ

☎ 01365 / pop 75,100

In the autonomous municipality of Orkhon, and not technically part of Bulgan aimag, Erdenet is a little slice of Russia in Mongolia. The reason for Erdenet's existence is the copper mine, which employs about 8000 people and is the lifeblood of the city.

Erdenet, Mongolia's second-largest city, is modern (built in 1974) and comparatively wealthy, so the facilities are the best outside of Ulaanbaatar. Up to one-third of the population of Erdenet was Russian during communist times, though now only about 1000 Russians still work as technical advisers at the mine. You'll hear plenty of Russian on the streets and will find restaurant menus featuring *peroshki* (meat-filled fried pastry) rather than *buuz* (steamed mutton dumplings).

There is evidence that Mongolians were making copper pots in the Erdenet area at least 200 years ago. Russian geologists initially recognised the area's potential during the 1940s. The copper was first seriously prospected during the 1960s, and by 1977 a train line to Ulaanbaatar was installed for hauling the ore. In 1981 an ore-processing plant was commissioned and Erdenet began exporting copper concentrate (30% copper), mostly to the former Soviet Union.

The **mine** (www.emc.erdnet.mn), a political teapot due to its close associations with the Mongolian People's Revolutionary Party (MPRP), has been plagued in recent years by mismanagement, corruption and a drop in the price of copper. It still accounts for around 40% of Mongolia's hard-currency earnings, producing some 25 million tonnes of copper/molybdenum ore per annum. The mining and processing operation consumes nearly 50% of Mongolia's electricity.

Orientation

Erdenet is a sprawling city, though everything you will need is along the main street, Sükhbaatar Gudamj. The train station is inconveniently located more than 10km east of the centre.

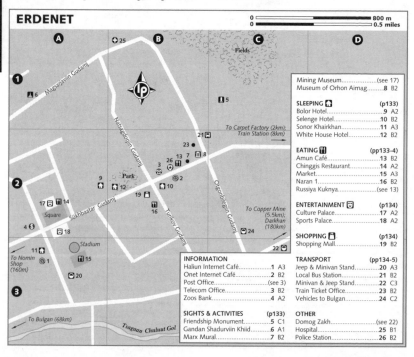

ERDENET

0 _____ 800 m
0 _____ 0.5 miles

	(see 17)
Mining Museum	(see 17)
Museum of Orhon Aimag	8 B2
SLEEPING	(p133)
Bolor Hotel	9 A2
Selenge Hotel	10 B2
Sonor Khairkhan	11 A3
White House Hotel	12 B2
EATING	(pp133-4)
Amun Café	13 B2
Chinggis Restaurant	14 A2
Market	15 A3
Naran 1	16 B2
Russiya Kuknya	(see 13)
ENTERTAINMENT	(p134)
Culture Palace	17 A2
Sports Palace	18 A2
SHOPPING	(p134)
Shopping Mall	19 B2
TRANSPORT	(pp134-5)
Jeep & Minivan Stand	20 A3
Local Bus Station	21 B2
Minivan & Jeep Stand	22 C3
Train Ticket Office	23 B2
Vehicles to Bulgan	24 C2
OTHER	
Domog Zakh	(see 22)
Hospital	25 B1
Police Station	26 B2

INFORMATION	
Haliun Internet Café	1 A3
Onet Internet Café	2 B2
Post Office	(see 3)
Telecom Office	3 B2
Zoos Bank	4 A2

SIGHTS & ACTIVITIES	(p133)
Friendship Monument	5 C1
Gandan Shadurviin Khiid	6 A1
Marx Mural	7 B2

Information
Haliun Internet Café (☎ 25806; per hour T400; ⊙ 8am-midnight) Behind the Sonor Khairkhan hotel.
Onet Internet Café (☎ 73977; per hour T400; ⊙ 9am-10pm) About 85m east of the Selenge Hotel.
Telecom Office (☎ 27427; ⊙ 24hr) The post office is also in this building.
Zoos Bank (☎ 21722; ⊙ 10am-7pm Mon-Fri 10am-3pm Sat & Sun) Changes US dollars and euros. An ATM machine is in the lobby of the Selenge Hotel.

Sights
COPPER MINE
The open-cut mine, easily seen to the north of the city, is one of the 10-largest copper mines in the world.

Open-cut mining is more damaging to the environment but infinitely safer than digging mine shafts below the surface. Also, since this particular mountain is almost solid copper and molybdenum ore, this is the only practical way to reach it. The mine operates 24 hours a day, 365 days a year.

The mine is worth a visit if you've never visited one like this before. You'll need to show your passport to the guard at the gate. Further up the hill, on the left, is the administration building where you could theoretically ask for a tour. There is nothing formal set up but somebody might show you around. On weekends there is hardly anyone around to ask. The views from the lookout over the gigantic open-cut mine, and of the city, are impressive. A taxi to the mine and back from the town centre costs about T4000, including waiting time.

FRIENDSHIP MONUMENT
This communist monument, about 200m northeast of the Selenge Hotel, is worth a quick look. On the way you pass a fine **Marx mural** and a picture of Lenin bolted to the wall. A little further to the east, the *ovoo* (a shamanistic collection of stones, wood or other offerings) is impressive if you haven't seen too many before. The hills north of the monument and south of the stadium are great for short hikes.

MINING MUSEUM
This Soviet-built **museum** (admission free; ⊙ 9am-6pm Mon-Fri) belongs to the copper-mining company, Erdenet Concern. It's on the 2nd floor of the Culture Palace, and is worth a look.

MUSEUM OF ORKHON AIMAG
Opened in 1983 and hidden in a concrete complex on the right side of the Marx mural, this small **museum** (admission T1000; ⊙ 9am-5pm) includes a few oddities including a model of the copper mine (you can see it in 'day' or 'night') and a model of a modern ger with a TV inside. Look out for the two-headed calf, which hopefully is no indication of what the mine is doing to the local water supply.

GANDAN SHADURVIIN KHIID
Opened in 1991, this small monastery (Гандан Шадурвийн Хийд) is located on the hill just north of downtown. The huge prayer wheels near the entrance, built in 2004, contain 100 million prayers each.

Sleeping
CAMPING
Although the city is comparatively large, it is still possible to camp near Erdenet. The best places to try are north of the Friendship Monument, or south of the stadium, over the other side of Tsagaan Chuluut Gol and among the pretty foothills.

HOTELS
Erdenet has the best choice of hotels outside Ulaanbaatar and is a good place to spoil yourself if on a long-distance expedition.

White House Hotel (☎ 28649; r US$35) White House is the best hotel in town, with good rooms, hot water and a sauna in the basement (T2000).

Sonor Khairkhan (☎ 28120; d 16,000, lux T25,000) This hotel in a blue building offers attractive, clean rooms, an excellent hot-water supply, phone, TV and the price includes breakfast in the room served promptly at 7.30am. It's near the outdoor market.

Selenge Hotel (☎ 27359; s/d T4000/8000, half-lux T6000/12,000, lux T15,000-40,000) This classic Soviet-style hotel has large, clean rooms with bathroom. It's moderately functional if you don't mind spotty hot water, box-spring beds and broken TVs.

Bolor Hotel (☎ 25361; r with/without bathroom T10,000-12,000/8000) Located in an apartment block behind the main arcade, this place has clean but unexciting rooms.

Eating
Naran 1 (☎ 20938; ⊙ 8am-midnight) If the Chinese chef is here, this place makes excellent

Chinese food. If he is on holiday, and you still want Chinese, try the restaurant in the Selenge Hotel.

Amun Café (☎ 23682; ⓒ 10am-midnight Mon-Fri, noon-midnight Sat & Sun) This decent place makes an attempt at spaghetti and beefsteak.

Next door to the Amun Café, the Russiya Kuknya sells *peroshkis*.

Casablanca Bar & Restaurant (☎ 9985 2898; ⓒ 8am-midnight) Various Russian and Mongolian dishes and beers are served to customers sitting in huge leather couches in this place that comes recommended by Erdenet's contingent of Mormon missionaries. It's located in the department store (Uilchilgeenii Töv).

Chinggis Restaurant (☎ 27400; meals T2800-5000; ⓒ 11am-midnight Mon-Sat, 3pm-midnight Sun) This elegant restaurant is a branch of the Chinggis in Ulaanbaatar, with a menu at slightly lower prices. After a long hard slog across the steppes, an excellent salad, pepper steak and cold beer are much appreciated by bedraggled travellers. Enter at the right side of the Cultural Palace.

The daily market behind the Sports Palace is surprisingly small and scrappy, though there's a good selection of (nonrefrigerated) dairy products here. Most locals buy their food from the selection of good shops along the main drag.

Entertainment
Culture Palace (Sükhbaatar Gudamj) There's always something on: a pop concert, some Russian and Chinese films, or a classical-music recital. There is even a disco on the weekends.

Sports Palace (Sükhbaatar Gudamj; ⓒ 8am-9pm) If you have some time to kill, check out this impressive place. You can take a hot shower (T500) or sauna (T1000 per hour), watch some wrestling or go ice-skating in winter at the stadium at the back. There's an indoor pool (T2500), open weekdays only, but the staff may make life difficult by insisting on a medical examination before they let you swim.

Shopping
Carpet Factory (☎ 20111) If a couple of tons of copper is a bit inconvenient to carry around, a carpet would make a good souvenir. The city's carpet factory produces over one million square metres every year using machinery from the former East Germany.

About 98% of the carpets are exported, mostly to Russia, but now increasingly to China and places beyond. The carpet factory is open year-round but production is low in summer (June to August) when supplies of wool are scarce. If you ask the guard it may be possible to take a tour of the entire operation. The factory is just off the main road to the train station, about 2km from the Friendship Monument.

Nomin Shop (☎ 21735; ⓒ 10am-7pm) You can also buy carpets and rugs here, about 500m west of the Sports Palace. A huge Chinggis Khaan wall carpet costs from T79,000 and smaller, towel-sized carpets are T3700 to T20,000.

For general goods (electronics, food and clothing) the best place to shop is Uilchilgeenii Töv (Үйлчилгээний Төв), the shopping mall adjacent to the Telecom office.

Getting There & Away
Travellers often bypass Erdenet and go straight from Ulaanbaatar to Mörön via Bulgan. If you have the time, and want a little luxury, take the sleeper train from Ulaanbaatar to Erdenet and catch a shared vehicle to Mörön; these wait at the container market (the taxi stand outside the Sports Palace is another place to ask). Don't make the mistake of first going to Bulgan and then trying to hitch to Mörön. Traffic to Mörön goes direct from Erdenet via Khutag-Öndor.

BUS, MINIVAN & JEEP
A daily bus departs at noon from Ulaanbaatar's Dragon bus stand for Erdenet (T6000, eight hours, 371km). Minivans and jeeps depart Dragon and Naran Tuul market each morning when full.

For shared vehicles to Mörön (T10,000, 10 hours), Bulgan (T3000, two hours), Tsetserleg (T7000, seven hours) and Uliastai (T12,000, 20 hours), the best place to look is at the container market (Domog Zakh) in the southeastern corner of town.

For Bulgan, vehicles might also wait at a lot 700m southeast of the Selenge Hotel. The best place to look for a vehicle to Ulaanbaatar is outside the Sports Palace. The local rate for a chartered minibus to Ulaanbaatar is T65,000.

The road between Erdenet and Darkhan (180km) is fully paved. The road between Erdenet and Bulgan city (68km) is unsealed and rough – or you could go via the more scenic Bugat route.

TRAIN

Train No 273 departs Ulaanbaatar for Erdenet at 7.20pm, arriving 11 hours later. It costs T2900/7200 for a hard-/soft-seat sleeper. The sleeper is definitely worth the extra tögrög: the hard-seat carriages are packed to the roof. The train returns to Ulaanbaatar from Erdenet at the same time (7.20pm). In summer a weekend train to/from Ulaanbaatar is added, though the schedule is a little unreliable, so check for times at the station.

The trip between Erdenet and Darkhan (5½ hours) goes through some lovely countryside, though most of the ride takes place in darkness. To Darkhan, the train costs T1700/4200 for a hard/soft seat. For Sükhbaatar in Selenge aimag, change in Darkhan.

The station has a small quota of tickets on the Trans-Mongolian Railway and sells tickets to Ulan Ude (T29,000, nine hours), Novosibirsk (T68,700, 49 hours) and Moscow (T109,200, 82 hours).

You can buy tickets at the train station, but it's better to queue on the day of, or before, departure at the **train ticket office** (☎ 22505; ☽ 9am-1pm & 2.30-6.30pm) in the northeast end of town. Look for the small train sign on the side of an apartment block, north of the local bus station. Line up as early as possible, the scrum waiting outside during the lunch break would put an All Blacks rugby scrimmage to shame.

If travelling hard seat, get to the station a couple of hours before departure, sharpen your elbows and huddle outside the train – the doors of the carriages open about 30 minutes before departure.

Buses meet arriving trains, but the stampede of passengers quickly fills these to overflowing. Also, not every bus you see at the train station is going to the centre – many are headed to industrial areas surrounding the city, so don't just get on any bus. It's best to get off the train as soon as you can and find a taxi (about T4000) before the crush starts.

It is more sedate going by bus *to* the train station. Buses (T300), cars (T500 per person) and taxis (T5000) leave from the local bus station, south of the train ticket office.

BUGAT БУГАТ

If you have rented a jeep with a driver, the best way to travel between Erdenet and Bulgan city is via Bugat village. It is rough going, but the 40km jeep trail goes through some of the most picturesque forests and gorgeous wildflowers in northern Mongolia (Bugat means 'Place of Elk'). You will have to ask directions to find the start of the trail from Erdenet as the trail can be tricky to follow; it's easier to find from Bulgan city.

BULGAN CITY БУЛГАН

☎ 01342 / pop 11,800 / elev 1208m

A small aimag capital, the Bulgan city has long been known to foreigners as an overnight stop between Ulaanbaatar and ever-popular Khövsgöl Nuur. If you've been travelling in central or southern Mongolia, Bulgan city may impress you with its conifers, log cabins and absence of gers. The daily market is small but interesting. Plenty of horses are hitched outside the market and around town, like a scene from a Wild West movie.

Information

Bathhouse (☽ Wed-Mon) Behind the pink government building.

Internet Café (☎ 24024; per hr T690; ☽ 9am-6pm Mon-Fri) In the same building as Telecom.

Mongol Post Bank (☎ 22169; ☽ 9am-1pm & 2-5pm Mon-Fri) Exchanges US dollars and will possibly give a cash advance on Visa.

Telecom Office (☎ 24117; ☽ 24hr) The post office is also here.

Sights

MUSEUMS

The **Aimag Museum** (☎ 22589; T1000; ☽ 9am-6pm) on the main street has some information on obscure sights in the aimag, a display on J Gurragchaa, Mongolia's first man in space, and some interesting old photos.

Next door, the **Ethnography Museum** (Ugsaatny Muzei; admission T1000; ☽ 9am-6pm) has a few interesting exhibits, such as ancient surgical instruments, *airag* churners and saddles.

DASHCHOINKHORLON KHIID

Like most monasteries in Mongolia, this one (built in 1992) replaces the original monastery, Bangiin Khuree, which was destroyed in 1937. About 1000 monks lived and worshipped at Bangiin Khuree before they were arrested and, presumably, executed. The

NOMADS TO NINJAS

Miners indulging in Mongolia's great new gold rush are turning verdant plains and pure rivers inside out in search of buried fortunes. But for once, it's not just the megacorporations from Ulaanbaatar who are to blame, it's the Ninjas.

When severe winters at the beginning of the millennium wiped out entire herds and family fortunes, many impoverished nomads turned to illegal gold mining in Bulgan, Töv and Selenge aimags. The green, shell-like buckets strapped to their backs, coupled with their covert, night-time operations, earned them the moniker 'Teenage Mutant Ninja Turtles' or Ninjas for short.

The Ninjas, who often pan what larger mining operations dredge from the flooded plains, attracted interest from businesspeople who sold them food and supplies. Soon 'Ninja ger-boomtowns' developed, each with ger-butchers, ger-shops, ger-karaoke bars, ger-sega parlours and ger-goldsmiths. Police have tried, often vainly, to break up the settlements, but the Ninjas return in larger numbers.

The Ninjas, who number over 100,000, pose a serious threat to the environment and themselves. Unlike the licenced mining companies they don't clean up after themselves; their work sites are often littered with discarded batteries and open pits. Mercury, which is used to separate gold from the rock, is another problem. Health workers report that miners who use this method have levels of mercury in their urine that are five to six times the safe limit.

Ninjas account for an incredible US$70 million in gold exports (although official bank figures say US$20 million), which represents over 7% of Mongolia's GDP. They receive US$270 per troy ounce, completely illegal and untaxed. Most Ninjas earn US$8 to US$12 per day. This kind of money, 10 times that of other rural salaries, has attracted more than out-of-work nomads. They've been joined by pensioners, redundant farm workers and poorly paid civil servants. Students who come in summer are able to finance their entire university education.

But this is dangerous business – 19 Ninjas were buried alive in mine shafts in 2003. Recognising that the Ninjas won't go away, the government has considered ways to legalise their activities, protect their health and clean up their mess, if for no other reason than to tax their cache, which is mostly smuggled to China.

remains of several stupas from the old monastery complex can be seen nearby.

The modern monastery of **Dashchoinkhorlon Khiid** (Дашчойнхорлон Хийд; GPS: N48° 47.821', E103° 30.687') contains statues of Tsongkhapa and Sakyamuni and features a painting of the old monastery layout. About 30 monks now reside there. The monastery is about 3km southwest of Bulgan city and is hidden behind some hills.

KHATANBAATAR MAGSARJAV MAUSOLEUM

Located 1km southwest of the Bulgan Hotel, across the stream and at the top of a hill, this curious blue building looks like a concrete ger but is actually a mausoleum (Хатанбаатар Магсаржавын Бунхан) in the shape of a hat. It allegedly contains the remains of Khatanbaatar Magsarjav, a key figure in the 1911 Revolution, who helped to liberate the city of Khovd from Chinese rule. There are some murals of battle scenes inside but to see them you'll need to get the keys from the caretaker. Ask at the Aimag Museum.

Sleeping
CAMPING

The best place to pitch your tent is over the southern side of the river, the Achuut Gol; go past the market and find a discreet spot. If you have your own transport, consider camping a few kilometres north of town, along the road to Mörön.

HOTELS

Khantai Hotel (☎ 22964; s/d T7000/14,000) This small B&B offers two spotless double rooms, one with a gorgeous balcony overlooking the park. The bathroom and shower are both downstairs and there is 24-hour hot water. The friendly owner usually has blueberries, cream and bread set out for breakfast.

Bulgan Hotel (☎ 22811; s/d T2500/3500, lux s/d T6500/12,000) This charmingly run-down Soviet hotel is in a peaceful location overlooking the park. The standard rooms lack a bathroom but the lux rooms include TV and cold-water shower. No-one seems to

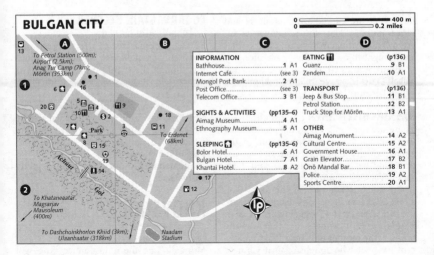

BULGAN CITY

0 ————— 400 m
0 ————— 0.2 miles

INFORMATION
Bathhouse...............................1 A1
Internet Café........................(see 3)
Mongol Post Bank...................2 A1
Post Office...........................(see 3)
Telecom Office........................3 B1

SIGHTS & ACTIVITIES (pp135–6)
Aimag Museum........................4 A1
Ethnography Museum...............5 A1

SLEEPING (pp135–6)
Bolor Hotel.............................6 A1
Bulgan Hotel...........................7 A1
Khantai Hotel..........................8 A2

EATING (p136)
Guanz.....................................9 B1
Zendem.................................10 A1

TRANSPORT (p136)
Jeep & Bus Stop.....................11 B1
Petrol Station.........................12 B2
Truck Stop for Mörön..............13 A1

OTHER
Aimag Monument....................14 A2
Cultural Centre.......................15 A2
Government House..................16 A1
Grain Elevator........................17 B2
Önö Mandal Bar......................18 B1
Police....................................19 A2
Sports Centre.........................20 A1

work on the front desk but you'll probably find someone in the bar and restaurant.

Bolor Hotel (per person T4000-6000) Has clean, dorm-style rooms, located on the main street above some shops in a black-and-white tile building.

Anag Tur Camp (☎ 22593; per person US$15) Located 13km northwest of Bulgan, this tourist camp (no gers) is popular with locals and is set in a beautiful area with wildflowers, pine trees and roaming yaks.

Eating
Close to the park, **Zendem** (☎ 23375; ⏰ 10am-9pm Mon-Sat) is a Chinese restaurant with a Mongolian chef, so the dishes tend to weigh in pretty heavy on the meat. The portions are huge so ask for a half size *(khagas)*.

Aside from one or two hole-in-the-wall *guanz* on the main street, the only other option is the restaurant in the Bulgan Hotel.

Getting There & Away
At the time of research there were no flights to Bulgan and there is little prospect these will resume in the near future.

HITCHING
As most tourist traffic between Ulaanbaatar and Mörön goes via Erdenet there is not too much traffic going through Bulgan, but if you ask around the jeep stand or petrol station (500m northwest of town) something will turn up.

MINIVAN & JEEP
When there is demand, direct vehicles go between Bulgan and Ulaanbaatar (T10,000, nine hours), but most people take a minivan to Erdenet (T3000, two hours, 68km) and then take the overnight train.

Vehicles to Mörön (or anywhere else) are very rare as these tend to leave from Erdenet. Usually on Monday a postal truck goes to Khutag-Öndör (T8000, four hours), but check details as the day is subject to change. Jeeps hang around the Önö Mandal Bar, northeast of the post office. You could charter one for about T250 per kilometre.

There are two routes between Ulaanbaatar and Bulgan city. The southern route is the most direct (318km), but it's mostly a dirt road, though not in bad condition as long as it isn't raining. Take this road if you are going straight to Khövsgöl Nuur.

The northern route (467km), through Darkhan (in Selenge aimag) and Erdenet, is on a good, sealed road – except for the Bulgan–Erdenet leg. If you want to visit Darkhan, Erdenet or Amarbayasgalant Khiid (north of the Darkhan–Erdenet main road), the northern route is the way to go.

Bulgan city is 248km from Darkhan and 353km from Mörön.

AROUND BULGAN
There are a couple of obscure historical monuments around Bulgan. About 20km south of Bulgan, just east of Orkhon are seven standing **deer stones**, so called because

NORTHERN MONGOLIA

the stones are carved with reindeers and other animals. The stones, known as Seeriyn Adigyn Bugan Khoshoo, mark what are thought to be Neolithic grave sites.

About 6km north of Bulgan is a 1m-tall **balbal** (Turkic grave marker), known as Zuun Turuuniy Khun Chuluu.

DASHINCHILEN AREA ДАШИНЧИЛЭН

There are a couple of minor monuments in Dashinchilen *sum*, in the south of the aimag, which might be of interest if you are travelling between Ulaanbaatar and Tsetserleg, via Ögii Nuur.

On the western side of the Tuul Gol, about 35km northeast of Dashinchilen, are the ruins of **Tsogt** (Tsogt Tayjiin Tsagaan Balgas), a 17th-century fort that was the home of the mother of Prince Tsogt, a 17th-century poet who fought against Chinese rule. There is a **stone stele** nearby.

About 12km west of the *sum* capital, the ruined **Khar Bukh Balgas** (Khar Bakhin Fortress; GPS: N47° 53.198′, E103° 53.513′) is worth exploring and easy to reach as it's just a few kilometres north of the main road. The fortress, inhabited by the Kitan from 917 to 1120, is sometimes known as Kitan Balgas. A small **museum** nearby is unlocked by a caretaker when visitors arrive.

URAN UUL & TOGOO UUL
УРАН УУЛ & ТОГОО УУЛ

About 60km west of Bulgan city is the extinct volcano of **Uran Uul** (GPS: N48° 59.855′, E102° 44.003′) and nearby Togoo Uul, part of the 1600-hectare Uran-Togoo Tulga Uul Natural Reserve in the *sum* of Khutag-Öndör.

Uran Uul is a pretty good place to break a journey to Khövsgöl, though the flies in this area can be intensely irritating. Trails to the top of the relatively unimpressive volcano lead up from the western side, which also has some nice camping areas. Jeep tracks lead to the volcano from the main road.

Another place to break your journey west is at a *guanz* near the bridge a few kilometres south of **Khutag-Öndör** – about 100km northwest of Bulgan city – you will be able to get some food and a bed for the night. A few trucks stop there, so it's a good place to hang around and ask for a lift.

Usually on Monday (the day can vary), a postal truck (T8000, four hours) from Bulgan city runs to Khutag-Öndör.

EG TARVAGTAIN BELCHER
ЭГ ТАРВАГТАЙН БЭЛЧЭР

This is a scenic area of rivers, forests and mountains, suitable for hiking and camping, though there are no tourist camps as yet. It is in Teshig *sum*, an area inhabited by Buriats.

To get there, head north towards Teshig and then east after you've crossed the Eg Gol. Roads on the more direct route are difficult. It could take 4½ to six hours from Bulgan depending on the weather.

Situated just southeast of Teshig is pretty **Khargal Nuur**.

KHÖVSGÖL ХӨВСГӨЛ

pop 121,500 / area 101,000 sq km

Mongolia's northernmost aimag, Khövsgöl is – with the possible exception of Arkhangai – the most scenic in Mongolia. This is a land of tall *taiga* forest, crystal-clear lakes, icy streams and lush grass. It does rain a lot during summer, but this only adds to the scenery: rainbows hang over meadows dotted with white gers and grazing horses and yaks. The best fishing is in the south, where the Ider, Bugsei, Selenge, Delger Mörön and Chuluut rivers converge.

The aimag is dominated by magnificent Khövsgöl Nuur, one of the most scenic spots in Mongolia. The lake is surrounded by several peaks of almost 3000m in height. To the west, there is the Darkhadyn Khotgor, with plentiful forests and lakes. In this region, around Tsagaannuur, live the fascinating, but fast disappearing, Dukha people, whose lives revolve around domesticated reindeer. Other ethnic groups include the Khalkh, Buriat, Uriankhai and Darkhad.

MÖRÖN МӨРӨН

☎ 01382 / pop 35,100 / elev 1283m

This rather scruffy aimag capital is cooler than most Mongolian cities, and has relatively few gers because nearby forests supply abundant timber. Mörön (which means river) has few sights and most travellers just drive through en route to Khatgal at the southern end of Khövsgöl Nuur.

Information

Bathhouse (per person T800; ⏰ 9am-10pm Tue-Sat) About 1km north of town.

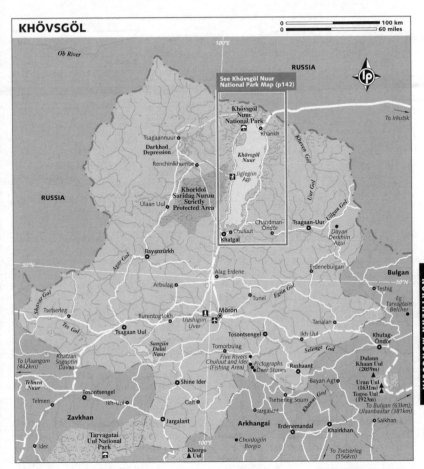

KHÖVSGÖL

See Khövsgöl Nuur National Park Map (p142)

Border Guard Office (☎ 22672, 24662; 🕑 9am-6pm Mon-Fri) Issues permits for border towns such as Tsagaannuur (T1000 per person).

Exchange Centre (☎ 23307; 🕑 9am-6pm Mon-Fri) Located upstairs of the Khadgalamjiin Bank, it will change US dollars and euros. Xac Bank, in the same building, says it can give a cash advance against Visa.

Internet Café (☎ 24706; per hr T600; 🕑 9am-11pm Mon-Fri, 10am-1pm Sat & Sun) Attached to the Telecom office. There is a message board here for travellers to post notices about shared vehicles.

Telecom Office (☎ 21034; 🕑 24hr) The post office is also located here.

Dangers & Annoyances
Mörön has always been a rough town and disgruntled locals have a habit of taking out their angst on foreign visitors. In particular, avoid the market and the hotels on its perimeter, where some travellers have reported being assaulted.

Sights
MUSEUM
Given the variety of wildlife in the aimag, stuffed animals are, not surprisingly, the main feature of the **museum** (☎ 24953; admission T1000) There's a large tusk from a woolly mammoth, but you won't see one of those in the flesh – they haven't inhabited this region for over 40,000 years. Photographic exhibits of the Dukha people are also intriguing. At the time of research the museum was being housed inside the Drama

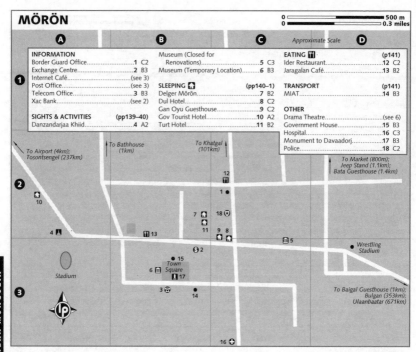

MÖRÖN

INFORMATION	Museum (Closed for	**EATING** (p141)
Border Guard Office.................1 C2	Renovations)................................5 C3	Ider Restaurant............................12 C2
Exchange Centre.......................2 B3	Museum (Temporary Location).........6 B3	Jaragalan Café.............................13 B2
Internet Café............................(see 3)		
Post Office...............................(see 3)	**SLEEPING** (pp140–1)	**TRANSPORT** (p141)
Telecom Office..........................3 B3	Delger Mörön.................................7 B2	MIAT...14 B3
Xac Bank..................................(see 2)	Dul Hotel......................................8 C2	
	Gan Oyu Guesthouse.....................9 C2	**OTHER**
SIGHTS & ACTIVITIES (pp139–40)	Gov Tourist Hotel.........................10 A2	Drama Theatre..............................(see 6)
Danzandarjaa Khiid...................4 A2	Turt Hotel....................................11 B2	Government House.........................15 B3
		Hospital.......................................16 C3
		Monument to Davaadorj................17 B3
		Police..18 C2

Theatre while renovations were made to the main building (located 150m east of the Dul Hotel).

DANZANDARJAA KHIID

The history of this monastery (Данзандаржаа Хийд) is unclear, but the original monastery (Möröngiin Khuree) was built around 1890 and was home to 2000 monks. It was rebuilt and reopened in June 1990, and now has 40 monks of all ages. It's a charming place, designed in the shape of a concrete ger, and contains a great collection of *thangka*.

The monastery is just back from the main road, on the way to the airport. Visitors are always welcome.

Sleeping
CAMPING

Mörön is not a great place to camp. If you must camp here, the best spots are by the river, the Delger Mörön Gol.

Twenty-seven kilometres east of Mörön, on the road to Bulgan city, a tiny, unmapped and unnamed lake offers good camping. A lush valley, 13km further east, is peppered with gers in summer and makes a great place to camp if you want to meet local herders.

GUESTHOUSES

Gan Oyu Guesthouse (☎ 22349, 9938 9438; dm T3000) This guesthouse is the best value in town, with a spotless dorm room and hot-water shower. It is on the 2nd floor of an apartment next to the Dul Hotel.

Bata Guesthouse (☎ 9138 7080; per person T2000) This guesthouse with English-speaking staff is a 20-minute walk from the centre. It's hard to find so call ahead for a pick up.

Baigal Guesthouse (☎ 9938 8408; baigal99mn@yahoo.com; dm T2500, hot shower T500) A similar option to the Bata, on the outskirts of town.

HOTELS

Dul Hotel (☎ 22206; s T5000, half-lux US$12-15, lux US$25) Although not the most inspirational name, this hotel has decent rooms; the more expensive ones come with bathroom. It is located 100m northeast of square.

Turt Hotel (☎ 9938 8569; per person T5000) Functioning toilets, hot-water showers and TVs make this place a comfortable option.

Delger Mörön (tw T7000) The Turt is a notch better than this requisite Soviet dinosaur next door, which has shabby rooms.

Gov Tourist Hotel (☎ 23479; per person US$18) Located on the northwest outskirts, this place is professionally run but overpriced and turns its nose up to independent travellers. There is the option of the outdoor cabins or rooms in the main building. The hotel is owned by the Gobi Cashmere Company.

Eating

The team of women who run **Jaragalan Café** (☎ 24409; meals T950; ☼ 9am-6pm) can serve up a pretty good schnitzel. Look for the cartoon sign above the entrance, just northwest of the square.

Otherwise, there is the Ider Restaurant next to the hotel of the same name, and several *guanz* by the market.

Getting There & Away

AIR

MIAT (Mongolian Airlines; ☎ 24095; ☼ 9am-1pm & 2-6pm Mon-Fri, 10am-1pm & 2-5pm Sat & Sun) is located in the Mongol Post Bank building. Another office opens at the airport when planes arrive. MIAT run direct daily flights between Ulaanbaatar and Mörön for US$80/143 one way/return. Aero Mongolia flies here on Tuesday, Thursday and Saturday for the same price as MIAT.

Mörön occasionally serves as a refuelling stop for flights headed further west, so you could theoretically combine a trip to the west with Khövsgöl Nuur. Check MIAT for details. Buy your ticket as early as possible.

Mörön airport is about 4km from the centre of town. You will have to take a jeep or taxi there (T1000), or hop on the crowded bus.

HITCHING

The Ulaanbaatar–Erdenet–Mörön road is fairly busy, so hitching a ride shouldn't be a problem. But be warned: the trip by truck between Ulaanbaatar and Mörön is a tough 30 or more nonstop hours (expect to pay T5000 to T10,000 for a lift). Some travellers do it one way for the 'experience' – and then gratefully fly back. It's best to fly here from UB as it's easier to get a seat.

To get information about hitching a ride from Mörön, hang around the market or the petrol station.

MINIVAN & JEEP

Minivans run between Ulaanbaatar and Mörön daily (T18,000, 25 hours, 671km). You can cut down on the time spent bumping around in a van by taking the sleeper train between UB and Erdenet.

Minibuses and jeeps leave most afternoons to Khatgal (T5000, four hours). There are occasional jeeps to Erdenet (T10,000, 10 hours) and Darkhan (T12,000, 13 hours).

Transport to Ulaanbaatar, Erdenet and Darkhan leaves from the southern side of the market. Transport to Khatgal and elsewhere leaves from north of the market.

From the city of Mörön it is 273km to Tosontsengel in Zavkhan aimag and 353km to Bulgan city.

UUSHIGIIN UVER УУШИГИЙН ӨВӨР

A Bronze Age site, **Uushigiin Uver** (GPS: N49° 39.205', E99° 55.425') contains 14 upright carved **deer stones**, plus **sacrificial altars** (*keregsuur*) scattered over a 6km plain. This remarkable collection is located 20km west of Mörön, and about 1km north of the Delger Mörön Gol. A caretaker living near the area can show you around and provide commentary. The charge to visit the site, T2000, goes towards its preservation.

KHÖVSGÖL NUUR NATIONAL PARK ХӨВСГӨЛ НУУР

Try to imagine a 2760-sq-km alpine lake, with sparkling water. Then add dozens of mountains 2000m high or more, thick pine forests and lush meadows with grazing yaks and horses, and you have a vague impression of Khövsgöl Nuur, Mongolia's top scenic attraction. In surface area, this is the second-largest lake (136km long and 36km wide) in Mongolia, surpassed in size only by Uvs Nuur, a shallow, salty lake in the western part of the country.

Khövsgöl Nuur is the deepest lake (up to 262m) in Central Asia, and the world's 14th-largest source of fresh water – containing between 1% and 2% of the world's fresh water (that's 380,700 billion litres!). Geologically speaking, Khövsgöl is the younger sibling (by 23 million years) of Siberia's Lake Baikal, 195km to the northeast, and was formed by the same tectonic forces.

The lake is full of fish, such as lenok and sturgeon, and the area is home to argali sheep, ibex, bear, sable and moose, as well

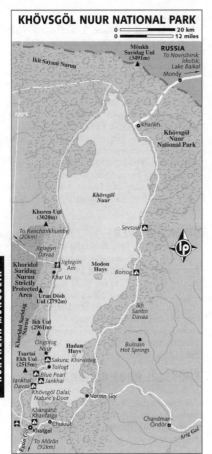

KHÖVSGÖL NUUR NATIONAL PARK

die each year because the lichen they feed on does not grow at lower elevations).

The lake is now part of the Khövsgöl Nuur National Park (established in 1992). Of its 838,000 hectares, 251,000 are forest (though tree cover is starting to disappear around the shore of the lake). The 188,634-hectare Khoridol Saridag Nuruu Strictly Protected Area was added to the park in 1997. Some 96 rivers flow into the lake, while the lone outlet – the Egiin Gol – flows into the Selenge Gol before reaching Lake Baikal in Siberia.

Visitors come to fish, swim in the icy water, watch the ducks, seagulls and other birdlife, hike or go on horseback treks along the shoreline, explore caves, or just find a comfortable spot to stay and soak in all the fresh air and natural beauty.

The lake water is still very clean but a rise in livestock using the area for winter pasture has led to some pollution of the shore and feeder rivers, so you are better off purifying your water.

Khövsgöl Nuur is a pristine but increasingly heavily visited part of Mongolia. Please read the boxed texts on p42 and pp230–1 for suggestions on how you can minimise your impact on this beautiful region.

Climate

The best time to visit the lake is in spring, when it rains less and the flowers and birdlife are often at their best – but it will still be very cold (there will be plenty of snow on the ground), and the lake may still be frozen.

The summer is a little more crowded (not so crowded that it would spoil your trip), but it can still be cold, and it often rains. The meadows around the lake are sprinkled with beautiful wildflowers during this time. Autumn is another good time to visit, when the leaves are changing colour.

Winter is amazingly cold, though blue skies are the norm. Locals say that the lake is at its most beautiful during this time. Khövsgöl Nuur freezes to a depth of 120cm (and may not completely thaw out until early June), allowing passenger trucks to cross the length of the lake in winter. Visitors enjoy the disorientating feeling of looking down through the ice to the lake floor. Oil trucks once made this journey in vast numbers but this practice was stopped in 1990 when it was determined that they

as over 200 species of birds, including the Baikal teal, bar-headed goose (*kheeriin galuu* in Mongolian), black stork and Altai snowcock.

The region hosts three separate, unique peoples: Darkhad, Buriat and Dukha (aka Tsaatan). Shamanism, rather than Buddhism, is the religion of choice in these parts.

One Dukha family has moved into the national park, drawn by the money created by tourism. The family offers tourists a shamanic consultation (for around US$5) and charges for any photos. Their camp keeps getting moved on by the park authorities, who don't like the disruption to the environment caused by their reindeer (which were polluting the water. About 40 trucks have fallen through the ice over the years.

Information
Discovery Initiatives produces a useful booklet on the park entitled *Lake Hovsgol National Park: A Visitors Guide,* which you can get in Ulaanbaatar and, maybe, in the national park office.

Information Centre (Мэдээллийн Төв; ⏰ 9am-8pm) Located near the Mönkh Saridag guesthouse in Khatgal. It has some interesting, museum-style displays on the lake but the staff speaks only Mongolian and has little practical information on touring the area. The caretaker (with the keys) can be found in a ger around the back.

Telecom Office (☎ 01382-26513/36; ⏰ 8am-8pm) Also in Khatgal; there're plans for an Internet café here but the only guaranteed place to connect is back in Mörön.

Permits
On the main road, 12km before Khatgal, you'll be required to pay an entrance fee at a gate to the national park. The cost is T3000/300 per person for foreigners/Mongolians. If there's no-one there you can buy permits at the information centre or from the ranger, who patrols the lakeside on horseback. With your permit you should receive a useful visitors pamphlet explaining the permits and how to limit your impact on the lake. Hang onto the ticket as you may be asked to show it more than once.

Festivals & Events
If for some strange reason you've come to northern Mongolia in winter, it is worth checking out the **Khatgal Ice Festival**, held eight days after Tsagaan Sar (January/February). The venue includes cross-country skiing, ice skating and horse-sledding competitions.

In late June or early July, the **'Sunrise to Sunset Ultra-marathon'** is held further up the lakeshore. Mongolian and international runners compete in 42km or 100km divisions; for more info, check the website: www.ultramongolia.org/.

Sights
KHATGAL
As the southern gateway to Khövsgöl Nuur, Khatgal (Хатгал) is the largest town on the lake. With some of the best budget accommodation in Mongolia, it is a good launching pad for the lake and most people spend at least a day here preparing for, or relaxing after, a

trip. The town is actually on the Egiin Gol, at the mouth of the lake, so you don't get much of an idea of the lake's size from here.

Khatgal used to be a busy depot for trucks headed to and from Russia, but the town's economy has since ground to a halt.

The national park rangers have set up a couple of marked walking trails starting from Khatgal. A shoreline trail leads 10km until it hits the jeep road. A 12km loop ridge trail branches off the shoreline trail and heads up and along a ridge, offering fine views of the lake. For an easier view of the lake just climb the hill immediately north of Nature's Door camp (p146).

WESTERN SHORE
From Khatgal, a reasonable road first heads southwest before swinging northeast across several dry riverbeds and over the pass, Jankhai Davaa, 17km from Khatgal, where you receive your first magical glimpse of the lake. The road continues past the gorgeous headlands of **Jankhai**, once a Russian scientist station, and **Toilogt** (GPS: N50° 39.266', E100° 14.961'), pronounced 'Toy-logt' but routinely mispronounced 'Toilet' by most travellers, where there is a rash of ger camps. The road then gradually deteriorates.

About 30km north of Toilogt is **Khar Us**, a series of springs surrounded by meadows of beautiful wildflowers. In June locals flock here to eat the bailius fish for its medicinal properties. This makes a great destination to reach on horseback.

A jeep can travel about 10km past Toilogt, after which the trail becomes overgrown and is best managed on horseback for the trip up to **Jiglegiin Am** (GPS: N51° 00.406', E100° 16.003'), almost exactly halfway up the western shore. From Jiglegiin Am you could take the western trail to Renchinlkhumbe, on the way to Tsagaannuur.

EASTERN SHORE
The eastern shore is not as good because the road rarely hugs the lake, the scenery isn't as pretty, there are only a handful of gers between Chuluut and Borsog, almost no wildlife, and the flies can be appalling. If that doesn't put you off, it might if we said that this is the worse stretch of road we encountered in 15,000km of overland travel! Recently built bridges along the trail are largely useless as most have already collapsed.

NORTHERN MONGOLIA

From Khatgal, head for the bridge over the Egiin Gol, where you may need to ask directions. The trail meanders over some hills and past a collection of huts known as **Chuluut** – if in doubt, follow the line of electricity poles. About 26km up the eastern side of the lake there's accommodation at **Nomin Sky ger camp** (☎ 354 121; with/without meals US$20/T4500). The trail continues past an interesting *ovoo* at the pass **Ikh Santin Davaa** (GPS: N50° 52.622′, E100° 41.185′) to a gorgeous spot called **Borsog** (GPS: N50° 59.677′, E100° 42.983′), six hours by jeep and 103km from Khatgal.

If your spine hasn't suffered permanent damage by now, you could carry on further to a couple of gers known as **Sevsuul**. The road actually improves a little here, then hugs the lake and is usually passable all the way to Khankh. Surprisingly, a few sand dunes dot the landscape.

From Khatgal, allow at least 12 hours by jeep to travel the 200km or so to **Khankh** (Turt), a former depot for oil tankers headed to and from Siberia. Khankh is more Buriat and Russian than Mongolian, because it is closer to its northern neighbour than to Ulaanbaatar. The **Last Frontier** (per person with meals US$20) ger camp is here. Don't stray too far from Khankh; nearby is the Russian border, where smugglers may be arrested or shot.

Remember that if you reach Khankh, you will have to come *all* the way back along the same bone-crunching, eastern road: there is no way any vehicle can get from Khankh to Jiglegiin Am, halfway up the western shore. At the moment going all the way around the lake is only possible by boat or horse. Locals say that the border crossing into Russia at Khankh will be open to foreign tourists by 2005. Check for updates at the border office in Ulaanbaatar or in Mörön.

Activities
CAVING
There are numerous caves around the lake, so speleologists are interested in the area, though finding a cave worth exploring in the thick forests will require a guide, considerable time and a lot of luck.

FISHING
If you love fishing, then you'll get excited about Khövsgöl Nuur. Bring your own fishing gear – or beg, borrow or steal some. Nature's Door and Mönkh Saridag can rent you some gear. A rod would be better, but you can still have success with a hand line and a simple lure. You can fish from headlands along the shore, from bridges or, if you are keen, wade into the lake for a few metres. After weeks of mutton you'll be desperate for some fish – incredibly, none of the *guanz* or restaurants in the aimag serve it.

Some of the best spots we found were the bridge at the southern end of Khatgal (which leads to the road going up the eastern shore), Borsog on the eastern shore, and at several coves where the eastern road meets the southeastern shore. Around a dozen species of fish inhabit the lake, including salmon, (bony) sturgeon, grayling and lenok.

A fishing permit costs T10,000 and is valid for two days or 10 fish, whichever comes first. You can get them from the park rangers, Khatgal government house or Mönkh Saridag guesthouse. Fishing is not allowed between 15 April and 15 June. The fine for fishing illegally is US$40.

HIKING
This is one of the best ways to see the lake and the mountains surrounding it. You will need to be self-sufficient, although there are a few gers in the area to buy some meat or dairy products from. The trails around the lake are easy to follow, or just hug the shoreline as much as you can.

Of the mountains in the southwestern region, the most accessible is Tsartai Ekh Uul (2515m), immediately west of Jankhai, where the hiking is excellent. Also try the numerous other mountains in the mountain range of Khoridol Saridag Nuruu, such as Khuren Uul (3020m), not far north of the trail to Renchinlkhumbe; Ikh Uul (2961m), a little northwest of Toilogt; and the extinct volcano of Uran Dösh Uul (2792m).

Longer treks are possible around the Ikh Sayani Nuruu range, which has many peaks over 3000m. It is right on the border of Russia, so be careful.

Both Garage 24 and Mönkh Saridag guesthouses (see opposite) have trained some local hiking guides in first aid, route finding and low-impact hiking and have scouted out some good treks in the surrounding mountains. Contact them for route ideas and/or guides.

HORSE RIDING

The only place to organise a horse trek around the lake is at Khatgal. The three main guesthouses can arrange everything within 24 hours. Prices are negotiable but reasonable at about US$5 per horse per day, and about US$5 to US$8 per day for a guide.

If you just want to hire a horse for a few hours you could arrange this with a family at the lake. All ger camps can arrange horse riding for anyone willing to pay high tourist prices of around US$10 to US$20 per day, plus a guide.

A guide is recommended for any horse-riding trips in the region and, in fact, park regulations stipulate that foreigners should have one local guide for every four tourists. Guides will expect you to provide food while on the trail.

A complete circuit of the lake on horseback will take from 10 to 15 days. A return trip by horse from Khatgal to Tsagaannuur, and a visit to the Dukha people, will take between 15 to 20 days. An interesting 10-day trip could take you east of the lake to Chandman-Öndör and Dayan Derkhiin Agui, a cave. You'll definitely need a guide for these last two trips.

Shorter trips include one to Toilogt, through the mountainous Khoridol Saridag Nuruu Strictly Protected Area, or up to Khar Us and back in a couple of days.

KAYAKING & BOATING

Travelling by kayak allows you to see the lake without the strain of driving along the appalling roads. The lake is full of glorious little coves, perfect for camping and fishing, and you could even check out **Modon Huys**, an island almost exactly in the middle of the lake. Nomadic Expeditions (p70) runs kayaking trips in the region.

Garage 24 has a Zodiac boat and can run travellers up to its camp and beyond to the island and the northern reaches of the lake. Mönkh Saridag also has a motor boat. Ask about the two-day boat trip to Jiglegiin Am (US$100 for up to six people, including meals).

Several large boats remain moored at Khatgal docks. They *very* occasionally take passengers up to Khankh but these days they will only move when chartered, which will cost an arm and a leg. If you do charter a boat to Khankh, you'll still have to share it with a boatload of nonpaying passengers who have been waiting for some tourist or trader to fork out the money.

Sleeping
KHATGAL

If you have a tent and are hanging around for a lift to the lake or to Mörön, you can camp in the forests along the shores of the Egiin Gol, either in town or in the beautiful valleys further south.

Mönkh Saridag (☎ 9979 6030; lake_hovsgol@yahoo .com; bed per person T4000, camping T500; meals T1200, hot shower T1000) This guesthouse (designed like a camp), in the extreme south of town, is the first collection of gers you see when arrive in town. Perhaps the most congenial of ger camps around Khatgal, the staff makes visitors feel at home, with communal meals and activities. Ask for Ganbaatar or Batzorig.

Sunway Guesthouse (☎ 9975 3824; per person T2000; meals T1500) If you're looking to save some tögrög, this place is inexpensive but still offers good value. It's on the northwestern part of town below the hills. Ask for Esee.

Garage 24 (☎ 011-323957, 99118652; www.4thworld adventure.com; dm US$5, camping US$2.50) Operated by Nature's Door travel company, this environmentally conscious backpackers hang-out is built from a reclaimed Soviet-era truck garage. The cosy lodge, warmed by a fireplace, has bunk beds and a dining area where you can get the best food in northern Mongolia. Mountain bikes, kayaks, horses and camping gear are rented out to suit your needs. The camp is in the north of town, at the base of the hill, not far from the storage drums of the petrol station.

Located near the shops, the run-down government **Blue Pearl Hotel** (☎ 113; dm T5000) has basic dorms, hot showers and a pit toilet. The **Tsagaan Uul Hotel** (☎ 110; dm T3000), near the post office, is really more of a bar and *guanz* but there are a couple of basic dorm rooms.

WESTERN & EASTERN SHORES
Camping

Khövsgöl Nuur is one of the best places in Mongolia to camp. There is endless fresh water, plenty of fish, and the hiking is outstanding. On the down side, it often rains in summer and flies abound.

There is some confusion as to whether tourists can camp anywhere. There are designated camp sites, marked by often-obscured blue signs, which read 'Хонох Цэг' (camping ground). There are camp sites near the Nature's Door camp, just past Jankhai camp and two in the bay between Jankhai and Toilogt. These seem to be aimed primarily at Mongolian tourists and groups.

Away from these areas you can pretty much pitch your tent anywhere you want, though try to stay 100m from other gers. You should never camp, wash or build fires within 50m of the shore.

The best camping spots on the western shoreline are anywhere between Jankhai and Ongolog Nuur, 10km north of Toilogt. If you have your own jeep, and want to experience one of the worst roads in Mongolia, the best spot to camp on the eastern shoreline is at Borsog.

Ger Camps

There are several ger camps in stunning locations on the western shore (only one or two on the east). Most have electricity, running water, toilets and showers, though many are dangerously near the shoreline and have little environmental regard for the lake. Most places will offer a lower price if you bring and cook your own food. The majority only open in mid-June.

Several families also accept guests in a guest ger. They are not registered with the park and so don't advertise, but if you ask around you can probably find a family who will let you stay for a couple of US dollars.

The Khangard and Khantaiga camps, 6km north of Khatgal, cater mostly to organised groups and suffer from loud generators. They are reached from the road north of Khatgal, not the main road which heads to the lake over Jankhai Davaa.

The main group of camps start where the road meets the lake, after descending from Jankhai Davaa.

Khövsgöl Dalai (GPS: N50° 35.518', E100° 10.685'; ☎ 01382-23762, 9929 3896; information@montravels .com; with/without meals T20,000/15,000, camping T1000) This relaxed and friendly ger camp is 5km past Jankhai Davaa, by the lakeside. Saunas and hot showers are available.

Nature's Door (☎ 9926 0919; with/without meals US$30/15) Although the reception is a bit chilly, this is one of the more professional ger camps on the lake, and has English-speaking staff and excellent Western-food options. Most people stay in the gers but if you are willing to shell out US$60, the flashy cabins are also an option. Nature's Door is associated with Garage 24 in Khatgal; it's about 250m past Khövsgöl Dalai ger camp.

Jankhai Ger Camp (with/without meals T25,000/ 15,000) Located 2km past Nature's Door, this place is a little disorganised and may not have food. But the location, on a tree-clad headland that extends into the lake, is perfect for camping.

About 2km past Jankhai ger camp, on the left, is the derelict Jankhai Resort, a former research station in Soviet times that was later converted into a holiday camp but was closed when we visited.

Blue Pearl (with/without food T30,000/15,000) This new place is 1km past Jankhai Resort. It's done in an attractive log-cabin style but is definitely aimed at Japanese, Korean and Chinese tour groups.

Camp Toilogt (☎ 011-460 368; with/without meals US$35/20) Run by Hovsgol Travel Company, this excellent camp is 5km north of Jankhai, and off the main road to the right. It is situated by a peaceful and lovely lake immediately adjacent to Khövsgöl Nuur. The camp sometimes has music shows for guests. It has a boat that can transfer you here from Khatgal but you'll need to give advance notice to the Ulaanbaatar office. Nearby, the affiliated Toilogt II camp handles overflow.

A couple of kilometres past here are the last two camps, Sakura Tour and Khirvisteg ger camps, both of which are fairly basic, with pit toilets.

Further on, Khövsgöl Lodge Company maintains a **lodge** (☎ / fax 011-310 852, 9911 5929; dm T4000) at Jiglegiin Am, the trailhead for Tsagaannuur. Jiglegiin Am is 90km from Khatgal.

Eating

There are a few basic shops in Khatgal selling things such as beer, soft drinks, chocolate bars and a limited selection of vegetables. If possible, stock up in Mörön or Ulaanbaatar. The following places are all in Khatgal.

Garage 24 (see p145) has a good Western-oriented menu that will come as a welcome break after a few days of hard trekking in the wilderness. The English breakfast (T6000) includes bacon, toast, beans and sausage. Lunch and dinner menu items include shepherds pie (T4800) and pizza (T5500). Give some advance warning as preparations take around an hour.

Mönkh Saridag guesthouse (see p145) is another good place to eat and will occasionally prepare *khorhog* (authentic Mongolian BBQ) for guests and visitors.

Orgil Restaurant (meals T900; ⏲ 9am-8pm), located amid the row of downtown shops, has an English-language menu that includes cream soup, goulash and *khuushuur* (mutton pancakes).

Getting There & Away

AIR
MIAT flies from Ulaanbaatar to Khatgal (via Mörön) on Monday, Wednesday and Friday for US$100/174. Flights are cut back in the off season, but extra flights might be added for the July peak season. Schedules are continually in flux so check with MIAT in Ulaanbaatar. There are no longer any flights to Khankh.

Boojum Expeditions occasionally operates helicopter trips from Ulaanbaatar to the lake and will sell travellers any remaining seats. Contact its office at the Khövsgöl Lodge Company (p70) in Ulaanbaatar.

HITCHING
For lifts from Mörön, hang around the market or the petrol station – and keep asking. Once in Khatgal, most trucks will stop in front of the post office.

From Khatgal, hitching a ride to Jankhai or Toilogt shouldn't be difficult in the summer, but you'll probably end up paying a fair bit for a lift anyway. You should be self-sufficient with camping gear and food.

Hitching around the eastern shore is much more difficult and you could wait for days for a lift to come along.

JEEP
Minivans and jeeps regularly make the trip between Mörön and Khatgal (three hours) for T5000 per person, or T50,000 for the jeep. Inquire at the stand at the northern end of the market in Mörön.

Transport also meets the Ulaanbaatar flight at Mörön airport to take passengers directly to Khatgal. Some jeep owners will try to charge foreigners up to US$50 for the run; local drivers with the 'ХӨА' licence plate are likely to be fairer. Nature's Door will normally pick up and drop off travellers at Mörön airport for T5000 per person.

A chartered jeep should not cost more than the normal T250 per kilometre. There are plenty of jeeps in Mörön but few in Khatgal, where it is best to ask at the guesthouses. In the peak season of July and August, it may be difficult to charter a jeep for a reasonable price. If you are headed north of Khatgal it is also important to find a reliable jeep that can handle the terrible roads on the eastern side of the lake. From Khatgal to Khankh, at the top of the lake, it is about 200km – then there's the trip back.

Khatgal is a rough 101km from Mörön – the valleys of the Egiin Gol, along the way, are particularly beautiful and worth a visit in their own right.

CHANDMAN-ÖNDÖR AREA
ЧАНДМАНЬ-ӨНДӨР

The village of Chandman-Öndör, a day's drive east of Khatgal, is in a beautiful area of wide meadows, alpine forests and wildflowers, which would make a good exploratory trip for hardy travellers.

There is no formal accommodation in town but a couple named Oyunchimeg and Enktuvshin operate two **wood cabins** (per person T4000) in their *khashaa* (fenced-in yard) on the southeastern edge of town. The town also has a decent **museum** and *guanz*.

Shared jeeps going to Chandman-Öndör (T8000) occasionally leave from the northern side of the market in Mörön. From Khatgal you need your own jeep, though the two- or three-day horse ride is said to be wonderful.

Surrounding sites include the **Bulnai hot springs** (Булнайн Рашаан), about 50km northwest of town, which offers simple cabins around a former Soviet resort. Further east, 30km southeast of Tsagaan-Uur, is the **Dayan Derkhiin Agui** (Даян Дэрхийн Агуй), a cave considered holy by local Buddhists and shamanists, and a nearby ruined monastery. According to legend, the monastery was founded here after the famed shaman Dayan Derkh turned to stone rather than be captured by Chinggis Khaan, whose wife the shaman had stolen.

With a few days up your sleeve this could make a rough but beautiful alternative route from Khövsgöl Nuur to Bulgan. Bear in mind that you'll need a border permit for Tsagaan-Uur and Dayan Derkhiin Agui, available in Mörön.

If you are travelling to/from Mörön, the *sum* (district) capital of **Erdenebulgan** has the basic **Burged Hotel** (Eagle Hotel; per person T3000).

In the northeast of the aimag, the area around the Khokh, Arig and Kheven rivers, is particularly good for **fishing**.

DARKHAD DEPRESSION
ДАРХАДЫН ХӨНДИЙ

About 50km west of Khövsgöl Nuur, behind a wall of mountains, sits a harsh but mystical landscape of prairie, forest, and about 300-odd lakes scattered over a wide plain called the Darkhad Depression. The depression is roughly the same size as Khövsgöl Nuur and was indeed originally formed as a glacial lake.

The difficulty in reaching the region ensures the unique Dukha (Tsaatan) people who inhabit the valleys (see below) are able to continue their traditional lifestyle – but tourism is slowly making an impact. Darkhad is one of Mongolia's strongest centres of shamanism.

This is one of the best-watered regions in Mongolia and the lakes are a vital part of Mongolia's very limited commercial fishing industry – white carp and trout are packed in salt and flown out to Ulaanbaatar to be served in the fancier hotels. Salmon and huge taimen can also be found in the region.

One definite drawback to visiting the region is the insects that invade the area. Be warned: these little critters have insatiable appetites for foreign skin and will ruin your trip if you are not fully prepared with mosquito nets and repellent.

Permits

Tsagaannuur and the region inhabited by the Dukha are not part of Khövsgöl Nuur National Park. However, authorities in Ulaanbaatar are currently considering a plan to limit the effects of tourism on the Dukha by implementing a permit system. At the time of writing, a temporary measure asks visitors to submit their name and travel dates to Dukha representatives in Ulaanbaatar. You can do this by emailing reindeer@hovsgol.org. The representative will inform you of the best travel dates and may even request that you bring certain items (ie foodstuffs) to the Dukha. Please respect the Dukha by dropping an email, you'll get a better welcome for it.

To visit Tsagaannuur (but not Renchinlkhumbe) you'll also need a border permit, available in Ulaanbaatar, or even easier, in Mörön. Border permits cost T1000 and are processed in one day. In a pinch, guesthouses can arrange the permit in Khatgal through their Mörön contacts.

THE REINDEER HERDERS

Not far from Khövsgöl Nuur live the Dukha people, who are commonly referred to by Khalkh Mongolians as Tsaatan (literally 'Reindeer People'). Their entire existence is based around their herds of reindeer, which provide milk, skins for clothes, horn for carving and medicine, transport and, occasionally, meat.

The Dukha are part of the Tuvan ethnic group, which inhabits the Tuvan Republic of Russia. There are only about 200 Dukha in total, spread over 100,000 sq km of northern Mongolia. They are truly nomadic, often moving their small encampments *(ail)* every two or three weeks, looking for special types of grass and moss loved by the reindeer. The Dukha do not use gers, but prefer *orts*, similar to Native American tepees, made from reindeer skin. The Dukha are strong practitioners of shamanism.

Visiting the Dukha is difficult and exhausting. The mosquitoes are legendary, the climate is exceedingly harsh, and it's easy to get lost without a good local guide. Plan to be self-sufficient with food and tents.

Irresponsible tourism, research and evangelical activities have put the Dukha culture and their reindeer at risk. In the past, tourist dollars have lured Dukha members down to Khövsgöl Nuur, an inhospitable elevation for their sensitive reindeer. Others have been subjected to bible-thumping sessions and Tarzan films shown by Korean missionaries. If you are intent on making the trip, read the Permits section (above).

Renchinlkhumbe & Tsagaannuur
Рэнчинлхүмбэ & Цагааннуур

Two villages in the region act as a supply base for locals and foreigners alike. Renchinlkhumbe is 42km west of the Jiglegiin Am trailhead on Khövsgöl Nuur, an adventurous two-day journey on foot or horseback. Most travellers heading further into the *taiga* will rest here for at least one night.

Renchinlkhumbe hosts an excellent local **Naadam** (National Day Celebration; July 11) complete with 'barrel racing' (horse racing around barrels) and mounted archery events, along with the usual wrestling, horse racing and standing archery.

The local ger camp, **Saridag Inn** (per person US$5) is run by Khövsgöl Lodge Company. As an income-generation project, the local school plans to open as a summer hotel for backpackers.

Another 40km of rough riding brings you to Tsagaannuur, the last stop before the Dukha encampments in the forests and valleys. Accommodation is at the basic **Taiga hotel** (per person T5000) and there are a few shops. A tent and your own food is a better idea.

Getting There & Away
AIR
Tiny chartered planes can land at the dirt runway at Tsagaannuur, but it will still take a couple of days on horseback to reach the Dukha. Staff from foreign embassies and development agencies in Ulaanbaatar sometimes take a helicopter directly to the Dukha encampments and land like some flying saucer from outer space.

HITCHING
Traffic between Mörön and Tsagaannuur is extremely sparse, but if you have your own tent and food, and don't mind waiting for a day or two, something may come along during summer – or it may not.

HORSE
There is really only one way to get to Tsagaannuur and the area: by horse. It is best to arrange things at Khatgal.

From Khatgal to Jiglegiin Am, about halfway up the western shore of Khövsgöl Nuur, will take five days (four hours' riding each day). From Jiglegiin Am, there are several easy-to-follow horse trails to Renchinlkhumbe – just make sure you are heading west. From the Jiglegiin pass (2500m), the trail to Renchinlkhumbe is easy; it then heads northwest to Tsagaannuur. From there, it will probably still take a couple of days to reach some Dukha encampments.

A return trip from Khatgal to Tsagaannuur, with a visit to the Dukha, will take from 15 to 20 days. You could go from Khatgal to Tsagaannuur on an easy trail in about five days (bypassing Jiglegiin Am), but your back would not appreciate the hard ride and you would miss Khövsgöl Nuur.

Another option recommended by guides in Khatgal is to make the trek to Renchinlkhumbe via Jiglegiin Am and back to Khatgal via the Khoridol Saridag mountains, and skip Tsagaannuur. On the way, you could stay at a warming hut at Ooliin Gol, 25km west of Jiglegiin Am. Check with Mönkh Saridag guesthouse for details on this trek.

JEEP
By chartered jeep, you can get to Tsagaannuur from Mörön (but not from Khatgal) in a bone-crunching 12 to 15 hours, depending on the state of the road. A seat should cost no more than T15,000, but you'll have to negotiate hard and long for a reasonable price. There are no scheduled public shared jeeps to Tsagaannuur.

FIVE RIVERS ТАВАН ГОЛ
About 50km south of Mörön, on the border with the Arkhangai aimag, is an area where the Ider, Bugsei, Selenge, Delger Mörön and Chuluut rivers converge (GPS: N49° 15.475', E100° 40.385'). In September and October this is one of the best **fishing** spots in the country. Another good camping and fishing area is the confluence of the Chuluut and Ider rivers (GPS: N49° 10.415', E100° 40.335'), about 15km south of the Five Rivers area. Four kilometres southeast of here is an area rich in **pictographs** (GPS: N49° 08.585', E100° 42.125') scattered across some 600 rocks. About 1km south of here are two **deer stones** (GPS: N49° 08.015', E100° 42.335').

Eastern Mongolia

Biologist George Schaller called eastern Mongolia 'one of the last great unspoiled grazing ecosystems in the world'. With gazelle bounding freely over the vast steppes, tall grasses waving in the breeze, and the occasional wood shack or ger (felt yurts), eastern Mongolia looks like Nebraska c 1810. Get there before it disappears.

Indeed, just as pioneers beat the American plains into submission, eastern Mongolia is coming under increasing pressure by mining companies, road builders and over-eager politicians. But for now, the steppes remain a quiet and unassuming place that offers plenty of scope for exciting jeep travel and ecotourism.

Besides the grasslands, the major feature of eastern Mongolia is the Khan Khentii mountains, Chinggis Khaan's boyhood stamping grounds. For Chinggisphiles, a pilgrimage to his birthplace in Dadal is a must, and there are several other sites associated with his life nearby. Archaeologists and historians are eagerly scouring this landscape in search of clues that might lead them to his undiscovered grave.

In the southeast of the region, Dariganga remains an unspoiled getaway for the adventurous. During the years under Manchu rule, this area served as the imperial grazing grounds for the emperor's best horses. This volcanic area is filled with craters, lava tubes, ancient stone figures and legendary stories about horse bandits that harassed the Chinese. The people of Dariganga represent just one of several ethnic minority groups in the region. Several villages in northern Khentii are inhabited by Buriats while in the extreme east there are Barga and Uzemchin peoples.

Travellers who head out east are rewarded with some stunning scenery, undisturbed grasslands and several important historical sites. All this is close to Ulaanbaatar.

EASTERN MONGOLIA

HIGHLIGHTS

- Follow in the footsteps of Chinggis Khaan by visiting his birthplace in **Dadal** (p157) and coronation site at **Khökh Nuur** (p156)

- Join the volunteers rebuilding the once-grand **Baldan Baraivan Khiid** (p156), an important, soon-to-be-reborn monastic institution

- Explore a landscape of extinct volcanoes around **Dariganga** (p168) and men can climb sacred **Shiliin Bogd Uul** (p170) for a great sunrise and awesome views

- Spot wildlife, including moose and huge herds of gazelle, at **Nömrög** (p166), the uninhabited eastern tip of Mongolia

★ Dadal

Baldan
★ Baraivan Khiid   Nömrög Strictly
★   Protected Area ★
Khökh Nuur

Shilin
Bogd Uul
★
Dariganga ★

- POPULATION: 201,900 | - AREA: 287,500 SQ KM

History

The Tamtsagbulag Neolithic site in Dornod, active more than 4000 years ago, is proof that agriculture predated nomadic pastoralism on the eastern steppes. But it was the Kitan, a Manchurian tribal confederation, who made the first big impression on the region, building forts and farming communities in the 10th century, including Bar Khot in Dornod.

Another Manchu tribe, the Jurchen, deposed the Kitan in the early 12th century, renamed itself the Jin, and returned eastern Mongolia to its warring ways. It wasn't until Chinggis Khaan united the fractured clans in 1206 that peace took over.

It was from Avarga (modern Delgerkhaan), that Chinggis launched expeditions south towards China. But he didn't stay long, moving the capital to Karakorum in 1220. With that the region withdrew into obscurity. It wasn't until 1939 that eastern Mongolia was again in the headlines, this time as a battlefield between Japanese and Soviet forces. Heavy Japanese losses forced their military machine south but the Khalkh Gol region is still littered with battle scars from the brief campaign.

Climate

Eastern Mongolia's climate and landscape has more in common with northeastern China than it does with Central Asia. Temperature extremes are less severe and winds less violent than the west. While the Khan Khentii mountains get a lot of rain in the summer, per-year precipitation on the steppes is around 250mm. Winter daytime temperatures fall to minus 20°C but skies are usually blue.

Getting There & Away

Daily jeeps and minivans connect Öndörkhaan with Ulaanbaatar's Naran Tuul jeep station. You can also get a ride with vehicles from Ulaanbaatar that go through Öndörkhaan on their way to Baruun-Urt and Choibalsan. Another route into the region is through northern Khentii – daily minivans from Naran Tuul travel to Dadal via Ömnödelger and Binder. During the rainy season this trip can take more than 25 hours.

With your own vehicle, it's possible to drive to eastern Mongolia from the Gobi.

You could even enter from Russia at the Erdeentsav–Borzya border crossing in Dornod aimag. If you are in Selenge aimag, the only direct way into Khentii is on foot or horseback; jeep travellers will need to go via Ulaanbaatar.

Getting Around

Public transport can get you to some places of interest, including Dadal and Dariganga. But if you want to maximise your time and see what the region really has to offer you'll need your own vehicle, either hired from Ulaanbaatar or from one of the aimag capitals. Make sure your guide and driver have some experience in the region, as this will make navigation easier (a GPS is a handy alternative). The best way to explore northern Khentii, including the Khan Khentii Strictly Protected Area, is on horseback – both Batshireet and Dadal are good places to launch an expedition.

KHENTII ХЭНТИЙ

pop 71,100 / area 82,000 sq km

Khentii is named after the impressive Khentii Nuruu mountain range, which covers the northwestern corner of the aimag (a province/state within Mongolia) and is part of the giant 1.2 million-hectare Khan Khentii Strictly Protected Area (most of which is in the adjoining Töv aimag). Although none of the peaks is over 2000m, these mountains are well watered and heavily forested. The aimag has over 70 rivers, including the Kherlen Gol, which flows through the aimag capital of Öndörkhaan, and the Onon Gol in the far northeast. There are also over 30 sources of mineral water.

All this means that the scenery is lush and travelling is very difficult. Jeeps have a hard time and often get bogged; access through the thickly forested regions is mainly on horseback or on foot. The water attracts an abundance of wildlife and is responsible for the stunning wildflowers that seem to carpet hills and valleys with a profusion of purple, red and yellow.

Khentii is the land of the ethnic Khalkh and Buriat groups, and also of the famed Chinggis Khaan. It is where he was born, grew up, rose to power, was crowned and (probably) where he was buried.

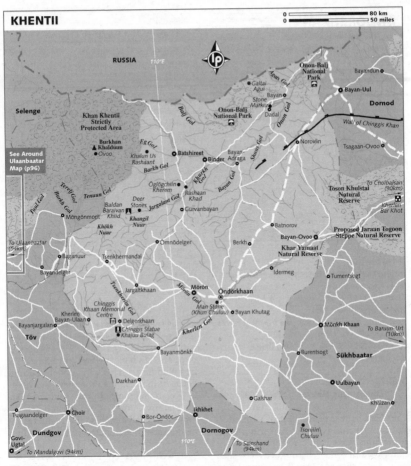

KHENTII

0 _____ 80 km
0 _____ 50 miles

RUSSIA 110°E

Selenge

Khan Khentii
Strictly
Protected Area

Burkhan
▲ Khalduun
• Ovoo

See Around
Ulaanbaatar
Map (p96)

Galtai
Agui
Stone
Marker

Onon-Balj
National
Park

Bayan

Onon-Balj
National
Park

Dadal

Bayandun •

• Bayan-Uul

Dornod

Wall of Chinggis Khan

• Norovlin

Tsagaan-Ovoo •

To Choibalsan
(90km)

EASTERN MONGOLIA

Eg Gol

Khalun Us
Rashaant

• Batshireet

Öglögchiin
Kherem

Baldan
Baraivan
Khiid

Deer
Stones

Binder

Bayan-
Adraga

Rashaan
Khad

Jargalant Gol

Guivanbayan

Khangil
Nuur

Khökh
Nuur

• Mönggönmort

• Omnödelger

Baganuur •

• Bayandelger

Tsenkhermandal

• Batnorov

Berkh •

Bayan-Ovoo •

Khar Yamaat
Natural Reserve

• Idermeg

Toson Khulstai
Natural
Reserve

Kherlen
Bar Khot

Proposed Jaraan Togoon
Steppe Natural Reserve

• Tumentsogt

To Ulaanbaatar
(54km)

Jargaltkhaan

Möron •

• Öndörkhaan

Man Stone
(Khun Chuluu)

• Bayan Khutag

Chinggis
Khaan Memorial
Centre

Bayanjargalan •

Kherlen
Bayan-Ulaan •

Töv

Delgerkhaan

Chinggis Statue
Khajuu Bulag

Bayanmönkh •

Darkhan •

Tsagaandelger •

• Choir

Dundgov

Govi-
Ugtal

To Mandalgovi (94km)

• Bor-Öndör

Ikhkhet •

Dornogov

• Galshar

110°E

To Sainshand
(94km)

• Mönkh Khaan

To Baruun-Urt
(10km)

• Burentsogt

Sükhbaatar

• Uulbayan

Khailzan •

Tsonjiin
Chuluu

The land is the source of the Kherlen and Onon rivers, both of which are mentioned extensively in the epic Mongol history of the life and deeds of Chinggis Khaan, *The Secret History of the Mongols*. Quests for knowledge about Chinggis Khaan, often conducted with international funding, have identified more than 50 historical sites relating to his life. Expect tourism officials to play up these sites with celebrations and events in 2006, the 800-year anniversary of Chinggis Khaan's unification of all Mongol clans.

This historical Mongol heartland, and specifically the town of Galshar in the far south of the aimag, is famed as the source of Mongolia's fastest horses.

ÖNDÖRKHAAN ӨНДӨРХААН

☎ 01562 / pop 16,700 / elev 1027m

The aimag capital of Öndörkhaan (which means 'High King') is in one of the flattest and driest parts of Khentii. However, the Kherlen Gol, flows through the southern part of Öndörkhaan, providing cattle with water and grass, and the locals (and brave foreigners) with a good swimming hole in the hot summer months. Most of the residents live in wooden buildings, so gers are relatively few.

A sleepy place, Öndörkhaan is far nicer than the other two eastern aimag capitals. It is perfectly located as a gateway to the region, so you may need to stay here to arrange onward transport or to break up a journey if you are heading to/from the east.

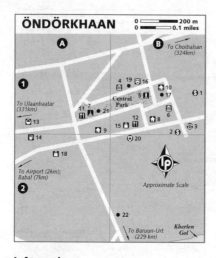

ÖNDÖRKHAAN

0 _____ 200 m
0 _____ 0.1 miles

To Choibalsan (324km)

To Ulaanbaatar (331km)

Central Park

To Airport (2km); Babal (7km)

Approximate Scale

To Baruun-Urt (229 km)

Kherlen Gol

Information

Internet Café (☎ 23695; per hr T710; ☼ 9am-10pm Mon-Fri, 9am-5pm Sat & Sun) In the Telecom office.

Khan Bank (☎ 22498; ☼ 9am-1pm & 2-4pm Mon-Fri) Changes US dollars and euros.

Post Bank (☎ 23091; ☼ 9am-1pm & 2-4pm) Changes dollars and offers cash advances on Visa.

Telecom Office (☎ 22838; ☼ 24hr) The post office is also here.

Sights

The **Ethnography Museum** (☎ 22187; admission T1000; ☼ 9am-1pm & 2-6pm Mon-Fri), next to the City Hall, is one of the best of its kind in the country and is certainly worth a look. It contains a few ethnic costumes, Mongolian toys and some religious artefacts, such as statues, *thangka* (scroll paintings) and books that must have been rescued from Stalin's thugs in the late 1930s. The four museum buildings were the 18th-century home of the Tsetseg Khaan, a Mongolian prince who governed most of eastern Mongolia during the Manchu reign. (As you enter the complex, the building on the left holds a portrait of the last Tsetseg Khaan, painted in 1923.) If the museum is closed ask someone at the hut at the back to open it up for you.

The small **Aimag Museum** (☎ 23834; admission T1000; ☼ 9am-1pm & 2-6pm Tue-Sat), north of the park, contains a mastodon tusk, a protoceratops skull, some Chinggis Khaan–era armour and the usual array of stuffed animals, including a saluting bear.

Shadavdarjaliin Khiid, in the western part of town near the Sports Palace, is a lively place with 13 monks. The original monastery in this area was built in 1660 and housed the first Buddhist philosophy school in Mongolia. At its peak, the monastery was home to over 1000 monks. In the spring of 1938, the Stalinist purge reached Khentii and the monks were all arrested. The buildings remained standing until the 1950s, when they were torn down.

A well-preserved Turkic-era **babal** (man stone or 'khunn chuluu'; GPS: N47° 16.722′, E110° 36.098′) is 7km west of Öndörkhaan, past the airport. The squat-figured statue, covered in blue silk *hadak*, has a disproportionately large head with pronounced eyebrows and deep-set eyes. His long hair is curled behind his ears, an unusual feature for this type of statue. Locals refer to the statue as 'Gelen', a religious title. Back in town, look out for the new **Chinggis Khaan statue**, dedicated in 2003, opposite the Government House.

Sleeping

CAMPING

If you want to camp, head south past the wrestling stadium, and walk along the Kherlen Gol to the west until you've found a quiet spot.

EASTERN MONGOLIA

HOTELS

Erdes Hotel (☎ 23007; s/d T5000/10,000, half-lux per person T6500-11,000, lux per person T19,000) Bright, renovated rooms make this the only sensible choice in town. The standard rooms use a shared bathroom but some of the half-lux rooms aren't much more expensive.

Jargalan Hotel (☎ 23722, 9910 2502; per person T5000-8000) Spacious but run-down rooms. The entrance is around the back of Government House.

Ganga Hotel (☎ 22344, 9909 1302; per person T5000) This small hotel, just off the main street, has small, non-attached rooms. They may be open to bargaining.

Eating

Tiger Cafe (☎ 9956 9191; meals T800-1000; ☽ 10am-9pm) Owned by the Khentii governor, this is one of the better places in town. The fried fish is among the more progressive menu items in this part of Mongolia. It's on the 2nd floor of a distinctive green building on the main street.

Erdes Restaurant (☎ 22537, 9956 9090; meals T800-1200; ☽ 9am-midnight) Located next to the hotel of the same name, this popular place has a kitsch Chinggis Khaan VIP room.

Khishig Café (meals T700-1000; ☽ 9am-8pm Mon-Fri, 10am-10pm Sat) Basic but clean café located next to the monastery.

Getting There & Away

AIR

On Wednesday MIAT (Mongolian Airlines) flies to/from Ulaanbaatar, en route from Baruun-Urt, for US$54 one way. Öndörkhaan's airport is 2km west of the city.

HITCHING

Öndörkhaan is the gateway for eastern Mongolia, so all vehicles heading to Dornod aimag and Sükhbaatar aimag will come through here. Getting a lift to Ulaanbaatar, Choibalsan and Baruun-Urt is comparatively easy. Hitching north is far harder. Like most aimag capitals your best bet is to wait at the petrol station, at the eastern edge of town. Alternatively, you could ask the drivers at the jeep stand or on the main street.

MINIVAN & JEEP

Daily jeeps and minibuses go between Ulaanbaatar and Öndörkhaan (T10,000, eight hours, 331km).

Postal trucks run to Dadal (T8820) on Thursday, to Delgerkhaan (T4410) on Friday, to Binder (T6170) on Tuesday and to Batshireet on Wednesday (T9000); they usually leave in the early morning. You could hire your own jeep at the stand, but many private cars also seem to hang around on the main street, near the food market.

Öndörkhaan is 324km southwest of Choibalsan and 229km west of Baruun-Urt. A paved road is being built from Baganuur to Öndörkhaan and the dirt trails further east are in good nick.

DELGERKHAAN ДЭЛГЭРХААН

Despite the historical significance of the area, there's little to actually see in Delgerkhaan, the *sum* capital, though it's an easy enough detour to or from Öndörkhaan.

Locals, and some historians, claim that Avarga, not Karakorum, was the first capital of the Mongolian empire. The ancient city is located on a 20km-wide plain, Khödöö Aral (Countryside Island), so named because the area is encircled by the Kherlen and Tsenkher *gols*.

Sights

The most impressive monument in the area is the **Chinggis Statue** (GPS: N47° 06.157', E109° 09.356'), 13km south of Delgerkhaan village. It was built in 1990 under the sponsorship of Unesco, to commemorate the 750th anniversary of the writing of *The Secret History of the Mongols*. The symbols on the side of the statue are the brands used by about 300 different clans in the area for marking their livestock.

One kilometre east of the statue is the **Avarga Toson Mineral Spring**, from which Ögedei Khaan drank and was cured of a serious stomach ailment. Locals claim the water can cure up to 13 known diseases including ulcers, hepatitis and any pancreatic problems, and acts as a male aphrodisiac (who says the Mongolians don't understand marketing?). The spring is covered by an *ovoo* (a shamanistic collection of stones, wood or other offerings to the gods, usually found in high places), and a pump house has been built near the site. A guard lives in the ger nearby and can open up the pump and sell you a litre of fizzy (slightly foul-smelling) spring water for T100 (bring some water bottles).

Between the statue and the spring lie the underground foundations of the ancient city of **Avarga**. Japanese researchers, using sonar equipment, claim an entire city lies underfoot, including nine temples and a palace. Where the walls and buildings of this 'city' disappeared to is anyone's guess.

About 7km west of the resort, the **Chinggis Khaan Memorial Centre** (GPS: N47° 11.188', E109° 05.416'; admission US$3; ⏲ 9am-sunset) is a kitsch exhibition of Chinggis memorabilia, housed in nine felt gers. The main ger contains a statue of Chinggis, surrounded by some amusing wooden dolls meant to be his top advisors and warriors.

If you've had enough of Chinggis, you can always go for a swim in the tiny lake, **Avarga Toson Nuur**, 4km west of Delgerkhaan.

Sleeping

CAMPING

You can camp anywhere near the lake, though it would help to have your own transport.

GER CAMPS

Khödöö Aral (☎ 011-57 855, 9915 8698; with/without food US$24/10) Run by Ikh Zasag University, it's not a particularly attractive ger camp, but it does have hot showers. It's next to the Chinggis Khaan Memorial Centre.

Avarga Resort (GPS: N47° 10.917', E109° 08.920'; per person/half-lux/lux T5800/9000/11,500) This is the place to come if you have a burning desire to join Mongolian families on holiday. The rather run-down resort offers hot-water baths or you could bury yourself in mud on the shores of the lake. The two small lakes behind the resort are said to contain curative properties. The resort is 4km west of Delgerkhaan.

Getting There & Away & Around

Delgerkhaan is close to the regional centres of Öndörkhaan (124km) and Baganuur (95km). However, there are no flights or public transport to Delgerkhaan or Avarga.

HITCHING

Delgerkhaan is popular with domestic tourists, so asking for a lift at the resort may be your best way out of town during summer. Getting to Delgerkhaan is equally a matter of luck. Some cars (and the Friday postal truck) come here from Öndörkhaan. Cars

from Ulaanbaatar turn off the main road at Erdene, or sometimes turn off at the bridge over the Kherlen Gol, 16km south of Baganuur. There is a road from Tsenkhermandal, but not many cars use it. The best idea is to get off the bus to Öndörkhaan at one of these turn-offs, or try the busier road junction of Jargalthaan. And wait…

JEEP

Chartering a jeep to Delgerkhaan from Ulaanbaatar, Öndörkhaan or Baganuur is easy – you could even go on day trips from the latter two places. You *might* be able to hire a jeep or motorbike to see the local sights around Delgerkhaan.

KHÖKH NUUR ХӨХ НУУР

About 35km northwest of Tsenkhermandal (which is just north of the Ulaanbaatar–Öndörkhaan road), the small **Khökh Nuur** (Blue Lake; GPS: N48° 01.150', E108° 56.450') is said to be where Temujin was crowned Chinggis Khaan in 1206. There is a small plaque that marks the **coronation spot**, which some say was attended by 100,000 soldiers. It's not a required stop on the Chinggis Khaan pilgrimage trail but it provides a nice place to break a jeep trip.

You'll need your own transport and a driver who knows where it is. Someone from nearby **Tsenkhermandal** might take you there by jeep or motorcycle, or you could organise an overnight horse trip if you or your driver/guide has some contacts in the area. The area is sometimes labelled Khar Zurkhen (Black Heart) on maps, which refers to a mountain behind the lake.

A further 30km away is the larger lake of **Khangil Nuur**.

BALDAN BARAIVAN KHIID
БАЛДАН БАРАЙВУН ХИЙД

This **monastery** (GPS: N48° 11.910', E109° 25.840') in Ömnödelger *sum* (district) was first built in 1700. At its peak it was one of the three largest monasteries in Mongolia and home to 5000 lamas. It was destroyed by thugs in the 1930s and by fire in the 1970s. Now only ruins remain.

The monastery is currently being restored by tourist-volunteers under the auspices of the American-based Cultural Restoration Tourism Project (CRTP). The project is due to be completed by 2007. For

details contact the **CRTP** (☎ 415-563 7331; www
.ctrp.net) in the USA.

The monastery is difficult to find on your
own, but most locals can point you in the
right direction (although there aren't many
gers to ask directions at). The area is perfect
for camping but the closest place to stay
is the **Bayangol Ger Camp** (GPS: N46° 09.621', E105°
45.590'; ☎ 9918 3067, 011-451 016; with/without food
US$30/15), 20km to the west.

About 17km past the monastery, on the
way to Binder, are two **deer stones** (GPS: N48°
11.916', E109° 35.712').

ÖGLÖGCHIIN KHEREM
ӨГЛӨГЧИЙН ХЭРЭМ

Literally 'Almsgivers Wall', but also known
as 'Chinggis Khaan's Castle' or 'Red Rock',
this 3.2km-long **stone wall** (GPS: N48° 24.443', E110°
11.812'), believed to date from the 8th century,
stretches around a rocky slope in Binder
sum. Once thought to be a defensive work or
a game preserve, recent archaeological digs
by a Mongolian–American research team
have identified at least 60 ancient graves
within the walls, indicating that it may have
been a royal cemetery. As you walk inside
the grounds you may see small red signs,
marking the location of graves excavated in
2002. The nearby wooden cabins, used by
the researchers, now lie dormant. The site
is 8km west of the road to Binder.

Close to the turn-off to Öglögchin
Kherem is **Rashaan Khad** (GPS: N48° 22.766', E110°
17.950') a huge rock with 20 different (barely
discernable) types of script carved upon
it. About 2km past the turn-off towards
Binder are more **deer stones** (GPS: N48° 25.098',
E110° 17.825').

BINDER & BATSHIREET
БИНДЭР & БАТШИРЭЭТ

At the confluence of the Khurkh and Onon
rivers, the village of **Binder** is a good place to
rest on your way to or from Dadal. There
are a couple of cafés, a **ger camp** (with food US$20)
7km from the village and a small **Chinggis
Khaan monument** 2km east of the village.

Batshireet, 45km northwest, is worth the
detour for some excellent camping, fishing
and horse-riding opportunities. From this
small Buriat community of 3000 souls you
can follow the Eg Gol to the Onon and
trek back to Binder. More challenging trails
lead west towards the **Khan Khentii Strictly**

Protected Area and Burkhan Khaldun (see
following). A seven-day loop in the protected area can also include the **Hot Water
Springs** (Khalun Us Rashaant).

There is good camping in Batshireet; the
best spots are 7km north of town on the Onon
Gol. Otherwise, the basic **Khunt Khas Hotel** (dm
T4000) is by the mayor's office. Camping is also
allowed behind the Protected Areas office.
The information officer, Tsetsegmaa, can arrange horses for a pack trip.

Because it's near Russia, you'll need a
permit for Batshireet from the Border
Protection Office in Ulaanbaatar. Expect a
visit from the police, who will want to see
your permit, original passport and trekking
route. If you've come without a permit you
can probably buy one for T2000 at the police office.

BURKHAN KHALDUUN БУРХАН ХАЛДУУН

This remote mountain, known as God's
Hill, in the Khan Khentii Strictly Protected
Area is one of the sites mooted as the burial
place of Chinggis Khaan. Over 800 burial
sites have been found in the region, though
the main tomb is yet to be found. Whether
or not Chinggis was buried here, *The Secret
History of the Mongols* does describe how
the khaan hid here as a young man and later
returned to give praise to the mountain and
give thanks for his successes.

Because of its auspicious connections,
Mongolians climb the mountain, which is
topped with many **ovoo** (sacred cairns; GPS: N48°
45.430', E109° 00.300'), to gain strength and good
luck. The hill is very remote, in the Khan
Khentii Strictly Protected Area. To get
there, head to Möngönmorit in Töv, then
travel north along the Kherlen Gol. This is
also a great place to reach by horse.

DADAL ДАДАЛ

As written in *The Secret History of the Mongols*, it is now generally accepted that the
great Chinggis was born at the junction of
the Onon and Balj rivers (though his date
of birth is still subject to great conjecture).
The assumed spot is in Dadal *sum*, near the
town of the same name.

Dadal is a gorgeous area of lakes, rivers,
forests and log huts (very few people live
in gers), reminiscent of Siberia, which is
only 25km to the north. Even if you are
not a Chinggisphile, there is no shortage

EASTERN MONGOLIA

CHINGGIS KHAAN STATUE

The statue at Chingissiin Gurvan Nuur is odd, if only because it was built at the time of the communist reign and managed to survive. Construction of the statue was authorised by Tomor-Ochir, a high-ranking member of the Central Committee of the Mongolian Communist Party in 1962. The statue was completed on the 800th anniversary of Chinggis' birth. The monument not only glorified Chinggis Khaan, it was also a response to the Chinese, who had just tried to one-up the Mongolians by constructing a 'Chinggis Khaan mausoleum' in Inner Mongolia (with vague hopes of luring Outer Mongolia back into the Chinese world). Tomor-Ochir was also instrumental in issuing a set of Chinggis Khaan stamps and organising the 1962 Chinggis Khaan symposium. He was considered a loyal communist and an ardent nationalist.

After the statue was finished, Tomor-Ochir was suddenly stripped of his official position. Davaatseren, the man who sculpted the monument, also lost his job and was jailed. Tomor-Ochir was sent to work in a timber mill in Bayankhongor and was then exiled again to Khankh in northern Khövsgöl to work as a customs official. He later became a museum director in Darkhan. In 1985 he was axed to death and the killer was never found.

It is thought that as officials in both Moscow and Ulaanbaatar grew nervous over the rising nationalistic pride in Chinggis Khaan, President Tsedenbal was told to clamp down on all those involved. Why the statue remained, and what exactly happened to those involved with the construction of the statue, remains a mystery.

of scenery to admire and hike around in. It wouldn't be hard to stay here a few days (which may be necessary anyway unless you have rented a jeep). The downside is that it often rains here in summer.

The 415,752-hectare **Onon-Balj National Park**, extending north from the village towards Russia, offers enticing camping spots, fishing holes and chances for spotting wildlife. National park charges will apply if you go hiking north of Dadal.

Information

Dadal is in a sensitive border area so it would be wise to register with the police (T2000). A few years back one British foreign-aid worker accidentally strayed across the border and ended up spending a week in a Russian jail. If you are heading any further out of town, it would also be a good idea to register with the border guards, on the western side of Dadal. Don't expect anyone to speak English.

Sights

About 3.5km north of Dadal village is a collection of hills known as **Deluun Boldog**. On top of one of the hills is a **stone marker** (GPS: N49° 03.158', E111° 38.590'), built in 1990 to commemorate the 750th anniversary of the writing of *The Secret History of the Mongols*. The inscription says that Chinggis Khaan was born here in 1162. Some historians may not

be entirely convinced about the exact date or location of his birth, but it's a great place to come into the world: the scenery and hiking around the valleys and forests are superb.

There's a more impressive **Chinggis Khaan Statue** (see the boxed text, above) in the Gurvan Nuur camp, built in 1962 to commemorate the 800th anniversary of his birth.

About 2.2km west of Deluun Boldog is the **Khajuu Bulag** (GPS: N49° 02.767', E111° 36.865') mineral water springs, where the great man once drank. Take your water bottles and fill them to the brim, because this is the freshest (flowing) spring water you will ever taste. You could also hike up into the hills behind town, where there is a large **ovoo**.

Activities

There are several **hiking** routes out of Dadal. Locals recommend the 30km hike to the junction of the Onon and Balj rivers, or the 45km trek further along the Onon Gol to the gorge at the confluence of the Onon and Agats *gols*. You'll need to inform the border patrol of your itinerary and it would be wise to take a guide (this is not a good place to get lost!). Ask at the ger camps or try to track down an English-speaking local.

Fishing is excellent in the entire Dadal region, with huge taimen growing up to 1.5m in length! Taimen are one of the largest freshwater fish on earth and can be very ferocious.

You should get a fishing permit (T500) from the town hall *(khotiin tov)*.

Sleeping & Eating
CAMPING
This is perfect camping country, so if you have your own tent and food supplies there is no need to stay in a hotel or ger camp. Just walk about 200m in any direction from the village and set up camp.

GER CAMPS
Chinggisiin Gurvan Nuur (Three Lakes; GPS: N49° 02.005', E111° 39.267'; 2-/4-bed cabin per person T6000/5000; meals T1000-1500) This resort has a good location on the shore of a lake about 2km from Dadal village. There are no gers. A good hiking trail starts from the back of the camp.

It's worth trying to track down a local named Dorjsuren, who runs a hostel next to his home. The classic Buriat-style **lodge** (per person about T5000) includes a toilet and hot-water shower block. There's a cast-iron stove for cooking and Dorjsuren can hunt down bread, eggs, milk, cream and vegetables. It is a 10-minute walk southeast of the centre, across the river, but there is no sign, so ask for directions from the Telecom office.

Between Gurvan Nuur and the village, by the monastery, is **Onon** (bed & 3 meals per person around US$30) ger camp, which locals assure us opens in summer, though it always seems to be closed when we visit.

Getting There & Away
AIR
Dadal's airfield, 14km from the village, has recently been improved with the hope that planes may someday fly here again. While this is unlikely, your best bet for info is to check with Aero Mongolia in Ulaanbaatar (see p85).

HITCHING
Getting a lift to Dadal from Ulaanbaatar is a difficult but fun experience. Quite a few vehicles travel between Baganuur, Tsenkhermandal and Ömnödelger daily, so this stretch shouldn't be too difficult. One good place to wait for a ride is the bridge over the **Kherlen Gol** (GPS: N47° 41.619', E108° 27.593'), 16km south of Baganuur, where traffic stops briefly at a checkpoint. There is also a *guanz* (canteen or cheap restaurant) here with basic **accommodation** (per person T5000).

From Ömnödelger (a pleasant village that has wooden huts and a hotel) fewer vehicles travel to Binder, which is another pretty, forested area, from where it's still 108km to Dadal.

Alternatively, you could try to hitch a ride from Öndörkhaan to Norovlin (also known as Ulz), where you can see the remains of the **Wall of Chinggis Khaan**, though traffic along this road is also sparse and there is nowhere to stay along the way.

THE SEARCH FOR CHINGGIS KHAAN'S GRAVE

Mongolians, and some historians, have agreed that the birthplace of Chinggis Khaan is at Deluun Boldog, in northern Khentii aimag – although the date of 1162 is not universally accepted. But where was he buried?

Chinggis' grave is probably in Khentii aimag, and not too far from his birthplace, but the exact location is not known. According to diaries kept by Marco Polo, at the time the Mongols wanted to keep the location of the grave a secret, which they have managed to do to this day. According to legend, the 2000 or so people who attended Chinggis' funeral were killed by 800 soldiers, who were in turn slaughtered themselves – so total secrecy was ensured. It is said that 1000 horsemen trampled the earth over the grave after the burial to conceal its location.

Various expeditions, often with Japanese and American assistance and technology, have failed to shed any light on the mystery. Chinese expeditions claim a site in the Altai region of Xinjiang province. An American expedition concentrates on central Khentii, while the Japanese claim the burial spot is near Delgerkhaan. His tomb may contain millions, if not billions of dollars worth of gold, silver, precious stones and other priceless religious artefacts (as well as many women, men and horses who were buried alive with the khaan), so the search is sure to continue.

However, the vast amount of money spent so far, which could be better used to assist regional development, and the fact that discovery of the grave is against the obvious wishes of Chinggis Khaan himself, has created resentment among many Mongolians.

JEEP

One minivan a day usually goes to Ulaanbaatar (T18,000, 515km). Jeeps take the quicker and more scenic road via Ömnödelger and Binder. The journey takes anywhere from 12 hours up to 35 hours after heavy rains.

A postal truck travels to Öndörkhaan (T8820) every Thursday morning at around 8.30am. Most traffic to Öndörkhaan takes the road via Norovlin, which is on the main road between Öndörkhaan and northern Dornod.

As there are virtually no vehicles available for hire in Dadal, the only option is to ask at the ger camps, which should be able to arrange something for around T250 per km.

Dadal is 254km northeast of Öndörkhaan and 301km northwest of Choibalsan.

GALTAI AGUI ГАЛТАЙ АГУЙ

Seventy kilometres northwest of Dadal is the Galtai Agui, a cave set in some beautiful countryside. It is an amazing 80m deep – apparently the deepest in Mongolia. There are also **healing rocks**, which are rich in shamanic lore, in the area called Tsagaan

Cholor. The cave is very close to the Russian border, hence you should get permission from the border guards (see p158). You'll need a good driver or guide to find it.

DORNOD ДОРНОД

pop 74,400 / area 123,500 sq km

Dornod, which means 'east', is not the most remote aimag in Mongolia, but it probably receives the fewest visitors. If you have the time, and a jeep to cross the vast treeless sparsely populated steppes, there are a few places of interest.

These include Buir Nuur and Khalkhin Gol, both the scenes of fierce fighting against the Japanese; Khökh Nuur, the lowest point in the country; and some lovely natural reserves. If you've already visited other more popular areas of Mongolia, Dornod offers good scope for some offbeat exploration.

The northern *sums* of Bayan Uul, Bayandun and Dashbalbar are home to the Buriats, who still practise shamanism. If you ask around you may be able to meet

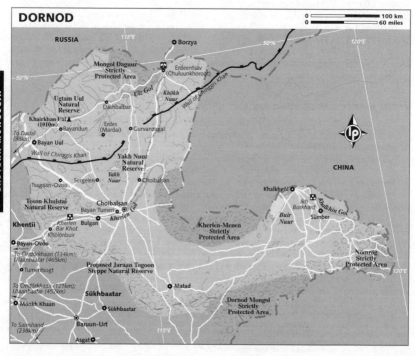

GAZELLE & ANTELOPE

One of the most magnificent sights in Mongolia, especially in the flat eastern provinces, is the thousands of white-tailed gazelle that almost seem to float across the plains. They collect in huge migratory herds that rival those in the Serengeti in Africa.

The wholesale slaughter of these creatures really kicked in during WWII, when 100,000 gazelle and saiga antelope were slaughtered for meat by Russian troops. Illegal poaching continues now at a rate of around 80,000 per year, about one tenth of their entire population. Habitat loss to mining and road construction further puts their numbers at risk.

Antelopes are especially prized by Chinese and Mongolians for meat, skins and their horns: each one fetches from Y70 to Y100 (US$8.50 to US$12).

---

a shaman or, if you are lucky, watch a shamanist ceremony in these areas.

National Parks

Thankfully, authorities have been convinced that the area's fragile environment and endangered fauna and flora need to be conserved. Dornod is currently the base of a multimillion dollar environmental protection project, which is researching everything from fires to field mice in an attempt to protect one of the world's last undisturbed grasslands. The Strictly Protected Areas (SPA) include:

Dornod Mongol (570,374 hectares) Holds one of the last great plain ecosystems on earth, protecting seas of feather-grass steppe and 70% of Mongolia's white-tailed gazelle, which roam in herds of up to 20,000.

Mongol Daguur (103,016 hectares) The reserve is divided into two parts; the northern half is hill steppe and wetland bordering on Russia's Tarij Nuur and Daurski Reserve, protecting endemic species such as the Daurian hedgehog; the southern area along the Ulz Gol protects *tsen togoruu* (white-naped crane) and other endangered birds. The area is part of a 1-million-hectare international reserve, linking the Siberian *taiga* with the inner Asian steppe.

Nömrög (311,205 hectares) An unpopulated area, which contains rare species of moose, cranes, otter and bears. Ecologically distinct from the rest of Mongolia, the area takes in the transition zone from the Eastern Mongolian steppe to the mountains and forest of Manchuria. There is a proposal to expand the park eastwards.

The aimag also has several natural reserves, including Ugtam Uul (46,100 hectares), Yakh Nuur (251,388 hectares) and also Toson Khulstai (469,928 hectares).

CHOIBALSAN ЧОЙБАЛСАН

☎ 01582 / pop 38,800 / elev 747m

Named after the Stalinist stooge Khorloogiin Choibalsan (see the boxed text, p163),

this charmless aimag capital is easily Mongolia's largest (after the autonomous cities of Ulaanbaatar, Darkhan and Erdenet). Centuries ago, the city was a trading centre and part of a caravan route across Central Asia. It grew into a town in the 19th century, and is now the major economic centre for eastern Mongolia.

Choibalsan is a poor city with the highest unemployment rate in Mongolia. From the ruins of many houses, it looks like Choibalsan has suffered a horrendous earthquake. In fact, the Russian buildings were abandoned after 1990 and the bricks, windows, gates and anything useable have been looted to help build new houses in the town's east.

The capital is inhabited by a large number of darker-skinned people, a legacy of centuries of intermarriages between Buriats, Bargas, Uzemchins and Chinese from Inner Mongolia.

Orientation

Although the city is spread out along a narrow 5km corridor north of the Kherlen Gol, most of the facilities needed by visitors are near the Kherlen Hotel. The market is 1.5km east of the main square, about halfway between the town and the train station.

Information

Eastern Mongolia Strictly Protected Areas Office
(☎ 23373; fax 22217; esbp@ magicnet.mn; ☽ 9am-5pm Mon-Fri) Next to the Tovan Hotel, this office has one or two English-speaking staff and can supply information on visiting protected areas in both Dornod and Sükhbaatar aimags. It can also arrange permits and sell tickets to protected areas and nature reserves.

Internet Centre (per hr T500; ☽ 8am-10pm Mon-Fri, 8am-7pm Sat & Sun) Next to the Telecom office, it has a slower connection.

EASTERN MONGOLIA

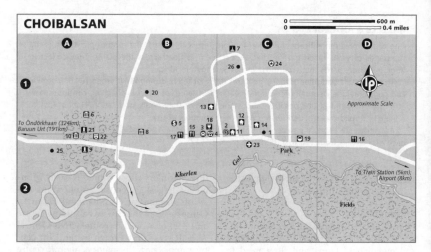

CHOIBALSAN

0 — 600 m
0 — 0.4 miles

Approximate Scale

To Öndörkhaan (324km);
Baruun Urt (?)

To Train Station (5km);
Airport (8km)

Kherlen

Gol

Park

Fields

Library Internet Café (☎ 9958 7290; per hr T500; ☻ 9am-8pm Mon-Fri, 10am-8pm Sat) Good Internet connection located in the public library.

Trade & Development Bank (T&D Bank; ☎ 23009; ☻ 9am-1pm & 2-4.30pm Mon-Fri) Changes dollars, euros, travellers cheques and gives cash advances against Visa and MasterCard.

Telecom Office (☎ 21861; ☻ 24hr) The post office is next door.

Sights

MUSEUMS & MEMORIALS

The **Aimag Museum & Gallery** (☎ 21940; admission T1000; ☻ 10am-7pm Mon-Fri), in the former Government House in the old part of town, is one of the best of its kind outside of Ulaanbaatar. It contains some interesting paintings, fascinating old photos, some Choibalsan memorabilia and a giant bowl, made in 1861, which is large enough to boil mutton for 500 people (the mind boggles, the stomach churns). The aimag map marks the location of the some ruined monasteries.

If you miss the requisite stuffed animals in the Aimag Museum, or simply want to see more, head for the **Natural History Museum** (☻ 10am-7pm Mon-Fri) on the western side of the square. It's free if you've already paid for the Aimag Museum.

The **GK Jukov Museum** (admission T1000) chronicles the war with the Japanese along the Khalkhin Gol in 1939. It's in the ger suburbs, about 1.5km northeast of the Drama Theatre and 200m north of the main road. The caretaker (with the key) lives next door.

Choibalsan's **Mongolian Heroes' Memorial** is one of the more dramatic pieces of Stalinist architecture in Mongolia. It is a large arch with a soldier on horseback charging towards the enemy. A Soviet tank next to the monument adds a quaint reminder of who really was boss.

EASTERN MONGOLIA

DANRIG DANJAALIN KHIID
According to the chief monk, this monastery (Данриг Данжаалин Хийд) was built around 1840 and was once very active. It contained three northern temples and four southern temples, but less than half the 800 monks could be accommodated at one time, so most had to pray outside. It was closed in 1937.

The monastery reopened in 1990 and has two small temples where about 15 monks worship. The monks are particularly friendly; we were warmly welcomed and allowed to watch a ceremony. The monastery is about 400m behind the Kherlen Hotel.

Sleeping
CAMPING
The best place to camp is anywhere south of the main street; walk for a few hundred metres and you will be sharing some great spots along the Kherlen Gol with a few curious cows.

HOTELS
Oilkhon Hotel (☎ 22835; s/d T3000/6000, per person half-lux/lux T9000/18,500) This clean and modern hotel is the best value in town. It is 250m north of the Telecom office.

Kherlen Hotel (☎ 29058; s/d without shower US$10/15, half-lux/lux US$20/30) This friendly hotel,

next to the library, has renovated rooms at slightly inflated prices. When the town has hot water you could use the common shower (T800). The sauna is an additional T2500.

Tovan Hotel (☎ 21551; dm US$5, half-lux s/d US$15/30, lux US$25/50) Rooms are nice and most have a shower and hot water, though it's grossly overpriced. Prices are per person.

Between the Kherlen and the Tovan, a local government office (Tamgiin Gazar) lets out large but somewhat creepy rooms in its annex for T6000 per person.

Eating & Drinking
Nice Café (10am-midnight Mon-Sat) has a pleasant atmosphere, and the pretty good goulash and *khuurag* (fried meat chunks) make this a better choice than the neighbouring Suld and Venera cafés.

Self-caterers can shop for groceries at the inexpensive **market** (9am-7pm) or the more pricey **Khishig Supermarket** (9am-10pm Mon-Fri, noon-7pm Sat), next to the post office. Both the Tovan and the Kherlen hotels have decent restaurants.

Stars Night Club (beer T1400; 7pm-midnight) is one of several nightclubs in Choibalsan; the entrance to this one is around the back of the Telecom building.

KHORLOOGIIN CHOIBALSAN

Choibalsan was born in Dornod aimag, northeast of what is now Choibalsan. A former monk at Gandantegchinlen Khiid and later a great hero of the 1921 revolution, he became Mongolia's leader in 1928, allegedly assassinating rivals in the process. Like his Russian mentor, Joseph Stalin, Choibalsan was ruthless, and is credited with launching the purge in 1937 that cost up to 27,000 lives. The victims, mostly monks, were forced to dig their own graves before being shot in the back of the head. Thousands of others were arrested and sent to Siberian labour prisons. Even after the purge, Choibalsan kept the country in a state of fear. Midnight arrests and executions for anyone suspected of treason continued for decades afterwards.

Although Choibalsan's regime has been heavily criticised by modern Mongolians, he is still surprisingly well regarded because of his efforts to protect Mongolia's independence. In 1945, against Stalin's orders, he launched an attack into Inner Mongolia. It was an attempt to reclaim the lost province during the political vacuum of the Japanese retreat near the end of WWII. The 80,000 Mongolian troops only withdrew after a strong rebuke from the Soviet Union.

Following the war, pressure was mounting for Mongolia to join the USSR. In 1944 Mongolia's northwest neighbour Tannu Tuva gave up its independence and joined the Soviet Union. The Tuvan leader Salchack Toka met Choibalsan and urged him to do the same. Choibalsan is said to have slapped Toka across the face for suggesting so and berated him for giving up Tuva's independence.

Choibalsan died of cancer in 1952, one year before Stalin. While images of Stalin have all but disappeared from Russian streets, statues of Choibalsan remain in Mongolia, and his name is still used for streets, cities and towns.

EASTERN MONGOLIA

Getting There & Away

AIR

Aero Mongolia (☎ 9958 8735) has an office in the Kherlen Hotel building. Aero Mongolia flies between Ulaanbaatar and Choibalsan on Monday, Wednesday and Friday (US$90/158 one way/return). Choibalsan boasts a top-notch runway (by Mongolian standards), the legacy of a large Soviet military base that existed until 1990. The airport is about 8km east of the centre; buses, jeeps and minivans sometimes go there.

HITCHING

Choibalsan is a large city by Mongolian standards, so hitching a ride on a truck or any other vehicle in or out of the city should not be difficult. Hang around the market and keep asking.

MINIVAN & JEEP

Minivans and jeeps run along the good road between Ulaanbaatar and Choibalsan daily (T15,000, 655km), departing UB from the Naran Tuul jeep station. Minivans depart Choibalsan in the morning from the Teeveriin Tovchoo parking lot at the eastern end of town. Daily vans and the odd jeep to Öndörkhaan (T9000, 324km), Baruun-Urt (T6000, 191km) and, less frequently, nearby *sums* such as Bayan Uul (T7000) leave from the same lot or from the market. It's relatively easy to charter a jeep here to visit the national parks and lakes in the aimag.

Postal minivans travel to Sümber (T9900, Wednesday), Matad (T4800, Friday), Dashbalbar (T5600, Monday), Bayandun (T5600, Tuesday) and Bayan Uul (T6200, Tuesday).

The roads in the northern part of Dornod are often buried under mud in late summer, but roads to the other eastern aimag capitals are OK. The border crossing into Russia from Erdeentsav was opened in 2004; get advice before crossing here.

TRAIN

A direct rail line from Choibalsan to Russia was built in 1939 to facilitate the joint Soviet–Mongolian war effort against Japan. It still functions, albeit only twice weekly. As a foreigner, you can go as far as Erdeentsav on the Mongolian side of the border (no permit is apparently required), but the train no longer carries passengers across the border and only travels to Russia to pick up fuel.

The train leaves Choibalsan at 7pm every Monday and Thursday and takes seven hours. The return trip leaves Erdeentsav at 11am on Tuesday and Friday. These times will almost certainly change and you may be told that the train takes only cargo. Call for more info at the **station** (☎ 21502). Tickets cost T2000 for hard seat (the only class). Take food and plenty of water as the carriage can get stiflingly hot during the day.

The train station is about 7km northeast of the centre. You can reach the station by bus, but go early, because close to departure time the buses make a sardine tin look spacious.

ERDES URANIUM MINE

Erdes (known locally as Mardai) was once a unique town in Mongolia. Built in the early 1980s for Russian miners brought in to work in the nearby Russian uranium mine, Mardai resembled a Western suburb – complete with footpaths, front lawns, quaint homes and lots of trees. The Russians wanted uranium for their warheads during the mid-1980s, so output at the mine was expected to hit one million tons a year by the year 2000. Simultaneously the population of Mardai was expected to reach 25,000. Despite its remoteness, the shops were stocked with new supplies from Moscow. The town and mine were kept a state secret until late in 1989 (even today it rarely appears on maps).

With the collapse of the Soviet economy in 1990, money for Mardai ran out. The Russian government pulled out and production stopped. In 1997 a Canadian–Mongolian–Russian consortium announced it would buy the mine, but in 1998 it too pulled out, leaving hundreds of Russians and Mongolians unpaid and unemployed.

By 1999 all the Russians had left and, amid much resentment and despair, the town was slowly stripped by vandals and looters. The Mongolian government assumed control of the mine and soldiers were dispatched to save what was left. It's a ghostly place now, inhabited by around 60 Mongolian families squatting in the hulking concrete remains.

KHERLEN BAR KHOT ХЭРЛЭН БАР ХОТ

Kherlen Bar Khot (GPS: N48° 03.287', E113° 21.865') is the location of some small-scale ruins and a 10m-high tower from a 12th-century city, once part of the ancient state of Kitan. You can see a picture of the tower in the Aimag Museum & Gallery in Choibalsan (p162).

Kherlen Bar Khot is about 90km west of Choibalsan, on the main road between Choibalsan and Öndörkhaan. It is worth a look if you have your own vehicle.

WALL OF CHINGGIS KHAAN
ЧИНГИСИЙН ХЭРЭМ

Stretching over 600km from Khentii aimag to China, and through all of Dornod, are the ruins of the Wall of Chinggis Khaan. This is not promoted by Mongolian tourist authorities because it was not built, or used, by Chinggis Khaan, but almost certainly created by the Manchu to (unsuccessfully) limit frequent raids from rampaging Mongolian hordes.

You will need a guide and jeep to find what little remains from the ravages of vandals and time, though it's doubtful whether it's worth the effort. Locals know it as the Chinggisiin Zam, or Chinggis' Rd, which gives some indication of just how worn down the wall has become. The best place to start looking is about two-thirds the way along the northern road from Choibalsan to the Russian border, near the village of Gurvanzagal (also known as Sümiin Bulag).

UGTAM UUL УГТАМ УУЛ

Ugtam mountain is part of the Ugtam Uul Natural Reserve (46,160 hectares), which also includes the nearby Khairkhan Uul and the ruins of some monasteries, one of which has recently reopened. The park is situated along the Ulz Gol in the northwest of the aimag, about 35km from the village of Bayandun.

KHÖKH NUUR ХӨХ НУУР

The lowest point in Mongolia is Khökh Nuur (Blue Lake), a medium-sized freshwater lake at an altitude of 560m. Other than the thrill of standing in the lowest part of the country, there isn't much to keep you here, though the lake has a subtle beauty and you could combine it with an exploration of the Wall of Chinggis Khaan. The lake is also an important migration point

for birds and you can spot many waders and shore birds here.

Khökh Nuur is visible from the railway line; you can get off the train at a stop near the lake, and then reboard the train the next day in the afternoon. There's no accommodation, so you'll need camping gear and all your food. Otherwise the lake is 45km south (an hour's drive) of **Erdeentsav**, the rail terminus, where you can hire a motorbike or jeep. There is no accommodation in Erdeentsav.

BUIR NUUR БУЙР НУУР

This beautiful lake is the largest in eastern Mongolia (the northern shore is actually in China). The surrounding countryside is mostly grassland, though there are a few trees. The lake has a maximum depth of 50m and, if you're equipped with the proper paraphernalia, is a good place to fish. The area is especially popular with mosquitoes so bring lots of repellent, or you'll need a blood transfusion. A dilapidated Sovietera tourist holiday camp here will probably open its creaking doors if a tourist ever turns up.

The only way to Buir Nuur is by chartered jeep from Choibalsan, 285km away over a flat dirt road, which occasionally gets flooded.

KHALKHYN GOL ХАЛХЫН ГОЛ

The banks of the Khalkhyn Gol, in the far eastern part of Dornod, are of particular interest to war historians because of the battles against the Japanese in 1939. The dry, unpolluted air ensures that most of the relics, which are just lying around, have been well preserved. The region is about a nine-hour drive east of Chibalsan.

Numerous **war memorials** line the banks of the river. The memorials are real socialist masterpieces, built to honour the Russian and Mongolian soldiers who died here. The largest memorial is the 10m-high **Khamar Davaa**. A **museum** in Sümber, and a smaller one in Choibalsan, offer some explanations (in Mongolian) about the history of the battles. Sümber's museum doubles as a **hotel** (per person T2500).

Another interesting site in the region is **Ikh Burkhant**, where there is a huge image of Janraisig (*Avalokitesvara* in Sanskrit) carved into the hillside. The carving was commissioned in 1864 by local regent Bat Ochiriin Togtokhtooriin, or Tovan (*van* means 'lord') and was reconstructed between 1995 and 1997. The carving is right on the roadside, halfway between Sümber and Khalkhgol village.

From here the spectacular but remote **Nömrög Strictly Protected Area** is around 100km southeast. The protected area only receives a handful of visitors each year, but those that go are rewarded with virgin fields and pine forests untouched by livestock or humans.

Permits

Khalkhin Gol is near the Chinese border and a military base and there are three military checks en route from Choibalsan. The border patrol in Choibalsan says you can get a permit at these checkpoints, but it's best to check the situation at the Eastern Mongolia Strictly Protected Areas office (p161).

It is possible that you'll need two permits: one at the checkpoints on the way to Khalkhin Gol (which shouldn't cost more than T1000) and probably one more if you are going to Nömrög (this one could cost T10,000 to T25,000).

The permit given at Sümber (for Nömrög) may be fake (ie some guards there sell fake permits and keep the money for themselves). If you have a border permit from the border office in Ulaanbaatar (which should be free) you could probably get past the border guards at Sümber, without risking having to buy a phoney permit.

WAR AT KHALKHIN GOL

After the Japanese moved into northeast China in 1931 to create the puppet state of Manchukuo, hundreds of thousands of Soviet troops moved into Dornod, along with 80,000 Mongolian soldiers. When the Japanese attacked the banks of the Khalkhin Gol in May 1939, the Russians were ready.

By September 1939 the tally was 61,000 Japanese, 10,000 Russians and over 1000 Mongolians killed, wounded or captured in battles involving tanks, bombers and ground troops. War historians believe the result probably prompted the Japanese generals to change their strategies, avoid further war with Russia, and concentrate on eastern Asia and the Pacific.

SÜKHBAATAR
СУХБААТАР

pop 56,400 / area 82,000 sq km

At the eastern edge of the Gobi Desert, Sükhbaatar aimag is almost pure grassland steppe, with no forests at all and only a few hills masquerading as mountains. The sparsely populated aimag is named after Sükhbaatar, the canonised hero of the communist revolution of 1921. Sükhbaatar did not actually live in this part of the country, it was his father who came from here. Ethnic groups residing here are the Khalkh, Dariganga and the Uzemchin.

The best thing about the aimag is the far southeastern region, known as Dariganga, and the nearby mountain, Shiliin Bogd Uul. Both are definitely worth a visit, but getting there will involve some effort.

BARUUN-URT БАРУУН-УРТ

☎ 01512 / **pop 14,300** / **elev 981m**

Baruun-Urt is a scruffy, dusty and sometimes rowdy town in the middle of absolutely nowhere. Most people live in large ugly apartment blocks and work in a new Chinese-invested zinc mine, or in a coal mine 7km to the northwest. The water in Baruun-Urt has high levels of sulphur so you are better off buying bottled water or filtering the tap water. Some maps refer to the town as Sükhbaatar, which is confusing because this is the name of a town to the east (see map).

Information

Anod Bank (☎ 22177; ☼ 9am-4.30pm Mon-Fri) Changes US dollars.

Internet Café (per hr T460; ☼ 8am-9pm Mon-Fri, 10am-3pm Sat & Sun) Inside the Telecom office.

Government House (City Square) Ask for the latest information about permits to border areas here.

Khaan Bank (☎ 21036; ☼ 8am-noon, 3-5pm Mon-Fri) Changes US dollars.

Post Bank (☎ 21034; ☼ 8am-noon & 1-5pm Mon-Fri) Also changes US dollars.

Telecom Office (☎ 21030; ☼ 24hr) The post office is also here.

Sights
MUSEUM

If you are stuck in Baruun-Urt, the **museum** (☎ 21486; admission T500; ☼ 8.30am-4.30pm) in the

SÜKHBAATAR

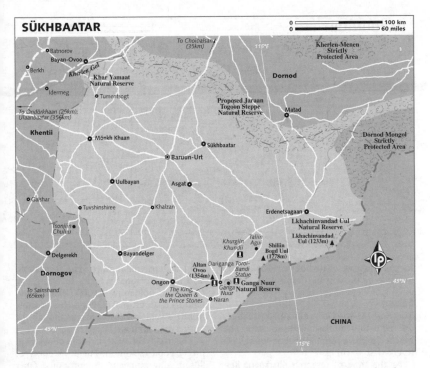

0 — 100 km
0 — 60 miles

To Choibalsan (35km)

115°E

Kherlen-Menen Strictly Protected Area

Batnorov
Bayan-Ovoo
Berkh

Kherlen Gol

Khar Yamaat Natural Reserve

Idermeg

Tumentsogt

Dornod

To Öndörkhaan (25km); Ulaanbaatar (356km)

Proposed Jaraan Togoon Steppe Natural Reserve

Matad

Khentii

Mönkh Khaan

Sükhbaatar

Dornod Mongol Strictly Protected Area

Baruun-Urt

Uulbayan

Asgat

Galshar

Tuvshinshiree

Khalzan

Erdenetsagaan

Lkhachinvandad Uul Natural Reserve

Tsonjin Chuluu

Khurgiin Khundii

Taliin Agui

Shiliin Bogd Uul (1778m)

Lkhachinvandad Uul (1233m)

Delgerekh

Bayandelger

Dornogov

Altan Ovoo (1354m)

Dariganga Toroi-Bandi Statue

To Sainshand (65km)

Ongon

The King, the Queen & the Prince Stones

Ganga Nuur

Ganga Nuur Natural Reserve

Naran

45°N

45°N

CHINA

115°E

dusty southern part of town is worth a look. It has a reasonable collection of costumes representing the three ethnic groups that inhabit the region: the majority Khalkh, Dariganga (30,000 live in the south of Sükhbaatar aimag) and Uzemchin (about 2000 live in Dornod aimag and Sükhbaatar aimag). Look out for the brass-studded Uzemchin wrestling jacket.

There are also fine examples of products from Dariganga's renowned silversmiths and blacksmiths, some stuffed gazelle (which is probably about as close as you will ever get to one), a map showing the locations of the 'man' and 'woman' *balbal* (stone figures believed to be Turkic grave markers) in the aimag, and some Sükhbaatar memorabilia.

ERDENEMANDAL KHIID

According to the monks at the monastery, Erdenemandal Khiid (Эрдэнэмандал Хийд) was originally built in 1830, about 20km from the present site. At the height of its splendour, there were seven temples and 1000 monks in residence, but the Stalinist purges

of 1938 had the same result as elsewhere. The monastery is about 200m west of the square.

Sleeping

CAMPING

Baruun-Urt is the only aimag capital where camping is not a good idea. The town is in the middle of dusty plains and there is no river nearby. The only passable option is by a creek in the northeast of town.

HOTELS

Sharga Hotel (☎ 21101; s/d/half-lux/4-bed lux T10,000/ 20,000/25,000/30,000) Next to the town square, this place has passable standard rooms and better deluxe rooms with sitting room, TV and private bathroom (but no hot water).

Ganga Hotel (☎ 21212; s/lux/d T4000/6000/8000) The rooms here are much cheaper than the Sharga, but you'll have to wait for the caretaker to find the owner, who keeps the keys. It's in a crimson building about a 10-minute walk northeast of the centre.

You can try the **Zotol Hotel** (☎ 9909 9515), across the square from Sharga Hotel; it was

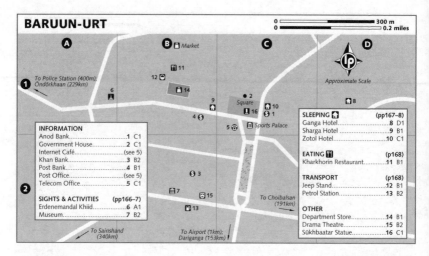

locked when we visited but is reckoned by locals to be the best in town.

Eating

The *guanz* in the Government House doles up regulation goulash with aplomb. The hotels also have restaurants but you'll have to give fair warning.

At the time of research **Kharkhorin Restaurant** (dishes T600-800; 9am-8pm Sun-Fri) was the only place in town that qualified as a restaurant, although the Zotol may be OK if it unlocks its doors. It's unlikely you'll be in town long enough to try both.

Getting There & Away

AIR

MIAT has flights to and from Ulaanbaatar every Wednesday for US$82/144, normally stopping in Öndörkhaan en route. The airport is 1km south of town.

HITCHING

This is difficult because few vehicles come here. Still, with some patience you'll get a lift to Choibalsan, Öndörkhaan, Dariganga and even Zamyn-Üüd. In Baruun-Urt, ask around at the jeep stand or the petrol station.

JEEP & MINIVAN

Shared jeeps and minivans leave Ulaanbaatar daily (T15,000, 560km) from the Naran Tuul jeep station. From Baruun-Urt, vehicles wait at a small jeep stand be-

hind a department store. The jeep stand also has occasional vehicles to Dariganga (T5000), Choibalsan (T6000, 191km) and Öndörkhaan (T7000, 229km). It's possible to hire a vehicle (T250 per km) though the options are limited.

The roads in eastern Mongolia are in pretty good condition, but the scenery in Sükhbaatar aimag is monotonous. Only the sight of thousands of gazelles galloping across the steppes can liven up a dull trip.

SÜKHBAATAR TOWN СУХБААТАР

This small *sum* centre is 48km east of Baruun-Urt. It's is not worth a trip in its own right but if you are passing through on your way to Dornod, there is an excellent museum dedicated to D Sükhbaatar. Exhibits include printing-press implements used by Sükhbaatar during his days as a typesetter in an Ulaanbaatar printing house. To get inside, you'll need to ask Mr Batjargal, a music teacher at the nearby elementary school, for the keys.

DARIGANGA ДАРЬГАНГА

Dariganga *sum* in the southeast of Sükhbaatar is by far the most interesting place in the aimag to visit. Famous for its silversmiths and blacksmiths, friendly Dariganga is also where the sand dunes of the Gobi and the grassy plains of the northern steppe converge to create what looks like thousands of hectares of perfect natural golf courses – but don't let any developer know!

To reach the sights in the area you will need a jeep and a good driver or guide. It's the only way to get to Dariganga village, and then to explore the lakes, volcanoes, mountains, sand dunes and ancient stones nearby. The sacred mountain of Shiliin Bogd is also not too far away.

Information

At the time of writing no permit was needed for Dariganga or Shiliin Bogd, despite their proximity to the Chinese border. Border permits have been required in the past so this could just be a lull in the action. Ask for the latest information at the Government House in Baruun-Urt or if you are in Choibalsan, at the Eastern Mongolia Strictly Protected Areas office (p161). If you are coming from Dornod you shouldn't have any trouble getting to Shiliin Bogd and on to Dariganga; this allows you to travel directly from the Khalkh Gol area and Dornod Mongol SPA, bypassing Choibalsan and Baruun-Urt.

Sights

The skyline of Dariganga is dominated by **Altan Ovoo** (Golden Ovoo), a wide former crater topped by a new **stupa**, which only men are allowed to visit. The stupa was built in 1990 on top of the ruins of the original Bat Tsagaan stupa, which was built in 1820 and destroyed in 1937.

In the area around Dariganga, there are dozens of broken *balbal* – mostly dating back to the 13th- or 14th-century Mongol period, although some are earlier. According to tradition, you should place an offering of food in the cup held in the statue's left hand. There are also three *balbals*, known as the **king, the queen and the prince** (GPS: N45° 18.540', E113° 51.224'), on the northern edge of town, near some hay sheds. In the village itself, you can visit the welcoming **Ovoon Monastery** (Овоон Хийд) which was built in 1990 and is served by three monks.

There are six lakes in the vicinity of Dariganga; all are part of the 28,000-hectare Ganga Nuur Natural Reserve. The three main lakes, Kholboo Nuur, Tsagaan Nuur and Ganga Nuur, are good for swimming, though a bit muddy.

The magnificent **Ganga Nuur** (Ганга Нуур; GPS: N45° 15.994', E113° 59.874') is about 13km southeast of Dariganga. From the end of Septem-

ber until mid-October, the lake is home to thousands of migrating swans. Along the shore, in a fenced compound, is delicious and safe spring water. Entry to the lake is T1000 per person and T500 per car (but you can park your car by the gate and walk).

The sand dunes in the region are known as **Moltsog Els** (Молцог Элс) and stretch for 20km, coming to within walking distance of Dariganga.

Sleeping

Dariganga has three ger camps, about 1.5km south of the village. There is little to differentiate the Dagshin Amaralt, the Zigistei Nuur and the Ovor Khurem ger camps, which all have ger accommodation and basic facilities for about T3000 per person. We preferred the Dagshin Amaralt, the middle of the three camps, if only for the breakfast of bread and *urum* (cream) served to us by the friendly caretaker.

There is nothing stopping you camping anywhere you want as long as you stay away from the ger camps. If you have a vehicle, camp on the shores of Ganga Nuur.

Shopping

Dariganga is renowned throughout Mongolia for the kettles, plates, jewellery and other products made by its blacksmiths and silversmiths. Examples of their excellent work can be seen in the museum in Baruun-Urt. There are only a couple of craftsmen left but they are easily found and can produce handmade jewellery for you to take home. Ask for Mr Bat-Khural who lives in a ger in the southeastern part of town. If you want extensive work done, bring your own silver from Ulaanbaatar as supplies are limited in Dariganga.

Dariganga has a few basic shops on the main road, alongside two or three *tsainii gazar* (tea houses/cafés).

Getting There & Away

The occasional chartered tourist flight comes to Dariganga but you'll be lucky to get on it.

Your best bet is to look out for the occasional shared jeep (T5000) that connects Dariganga with Baruun-Urt (four hours). A postal truck runs every Thursday from Baruun-Urt; ask the post office for timings.

One or two jeeps and even motorbikes are available for charter in Dariganga.

EASTERN MONGOLIA

Travellers report being able to hire horses through one of the ger camps.

SHILIIN BOGD UUL ШИЛИЙН БОГД УУЛ

At 1778m, **Shiliin Bogd Uul** (GPS: N45° 28.350', E114° 35.349'), about 70km east of Dariganga, is the highest peak in Sükhbaatar aimag. The extinct volcano is sacred to many Mongolians: the spirit of any man (and man only!) who climbs it, especially at sunrise, will be revived. The region is stunning, isolated and close to the Chinese border – so be careful.

A jeep can drive about halfway up the mountain, and then it's a short, but blustery, walk to the top. There are plenty of *ovoos* and awesome views of craters all around. About 3km to the south, the fire break that squiggles into the distance is border with China. If you are camping, Shiliin Bogd offers one of the greatest sunrises in a country full of great sunrises.

On the road between Dariganga and Shiliin Bogd, 8km past Ganga Nuur, look out for the new statue of **Toroi-Bandi** (GPS: N45° 17.308', E114° 04.466'), the Robin Hood of Mongolia, who had a habit of stealing the horses of the local Manchurian rulers, then eluding them by hiding near Shiliin Bogd Uul. The statue, dedicated in 1999, pointedly faces China.

The only two roads to Shiliin Bogd start from Erdenetsagaan (70km) and Dariganga (70km). It's better to go to Dariganga first, where you are more likely to find a jeep for rent or a lift.

MILLENNIUM ROAD

Mongolia's road network, little more than a series of dirt tracks that squiggle haphazardly across the plains, is taking a great leap forward. The Millennium Road project, launched by the Mongolian government in 2000, envisions a paved road running the length of the country, from Dornod to Bayan-Ölgii, plus several north–south roads, including one alongside the Trans-Mongolia railway line.

Defenders of the controversial project compare it to America's interstate system of the 1950s or Germany's autobahn, and claim boosts in trade and tourism. Builders point out that one road will reduce land degradation as drivers will end the practice of creating multiple tracks across the steppe. But a cash deficit has slowed progress and political opponents say it's called the Millennium Road because it will take 1000 years to build.

Around 20% of the 2640km road has already been constructed, mostly with loans from international lenders and far-flung countries such as Kuwait, whose royal family imports Mongolian falcons en masse.

Conservationists and economists discredit the road as a waste of time and money, saying it goes from nowhere to nowhere. (The current proposal seeks to end the road on a remote plain near the village of Sümber, hundreds of kilometres from the nearest urban area.) They argue that the money would be better spent on building roads and infrastructure in sprawling Ulaanbaatar.

There is some credibility in the dissent, particularly in Dornod aimag, where plans show the road east of Choibalsan cutting into important gazelle migration routes and heading towards an oil field at Tamsagbulag.

Mining companies, oil men, cashmere traders, marmot-skin smugglers and gazelle poachers (both Chinese and Mongolian) may enjoy the benefits of the proposed route, but biologists would prefer to keep this pristine wilderness, and the gazelle migration route, untouched. An alternative route northeast of Choibalsan, favoured by conservationists, has so far been overlooked by developers.

The situation was rather unclear at the time of writing. In 2004, the Ministry of Nature and Environment had rejected feeble environmental reports on this section of the road and talks with donor agencies had stalled on whether or not to extend the highway though the sensitive Nömrög Strictly Protected Area.

Special interest groups, conservationists, politicians and economists (not to mention local herders, traders, and border-guard generals) remain locked in battle over the Millennium Road's eastern terminus. But if the project procedes in its current ill-planned manner, it could be a knock-out punch for the majestic gazelle, a species already threatened by hunting and poaching.

AROUND SHILIIN BOGD UUL

Assuming that you have a jeep to get to Shiliin Bogd Uul in the first place, you can make a good loop from Dariganga, to take in Ganga Nuur on the way to Shiliin Bogd Uul, and Taliin Agui and Khurgiin Khundii on the way back to Dariganga.

Taliin Agui (Талын Агуй; GPS: N45° 35.405′, E114° 30.051′), 15km northwest of the mountain, is one of the largest caves in Mongolia. If the ice covering the entrance has melted (it's normally covered until August) you can squeeze through the narrow entrance. The large, icy cavern has three chambers to explore (the back wall looks like a dead end but you can squeeze under the overhang). You'll need a torch (flashlight) to see anything, and be careful on the slippery floor.

Khurgiin Khundii (Хургийн Хөндий; GPS: N45° 33.165′, E114° 13.970′), a pretty valley 40km west of Shiliin Bogd Uul, once contained seven stone statues that date back to the 13th or 14th century (only three statues can be found today). Although there are various legends to describe the origins of the stones, the most prominent recalls a certain khaan who, on a hunting trip, drove a herd of gazelle over a cliff, killing hundreds of them. Angered by this senseless slaughter, the sky god (Tenger) struck down the king's family members with disease and natural calamity. The statues in Khurgiin Khundii were erected in memory of the king and his family, and as a reminder for people to respect nature. Because the valley is considered to be haunted by the ghosts of the royal family, herders do not put their gers here. You will have to rely on your driver to find the statues and to locate **Bichigtiin Khavtsal** (Бичигтийн хавцал), a pretty canyon about 2km away.

LKHACHINVANDAD UUL NATURAL RESERVE ЛХАЧИНВАНДАД УУЛ

If you are visiting Shiliin Bogd by jeep, you may wish to carry on east for another 120km to the 58,500-hectare Lkhachinvandad Uul Natural Reserve, on the border with China. This reserve contains Lkhachinvandad Uul (1233m) and is full of **gazelle** and **elk**. Access is through the town of Erdenetsagaan, where there is a basic hotel.

The Gobi

CONTENTS

'Only a fool crosses the great Gobi without misgivings.'

Mildred Cable, Gobi traveller, 1926

There is a terrific bleakness about the Gobi that few places on Earth can rival. The cruel landscape of bone-dry plains, salt lakes and sandy wastes has been plaguing travellers for centuries, but, somehow, the Mongols have made a home of it.

In centuries past the Gobi was mainly the domain of brigands. In more recent decades the two-humped Bactrian camel, and its valuable wool, has taken over the economy. But new trades, namely mining and tourism, are diversifying the economy. The massive Oyu Tolgoi copper mine, in Ömnögov, is on everyone's lips as Mongolia's great economic saviour.

While most envision the Gobi as endless sand dunes, dunes cover just 3% of the landscape. The Gobi, which literally means 'desert', consists mainly of stony plains, rugged treeless mountains and scrubland. It is still one of the least populated regions on Earth, with less than 0.5 people per square kilometre. The spectacular scenery should be enough to entice visitors, but another reason to come is to follow in the footsteps of Roy Chapman Andrews, whose expeditions to the Gobi in the 1920s uncovered a wealth of dinosaur bones and scientific findings.

The Gobi aimags (provinces) of Bayankhongor, Dornogov, Dundgov, Gov-Altai and Ömnögov are surprisingly alive with wildlife. You will see thousands of wild and domesticated camels, cranes, hawks and gazelles. It's awe-inspiring territory but transportation and infrastructure are sparse and distances great. Water is scarce but gers (traditional felt yurts) are a sure sign of a spring or well. If the spring or well has a trough, fill it with water; by evening, parched gazelles and camels will come out of nowhere looking for water – a great sight.

HIGHLIGHTS

- Explore the caves and climb the boulders at magical **Baga Gazrin Chuluu** (p177)
- Hike though the dramatic **Yolyn Am** (p190), a remarkable desert gorge that contains ice for most of the year
- Scramble up and slide down the dunes at **Khongoryn Els** (p191), perfect for camel riding
- Get lost in the **Bayangovi area** (p195), a forbidding landscape of colourful canyons and rocky escarpments
- Hike up the remote but stunning **Eej Khairkhan** (p198), Mongolia's version of Uluru (Ayer's Rock)

Eej Khairkhan ★
Baga Gazrin Chuluu ★
Bayangovi ★
Khongoryn Els ★
★ Yolyn Am

THE GOBI

- POPULATION: 293,900
- AREA: 612,000 SQ KM

Climate

While daytime temperatures in summer can range from pleasant to stifling hot, nights are almost always cold, so take a sleeping bag. Dust storms can rock the region at any time but are especially common in April and May. The tourist season lasts longer here than northern areas; even October is not too late to see the sights. By December the desert will be blanketed by snow and daily maximum temperatures will fall to -15°C.

Getting There & Away

There is plenty of public and private transport heading from Ulaanbaatar to all the Gobi aimag capitals, so it's easy enough to reach Altai, Bayankhongor, Mandalgov, Sainshand and Dalanzadgad. You can fly to all of these cities, with the exception of Sainshand, which is on the main railway line. If you are travelling on local trains in China, it's possible to enter Mongolia at Dornogov aimag, get a ride with a jeep in Zamyn Üüd or Sainshand, and head straight across the desert to Dalanzadgad. There is little infrastructure in Dornogov to organise a proper Gobi tour, though, so it's best to contact a tour operator in Ulaanbaatar that can send a jeep, driver and (at the very least) a guide to meet you when you get off the train.

Getting Around

Gobi infrastructure is almost nonexistent, but the lack of roads does not prevent vehicles from getting around. On the contrary, the rock-hard jeep trails are the best in the country and along main routes it's possible for jeeps to reach speeds of 100km/h. But breakdowns in the Gobi can be deadly.

Travel in this region is serious business and you shouldn't think of setting off without a reliable jeep and driver, plenty of water and supplies, and a good sense of direction. A map and a GPS unit would not go astray if your driver is inexperienced. Hitchhiking is not recommended, though we have mentioned instances in this chapter when it might be possible. Otherwise, there are few vehicles and a breakdown can leave you stranded for days.

DUNDGOV ДУНДГОВЬ

pop 50,500 / area 78,000 sq km

Dundgov (Middle Gobi) consists of flat, dry plains, occasional deserts, rock formations and little else. The northern part of Dundgov is relatively green, but the southern and eastern areas are mostly bone-dry. The aimag was hit harder than any other during the *zud* (severe winter) years of 1999–2002, when drought and heavy snowfall was exacerbated by a plague of voles that devoured huge areas of grassland. Around half of Dundgov's livestock perished.

Dotted around Dundgov (and Arkhangai aimag) are hundreds of ancient graves of re-

---

THE GOBI DESERT

Stretching from the southern Khovd aimag to the Dariganga region in Sükhbaatar, and including parts of northern China, the Gobi covers a third of Mongolia. Fossil finds have revealed that the Gobi basin was once part of a large inland sea, though some Mongolians will tell you that the Gobi was formed by the trampling of Chinggis Khaan's army.

Contrary to common preconceptions, most of the Gobi consists of stony, scrubby wasteland: sandy dunes only cover about 3% of the Gobi. The word *gobi* simply means 'desert' in the Mongolian language, but Mongolians actually differentiate between 33 types of desert.

The Gobi is a land of extremes: decent rain only falls every two or three years; it can be well over 40°C during the summer, and below -40°C in winter; and storms of dust and sand are fearsome in spring. The few lakes that exist are in constant threat of dying up but springs and wells continue to provide vital water.

The Gobi is understandably very sparsely populated, but the desolate landscape is home to gazelle, *khulan* (wild ass), Bactrian two-humped camels, *takhi* (the Mongolian wild horse), rare saiga antelope and the world's only desert bear – the Gobi bear, of which there are only 25 left in the wild. The appropriately named desert warbler and saxaul sparrow hide in saxaul (*zag* in Mongolian), a stubby shrub that produces wood so dense that it sinks in water. For a detailed account of this mystical desert, read John Man's *Gobi: Tracking the Desert*.

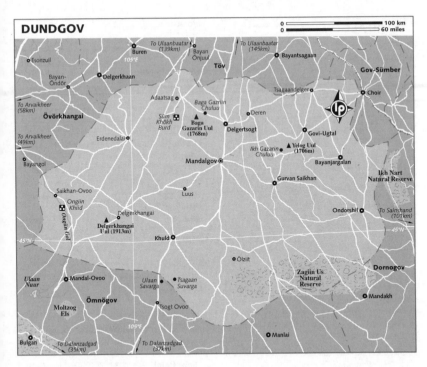

DUNDGOV

0 ——————————— 100 km
0 ——————————— 60 miles

vered Mongolian warriors. Little is known about these graves, but they probably predate Chinggis Khaan. The graves are about 3m deep and often contain gold and bronze, but are sacred and therefore left untouched. They are identifiable by an unnatural collection of large rocks on a small hump.

The advantages of travelling around Dundgov are its proximity to Ulaanbaatar, the good network of jeep trails and the flat ground that makes it easy to get around. Most visitors, however, ignore Dundgov and fly or drive straight through to the more developed and tourist-oriented Ömnögov aimag. If you are travelling overland to Ömnögov, it is worth taking the road via Erdenedalai, rather than directly to Dundgov's capital, Mandalgov.

MANDALGOV МАНДАЛГОВЬ
☎ 01592 / pop 14,000 / elev 1427m

Mandalgov came into existence in 1942, when the town consisted of just 40 gers. Today, it's a sleepy town that offers the usual amenities for an aimag capital: an airport, a hotel, a monastery, a museum and a few shops. A walk to the top of Mandalin Khar Ovoo, just north of the town centre, affords sweeping views of the bleak terrain. There is more to see in western Dundgov, but Mandalgov is a useful stopoff on the way to Dalanzadgad in Ömnögov.

Information
Internet Café (per hr T480; ⊙ 9am-6pm Mon-Fri) In the Telecom office.
Khan Bank (☎ 23881; ⊙ 9am-noon & 1-6pm Mon-Fri) Can change US dollars and give a cash advance on Visa or MasterCard.
Telecom Office (☎ 21212; ⊙ 24hr) The post office is also located here.

Sights
AIMAG MUSEUM
The renovated **Aimag Museum** (☎ 23690; Buyan Emekhiin Gudamj; admission US$1; ⊙ 9am-6pm) is divided into two main sections: a natural history section and a more interesting ethnography and history section. Among the displays is a bronze Buddha made by Zanabazar (see the boxed text, p130). There's also a collection of priceless *thangka* (scroll

THE GOBI

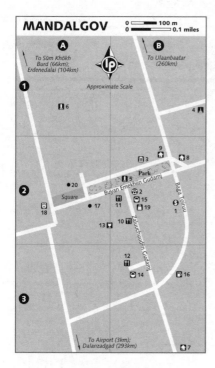

paintings), old flintlock rifles, bronze arrowheads, silver snuffboxes, pipes, and chess sets carved out of ivory.

DASHGIMPELIIN KHIID
In 1936 there were 53 temples in Dundgov. A year later, nearly all were reduced to ashes and rubble by the Mongolian KGB. In 1991 Dashgimpeliin Khiid (Дашгимпэлийн Хийд) was opened to serve the people of Mandalgov.

Faulty wiring caused a fire in June 2004 but within two months funds were raised for a new temple next door. The monastery is now served by 30 monks and services are held most mornings from 10am. It's 450m northeast of the Lenin statue.

Sleeping
Like other Gobi aimag capitals, Mandalgov has no great camping spots; the city has no river, and it's flat and dusty. Perhaps walk north of town and find somewhere past Mandalin Khar Ovoo or the monastery.

Mandal Hotel (☎ 22100; Buyan Emekhiin Gudamj; dm/half-lux T3000/4000) This place is a bit run-

down but offers good-value rooms. The half-lux room, with bathroom, is probably the best deal in town. Prices are per person.

Gobi Hotel (☎ 22137; Buyan Emekhiin Gudamj; dm US$5-6, half-lux/lux per person US$8/10) The foreigner-priced rooms are clean and fairly comfortable, though the Mandal is still a better deal unless you are really craving a hot shower. There's an excellent restaurant downstairs.

Builder's Hotel (☎ 22267, 9909 7765; Zaluuchidiin Gudamj; dm/s/d US$6/8/16, half-lux/lux US$12/15) It's a clean, monstrous and terribly overpriced hotel in the south of town.

Eating & Drinking
Mandalgov's café scene is a bit behind the times, but the restaurant in the Gobi Hotel (see earlier) has good *chinjuurte khuurag* (meat and pepper) or *moogtei khuurag* (meat and mushroom) dishes, plus much-needed cold beer.

Delgerkhangai Restaurant (Zaluuchidiin Gudamj; 🕙 10am-7pm Mon-Sat) A canteen-style place that slops up decent goulash, salad and soup out of huge steel vats.

Gobiin Chonos Bar (🕙 11am-11pm Mon-Sat) This place serves up *tsuivan* (fried flat noodles with meat) for T700, but mostly as a chaser for its draught beer.

Self-caterers can pick up food items at the local market or **Gandalai Supermarket** (Buyan Emekhiin Gudamj; 10am-10pm) on the main street.

Getting There & Away
AIR
MIAT flies between Mandalgov and Ulaanbaatar every Tuesday, en route to Dalanzadgad. Tickets are comparatively cheap (US$41), but the flights are a bit unreliable as Mandalgov is only a transit stop, and few people travel here. It might be possible to get on the plane at Mandalgov for the second leg to Dalanzadgad (US$48), though there's a risk that you'll get bumped if there are no seats. The airport at Mandalgov is 3km south of the city.

HITCHING
As the main road from Ulaanbaatar to Dalanzadgad goes through Mandalgov, hitching is the major form of transport to either place. Getting to Ulaanbaatar or Dalanzadgad on a truck, or another type of vehicle, won't take too long if you are prepared to ask around at the market and wait a while.

JEEP & MINIVAN
Mandalgov is a poor city and finding a jeep to charter will create a headache – Dalanzadgad is a far better place to look. Daily share jeeps to Ulaanbaatar (T11,000, six hours) and Choir (T8000, four hours) leave when full from the jeep stand outside the Telecom office. You're unlikely to find a share jeep to Dalanzadgad (T11,000, six hours), but Dalanzadgad-bound jeeps coming from Ulaanbaatar might be able to squeeze you in. Wait for these at the petrol station in the south of town. The jeep stand outside the market is another place to look.

BAGA GAZRIN CHULUU
БАГА ГАЗРЫН ЧУЛУУ
This granite rock formation in the middle of the dusty plains sheltered Zanabazar during conflicts between the Khalkh and Oirat Mongols. Later it was home to two 19th-century monks who left **rock drawings** in the area. The rocks are worshipped by locals who sometimes make pilgrimages here. Naturally, there is a legend that Chinggis Khaan grazed his horses here.

Five kilometres away, the highest peak in the area, **Baga Gazrin Uul** (1768m), will take about five hours to climb. The mountain also contains a **cave** with an underground lake. The **mineral water springs** and trees in the region make it a great spot to camp, and there are plenty of rocky hills, topped by *ovoo* (sacred pyramid-shaped collections of stone and wood), to explore.

The **Bayan Bulag ger camp** (GPS: N46° 13.827', E106° 04.192'; 9989 8338; with/without meals US$27/15) is one of the Gobi's more attractive ger camps and it offers good food and hot showers.

Baga Gazrin Chuluu is in a very remote area, about 60km to the northwest of Mandalgov, and about 21km east of Süm Khökh Burd. Although not an official protected area, you may encounter a local ranger who charges a dubious T3000 entry fee.

SÜM KHÖKH BURD СУМ ХӨХ БУРД
The temple **Süm Khökh Burd** (GPS: N46° 09.621', E105° 45.590'), which sits on an island in the middle of a tiny lake, was built in the 10th century. Remarkably, the temple was built from rocks that can only be found over 300km away. It was abandoned and in ruins a few centuries after being built.

Three hundred years ago, a **palace** was built here, and 150 years later, the writer Danzan Ravjaa (p182) built a stage on top of the ruins. Enough of the temple and palace remain to give you some idea of what a magnificent place it once must have been.

The lake itself, **Sangiin Dalai Nuur**, only encircles the palace after heavy rains; most of the time you can skip over a rock pathway to the palace (take off your shoes for the slog through the muddy bits). There is good bird-watching here; various species of eagles, geese and swans come to this spring-fed lake in summer and autumn.

There is no shortage of camping spots in the area. There is also a small, scruffy hotel with **ger accommodation** (ger bed T5000, hotel bed T8000) and a restaurant, but you'll find nicer ger camps in Baga Gazrin Chuluu. Prices are per person.

The temple is 72km east of Erdenedalai, 65km northwest of Mandalgov and 21km west of Baga Gazrin Chuluu. You will need an experienced driver to find it. There is no hope of getting here on public transport or by hitching.

THE GOBI

ERDENEDALAI ЭРДЭНЭДАЛАЙ

This sometime camel-herding community in the middle of nowhere, 114km northwest of Mandalgov, is a good place for to refuel before visiting nearby attractions if you have your own vehicle. Erdenedalai is also a useful halfway stop between Arvaikheer (in Övörkhangai aimag) and Mandalgov, or between Ulaanbaatar and Dalanzadgad.

Gimpil Darjaalan Khiid
Гимпил Даржаалан Хийд

This monastery, with its temple **Damba Darjalan Süm** (admission T1000), is a very pleasant surprise after travelling around the dusty and dull countryside. Built in the late-18th century to commemorate the first ever visit to Mongolia by a Dalai Lama, the monastery was once used by about 500 monks. It was the only monastery out of nine in the immediate vicinity to survive the Stalinist purges – by becoming a warehouse and shop.

The monastery was reopened in 1990 and the current Dalai Lama visited in 1992. If no-one is there, wait a few minutes and some boys will materialise with the keys and admission ticket. The spacious temple has a central statue of Tsongkhapa, some large parasols and some huge drums. Photos are permitted outside the temple but not inside.

Sleeping & Eating

Erdenedalai is dusty and very small. Walk about 100m in any direction from the monastery and pitch your tent. A few inquisitive locals, or a camel or two, may visit.

Hotel (r per person T2500) Like most *sum* (district) capitals, Erdenedalai has a nameless hotel with a few different types of rooms, so ask to look at a few. There is certainly no style or comfort, but you will probably have the place to yourself. Look for the decrepit building with yellow paint and blue windows. If it's locked, ask at the shop outside.

Middle Gobi Camp (☎ 9912 8783, 011-367 316; with/without meals US$25/14) About 25km north of Erdenedalai, it's not a bad place to spend the night if you are headed in this direction.

Getting There & Away

Every Wednesday and Saturday, a post office truck leaves Erdenedalai for Ulaanbaatar, returning the next day. On Tuesdays, a postal truck travels to Erdenedalai from Mandalgobi.

Otherwise you will have to hitch a ride. Although the village is small, it is on a major jeep trail, so a few vehicles come through here every day.

ONGIIN KHIID ОНГИЙН ХИЙД

This small mountainous area along the river, the Ongiin Gol, in the western *sum* of Saikhan-Ovoo, makes a good resting place to break a trip between the south Gobi and either Ulaanbaatar or Arvaikheer. The bend in the river marks the remains of two ruined monasteries, the **Barlim Khiid** on the north bank, and the **Khutagt Khiid** on the south. Together the complex is known as **Ongiin Khiid** (GPS: N45° 20.367', E104° 00.306'; admission US$1, photos US$1, video US$2). A contingent of 13 monks has set up shop amid the ruins, completing a new temple in 2004. The ger in front of the temple is a '**museum**' (admission US$1) that houses some unimpressive artefacts found at the site. Despite it being illegal, locals may try to sell you some of the artefacts or dinosaur eggs.

There are plenty of places to camp along the forested riverside and there are five ger camps in the vicinity. Otherwise, a shop-cum-hotel in Saikhan-Ovoo *sum* centre has beds for T3500.

Ongi Tour (☎ 011-211 238; 9191 6184; ongi-tour@magicnet.mn; bed with/without meals US$27/12-15) camp is right on the riverside. It's a friendly place with an English-speaking staff. Amenities include a sauna, basketball court (!) and camel riding (US$3 per hour, US$10 per day).

Just past Ongi Tour is the very basic **Ongiin Khiid ger camp** (bed with/without meals T15,000/10,000), which has beds without food for T10,000. About 1km away from here is the neglected and overpriced Möngke Khan ger camp.

Next to Ongi Tour, **Tsagaan Ovoo** (☎ 011-318 167; bed with/without meals US$25/10) is a bit cheaper but the gers aren't as nice and there's no English spoken.

The well-run **Saikhan Gobi** (GPS: N45° 23.114', E103° 58.328'; ☎ 011-367 316, 9912 8783; adiya49@yahoo.com; bed with/without meals US$25/10) camp is 11km before Ongiin Khiid, on the road from Saikhan-Ovoo.

There is no public transport to Ongiin Khiid.

IKH GAZRYN CHULUU ИХ ГАЗРЫН ЧУЛУУ

This area of unusual rock pinnacles is about 70km northeast of Mandalgov in Gurvan

Saikhan *sum*. You'll probably pass through it if you're on the Mandalgov–Choir road. You can overnight at the comfortable **Töv Borjigan ger camp** (☎ 9916 5120; ganaa36_2002@yahoo.com; with/without food US$25/9).

ULAAN SUVRAGA УЛААН СУВРАГА

In the southernmost *sum* of Ölziit is Ulaan Suvraga, an area that might be described as a 'badlands' or a 'painted desert'. The eerie, eroded landscape was at one time beneath the sea, and is rich in marine fossils and clamshells. There are also numerous **ancient rock paintings** in the region.

The museum in Mandalgov has a photograph of Ulaan Suvraga, which you might want to look at to decide whether it's worth

travelling 115km to get there. About 20km east of Ulaan Suvraga is the equally stunning **Tsagaan Suvraga**, an area of 30m-high white limestone formations.

The best place to stay in the area is the **Tsagaan Suvraga ger camp** (GPS: N44° 34.405′, E105° 48.542′; ☎ 01592-23058 or 9959 9602; with food US$25), 8km west of Tsagaan Suvraga.

DORNOGOV ДОРНОГОВЬ

pop 52,100 / area 111,000 sq km

Dornogov (East Gobi) is classic Gobi country – flat, arid and with a sparse population. In a good year, the aimag sprouts short grass, which sustains a limited number of

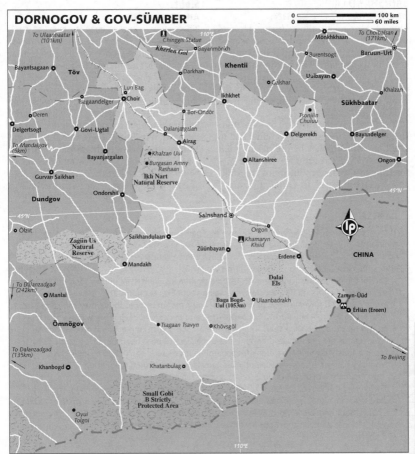

sheep, goats and camels for their ethnic Khalkh owners. In a bad year, the wells go dry, the grass turns brown and the animals die. Unless there is a sudden demand for sand, Dornogov's economic future will continue to be based on the international rail line to China – though recent US interest in local oil reserves may improve things.

If travelling on the train to or from Beijing or Hohhot, you will see a lot of the desolate landscape from the window. If travelling around the Gobi independently, there is little need to come to Dornogov: there are very few interesting attractions, the roads are bad or nonexistent, water is scarce and the facilities are poor.

SAINSHAND САЙНШАНД
☎ 01522 / pop 18,640 / elev 938m

One of Mongolia's most dusty, dry and windblown aimag capitals, Sainshand (Good Pond) is important primarily because of its location. The city was founded in 1931 and was called Tüsheet Khaan aimag during Manchu rule. It is on the main rail line to China, and not far from the Chinese border.

If you are travelling around by jeep, Sainshand makes a useful place to refuel and to stock up with supplies before heading out into the Gobi. There are a few jeeps for hire for trips to the desert, but more are available in Dalanzadgad in Ömnögov aimag.

Sainshand is handy because it is the only aimag capital in the Gobi to be linked by train to Ulaanbaatar.

Orientation & Information
Most things needed by the traveller are located around Danzan Ravjaa Park. The train station is 2km to the north.

Internet Café (☎ 22289; per hr T500; ⏱ 9am-10pm Mon-Fri, 9am-5pm Sat & Sun) In the Telecom office.

Trade & Development Bank (☎ 22298; ⏱ 9am-4pm Mon-Fri) Changes US-dollar travellers cheques and gives cash advances on MasterCard and Visa. The Mongol Post Bank is in the same building.

Telecom Office (☎ 22722; ⏱ 24hr) The post office is located here.

Sights
AIMAG MUSEUM
The well-appointed **Aimag Museum** (☎ 22657; admission T1000; ⏱ 9am-1pm & 2-6pm) houses plenty of stuffed Gobi animals, a collection of sea shells and marine fossils (Dornogov was once beneath the sea) and some dinosaur fossils. The history section includes some eulogies to Manzav, the local *baatar* (hero) who distinguished himself fighting for Mongolian independence during the 1921 revolution. Look out also for the 13th-century wooden breastplate worn by a Mongol soldier in Korea and the *morin khuur* (horsehead fiddle), from 1940, decorated with carved images of Lenin and

---

CAMELS

Throughout Mongolia, you will see the two-humped Bactrian camel. They were domesticated thousands of years ago, and are closely related to the rare wild camel known as the *khavtgai*. Of the 256,700 camels in the country, two-thirds can be found in the five aimags that stretch across the Gobi – 80,000 in Ömnögov aimag alone.

One of the five domesticated animals revered by nomads, camels are perfect for long-distance travel in the Gobi (though they are slow, averaging about 5km per hour). They are easy to manage (a camel can last for over a week without water, and a month without food); they can carry a lot of gear (up to 250kg – equal to 10 full backpacks); and they provide wool (an average of 5kg per year) and milk (up to 600L a year). They are also a good source of meat, and produce 250kg of dung a year! If the humps are drooping, the camels are in poor health, or need some food or water (if a thirsty camel hasn't drunk for some time it can suck up 200L in a single day).

Normally relaxed, if somewhat aloof, male camels go crazy during the mating season in January and February – definitely a time to avoid approaching one.

The current number of camels is considerably lower than it was just 40 years ago. The decline could be because they are being killed for their meat, and because many nomads are leaving the harsh Gobi and breeding other livestock. In an attempt to stop the decline in numbers, several national parks in the Gobi have been established to protect the 300 or so remaining wild *khavtgai*.

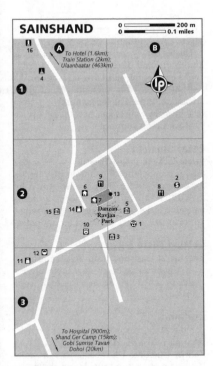

SAINSHAND

0 —————— 200 m
0 —————— 0.1 miles

Sükhbaatar. The museum is in the centre of town, a little west of the Telecom office.

MUSEUM OF DANZAN RAVJAA

Noyon Khutagt Danzan Ravjaa (1803–56), a well-known Mongolian writer, composer, painter and medic, was born about 100km southwest of Sainshand. The **museum** (☎ 23221; www.danzanravjaa.org; admission T1000, photos per shot T5000; ☟ 9am-1pm & 2-6pm) has a collection of gifts presented to Danzan Ravjaa by Chinese and Tibetan leaders, costumes used in his plays, Buddhist statues presented to him by the 10th Dalai Lama, and some of his paintings. He was also very interested in traditional medicine, so the museum has a collection of herbs.

Look out for the jar in front of his statue, which contains the Danzan Ravjaa's bones; the poet's mummified body was burned along with his monastery in the 1930s.

DECHINCHOINKHORLIN KHIID

This **monastery** (Дэчинчойнхорлин Хийд; ☟ 10am-5pm Mon-Fri), which opened in 1991, is in a large walled compound at the northern end of the central district. There is an active temple, and though visitors are welcome, photographs are not allowed inside. The 25 monks are very friendly. The best views are from the tank monument located behind the monastery.

Sleeping
CAMPING

Sainshand, like most aimag capitals in the Gobi, does not offer anywhere decent to pitch a tent. There is no river and it's spread out, so getting away from the ger suburbs will involve some walking. The best place to head for is the cliffs north of the monastery.

GER CAMPS

Gobi Sunrise Tavan Dohoi (GPS: N44° 45.418′, E110° 11.236′; ☎ 23086, 9909 0151; www.magicnet.mn /~gobisunrise; with/without meals US$25/10) is about 20km south of Sainshand, on the road to Khamaryn Khiid (p183). A well-run ger camp, it has a restaurant, flush toilets and clean showers with hot water. To arrange transport to the camp, ask Altangerel, the curator at the Danzan Ravjaa museum.

Shand Ger Camp (☎ 9925 7883; with 3 meals US$27) Located 15km south of Sainshand, this camp is more expensive but not as nice as the Gobi Sunrise. Arrange transport through the Shand Plaza.

THE GOBI

HOTELS

Shand Plaza (☎ 9914 8352; d/tr/half-lux/lux T20,000/18,000/35,000/65,000) One of the better countryside hotels, this place has clean, modern rooms at higher-end prices. The triple room has no shower but the basement has a shared shower (T500) and sauna (T5000) that can be used even if you aren't staying here. The hotel also has a restaurant, disco, billiard room and local branch of the Anod Bank where you can receive a money transfer.

Ikh Goviin Naran Hotel (Great Gobi Sun Hotel; ☎ 22473; per person T6000) In the building of the Mongolian People's Revolutionary Party (MPRP), the simple rooms with bathroom are spacious but don't expect any hot water. It's just north of the Od Hotel.

Od Hotel (Star Hotel; ☎ 23245; dm T4500-5500) In the west wing of the Government House, it has a hot-water shower room and a grumpy matron. Enter the hotel from the north side.

If it's late, you may want to try the nameless **hotel** (☎ 9909 0729; r T10,000-15,000) a five-minute walk from the train station. It's the white-blue building on the right side of the cultural palace.

Eating

Zeegiin Ogloo Restaurant (☎ 9620 6864; 🕐 9am-9pm) Located in the Shand Plaza, this place receives top marks for its goulash and *on-dogtei beefshteks* (beefsteak with egg).

Chinese Guanz (dishes T1000-2500; 🕐 10.30am-8pm) Next to a supermarket just past the Danzan Ravjaa museum on the left, this place serves authentic Chinese meals.

Ergeliin Zoo (🕐 9am-6pm) This *guanz* serves *khuushuur* and fizzy drinks.

Otherwise, the Ikh Goviin Naran or the Od hotels can whip something up if given advance notice. The **indoor market** (🕐 10am-6pm) near the Sports Palace is the best place to stock up on supplies.

Entertainment

Saran Khökhöö Drama Theatre (☎ 22796, 9952 6566) is named after the famous play by the local hero Danzan Ravjaa, who would be proud that this Sainshand theatre group is considered the best outside of Ulaanbaatar. Unfortunately, performances are sporadic.

Getting There & Away

Because at least one train links Sainshand with Ulaanbaatar every day, there are no flights or scheduled bus services to or from Sainshand.

HITCHING

For the same reasons that jeeps are scarce, hitching is also hard. You will get a lift to Zamyn-Üüd or to Ulaanbaatar, but the train is quicker, more comfortable and cheap.

JEEP

Share jeeps park themselves at a stop south of the Sports Palace. There is little demand for long-distance shared jeeps as most locals travel to places connected by train, and

---

DANZAN RAVJAA

Danzan Ravjaa was a hot-headed, rebellious monk, a writer and popular leader of Mongolia's Red Hat Buddhists. He was recognised as a child prodigy by local people (he began composing and singing his own songs at the age of four) and was proclaimed the Fifth Gobi Lord in 1809. The Manchu had executed the Fourth Gobi Lord and forbade another and it was only by the narrowest of chances that the Manchu court allowed the young Gobi king to live.

Danzan Ravjaa's fame as a writer, artist and social critic spread far and wide. He received foreign students at his monastery and travelled to foreign countries, bringing his acting troupe with him to study drama.

He was also an expert at martial arts, Tantric studies, yoga and traditional medicine. He spent months in solitude, in caves or in his ger, writing. It is said that he so hated being disturbed that he built himself a ger with no door. Danzan Ravjaa, however, had a lousy temper that was often exacerbated by protracted bouts of drinking.

Danzan Ravjaa's mysterious death came either at the hands of the rival Yellow Hat Buddhist sect or a jealous queen who failed to gain his love. The people of Dornogov still know many tall tales about his supernatural powers and heroic feats, and locals dream of rebuilding his theatre (see opposite) to again perform his famous play, *Life Story of the Moon Cuckoo*.

THE GOBI

almost no tourists come here. Sainshand is 463km southeast of Ulaanbaatar, and 218km northwest of Zamyn-Üüd.

TRAIN

Local train No 286 from Ulaanbaatar (daily except Tuesday and Saturday), goes through Choir, departing at 9.50am and arrives at 7.30pm. It returns to UB at 8.50pm, arriving 8.20am. A second option is local train No 276 to Zamyn-Üüd, which leaves Ulaanbaatar at 4pm arriving at Sainshand at the inconvenient time of about 2am – not a great time to find a hotel. This train departs Sainshand at 10.30pm and arrives in UB at 9am. There may be other departure times so check when you book your ticket. Tickets from Ulaanbaatar cost T3200 for a hard seat and T7600 for a soft seat. While hard seat is not unbearable, the coupé cabin is your only chance for a good sleep.

The Trans-Mongolian Railway and the trains between Ulaanbaatar and Hohhot (in Inner Mongolia) and Ereen (just over the Chinese border) stop at Sainshand, but you cannot use these services just to get to Sainshand, unless you buy a ticket all the way to China. You must take the local daily train.

Getting *on* the Trans-Mongolian at Sainshand for China is fraught with complications unless you have bought your Ulaanbaatar–Beijing/Hohhot ticket beforehand in Ulaanbaatar, and have arranged for someone to tell the train steward at Ulaanbaatar station not to sell your seat. In Beijing, you can only buy a Beijing–Ulaanbaatar ticket, but you can get off at Sainshand.

SOUTH OF SAINSHAND

Khamaryn Khiid Хамарын Хийд

This reconstructed **monastery** (GPS: N44° 36.038', E110° 16.650'), an hour's drive south of Sainshand, has grown up around the cult of Danzan Ravjaa (opposite), whom many local people believe to have been a living god. His image is sewn into a carpet that hangs in the main hall. The original monastery and three-storey theatre, built by Danzan Ravjaa in 1821, was destroyed in the 1930s. The surroundings hold meditation caves and retreats used by Danzan Ravjaa and his students. Water from the spring nearby (surrounded by a concrete building) is said to hold curative properties.

Altangerel, the curator of the Museum of Danzan Ravjaa in Sainshand (and the fifth generation in the hereditary line of Danzan Ravjaa's personal protectors, which extends from Danzan Ravjaa's assistant Balchinchoijoo) can help with accommodation. Contact him at the museum in Sainshand if you are thinking of heading to Khamaryn Khiid. The shack that serves as a hotel near the monastery is pretty grim, but the Tavan Dohoi ger camp (p181) is a 30-minute (20km) drive back towards Sainshand.

Burdene Bulag & Khatanbulag
Бүрдэнэ булаг & Хатанбулаг

Some of the largest and most accessible sand dunes in the Gobi are at **Burdene Bulag**. There are also cold-water springs in the area, but you will need a guide to find them. The dunes and springs are 30km southwest of Erdene, which is about halfway along the main road between Sainshand and Zamyn-Üüd.

The region around **Khatanbulag** (also known as Ergel) is noted for its cliffs, ancient archaeological artefacts and rare Gobi animals. A jeep trail from here links Dornogov with Khanbogd *sum* in eastern Ömnögov where you could hunt for the remains of **Demchigiin Khiid** (Дэмчигийн Хийд), a ruined monastery made from mud-brick.

ZAMYN-ÜÜD ЗАМЫН-УУД
☎ 025245

This town has only two claims to fame: it's right on Mongolia's southern border and it is the hottest place in the country. The only reasons to come here are to save money by travelling from Ulaanbaatar to China on local trains, rather than on the dearer international Trans-Mongolian Railway; or if you are planning to visit obscure villages by train in Inner Mongolia. Desertification is a real problem here and sand dunes are starting to pile up between buildings. Locals, with Japanese aid, are trying to keep the dunes at bay with a massive tree-planting campaign.

Information

Telecom Office (☎ 5109; ⏱ 24hr) This office has an Internet café charging T600 per hour.

Trade & Development Bank (☎ 53605; ⏱ 9am-4pm Mon-Fri) On the 1st floor of the train station (look for the sign in English), this handy bank changes cash and travellers cheques, and gives a cash advances against Visa and MasterCard. You can also use the moneychangers outside the station.

Sleeping & Eating

Thanks to cross-border trade, Zamyn-Üüd has become something of a boom town and Mongolia's wealthiest *sum* centre, translating into better hotels, shops and restaurants compared with villages of similar size. There has even talk of building a hotel/casino to feed China's appetite for gambling.

There are three main places to stay.

Zamyn-Üüd Hotel (☎ 21265; dm/half-lux/lux T3000/12,000/20,000) The better rooms here have attached bathroom. It's a five-minute walk west of the station.

Khaan Shonkhor Hotel (☎ 21508; dm T5000, half-lux/lux T6000/20,000) The 'King Falcon', another good choice, has cheaper rooms and 24-hour hot water. The staff is friendly and don't mind if you hang around the restaurant while waiting for a train. All prices are per person.

Jintin Hotel (☎ 025245-53289; dm US$8, half-lux/lux US$12/30) Located next to the train station, this modern hotel has rooms with private bathroom. Hot water is spotty, which is not a great loss when the temperature is soaring. There's a good restaurant here. All prices are per person.

There are several hotels in Ereen (Érliàn) on the Chinese side of the border.

Getting There & Away

The daily train (No 276) to Zamyn-Üüd, via Choir and Sainshand, leaves Ulaanbaatar every day at 4.30pm, arriving around 7.10am. Tickets cost T4100/9700 for hard/soft seat. The train returns to Ulaanbaatar at 5pm, arriving the next morning at 8.35am. Tickets cost T1800/4700 to Sainshand and T3000/7300 to Choir.

From UB you can also take the No 34 express train, departing Tuesday, Thursday and Saturday at 8.10pm, arriving in Zamyn-Üüd at 8.03am for T15,5000. It returns at 9pm.

To cross the border, most people take the frequent minivans (T8000) that run the 7km between the train stations of Zamyn-Üüd and Ereen. The minivans are generally quicker than the train. This price includes a T6000 departure tax. The border is open from 10am to 6pm daily except Sunday.

If you are on the Trans-Mongolian train, or the service between Ulaanbaatar and Hohhot or Ereen, you will stop at Zamyn-Üüd for an hour or two while Mongolian customs and immigration officials do their stuff – usually in the middle of the night. See p255 for details.

Make sure that your passport and Mongolian and Chinese visas are all in order – bureaucracy moves mighty slow in this part of the world. In 1999 a Nigerian man was arrested here for travelling on a dodgy passport; he spent two years in the local jail before Zamyn-Üüd officials finally figured a way to send him home.

NORTH OF SAINSHAND

Probably the best sight in Dornogov, **Senjit Khad** is a natural rock formation in the shape of an arch. It is about 95km northeast of Sainshand in Altanshiree *sum*.

The volcanic rock formation of **Tsonjiin Chuluu** looks rather like a set of hexagonal organ pipes. It's in the extreme northeast corner of Dornogov, in Delgerekh *sum*, about 160km along the northeast road from Sainshand.

Both sites can be visited only with your own vehicle en route between Dornogov aimag and eastern Mongolia.

KHALZAN UUL ХАЛЗАН УУЛ

Khalzan Uul is an area of natural springs about 50km south of Choir. Locals are crazy about its mineral water, claiming it can cure everything from hangovers to HIV. Local entrepreneurs plan to bottle the water and sell it. You'll need your own vehicle to get here.

Burgasan Amny Rashaan is another mineral spring just a few kilometres south.

CHOIR ЧОЙР

Choir, about halfway between Sainshand and Ulaanbaatar, is a town with one foot in the past and the other in the future. Unfortunately the present is pretty grim. The only reason to visit Choir is to explore the nearby springs at Khalzan Uul, or to refuel between Ulaanbaatar and Sainshand.

Around 15km north of the town is the village of **Lun Bag**, the site of the largest **Soviet air base** in Mongolia. The Russians departed in 1992, leaving behind an eerie ghost town of concrete buildings and statues of MiG fighters. Some of the flats, which formerly housed military personnel, are now occupied by Mongolian families, but many sit empty, the windows broken, the plumbing ripped out and the walls scrawled with graffiti. The Russians left behind something else: the best paved runway in Mongolia.

To promote rapid economic growth, Choir formally seceded from Dornogov (it is now an autonomous municipality called Gov-Sümber, with a population of 12,200) and was declared a Free Trade Zone. Nothing much was done to promote the area and it continues to languish in neglect.

There are a couple of hotels near the train station. The **Ortoo Hotel** (Station Hotel; ☎ 02542-50521; dm/lux T4500/12,000) is right next to the station. The **Oron Tsootsnii Hotel** (☎ 02542-50438; dm T4000), 400m east of the station, has larger, cleaner rooms with a shower.

To Choir, a train leaves Ulaanbaatar daily at 4.30pm and arrives at 9.26pm. Another train departs at 9.50am (daily except Tuesday and Saturday). Tickets cost T2000/5300 for a hard/soft seat. The train departs for Ulaanbaatar at the unspeakable time of 3.48am. On Thursday, Saturday and Monday another train departs at 2.16am. If you are a day person you could take the paved road to UB.

The Trans-Mongolian Railway briefly stops in Choir but you won't be able to buy a ticket to get off here (the situation is the same as for Sainshand, p183).

ÖMNÖGOV ӨМНӨГОВЬ

pop 46,700 / area 165,000 sq km

Ömnögov (South Gobi) is the largest but least populated aimag in Mongolia, with a population density of only about 0.3 people per square kilometre. It's not hard to see why humans prefer to live elsewhere: with an average annual precipitation of only 130mm a year, and summer temperatures reaching an average of around 38°C, this is the driest, hottest and harshest region in the entire country.

The Gurvan Saikhan Nuruu range in the centre provides the main topographic relief in this pancake-flat region. These mountains reach an altitude of 2825m and support a diverse range of wildlife, including the extremely rare snow leopard (see p198). The mountains also make human habitation marginally possible by capturing snow in winter, which melts and feeds springs on the plains below, providing water for some limited livestock.

Ömnögov supports thousands of black-tailed gazelle, which you may see darting across the open plains. The aimag also is home to one-quarter (80,000) of Mongolia's domesticated camels. The 2-million-hectare Gurvan Saikhan National Park protects a lot of wildlife and is home to dinosaur fossils, sand dunes and rock formations. The 1,839,176-hectare Small Gobi Strictly Protected Area, in the southeastern section of the aimag, is the last great bastion of the *khulan* (wild ass).

Tourism has taken off since the mid-1990s and is becoming an important part of the economy, so much so that an international airport is being built in Dalanzadgad. Of more controversial moneymakers is the

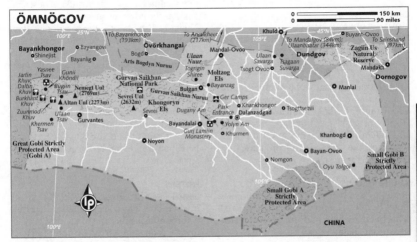

THE GOBI

Oyu Tolgoi copper deposit, located near the Chinese border in Khanbogd *sum*, where a Canadian company is on the verge of unearthing a deposit that will make the one at Erdenet resemble an ant hill.

DALANZADGAD ДАЛАНЗАДГАД

☎ 01532 / pop 15,300 / elev 1465m

The capital of Ömnögov aimag, Dalanzadgad is a speck of civilisation in the desert, sitting in the shadow of the Gurvan Saikhan Nuruu range. The town has reasonable facilities and regular transport, so it's a good base for explorations into the desert. Besides the museum – which is not as good as the one at Yolyn Am – there is little to see or do.

Information

Bathhouse (per person T800; ☺ 10am-9pm) One street north of the Strictly Protected Areas office.

Gobi Tour (Enkhe's Guest House; apt 15, entrance 3, door 19) Arranges jeep tours and camel treks.

Internet Café (per hr T690; ☺ 9am-10pm Mon-Fri, 10am-10pm Sat & Sun) In the Telecom office.

Khan Bank (☎ 22216; ☺ 9am-1pm, 2-4pm) Changes dollars and can give a cash advance against Visa or MasterCard.

Strictly Protected Areas Office (☎ 23973; gtzgobi@magicnet.mn) In the southwest of town, this office mostly deals in bureaucratic affairs. For information, you are better off at the information ger at the gate to the Gurvan Saikhan National Park.

Telecom Office (☎ 24110; ☺ 24hr) A one-minute call to the USA or Europe costs T772.

Sights

SOUTH GOBI MUSEUM

Surprisingly, this **museum** (☎ 22154; admission T1000, photos T5000, video T10,000; ☺ 10am-6pm) has little on dinosaurs – just a leg, an arm and a few eggs. (All of the best exhibits are in Ulaanbaatar, or in any of a number of museums around the world.) There are a few nice paintings, a huge stuffed vulture and a display of scroll paintings and other Buddhist items. The museum is on the main street, on the other side of the park from the pink Drama Theatre.

MAANIIN KHIID

Built in 2002, this stands as Ömnögov's lone Buddhist monastery (Маанийн Хийд). The 10 lamas here perform morning rituals around 10am.

Sleeping

CAMPING

Like other Gobi capitals, there is no river or any decent place to camp in Dalanzadgad. You will just have to walk one or two kilometres in any direction from town, and pitch your tent somewhere secluded.

GER CAMPS

Mazaalai Hotel (☎ 22076, 23040; per person T5000) This small ger camp is on the eastern end of town near the Nomin Gov store.

Juulchin-Gobi Camp (GPS: N43° 45.236', E104° 07.578'; ☎ 26522; jgobi@magicnet.mn; with/without meals US$35/16) This huge camp 35km from town, with an airstrip attached, is popular with organised tours. If you rock up with a tent it's possible to camp here for US$5. It is about the same standard as the others, but the location isn't as good. Planes fly here direct in summer and sometimes continue on to the Juulchin 2 camp in Khongoryn Els for an extra US$30 or so.

Tovshin Resort 1 (GPS: N43° 45.841', E104° 02.838'; ☎ /fax 322 728, 9911 4811; with/without meals US$30/15) Located 7km away from Juulchin, this camp has good hot showers and toilets, and a decent restaurant and bar, but the location is uninteresting and the buildings are ugly.

Three Camels Lodge (GPS: N43° 53.603', E103° 44.435'; in UB ☎ 011-313 396, in Dalanzadgad ☎ 23232; www.threecamellodge.com; with/without meals US$70/35) A veritable oasis in the desert 90km northeast of Dalanzadgad, overlooking a great grassy plain and spectacular mountains, with first-rate facilities and food, this place raises the bar for the Mongolian ger camp. Run by Nomadic Expeditions, the cosy lodge offers nightly performances of folk singing and dancing. Asian/European meals are buffet-style and tasty. Lunch (US$12) is the main meal of the day; the dessert, a baked apple with raisins and custard cream, is reason enough to splurge. Visitors stay in luxurious gers that have easy access to a good-quality shared bathroom. It is a great way to break up a long journey. If you don't want to stay here, you could stop by for a drink on the terrace.

HOTELS

Devshil Hotel (☎ 23786; s/d T4000/8000) Clean and bright rooms at a good price and with private bathroom make this one of the best deals in town. It's on your left as you enter town.

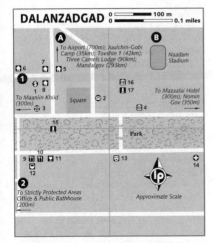

Gobi Gurvan Saikhan Hotel (☎ 23830; d with bathroom T5000, tr T4000) This place is homely and bright, but not as good value as the Devshil. Prices go up by 20% in winter. Prices are per person.

Enkhe's Guest House (☎ 22003, 9982 1598; http ://gobitour.tripod.com; apt 15, entrance 3, door 19; per person US$4). This apartment-style guesthouse makes for good accommodation if you've turned up in a group. English-speaking Enkhe has a five-bed room and a smaller single room. The kitchen is available for cooking and there's a washing machine, but no hot water. She can also provide meals for between T1200 and T1600 a go. To find Enkhe, phone in advance (she will meet your plane) or head for the apartment (look for the blue sign above the door), a block west of the Devshil Hotel. The guesthouse can also arrange jeep hire and tours of the national park.

The nearby **Tuvshin Hotel** (☎ 22240; per person T5000), in the same building as the Mongol Bank, is another option.

Eating & Drinking

Dalanzadgad offers little in the way of cooked food, but you could put together salad from the fresh vegetables on sale in the market (Gobi vegetables are renowned in Mongolia for their sweet taste). Nearby, you'll also see women selling jars of lovely *tarag* (yogurt; T500) and packets of sugar.

Naran Café (☎ 22668; dishes T1100-1200; ⌚ 9am-9pm) A conveniently located *guanz* with the standard meat and potatoes menu.

If you need to stock up for an expedition, the best place is **Nomin Gov** (☎ 24003; ⌚ 8am-11pm), a smaller version of Ulaanbaatar's State Department Store, at the eastern end of town.

Mazaalai Bar (☎ 23040; beer T900; ⌚ 9am-midnight) This unsigned bar has entertained travellers for quite a few years. They no longer cook food but in the same entryway is a tiny *guanze* (canteen or cheap restaurant) that serves hot *khuushuur* (fried, flat meat pancake; T120) until 6pm.

Getting There & Away
AIR

MIAT flies between Dalanzadgad and Ulaanbaatar on Tuesday and Friday for US$81/140 one way/return. During the peak tourist season – July to mid-September – MIAT also schedules extra daily flights between Ulaanbaatar and the Juulchin-Gobi ger camp for the same price. Even if you have a ticket to Dalanzadgad, check that you are going to Dalanzadgad city and not just the ger camp. The airport is a dirt field a few hundred metres north of the town.

Aero Mongolia flies to Oyu Tolgoi, the copper mine in the southwestern part of the aimag, twice a week.

HITCHING

Hitching around the Gobi Desert, including to the attractions in Gurvan Saikhan

THE GOBI

National Park, is totally impractical and dangerous. Hitching between aimag capitals and out to some *sum* centres is possible but not easy. But there won't be anything of interest on the way so you'll still need to hire a jeep at some point to visit the attractions. Make sure you carry plenty of water, food and a tent and sleeping bag for the inevitable breakdowns.

JEEP

Daily postal cars run from Dalanzadgad to Ulaanbaatar (T14,000, 553km); for details call ☎ 23708. The cheapest way to see the attractions in Gurvan Saikhan National Park is to take a bus or hitch to Dalanzadgad, where you can hang around for a few days and ask other independent travellers to share a jeep.

Dalanzadgad is the natural starting point for trips into this part of the Gobi, and there are a few (but not many) jeeps for hire. Most jeep drivers hang around the market area. Alternatively, leave a message with the post office or bus station. We were quoted a reasonable price of about T250 per km. The main headaches are the language barrier and finding a driver that is experienced in taking foreigners.

If travelling independently and staying at a ger camp in the national park, most camps rent jeeps for tourist rates of T400 per km, including a driver/guide. This is higher than normal, but in a remote yet touristed area this is not too expensive, especially if you are sharing costs.

Public shared jeeps run occasionally to Ulaanbaatar but rarely anywhere else; most people fly or hitch on a truck.

BULGAN БУЛГАН

There is little to see in this ramshackle village, 95km northwest of Dalanzadgad, but you may end up here as it is located along the main tourist route between Bayanzag and points south.

By virtue of its position, this small village is now home to large-scale **Tsagaan Sar** (Lunar New Year) festivities, which take place in January or February. The two-day festival includes camel racing, camel polo and a camel beauty contest (unfortunately, good breath is not a key category). During the event, temporary ger camps pop up to house tourists.

If it's late, you could stay with a friendly local named Paul, who speaks English and has two **guest gers** (T1500-2000). Look for his brightly coloured sign.

Nearby is **Ulaan Nuur** (Red Lake), the largest and just about the only lake in Ömnögov. It may not be there when you visit because it often dries out; it won't quench your thirst either – it is very salty.

BAYANZAG БАЯНЗАГ

Bayanzag, which means 'rich in saxaul shrubs', is more commonly known as the 'Flaming Cliffs', penned by the palaeontologist Roy Chapman Andrews (see the boxed text, opposite). First excavated in 1922, it is renowned worldwide for the number of dinosaur bones and eggs found in the area, which you can see in the Museum of Natural History in Ulaanbaatar or, mostly, in other museums around the world.

Even if you are not a 'dinophile', the eerie beauty of the surrounding landscape is a good reason to visit. It's a classic desert of rock, red sands, scrub, sun and awesome emptiness. There's not much to do once you're here except explore the cliffs.

Bayanzag Tourist Camp (GPS: N44° 10.466', E103° 41.816'; ☎ 9953 9988; with meals US$20-25, without meals US$5-10), about 5km from the cliffs, is the only ger camp in the immediate vicinity. Camel rental here is T3000 per hour. A local family near the ger camp might have a bed for T3000, or you could camp near the *zag* (scrub) forest.

Bayanzag (GPS: N44° 08.311', E103° 43.667') is 105km northwest of Dalanzadgad and 18km northeast of Bulgan. It can be surprisingly hard to find so you really need to take a driver or guide who's been there before, or ask directions regularly from the few people who live in the area.

A further 22km northeast of Bayanzag is an area of sand dunes called **Moltzog Els**, which might be worth a visit if you aren't planning to visit Khongoryn Els.

GURVAN SAIKHAN NATIONAL PARK
ГУРВАН САЙХАН

Stretching from the border with Bayankhongor almost to Dalanzadgad, the 2.7 million-hectare Gurvan Saikhan National Park is the highlight of the aimag, and the overwhelming reason why any tourist comes here. Unlike other national parks in the Gobi, the Gurvan Saikhan does contain a few attractions, and its ger camps and roads are reasonably good.

Gurvan Saikhan (Three Beauties) is named after its three ridges (though there are four).

It contains mountains, dinosaur fossils, sand dunes, rock formations and a valley which, incredibly, has ice for most of the year.

The park also contains over 200 species of birds, including the Mongolian desert

DINOSAURS

In the early 1920s, newspapers brought news of the discovery of dinosaur eggs in the southern Gobi Desert by American adventurer Roy Chapman Andrews. Over a period of two years Andrews' team unearthed over 100 dinosaurs, including Protoceratops Andrewsi, which was named after the explorer. The find included several Velociraptors (Swift Robber), subsequently made famous by *Jurassic Park*, and a parrot-beaked Oviraptor (Egg Stealer). Most valuable in Andrews' mind was the discovery of the earliest known mammal skulls, 'possibly the most valuable seven days of work in the whole history of palaeontology to date'.

Subsequent expeditions have returned to the Gobi and added to the picture of life in the late Cretaceous period (70 million years ago), the last phase of dinosaur dominance before the mammals inherited the earth.

One of the most famous fossils so far unearthed is the 'Fighting Dinosaurs', discovered by a joint Polish-Mongolian team in 1971 and listed as a national treasure. The remarkable fossil is of an 80 million-year-old Protoceratops and Velociraptor locked in mortal combat. The raptor's claws remain hooked in the Protoceratops' belly, which is fighting back by clamping the raptor's right arm in its mouth. It is thought that this and other fossilised snapshots were entombed by a violent sand storm or by collapsing sand dunes. One poignant fossil is of a fossilised Oviraptor protecting its nest of eggs from the impending sands.

A picture of the Gobi has emerged as a land of swamps, marshes, rivers and lakes, with areas of sand studded with oases. The land was inhabited by a colourful cast of characters, which included huge duck-billed Hadrosaurs, and also Anklysaurs, which was up to 25 feet tall, armour-plated and had a club-like tail that acted like a giant mace. Also on the list is the sheep-sized Protoceratops, with a distinctive frilled head. Huge long-necked sauropods like Nemegtosaurus, which may have grown to a weight of 90 tonnes, were hunted by three-toed therapods such as the mighty Tarbosaurus ('Alarming Reptile'), a carbon copy of a Tyrannosaurus Rex, with a 1.2m-long skull packed with razor sharp teeth up to 15cm long.

Other weird and wonderful beasts that once roamed the South Gobi include the bone-headed Pachycephalosaurs, which used their reinforced skulls as battering rams; Ebolotherium, with a periscope-style nose that allowed it to breathe while the rest of it was underwater; and Therizinosaurus, a fierce carnivore with massive claws over 60cm long. Huge rhinos, over four times the size of an adult elephant and thought to be the largest land mammals ever to have lived, shared the land with tiny rodents, the forerunners of modern-day mammalian life.

Less dramatic (but equally important) modern fossil finds such as Mononykus, a flightless bird with claw-like limbs instead of wings, have linked the evolution of birds to dinosaurs (Jurassic Park's Velociraptors are now depicted as feathered). The recent discovery of fossilised Gobi marsupials has shown that these animals originate from Asia, not Australia.

With a bit of digging, you may be able to find some dinosaur fossils in the southern Gobi – but please be aware that these fossils are very precious, and far more useful to palaeontologists. Locals may approach you at Bayanzag, the ger camps and even Dalanzadgad to buy some dinosaur bones and eggs. Remember that it is *highly* illegal to export fossils from Mongolia. If you get caught, you'll be in serious trouble.

Apart from the famous sites of Bayanzag and nearby Togrigiin Shiree, the richest sites of Bugiin Tsav, Ulaan Tsav, Nemegt Uul and Khermen Tsav are all in the remote west of Ömnögov aimag and impossible to reach without a dedicated jeep and driver.

Today, the best places to come face to face with the dinosaurs of the Gobi are the Museum of Natural History in Ulaanbaatar and the American Museum of Natural History in New York. The latter has a fine website (www.amnh.org) of the discoveries made during the 1920s.

THE GOBI

finch, cinereous vulture, desert warbler and houbara bustard. Spring brings further waves of migratory birds.

The park also has maybe 600 or more types of plants (a lot of which only bloom after very infrequent heavy rain). The sparse vegetation does manage to support numerous types of animals, such as the black-tailed gazelle, Kozlov's pygmy jerboa and wild ass, and endangered species of wild camel, snow leopard, ibex and argali sheep. In 2000, the park was expanded by over half a million hectares, stretching into Bayankhongor aimag.

Information

There is a national park entry fee of T3000 per person. You can pay the fee and get a permit at the park office in Dalanzadgad, at the entrance to Yolyn Am or from the ranger at Khongoryn Els. In theory, this permit covers the entire park, so if you pay to enter Yolyn Am in the morning and then drive to Khongoryn Els that same day your permit covers you for both sites. Keep your entry ticket as you may need to show it to rangers later in your trip.

You can camp in most accessible areas of the park (though not the remote core areas), as long as you stay a fair distance from the ger camps and have your own food and water.

Sights & Activities

YOLYN AM

Yolyn Am (Ёлын Ам; Vulture's Mouth) was originally established to conserve the birdlife in the region, but it's now more famous for its dramatic and very unusual scenery – it is a valley in the middle of the Gobi Desert, with metres-thick ice for most of the year.

The small **Nature Museum** (GPS: N43° 32.872', E104° 02.257'; admission US$1; ☼ 8am-9pm) at the gate on the main road to Yolyn Am has a collection of dinosaur eggs and bones, stuffed birds and a snow leopard. They also sell the excellent booklet *Gobi Gurvan Saikhan National Park* by Bern Steinhauer-Burkhart. More information in English on the park and its facilities can be found in an 'information ger', which also sells park entry tickets. There are several souvenir shops as well as the **Tavan Erdene guesthouse** (☎ 9953 9297; per person US$8).

Look out for the remarkable petrified wood lying by the roadside. The ranger

ROY CHAPMAN ANDREWS

An American zoologist from Wisconsin, Roy Chapman Andrews (1884–1960) explored the Gobi in the 1920s, and found the first dinosaur eggs, jaws and skulls in Central Asia. Andrews' most famous expeditions were based at Bayanzag, which he famously renamed the 'Flaming Cliffs'.

Andrews had actually come to Mongolia to find the missing link between apes and man and to prove his boss Henry Osborn's theory that Central Asia was the dispersal point for mammalian life. He never found evidence of this, though he did uncover traces of a 20,000-year-old people, which he dubbed the Dune Dwellers. As Chinese bandits and Soviet secret police placed unbearable strains on field work, he abandoned his incomplete excavations after about five expeditions.

From his books and biographies, he was a real-life adventurer, who took the expedition's ambushes, raids, bandits, rebellions and vipers in his stride (the camp killed 47 vipers in their tents one night). He was never one for understatement; as one expedition member said, 'the water that was up to our ankles was always up to Roy's neck'. In reality, one of the few times an expedition member was seriously injured was when Andrews accidentally shot himself in the leg with his own revolver.

Andrews worked for US intelligence during WWI and also explored Alaska, Borneo, Burma, Korea and China. He wrote such Boys' Own classics as *Whale Hunting with Gun and Camera* (1916), *Across Mongolian Plains* (1921), *On the Trail of Ancient Man* and *The New Conquest of Central Asia*. Always kitted out in a felt hat, khakis and a gun by his side, Andrews is widely regarded as the model on which the Hollywood screen character Indiana Jones was based.

On his return to the US Andrews took the directorship of the American Museum of Natural History but was asked to resign in 1941 after a difficult tenure during the depression years. His death in California in 1960, at the age of 76, went almost unnoticed. For more information on RC Andrews, read *Dragon Hunter*, a biography by Charles Galenkamp.

office and museum sells some good souvenirs, including landscape paintings and, amazingly, one of the best collections of Mongolian stamps in the country.

From the museum, the road continues for another 10km to a car park. From there, a pleasant 2km walk, following the stream, leads to an ice-filled **gorge** (GPS: N43° 29.332', E104° 04.000') and one or two lonely souvenir salesmen. Locals also rent horses and camels for about T6000 for the trip.

In winter, the ice is up to 10m high, and continues down the gorge for another 10km. Sadly, the ice is not particularly accommodating for tourists, and only appears in the off season (November to May)

The surrounding hills offer plenty of opportunities for some fine, if somewhat strenuous, day **hikes**. If you are lucky you might spot ibex or argali sheep along the steep valley ridges.

Yolyn Am is in the Zuun Saikhan Uul range, 46km west of Dalanzadgad. The turn-off to the entrance is signposted, about 40km from Dalanzadgad.

If you are headed from Yolyn Am to Khongoryn Els, an adventurous and rough alternative route takes you through the **Dugany Am** (GPS: N43° 29.521', E103° 51.586'), a spectacular and narrow gorge. The gorge is blocked with ice until July and can be impassable even after the ice has melted, so check road conditions with the park ranger's office at the park entrance. At the end of the gorge are the minor ruins of a monastery, the **Gurj Lamiin Khiid** (GPS: N43° 29.030', E103° 50.930'). It is 165km from Yolyn Am to Khongoryn Els.

KHONGORYN ELS

The Khongoryn Els (Хонгорын Элс) are some of the largest and most spectacular sand dunes in Mongolia. Also known as the *duut mankhan* (singing dunes), they are up to 300m high, 12km wide and about 100km long. The largest dunes are at the northwestern corner of the range. You can climb to the top of the dunes with a lot of effort and then slide back down if you have a garbage bag handy. The views of the desert from the top are wonderful. There is an information ger near the parking area at the base of the dunes.

To properly explore the area, you will need to stay the night in the desert before returning to Dalanzadgad. There are plenty of camping spots near the dunes (you'll need your own water) and a handful of ger camps.

Tovshin 2 (GPS: N43° 49.415', E102° 23.489'; with/without meals US$25/12) is a welcoming ger camp, 10km north of the dunes. **Juulchin Gobi 2** (☎ 26522, 9914 8115; jgobi@magicnet.mn; with/without meals US$35/17) is about 2km from the dunes. A third camp, Duut Mankhan, charges about US$25 for a bed and three meals.

The dunes are about 180km from Dalanzadgad and the ger camps. There is no way to get there unless you charter a jeep or are part of a tour.

From Khongoryn Els it is possible to follow desert tracks 130km north to Bogd in Övörkhangai, or 215km northwest to Bayanlig in Bayankhongor. This is a remote and unforgiving area and you shouldn't undertake either trip without an experienced driver and full stocks of food, water and fuel.

BAYANKHONGOR
БАЯНХОНГОР

pop 83,200 / area 116,000 sq km

This strangely shaped aimag is dominated by the mighty Khangai Nuruu range to the north. Its southern part passes through the Gobi to the Chinese border and includes part of the Mongol Altai Nuruu range. Although somewhat higher than the Khangai Nuruu, the Mongol Altai is a bleak desert range where life is hard even for the durable argali sheep and ibex.

By contrast, the Khangai is lush, providing sufficient snowmelt to make livestock raising and human existence a viable proposition. Bayankhongor, which means 'rich chestnut' (named after the colour of the horses – or your skin after a couple of hours in the sun), is home to wild camels and asses and the extremely rare Gobi bear.

The aimag was hard hit by the 1999–2002 *zud*, especially in the northern sums where families were trapped for weeks amid deep snows.

Most travellers bypass the aimag while travelling along the major southern Ulaanbaatar–Khovd road, but Bayankhongor does have some interesting, albeit remote, attractions. Some adventurous travellers have ridden horses from Bayankhongor over the Khangai Nuruu to Tsetserleg in

THE GOBI

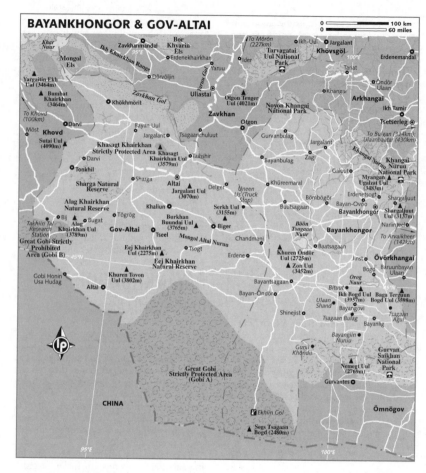

BAYANKHONGOR & GOV-ALTAI

Arkhangai. Getting to these remote places is as much expedition as common travel, but if you are well prepared the area offers some magical trips off the beaten track.

BAYANKHONGOR CITY БАЯНХОНГОР

☎ 01442 / pop 26,100 / elev 1859m

The broad avenues, cantonment-style apartment blocks and parade ground in front of a monolithic Government House are straight out a Soviet planner's briefcase. But Bayankhongor city, built in 1942 as a pit stop on the southern highway to Khovd, was never given a soul. Waste ground and concrete mingle in depressing shades of grey and brown, but the Khangai Nuruu, with several peaks of 3000m or more, is

not too far away. You'll probably have to stay here if on a long haul to or from the west, to start explorations to more remote regions in the south, or to go on a day trip to the nearby springs at Shargaljuut.

Information

Bathhouse (☎ 22652; per person T800, sauna T1500; ◷ 9am-11pm) Located 650m north of the Telecom office.
Internet Café (per hr T710; ◷ 10am-5pm) Inside the Telecom office.
Internet Café (per hr T600) On the 3rd floor of Government House.
Khan Bank (☎ 22981; ◷ 9am-1pm & 2-5pm Mon-Fri) Changes US dollars.
Telecom Office (☎ 24105; ◷ 24hr) The post office is also here.

Sights

The skyline of the city is dominated by a **stupa** on a hill to the west of the square. If you are staying for a while, take a walk up there for views of the town and nearby countryside.

LAMYN GEGEENII GON GANDAN DEDLIN KHIID

There was no ancient monastery on this particular site, but 20km to the east of Bayankhongor city a monastery existed with the same name. This monastery complex once housed up to 10,000 monks, making it one of the largest in the country. As elsewhere in Mongolia, the communist police descended on the place in 1937 and carted off the monks, who were never seen again. The temple was levelled and today nothing remains.

The current monastery (Ламын Гэгээний Гон Гандан Дэдлин Хийд), built in 1991, is home to only 40 monks. The main temple is built in the shape of a ger, although it's actually made of brick. The main hall features a statue of Sakyamuni flanked by a green and white Tara. The monastery is on the main street, 700m north of the square.

MUSEUMS

The **Aimag Museum** (☎ 22339; admission T1000, photos T1000; ☼ 9am-5pm Mon-Fri), inside the sports stadium in the park, is well laid out and worth a visit, though there are no English captions as yet. There is a good display on Buddhist art, featuring two lovely statues of Tara, some fine old scroll paintings and *tsam* (lama dance) masks and costumes. Other exhibits fall into the standard mould of communist history and model gers.

Disappointed by the lack of badly taxidermal creatures? Head across the street to the **Natural History Museum** (T1000; ☼ 9am-5pm Mon-Fri). The highlights here are some dinosaur fossils, a replica Tarbosaurus skeleton and a 130 million-year-old fossilised turtle.

Sleeping

The best place is to camp probably by the Tüin Gol, a few hundred metres east of the city.

Negdelchin Hotel (☎ 22278; d/tr/lux per person T3600/3000/5000) Located at the southern end of the main street, this is Bayankhongor's typically antiquated main hotel. All rooms have a toilet but only the lux rooms have a shower. Prices are per person.

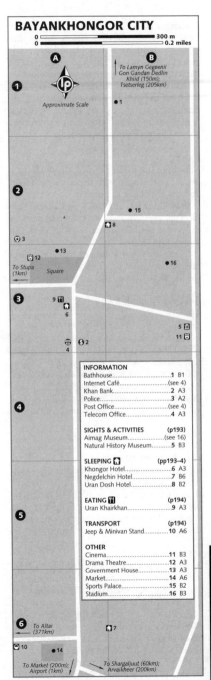

THE GOBI

Khongor Hotel (☎ 22300, 9944 8732; q per person T4500, lux T10,000) Above a restaurant on the main road, this small hotel has clean, modern rooms with TV, fridge and attached bathroom, though hot water is unlikely.

Uran Dosh Hotel (☎ 23139; dm/s/d T4500/5000/10,000, half-lux T8000) This funky, light-blue tile building near the Sports Palace houses a restaurant and small hotel. Common rooms share a bathroom down the hall.

Eating

The three hotels mentioned above all have decent restaurants, with the Khongor Hotel being a cut above the others.

Uran Khairkan (☎ 22062; ⏲ 11am-9pm Mon-Fri) This creatively decorated restaurant in the centre of town serves passable meat, egg and potato dishes.

There are a few *guanz* nearby, including one just south of the Telecom office. Look for the sign: Зоогийн Газар.

Getting There & Away

AIR

On Tuesday and Saturday, MIAT flies between Ulaanbaatar and Bayankhongor for US$82/143. It departs UB at about 6.35pm and returns from Bayankhongor at 7.45pm and stops are made each way in Arvaikheer. Aero Mongolia flies here nonstop on Monday, Wednesday and Friday at 2.15pm. The airport is about 1km south of the city.

HITCHING

Bayankhongor is on the main southern road between Ulaanbaatar and Khovd. A lot of vehicles going in either direction stop here, so getting a ride to Altai or Arvaikheer shouldn't be difficult. South of Bayankhongor, or to Shargaljuut, you will have far less success. Ask around at the market, which doubles as a bus and truck station.

JEEP & MINIVAN

As a central point in southern Mongolia, Bayankhongor is well connected by bus, or better still by minivan to Ulaanbaatar, making this an interesting and cheap, if somewhat uncomfortable, way to reach the western Gobi. Minivans leave daily and go via Arvaikheer. They stop at the market in Bayankhongor, about 300m south of the square.

If you ask around the market you should be able to find a minivan or jeep headed to

Altai (T10,000, 10 hours, 400km) or even Khovd (T20,000, 24 hours).

GALUUT ГАЛУУТ

The 25m-deep Galuut canyon is worth a visit if, for some bizarre reason, you are in the region. The **canyon** is only about 1m wide in places. It is 20km southwest of Galuut *sum* centre, which is about 85km northwest of Bayankhongor town. The ruins of **Mandal Khiid**, destroyed in 1937, are in the vicinity.

SHARGALJUUT ШАРГАЛЖУУТ

The major attraction in Bayankhongor aimag is the 300 or so hot- and cold-water **springs** at Shargaljuut. About 60km northeast of Bayankhongor city, the springs are one of the few natural attractions in the Gobi region that are easily accessible from an aimag capital.

The springs and bathhouses cover the banks of the river between the peaks of Myangan Ugalzat Uul (3483m) and Shargaljuut Uul (3137m). The hot water, which can reach 50°C, is supposed to cure a wide range of complaints and many Mongolians come for treatment at the neighbouring **sanatorium** (⏲ 9am-6pm Mon-Sat Apr-Dec).

Foreign guests can stay at the **ger camp** or a **hotel** (☎ 26503; d/half-lux/lux per person T5000/7000/10,000) at the sanatorium, but you should try to reserve in advance by calling the manager, Mr Yadmaa. Alternatively, you can camp further down from the springs along the valley, but you may be charged T1000.

Occasional shared jeeps or minivans leave Bayankhongor's market for Shargaljuut (per person T2500). Chartering a minivan costs around T30,000 return. Alternatively, try the airport on Tuesday and Saturday, when a minivan bound for the springs meets incoming passengers from Ulaanbaatar.

OROG NUUR ОРОГ НУУР

The saltwater **Orog Nuur** (GPS: N45° 02.692', E100° 36.314') is at the end of the Tüin Gol, which passes through Bayankhongor city. Also referred to as Shar Burd Nuur, the lake is a good place to watch birdlife. It is nestled in the foothills of Ikh Bogd Uul (3957m) in Bogd *sum*, a four-hour, 110km drive south of Bayankhongor city. With a jeep and local guide it is possible to drive to the top of Ikh Bogd for stupendous views. You can use the lake as a base to visit sights further south. Easily recognisable ger camps sometimes pop up here in summer but you should be prepared to camp if nothing has been set up.

BAYANGOVI БАЯНГОВЬ
The small town of Bayangovi is about 100km south of Orog Nuur in a beautiful valley dominated by the Ikh Bogd range. While there is nothing of special interest in Bayangovi itself, the surrounding countryside offers some intriguing desert sites, which can be visited on a one- or two-day excursion with the aid of a jeep and a local guide.

Gobi Camels (☎ 011-310 455; with/without food US$35/15) ger camp, 6km northwest of town, offers hot showers, satellite TV and comfortable gers. The other alternative is the unmarked and very basic **hotel** (per person T5000) within a compound on the southern edge of the town 'square'. It is usually deserted so you'll have to ask around the shops for the keyholder, Ms Dolumsuren.

The best way to get to Bayangovi and its surrounding attractions is in your own rented transport, either from Bayankhongor or as part of a longer trip.

Failing this, shared minivans or jeeps occasionally run to Bayangovi from outside the central market at Bayankhongor. There is also a postal truck (T7500) that leaves for Bayangovi from Bayankhongor on Wednesday; inquire at the post office in Bayankhongor. To get to Bayankhongor ask at the post office or petrol station, and wait.

Once you get to Bayangovi your only option to see the surrounding sites is to hire a jeep from the Gobi Camels camp.

AROUND BAYANGOVI
About 90km east of Bayangovi lies **Tsagaan Agui** (GPS: N44° 42.604', E101° 10.187'). Situated in a narrow gorge, the cave once housed Stone Age human beings 700,000 years ago. It features a crystal-lined inner chamber. Entrance to the cave costs T1000 (including a local guide), which is paid at the nearby ger.

Also near Bayangovi are several intriguing rock inscription sites. At **Tsagaan Bulag** (GPS: N44° 35.156', E100° 20.733'), 18km south, a white rock outcrop has the faint imprint of a strange helmeted figure, which locals believe was created by aliens. The area is also home to many herds of camel, attracted to the springs at the base of the outcrop.

Other noteworthy sites which you could add on to make a full day trip include the vertical walls of the 4km-long **Gunii Khöndii** gorge, about 70km southwest of Bayangovi, and the beautiful **Bituut rock**, west of Bayangovi on the southern flank of Ikh Bogd, formed after an earthquake in 1957.

Further afield at **Bayangiin Nuruu** (GPS: N44° 17.218', E100° 31.329'), 90km south of Bayangovi, is a canyon with well-preserved rock engravings and petroglyphs dating from 3000 BC. The engravings depict hunting and agricultural scenes in a surprisingly futuristic style.

Travelling further south the landscape slowly descends into the Gobi Desert proper, along the border with Ömnögov aimag. Just over the border are numerous **oases**, among them **Jartiin Khuv, Daltin Khuv, Burkhant** and **Zuunmod**. Look out for the wild horses and camels, black-tailed gazelle, antelope and *zam* lizards, which inhabit the area.

This region is rich in fossil sites. **Bugiin Tsav** (GPS: N43° 52.869', E100° 01.639') is a large series of rift valleys running parallel to the Altan Uul mountain range. A number of dinosaur fossils have been found here, which are now housed in the Museum of Natural History in Ulaanbaatar. The other fossil site is at **Yasnee Tsav**, an eroded hilly region with some impressive buttes. Local guides claim they can point out authentic fossils at this site.

Continuing south will lead to the other famous fossil site of **Khermen Tsav** (GPS: N43° 28.006', E99° 49.976'), arguably the most spectacular canyons in the Gobi. From here one could continue east into the Gobi towards Gurvantes, Noyon and Bayandalai, but be warned that this section of road is notoriously treacherous. Don't go without plenty of water and well-equipped 4WD vehicles.

Getting There & Around
All of the sites mentioned above are very difficult to find without a good local guide. Bodio, the manager of the Gobi Camels ger camp (see left), can organise local guides for US$15 per day (though few of these speak English so you really still need your own translator). He also hires out jeeps for T300 per kilometre, which includes driver, petrol and local guide, and can arrange horse and camel tours for US$5 per person per day, plus US$5 per day for a guide.

BÖÖN TSAGAAN NUUR
БӨӨН ЦАГААН НУУР

This large saltwater **lake** (GPS: N45° 37.114′, E99° 15.350′), at the end of Baidrag Gol, is popular with birdlife, especially the relic gull, whooper swan and geese. It is possible sleep in the abandoned cabins by the lake. A caretaker at the nearby ger will unlock one for T1000. The lake is about 90km southwest of Bayankhongor city, and 18km west of Baatsagaan.

GOV-ALTAI ГОВЬ–АЛТАЙ

pop 61,400 / area 142,000 sq km

Mongolia's second-largest aimag is named after the Gobi Desert and the Mongol Altai Nuruu range, which virtually bisects the aimag to create a stark, rocky landscape. There is a certain beauty in this combination, but there is considerable heartbreak too. Gov-Altai is one of the least suitable areas for raising livestock, and therefore one of the most hostile to human habitation. Severe winters (*zud*) from 1999 to 2001 destroyed half the aimag's livestock population and forced more than 12,000 people to leave the area for better opportunities in the city. It is hoped that an ambitious Kuwaiti-funded hydroelectric power project and dam on the Zavkhan Gol (near Taishir) will bring an economic upturn to the region.

Somehow a few Gobi bears, wild camels, ibexes and even snow leopards survive, protected in several remote national parks. Most of the population live in the northeastern corner, where melting snow from the Khangai Nuruu feeds small rivers, creating vital water supplies.

Gov-Altai is famous for its oases, and contains some remote sections of several national parks, but most travellers head further west to the more beautiful and interesting aimags in western Mongolia.

Mountaineers and adventurous hikers with a lot of time on their hands might want to bag an Altai peak. Opportunities include Khuren Tovon Uul (3802m), in Altai *sum*, Burkhan Buuddai Uul (3765m) in Biger *sum*, or the permanently snowcapped peak of Sutai Uul (4090m), the highest peak in Gov-Altai. Most climbers approach Sutai Uul from the Khovd side.

National Parks

The beauty of Gov-Altai's diverse and sparsely populated mountain and desert environment has led to the allocation of a large portion of the aimag as national parks:

Alag Khairkhan Natural Reserve (36,400 hectares) Protects Altai habitat, rare plants, snow leopards, argali and ibex.

Eej Khairkhan Natural Reserve (22,475 hectares) About 150km directly south of Altai, the reserve was created to protect the general environment.

Great Gobi Strictly Protected Area It's divided into 'Gobi A' (Southern Altai Gobi) and 'Gobi B' (Dzungarian Gobi). 'Gobi A' is over 4.4 million hectares in the southern part of the aimag. 'Gobi B' is 881,000 hectares in the southwest of Gov-Altai and in neighbouring Khovd. Together, the undisturbed area is the fourth-largest biosphere reserve in the world and protects wild ass, Gobi bears, the wild Bactrian camel and jerboa, among other endangered animals.

Khasagt Khairkhan Strictly Protected Area (27,448 hectare) The area protects endangered argali sheep and the Mongol Altai mountain environment.

Sharga Natural Reserve Like the Mankhan Natural Reserve in Khovd aimag, it helps to preserve highly endangered species of antelope.

Takhiin Tal On the border of the northern section of Gobi B (Dzungarian Gobi). *Takhi* (the Mongolian wild horse) have been reintroduced into the wild here since 1996 through the Takhi Research Station. Experts hope they will survive and flourish in this remote area of the Gobi.

ALTAI АЛТАЙ

☎ 01482 / pop 19,800 / elev 2181m

Nestled between the mountains of Khasagt Khairkhan Uul (3579m) and Jargalant Uul (3070m), the aimag capital is a pleasant tree-lined place, with friendly people. With an interesting museum and a well-stocked market, Altai is a good place to stop on the way to somewhere else – either to or from Khovd, or the national parks to the south.

Information

Internet Café (per hr T800; ☼ 10am-8pm Mon-Sat) Inside the Telecom office.

Khan Bank (☎ 23773; ☼ 9am-1pm & 2-6pm Mon-Fri) Changes cash and, if you are persistent, travellers cheques.

Telecom Office (☎ 24117; ☼ 24hr) The post office is also here.

Sights
DASHPELJEELEN KHIID

This small, attractive monastery (Дашпэлжээлэн Хийд) was built in 1990 and is home to 30 monks. Unlike most others, there was no

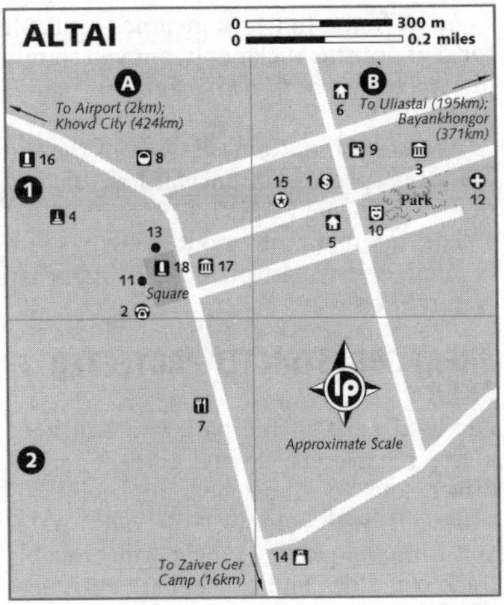

INFORMATION
Internet Café .... (see 2)
Khan Bank 1 B1
Post Office .... (see 2)
Telecom Office 2 A1

SIGHTS & ACTIVITIES (pp196–7)
Aimag Museum 3 B1
Dashpeljeelen Khiid 4 A1

SLEEPING (p197)
Altai Hotel 5 B1
Birj Hotel 6 B1

EATING (p197)
Sutai Restaurant 7 A2

TRANSPORT (pp197–8)
Jeep & Minivan Stand 8 A1
Petrol Station 9 B1

OTHER
Drama Theatre 10 B1
Government House 11 A1
Hospital 12 B1
Information & Technology Centre (Under Construction) 13 A1
Market 14 B2
Police 15 B1
Russian-Mongolian Friendship Monument 16 A1
Sports Palace 17 A1
Statue of Magsaryn Janchiv 18 A1

previous structure on this site. On most days from 10am, you can witness a ceremony. The monastery is a short walk northwest of the town square.

AIMAG MUSEUM

The barely functioning **Aimag Museum** (☎ 24213; admission T1000; 9am-1pm & 2-6pm Mon-Fri) includes some excellent bronze statues, scroll paintings, some genuine Mongol army chain mail, and an interesting shaman costume and drum. Unfortunately there is very little English text, the electricity is usually off and the caretaker will probably need to go find the keys before you can get inside.

Sleeping & Eating

CAMPING

The road from Altai to Khovd goes through a surprisingly lush plain for about 10km. So, if you have a tent and your own vehicle, head out there. A great patch of ground, which you will have to share with a few cows, is only a 20-minute walk northwest of town.

Zaiver ger camp (☎ 9948 9718; per day US$10) Another option is this ger camp, 16km from Altai. The staff will pick you up from town if you call ahead.

HOTELS

Altai Hotel (☎ 24134; s/d T6000/12,000, half-lux/lux per person T9100/15,000) This unexciting relic from the Soviet past, smack in the centre of town and close to the drama theatre, is where most visitors to Altai lay their heads. The staff is friendly enough, and all rooms come with toilets, but only the half-lux and lux rooms have shower (with ice-cold water).

Birj Hotel (☎ 23546; s/d T2500/5000, half-lux per person T5000) Simple but clean and bright rooms, although the pit toilets outside are a tad basic.

Eating

The Altai Hotel manages to feed guests with a decent selection of *buuz* (steamed meat dumplings), *tsuivan* and goulash for around T800. The two *guanzes* on the street south of the Altai hotel are both pretty dire. Your best bet for a square meal is the Sutai Restaurant, south of the Telecom office, which was closed for renovation at the time of research.

Getting There & Away

AIR

MIAT flies from Ulaanbaatar to Altai and back on Tuesday, Thursday and Saturday for US$120/210. The airport and **reservation office** (☎ 23544, 9948 9665) is 2km northwest of the centre.

HITCHING

There is some traffic along the main road towards Khovd and Bayankhongor, but you may have to wait a few hours for something suitable. Very few vehicles travel between Altai and Uliastai; you will probably have to wait for something to arrive from Uliastai first. Almost no vehicles venture into the south of Gov-Altai.

The best place to ask around for a shared jeep is at the southern entrance to the market. Expect to pay around T10,000 to T15,000 for a ride to Khovd or Bayankhongor.

MINIVAN & JEEP

Altai is a stop on the road to Khovd and you'll find minivans (T30,000) departing every morning from Ulaanbaatar's Dragon and Naran Tuul stations.

Altai is not somewhere you should expect to find any reliable jeeps for hire. You are more likely to have success in Uliastai and Khovd city. Shared minivans for Ulaanbaatar and Khovd leave from the roadside near the monastery.

The road from Altai to Khovd city (424km) starts off through a lush plain, then becomes desolate and boring. Altai is also 371km west of Bayankhongor city and 195km south of Uliastai.

EEJ KHAIRKHAN UUL ЭЭЖ ХАЙРХАН УУЛ

Near the base of the Eej Khairkhan Uul (2275m), just north of 'Gobi A' National Park, you could camp at some delightful **rock pools** and explore the nearby **caves**. You will need a guide to show you around. Almost no suitable drinking water is available, so take your own into the area.

An A-frame hut is sometimes available for rent near the rock pools, but you should always bring your own camping equipment.

About 30 minutes' walk west of the hut are some spectacular, ancient **rock paintings** of ibex, horsemen and archers.

The mountain is about 150km south of Altai, and is part of the Eej Khairkhan Natural Reserve.

GREAT GOBI STRICTLY PROTECTED AREA

For both parts of the park you will need a very reliable vehicle and an experienced driver, and you must be completely self-sufficient with supplies of food, water and camping gear. A ranger will probably track you down and collect park entry fees (T3000 per person).

Gobi B (Dzungarian Gobi)

Although the majority of this 881,000-hectare park lies in neighbouring Khovd aimag, most travellers enter from the Gov-Altai side, where a **research station** (GPS: N45° 32.197', E93° 39.055') has been set up to protect reintroduced *takhi* (Przewalski's) horse. Most of the *takhi* now run free, although a few still live in enclosures near the research station, which is about 15km southwest of Bij-Altai village. For more on the *takhi*, see the boxed text on p103.

SAVING THE SNOW LEOPARD

The mountain regions of Gov-Altai are home to the beautiful and elusive *irbis* (snow leopard). Up to 50kg in weight, and about 1m long (the tail is an extra 70cm), snow leopards can easily kill an ibex three times its size. They remain solitary except during the brief mating season.

An estimated 7500 snow leopards live in an area of 1.5 million sq km across China, Pakistan, Afghanistan, India, Nepal and Mongolia (where 1000 to 1500 live). The principal threats are poaching, habitat loss and wild prey loss. Declining numbers of Argali sheep and ibex have forced snow leopards to kill livestock and brought them into conflict with local herders.

It is hoped that the establishment of several national parks, education programmes and local income-generation projects can help save the snow leopard. Otherwise, the few pelts on display in local museums and even the odd ger camp will be all that is left of this beautiful creature.

Irbis is a local organisation that protects snow leopards in Mongolia by providing alternative sources of income to herders in snow-leopard habitat. The company sells and markets locally made handicrafts, such as felt mats and camel and cashmere goods, with proceeds going jointly to producers and a conservation fund.

If you would like more information about the protection of the snow leopard, contact the **International Snow Leopard Trust** (in the USA ☎ 206-632-2421; www.snowleopard.org; 4649 Sunnyside Ave N, Seattle, Washington, 98103). In Ulaanbaatar, contact **Ms Bayara** (bayar_drew@hotmail.com) or **Mr Munkh-Tsog** (☎ 011-329 632; isltmon@magicnet.mn).

The scientists based here can provide information on tour options and the best places to camp. Besides the *takhi*, you stand a good chance of seeing argali sheep, ibex and wild ass. The park also protects wild the Bactrian camel, and a handful of elusive Gobi bears.

Gobi A (Southern Altai Gobi)

The majority of this 4.4 million-hectare national park, also known as 'Gobi A', lies in the southern Gov-Altai. Established over 25 years ago, the area has been nominated as an International Biosphere Reserve by the UN.

The park is remote and very difficult to reach, which is bad news for visitors but excellent news for the fragile flora and fauna.

There are a few mountains over 1200m, and several springs and oases, which only an experienced guide will find. To explore the park, start at Biger, turn southwest on the trail to Tsogt, and head south on any jeep trail you can find.

Western Mongolia

CONTENTS

Stretching towards Inner Asia – with glacier-wrapped mountains, sparkling alpine lakes and coloured deserts – western Mongolia is the most remote and magical slice of Mongolia.

The diversity of the landscape is matched only by the ethnic groups that inhabit the three aimags (provinces or states) that make up this territory: Bayan-Ölgii, Khovd and Uvs. Only half the population in the west is Khalkh; the remainder are made up of ethnic Kazakhs, Dorvods, Khotons and Myangads. Bayan-Ölgii is in fact designated as a 'Kazakh province' and it is here that their culture persevered despite communist oppression for much of the 20th century.

The dominant feature of western Mongolia is the Mongol Altai Nuruu, Mongolia's highest mountain range, which stretches from Russia through Bayan-Ölgii and Khovd, and on to the adjacent Gov-Altai aimag. It contains many challenging and popular peaks for mountain climbers, and is the source of several rivers which eventually flow into the Arctic and Pacific Oceans.

Western Mongolia is an anachronistic part of the world where conservative and communist values still hold sway. Travellers have even been arrested and jailed for not carrying border permits in Altai Tavan Bogd National Park. There are areas of lawlessness: the Russian border in Uvs sees occasional attacks by Tuvan cattle rustlers. And infrastructure is poor – electricity mostly comes from Russia and when bills go unpaid the Russians pull the plug.

Despite the hardships, western Mongolia's attractions, both natural and cultural, are well worth the effort. With time and flexibility, the region may well be the highlight of your trip.

HIGHLIGHTS

- Trek around **Tsambagarav Uul National Park** (p215), a stunning area of glaciers, traditional Kazakh culture, forests and streams, in the shadow of snowcapped peaks
- Camp by the shores of **Üüreg Nuur** (p220), a lovely, accessible freshwater lake filled with fish
- Explore **Uvs Nuur** (p219), Mongolia's largest lake, with impressive (but hard to find) birdlife
- Venture to the blue lakes and 4000m peaks of **Altai Tavan Bogd National Park** (p208), on the border with Russia and China
- View the towering mountain **Otgon Tenger Uul** (p225), abode of the gods and Mongolia's holiest peak

- POPULATION: 270,200
- AREA: 191,000 SQ KM

Climate

Weather can be extremely temperamental in the Altai mountains. Brief snowstorms are common even in summer. These don't last long; usually within an hour the sun will be out again, but have a jacket ready. With the exception of the mountaintops, Uvs Nuur is the coldest part of the country in winter – temperatures of -50°C are not unknown. The low-lying lakes and rivers of western Mongolia also attract some appalling packs of mosquitoes; arm yourself with serious bug repellent.

Language

In some parts of western Mongolia, especially Bayan-Ölgii, Kazakh is the dominant language. Other dialects are also spoken; the 1500 Tuvans in the Tsengel *sum* (a district; the administrative unit below an aimag) of Bayan-Ölgii have their own language. With the exception of small Kazakh children, most people will understand some Mongolian and possibly Russian.

Getting There & Away

Transport between western Mongolia and Ulaanbaatar is mainly by plane – so flights are often very full. Transport by land from Ulaanbaatar is a rough and tedious six days. The northern route via Arkhangai has several points of interest en route, but most shared vehicles travel along the mind-numbingly dull southern route via Bayankhongor and Altai to Khovd.

Though not a main traveller route yet, it is possible to enter or leave Mongolia at the Tsagaannuur border crossing. With a bit of planning (you'll need a Russian visa; see p239), it's possible to tour the area and exit to Russia without hightailing it back to the capital.

Note that western Mongolia is on a different time zone from Ulaanbaatar – one hour behind the rest of the country.

Getting Around

Hiring a jeep is relatively easy in any of the three western aimag capitals, and all three cities are linked by decent roads. You'll waste a lot of time if hitchhiking in the area; trucks will be most likely headed for the nearest border post and jeeps will be packed full of people. Your best chance of finding a lift is to ask for a shared jeep at the mar-

kets. You'll save the anguish of sitting in the jeep all day by telling the driver to pick you up at your hotel. If you are determined to hitch, bring water, food, a tent and plenty of patience. Travelling by mountain bike or horse is great if you have the time.

BAYAN-ÖLGII
БАЯН-ӨЛГИЙ

pop 100,800 / area 46,000 sq km

The Mongol Altai Nuruu is the backbone of Bayan-Ölgii. The highest peaks, many over 4000m, are permanently covered with glaciers and snow, while the valleys have a few green pastures that support about two million livestock, as well as bear, fox and lynx. These valleys are dotted with small communities of nomadic families enjoying the short summer from mid-June to late August, as well as some beautiful alpine lakes.

The ethnic groups who call Bayan-Ölgii home comprise the Kazakh, Khalkh, Dorvod, Uriankhai, Tuva and Khoshuud. Unlike the rest of Mongolia, which is dominated by the Khalkh Mongols, about 90% of Bayan-Ölgii's population are Kazakh, almost all of them Muslim. The remaining 10% are mostly small minority groups.

Trading heavily with Russia and China, and utilising increased cultural ties with Kazakhstan, it's a region apart from the rest of Mongolia. When the economy goes bad it's Almaty and Astana that workers migrate to, rather than Ulaanbaatar. More than 10,000 people left for Kazakhstan in the 1990s, though some have returned.

The aimag has a rich collection of archaeological sites, with many *balbal* (Turkic stone figures believed to be grave makers), deer stones, *kurgans* (burial mounds) and a remarkable collection of 10,000 petroglyphs near the Russian border at Tsagaan Sala (also known as Baga Oigor). If you are particularly interested in these remote and obscure sites, contact the Mongol Altai Nuruu Special Protected Area office in Ölgii (see p204).

National Parks

Most parks come under the jurisdiction of the Mongol Altai Nuruu Special Protected Area. Environmentalists hope that further sections of Bayan-Ölgii will become na-

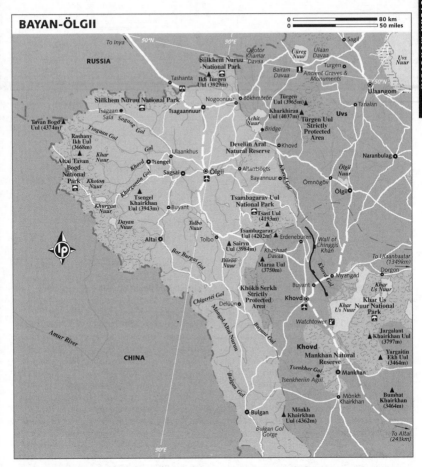

BAYAN-ÖLGII

tional parks to preserve the argali sheep, ibex and snow leopard, as well as the important sources of lakes and rivers in the Great Lakes Depression in the Uvs and Khovd aimags.

Altai Tavan Bogd National Park (636,161 hectares) Takes in Tavan Bogd Uul, Mongolia's highest mountain, and the stunning lakes of Khoton, Khurgan and Dayan. Fauna includes argali sheep, ibex, maral (Asiatic red deer), stone marten, deer, elk, Altai snowcock and eagles.

Develiin Aral Natural Reserve (10,300 hectares) A remarkable habitat around Develiin Island in the Usan Khooloi and Khovd rivers. It is home to pheasants, boars and beavers.

Khökh Serkh Strictly Protected Area (65,920 hectares) A mountainous area on the border with Khovd, which protects argali sheep and ibex.

Siilkhem Nuruu National Park (140,080 hectares) This park has two sections, one around Ikh Türgen Uul, the other further east.

Tsambagarav Uul National Park (110,960 hectares) Established in 2000 to protect glaciers and the snow-leopard habitat; borders on Khovd.

ÖLGII ӨЛГИЙ

☎ 01422 / pop 28,500 / elev 1710m

Ölgii, the capital of the aimag, is an ethnically Kazakh city that happens to be in Mongolia. You can certainly feel that you are in a Muslim-influenced Central Asian region: many places have squat toilets; there are signs in Arabic and Kazakh Cyrillic; and the market, which is called a bazaar rather than the Mongolian *zakh*, sells the odd *shashlyk*

WESTERN MONGOLIA

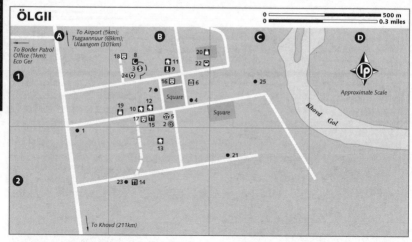

(kebab) and is stocked with goods from Kazakhstan. Ölgii is 1645km from Ulaanbaatar but only 225km from Russia.

The town itself is a squat, concrete affair, meandering along the river, Khovd Gol, and surrounded by ger (traditional circular felt yurt) districts and rocky escarpments. Thunderclouds brew in the mountains above town, making for some dramatic climatic changes throughout the day and brilliant shows of light in the late afternoon. A friendly local population makes the place a welcome break on a long road journey and the logical place to launch an expedition into the Altai mountains.

Information

Bathhouse (☎ 22442; per person T800; ☽ 9am-10pm) Hot-water showers, sauna and barbershops. *Monsha* is 'hot water' in the local Kazakh dialect.

Jarag Internet Café (☎ 23732; per hr T900; ☽ 11am-7pm Mon-Sat) Good computers and a decent connection. The Telecom office also has an Internet café that opens earlier and on Sunday, but its connection is slower and costs T950 per hour.

Khadgalamj Bank (☎ 22493; ☽ 8am-noon & 1-4.30pm Mon-Fri) Changes dollars and euros. Private moneychangers can also be found in the market.

Protected Areas Office (☎ 22111, 23518; atai_a@ yahoo.com; ☽ 9am-noon & 1-6pm Mon-Fri) The Protected Areas office doubles as an information centre, with informed English-speaking staff plus photos, maps and heaps of reading material on the park. The office can help with your border permit, sell national park tickets, provide itineraries for your trip depending on how much time you have, and recommend drivers and guides. The director, Atai, has years of mountaineering experience in the area and may be able to hire out some climbing equipment. The office is located in the MPRP building at the southeastern corner of the main square.

Telecom Office (☎ 24117; ☽ 24hr) The post office is also located here.

Sights

The **Aimag Museum** (admission T2000; ☽ 9am-1pm & 2-6pm Mon-Fri) gives an excellent overview of Kazakh culture and of the geography of Bayan-Ölgii. The 2nd floor is devoted to history, and the 3rd floor has some interesting ethnographic displays.

Ölgii's **mosque** and *madrasah* (Islamic place of learning) is worth a quick look, especially on Friday at lunchtime when weekly prayers are held, though you may not be allowed inside. The mosque holds the offices of the Islamic Centre of Mongolia. Its unusual angle is due to its orientation to Mecca.

ESSENTIAL KAZAKH

Peace be with you.	*asalam aleykum.*
Hello.	*salamatsyz be.*
Goodbye.	*qosh-sau bolyngdar.*
Thank you.	*rakhmet.*
Yes/no.	*ia/zhoq.*
Where is...?	*...qayda?*
How much?	*qansha?*
Tea.	*shay.*

Courses

Mr Cheryazdan (☎ 23358), a music instructor at the Teacher's College, gives *dombra* (two-stringed lute) lessons for a fee. The college is east of downtown, near the Khovd Gol.

Tours

Bayan-Auul Tour (☎ 9942 9935; ba-tours@chinggis.com)
Blue Wolf Tours (☎ 9909 2401, 9911 0303, 22772) Run by experienced tour operator Khanat, Blue Wolf has been in the business for about 10 years and runs quality trips including winter eagle-hunting tours. Khanat has a ger camp at Sagsai, charging US$5 per night, US$3 for a hot shower and US$5 per meal. The Ölgii office is about 400m south of the ochre-coloured National Theatre.
Kazakh Tour (☎ 9942 8304)

Festivals & Events

The annual **Eagle Festival** (admission plus photography US$30, admission plus video & photography US$50), held on the first Sunday and Monday in October, has been running since 2000. This is

a good time to shop for arts and crafts and watch eagle-hunting competitions (though animal-lovers may find it somewhat cruel as live foxes and wolves are used as bait). Contact Nomadic Expeditions (p70) for details. A smaller Eagle Festival is held two days earlier in Sagsai *sum*; contact Blue Wolf Tours (left).

On 22 March, the spring festival and family event of **Navrus** is held. Family visits and feasting are common.

Sleeping
CAMPING
If you want to camp, walk east of the square to Khovd Gol and then head southeast, away from the market and ger suburbs.

GER CAMPS
Aulum Sayajim (Green Garden; ☎ 23983, 9942 9094; zoz_avil@chinggis.com; per person T5000) A Kazakh ger camp located in the centre of town, this place offers comfortable beds in traditional gers decorated with wall hangings and carpets. It has a pit toilet in the back and water spigot for washing, but the attached beer garden can get a bit noisy.

The city's Protected Areas office runs a backpacker-friendly **Eco Ger** (☎ 22502; per person T3000) in the suburbs near the border-patrol office. Ask for Dagas or contact the Protected Areas office for details.

HOTELS
Hotels in Ölgii want to keep your passport for the duration of your stay. It is much better to give a photocopy of your passport – there is less to worry about if you forget to pick it up when checking out.

Duman (☎ 9942 8174; s/d T5000/10,000, lux T15,000-17,000) This place has good-looking rooms and the reasonably priced lux options are the best in town, complete with TV, comfy beds and 24-hour hot-water showers.

Altan Orda (☎ 22258, 9942 8877; s/d/q T6000/9000/16,500, 2-bed lux T19,000) Another place with a hotchpotch of rooms; it's a little better than the Bastau as the 2nd-floor rooms come with attached bathroom. It has a decent restaurant that turns into a thumping disco by night.

Bastau Hotel (☎ 23629; dm/s/d T3000/3000/6000, half-lux s/d T3500/7000, lux per person T7000) This welcoming hotel has a variety of rooms including a handy three-bed dorm with two

KAZAKHS

Kazakh nomads have lived in Central Asia for 400 years, but first started to come to the Bayan-Ölgii area in the 1840s to graze their sheep on the high mountain pastures during summer. They then returned to Kazakhstan or Xinjiang for the winter. After the Mongolian Revolution in 1921, a permanent border was drawn by agreement between China, Russia and Mongolia, but the Kazakhs remained nomadic until the 1930s, crossing the border at will.

The word 'Kazakh' is said to mean 'free warrior' or 'steppe roamer'. Kazakhs trace their roots to the 15th century, when rebellious kinsmen of an Uzbek khaan (king or chief) broke away, and settled in present-day Kazakhstan.

Traditional costume for Kazakh women is a long dress with stand-up collar, or a brightly decorated velvet waistcoat with heavy jewellery. Older married women often wear a white head-scarf. The men still wear baggy shirts and trousers, vests, long black cloaks (not the traditional Mongolian *del*, the all-purpose, traditional coat or dress worn by men and women), and a skullcap or a *loovuuz* (fox-fur hat). The Kazakh culture of Mongolia is far more intact than that of strongly Russified Kazakhstan.

Kazakh culture is quite different from Mongolian; even Kazakh saddles are a different shape. Music is commonly sung by bards who accompany their singing with a *dombra*, a two-stringed lute. Kazakh gers (traditional circular felt yurts) are taller, wider and more richly decorated than the Mongolian version. *Tush* (wall hangings) and *koshma* (felt carpets), decorated with stylised animal motifs, are common. *Chiy* (traditional reed screens) are becoming less common.

Kazakhs generally adhere rather loosely to Sunni Islam, but religion is not a major force. This is because of their distance from the centre of Islam, their nomadic lifestyle and the suppression of Islam by Stalinism. Islam is making a comeback in Bayan-Ölgii, thanks to the lifting of restrictions against religion, aid packages from other Muslim countries, the construction of a mosque in Ölgii, and the first hajj or pilgrimage to Mecca in 1992. Islamic law has always sat lightly with the many Kazakhs, however, who enjoy a bottle of vodka as much as the next Mongolian. The main Kazakh holiday is the pre-Islamic spring festival of Navrus, celebrated on 21 March.

Kazakhs speak a Turkic language with 42 Cyrillic letters, similar to Russian, and a little different from Mongolian. The Mongolian government is trying to placate the Kazakh minority, and stop them returning to Kazakhstan, by encouraging the Kazakh language in schools in Bayan-Ölgii.

couches and a TV. The lux room includes a cosy living room and attached bathroom. Other rooms use a shared bathroom with luke-warm shower.

Eating

Big Dog (☎ 9909 2401) Run by the folks at Blue Wolf Tours, this exciting idea is located 400m south of the National Theatre. It was under construction at the time of research but is definitely worth checking out – the owner makes far-reaching promises of Mexican and French dishes (?!).

Duman (☎ 21666; meals T600-2000; ❧ 10am-8pm) One of the newer cafés in town, this modern place serves an adequate goulash, cutlet (meat patty with sauce) and *tsuivan* (fried noodles). It's in the hotel of the same name.

Both the Altan Orda and the Bastau have good restaurants. Otherwise, try the five or six *shaykhana* (teahouses) or *ashkhana* (restaurants) in abandoned train wagons around the market and town squares. They usually serve delicious tea (*shay* in the Kazakh language) – not the milky and salty stuff loved by Mongolians. They also serve some *khuushuur* (fried meat pancakes) with a delicious *khaluun nogoo* (chilli sauce). There is the decent **Toganai shaykhana** (buuz T100, khuushuur T120) opposite the Bastau Hotel run by three Kazakh sisters. If you give some advance warning, one of these restaurants should be able to prepare *besbarmak* (literally 'five fingers'), a traditional Kazakh dish of meat and pasta squares.

Entertainment

The incongruous ochre-coloured Kazakh National Theatre used to have *dombra* recitals, though it seems to be permanently closed now. You could try the BU Palace on the square.

Nur Danesca (☎ 23720; admission T300; ❧ 6pm-1am) A modern disco club behind the mosque.

For a beer in a quieter atmosphere, try the **Aulum Sayajim beer garden** (☎ 23983, 9942 9094), near the police station.

Shopping

The **market** (⊗ 11am-5pm) has a decent selection of food supplies imported from Russia and China. Traditional Kazakh skullcaps and boots can also be found amid the chaos. There's a small charge to get into the enclosed part of the market where all the food is.

If you are on the hunt for Kazakh wall hangings and felt rugs, check out the shop next to the Special Protected Area office and the two shops in the lobby of the Aimag Museum. Everything is up for negotiation.

For general goods, such as food products and Kodak film, try the 2nd-floor 'Delguur' (shop) just east of the Altan Orda Hotel.

Getting There & Away
AIR

MIAT (Mongolian Airlines) has flights between Ölgii and Ulaanbaatar, with a refuelling stop (often at Mörön), every Wednesday, Thursday and Saturday for US$185/323 one way/return. The four-hour flight provides breathtaking views of glacier-capped peaks as you approach Ölgii.

The airport is 6km north of the centre, on the opposite side of the river. There is no bus, but it's usually possible to hitch a ride in a truck or on the back of a motorcycle.

MIAT is located in the same building at the Protected Areas office, though the staff can be difficult to find. A smaller office opens at the airport on the mornings when a flight arrives.

To Kazakhstan

Each Wednesday afternoon, Air Irtysh (a Kazakh airline) flies between Almaty and Ölgii via Üst Kamenogorsk in eastern Kazakhstan. This flight (US$200 plus T5500 tax) is a little unreliable and you can only buy a ticket in Ölgii, which means there is no guarantee you'll get on the flight. The ticket agent is in the Red Cross building, a five-minute walk southeast of the square. You may also want to inquire about the latest details with tour operators in Almaty and Üst Kamenogorsk (see Lonely Planet's *Central Asia* for details).

Your biggest obstacle to this flight is immigration procedures, which will have to be cleared at the airport. Foreign travellers are not allowed to go through customs in Üst Kamenogorsk so you need to buy a ticket all the way through to Almaty. Those that have tried to get off the plane in Üst Kamenogorsk found themselves stuck in the airport for 24 hours, forced to wait for the next plane to Almaty. Likewise, coming the other way, you'll need to board the plane in Almaty.

HITCHING

A few vehicles, most of which are petrol tankers, travel the road between Ölgii and Khovd city. The Ölgii–Ulaangom road is not as busy because most vehicles head east towards Ulaanbaatar and use the southern road via Khovd city. Most vehicles travelling between Ölgii and Ulaangom bypass Tsagaannuur and take the shortcut via Achit Nuur.

Listen to the loudspeaker at the market for information (this could be a challenge as you'll hear it in Mongolian, Kazakh or Russian) about lifts around the aimag. Check out the noticeboard there too. If you can't read the notices, just ask around anyway. A lot of Russian trucks hang around the market, waiting for cargo to take to Russia via Tsagaannuur. There is also quite a lot of traffic, with jeeps being driven from Russia and sold locally.

JEEP

Public shared jeeps to Khovd (T8000), Ulaangom (T10,000) and Tsengel *sum* (T2500) leave from Ölgii market. Drivers may try to charge foreigners double here, so check to see what others are paying. There are more frequent shared jeeps to Tsagaannuur (T3000), the last town before the Russian border. Travellers have recomended a local driver named **Dosjan Khabyl** (dosjan@yahoo.com) who speaks English, Mongolian, Russian and Kazakh. He has a new jeep and can get you out to places such as Tavan Bogd.

The road from Ölgii to Khovd city (211km) is pretty good. The 300km road to Ulaangom, via Achit Nuur, is also good. The road passes the surprisingly lush riverside forests of the Develiin Aral Natural Reserve. Look out for the canyon to the left, marked by ancient graves, some 21km from Ölgii.

TSAST UUL ЦАСТ УУЛ

The two *sums* of Altantsögts and Bayannuur are about 50km southeast of Ölgii, on the border with Khovd aimag. They are full of lush valleys with friendly Kazakh and Mongol nomads in summer, dozens of tiny unmapped lakes and soaring, permanently snowcapped peaks, such as Tsast Uul (Mountain of Snow; 4193m).

If you have your own vehicle and tent, take a detour between Khovd city and Ölgii and spend a few peaceful days around Tsast Uul. It is always cold up here (it only stops snowing between about mid June and late August), so be prepared. Just to the south, in Khovd aimag, Tsambagarav Uul (4202m) is slightly higher and equally as stunning (see p215).

TOLBO NUUR ТОЛБО НУУР

Tolbo Nuur (GPS: N 48° 35.320', E 090° 04.536') is about 50km south of Ölgii, on the main road between Ölgii and Khovd city, so it's an easy day trip or stopover. The freshwater lake is high (2080m), expansive and eerie, but a bit disappointing because the shoreline is treeless and there are a few mosquitoes (camp away from the marshy shoreline). There are a few gers around the lake, and the water is clean enough for swimming if you don't mind icy temperatures. If you want to see, and camp at, some better lakes, keep travelling on north to Uvs aimag.

A major battle was fought here between Bolshevik and White Russians, with the local Mongolian general, Khasbaatar, siding with the Bolsheviks. The Bolsheviks won and there are a couple of memorial plaques by the lake.

TOLBO TO BULGAN

The southern road through the spine of the Mongol Altai Nuruu, one of the most remote roads in the country, is the back door into Khovd aimag. From Tolbo *sum* centre, which has an interesting mosque, it's an easy detour to Dööröö Nuur and nearby Sairyn Uul, an increasingly popular place for horse trekking.

The next *sum* south of Tolbo is Deluun, famed for its eagle-hunters, and starting point for a horse trek through the Khökh Serkh Strictly Protected Area to Khovd city. Further south, the road winds through the spectacular canyon lands of Bulgan *sum*, on the western flank of 4362m Mönkh Khairkhan Uul. From here it's a very rough six-hour drive through the Bulgan Gol

gorge, which is navigable by kayak at the end of June, if you can stand the mosquitoes and happen to have a kayak. Confusingly, the road comes out of the gorge at Bulgan *sum* in Khovd aimag. The mosquito-infested Mongolian–Chinese border post sees many petrol tankers but is closed to foreign travellers.

ALTAI TAVAN BOGD NATIONAL PARK
АЛТАЙ ТАВАН БОГД

This stunningly beautiful park stretches south from Tavan Bogd Uul and includes the three stunning lakes of Khoton Nuur, Khurgan Nuur and Dayan Nuur. It's a remote area, divided from China by the high wall of snowcapped peaks, and known to local Kazakhs as the Syrgali region.

All three lakes are the source of the Khovd Gol, which eventually flows into Khar Us Nuur in Khovd aimag. It's possible to make rafting trips down river from Khoton Nuur. No agencies offer rafting trips at present, but you could check with the Protected Areas office.

Tsengel, Mongolia's westernmost town, is the jumping-off point for the park. It occupies a nice setting amid the mountains and there is good camping away from town, by the river. There are a couple of *guanz* (canteens or cheap restaurants) and a small market, but no hotel. Hiring a jeep could be difficult; you are better off bringing one from Ölgii.

You won't be let inside the park on your own and will need a guide or local Kazakh to help you out.

Permits

Park entry fees are the standard T3000 per person per day. Fishing permits cost T500 per day, but fishing is not permitted between 15 May and 15 July (there is a US$50 fine). The main entry to the park is by the bridge over the Khovd Gol, south of Tsengel. You can pay for permits here, or at the Mongol Altai Nuruu Special Protected Area office in Ölgii or from rangers around the lake.

You definitely need to get a border permit from the **Border Patrol office** (Khiliin Tserenk Alban; ☎ 22341; ⏰ 8-11am & 2-5pm Mon-Fri) in Ölgii, located a couple of kilometres from the centre. The permit will be checked by the border guards at Dayan Nuur, Tavan Bogd base camp, Aral Talgai (western end of

EAGLE-HUNTERS

While travelling around Bayan-Ölgii, you may come across Kazakh eagle-hunters. If you ask gently, the Kazakhs may proudly show you their birds, though actual hunting only takes place in winter.

Eagle-hunting is a Kazakh tradition dating back about 2000 years (Marco Polo mentions it in his *Travels*). Female eagles are almost always used as they are one-third heavier than the males and far more aggressive. Young birds, around two years old, are caught in nearby valleys, fattened up and then 'broken' by being tied to a wooden block so that they fall when they try to fly away. After two days they are exhausted and ready for training, which involves being kept on a pole called a *tugir*, and catching small animal skins or lures called *shirga*. The eagles are trained to hunt marmots, small foxes and wolves (eagles have vision eight times more acute than humans), and release them to the hunter, who clubs the prey to death. Part of the meat is given to the eagles as a reward.

Tools of the trade include the *tomaga* (hood), *bialai* (gloves) and *khundag* (blanket to keep the bird warm). If well trained, a bird can live, and hunt, for about 30 years. Most hunters train several birds during their lifetime and release their birds into the wild after eight years.

The most likely places to find a Kazakh eagle-hunter are in the mountain region of Tsast Uul between Khovd and Bayan-Ölgii, and the Deluun, Tsengel and Bayannuur regions of Bayan-Ölgii aimag. For an up close and personal look at the sport, try the Eagle Festival (p205).

Khoton Nuur) and Syrgal (the point where Khoton Nuur meets Khurgan Nuur). If you don't have a permit you will be fined about US$100 and given 72 hours to leave the area. The soldiers have nothing to do with the national park and cannot be negotiated with. In 2004, one Australian traveller was jailed for five days and had all his film destroyed after hiking too close to the border. Hikers that are escorted out of the park in a border-patrol jeep are charged T600 per kilometre. Note that your guide and driver will need their Mongolian passports.

At the time of research the price of a group permit was T3000, but this may increase. Processing the permit takes between 10 minutes and an hour depending on the guards' mood. You must bring your original passport (no photocopies accepted) and be prepared to describe your itinerary.

Sights

There are many archaeological sites in the region. As the main road through the region swings towards the southern shore of Khurgan Nuur you can see a stupa-like construction and several burial sites. Nearby is a **balbal** (Turkic stone statue) and the remains of a **processional pathway** (GPS: N48° 31.908′, E86° 28.926′). Further along the road is a wooden **Kazakh mosque**, with a ger-shaped roof. More *balbals* can be found in the Mogoit (Snake) valley, north of Khurgan Nuur.

The best **petroglyphs** in the area, if not all of Central Asia, can be found at Tsagaan Sala (aka Baga Oigor), on the route between Ulaankhus and Tavan Bogd. The drawings, more than 10,000 of them, are scattered over a 15km area; you'll need a guide to find the best ones.

Going further northwest, along the southwestern shore of Khoton Nuur, the road deteriorates and there are several rivers to cross as they flow into the lake. Northwest of Khoton Nuur the mountains close in and there's some fine hiking possibilities. For experienced backcountry walkers, it is even possible to travel up river for 90km all the way to Tavan Bogd. It is a five-day walk and you'll need to be completely self-sufficient. About 25km north of Khoton Nuur you can also visit Rashany Ikh Uul, an area of 35 **hot springs**.

TAVAN BOGD UUL

Tavan Bogd (Таван Богд Уул; Five Saints) mountain rises 4374m above the borders of three nations, and for this reason it is also known as Nairamdal (Friendship) Peak. If you sit on the summit, you can simultaneously be in Mongolia, China and Russia (though you won't need a visa for all three).

Tavan Bogd is one of Mongolia's most spectacular peaks, of interest to professional climbers, and the only one in Bayan-Ölgii to be permanently covered with large glaciers (including the 19km-long Potanii glacier, the longest in Mongolia). It's fairly dangerous, and to climb it you need to be with an experienced group properly equipped with ice axes, crampons and ropes. Don't even consider attempting it solo. The best time to climb is August and September, after the worst of the summer rains.

Even if you are not a climber, it's worth making it here for the views and hiking potential.

From the end of the road, it's a 17km trek to the first glacier, where most climbers set up base camp. The climb up the glacier is about 25km, and you can expect to encounter icy temperatures, crevasses and very volatile weather.

The massif is made up of five peaks (the 'five saints') – Khuiten, Naran, Ölgii, Burged and Nairamdal – the highest of which is Khuiten (meaning 'cold') at 4374m.

Sleeping & Eating

The Protected Areas office runs **Eco Ger** (per person T5000; meals T2000) at the Tavan Bogd base camp. Another Eco Ger is planned for somewhere between the two lakes.

There are beautiful camping spots all around the lakes. Dayan Nuur has some nasty mosquitoes, but the other two lakes are largely bug-free. The lakes teem with fish.

Getting There & Away

The main road from Tsengel leads 50km south to the bridge over the Khovd Gol (there's a T300 toll) and then continues 33km to the junction of the Khoton and Khurgan *nuurs*, where there is a bridge across the wide water channel between the two lakes.

A more scenic route takes you from Sagsai, over a pass and up the beautiful Khargantin Gol valley, past the 3943m-high Tsengel Khairkhan Uul and Khar Nuur, and then down to Dayan Nuur. A good option would be to enter the park this way and exit via the main road. It's possible to drive from Dayan Nuur to Buyant by jeep, but you'd need a good driver who knows the way.

To get to the Tavan Bogd Uul, you should be able to hitch a ride to Tsengel, but from there you will have to hike about 110km along the Tsagaan Gol. If you have your own vehicle, you can drive to within about 40km of the base of the mountain, where there are fine views of the glaciated mountains.

It is also possible to access the mountain by road along the Sogoog Gol and, in fact, in rainy weather this is often the most reliable route. For advice on access and climbing, talk to the staff at the Mongol Altai Nuruu Special Protected Areas office in Ölgii city (p204). You will need border permits to visit the mountain (p208) and will have to pay national park fees.

KHOVD ХОВД

pop 87,500 / area 76,000 sq km
Khovd is one of Mongolia's most heterogeneous aimags, with a Khalkh majority and minorities of Khoton, Kazakh, Uriankhai, Zakhchin, Myangad, Oold and Torguud peoples. Except for the Mongol Altai Nuruu range, which cuts the aimag in half, the territory is a barren semidesert dotted with salt lakes and smaller mountains. The melting snow from the mountains recharges the water table every spring, providing Khovd with more than 200 fast-moving rivers (and dozens of lakes), none of which has an outlet to the sea. All the rivers simply disappear beneath the sands or run into large saltwater marshes, which serve as giant evaporating ponds.

Khovd is worth a few days of your time, and has some logical stops on a loop tour around the west. There are good ecotourism opportunities around Khar Us Nuur and fantastic hiking opportunities around Tsambagarav Uul.

National Parks

There are several important protected areas in Khovd aimag. Mönkh Khairkhan Uul is expected to become a protected area in 2005.

Bulgan Gol Natural Reserve (1840 hectares) On the southwestern border with China, it was established to help preserve *minj* (beavers), sable and stone marten. A border permit is required.

Great Gobi Strictly Protected Area (also known as 'Gobi B') Created to protect *khulan* (wild asses), gazelles, jerboas and *takhi* (wild horses).

Khar Us Nuur National Park (850,272 hectares) Protects the breeding grounds for antelopes and rare species of migratory pelicans, falcons and bustards.

Khökh Serkh Strictly Protected Area (65,920 hectares) On the northwestern border with Bayan-Ölgii, it helps protect argali sheep, ibex and snow leopards.

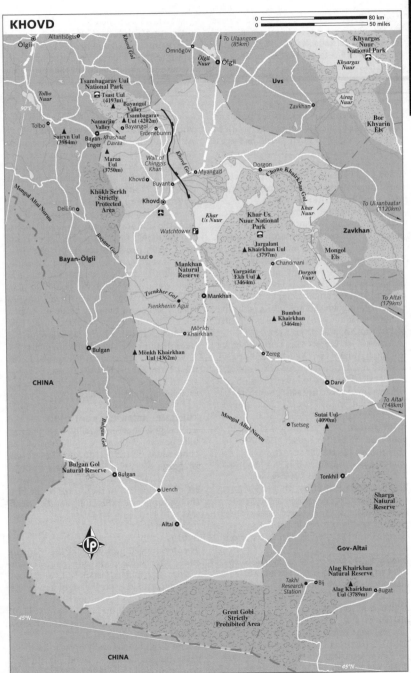

KHOVD

| 0 | 80 km |
| 0 | 50 miles |

Altantsögts

Ölgii

To Ulaangom
(85km)

Ömnögöv

Ölgii
Nuur

Ölgii

Khyargas
Nuur
National Park

Khyargas
Nuur

Uvs

Tsambagarav Uul
National Park

Tsast Uul
(4193m)

Tolbo
Nuur

Bayangol
Valley

Tsambagarav
Uul (4202m)

Zavkhan

Airag
Nuur

Bor
Khyarin
Els

90°E

Tolbo

Namarjin
Valley

Bayangol

Sairyn Uul
(3984m)

Bayan-
Enger

Khashaat
Davaa

Erdeneburen

Maraa
Uul
(3750m)

Wall of
Chinggis
Khan

Khovd Gol

Myangad

Dorgon

Chono

Khairkhan Gol

Chono

Khar
Nuur

To Ulaanbaatar
(1120km)

Khovd

Buyant

Mongol Altai Nuruu

Delüün

Khökh Serkh
Strictly
Protected
Area

Khovd

Watchtower

Khar
Us Nuur

Khar Us
Nuur National
Park

Zavkhan

Bayant Gol

Bayan-Ölgii

Duut

Mankhan
Natural
Reserve

Jargalant
Khairkhan Uul
(3797m)

Mongol
Els

Dorgon
Nuur

Chandmani

To Altai
(179km)

Tsenkher Gol

Tsenkheriin Agui

Mankhan

Yargaitin
Ekh Uul ▲
(3464m)

Mönkh
Khairkhan

Bumbat
▲ Khairkhan
(3464m)

CHINA

Bulgan

Mönkh Khairkhan
Uul (4362m)

Zereg

Darvi

To Altai
(148km)

Bulgan Gol

Mongol Altai Nuruu

Sutai Uul
(4090m)

Tsetseg

Bulgan Gol
Natural Reserve

Bulgan

Tonkhil

Sharga
Natural
Reserve

Uench

Altai

Gov-Altai

Alag Khairkhan
Natural Reserve

Takhi
Research
Station

Bij

Alag Khairkhan
Uul (3789m)

Bugat

45°N

Great Gobi
Strictly
Prohibited Area

CHINA

45°N

Mankhan Natural Reserve Directly southeast of Khovd city, it preserves an endangered species of antelope.
Tsambagarav Uul National Park (110,960 hectares) Established in 2000, on the border with Bayan-Ölgii, it protects the snow-leopard's habitat.

KHOVD CITY ХОВД

☎ 01432 / pop 31,000 / elev 1406m

Once a Manchurian military outpost and later a centre for manufacturing and trade in western Mongolia, Khovd is still the largest city in western Mongolia. It was one of the last cities to be liberated from the Chinese, in 1912 (and again in 1921), by the forces of the Mongolian commanders Dambijantsan, Magsarjav and Damdinsüren.

A pleasant and easy-going city built near the fast-flowing Buyant Gol, Khovd is a good place to start a trip around western Mongolia. The city is not prosperous but survives on an agricultural economy, food processing and some light manufacturing of building materials. It also boasts an agricultural institute and the main university in western Mongolia. About 600 Kazakhs live in the town and more live in the *sum* centre of Buyant, 25km north of Khovd.

A small statue in the central square honours Aldanjavyn Ayush (1859–1939), a local revolutionary hero who agitated against the Manchus to lower taxation and who was made head of Tsetseg *sum* after the 1921 revolution.

Information

Bathhouse (☎ 23690; shower/sauna T580/1200; ⏱ 9am-10pm) Just north of the market.
Internet Café (☎ 23901; per hr T476; ⏱ 8am-1pm & 2-10pm Mon-Fri) Inside the Telecom office.
Khar Us National Park Office (☎ /fax 22359, 22334; kharus@magicnet.mn; ⏱ 8am-5pm Mon-Fri) Opposite the Telecom office, this office can give information on, and permits for, nearby Khar Us Nuur National Park.
Telecom Office (☎ 24107; ⏱ 24hr) The post office is also located here.
Zoos Bank (☎ 24004; ⏱ 8am-5pm Mon-Fri) Changes dollars but not travellers cheques. Claims to be able to give a cash advance from a MasterCard.

Sights & Activities

MUSEUM

The **museum** (admission T2000; ⏱ 8am-noon & 1-5pm Mon-Fri) has the usual collection of stuffed wildlife, some excellent ethnic costumes, Buddhist and Kazakh art, and a snow-leopard pelt tacked up on the wall. One of the more interesting exhibits is the re-creation of cave paintings at Tsenkheriin Agui (p216), which is now better than the original. There are also several examples of the many deer stones scattered around the aimag, plus a model of the original Manchurian fortress. It is on a corner, near the police station.

SANGIIN KHEREM (MANCHU RUINS)

At the northern end of the city are some rapidly disappearing walls built around 1762 by the Manchu (Qing dynasty) warlords who once conquered and brutally governed Mongolia. The 40,000-sq-metre walled compound (Сангийн Хэрэм) once contained several temples, a Chinese graveyard and the homes of the Manchu rulers, though there's little left to see. Three enormous gates provided access. At one time, there was a moat (2m deep and 3m wide) around the 4m-high walls, but this has been completely filled in. The 1500-man Chinese garrison was destroyed after a 10-day siege and two-day battle in August 1912. The one legacy of Manchurian rule which has remained are the 200-year-old trees that line the streets of Khovd city.

While you are around this part of town, the nearby **Akhmet Ali Mejit** (mosque), constructed in 2000, is worth a look. Friday services are held at 2.30pm.

TÜREEMEL AMARJUULAGAI KHIID

The original Shar Süm (Yellow Temple) was built outside of Khovd in the 1770s but was completely destroyed during the Stalinist purge of 1937. The **monastery** (Түрээмэл Амажуулагай Хийд; admission T2000; ⏱ 9am-5pm) was recently relocated to the centre of the city (in the former billiards club) but it's not all that active.

HIKING

The dry, rugged hills north of the Manchu ruins offer some good opportunities for hiking. Try Yamart Ulaan Uul (Red Goat Mountain) to the northeast of town; it's a difficult six- to seven-hour return hike. An easier option is the small mountain just south of the airport with the *soyombo* national symbol carved on it.

The views are naturally great from these peaks but be careful – if you slip, there's no-one around to help you.

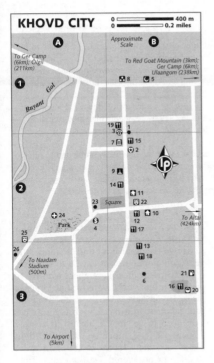

The Buyant Gol is a swift river on the western side of town. The locals go swimming here, and it's a great place to hike around, either upstream or downstream.

Sleeping
CAMPING
Some of the best camping in western Mongolia is along the Buyant Gol. Just walk south from the town for about 10 minutes (or take a jeep) to the interesting, Islamic-influenced Naadam Stadium. The area is fairly crowded with cows and gers, but you will be left alone. From around mid-September until the cold weather sets in, clouds of mosquitoes descend on the area, so make sure you plenty of insect repellent handy.

If you have your own vehicle, try further along the Buyant, on the road to either Ulaangom or Ölgii.

HOTELS
Eco Ger (☎ 22359; dm T3000) Two gers set up behind the National Park office are available for tourists. The toilet is 'long drop' variety and a hot-water flask is available for wash-

ing. A second ger camp (US$5 per person) is located about 6km from town; ask for directions from the National Park office.

Buyant Hotel (☎ 23860; dm/s/d T6000/6000/10,000, half-lux s/d T10,000/16,000, lux T15,000/20,000) Though nothing extravagant, this is the best hotel in town. The lux room has a huge living room with fridge and TV plus hot-water shower. The half-lux rooms include toilet and cold-water shower. The dorm beds are overpriced, considering the location of the bathroom, two floors below.

Khovd Hotel (☎ 23063; s/d T3000/6000, half-lux s/d T6000/12,000, lux T8000/16,000) This scruffy, communist-era hotel near the Drama Theatre is the other option for budget travellers. One look at the shared, co-ed toilets may induce you into upgrading to a half-lux room.

Eating
Both the Buyant and Khovd hotels have restaurants, though you may have better luck at a *guanz* on the main drag.

Naran Restaurant (☎ 9943 5000; chicken T2500, goulash T1200; ☻ 10am-11pm) The orange tablecloths and plastic flowers were a nice touch

DAMBIJANTSAN

Also known as Ja Lama, Dambijanstan was the self-proclaimed leader of western Mongolia from 1912–14. A Kalmuk lama from the Russian Volga, historical records describe Ja Lama as an 'insane and cruel genius', who would beat to death anyone who disobeyed him, even gouging out the eyes of live men. Many locals held him in awe, believing him to be the bulletproof reincarnation of the Oirad warrior leader.

He was finally arrested by the Russians while trying to set up his own kingdom at Münjig in southern Khovd, and was exiled to Yakutsk in Siberia. In 1918 he somehow managed to make it back to western Mongolia. His first task was to build himself a stone palace, which he financed through a series of highway robberies.

Eventually the central government ran out of patience with the renegade, pretended to offer him a government post and then had him shot. When no-one believed that he had actually been killed, his head was displayed in Uliastai and then Urga (Ulaanbaatar), before it was smuggled to St Petersburg and bizarrely found its way into the private collection of Peter the Great.

and there was cold beer too. The food is said to be the best in town and if you ask there might be fish on the menu.

Altan Khökhii (☎ 25164; ☽ 10am-9pm Mon-Sat) This local favourite serves *banshtei tsai* (small dumplings in milk tea) for T800 and warm goat's milk for T150 per glass.

SELF-CATERING

The daily market, south of the town centre, is large, lively and well stocked. Khovd aimag is justifiably famous for its miniature watermelons (normally best in late summer), which are available at the market.

One or two shops in the town sell some pricey imported foods at prices about 50% higher than in Ulaanbaatar. The best shops are currently the Altan Luu shop and the 'miini delguur' (my-shop) along the road between the market and the central square. Tenger shop, near the Telecom office, is also good.

Getting There & Away
AIR

The airport is 5km south of the city. There may be a bus there when you arrive, but otherwise you will have to get a ride on a jeep for T500 per person or T2000 per jeep. Jeeps leave for the airport from outside the Magsarjav Theatre.

The four-hour MIAT flight between Ulaanbaatar and Khovd city (via Tosontsengel) leaves on Monday and Friday and costs US$168/294. You may be able to just get a ticket for the Khovd–Tosontsengel leg, but only if the flight isn't full. Aero Mongolia flies between Ulaanbaatar and Khovd and

back on Monday, Wednesday and Friday (US$146/256 one way/return).

Khovd–Ulaanbaatar flights (and vice versa) are popular, so it is vital to buy tickets well in advance. Foreigners who try to buy last-minute tickets are routinely turned away. If you have a return ticket from Ulaanbaatar, reconfirm it as soon as you arrive. You need to get to the airport at around 8.30am on the morning of your flight (which normally leaves at 2pm!) in order to get your numbered boarding card. Then you can wait the remaining four hours until boarding, or return to the city for lunch.

HITCHING

Hitching to anywhere from Khovd is a hassle and not recommended. Your time will be spent more wisely slugging it out on a shared Furgon or jeep. If you do hitch, the easiest destination is probably Ölgii and you might get a lift from other tourists. Although it's the main highway to Ulaanbaatar, hitching to Altai (in Gov-Altai aimag) isn't easy and you may end up stranded halfway in **Darvi** (Дарви). Darvi has a **hotel** (per person T1000), but you'll need to wait by the petrol station should the rare vehicle pass through.

MINIVAN & JEEP

Furgons (Russian-made minivans) wait at the market. You should be able to get a ride somewhere within a day, or maybe two. Approximate fares at the time of research were T15,000 to Altai, T25,000 to Bayankhongor and T35,000 to Ulaanbaatar. At least one Furgon per day will travel to Ulaanbaatar. As usual, these vans leave around four hours after the stated departure time; ask the driver to pick you up at your hotel when he is ready.

There's less traffic headed to Ölgii (T8000), and less still to Ulaangom, but again something should come up. Jeeps cost around T250 per kilometre, including petrol, but you'll have to negotiate hard. Ask around at the market.

The road from Khovd city to Ölgii (211km) is pretty good; to Altai (424km) it is rough and boring in patches; and to Ulaangom (238km) the road is often marred by broken bridges and flooded rivers after heavy rain.

TSAMBAGARAV UUL NATIONAL PARK
ЦАМБАГАРАВ УУЛ

Tsambagarav Uul, in the far northwestern *sum* of Bayannuur, is one of the most glorious snowcapped peaks in Mongolia. Despite its altitude of 4202m, the summit is relatively accessible and easy to climb compared with Tavan Bogd, but you'd need crampons and ropes.

One excellent possible jeep route in this region is to travel northwest from the main Khovd–Ölgii road to the **Namarjin valley**, where there are outstanding views of Tsambagarav. From here you can head west and then south to rejoin the main Khovd–Ölgii road, via several **Kazakh settlements** and a beautiful turquoise lake. You'll need to be completely self-sufficient for this trip.

The other main area to visit is the **Bayangol valley**, to the east of Tsambagarav, 100km and three hours of difficult driving from Khovd. A jeep road leads from Erdeneburen *sum* centre (where you can see a **deer stone** dating back to the pre-Mongol era) up the mountainside, following dozens of rocky switchbacks. The valley itself is nothing special but there are fine views southeast to Khar Us Nuur and you might be able to rent a horse for the hour ride to the Kazakh-populated **Marra valley**. With help you could do a fine three- or four-day horse trek circling Tsambagarav Uul, or to the Namarjin valley.

To explore the area, you'll definitely need a driver who knows the region well. Nomads in Ulaanbaatar are a good source of guides and information on this area. The area lies in a national park zone so you can expect standard park entry fees to apply.

KHAR US NUUR NATIONAL PARK
ХАР УС НУУР

About 40km to the east of Khovd city is Khar Us Nuur (Black Water Lake), the second-largest freshwater lake (15,800 sq km) in Mongolia – but with an average depth of only 4m. Khovd Gol flows into this lake, creating a giant marsh delta. Khar Us Nuur is the perfect habitat for wild ducks, geese, wood grouse, partridges and seagulls, including the rare relict gull and herring gull – and by late summer a billion or two of everyone's friend, the common mosquito. Be prepared for the blighters, otherwise your life will be a misery. The best time to see the birdlife is in May and late August.

As at Uvs Nuur (p219), bird-watchers may be a little disappointed: the lake is huge, difficult to reach because of the marshes, and locals know very little, if anything, about the birdlife. The best idea would be to go with one of the national park workers and to head for the delta where the Khovd Gol enters the lake. You'll need several litres of drinking water and mosquito repellent.

The easiest place to see the lake is from the main Khovd–Altai road at the southern tip of the lake, where a metal **watchtower** (GPS: N 47° 50.541′, E 092° 01.541′) has been set up to view the nearby reed islands.

The outflow from Khar Us Nuur goes into a short river called Chono Khairkhan, which flows into another freshwater lake, **Khar Nuur** (Black Lake), home to some migratory pelicans. See this area while you can: a Chinese firm has started construction of a hydropower dam on the Chono Khairkhan that will inundate canyons and huge tracts of grassland.

The southern end of Khar Nuur flows into **Dorgon Nuur**, which is a large alkaline lake good for swimming. The eastern side of Dorgon Nuur is an area of bone-dry desert and extensive sand dunes.

Just to the south, and between, the Khar and Khar Us lakes, are the twin peaks of **Jargalant Khairkhan Uul** (3796m) and **Yargaitin Ekh Uul** (3464m). You can see the massif as you drive to Ölgii from Altai in Gov-Altai aimag. With the help of a guide you'll find numerous springs in these mountains.

If you are driving in a loop through the park, the village of **Chandmani** makes a logical place to camp. There are good camp sites, a few shops and, for once, no mosquitoes.

KHÖÖMI

Khöömi (throat singing) is one of the most enigmatic arts of Mongolia, redolent of the vast steppes of Central Asia and the remote mountain forests of Siberia. The style of singing produces a whole harmonic range from deep in the larynx, throat, stomach and palate, and has the remarkable effect of producing two notes and melodies simultaneously: one a low growl, the other an ethereal whistling. Throat singing is traditionally centred on western Mongolia (particularly Chandmani in Khovd) and the neighbouring republic of Tuva.

Several recordings of throat singing are available abroad, though most are from Tuva, and there have even been some bizarre throat-singing fusions, with artists such as Frank Zappa, the Chieftains and Afro Celt Sound System incorporating samples. To check out some throat singing try the CDs *Spirit of the Steppes: Throat Singing From Tuva & Mongolia*, or *Voices from the Distant Steppes* by Shu-De (Real World).

Chandmani is also renowned as a centre for Khöömi singers (see above) and Westerners sometimes come here for informal study from the old masters.

TSENKHERIIN AGUI ЦЭНХЭРИЙН АГУЙ

The **Tsenkheriin Agui** (GPS: N 47° 20.828', E 091° 57.225') are located in an attractive setting next to a stream in Mankhan *sum*, 100km southeast of Khovd city. Until just a few years ago the walls of these caves were strewn with dozens of 15,000-year-old wall paintings. For reasons that we cannot fathom, vandals have wrecked all but a couple of the drawings. The museum in Khovd city (see p212) has re-creations of how the cave paintings looked before their destruction.

MÖNKH KHAIRKHAN UUL
МӨНХ ХАЙРХАН УУЛ

At 4362m, this mountain is the second highest in Mongolia. You can walk up the peak if you approach from the northern side. There is plenty of snow and ice on top, so you'll need crampons, an ice axe and rope, but the climb is not technically difficult. A jeep trail runs to the base from Mankhan. The peak is known locally as Tavan Khumit. At the time of research, plans were being laid to turn the mountain into a Strictly Protected Area, in which case park fees will apply.

UVS УВС

pop 81,900 / area 69,000 sq km
One of Mongolia's most geographically diverse aimags, Uvs is dominated by the Ikh Nuuruudin Khotgor: the 39,000-sq-km Great Lakes Depression stretching from the enormous Uvs Nuur to the Khovd and Zavkhan aimags. Other physical features of Uvs aimag, which are definitely worth exploring, are the **Böörög Deliin Els sand dunes**, east of Uvs Nuur; a cluster of other lakes (which are nicer than Uvs Nuur) comprising Achit, Khyargas and Üüreg; the 4037m-high Kharkhiraa Uul; and the gorgeous **Kharkhiraa valley**. The basin is also one of Mongolia's most seismically active regions. In 1905 an earthquake measuring greater than 8.0 ripped through the province and left a distinct fault line in the eastern part of the aimag.

Uvs aimag was originally named Dorvod after the main ethnic group that inhabited the area. The Dorvod people, who still represent just under half of the population of Uvs, speak their own dialect. Other minority ethnic groups include the Bayad, Khoton and Khalkh.

Uvs is a good place to organise and start a trip around western Mongolia. If you're on a tight budget, it's one of the few places where you could justify renting a jeep to explore the lakes, mountains, valleys and sand dunes, all within a day or so by jeep from Ulaangom.

Be careful if you are headed anywhere near the Tuvan/Russian border. Cattle rustling has turned violent in recent years, with armed gangs of Mongolians and Tuvans crossing the border at night to steal cattle and horses from each other. You may be stopped by the army if you get too close to the border areas of Tes or Davst *sums*.

National Parks

The Great Lakes Depression is a globally important wetland area for migratory birds and is a Unesco World Biosphere Reserve. Many other parks have been established in the

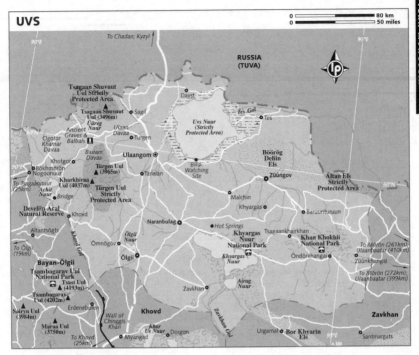

UVS

0   80 km
0   50 miles

To Chadan; Kyzyl

RUSSIA
(TUVA)

90°E   95°E

Tsagaan Shuvuut
Uul Strictly
Protected Area

Davst

Tsagaan Shuvuut   Sagil
Uul (3496m)   Tes-Gol   Tes
Üüreg   Ulaan
Ancient Nuur Davaa   Uvs Nuur
Ogotor Graves &   (Strictly
Khamar Balbals   Protected Area)
Davaa   Turgen
Bairam   Böörög
Khotgor   Davaa   Ulaangom   Delin
Els
90°E Bökhmörön   Türgen Uul   Züüngov   Altan Els
Nogoonuur   (3965m)   Tanalan   Strictly
Kharkhiraa   Protected Area 50°N
To Tsagaannuur Uul (4037m)   Bird-
(25km) Achit   Bridge Türgen Uul   Watching
Nuur   Strictly   Site   Malchin
Protected Area   Khyargas
Develiin Aral   Baruunturuun
Natural Reserve   Khovd   Naranbulag   Hot Springs
Altansögts   Khyargas Tsagaankhairkhan Khan Khokhii
Ölgii   Nuur   National Park
To Ölgii   Ömnögov Nuur   Ölgii   National Park Öndörkhangai
(19km)   Khyargas
Bayan-Ölgii   Nuur   To Mörön (261km);
Tsambagarav Uul   Ulaanbaatar (410km)
National Park   Tsast Uul   Züünkhangai
(4193m)   Zavkhan   Airag   To Mörön (272km);
Tsambagarav   Nuur   Ulaanbaatar (399km)
Uul (4202m)
Sairyn Uul Erdenebüren   Zavkhan
(3984m)   Wall of
Maraa Uul   Chinggis
(3750m)   Khan   Khar   Urgamal Bor Khyarin   Santmargats
To Khovd Myangad Us Nuur Dorgon   Els   95°E
(25km)

aimag, which, together with parks in Russia, Tuva, China and Kazakhstan, form a Central Asian arc of protected areas including:

Khan Khökhii National Park (220,550 hectares) An important ecological indicator and home to snow leopards, wolves and musk deer.

Khyargas Nuur National Park (332,800 hectares) An area of hot springs and rocky outcrops that harbours abundant waterfowl.

Uvs Nuur Strictly Protected Area (712,545 hectares) Consists of four separate areas: Uvs Nuur, Türgen Uul, Tsagaan Shuvuut and Altan Els. Between them, the protected area contains everything from desert sand dunes to snow-fields, and marsh to mountain forest. Snow leopards, wolves, fox, deer and ibex are among the animals protected. The area has been nominated as a World Heritage Site.

ULAANGOM УЛААНГОМ
☎ 01452 / pop 26,900 / elev 939m
Ulaangom, which means 'red sand', is a weather-beaten slab of concrete in the middle of the desert. Still, it's not a bad place to hang around while you explore the countryside or plan a trip around western Mongolia: there are good shops, a fantastic market and mountain views.

The bronze statue in front of Government House is of Yumjaagiin Tsedenbal, who ruled Mongolia for about 40 years until 1983, and was born near Ulaangom. Opposite the town square, another statue honours Givaan, a local hero who was killed in 1948 during clashes with Chinese troops.

Information
Border Patrol Office (Khiliin Tserenk Alban) Opposite the market, ask about a border permit here.
Democratic Party Internet Café (☎ 23370; per hr T600; 9am-8.30pm) Inside the Democrat Party HQ behind Government House.
Eco Ger (Airport) This small tourist-information ger has details on good horse trekking and hiking areas, and should be able to find you an experienced driver. It opens when an aeroplane arrives from Ulaanbaatar.
Internet Café (☎ 23370; per hr T500; 9am-9pm Mon-Sat) At the Telecom and post office.
Strictly Protected Area Office (☎ 22184, 22177; 9am-5pm Mon-Fri) Located at the western end of the main road, this office can provide information on, and permits to, the protected areas in the aimag.
Xac Bank (☎ 24120; 9am-6pm Mon-Fri)
Zoos Bank (8am-5pm) Next door to Xac.

WESTERN MONGOLIA

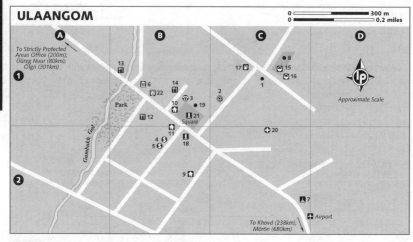

ULAANGOM

0   300 m
0   0.2 miles

A   B   C   D

To Strictly Protected
Areas Office (200m);
Üüreg Nuur (80km);
Ölgii (301km)

13

● 8

17

● 15
● 16

Approximate Scale

6
22

14

3   ● 19

2
●1

Park

12

10

21
Square

11

4
5

18

20

9

Gumbukh Gol

7

Airport

To Khovd (238km);
Mörön (680km)

Sights

The comprehensive **Aimag Museum** (admission T1500; ⏰ 9am-5pm Mon-Sat, noon-5pm Sun) has the usual stuff plus a section on the 16th-century Oirat leader Amarsanaa (the chain-mail jacket is supposedly his). There's a mind-numbing room dedicated to the communist dictator Yu Tsedenbal, but a useful aimag map indicates the location of deer stones and *balbals*.

The **market** (⏰ 9am-5pm) is the biggest show in town. Between the usual Russian and Chinese imports you'll find dusty nomads haggling for traditional hats (T4000) and boots (T50,000). Near the entrance you can try your luck at computer roulette (minimum bid T100).

Dechinravjaalin Khiid, on the eastern end of town near the airport, was originally founded on this spot in 1738. It contained seven temples and 2000 monks; an artist's rendition hangs inside the office of the head monk. The place was pulverised in 1937 and its current incarnation consists of a concrete ger and about 20 welcoming monks.

Sleeping

CAMPING

The only place to camp nearby is along Gumbukh Gol, which you cross as you come from Ölgii. Walk about 300m northwest of the town square and find a spot. If you have your own vehicle, camping is far better along the Kharkhiraa Gol or anywhere south of the city on the road to Khovd.

HOTELS

Bayalag Od Hotel (s/d $8/16, lux s/d $10/20) Located in an unexciting brick heap, this place has en-suite lux rooms with TV. Hot water comes in fits and starts.

Uvs Nuur Tsogtsolbor Hotel (☎ 24614; d/lux T25,000/30,000) This modern hotel is the nicest in town and has the most reliable hot water and plumbing, though both remain a bit dicey. The lux rooms come with TV and twin beds while the ordinary rooms have king-size beds but no TV.

Khyargas Nuur Hotel (s/d T7000/14,000, dm T10,000) There's no chance for hot water, and the management can be gruff, but the rooms are fairly clean. The 'lux' room is actually a grossly overpriced dorm. Pay up first or you may find extra charges upon checkout.

Eating

All three hotels mentioned earlier have restaurants. The classiest is at the Tsogtsolbor, although Bayalag is the local favourite. If you are looking for some really cheap *khuushuur* (mutton pancakes) or *buuz* (steamed dumplings) and are not fussy about hygiene, try the train-car *guanz* outside the market.

Khankhökhii Restaurant (☎ 22544; ⏰ 9am-midnight) Northwest of the Khyargas Nuur Hotel, this upstairs place serves a surprisingly edible plate of mutton, rice and vegetables for T800.

Otherwise, try **Az Café** (soup T600, goulash T1000; ⏰ 9am-7pm Mon-Sat), just off the main road.

INFORMATION	
Border Patrol Office	**1** C1
Democratic Party Internet Café	**2** C1
Internet Café	(see 3)
Post Office	(see 3)
Telecom Office	**3** B1
Xac Bank	**4** B2
Zoos Bank	**5** B2

SIGHTS & ACTIVITIES	(p218)
Aimag Museum	**6** B1
Dechinravjaalin Khiid	**7** C2
Market	**8** C1

SLEEPING 🏠	(p218)
Bayalag Od Hotel	**9** B2
Khyargas Nuur Hotel	**10** B1
Uvs Nuur Tsogtsolbor Hotel	**11** B2

EATING 🍴	(p218)
Az Café	**12** B1
Guanzs	**13** B1
Khankhökhii Restaurant	**14** B1

TRANSPORT	(p219)
Jeep/Truck Station	**15** C1
Minivans for Ulaanbaatar	**16** C1
Petrol Station	**17** C1

OTHER	
Givaan Statue	**18** B2
Government House	**19** B1
Hospital	**20** C2
Statue of Tsedenbal	**21** B1
Theatre	**22** B1

Getting There & Away

AIR

MIAT flies both ways between Ulaanbaatar and Ulaangom (with a possible refuelling stop in Tosontsengel) on Sunday and Wednesday. Aero Mongolia flies nonstop on Tuesday, Thursday and Saturday. Tickets cost US$144/252 single/return. The airport is a dirt field just 1km from the town centre.

HITCHING

Getting to and from Ulaangom is fairly difficult and you'll need time and patience on your side. For points east most vehicles are going to and from Tosontsengel (Zavkhan), though some will head to/from Mörön.

Fewer vehicles travel to/from Ölgii, though this is a popular tourist route and you may be able to find other travellers going your way. If you can get as far as Bohmörön from Ulaangom, then it is just a 9km walk to Nogoonuur *sum* in Bayan Ölgii province, from where you can get a ride to Ölgii city. The difficulty here is crossing the wide river, the Boh Mörön; you'll definitely need a guide and pack horse to get you across.

From Ulaangom to Khovd, and to the Kharkhiraa Valley, hitching is even harder. In Ulaangom, ask around the modern and busy petrol station near the market, and at the market itself.

JEEP & MINIVAN

A few public shared jeeps leave for Ölgii (T9000) and Khovd (T6000) when there are enough people to pack a jeep to bursting point. Ask around the truck/jeep station by the market.

Share vans to Ulaanbaatar (T35,000, via Tosontsengel and Tsetserleg) and to Erdenet (T30,000, via Mörön) wait by the road near the market.

The reasonable road between Ölgii and Ulaangom goes past delightful Üüreg Nuur, a good place to camp if it's late. From here drivers have two choices: the longer, less-rugged route (301km) favoured by truckers via Bohmörön *sum* (where you can check out the 8th-century Turkic *balbal*) or the short cut (254km) over Bairam *davaa* (pass) and past the coal-mining village of Khotgor.

The Khovd city–Ulaangom road (238km) sometimes suffers from flooded rivers and collapsed bridges after heavy rain.

UVS NUUR STRICTLY PROTECTED AREA
Uvs Nuur Увс Нуур

Uvs Nuur is a gigantic inland sea in the middle of the desert. The lake's surface occupies 3423 sq km, making it Mongolia's largest lake, though it's very shallow at an average depth of 12m. (Legend has it that the lake is bottomless.) Many textbooks claim that Khövsgöl Nuur is the largest lake in the country, but that only applies to water volume, not surface area. Uvs Nuur is large enough for you to stand on one shore and not see the other side, creating the impression that you have indeed reached the sea.

Uvs Nuur is five times saltier than the ocean, and devoid of edible fish, but this doesn't mean the lake is dead. The lake's surface is at an altitude of 759m, making it the lowest point in western Mongolia. It has no outlet, so a lot of the shoreline is quasi-wetland, making it difficult to reach.

Except for Mongolia's highest peaks, this is the coldest part of the country: in 1974 a temperature of -57°C was recorded. Summer temperatures typically climb to over 40°C, and these extremes are one reason why the lake was chosen as one of 10 locations globally to be studied for climate change by the international Geo-Biosphere Program. The lake is part of the Uvs Nuur Strictly Protected Area.

Despite the superlatives, compared with other lakes in western Mongolia, Uvs Nuur is disappointing: it is extremely large and contains high levels of saltwater. It is also not great for swimming or camping, though there is a small beach and camping area on the southwestern shore, near Ulaangom. Camping can be hell thanks to the mosquitoes. If you have a jeep, an interest in birdlife and a tolerance for mosquitoes then it may be worth your time. Otherwise it's best to head for the prettier, smaller and more accessible Üüreg freshwater lake.

BIRD-WATCHING

Ornithologists have documented over 200 species of birds around Uvs Nuur, including cranes, spoonbills, geese and eagles, as well as gulls that fly thousands of kilometres from the southern coast of China to spend a brief summer in Mongolia.

Bird-watchers, however, could be disappointed: the birdlife is there and *is* impressive, but it is extremely difficult to find. The lake is huge; public transport around it is nonexistent; trails often turn into marsh and sand; only park officials know anything about the birdlife; and you may not be there at the right time anyway. The easiest place to start looking for birdlife is where the rivers enter the lake, but real enthusiasts will have to make it out to the northeastern delta around **Tes**. Note that Tes is a border area and you'll need a permit from the border office in Uvs. Contact the Uvs Nuur Strictly Protected Area office in Ulaangom (see p217) for a list of visiting species and ideas on how to spot them.

GETTING THERE & AWAY

Approaching from the west, the lake is an awesome sight from the 2533m Ulaan *davaa*. You could hitch a ride *to* the lake, and get off along the relatively busy Ulaangom–Mörön road nearby, but you will still need a jeep to get *around* the lake, unless you plan to do a helluva lot of hiking.

Uvs Nuur is only 28km from Ulaangom, but in reality the trails along the southern and eastern sides skirt around the lake, and very few actually lead *to* the lake because of sand dunes, creeks and vegetation. The lake is more accessible if you park the jeep or pitch your tent on a trail, and walk about 1km or so to the lake.

If you are travelling between Ulaangom and Mörön you can get decent views from the road (about 1km from the shore) and maybe persuade your driver to veer off the road for closer look. If you've got a GPS and are equipped for mozzies, N 49° 59.406', E 092° 41.516' is a good spot to shoot for.

Üüreg Nuur Үүрэг Нуур

Large and beautiful **Üüreg Nuur** (GPS: N 50° 05.236', E 091° 04.587'), at an elevation of 1425m, is surrounded by stunning 3000m-plus peaks, including Tsagaan Shuvuut Uul (3496m), which are part of the Uvs Nuur Strictly Protected Area. The freshwater Üüreg Nuur has some unidentified minerals and is designated as 'saltwater' on some maps, so it's best to boil or purify all water from the lake. There is a freshwater well on the southeastern edge of the lake near some deserted buildings.

The lake is great for swimming (albeit a little chilly) and locals say there are plenty of fish. The surrounding mountains are just begging to be explored. One added attraction is that it's one of the few bug-free lakes in the region.

If you are travelling to/from the lake over Bairam *davaa* (in the direction of Achit Nuur) look out for several **ancient graves and balbals** (GPS: N 50° 00.484', E 091° 02.932') by the road, a few kilometres south of Üüreg Nuur.

Camping is naturally the only sleeping option. The ground is a bit rocky and there is no shade, but you do have access to squillions of gallons of drinking water. There are only a few gers in the area, so you feel like you have the lake to yourself.

One definite attraction of the lake is its accessibility: it's just a little off the main road between Ulaangom and Ölgii. You could hire a jeep and driver from Ulaangom, and maybe arrange to be picked up later, or you could hitch a ride there fairly easily.

Along the road south towards Achit Nuur, you can see the permanently snow-capped twin peaks of Kharkhiraa Uul and Türgen Uul.

KHARKHIRAA ХАРХИРАА

First off, there are several Kharkhiraas. For information on Kharkhiraa Uul and Kharkhiraa Gol see opposite. A more accessible valley, also known as Kharkhiraa, lies further northeast, about 30km southwest of Ulaangom. Bear in mind that Kharkhiraa is also the name of a *sum* centre, 23km south of Ulaangom. There's plenty of scope for confusion here, so make sure you and your driver know exactly where you are going.

The Kharkhiraa Gol valley is surrounded by dense pine forests, has a crystal-clear river (from which it's safe to drink) and is often carpeted with flowers. It is a fine place for some day hikes. The valley is not in any protected area so it's free to visit, although some locals insist otherwise and you may encounter a caretaker who asks for a dubious T3000 entry fee.

The only place to stay in the region is the run-down **Kharkhiraa Resort** (dm T3000, per bed in 4-bed cabin T6000), a collection of quaint log cabins and huts hidden among the pine forests. Meals cost T500 to T700 each. The resort is managed by the park office.

If you don't have your own vehicle, you could charter a jeep from Ulaangom and arrange for the driver to pick you up later. The cheapest, but most exhausting, way is to get a lift to the turn-off at the transformer (electric) station, 11km west on the main road from Ulaangom. From the station, a gentle, easy-to-follow, 25km trail leads to the gate of the resort. Hitching is not an option; almost no vehicles make it up here.

KHARKHIRAA UUL & TÜRGEN UUL
ХАРХИРАА УУЛ & ТҮРГӨН УУЛ

The twin peaks of Kharkhiraa Uul (4037m) and Türgen Uul (3965m), which dominate the western part of the aimag, are curiously almost equidistant between Achit, Üüreg and Uvs lakes. As vital sources of the Uvs Nuur, the mountains are part of the Uvs Nuur Strictly Protected Area.

The river valley between the two mountains is the Kharkhiraa Gol, which flows into Uvs Nuur. This valley is the start of some excellent **hiking** routes, which lead up to both mountains, and you could also do some fine day hikes around here with your own jeep and camping equipment. The area is mostly populated by Khoton people, famous throughout Mongolia as shamans.

The Kharkhiraa Gol is accessed via the *sum* centre of Tarialan, 31km south of Ulaangom. To get there, you will have to charter a jeep from Ulaangom or Ölgii city, and be prepared for a rough, but scenic, trip. There are remains of some Uighur statues in the region, but you'll need a guide to find them.

ÖLGII NUUR ӨЛГИЙ НУУР

To confuse things a little, another freshwater lake in the region is called Khar Us Nuur, but it is sometimes referred to as Ölgii Nuur. The 20km-long lake is accessible, but is not quite as scenic as Üüreg and Achit lakes. You can swim and fish in Ölgii Nuur, but the camping is not as good – the winds can be horrendous, so pitch your tent securely.

The lake is a welcome place to stop between Ulaangom and Khovd city if you have your own vehicle. Traffic between Ulaangom and Khovd is generally sparse, but you could hitch to and from the lake if you are self-sufficient, have a tent and don't mind waiting.

ACHIT NUUR АЧИТ НУУР

The largest freshwater lake in Uvs, Achit Nuur is on the border of Uvs and Bayan-Ölgii aimags, and is an easy detour between Ulaangom and Ölgii. It offers stunning sunsets and sunrises and good fishing. If you don't have your own fishing gear, you can probably buy some from the Russian and Tuvan fishermen who work there in the summer.

The lake is home to flocks of geese, eagles and other **birdlife**. One drawback is the absolute plethora of mosquitoes during the summer. Some camping spots are better than others for mozzies, so look around. Locals claim they are almost bearable by October.

The small Kazakh encampment on the southeastern edge has a *guanz*.

A **bridge** (GPS: N 49° 25.446', E 90° 39.677') just south of the lake allows for relatively steady traffic between Ulaangom and Ölgii. You can hitch a ride or charter a jeep to the lake from either city without too much trouble. The trail from Ölgii is reasonably good and pretty, while the trails from Achit Nuur to Ulaangom and Üüreg Nuur are often tough, but also dramatic.

KHYARGAS NUUR NATIONAL PARK
ХЯРГАС НУУР

Khyargas Nuur, a salt lake amid desert and scrub grass, provides an attractive summer home for birds, but it is not as scenic or as accessible as other lakes in the region. It is still worth a stopover if you are travelling between Uvs Nuur and Khar Us Nuur in Khovd aimag, or driving or hitching through the mideastern part of Uvs aimag towards Tosontsengel in Zavkhan.

On the northwestern side of Khyargas Nuur, there are some fantastic **hot springs**. Head for the abandoned village where the road leaves the lake, or ask directions at Naranbulag. A national park fee of T3000 applies around the lake, though you'd be lucky (or unlucky) to find a ranger to pay it to.

South of Khyargas Nuur, but still in the national park, is the freshwater lake **Airag Nuur** (GPS: N 48° 57.126', E 093° 22.011'), at the end of the mighty Zavkhan Gol. Despite the name, the lake is not full of fermented mare's milk, but it does have about 10 breeding pairs of migratory **Dalmation pelicans**. There were about 400 pelicans in the 1960s, but the numbers are tragically decreasing because poachers kill them for their beaks, which are used to make a traditional implement for cleaning horses, called a *khusuur* (currycomb), which you may see in use at the Naadam Festival, held on 11 and 12 July.

ALTAN ELS STRICTLY PROTECTED AREA АЛТАН ЭЛС

The road between Ulaangom and Mörön passes the sand dunes of **Böörög Deliin Els**, which apparently form the northernmost desert on earth. The dunes lead to Altan Els (Golden Sands), part of the Uvs Nuur Strictly Protected Area. Altan Els is another wonderful area for wildlife, if you can find any. You'll need a good jeep and driver, and you must be self-sufficient in everything before exploring this hot and remote region. The Altan Els are on the border of Uvs and Zavkhan aimags, and are an easy detour from the Ulaangom–Mörön road.

ZAVKHAN ЗАВХАН

pop 82,900 / area 82,000 sq km

The eastern edge of Zavkhan aimag is the western flank of the Khangai Nuruu, the second-highest mountain range in Mongolia, and a spectacular area of forests and lakes, dotted with snow-clad peaks, white-water streams and hot and cold springs.

Southern and western Zavkhan is usually ignored by travellers and Mongolians because of poor roads and transport. This part is one of sharp contrasts – a land of vast deserts, salt lakes and sand dunes where rain falls once or twice a year. Most of the border with Gov-Altai aimag is the Zavkhan Gol,

which flows from Khangai Nuruu northwest to Khyargas Nuur in Uvs aimag and drains an area of over 71,000 sq km.

Zavkhan is in an awkward location and very few travellers are likely to pass through much or any of the aimag. This is a pity because the scenery is some of the most dramatic and varied in the country; one minute you are travelling through lush valleys and hills, and then a few kilometres further you are in a place reminiscent of a desert from *Lawrence of Arabia*. If going from Khövsgöl to the western provinces, you'll quickly pass through the northern part of Zavkhan, via Tes; travelling from Ulaanbaatar to the west along the better, southern roads, you'll miss the aimag entirely; and if heading from Khövsgöl to the Gobi region, it's far better to go through Arkhangai and Övörkhangai aimags.

If you are looking for some off-beat travel, fly to Uliastai, explore Otgon Tenger, and continue your travels north to Khövsgöl or west to Khovd.

ULIASTAI УЛИАСТАЙ

☎ 01462 / pop 19,100 / elev 1760m

Located at the confluence of the Chigistei and Bogdiin *gols*, Uliastai is wedged in by mountains on all sides, and has a brisk but dry climate. It is one of the most remote aimag capitals in Mongolia, but pleasant and quiet, and a logical place to stay while you consider the direction of your plunge into the Mongolian wilderness.

History

Manchurian generals established a military garrison here in 1733 to keep one eye on the Khalkh Mongols to the east and the other on the unruly Oirad Mongols who lived west of the Khangai mountains. The fortress (the remains of which are visible 3km northeast of town) contained up to 3500 soldiers and was surrounded by an inevitable Chinese trading quarter called Maimaicheng. Chinese farmers tilled the lands along the Bogdiin Gol and, as Russian ethnologist Alexei Pozdneev noted during his 1890 visit, a large contingent of local women were on hand to 'serve' the soldiers.

The fort was emptied in 1911 with the disintegration of the Manchu dynasty, but Chinese troops came slithering back four years later, only to be booted out once and

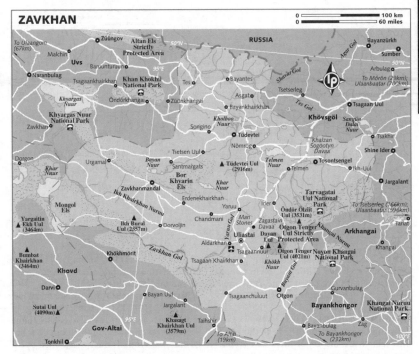

ZAVKHAN

for all in March 1921, following the capture of Urga (Ulaanbaatar) by White Russian forces. One of the few traces left visible of the Manchu era are the shackles and torture devices used by the Manchus, now on display in the History Museum.

Orientation

The town is divided into two main districts: west of the Chigistei Gol is the central area with the hotels, restaurants and other life-support systems; across the bridge on the eastern bank is the industrial area, which you are unlikely to visit. The airport is close to the town of Aldarkhaan, 35km west of Uliastai.

Information

Internet Café (☎ 21120; per hr T690; ☺ 9am-11pm Mon-Fri & 4-9pm Sat-Sun) In the Telecom office.

Khaan Bank (☎ 22587; ☺ 9am-6pm Mon-Fri) Changes dollars and travellers cheques. It's possible to get a cash advance on Visa or MasterCard.

Post Bank (☎ 23686; ☺ 9am-6pm Mon-Fri) Can also change dollars and travellers cheques.

Strictly Protected Areas Office (☎ 9946 9629; ☺ 9am-1pm & 2-5pm) This office contains a small

information room with brochures and pictures, though no English is spoken. The staff can also sell you entry tickets to Otgon Tenger Strictly Protected Area.

Telecom Office (☎ 24117; ☺ 24hr) The post office is also located here.

Sights
MUSEUMS

The **History Museum** (admission T1500; ☺ 9am-1pm & 2-5pm Mon-Fri), on the main street, contains a mammoth bone, some fine religious art and a *tsam* mask, worn during lama dances, made from coral. Next door, the **Museum of Famous People** (admission T1500; ☺ 9am-1pm & 2-5pm Mon-Fri) features well-known Zavkhan-ites, including Mongolia's first two democratically elected presidents, P Ochirbat and N Bagabandi.

TÖGS BUYANT JAVKHLANT KHIID

This small, well-appointed monastery (Төгс Буянт Жавхлант Хийд) was relocated from its place in the suburbs in 2003 and now has around 25 monks. You are allowed to watch their ceremonies, which start at about 10am every day. The monastery is on the eastern

WESTERN MONGOLIA

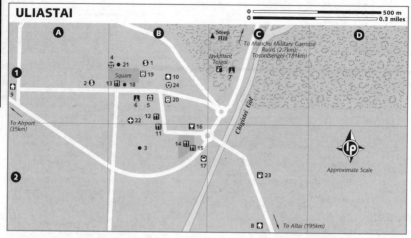

side of Javkhlant Tolgoi. A second temple, Ochirpurev Tsogt Khiid, a Nyingmapa monastery with five lamas, is near the museums and signposted in English.

JAVKHLANT TOLGOI

This hilltop (Жавхлант Толгой), near the river and just to the north of the main street, features a pavilion, nine stupas and the concrete likenesses of an elk, ibex and argali sheep. The views from the top are good. To the northeast, about 3km away, you can barely make out the remains of the old **Manchurian military garrison**. It is possible to walk to the garrison in about 30 minutes, though there's not much to see and it is generally regarded by locals as a waste dump.

Sleeping
CAMPING

Along the lush valley that hugs the Chigistei Gol for 15km from town, and parallel to the northern road to Tosontsengel, there are some gorgeous (though a little busy) camping spots. Just get off the bus, truck or jeep at somewhere you like.

HOTELS

Uliastai Hotel (☎ 22414; s/d US$8/16, half-lux/lux per person US$10/12) This slightly decrepit pile is moderately clean though overpriced. All rooms have toilet and basin but no shower.

Uran Baigal Hotel (☎ 9946 9582; dm per person T4500-5000) Cheaper than the Uliastai, this hotel has reasonable rooms but none with an attached toilet. It is located north of the police station and has a decent restaurant on the 1st floor.

Bayalag Centre Hotel (☎ 23039; r T2000-5000, half-lux/lux T8000/15,000) On the southeastern edge of town, about 400m from the bridge, this large hotel has rooms catering to all budgets, but no-one was around when we stopped by.

Eating & Drinking

Jinst Café (meals T700-1000; ☺ 9am-7pm) The goulash is a bit fatty but the *khuushuur* is probably the best in town.

Chigistei Restaurant (☺ 8.30am-11pm Mon-Fri, 8.30am-8pm Sat & Sun) Offers the usual menu items but can also procure fresh yogurt if requested.

Next door, the Ekhlel Café has a similar menu. The owner, an English-speaking local woman named Tuya, has helped independent travellers find guides and horses for countryside trips.

Self-caterers can explore the busy market or try the **Tesiin Gol Supermarket** (☺ 10am-6pm) near the roundabout.

Great Land Disco (☺ 6am-midnight) Local expatriates recommend this bar and nightclub as *the* place to kick your hiking boots together. It's just off the main roundabout.

Getting There & Away
AIR

MIAT (☎ 22141; ☺ 10am-6pm Tue, Wed & Fri) flies between Ulaanbaatar and Uliastai on Monday and Thursday for US$124/217 one way/

return. The airport is about 35km west of Uliastai; a taxi will cost about T9000.

HITCHING
The road between Uliastai and Tosontsengel is fairly busy, so hitching shouldn't be difficult, but because it rains a fair bit in summer, hanging around for a lift may not be pleasant. Hitching to anywhere else from Uliastai is really hard – Zavkhan's isolated location ensures that few vehicles come this way.

MINIVAN & JEEP
Several minivans and jeeps leave each day for Ulaanbaatar (T30,000) via Tosontsengel (T8000, 181km) Tariat (T11,000, 399km, for Terkhiin Tsagaan Nuur) and Tsetserleg (T15,000). If you are lucky you might find a minivan or jeep headed north to Mörön (389km), but very little traffic heads south to Altai. Almost all traffic leaves from the jeep station between the river and the market. In the last week of August it is easy to get a ride to Khovd (T8000) when vans fill up with students headed back to university.

The road between Uliastai and Tosontsengel is unpaved, but pretty reasonable and

easy to follow. The turn-off to Tosontsengel is 148km north of Uliastai and 33km west of Tosontsengel.

Every Wednesday, postal vans depart from Uliastai to the *sums* of Zavkhan, including Tosontsengel (T5000).

ZAGASTAIN DAVAA ЗАГАСТАЙН ДАВАА
Forty-eight kilometres northeast of Uliastai on the Uliastai–Tosontsengel road is a spectacular mountain pass with the unusual name of **Fish Pass** (GPS: N 48° 04.157', E 097° 09.900'). At the top, there are good views, a large *ovoo* (a shamanistic collection of stones, wood or other offerings to the gods, usually found in high places) and the largest collection of flies in western Mongolia. There is good camping and hiking on the stretch of road between the pass and Uliastai. Look out for the two **balbals** (GPS: N 47° 56.396', E 097° 00.824') and burial mounds 20km south of the pass.

OTGON TENGER UUL STRICTLY PROTECTED AREA ОТГОН ТЭНГЭР УУЛ
Hard-core mountaineers and alpine explorers may want to travel to Otgon Tenger Uul, about 60km east of Uliastai. At 3905m, it is the highest peak in the Khangai Nuruu range and is now part of the 95,510-hectare Otgon Tenger Strictly Protected Area. Normal park fees of T3000 per person per day apply; pay just past the children's camp, about 45km from Uliastai. From the base of the mountain it's a gruelling 11-hour return hike; however, there is currently a ban on climbing the mountain until 2007 (though no-one at the SPA office in Uliastai seemed to know why). Locals consider the mountain holy and are particularly irritated when Westerners inquire about scaling its heights.

For now, your best bet is to view Otgon Tenger from **Dayan Uul**, a 30-minute drive past the children's camp (passing pretty Tsagaannuur en route), where you'll also get views of lovely **Khökh Nuur** (GPS: N 47° 37.207', E 97° 20.546'). Taxi drivers will take you to Dayan Uul for petrol money plus T10,000.

A second route into the area is via the town of **Otgon**, 138km from Uliastai, where a decent road heads up the Buyant Gol towards the southeastern flank of the mountain. The route from Uliastai to Otgon is littered with impressive pre-Mongol-era burial mounds.

TOSONTSENGEL ТОСОНЦЭНГЭЛ

☎ 014546 / elev 1716m

Occupying a pretty valley along the Ider Gol, with forested mountains on all sides, Tosontsengel is Zavkhan's second-biggest city and a transit hub for west-bound traffic. Tosontsengel once supported a booming timber trade and its many wood-fronted buildings, coupled with unpaved lanes and wandering horsemen, give a Wild-West atmosphere. The oriental-looking green-roofed building south of the main square is the **Wedding Palace**. There's also a small **monastery** 500m north of the town centre.

Sleeping

Tosontsengel is another reason why you should have a tent with you. From the town square, head south for a few hundred metres to the Ider Gol, on which the town is based, and find a quiet spot. If you have your own transport there are also some lovely valleys, including the beautiful Telmen Khurren Tal, about 10km west of Tosontsengel.

Rashaant Hotel (☎ 22522; per person T2500), on the eastern side of the square, has musty, crumbling rooms and basic facilities.

Other nearby options include a billiard hall-cum-bunkhouse across the street or the Od (Star) hotel 150m southwest. Both were locked when we visited so you may need to poke around for the keyholders.

Eating

The main road is piled up with truck-stop style cafés and canteens. Outside the Mandal restaurant it is possible to buy fresh blueberries and cranberries for T800 per litre. Many of the *guanz*, including **Mandal** (☎ 22532), also double as bunkhouses and you could get a bed for T2000. There's no market but plenty of shops on the main road.

Getting There & Away

AIR

MIAT flies between Ulaanbaatar and Tosontsengel on Tuesday and Friday for US$100/176. Planes from Ulaanbaatar to Khovd, Ölgii and Ulaangom normally stop in Tosontsengel for refuelling so it might be possible to get a seat here.

HITCHING

If you hang around the petrol station in Tosontsengel, you should be able to get a lift to Uliastai. Ask around the main road for lifts to Tariat or Tsetserleg.

JEEP

The only transport to/from Tosontsengel is the occasional minivan to/from Uliastai (T5000) and the odd vehicle headed between Ulaanbaatar and Uliastai. In Tosontsengel, minivans and jeeps hang around on the main road by the shops and canteens.

From Tosontsengel, it's 181km southwest to Uliastai (the turn-off to the south is at the 33km point), 273km northeast to Mörön, and a *long* 533km northwest to Ulaangom.

There are two main roads between Mörön and Tosontsengel: one heads west via Tsagaan-Uul in Khövsgöl aimag, and the other goes via Jargalant in Arkhangai aimag. These two roads are rough, but extremely pretty and worth exploring if you have a good jeep and tent.

TELMEN NUUR ТЭЛМЭН НУУР

This beautiful salt lake is accessible from the town of Telmen, 20km southeast of the lake, on the main Uliastai–Tosontsengel road, or by heading west 25km from the main Mörön–Uliastai crossroads. There is good **camping** (GPS: N48° 48.889′, E97° 31.068′) at the eastern end of the lake, but bring your own water.

ERDENEKHAIRKHAN AREA

The village of Erdenekhairkhan, around 100km northwest of Uliastai, is nothing special but within the region there are several places of natural beauty worth exploring if you have your own jeep. **Khar Nuur** (Хар Нуур), northeast of Erdenekhairkhan, is a pretty freshwater lake bordering on alpine and desert zones. Southwest of Erdenekhairkhan, you stand a good chance of spotting ibex and wolves if you hike around the cliffs of the **Ikh Khairkhan** mountains (Их Хайрхан). There are caves in the area, but you'll need a local guide to find them.

Continuing west, close to the border of Uvs aimag, **Bayan Nuur** (Баян Нуур) is a difficult-to-reach salt lake amid extraordinary scenery. Locals say the fishing is good here. South of the lake, **Khomyn Tal** (Хомын Тал) is the newest rehabilitation area for *takhi* horses. Twelve *takhi* were sent here from France in September 2004 and more are expected. Khomyn Tal is in the buffer zone of Khar Us Nuur National Park in Dorvoljin *sum*.

Directory

CONTENTS

ACCOMMODATION

Like most things about Mongolia, the accommodation situation in Ulaanbaatar is vastly different from what you will find anywhere outside of the capital city. In Ulaanbaatar, there is a wide range of accommodation, from dorm-style places for US$4 a night to suites in the Chinggis Khaan Hotel, which cost almost as much as Mongolia's gross domestic product. Yet only 30 minutes by bus from the capital city, the hotels are decrepit, closed or offer very little comfort or service. Many accommodation options have no telephone.

One unique option, particularly popular with organised tours, is to stay in tourist gers, which are like those used by nomads – except for the hot water, toilets, sheets and karaoke bars. Also seriously consider bringing your own tent and camp – it is free, and you really experience what Mongolia has to offer.

Payment for accommodation is usually made upon checkout, but some receptionists will ask for money up front. Always check for taxes and hidden extras. Remember that most hotels in the countryside will charge you a 'foreigners' price' (which is sometimes double the local rate).

If you negotiate a reasonable price with the management, try to pay immediately and get a receipt. Asking for a receipt sometimes drops the price dramatically; in some cases the staff will officially register you as a Mongolian, charge you the 'Mongolian price' on paper, charge you the 'foreigners' price' in reality, and pocket the difference themselves.

Hotel staff may ask to keep your passport as 'security'. This is not a good idea, for three reasons: staff often do not show up for work (so the person with your passport cannot be found when you want to depart); once staff have your passport, it leaves you open to possibly being asked to pay more for your room while a taxi waits for you outside; or you may simply forget to pick it up and be 300km away before you realise it. An expired passport, student card or some other ID with your photo is a great alternative to leaving your real passport.

Security should be a consideration. Always keep your windows and door locked (where possible). Because staff may enter your room while you're not around, take any valuables with you or at least keep them locked inside your luggage and don't leave cameras and money lying around your room. Most hotels have a safe where valuables can be kept. When you retrieve things from it, they are often as anxious as you that you check everything on the spot, lest they be accused of sticky fingers.

Apartments

Apartment rental is only really an option in Ulaanbaatar; see p71 for details.

DIRECTORY

PRACTICALITIES

■ The weekly English-language newspapers are the **Mongol Messenger** (Map pp56-8; www
.mongolmessenger.mn) and the **UB Post** (http://ubpost.mongolnews.mn). Both have good articles,
events listings and classified sections.

■ Major private dailies in Mongolian include *Ardiin Erkh* (People's Right), *Zunny Medee* (Century
News), *Odriin Sonin* (Daily News) and *Önöödör* (Today).

■ BBC World Service has a nonstop service at 103.1FM. Local stations worth trying include Jag
(107FM), Blue Sky (100.9FM) and Radio Ulaanbaatar (102.5FM). Voice of America news programmes are occasionally broadcast on 106.6FM.

■ MNTV has a 10-minute news bulletin in English at 10pm on Monday, Wednesday and Friday.
Local TV stations don't start broadcasting until the afternoon and switch off around 11pm.
All the stations have political allies; Channel 25 favours the democrats, Channel 9 prefers the
MPRP and the others go with whoever is in power.

■ The predominant video format in Mongolia is Secam, a system compatible with France and
Greece but incompatible with that used in most of Europe, Australia, China and the USA.

■ Electric power is 220V, 50Hz. The sockets are designed to accommodate two round prongs in
the Russian/European style.

■ Mongolia follows the metric system.

■ As in the USA, the ground floor is called the 1st floor, as opposed to the UK system, where
the next floor above ground level is the 1st floor.

Camping

Mongolia is probably the greatest country in
the world for camping. With 1.5 million sq
km of unfenced and unowned land, spectacular scenery and freshwater lakes and rivers,
it is just about perfect. The main problem
is a lack of public transport to great camping sites, though there are some accessible
sites near Ulaanbaatar, such as in Gachuurt,
Khandgait and Terelj. Camping is also well
worth considering given the poor choice of
hotels and the expense of ger camps.

Local people (and even a few curious
cows or horses) may come to investigate
your camping spot, but you are very unlikely to encounter any hostility. Your jeep
driver will have ideas about good places to
stay, otherwise look for somewhere near
water, or in a pretty valley. If you're hitching, it is not hard to find somewhere to
pitch your tent within walking distance of
most aimag capitals and towns. You will
need to bring your own tent, as well as
cooking equipment, if you want to camp
away from the main towns or want to avoid
the local *guanz* (canteens).

To wash yourself, you'll probably need
to use the local town's bathhouse. Many
are listed under the Information entries in

this book. Be aware, though, that the bathhouses won't be like what you'd expect to
find in Turkey; in Mongolia they are simply
for getting a hose-down.

Be mindful of your security. If drunks
spot your tent, you could have a problem.
If the owners (and their dog) give you permission, camping near a ger is a good idea
for extra security; otherwise camp at least
300m from other gers. Mongolians have little or no idea of the Western concept of privacy, so be prepared for the locals to open
your tent and look inside at any time –
no invitation is needed.

You can often get boiled water, cooked
food, uncooked meat and dairy products
from nearby gers in exchange for other goods,
but don't rely on nomads, who may have
limited supplies of food, water and fuel. It is
best to bring a portable petrol stove (petrol
is the only widely available fuel in Mongolia)
rather than use open fires, which are potentially dangerous, use precious wood and may
not be possible where wood is scarce.

Here are a few extra tips:

■ Burn dried dung if you are being eaten
alive by mosquitoes (you may then have
to decide which is worse: mozzies or
burning cow shit) and bring strong re-

pellent with as much DEET as possible. Other anti-mosquito measures include: wearing light-coloured clothing, avoiding perfumes or aftershave, impregnating clothes and mosquito nets with permethrin (nontoxic insect repellent), making sure your tent has an insect screen; and camping away from still water or marshes.

- Make sure that your tent is waterproof before you leave home and always pitch it in anticipation of strong winds and rain.
- Ensure your gear is warm enough for sub-zero temperatures, or you'll freeze.
- Store your food carefully if you don't want a midnight visit from a bunch of ravenous marmots (or worse).
- Don't pitch your tent under trees (because of lightning), or on or near riverbeds (flash floods are not uncommon).

For some more advice on camping responsibly in Mongolia, see the boxed text on p230.

Gers

For information of ger etiquette, see the boxed text on p27.

TOURIST GER CAMPS

Tourist ger camps are springing up everywhere. They may seem touristy, and are usually poor value, but if you are going into the countryside, a night in a tourist ger is a great way to experience a Western-oriented, 'traditional Mongolian nomadic lifestyle' without the discomforts or awkwardness of staying in a private ger. If on an organised tour, you will certainly stay in one for a few nights; if travelling independently, one or two nights in a tourist ger is often worth a splurge, particularly at somewhere as remote as the south Gobi or as beautiful as Terelj in central Mongolia.

A tourist ger camp is a patch of ground with up to two dozen traditional gers, with separate buildings for toilets, hot showers (!) and a ger-shaped restaurant/bar. Inside each ger, there are usually two to three beds, an ornate table, four tiny chairs and a wood stove that can be used for heating during the night – ask the staff to make it for you (though it may be with dried dung). The beds are really just smallish cots – if you are built like an NBA

basketball player or a sumo wrestler, you'll need to make special arrangements.

Toilets are usually the sit-down types, though they may be (clean) pit toilets.

Expect to pay about US$20 to US$30 per person per night, including meals. Occasionally this price may include a trip to a nearby attraction, but normal activities, such as horse or camel riding, will cost extra. A surprising amount of the charge goes to the food bill, so you may be able to negotiate a discount of 50% to 65% by bringing your own food. This is pretty reasonable for a clean bed and a hot shower.

Meals are taken in a separate restaurant, which is often in a ger and can be quite opulent (some gers even have chandeliers!). Although the food is Western, and definitely better than in any restaurant anywhere in the countryside, it is rarely a culinary delight. Most camps have a bar (and, sometimes, even satellite TV and a blasted karaoke machine). There's often little to differentiate ger camps; it's normally the location that adds charm and makes your stay special.

If you plan to stay in a ger camp you may want to bring a torch for nocturnal visits to the outside toilets, candles to create more ambience than stark electric lights (not all have electricity), towels (the ones provided are invariably smaller than a handkerchief), and toilet paper (they usually run out).

If travelling independently and you want to stay in a ger camp, it is best to book ahead to ensure that the camp is open and has decent food. Ger camps rarely have their own phone, so the numbers listed in this book are usually for an Ulaanbaatar office, which will somehow get the message out that you are headed for the camp.

Except for a handful of ger camps in Terelj catering to expat skiers, most ger camps are only open from June to mid-September, although in the Gobi they open a month earlier and close a little later.

In a few touristed places, such as Terelj, Terkhiin Tsagaan Nuur and Khövsgöl Nuur, private families often have a guest ger and take in paying guests. In this case the advice of offering gifts as payment does not apply – this is a commercial transaction. These families are rarely registered with local authorities so they don't advertise, so you'll have to ask around (any ger set up next to a road is a good bet).

RESPONSIBLE CAMPING & HIKING

To help preserve the fragile ecology and beauty of Mongolia, consider the following tips when camping and hiking.

Rubbish

■ Carry out all nonbiodegradable items and deposit them in rubbish bins in the nearest town. Don't overlook easily forgotten items, such as silver paper, orange peel and cigarette butts. Make an effort to carry out rubbish left by others.

■ Never bury your rubbish: digging disturbs soil and ground cover, and encourages erosion. Buried rubbish will likely be dug up by animals, who may be injured or poisoned by it. It may also take years to decompose.

■ Minimise waste by taking minimal packaging and no more food than you will need. Take reusable containers or stuff sacks.

■ Sanitary napkins, tampons and condoms should be carried out despite the inconvenience. They burn and decompose poorly.

■ Don't rely on bought water in plastic bottles. Disposal of these bottles can be a major problem. Use iodine drops or purification tablets instead.

Human-Waste Disposal

■ Contamination of water sources by human faeces can lead to the transmission of all sorts of nasties. Where there is no toilet, choose a spot at least 100m (320 ft) from any water source, bury your waste at least 15cm (6 in) deep, and bury or burn toilet paper, if possible. Cover the waste with soil and a rock. In snow, dig down to the soil.

■ Ensure that these guidelines are applied to a portable toilet tent if one is being used by a large hiking party. Encourage all party members, including porters, to use the site.

Washing

■ For personal washing and teeth cleaning, use biodegradable soap or toothpaste and a water container at least 50m (160ft) away from the watercourse. Disperse the waste water widely to allow the soil to filter it fully before it seeps back to the watercourse.

■ Don't use detergents within 50m of watercourses, even if they are biodegradable. Try to wash cooking utensils 50m from watercourses, and use a scourer, sand or snow instead of detergent.

TRADITIONAL GERS

If you are particularly fortunate, you may be invited to spend a night or two out on the steppes in a genuine ger, rather than a tourist ger camp. This is a wonderful chance to experience the 'real' Mongolia.

If you are invited to stay in a family ger, only in very rare cases will you be expected to pay for this accommodation. Leaving a gift is strongly recommended, though. While cash payment is usually OK as a gift, it's far better to provide worthwhile gifts for the whole family, including the women (who look after the guests). Cigarettes and vodka are appreciated by men, but are rarely enjoyed by women. Sweets for young children aren't going to do their teeth any good. Constructive presents include needles (with large eyes) and thread, lighters, toothbrushes, strong string, candles, scotch tape, notebooks, recent editions of Mongolian newspapers, hand mirrors and AA- or D-size batteries for the radio. Children will enjoy colouring books, pens, paper and puzzles.

Your host may offer to cook for you; it is polite for you to offer to supply some food, such as biscuits, fruit, salt, rice, pasta and noodles. Don't offer tinned goods, because they may not have a tin opener, and they certainly won't have any suitable means of disposing of the can. If you have noth-

Erosion

■ Hillsides and mountain slopes, especially at high altitudes, are prone to erosion. Stick to existing trails and avoid short cuts.

■ If a well-used trail passes through a mud patch, walk through the mud so as not to increase the size of the patch.

■ Avoid disturbing the plant life that keeps topsoils in place.

Fires & Low-Impact Cooking

■ Don't rely on open fires for cooking and use a petrol stove whenever possible. Avoid stoves powered by disposable butane gas canisters. If you *have* to make an open fire use existing fire rings wherever possible; only use dead, fallen wood and remember that it is sacred to Mongolians. Use minimal wood – just enough for cooking purposes. Dried dung burns with great efficiency.

■ Ensure that you fully extinguish a fire after use. Spread the embers and douse them with water.

■ If you are hiking with a guide and porters, supply stoves for the whole team. In alpine areas, ensure that all members are outfitted with enough clothing so that fires are not a necessity for warmth.

■ If you patronise local accommodation, select those places that do not use wood fires to heat water or cook food.

Wildlife Conservation

■ Do not feed the wildlife as this can lead to unbalanced populations, to diseases and to animals becoming dependent on hand-outs.

■ Discourage invasions by wildlife by not leaving food scraps behind. Place gear out of reach and tie packs to rafters or trees.

Environmental Organisations

■ **WWF** (Map pp56-8; World Wide Fund for Nature; ☎ 011-311 659; fax 011-310 237; wwfmon@magicnet.mn; Meteorological bldg, Julchin Gudamj 5, Ulaanbaatar)

■ **Information & Training Centre for Nature and Environment** (☎ 011-318 586; itcne@ mongol.net)

ing to spare, at least offer to photograph your host's family and send the photos to them later. Be sure to get their address and, *please*, keep your promise.

If you stay longer than a night or two (unless you have been specifically asked to extend your visit), you will outstay your welcome and abuse Mongolian hospitality, making it less likely that others will be welcome in the future. (Never rely on families to take you in; always carry a tent as a back up.)

Guesthouses

Ulaanbaatar now has around 10 guesthouses firmly aimed at foreign backpack-

ers. Most are in apartment blocks and have dorm beds for around US$4, cheap meals, a laundry service, Internet connection and travel services. They are a great place to meet other travellers to share transportation costs, but can get pretty crowded during Nadaam (11 and 12 of July).

Outside Ulaanbaatar only Dalanzadgad in the Gobi and Khövsgöl Nuur have accommodation aimed at backpackers.

Hotels

Hotels in Ulaanbaatar are generally pretty good, though they are all chronically overpriced. Most places not in the budget range cost at least US$35 per single room. (Expect far fewer facilities than you'd get for the same price in most Western countries.) These rooms will be comfortable and clean and perhaps have satellite TV. Hot water and heating is standard for most buildings and hotels in Ulaanbaatar, and air-conditioning is never needed. The staff in mid-range and top-end places will speak English.

Staff at budget places in Ulaanbaatar and anywhere in the countryside (except for ger camps) will speak no English. The 'foreigners' price in this book may be quoted in US dollars because the exchange rate fluctuates, but you should pay in tögrög because it is now the law.

A sleeping bag is generally not needed if you are staying in mid-range or top-end places or ger camps, though it's an added luxury (and useful if the heating breaks down outside of summer, which is not uncommon). If you plan to stay in budget hotels in the countryside you should bring a sleeping bag. An inner sheet (the sort used inside sleeping bags) is also handy if the sheets are dirty. Blankets are always available, but are generally dirty or musty.

Most hotels (*zochid budal*) in the countryside (and budget hotels in Ulaanbaatar) have three types of rooms: a 'deluxe' (*lux*) room, which includes a separate sitting room, usually with TV, and a private bathroom; a half-deluxe (*khagas lux*), which is much the same only a little smaller but often much cheaper; and a 'simple' (*engiin*) room, usually with a shared bathroom. Sometimes, dorm-style (*niitiin bair*) beds are also available. Invariably, hotel staff will initially show you their deluxe room, which usually costs a ridiculous foreigners' price of up to T15,000 per person per night. Simple rooms are cheaper but generally still overpriced at about T5000 per person per night. Unless the hotel offers satellite TV, don't bother paying extra for a TV – it will only show distorted and incomprehensible Mongolian and Russian programs.

In the countryside, the hotels are generally empty and falling apart, though a few aimag capitals such as Tsetserleg, Erdenet and Darkhan have new private hotels that are quite good. They will normally be very cheap (if you can get the Mongolian price (about T2500 per person per night), but have few facilities. The newer private hotels are normally owned by a local business and

may not be advertised. You may have to find out where the manager lives to get the hotel opened, the hotel may have no food, the toilets may be unbearable pit toilets or may be locked, and the electricity will probably be turned off by midnight or may not work at all. The quality of hotels in the countryside is reason enough to take a tent and go camping.

As for service, it is generally poor, except for top-end places in Ulaanbaatar. You'll gain little by getting angry – just be businesslike and eventually you'll get what you want. If the staff haven't seen guests for a long time (very possible in the countryside), they might have to search for some sheets, blankets, even a bed, washstand and water, and then rouse a cook to light a fire to get some food ready a few hours later.

If the hotel has no hot water (most likely outside UB), or no water at all, it's worth knowing that most aimag capitals have a public bathhouse.

ACTIVITIES

Mongolia is all about getting out into the countryside; there are a host of active options for you to pursue. For details of overseas companies that organise activities, see p257; for Mongolian companies see p59.

Birding

The best places to get out your binoculars and telephoto lens are the following areas:
Airag Nuur (p222) Migratory pelicans.
Ganga Nuur (p169) Migratory swans.
Khar Us Nuur and Khar Nuur (p215) Geese, wood grouse and relict gull, and migratory pelicans.
Mongol Daguur Special Protected Area (p161) White-napped crane and other waterfowl.
Sangiin Dalai Nuur (p177) Mongolian lark, eagles, geese and swans.
Uvs Nuur (p219) Spoonbills, cranes and gulls.

Fishing

With Mongolia's large number of lakes (*nuur*) and rivers (*gol*), and a sparse population that generally prefers red meat, the fish are just waiting to be caught. The best places to dangle your lines are at Khövsgöl Nuur (p141) in summer (June to September) and the nearby Five Rivers area (p149) in September and October. The rivers and lakes in the Tsagaannuur region (p149) west of Khövsgöl Nuur, Orkhon Gol in Övörkhangai (p104), and Chuluut Gol in Arkhangai aimag (p114) are also excellent.

Tourists must have a special permit authorised by the **Ministry of Nature & Environment** (☎ 011-326 617; fax 011-328 620; Baga Toiruu 44, Ulaanbaatar). It's difficult to get a permit unless you sign up with a company that has agreements to fish specific rivers. But, before signing up, make sure your outfitter has the necessary agreements and permits – some cut corners. If you fish without a permit, you may be fined, have your fishing gear confiscated, or worse.

Take caution when approaching tour operators about a fishing trip, as many do not use sustainable fishing techniques, and Mongolia's rivers have suffered because of it. Weekend warriors from Ulaanbaatar, plus local guides with foreign anglers have cleaned out many fishing areas, and Mongolia's Ministry of Nature & Environment has done little to curb the onslaught. However, the **Association of Mongolian Angling Guides** (www.taimen.mn) is doing its bit to improve the situation.

Catch and release is standard practice.

Equipment is hard to rent anywhere in the country, so bring your own gear (but use barbless hooks to protect the fish). In many places, all you need is a strong handline and a lure. Fishing is officially permitted only from mid-June to December, although a few outfitters have special permission for spring fishing.

A few pockets of world-class fly-fishing areas remain, safeguarded by responsible, joint-venture companies with exclusive rights to fish them.

Three responsible fly-fishing tour operators include **Mongolia River outfitters** (www.mongoliarivers.com), **Fish Mongolia** (www.fishmongolia.co.uk) and **Sweetwater Travel** (www.sweetwatertravel.com/mongolia.htm). For more details, look out for *Fishing in Mongolia* published by the US-based Avery Press.

Golf

In the summers of 2003 and 2004, an eccentric American named Andre Tolme golfed his way across Mongolia, designating 18 cities and towns as 'holes'. Andre shot the round in 12,170 strokes, but lost over 500 golf balls en route. He called it 'extreme golfing', but unsurprisingly no-one has

golfed in his footsteps. You can read more about his adventure at www.golfmongolia.com. If you don't fancy slugging it out of sand traps the size of the Netherlands, you could try the UB Golf Club or the newly built driving range (see p67).

Hiking

Mongolia has many outstanding opportunities for hiking, though very few locals do it and think foreigners are crazy for even thinking about it. The biggest obstacle faced by hikers is finding transport to the mountains once they get far afield from Ulaanbaatar. However, in the regions around Bogdkhan Uul and Terelj, which are not far from Ulaanbaatar, there are mountains enough to keep hikers busy for a few days.

Way out west, you can break out the expedition gear and scale a handful of mountains with glaciers. Warm-weather hikers can head for the Gobi Desert, which despite its vast flatness also harbours a few rugged mountain ranges.

Pay any fees and procure any permits required by local authorities. Be aware of local laws, regulations and etiquette about wildlife and the environment.

Some good hiking areas include:

Altai Tavan Bogd National Park (p208) Soaring mountains, stunning lakes and plenty of wildlife.

Gorkhi-Terelj National Park (p99) Beautiful area, close to Ulaanbaatar.

Khan Khentii Strictly Protected Area (p157) Lush area of dense forests and wildflowers.

Kharkhiraa Valley (Uvs) (p220) A crystal clear river surrounded by wildflowers and dense pine forest.

Khövsgöl Nuur area (p141) A huge lake that is just perfect for exploring.

Decent maps are hard to come by. The ONC/TPC series or the 1:1,000,000 topographic maps available in Ulaanbaatar are your best bet. It will also be handy to have a working knowledge of appropriate phrases such as: 'Where am I?' (*'En yamar nertei gazar ve?'*) and 'Is that dog dangerous?' (*'En nokhoi ayultai uu?'*).

Mosquitoes and midges are a curse. The situation is at its worst during spring and early summer, with the marshy lakes and canyons in the western deserts the most troublesome areas.

For some ideas on responsible hiking, see the boxed text on pp230–1.

SAFETY GUIDELINES FOR HIKING

Before embarking on a walking trip, consider the following points to ensure a safe and enjoyable experience:

- Be sure you are healthy and feel comfortable about hiking for a sustained period.
- Obtain reliable information about physical and environmental conditions along your intended route (eg from park authorities).
- Walk only in regions, and on trails, within your realm of experience.
- Be aware that weather conditions and terrain vary significantly from one region (or even one trail) to another. Seasonal changes can significantly alter any trail. These differences influence the way hikers dress and the equipment they carry.
- Don't forget about Mongolia's notoriously changeable weather – a sudden wind from the north will make you think you're in the Arctic rather than the Gobi. Only from June to August can you usually expect balmy temperatures, but this is also when it rains the most.
- Essential survival gear includes emergency food rations and a leak-proof water bottle (take a minimum of two litres of water a day, and more during summer).
- It's best to hike with at least one companion, always tell someone where you're going and refer to your compass frequently so you can find the way back. A GPS is also a handy tool.
- Unless you're planning a camping trip, start out early in the day so that you can easily make it back before dark.

Horse & Camel Riding

Riding on horses and camels (and even yaks) is part of many organised tours and great fun – if only for a few minutes. (Mongolians watching you will probably enjoy it even more.) Most ger camps can arrange horse riding – the prettiest (but not cheapest) places to try are the camps at Terelj and Khövsgöl Nuur, where you can normally hire a horse and guide for less than US$20 a day.

If you want to do some serious exploration on horseback read the advice on p262. Of the dozens of possible horse treks, several are popular and not difficult to arrange:

Bayankhongor to Tsetserleg You'll need a good guide for this wilderness trip, which crosses a series of alpine passes.

Binder area (p157) From Binder in Khentii aimag to Khan Khentii or possibly as far as Dadal, near the Siberian border.

Khövsgöl Nuur (p141) Circuiting the lake or the region around it.

Terelj to Bogdkhan Uul Via Gachuurt and Manzushir Khiid, near Ulaanbaatar.

Tsast Uul and Tsambagarav Circuit (p207 and p215) Starting in the Namarjin or Bayangol valleys, taking in Mongolian and Kazakh encampments.

Tsetserleg to Khujirt In Central Mongolia.

At touristy places such as the ger camps at Terelj and in the south Gobi you can ride a camel, though these are more like photo sessions rather than serious sport. Some of the ger camps at Ongiin Khiid (p178) can arrange a multiday camel trek.

Ice Skating

In winter, you won't have to worry about falling through the ice, as many lakes and rivers freeze right down to the bottom. Many Mongolians are keen ice skaters – at least those who live near water, or in big cities with rinks. The soccer stadium in Nairamdal Park becomes an ice rink in winter but it is not maintained so the ice gets pretty chewed up. You can rent skates here, but the quality is terrible so if you're serious about this sport, bring your own equipment.

Kayaking & Rafting

Mongolia's numerous lakes and rivers are often ideal for kayaking and rafting. Rafting is organised along the Tuul and Khovd Gols by agencies based in Ulaanbaatar, including:

Juulchin travel agency (☎ 011-328 428; fax 011-320 246; www.mongoljuulchin.mn; Bayangol Hotel, 5B)

Khövsgöl Lodge Company (☎ /fax 011-310 852; ☎ 9911 5929; Room 16, Bldg 13, Sukhbaatar District) A branch of Boojum Expeditions, it has started kayaking trips on Khövsgöl Nuur.

Nomadic Journeys (☎ 011-328 737; fax 321 489; www
.nomadicjourneys.com; Sükhbaataryn Gudamj 1) Another
good agency; it does everything from local trips on the Tuul
to remote adventures that require helicopter drops.

There is nothing stopping you from heading out on your own. The **UB Outdoor Equipment Centre** (☎ 9917 7029, 011-321 276; info@active
adventures.com) rents inflatable kayaks for
about $25 a day.

The best time for kayaking is in summer
(June to September); for rafting, the best
time is July and August after some decent
rain. River enthusiasts should read Colin
Angus' *Lost in Mongolia*, a description of the
author's decent of the Ider-Selenge system.

Mountain Biking

Mongolian roads are made for strong
mountain bikes and masochistic riders –
villages and people are few and far between,
and Mongolian dogs just *hate* bikes, but it's
still a great way to travel. The best places
to try are:
Darkhan to Erdenet Via Amarbayasgalant Khiid and
Bugant.
Kharkhorin to Orkhon Khürkhee Via Khujirt.
Khövsgöl Nuur Along either side of the lake from
Mörön or Khatgal.
Ulaanbaatar area To Terelj, Khandgait and/or
Manzushir Khiid.

Mountaineering

Mongolia also offers spectacular opportunities for mountain climbing. In the western provinces, there are dozens of glaciers,
and 30 to 40 permanently snowcapped
mountains. You must have the necessary
experience, be fully equipped and hire local
guides. The best time to climb is July and
August.

While you don't need permits from the
Ministry of Nature & Environment unless
the mountain is in a national park, you
should consult the undisputed experts in
mountain climbing, the **Mongol Altai Club**
(☎ 011-455 246; anji@mongol.net; PO Box 49-23, Bayanzurkh, Ulaanbaatar). The club runs specially
designed mountain-climbing trips. The office is in room 405 of the Physical Training
Institute, opposite the Indian Embassy.

Mongolia's highest peaks in ascending
order are:
Türgen Uul (3965m; p221) One of the most easily
climbed and spectacular, in Uvs.

Otgon Tenger Uul (4021m) Mongolia's holiest moun-
tain, located in Zavkhan aimag. Current regulations forbid
foreigners from climbing it.
Kharkhiraa Uul (4032m; p220) In Uvs; a great hiking area.
Sutai Uul (4090m; p196) On the border of Gov-Altai and
Khovd aimags. This awesome mountain is accessible and
dominates the road between Altai and Khovd city.
Tsast Uul (4193m; p207) On the border of Bayan-Ölgii and
Khovd aimags. It's accessible and the camping here is great.
Tsambagarav Uul (4202m; p215) In Khovd; it is rela-
tively easy to climb with crampons and an ice axe. In 1996
a Japanese man skied down this mountain in 24 minutes.
Mönkh Khairkhan Uul (4362m; p216) On the border of
Bayan-Ölgii and Khovd aimags. You will need crampons,
ice axe and ropes.
Tavan Bogd Uul (4374m; p209) In Bayan-Ölgii, on the
border of Mongolia, China and Russia. It is full of permanent and crevassed glaciers.

Skiing

If you can bear the cold, Mongolia is a great
place for cross-country skiing. The snow is
often thin, but it's blanketed sometimes for
six months a year. The Juulchin travel agency
(p70) runs skiing tours near Ulaanbaatar,
or if you have your own gear go to Terelj,
the best and most accessible place, and ask
about some safe trails. In winter you can hire
Russian-made cross-country (but not downhill) skis and sleds in Khandgait; see p102.

The best months for skiing are January
and February, although be warned: the
average temperature during these months
hovers around a very chilly –25°C.

BUSINESS HOURS

Government offices are usually open from
9am to 5pm on weekdays. Banks stay open
later (many until 7pm) and in Ulaanbaatar
there are several offering 24-hour banking.
Most private and state-run businesses open
at about 10am and close sometime between
5pm and 8pm. Many open on Sundays.

Most shops and businesses will close for
an hour at lunch, sometime between noon
and 2pm. Some supermarkets and banks in
UB are open 24 hours.

Outdoor markets are usually open from
9am to 7pm daily (or sunset in winter), while
indoor markets open from 10am to 8pm.

Museums have reduced hours in winter
and are normally closed an extra couple of
days a week.

For details on the opening hours of places
to eat, see p47.

DIRECTORY

CHILDREN

Children can be a great icebreaker and are a good avenue for cultural exchange with the local people; however, travelling in Mongolia is difficult for even a healthy adult. Long jeep rides over nonexistent roads are a sure route to motion sickness and the endless steppe landscape may leave your children comatose with boredom. Mongolian food is difficult to stomach no matter what your age. That said, children often like the thrill of camping, for a night or two at least. For a child-friendly experience, try the very tame rides at Nairamdal Park (p67) in Ulaanbaatar. Check out LP's *Travel with Children* for general tips.

Practicalities

Items such as formula, baby food, nappies (diapers) can be found at the State Department Store and Sky Shopping Centre in Ulaanbaatar, but nowhere else. Few cars in Mongolia even have working seat belts so you can pretty much rule out finding a car seat. You'll have to bring your own if you have very small children. When travelling in the countryside, deluxe hotel rooms normally come with an extra connecting room, which can be ideal for children.

CLIMATE CHARTS

It is said that Mongolia can experience four seasons in a single day. This seems especially true in spring when changeable weather creates snowstorms intermixed with bouts of wind and sun. The four seasons are distinct – winter lasts from November to February, spring from March to mid-May, summer from mid-May until late August, and autumn is during September and October. The cold weather in the far north can last a month or two longer than the Gobi areas. The highest amount of rain falls in the *taiga* (southern reaches of Siberia) areas along the northern border, especially Khentii and Khövgöl. See p9 for advice about the best times to visit.

CUSTOMS

Customs officials want to keep out pornography, drugs and expensive imports that might be sold to Mongolians; and want to keep in old paintings, statues, fossils, works of art and mineral samples. Baggage searches of foreigners exiting Mongolia by air are sometimes rigorous, but are less rigorous at border crossings by train to China or Russia, when most passengers are asleep.

When you enter Mongolia, you must fill out an English-language Customs Declaration form to declare any prohibited items, all precious stones and all 'dutiable goods'. You are also asked to list all 'money instruments' – ie currencies – that you bring into the country. There is no need to be too accurate; this form is rarely checked on your way out. You should, nevertheless, keep all receipts when

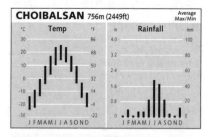

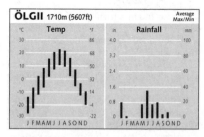

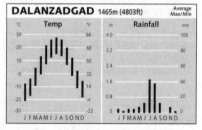

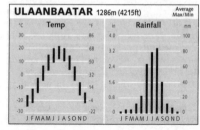

you change money at banks, though changing money with licensed moneychangers (who will not issue receipts) is legal.

The Customs Declaration is checked by the customs official and then returned to you. When you leave Mongolia, you will be asked to hand in the form – so keep it safe during your trip.

You can bring 1L of spirits, 2L of wine, 3L of beer, three bottles of perfume and 200 cigarettes into Mongolia duty-free.

If you are legally exporting any antiques, you must have a receipt and customs certificate from the place you bought them. Most reliable shops in Ulaanbaatar can provide this. If you don't get one of these you'll need to get one from the **Centre of Cultural Heritage** (☎ 011-312 735, 323 747) in the Cultural Palace in Ulaanbaatar. You'll need to fill in a form giving your passport number, where the antique was purchased and two photos of the antique itself.

If you have anything that even *looks* old, it is a good idea to get a document to indicate that it is not an antique. That goes for Buddha images and statues as well.

During your trip you will probably be offered furs of rare animals, antique items such as snuffboxes, bits and pieces from Erdene Zuu Khiid, and even fossilised dinosaur bones and eggs. Please do not take up these offers. These items are precious to Mongolia's history and the fine for illegally exporting fossils is from US$100 to US$150, or five years in jail.

DANGERS & ANNOYANCES

Before you get angry and complain about why things just don't work as well as they could or should, take a second to think about what Mongolia has experienced and is still enduring: years of Chinese domination and Soviet communism; a perverse climate; a terrible road and transport system; a sparse population that suffers from poverty and poor health; a lifestyle based on nomadism, which rarely complements Western thinking, economics and the needs of tourists; and unrestrained capitalism and development since 1990.

Alcoholism

Alcoholism is a real problem but is far worse in the cities than in the countryside. Drunks are more annoying than dangerous,

except when they are driving your vehicle. Drivers who work for tour companies have been disciplined to hold their alcohol on trips, but hitchhikers may encounter drunk drivers.

If camping, always make sure that you have pitched your tent somewhere secluded, and that no drunks have seen you set up camp – otherwise, they will invariably visit you during the night.

Corruption & Greed

Mongolians complain loudly because they suffer the consequences of corruption daily – aid money doesn't reach its intended beneficiaries, the old elite still controls everything and no-one believes many senior politicians survive just on their official salary. Anyone trying to do business in Mongolia will soon discover that corruption is rampant and growing.

Out on the highways and in city streets, the chances are good that your driver will be stopped by police for no reason. These random checks are an attempt to find drivers using an expired or phoney license. These shouldn't affect you, but your driver may have to fork out the occasional fine.

At Terkhiin Tsagaan Nuur, we have heard reports of locals demanding 'fines' for fishing or 'fees' for camping, among other such things. Problems such as this are often due to frustration about the lack of income reaching locals, in spite of increasing tourism. If someone says that they are a ranger or government official, ask to see identification and get a receipt for all monies paid. The main problem in protected areas is that park rules, such as the system of issuing fishing permits, are often vague and hard to implement. Rangers can be devilishly hard to find until you commit the smallest infraction and then five jump on you at once.

Dogs

Stray dogs in the cities and domestic dogs around gers in the countryside can be vicious, and possibly rabid. In the countryside, some dogs are so damn lazy that you are unlikely to get a whimper if a hundred lame cats hobbled past; others may almost head-butt your vehicle and chase it for 2km or 3km while drooling heavily. Before approaching any ger, especially in the countryside, make sure the dogs are friendly or under control and shout the phrase '*Nokhoi khor*', which roughly translates as 'Can I come in?', but literally means 'Hold the dog!'.

If you need to walk in the dark in the countryside, perhaps for a midnight trip to the toilet, locals have suggested that if you swing a torch in front of you it will stop any possible dog attack.

Scams

Professional scamming is not common, but the main thing to be aware of are dodgy tour companies that don't deliver on their promises. We get letters from readers who booked a tour with promises of particular accommodation, food and service standards that fell short of expectations. (More often than not these are onward trips to Russia booked from Mongolia.) It might be good to get in writing exactly what is offered, and ask about compensation if things don't work out as planned.

Theft

Mongolia is a very safe country and Mongolians are some of the friendliest and most helpful people in Asia. Most Mongolians are very poor and foreign goodies are a real temptation, but theft is seldom violent against foreigners, just opportunistic. In the countryside, keep an eye on your gear and don't leave valuables lying around your camp site if you wander off. Lock up your kit inside your jeep or hotel when possible. When horse trekking, be wary of Mongolians who seem to be following you; they may be after your valuables or even your horses, which are easily stolen while you sleep. For information on the dangers of theft in Ulaanbaatar, see p59.

Other Annoyances

Electricity, heating and hot water shortages and blackouts are common in aimag capitals. Some villages go for months without any utility services at all. Although official policies have relaxed considerably since the arrival of democracy, some of the old KGB-inspired thinking still occurs among the police, especially in rural backwaters and border areas.

Quarantine sometimes affects travel in Mongolia. Foot and Mouth disease, malignant anthrax and the plague pop up all the time and may prevent you from trav-

elling to certain areas. Some regions that have been hit by Foot and Mouth require drivers to decontaminate their cars when they enter and leave cities. This requires the spraying of tyres (or the whole car) and could cost a few thousand tögrög.

DISABLED TRAVELLERS

Mongolia is a difficult place for wheelchair travellers as most buildings and buses are not wheelchair accessible, and in addition there are rough roads and generally poor standards of accommodation. Still, travel to Ulaanbaatar, and jeep trips to places such as Kharkhorin shouldn't cause insurmountable problems.

If any specialised travel agency might be interested in arranging trips to Mongolia, the best bet is the US company **Accessible Journeys** (☎ 800-846-4537; fax 610-521 6959; www.disability travel.com) in Pennsylvania. At the very least, hire your own transport and guide through one of the Ulaanbaatar agencies (see p69). If you explain your disability, these agencies may be able to accommodate you.

The following organisations offer general travel advice for the disabled but provide no specific information on Mongolia.

Australia
Nican (☎ 02-6285 3713; www.nican.com.au; PO Box 407, Curtin, ACT 2605) Provides information on recreation, tourism, sports and the arts for disabled people.

UK
Holiday Care Service (☎ 0845-124 9974; www .holidaycare.org.uk; Sunley House, 7th fl, 4 Bedford Park, Croydon, Surrey CRO 2AP)

USA
Mobility International USA (☎ 541-343-1284; www .miusa.org; PO Box 10767, Eugene, OR 97440) Organises international exchanges.
SATH (Society for the Advancement of Travel for the Handicapped; ☎ 212-447-0027; www.sath.org) Website contains tips on how to travel with diabetes, arthritis, visual and hearing impairments, and wheelchairs.

For general advice, bulletin boards and searchable databases on the Internet try the following websites.
Access-able Travel Source (www.access-able.com) Provides access information for mature and disabled travellers.
New Mobility Magazine (www.newmobility.com) An excellent online resource for disability culture and lifestyle.

DISCOUNT CARDS

An ISIC student card will get a 25% discount on train tickets plus discounts with some tour operators. Check the ISIC website (www.isiccard.com) for updates. **SSS Travel** (☎ 011-328 410; fax 011-311 915; Sükhbaataryn Gudamj 1) can sell these cards if you can prove you are a student.

EMBASSIES & CONSULATES
Mongolian Embassies & Consulates

You'll find a full listing of Mongolia's embassies and consulates at www.extmin.mn. The following are embassies unless noted. For information on Mongolian visas, see p246.

Austria (☎ 01-535 3012; fax 01-535 3006; office@embassymon.at; Teinfaltstr, 3/6 1010 Vienna)

Belgium (☎ 02-344 6974; fax 02-344 3215; brussels.mn .embassy@chello.be; Besme 18, 1190 Forest, Brussels)

Canada (☎ 613-569-3830; www.mongolembassy.org; 151 Slater St, suite 503, Ottawa, ON K1P 5H3)

China (☎ 010-6532 6216; www.mongolianembchina .org.cn; 2 Xiushui Beilu, Jianguomenwai Dajie, Beijing); Consulate (☎ 0471-430 3254; fax 0471-430 3250; Xincheng Gu Wulanxiagu, Bldg No 5, Hohhot)

France (☎ 01 46 05 23 18; fax 01 46 05 30 16; info@ambassademongolie.fr; 5 Ave Robert Schumann, 92100 Boulogne-Billancourt, Paris)

Germany (☎ 030-447 35122; fax 030-474 80616; mongolbot@aol.com; Dietzgen-Str 31, 13156, Berlin)

Japan (☎ 033-469 2088; fax 033-469 2216; embmong@gol.com; 21-4 Kumiyama-cho, Shibuya-ku, Tokyo 150-0047)

Kazakhstan (☎ 3272-200 865; fax 3272-581 727; monkazel@kazmail.asdc.kz; Ul Aubakerova 1/1, Almaty)

Russia (☎ 095-290 6792; fax 095-291 4636; bayar@msk .tsi.ru; Borisoglebskaya pereulok 11, Moscow) The embassy is close to Smolenskaya metro station. Visas are obtained from the consular section (☎ 095-244 7867; Spasopeskovsky pereoluk 7, Moscow; ☯ 9am-1pm Mon-Fri); Consulate (☎ 3952-342 145; fax 3952-342 143; irconsul@ angara.ru; ulitsa Lapina 11, Irkutsk); Consulate (☎ 3012-220 499; fax 3012-214 188; mnc@ burnet.ru; Hotel Baikal, ulitsa Erbanova-12, Ulan Ude)

South Korea (☎ 02-794 1350; fax 02-794 7605; monemb@uriel.net; 33-5 Hannam-Dong Yongsan-gu, Seoul)

Switzerland (☎ 022-774 19 74; fax 022-774 32 01; mongolia@ties.itu.int; 4 Chemin des Mollies, 1293 Bellevue, Geneva)

VISAS FOR ONWARD TRAVEL

China

The consular section of the Chinese embassy in Ulaanbaatar is a good place to get a visa for China. It is open from 9.30am to noon Monday, Wednesday and Friday. Transit visas (single or double entry) last up to seven days from each date of entry. Single- and double-entry tourist visas are valid for 30 days from the date of each entry and you must enter China within 90 days of being issued the visa. Single-/double-entry tourist visas cost US$30/60 and take a week to issue. For three-day or same-day service, you'll have to fork out an extra US$50 or US$60. You must pay in US dollars. Single-/double-entry tourist visas for US citizens are US$50/75 for the one-week service. Transit visas cost about the same as a single-entry visa.

Kazakhstan

The Kazakhstan embassy is open from 9.30am to 1pm and 2.30pm to 6pm weekdays. Single-entry, one-month visas cost US$70 and take seven days to process. A double-entry, three-month visa costs US$100. A multiple-entry visa valid for one year costs US$210.

Russia

If at all possible get your Russian visa somewhere else; getting it in Ulaanbaatar will give you severe headaches. The consular section is open for visas from 2pm to 3pm daily; pick-up time is from 11.15am to 12.30pm. Almost everyone ends up paying a different price for their visa; costs vary between US$25 and US$200 depending on your itinerary and nationality. You will need three photos and an invitation or sponsor. You will also need 'health insurance', which local agents can organise for about US$1 per day. A visa normally takes a couple of days to issue or, if 'urgent', it can be issued on the spot for double the normal cost. However, your tour agent will need around 10 days to get the vouchers, so start the process early. The embassy will also issue visas for former Soviet Central Asian republics that are not represented individually in UB. If you need vouchers the consular will give you directions to a travel agent (usually Legend Tours; see p59).

UK (☎ 020-7937 0150; www.embassyofmongolia.co.uk; 7-8 Kensington Ct, London W8 5DL)
USA (☎ 202-333-7117; www.mongolianembassy.us; 2833 M St NW, Washington, DC 20007); Consulate (☎ 212-472 6517; fax 212-861 9464; 6 East 77th St, New York, NY 10021)

Embassies in Mongolia

A few countries operate embassies in Ulaanbaatar, though for most nationalities, the nearest embassies are in Beijing and/or Moscow. If your country has an embassy in Ulaanbaatar, it's a good idea to register with it if you're travelling into the remote countryside, or in case you lose your passport.

Note that the German embassy also looks after the interests of Spanish, Dutch, Belgian, Greek and Portuguese citizens. The British embassy handles normal consular duties for most Commonwealth countries.

For details on getting visas for China, Kazakhstan and Russia, see p239.

Austria (Map pp56-8; ☎ 324 804; hk_at_ub@ magicnet.mn; Peace Ave 7)
Canada (Map pp56-8; ☎ 328 285; fax 328 289; canada@mongolnet.mn; Bodicom Tower, 7th fl, Sükhbaataryn Gudamj)
China (Map pp56-8; ☎ 320 955; fax 311 943; 5 Zaluu-chuudyn Örgön Chölöö) The consular section is to the left of the embassy's front gate.
France (Map pp56-8; ☎ 324 519; www.ambafrance-mn .org in French; Apt 48, Diplomatic Services Corps Bldg 95)
Germany (Map pp56-8; ☎ 323 325; fax 312 118; Negdsen Undestnii Gudamj 7)
Japan (Map pp56-8; ☎ 320 777, 313 332; Olympiin Gudamj 6)
Kazakhstan (Map pp56-8; ☎ 312 240; kzemby@ mbox.mn; Apt 11, Diplomatic Services Corps Bldg 95)
Russia (Map pp56-8; ☎ 326 836; fax 327 018; Peace Ave A6)
South Korea (Map pp56-8; ☎ 321 548; fax 311 157; Olympiin Gudamj 10)
UK (Map p53; ☎ 458 133; fax 458 036; britemb@ magicnet.mn; Peace Ave 30)
USA (Map p53; ☎ 329 095; www.us-mongolia.com; Ikh Toiruu 59/1)

FESTIVALS & EVENTS

With the exception of Naadam (p71), held on 11 and 12 July, Mongolia has few genuine festivals. The **Maidar Ergekh** festival, held at a date according to the lunar calendar (usually August), is a religious festival that used to draw thousands of monks and spec-

tators before it was banned in the 1920s by the communist government. Since being reinstated in 1990, the festival has been held in a different monastery each year. It involves *tsam* mask dancing and the parading of a statue of the future Buddha (Maitreya) around the monastery. Although small and unpublicised, it's worth asking about, especially if you have an interest in Buddhism.

Ikh Duichin, or Buddha's Birthday, is held on 18 May and marked by *tsam* dancing in Gandantegchinlen Khiid in Ulaanbaatar and by special services in most other monasteries.

In an effort to boost tourism, travel companies and tourist officials have launched a series of festivals in countryside areas. Some are fairly obscure, such as the **Airag Festival** in Dundgov aimag, which is held in late August, and the **International Gobi Marathon**, held in September (which drew seven runners in 2004). Others are catching on with both locals and foreigners. The **Yak Festival** (Arkhangai; early August), the **Eagle Festival** (Bayan-Ölgii; early October), the **Camel Festival** (Ömnögov; one week after Tsagaan Sar) and the **Sunrise to Sunset** 100km run (Khövsgöl Nuur; late June) are worth checking out, especially if you've missed Naadam. See the website of the **Tourism Board** (www.mongoliatourism.gov.mn) for a list of events.

FOOD

See the Food & Drink chapter (p44) for details on what is on offer, the type of eateries and costs. For this book, expect main dishes to cost T800 to T1500 in budget joints, T2000 to T3000 in mid-range places and T4000 to T8000 in most top-end restaurants.

GAY & LESBIAN TRAVELLERS

Mongolia is not a gay-friendly place and not a place to test local attitudes towards homosexuality, which is apparently illegal. Ulaanbaatar has a small gay community that will occasionally convene at a tolerant restaurant or bar, but it moves around every few months, so you'll need to quietly tap into the scene and ask. For more information, see p81. As you never know what sort of reaction you'll get from a Mongolian, try making contacts through the web. Insight can be found at www.globalgayz .com/g-mongolia.html and travel info at www.geocities.com/gaytomongolia/.

HOLIDAYS

Mongolians do not get many holidays. The Naadam festival and Tsagaan Sar warrant three days off each, plus a day off for New Year's. Most tourist facilities remain open during holidays, but shops and offices will close down. The following public holidays are observed:

Shin Jil (New Year's Day) 1 January.

Constitution Day 13 January; the adoption of the 1992 constitution (generally a normal working day).

Tsagaan Sar (Lunar New Year) January/February; a three-day holiday celebrating the Mongolian New Year (for more information see p46).

Women's Day 8 March (generally a normal working day)

Mother & Children's Day 1 June; a great time to visit parks.

National Day Celebrations 11-12 July; more famously celebrated as the Naadam Festival.

Mongolian Republic Day 26 November (generally a normal working day).

INSURANCE

A policy covering loss, theft and medical expenses, plus compensation for delays in your travel arrangements, is essential for Mongolia. If items are lost or stolen you'll need to show your insurance company a police report. You may also need to prove damage or injury so take photos. All policies vary so check the fine print. For more on insurance, see p270.

INTERNET ACCESS

There are Internet cafés on nearly every street in downtown Ulaanbaatar; most are identified with English-language signboards. Nearly all aimag capitals have an Internet café in the central telephone office, and some of the bigger cities may also have private Internet cafés. Virtually none of the *sum* (district) centres have Internet access, though this is bound to change. In Ulaanbaatar, Internet access is T800 per hour, while in the aimags the prices range between T400 and T700. Some hotel business centres and guesthouses have Internet access for guests, but prices are more expensive.

If you have your own laptop it is easy to sign up for an Internet account at one of the major ISPs (Magicnet, Bodicom or Micom). If you are not in Mongolia long term, it is easier to get an Internet card (sold at the exchange kiosks in the State Department Store). A 10-hour Internet card costs just T5000.

Wifi (wireless) access is not yet available, but at the time of research **Magicnet** (☎ 011-312 061; National Information Technology Park, 2nd fl) was planning to wire the Chinggis Khaan, Ulaanbaatar and Bayangol hotels. A high-speed connection is possible, but for the moment this is prohibitively expensive for ordinary users (around US$500 per month).

LEGAL MATTERS

Foreigners' rights are generally respected in Mongolia, although you may bump into the occasional bad cop or customs inspector who won't be satisfied unless they've gotten a piece of what's inside your wallet. If caught, drug use will give you a peek into Mongolia's grim penitentiary system.

The most common offence committed by foreigners is straying too close to a border without a permit. Violators end up paying a fine and a few unlucky souls have been imprisoned for a few days. If you run into serious trouble, ask to contact your embassy.

Making life difficult is that police often blame the victim; don't expect any sympathy if you've been a victim of crime or a road accident. You're more likely to be scolded about how careless you've been, which can be demoralising. Overall, police are harmless, but unreliable when you really need one.

MAPS

If you are on an organised tour (especially if it's combined with a trip to China), the following maps provide some detail but are not good enough for independent travel: *China & Far East* (1:6,000,000) by Hallway, *China* (1:5,000,000) by Kümmerly & Frey and *China* (1:6,000,000) by Cartographia – the latter is probably the best of the lot.

If you are travelling independently, the best country maps are available in Ulaanbaatar only. The best map for jeep travel is the 1:2,500,000 *Road Map of Mongolia* (2004; T6000). It has the most accurate road layout and town names and usefully marks the kilometres between all towns.

Another useful tourist map is the *Tourist Map of Mongolia* (2004; T5500), which marks a host of obscure historical, archaeological and natural sights and has a 1:500,000 insert of Around Ulaanbaatar. Similarly, the *Tourist Map of Ulaanbaatar* (2004; T5500) is updated regularly and has cultural info on the back.

Explorers will want to check out the 1:500,000 series of topographic maps, which cover Mongolia in 37 maps. The cost of each varies between T4500 and T7000, but don't count on all being available. The topographic maps are particularly useful if you are travelling by horse or foot, or using a GPS (global positioning system), but they can get expensive. A cheaper alternative is a series of all 21 aimag maps (T23,000).

All these maps are available from the Map Shop in Ulaanbaatar, see p52. It also sells handy regional maps (T3500 each) to the most popular tourist areas, including Khövsgöl Nuur (1:200,000), Gobi Gurvan Saikhan (1:200,000), Terelj (1:100,000) and the stretch of road between Ulaanbaatar and Kharkhorin (1:500,000).

Chinggis Khaan junkies will want to check out the *Chinggis Khaan Atlas,* available around Ulaanbaatar for about T8000, which maps his every presumed movement in obsessive detail. The *Welcome to the Land of Chinggis Haan* tourist map is a more reasonable survey of Khentii aimag, with good historical detail.

In many Western countries, you can buy the ONC and TPC series of topographical maps published by the Defense Mapping Agency Aerospace Center in the USA. The maps are topographically detailed but dated and are not reliable for place names or road layout. Mongolia is covered by ONC (1:1,000,000) and TPC (1:500,000) map Nos E-7, E-8, F-7 and F-8.

MONEY

The Mongolian unit of currency is the tögrög (T), which comes in notes of T5, T10, T20, T50, T100, T500, T1000, T5000 and T10,000. (T1 notes are basically souvenirs). There are also T50 and T100 coins. The highest-value note is worth around US$9 so when changing a lot of cash you'll be given a stack of machine-collated bills.

Banks and exchange offices in Ulaanbaatar will change money with relative efficiency. Those in provincial centres have also gotten better, though it's still a good idea to change the bulk of your travel expenditure before leaving the capital.

Every year the tögrög loses a little bit of value against the US dollar; the result is that many guesthouses, hotels and tour operators will try to demand payment in

MONGOLIA'S CURRENCIES

Mongolia's various rulers have ensured a constant change of currencies. During Chinggis Khaan's time, coins or *sükh,* made from gold and silver, were used as currency. During the Manchurian rule, Chinese currency was used, but Mongolian traders preferred to use Russian gold, British notes and goods such as tea, silk and furs.

In 1925, four years after independence from China, the tögrög was first introduced. At that time, one tögrög was worth US$0.88 cents; by 1928, one tögrög was worth up to US$52! Currently, about 1200 tögrög are worth just US$1.

US dollars. But, if you only have tögrögs, they'll accept them. Other forms of currency aren't usually accepted, although the euro is probably second best. Cash offers the best exchange rates and you won't be paying any commission charge, but for security purposes you can also use travellers cheques and debit cards.

Moneychangers who hang around the markets may or may not be legal. They offer the best rates for US dollars and are usually safe, but the risks are obvious. Remember to change all your tögrög when leaving the country as its worthless elsewhere.

See the inside front cover for exchange rates at the time of publication and p10 for the costs of everyday items.

ATMs

The Trade and Development Bank has plonked down ATMs at a few key locations in Ulaanbaatar, Darkhan and Erdenet. These ATMs accept Visa cards and work most of the time, allowing you to withdraw up to T400,000 per day. Because most of the Golomt Bank branches are open 24 hours, they don't have ATM machines. Ordinary ATM cards issued from your bank at home probably won't work; try to get a 'Debit' card linked to your bank account. It should be associated with a credit card company.

Credit Cards

You can't rely on plastic for everything, but credit cards are becoming more widely accepted in upmarket hotels, travel agencies and antique shops. Most of these, however, charge an additional 3% if you use a credit card. Banks can give a cash advance off a credit card, often for no charge if you have Visa, but as much as 4% with MasterCard.

PHOTOGRAPHY & VIDEO

Mongolia is a very photogenic country so take loads of film with you, especially if you are there during the Nadaam Festival period. Major brands of print and even Polaroid film are available in photo processing studios in Ulaanbaatar (but are rare in the countryside). Several places around Sükhbaatar Square will process print film cheaply, but the quality may not be great; it's best to wait until you get home.

Slide film is rare and expensive, so bring what you need and get it developed when you get home. There are one or two places to buy a decent camera, but selection is limited.

In summer, days are long, so the best time to take photos is before 10am and between 6pm and 8pm, when Mongolia basks in gorgeous light. As bright, glaring sunshine is the norm, a polarising filter is essential. If you do a jeep trip on an unsurfaced road, you can expect plenty of dust, so keep the camera well sealed in a plastic bag.

Keep your film out of the Gobi's summer sun and Mongolia's winter freeze, when your automatic cameras and batteries may not work properly. Bring a spare camera battery, as these can stop working because of the cold, even in summer.

For professional tips on how to take better photos, check out LP's *Travel Photography*, by Richard I'Anson.

Photographing People

Always ask before taking a photograph. Keep in mind that monks and nomads are not photographic models, so if they do not want to be photographed, their wishes should be respected. Point a camera at an urban Mongol on the street and chances are they will cover their face. Don't try sneaking around for a different angle as this may lead to an argument. Markets are often a place where snap-happy foreigners are not welcome. Some visitors have even been stoned after taking photos at markets in Ulaanbaatar and Mörön.

On the other hand, people in the countryside are often happy to pose for photographs if you ask first. If you have promised to send them a copy, *please* do it, but explain that it may take several months to reach them – some nomads believe that all cameras are (instant) Polaroids. Several nomads also told us how devastated they were because they had not received photos as promised by foreigners. To simplify matters, bring blank envelopes and ask them to write their address on the outside. On the inside, make a note to yourself about who they were in case you forget.

When Mongolians pose for a portrait they instantly put on a face that looks like they are in mourning at Brezhnev's funeral. You may need to take this Soviet-style portrait in order to get a more natural shot later. 'Can I take your photograph?' in Mongolian is *'Bi tany zurgiig avch bolokh uu?'*

Restrictions

Photography is prohibited inside monasteries and temples, although you may photograph the exterior building and the monastery grounds. Also you can sometimes obtain special permission to take photographs for an extra fee.

In most museums throughout the country you need to pay an (often outrageously high) extra fee to use your still or video camera. It is best to have a look around first before you decide whether to fork out the extra tögrög.

Don't photograph potentially sensitive areas, especially border crossings and military establishments.

POST

The postal service is reliable but can often be *very* slow. Allow *at least* a couple of weeks for letters and postcards to arrive home from Mongolia. Foreign residents of Ulaanbaatar find it much faster to give letters (and cash to buy stamps) to other foreigners who are departing.

You won't find letter boxes on the streets. In most cases, you will have to post your letters from the post office. You can buy stamps in post offices (and top-end hotels) in Ulaanbaatar and aimag capitals.

Postal rates are often relatively expensive, especially for parcels, for which there is only an 'airmail' rate – yet they often arrive months later (probably by sea). Normal-sized letters cost T640 and postcards cost T460 to all countries. A 1kg airmail parcel to the UK will cost T14,000, or T18,000 to the USA.

The poste restante at the Central Post Office in Ulaanbaatar seems to work quite well; bring along your passport as proof of identification. Don't even think about using poste restante anywhere else in the country.

Contact details for the more reliable courier services, including DHL and FedEx, are found on p56.

SHOPPING

Mongolia has a number of unique items that are worth bringing home. Cashmere and wool products are usually at the top of the list, but there are many fine antiques and crafts too. Try shopping for Buddhas, *thangkas* (scroll paintings) and marvellous silver jewellery in the antique stores. You could even go down to the black market and buy all the pieces needed for a ger. The problem, of course, is how to ship one home. For this try asking Christo at the **El Latino restaurant** (☎ 011-311 051; Peace Ave 3). Mongolian clothes including *dels* (traditional coats), *hurrum* (jackets) and boots are nice to take home, as are the wonderful embroidered products made by hand in the Kazakh province of Bayan-Ölgii. No matter how many times you're offered them, dinosaur bones and eggs are definitely not souvenirs (legal ones anyway); please say 'no'.

SOLO TRAVELLERS

The high costs of jeep hire means that solo budget travellers will need to hook up with others for countryside trips. This usually isn't too much of a problem in summer, when van loads of backpackers depart daily from the guesthouses in Ulaanbaatar.

In Ulaanbaatar, single travellers on a budget will probably have to go for a dorm bed in a guesthouse, or find another single traveller to share the cost of a double room. Countryside hotels usually have a per bed option. Cycling, camping and hiking trips into the wilderness are safer in twos. If you do go off alone make sure to tell someone of your route and expected time of return. See p247 for information for solo women travellers.

TELEPHONE

It's easy to make international or domestic calls in Ulaanbaatar. Outside the main cities, making phone calls is a challenge. Aimag capitals are upgrading their systems but in the *sum* (district) centres you'll run head on with WWII-era technology, complete with wind-up phones and operators languishing behind massive metal boards, busily plugging and unplugging wires and shouting '*bain uu?!*' (is anybody there?!), into the receiver.

Ulaanbaatar landline phone numbers have six digits while most countryside numbers have five. Every aimag has its own area code; we have listed them in this book under the aimag capital headings.

If you are calling out of Mongolia, and are using an IDD phone, just dial ☎ 00 and then your international country code. On non-IDD phones you can make direct long-distance calls by dialling the international operator (☎ 106), who may know enough English to make the right connection (but don't count on it).

The other options are making a call from a private international phone office (Olon Ulsiin Yariin), which are becoming common in Ulaanbaatar but not in other cities. These charge reasonable rates to call abroad: T100 to the USA or T150 to Europe, on a per minute basis. Calls from the central Telecom offices in any city will be more expensive, but not outrageous: T560 per minute to the USA and UK, T820 per minute to Australia. To make the call, you need to pay a deposit in advance (a minimum equivalent of three minutes). The most expensive, but often the most hassle-free, is to call from the business centres or reception desks at the top-end hotels.

A couple of the top-end hotels have Home Country Direct dialling, where the push of a button gets you through to international operators in the USA, Japan and Singapore. You can then make a credit-card, charge-card or reverse-charge (collect) call.

Making a call *to* Mongolia is a lot easier, with one catch. Dial the international access code in your country (normally ☎ 00) and the Mongolian country code (☎ 976). Then, for a landline number dial the local code (minus the '0' for Ulaanbaatar, but include the '0' for all other areas) and then the number. Be aware, though, that there are different requirements for area codes if using/phoning a mobile phone; see p245.

In Ulaanbaatar, the domestic operator's number is ☎ 111 between 9am and 9pm. From 9pm to 9am it's ☎ 1109.

Mobile & Satellite Phones

The two main companies are Mobicom and Skytel. The mobile-phone network is GSM. If you bring a GSM phone you can get a new SIM card installed in Mongolia. The process is simple – just go to a mobile-phone office (a Mobicom office is conveniently located on the 3rd floor of the State Department Store), sign up for basic service (around T15,000), and buy units as needed. Cards come in units of 10 (T2500), 30 (T6600), 50 (T10,250) and 100 (T19,000). It is free to receive calls and text messaging charges are almost negligible. If you are abroad, and calling a mobile-phone number in Mongolia, just dial the country code (☎ 976) without the area code. Note that you drop the '0' off the area code if dialling an Ulaanbaatar number *from* a mobile phone but you retain the '0' if using other area codes.

Every aimag capital (and a few *sum* capitals including Kharkhorin and Khujirt) has a mobile-phone service, and calls are fairly cheap, making this a good way to keep in touch with home.

Mongolians loathe out-of-fashion mobile phones, so older models can be bought at reasonable prices (US$30 to US$50). Be wary of flimsy, worn-out models as quality will probably be inferior. Most mobile-phone shops (and there are plenty in Ulaanbaatar) sell used models.

If you are planning a serious mountaineering or horse-trekking expedition, considering bringing or renting a satellite phone, which aren't too bulky and can be used anywhere. A local company, **Monsat** (☎ 011-323 705, 9120 6050; MCS Plaza, Seoul St, Ulaanbaatar), rents 'sat' phones for US$5 to US$10 per day depending on the model. Calls are an additional US$1.65 per minute to the USA or Europe.

Phone Cards

If you have access to a private phone and need to make international calls, the easiest option is to buy an international phone card, sold in various outlets including the post office, State Department Store or mobile-phone shops. Instructions for the card are in Mongolian, but you can ask at the post office for English instructions. The Personal Identification Number (PIN) for these cards is the last four digits of the code on the card. Be careful where you scratch off the code,

---

MARGASH & YOU

There is another form of 'Mongolian time' – add two hours waiting time to any appointments you make. Mongolians are notorious for being late, and this includes nearly everyone likely to be important to you, such as jeep drivers, your guide or the staff at a museum you want to visit. You could almost adjust your watch to compensate for the difference. The Mongolian version of *'mañana'* (tomorrow) is *margash*.

---

poachers can peek over your shoulder, steal the code and use it before you do (which has happened at the post office).

There are a variety of phone cards available, and you usually get what you pay for – the cheaper ones (such as Bodicom) have terrible sound quality and echo, but cost less than US$0.10 per minute.

TIME

Mongolia is divided into two time zones: the three western aimags of Bayan-Ölgii, Uvs and Khovd are one hour behind Ulaanbaatar and the rest of the country. Mongolia observes daylight-saving time.

The standard time in Ulaanbaatar is UTC/GMT plus eight hours. When it is noon in Ulaanbaatar, it is also noon in Beijing, Hong Kong, Singapore and Perth; 2pm in Sydney; 8pm the previous day in Los Angeles; 11pm the previous day in New York; and 4am in London. See the world timezone map on pp276–7. The 24-hour clock is used for plane and train schedules.

TOILETS

In most hotels in Ulaanbaatar, aimag capitals and in most ger camps, toilets are the sit-down European variety. Strangely, there are only about three intact toilet seats in the entire country. In other hotels, and some more remote ger camps, you will have to use pit toilets and hold your breath.

In the countryside, where there may not be a bush or tree for hundreds of kilometres, modesty is not something to worry about – just do it where you want to, but away from gers. Also, try to avoid such places as an *ovoo* (a sacred cairn of stones), rivers and lakes (water sources for nomads) and marmot holes.

The plumbing is decrepit in many of the older hotels, and toilet paper can easily jam up the works. If there is a rubbish basket next to the toilet, this is where the waste paper should go. The hotel management will get quite upset if you plug things up. Most of the toilet paper in hotels resembles industrial-strength cardboard, or may be pages torn from Soviet-era history books or recently distributed bibles. To avoid paper cuts, stock up on softer brand bog rolls, available in the larger cities.

TOURIST INFORMATION

Juulchin, once the sole agency responsible for the entire tourist industry, has now been privatised. It is just another travel agency, but still the biggest (see p70). The Mongolian Tourism Board (see p59) is the government agency that deals with tourism, but its main duties are planning and infrastructure. The US Agency for International Development (USAID) has allocated funds to open a tourist information centre in Ulaanbaatar, supposedly in the Urt Tsagaan pedestrian mall. About 50m east of the mall, Skyland Travel has set up a tourist information office, which has little to offer.

Oddly enough, the only dedicated, legitimate tourist information office in the entire country is in Ölgii in far off Bayan-Ölgii aimag, where the Kazakhs are showing the Mongols how it's done.

VISAS

Currently, a 30-day tourist visa is easily obtained at any Mongolian embassy consulate, consulate-general or honorary consuls.

To get a visa for longer than 30 days, you must be invited or sponsored by a Mongolian, a foreign resident or a Mongolian company, or be part of an organised tour.

If you absolutely cannot get to a Mongolian consulate, it is theoretically possible to get a 30-day tourist visa on arrival at Ulaanbaatar airport. To do this you will need an invitation from a Mongolian travel company. It's best that a representative from this company meets you at the airport on arrival to liaise with visa officials.

It is also theoretically possible to get a visa at the land entry points at Zamyn-Uud and Sükhbaatar train stations, but there are many hassles with this, and for peace of mind it's best to have the visa before you

go. If you can get a visa at the airport or border crossing, you will need US$50 and two passport photos.

Israeli and Malaysian citizens can stay visa-free for up to 30 days and Hong Kong and Singaporean citizens can stay visa-free for up to 14 days.

US citizens can stay in Mongolia for up to 90 days without a visa. If you stay less than 30 days nothing needs to be done, other than having your passport stamped when you enter and leave the country.

All visitors who plan to stay *more* than 30 days must be registered within seven days of your arrival (see Registration opposite).

Mongolian honorary consuls (see www .extmin.mn for a list) can issue transit visas and nonextendable tourist visas but only for 14 days from the date of entry. However, these visas are for entry only; they cannot issue normal entry/exit visas, so you will have to spend some of your precious time in Ulaanbaatar arranging an exit visa (see opposite) from the **Office of Immigration, Naturalization & Foreign Citizens** (INFC; ☎ 011-315 323; ☺ 9am-1pm & 2-5pm Mon-Fri), on the west side of Peace Bridge, opposite NIC petrol station.

To check current regulations, try the website of the Ministry of External Relations at www.extmin.mn.

For information on getting visas to China, Kazakhstan or Russia from Mongolia, see p239.

Tourist Visas

Standard tourist visas generally last 30 days from the date of entry and you must enter Mongolia within three months of issue. Tourist visas cost US$25 for a single entry/exit, though there may be a 'service fee'. Visas normally take several days, or even up to two weeks, to issue. If you want your visas quicker, possibly within 24 hours, you will have to pay an 'express fee', which is double the normal cost. If you want to stay longer than 30 days, tourist visas can be extended in Ulaanbaatar (see opposite).

Multiple-entry/exit tourist visas (which cost US$65 and are valid for six months after the date of issue) are usually only issued to foreign residents who do a lot of travel.

Transit Visas

These visas last 72 hours from the date of entry. This period will only allow you to get off the Trans-Mongolian train for a very short time before catching another train to Russia or China. A single-entry/exit transit visa costs US$15 (US$30 for express service), but cannot be extended. You will need to show the train or plane ticket and a visa for the next country (Russia or China).

Visa Extensions

If you have a 30-day tourist visa you can extend it by another 30 days. For extensions, go to the INFC office (p246). The only catch is that if you stay longer than 30 days you have to be registered at this office (see below).

If you are having trouble getting stuff done at INFC, you could try asking at the main visa office of the **Ministry of External Relations** (cnr Peace Ave & Olympiin Gudamj; ☺ 9.30am-noon Mon-Fri) – enter from the back. The folks here are even grumpier than those at the aforementioned INFC office, though.

If you have already registered, you should apply for an extension about a week before your visa expires. It officially costs US$15 for the first seven days and a further US$2 per day for up to an additional 23 days. You will need a passport-sized photo and must pay a T5000 processing fee. It should take two or three days to process. Several guesthouses in Ulaanbaatar will take care of visa extensions (and registration) for a small fee.

Exit Visas

Transit and tourist visas are good for one entry and one exit (unless you have a double or multiple-entry/exit visa). If you are working in Mongolia, or if you obtained your visa at an honorary consul, you are usually issued a single-entry visa (valid for entry only). In this case, another visa is required to *leave* the country. These visas are available from the INFC office (see p246). For most nationalities the exit visa costs US$20, and for US citizens it is US$100. It is valid for 10 days, which means that you can stay 10 days after your normal visa has expired.

Registration

If you intend to stay in Mongolia for more than 30 days you must register with the police in Ulaanbaatar within seven days of arriving in the country.

Registration takes place at the INFC office (p246). The process is free, but you have

to pay T1000 for the one-page application. You'll need one passport-sized photo. Most guesthouses can rustle up an invitation to Mongolia for you if you require one.

As a formality, the registration also needs to be 'closed', however, the official you are dealing with will usually do this when you register so you won't have to come back.

Be aware that you won't be able to register on arrival in places such as Ölgii or Ulaangom. Call the INFC office for assistance or have someone in UB visit on your behalf. Chances are the INFC will give a grace period if you can show that you entered at Bayan-Ölgii aimag. (After all, the new border crossings were opened specifically to benefit tourists.) But you never know.

If you don't register, you are liable for a fine (theoretically from US$100 to US$300) when you leave the country.

Long-Term Stays

The only way to remain in Mongolia on a long-term basis (ie more than three months) is to get a work or study permit. The company or organisation you are working for should handle this for you, but if you are working independently you need to go it alone. In most cases, with a letter from your employer, you can get your stuff done at the INFC office. The staff may send you to the **Labour Regulation Department** (☎ 011-260 376, 260 363) in the Supreme Court building on Sambuugiin Örgön Chölöö. Independent researchers and students are usually registered through the Ministry of Enlightenment (in Mongolian 'Shinjileh Uhaan Bolovsroliin Yam'), in a building behind the Ulaanbaatar Hotel.

WOMEN TRAVELLERS

Mongolia doesn't present too many problems for foreign women travelling independently. The majority of Mongolian men behave in a friendly and respectful manner, without ulterior motives. However, you may come across an annoying drunk or the occasional macho idiot. There are occasional incidents of solo female travellers reporting being harassed by their male guide. If your guide is male, it is best to keep in touch with your tour agency in Ulaanbaatar, perhaps making contingency plans with them if things go awry. Better yet, take a female guide whenever possible.

DIRECTORY

Tampons and pads are available in Ulaanbaatar and other main cities such as Darkhan and Erdenet, though these will be very hard to find the deeper you go into the countryside. Many women also find it useful to wear long skirts while in the countryside, so that they can relieve themselves in some semblance of privacy on the open steppes.

Although attitudes towards women are more conservative in the mostly Muslim Bayan-Ölgii aimag, you don't need to cover up as you would in other areas of Central Asia.

WORK

Mongolia is certainly not somewhere you can just turn up and expect to get paid employment – the demand is not high even for teaching English. Also, if you do get work the pay will be poor (possibly the same as the locals), unless you can score a job with a development agency, but these agencies usually recruit their non-Mongolian staff in their home country, not from within Mongolia.

If you are keen to work in Mongolia and are qualified in teaching or health, contact the organisations listed below, network through the Internet, or check the English-language newspapers in Ulaanbaatar,

Permission to work is fairly easy to obtain if you have been hired locally. In most cases, your employer will take care of this for you. See also Long-Term Stays on p247.

Language Teaching

Some Mongolians want to forget Russian and learn a useful European language, particularly English, so there is a demand (albeit low) for teachers. Colleges and volunteer agencies are, however, on the lookout for qualified teachers who are willing to stay for a few terms (if not a few years), but not just for a week or two. Contact the voluntary-service agencies in your home country or the ones listed below.

Informal, short-term work may be possible through smaller organisations, such as the many private universities that have sprung up, or you may be able to do freelance tutoring for a while, but don't expect to make much money. In Ulaanbaatar try the **Mongolian Knowledge University** (☎ 011-327 165; fax 011-358 354), the **Ikh Zasag University** (☎ 011-457 855), the **International School** (☎ 011-452 959), the **Turkish School** (☎ 9978 0173) or **Orchlon** (☎ 011-353 519; www.orchlon.mn).

Volunteer Work

Some organisations are anxious to receive help from qualified people, particularly in education and health. Unless you are particularly well qualified, or your expertise is in desperately short supply, you are asked to contact these agencies *before* you come to Mongolia.

Agencies are more interested in committed people who are willing to stay two years or more. In most instances, you will be paid in local wages (or possibly a little more).

Australian Volunteers Abroad (AVA; ☎ 03-9279 1788; fax 03-9419 4280; osb@osb.org.au; PO Box 350, Fitzroy Vic 3065) AVA has a handful of Australian volunteers in Mongolia.

Khustain National Park (www.ecovolunteer.org) The park runs a three-week eco-volunteer programme where you can help with research.

Peace Corps (Map pp56-8; Enkh Tavnii Korpus; ☎ 011-311 520) The organisation is well represented throughout the country. Alternatively, contact your local Peace Corps office in the USA (☎ 1-800-424 858, 202-606 3970; fax 606 3110; www.peacecorps.gov).

UN Development Program (UNDP; ☎ 011-327 585; fax 011-326 221; PO Box 46/1009, Ulaanbaatar, Negdsen Undestnii Gudamj 12) The UNDP is always on the lookout for committed and hard-working volunteers but normally recruits abroad.

Voluntary Service Overseas (VSO; ☎ /fax 011-313 514; vsomongolia@magicnet.mn; PO Box 678, Ulaanbaatar) This British-run organisation is set up mainly for Brits. It prefers you to contact the organisation through its head office in the UK (☎ 020-8780 2266; fax 020-8780 1326; 317 Putney Bridge Rd, London SW15 2PN).

Transport

CONTENTS

GETTING THERE & AWAY

ENTERING THE COUNTRY

When entering Mongolia, by land or air, you should fill out straightforward immigration and customs forms. You shouldn't have to pay anything if your visa is in order (see p246 for visa information). You'll have to register if you plan to be in Mongolia for more than 30 days; see p247 for details. Registration is a hang-up if arriving at a distant point in Mongolia as you must register within seven days of arrival. Registering in Ulaanbaatar is fairly straightforward, but it's not possible in a town such as Ölgii or Ulaangom.

Passport

Make sure that your passport is valid for at least six more months from the date of arrival. If you lose your passport, your embassy in Ulaanbaatar can replace it, usually in one day. Before leaving Mongolia, check whether you'll need an exit visa from the Immigration, Naturalization and Foreign Citizens (INFC) office (p246).

AIR
Airports & Airlines

Ulaanbaatar's **Buyant Ukhaa airport** (☎ 198, 011-983 005) is Mongolia's major international airport; the code is ULN. Because the runway was built on a slope, landings are one-shot deals for modern jets. The somewhat limited runway has convinced authorities to build a new airport, which is expected to be finished by 2009.

The only other airport with international flights is Ölgii, which is connected to Almaty (Kazakhstan).

With the help of an Irish team of consultants, which managed the airline from 2002 to 2004, the Mongolian national airline, MIAT, improved its safety practices for international flights to near Western standards. Mechanics from Lufthansa were brought in to maintain the aircraft and readers have reported good things about this once-notorious airline.

At the time of writing, MIAT was setting up an e-ticketing scheme, which will allow travellers to buy and print their ticket through the Internet. This way, you could book a ticket to from your home country to Beijing through a travel agent, and then

---

THINGS CHANGE

The information in this chapter is particularly vulnerable to change: prices for international travel are volatile, routes are introduced and cancelled, schedules change, special deals come and go, and rules and visa requirements are amended. At the time of research MIAT (Mongolian airlines) was in the process of retiring its aged domestic fleet. It's not known if these planes will be replaced, so many domestic routes listed in this book may not be available.

You should check directly with the airline or a travel agent to make sure you understand how a fare (and ticket you may buy) works and be aware of the security requirements for international travel. Shop carefully. The details given in this chapter should be regarded as pointers and are not a substitute for your own careful, up-to-date research.

TRANSPORT

book your own connecting flight through MIAT. On international flights, MIAT allows 30kg baggage for business travellers and 20kg for economy travellers.

Most people fly in from Beijing, Berlin or Moscow; there are additional nonstop flights from Osaka and Seoul. Current airline schedules also allow you to fly from Ulaanbaatar to Irkutsk, on Lake Baikal in Russia, and Hohhot (Khokh Khot), the capital of the 'autonomous region' of Chinese Inner Mongolia.

In July and August, most flights are full, so book ahead, and confirm – and then confirm again.

Airlines flying to and from Mongolia are:
Aero Mongolia (airline code MNG; ☎ 9191 2903; www.aeromongolia.mn)
Aeroflot (airline code SU; ☎ 011-320 720; www.aeroflot .com)
Air China (airline code CA; ☎ 011-328 838; www.air -china.com)
Korean Air (airline code KE; ☎ 011-326 643; www .koreanair.com)
MIAT (airline code OM; ☎ 011-322 144; www.miat.mn)

Tickets

Full-time students and people aged under 26 years (under 30 in some countries) have access to better deals than other travellers. You have to show a document proving your date of birth or a valid International Student Identity Card (ISIC) when buying your ticket.

Most travel agencies will offer discounted tickets to Beijing and Moscow but not to Ulaanbaatar. In fact, unless you buy a through-ticket with Aeroflot or Air China you will find it hard to even book a Moscow–Ulaanbaatar or Beijing–Ulaanbaatar ticket from abroad. For these it's best to book with a travel agency in those cities. MIAT's proposed e-ticketing option (see p249) may be the solution.

DEPARTURE TAX

The departure tax at Buyant-Ukhaa International Airport is T12,500 (around US$10). It is paid at a small booth in the terminal, but is usually included with the price of the ticket. If you have run out of tögrög there is an exchange booth nearby. The departure tax for Öglii airport is T5500.

Australia & New Zealand

Flights to Mongolia go via Seoul or Beijing. The cheapest return flights from Sydney to Ulaanbaatar, on Korean Air, go for A$1970. Low-season return fares to Beijing from the east coast of Australia start at around A$1100. The lowest fares are offered by Vietnam Airlines.
Flight Centre (in Australia ☎ 133 133, in New Zealand ☎ 0800 243 544; www.flightcentre.com)
STA Travel (in Australia ☎ 1300 733 035, in New Zealand ☎ 0508 782 872; www.statravel.com)

China

From Beijing there are daily flights on either Air China or MIAT. Between 15 April and 15 September MIAT flies to Beijing daily except Friday for US$225/426 one way/return. At other times flights are limited to Monday, Wednesday and Friday. Air China has six flights per week (three in winter) from Beijing for the same price.

Note that you'll need a double-entry visa to return to China, or you'll have to buy one in Ulaanbaatar. Travellers without a Chinese visa have been refused boarding flights to Beijing. **MIAT** (in Beijing ☎ 8610-6507 9297) has an office on the 7th floor, Sunjoy Mansion, Room 705, opposite the Beijing International Club, just off Jianguomenwei Daijie.

Aero Mongolia flies to/from Hohhot in China on Monday and Thursday for US$167/ 251.

There is talk of starting up a (summer only) flight between Ulaanbaatar and Shanghai and possibly Hong Kong. Travel agents include:
STA Travel (☎ 2736 1618; www.statravel.com.hk)
Four Seas Tours (☎ 2200 7760; www.fourseastravel .com/english)

Continental Europe

Most Europeans generally fly to Mongolia from Moscow (see Russia opposite) or Berlin on either MIAT or Aeroflot. The fare to/from Berlin is US$601/929 one way/return on MIAT and US$886/971 on Aeroflot.

Fares to Beijing from Western Europe are similar to those from London (see UK, opposite).

Some travel agencies to check out are:
CTS Viaggi (☎ 06-462 0431; www.cts.it) Italian company that specialises in student and youth travel.
NBBS Reizen (☎ 0900 10 20 300; www.nbbs.nl in Dutch) Branches in most Dutch cities.

Nouvelles Frontiéres (☎ 08 25 00 07 47; www
.nouvelles-frontieres.fr in French) Many branches in Paris
and throughout France.
STA Travel (in Paris ☎ 01 43 59 23 69, in Frankfurt
☎ 069-430 1910; www.statravel.com) Branch offices
across Europe.

Japan & Korea

In summer, MIAT flies to/from Tokyo on
Monday, Wednesday and Saturday (US$446/
867 one way/return), to/from Osaka on Friday (US$406/794), and to Seoul daily except
Saturday for US$375/594. Korean Air flies
daily to Seoul, for US$379/493. For travel
agents try:
No 1 Travel (☎ 03-3205 6073; www.no1-travel.com)
STA Travel (☎ 03-5391 2922; www.statravel.co.jp)

Kazakhstan

Border junkies may be interested in this obscure route into Mongolia. Air Irtysh flies
from Almaty to Ölgii via Üst Kamenogorsk
on Wednesday morning. One-way flights
cost about US$200. For information on
flying in the other direction, see p207. Remember that after arriving in Ölgii, you'll
need to get your passport registered within
seven days if you plan on staying in Mongolia for more than 30 days. The police in
Ölgii *may* be able to do this.

Russia

Aeroflot has four flights a week between
Ulaanbataar and Moscow (US$450/580 one
way/return). MIAT flies to Moscow (US$330/
660) on Tuesday, Friday and Sunday, continuing to Berlin and returning the same day.
MIAT also flies to/from Irkutsk on Monday,
Wednesday and Friday for US$91/181.
    Aero Mongolia flies to Irkutsk on Tues-
day and Friday (US$90/160).

UK & Ireland

To Beijing, low-season return fares from
London start at £430 with Air China (flying direct). Aeroflot flies Ulaanbaatar to
London on Friday for £390 return, with
a change of planes but no overnight stay
or airport transfer required. The Saturday
connection is not as convenient as it entails
a night in Moscow at your own expense.
    Agencies to try include:
Bridge the World (☎ 0870 814 4400; www.b-t-w.co.uk)
Flightbookers (☎ 0870 814 4001; www.ebookers.co.uk)
STA Travel (☎ 0870 160 0599; www.statravel.co.uk)

USIT Campus Travel (☎ 020-7730 3402; www.usit
campus.com)

USA & Canada

The cheapest fares to Beijing are from San
Francisco, Los Angeles and New York on
Korean Air, Air China, Northwest Airlines
and United Airlines. From the US west/
east coast, return fares start at US$750/890.
The cheapest return flight to Moscow from
New York will probably weigh in around
US$900 return.
    In general, fares from Canada to both
Beijing and Moscow cost 10% more than
from the USA. Return low-season fares be-
tween Toronto and Beijing start at around
C$1850. Agencies include:
Orbitz (☎ 888-656-4546; www.orbitz.com) Discount
Internet website.
STA Travel (☎ 800-777-0112; www.statravel.com)
Offices in Boston, Chicago, Miami, New York, Philadelphia,
San Francisco and other major cities.
Travel CUTS (☎ 1-866-246-9762; www.travelcuts.com)
Canada's national student travel agency, which has offices
in all major cities.

LAND

There are two main land border crossings
open to foreigners; Ereen (Erenhot or Érliàn in Chinese) and Zamyn-Üüd, on the
Chinese–Mongolian border, and Naushki
and Sükhbaatar, on the Russian–Mongolian
border. It's possible to cross borders by
minivan or train, though the latter is the
more common and convenient. In 2004,
three border crossings were opened with
Russia (see p253).
    If you plan on staying over 30 days in
Mongolia you will need to register within
seven days of arrival. This can be a problem
if you arrive a long way from Ulaanbaatar.
See p247 for more details.

China
BORDER CROSSINGS

The only border open to foreigners is the one
between Zamyn-Üüd and Ereen. Note that
the border is closed on weekends.
    Heading into China, it *might* be possible
to get an emergency 72-hour transit visa if
you can prove that you have a flight out of
the country. If you are heading for Mongolia, an office on the 3rd floor of the Erlian
Fandian (Ereen Hotel), can issue Mongolian
visas. For more info on visas, see p246.

TRANSPORT

If you are taking the direct train between China and Mongolia you will have up to three hours to kill in Ereen. You can buy snacks for the train at the market or one of the well-stocked shops. Many of the shop signs are in Cyrillic Mongolian for the benefit of the many traders that come here. There are moneychangers and banks in and around the station. If going *to* China and still have tögrög, change it here or you'll be keeping it as a souvenir.

Zamyn-Üüd, on the Mongolian side, is not an interesting place, so you aren't missing anything if the train stops in the middle of the countryside (usually in the middle of the night), and not at Zamyn-Üüd. Mongolian customs and immigration officials take about two hours to do their stuff.

CAR & MOTORCYCLE
Foreigners are not allowed to drive their own vehicle around China yet, so driving across the Chinese border is currently out of the question.

MINIVAN
Minivans shuttle between the train stations of Zamyn-Üüd, on Mongolia's southern border, and Ereen, the Chinese border town, for T8000 (which includes an exit tax of T6000). Because most travellers are trying to connect with onward morning trains, there is a big rush for the vans when the Ulaanbaatar to Zamyn-Üüd train arrives. Going the other way, a minivan will cost Y108.

TRAIN
Refer to the table 'Trains to/from Mongolia' (opposite), which outlines international train services. There is no departure tax if travelling on the train.

Direct Trains
Most travellers catch the direct train between Beijing and Ulaanbaatar.

There are two direct trains a week each way between Beijing and Ulaanbaatar. One of these (No 3 and 4) is the Trans-Mongolian train, which runs between Beijing and Moscow. The other (No 23 and 24) is easier to get tickets for. For more details on the Trans-Mongolian see p255.

It is also possible twice a week to travel directly between Ulaanbaatar and Hohhot, allowing you to either bypass Beijing com-

pletely or catch a train or flight (US$80) on to Beijing from there.

The costs in tögrög for destinations in China from Ulaanbaatar are found in the following table.

Destination	2nd class (hard sleeper)	1st class (soft sleeper)	Deluxe* (coupé)
Beijing	61,650	88,270	108,990
Datong	50,920	73,350	90,150
Ereen		35,100	
Hohhot	42,810	60,870	79,000

* Prices are for Chinese trains. Mongolian trains are about 15% to 20% cheaper for deluxe (coupé) class.

Local Trains
If you are on a tight budget it is possible to take local trains between Ulaanbaatar and Beijing. This will save you some money but involves more hassle and uncertainty and requires more time. During the summer travel season from mid-June to mid-August, international train bookings are almost impossible to get, unless you have booked your seats weeks or even months in advance. The local train may be your only option.

The first option is train No 22 or 21, which runs between Ulaanbaatar and Ereen just inside China. This Mongolian train leaves Ulaanbaatar at 9.15pm on Monday and Thursday and arrives in Ereen at about 11.30am the next morning, after passing through immigration and customs formalities. In reverse, No 21 leaves Ereen on Tuesday and Friday evenings and arrives the next day. Tickets from Ulaanbaatar for soft-sleeper (1st class) cost T32,100. The schedules for this train change regularly.

The second option is to take local trains to Zamyn-Üüd in Mongolia (see p87) and then cross the border by minivan or jeep. From Ereen you can take a local train to Jining and then on to Beijing.

From Beijing, the local train for Jining departs at 11.42am and takes about nine hours. A second train departs at 9.20pm and continues to Hohhot. The train (Y44) from Jining to Érliàn (Ereen) departs around noon and takes six hours. (Alternatively, a 7am bus takes just four hours). If you have to stay the night in Jining there's a budget hotel on the right (south) side of the plaza as you walk out of the train sta-

TRANS PORT

TRAINS TO/FROM MONGOLIA

Schedules change from one summer to another, and services reduce in winter, and can increase in summer. The duration below refers to the journey time to/from Ulaanbaatar.

Train	Train no	Day of departure	Departure time	Duration
China-Mongolia				
Beijing-Ulaanbaatar	23	Tue	7.40am*	30hrs
Beijing-Ulaanbaatar-(Moscow)	3	Wed	7.40am*	30hrs
Hohhot-Ulaanbaatar	215	Sun, Wed	10.40pm	30hrs
Mongolia-China				
Ulaanbaatar-Beijing	24	Sun	8.50am	30hrs
(Moscow)-Ulaanbaatar-Beijing	4	Thu	8.50am	30hrs
Ulaanbaatar-Hohhot	34	Mon, Fri	8.00pm	24hrs
Mongolia-Russia				
Ulaanbaatar-Irkutsk	263	daily	8.45pm	36hrs
Ulaanbaatar-Moscow	5	Tue, Fri	1.50pm	70hrs
(Beijing)-Ulaanbaatar-Moscow	3	Thu	1.15pm	100hrs
Russia-Mongolia				
Irkutsk-Ulaanbaatar	264	daily	7.10pm	36hrs
Moscow-Ulaanbaatar	6	Wed, Thu	9pm	70hrs
Moscow- Ulaanbaatar-(Beijing)	4	Sun	7.55pm	100hrs

* Trains Nos 3 and 23 pass through Datong at approx 2.15pm, Jining at 4.15pm, Ereen at 8.45pm and Zamyn-Üüd at 11.45pm.

tion. Most transport between Ereen and the border takes place in the morning.

Russia
BORDER CROSSINGS
Most travellers go in and out of Russia at the Naushki–Sükhbaatar train border crossing. Until recently this was the only option open to foreigners. In 2004, three road crossings were opened up: Tsagaannuur–Tashanta in Bayan-Ölgii aimag, Altanbulag–Kyakhta in Selenge and Erdeentsav–Borzya in Dornod. Travellers have only recently begun getting vehicles across, so we can't offer much in the way of advice. The crossings are open 9am to noon and 2pm to 6pm Monday to Friday.

From Ulan Ude, you could take the 8am bus (160 roubles) to Altanbulag, but there are no public transport options across the other new crossings.

There is hope that the Khankh–Mondy border in northern Khövsgöl will be opened in 2005; check the situation before heading out this way.

Both the road and rail crossings can be agonisingly slow, but at least on the road journey you can get out and stretch your legs. Train travellers have been stranded for up to 10 hours on the Russian side, much of this time locked inside the train cabins. Procedures on Ulaanbaatar–Moscow train are faster than on the local trains.

We have received a number of complaints about scams and problems with customs at the Russian side of the border, so be ready for anything.

One thing to be careful about is the Russian exit declaration form. The currency you list on the form must match the currency you listed on the customs form you

TRANSPORT

BOGIES

Don't be concerned if you get off at Ereen (on the Chinese side of the border), and the train disappears from the platform. About two hours are spent changing the bogies (wheel assemblies) because the Russians (and, therefore, the Mongolians) and the Chinese use different railway gauges. Train buffs may want to see the bogie-changing operation. Stay on the train after it disgorges passengers in Ereen. The train then pulls into a large shed about 1km from the station. Get off immediately before the staff lock the doors – they really don't want you in the train anyway. It's OK to walk around the shed and take photos, but don't get in anybody's way.

---

received when you entered the country. If the form shows that you are leaving with more dollars or euros than you had when you arrived, you will have to get off the train and change all the excess money into roubles. Further, if the entry form was not stamped when you arrived in Russia (or if you never received one) it will be considered invalid, so have the form stamped even if you have nothing to declare.

The problem gets more complex if you have to change the cash, because there is no place to change in Naushki; the nearest bank is 35km away in Kyakhta (which doesn't change euros anyway). If you do end up in Kyakhta, you might as well ditch the train and travel to Ulaanbaatar by road. To avoid these problems, either don't cross the border with foreign currency (roubles are ok) or be vigilant with that exit declaration form. Lying about not having foreign cash is one option, but you run the risk of being searched. Telling the border guard you plan to use a credit card may work.

Russian–Mongolian Border Towns

Customs and immigration between Naushki and Sükhbaatar can take at least four hours. You can have a look around Naushki, but there is little to see and the border crossing usually takes place in the middle of the night. Surprisingly, you may have difficulty finding anyone at the Naushki station to change money, so wait until Sükhbaatar or Ulaanbaatar, or somewhere else in Russia.

(Get rid of your tögrög before you leave Mongolia, as almost no-one will want to touch them once you are inside Russia.)

The train may stop for one or two hours at, or near, the pleasant Mongolian border town of Sükhbaatar, but there is no need to look around. You may be able to buy some Russian roubles or Mongolian tögrög from a moneychanger at the train station, but the rate will be poor. If there aren't any moneychangers, you can use US dollars cash to get by until you change money elsewhere.

CAR & MOTORCYCLE

In 2004 the Mongolian and Russian government agreed to relax border regulations and allow people other than Russians or Mongolians to drive between the two countries at Tsagaannuur (Bayan-Ölgii), Altanbulag (Selenge) and Erdeentsav (Dornod).

However, these new road crossings can be difficult. Travellers crossing into Bayan-Ölgii aimag reported that the guards wanted to see special written permission from the government of Mongolia. One group was able to produce a letter written by the Mongolian embassy in London, stating that they could pass through the border, which did the trick. The process of getting through these borders could take up to six hours.

The situation will probably get easier over time, but it won't hurt to have a letter written by the Mongolian consular when you get your visa. (Or Russian if you are headed that way.) US citizens may want to bring documentation stating that visas are not needed as proof to inexperienced border guards.

Foreigners are currently not allowed to 'walk' across the Kyakhta–Altanbulag border, but they are allowed to pass through in a car or even on a motorcycle, so you may have to pay someone to drive you across, which could cost up to 200 roubles. Things continue to change so it's worth asking if you can walk across the border.

TRAIN

Besides the Trans-Mongolian Railway connecting Moscow and Beijing (see p255), there is a direct train twice a week connecting Ulaanbaatar and Moscow, which is easier to book from Ulaanbaatar. The epic trip takes four days.

If you are headed to Lake Baikal, there is a daily train between Ulaanbaatar and

Irkutsk, which stops en route in Darkhan. These trains stop at every village, however, and the No 263 travels past Lake Baikal at night, so if you are in a hurry or want to see the lake, take the Ulaanbaatar–Moscow (No 5) as far as Irkutsk. Note that departure and arrival times at Irkutsk are given in Moscow time, although Irkutsk is actually five hours ahead of Moscow.

When entering or leaving Russia by train, be careful of official-looking rogues that try to sell a phoney insurance card for US$10. They can be pretty persistent, saying you can't cross the border without it, but don't be fooled. They may stop bothering you if you wave a card (student card or other) that looks like an insurance card.

This trip can be done more cheaply by travelling in stages on local trains (eg from Ulan Ude to Naushki, Naushki to Sükhbaatar, and Sükhbaatar to Ulaanbaatar) but it would involve more hassles, especially as Russian visas are more difficult to arrange than Chinese due to Russian officials wanting full details of your itinerary.

Approximate costs (in tögrög) for major destinations in Russia from Ulaanbaatar are listed below. Exact costs depend on whether the train is Russian, Chinese or Mongolian; we have listed the most expensive.

Destination	2nd class (hard sleeper)	1st class (soft sleeper)	Deluxe (coupé)
Naushki	21,450	24,970	35,750
Ulan Ude	28,970	34,260	45,800
Irkutsk	41,790	49,020	65,430
Krasnoyarsk	60,540	74,220	99,220
Novosibirsk	69,210	84,860	113,280
Omsk	77,020	94,370	126,220
Yekaterinburg	91,020	110,350	148,080
Perm	94,220	114,400	152,130
Moscow	111,360	134,810	180,870

Trans-Mongolian Railway

Most people travel from Russia or China to Mongolia directly on the Trans-Mongolian Railway line. The following gives general information on this travelling route.

The names of the rail lines can be a bit confusing. The Trans-Mongolian Railway goes from Beijing through Ulaanbaatar and onto a junction called Zaudinsky, near Ulan Ude in Russia, where it meets the Trans-Siberian line and continues on to Moscow. The Trans-Siberian Railway runs between Moscow and the eastern Siberian port of Nakhodka – this route does not go through either China or Mongolia. The Trans-Manchurian Railway crosses the Russia–China border at Zabaikalsk–Manzhouli, also completely bypassing Mongolia.

GENERAL TRAIN INFORMATION

At the stations in Mongolia and Russia, there may be someone on the platform selling food; in the more entrepreneurial China, someone on the platform will have some delicious fruit and soft drinks for sale.

The restaurant cars on the Russian and Chinese trains have decent food (US$2 to US$4) and drinks in their restaurant cars. Staff on the Russian train to Moscow have a tendency to sell off all the food at stops in Siberia, so you may find food supplies have dwindled by Novosibirsk.

Note that toilets are normally locked whenever you are in a station and for five minutes before and after. Showers are only available in the deluxe carriages. In 2nd and 1st class, there is a washroom and toilet at the end of each carriage – which always get progressively filthy. It's a good idea to bring a large enamel mug (available in most Chinese railway stations) and use it as a scoop to pour water over yourself from the washbasin.

Generally you are only allowed to take 35kg of luggage, but for foreigners this is rarely checked, except perhaps when departing Beijing. A lot of smuggling is done on this train, so never agree to carry anything across the border for anyone else.

Don't leave unattended baggage in your cabin. A few years ago, the Trans-Mongolian had a bad reputation for theft, but militia now ride the trains and security has improved. For added safety, lock your cabins from the inside and also make use of the security clip on the upper left-hand part of the door. The clip can be flipped open from the outside with a knife, but not if you stuff the hole with paper.

If you want to get off or on the Trans-Mongolian at Sükhbaatar, Darkhan (travelling from Russia) or Sainshand (from China), you will still have to pay the full Ulaanbaatar fare. If you are not actually getting *on* the train in Ulaanbaatar, you should arrange for someone in UB to tell the attendant

TRANSPORT

that you will catch the train at a later stop, so your seat is not taken.

Tickets list the departure times. Get to the station at least 20 minutes before *arrival* to allow enough time to find the platform and struggle on board, as the train only stops in Ulaanbaatar for about 30 minutes.

For detailed information on the Trans-Mongolian and Trans-Siberian trains, try Lonely Planet's *Trans-Siberian Railway*.

What to Bring

US dollars in small denominations are useful to buy meals and drinks on the train, and to exchange for the local currency, so you can buy things at the train stations. It's a good idea to buy some Russian roubles or Chinese yuan at the licensed moneychangers in Ulaanbaatar before you leave Mongolia.

Stock up on munchies such as biscuits, chocolate and fruit, and bring some bottled water or juice. You'd be wise to purchase your own alcohol before boarding the train because it is expensive on the train and the choice is limited.

A small samovar at the end of each carriage provides constant boiling water; a godsend for making tea and coffee, as well as instant packet meals of noodles or soup.

Other essential items include thongs (flip flops) or slippers, an enamel mug, a flannel, toilet paper, plenty of reading material and loose, comfortable long pants.

CLASSES

With a few exceptions, all international trains have two or three classes. The names and standards of the classes depend on whether it is a Mongolian, Russian or Chinese train.

On the Russian (and Mongolian) trains, most travellers travel in 2nd class – printed on tickets and timetables as '1/4' and known as 'hard-sleeper', 'coupé' or *kupeynyy* in Russian. These are small, but perfectly comfortable, four-person compartments with four bunk-style beds and a fold-down table.

First class (printed as '2/4') is sometimes called a 'soft-sleeper', or *myagkiy* in Russian. It has softer beds but hardly any more space than a Russian 2nd-class compartment and is not worth the considerably higher fare charged. On Chinese trains it is non smoking, which can be a godsend.

The real luxury (and expense) comes with Chinese deluxe class (printed as '1/2'):

it involves roomy, wood-panelled two-berth compartments with a sofa, and a shower cubicle shared with the adjacent compartment. The deluxe class on Russian trains, which is slightly cheaper than the Chinese deluxe, has two bunks but is not much different in size from 2nd class and has no showers.

CUSTOMS & IMMIGRATION

There are major delays of three to six hours at both the China–Mongolia and Russia–Mongolia borders. Often the trains cross the border during the middle of the night, when the alert Mongolian and Russian officials maintain the upper hand. The whole process is not difficult or a hassle – just annoying because they keep interrupting your sleep.

Your passport will be taken for inspection and stamping. When it is returned, inspect it closely – sometimes they make errors such as cancelling your return visa for China. Foreigners generally sail through customs without having their bags opened, which is one reason people on the train may approach you and ask if you'll carry some of their luggage across the border – *this is not a good idea.*

During these stops, you can alight and wander around the station, which is just as well because the toilets on the train are locked during the inspection procedure.

TICKETS

The international trains, especially the Trans-Mongolian Railway, are popular, so it's often hard to book this trip except during winter. Try to plan ahead and book as early as possible.

If you are in Ulaanbaatar and want to go to Irkutsk, Beijing or Moscow, avoid going on the Beijing–Moscow or Moscow–Beijing trains; use the other trains mentioned on p252 and p254, which *originate* in Ulaanbaatar. In Ulaanbaatar, you cannot buy tickets a few days in advance for the Beijing–Moscow or Moscow–Beijing trains, because staff in UB won't know how many people are already on the train. For these trains, you can only buy a ticket the day before departure, ie on Wednesday for trains from Ulaanbaatar to Moscow, and on Saturday for trains from Ulaanbaatar to Beijing. You will need to get to the ticket office early and get into the Mongolian scramble for tickets.

For details on buying tickets in Ulaanbaatar see p87.

From China (& Hong Kong)

Trains leave from Beijing Railway Station. You will need to get your baggage x-rayed and your ticket stamped before you can board the train. So make sure you arrive early.

If your luggage weighs over 35kg, on the day before departure you'll have to take it to the Luggage Shipment Office, which is on the right-hand side of the station. The excess is charged at about US$11 per 10kg, with a maximum excess of 40kg allowed.

The best place to buy tickets in China is the **China International Travel Service** (CITS; in Beijing ☎ 010-6512 0507; www.cits.net/index.jsp; ✆ 8.30am-noon & 1.30-5pm Mon-Fri), in the International Hotel, Jianguomenwai Dajie, Beijing. Tickets are also available at the **CITS**

TRAVEL AGENCIES & ORGANISED TOURS

In this section we list reliable agencies outside Mongolia that can help with the logistics of travel in Mongolia, including visas, excursions or the whole shebang. These include travel agencies, adventure tour operators and homestay agencies. The following agencies can hook you up with tickets, individual itineraries or group packages. For Ulaanbaatar-based travel companies, see p69.

The largest travel company specialising in Mongolia is **Juulchin** (www.juulchin.com), the former state company that has gone private. Juulchin has offices in Beijing, Berlin, Tokyo, Seoul and New Jersey.

Australia
Intrepid Travel (☎ 03-9473 2626; www.intrepidtravel.com.au; 11 Spring St, Fitzroy, Victoria 3065)
Peregrine Adventures (☎ 03-9663 8611; www.peregrine.net.au; 258 Lonsdale St, Melbourne, Victoria 3000)

USA & Canada
Boojum Expeditions (☎ 1-800-287 0125; 406-587 0125; www.boojum.com; 14543 Kelly Canyon Rd, Bozeman, MT 59715) Offers horse riding, mountain biking, fishing and trekking trips. Also organises eagle-hunting in November and December. In Ulaanbaatar, Boojum's local office is called Khövsgöl Lodge Company.
Geographic Expeditions (☎ 415-922 0448, 1-800-777 8183; www.geoex.com; 1008 General Kennedy Ave, 2nd floor, San Francisco, CA 94129) Horse-riding trips to Khentii and jeep trips combining western Mongolia and Tuva in western Siberia.
Hidden Trails (☎ 604-323 1141; www.hiddentrails.com; 202-380 West 1st Ave, Vancouver BC, V5Y 3T7) Horse-riding tours to Terelj and Darkhad Depression, in conjunction with Equitour.
Mir Corporation (☎ 1-800-424 7289; www.mircorp.com; 85 South Washington St, Suite 210, Seattle WA 98104)
Nomadic Expeditions (☎ 609-860 9008, 1-800-998 6634; www.nomadicexpeditions.com; 1095 Cranbury-South River Rd, Suite 20A, Jamesburg, NJ 08831) One of the best Mongolia specialists, offering everything from palaeontology trips to eagle-hunting, kayaking and camel trekking. It also has an office in Ulaanbaatar.
Turtle Tours (☎ 888-299-1439; www.turtletours.com; PO Box 1147, Carefree, AZ 85377)

UK & Continental Europe
Discovery Initiatives (☎ 01285-643333; www.discoveryinitiatives.com; The Travel House; 51 Castle St, Cirencester, GL7 1QD UK) Runs environmentally friendly conservation trips to Khövsgöl, the Gobi and elsewhere in cooperation with local scientists.
Equitour (☎ 061-303 3108; www.equitour.com; Herrenweg, 60 CH-4123 Allschwil, Switzerland) Specialises in horse-riding tours.
Exodus (☎ 020-8675 5550; www.exodus.co.uk; 9 Weir Rd, London SW12 0LT, UK)
In the Saddle (☎ 01299-272 997; www.inthesaddle.co.uk; Reaside, Neen Savage, Cleobury Mortimer, Shropshire DY14 8ES UK) Runs horse-riding tours.
KE Adventure (☎ 017687-73966; www.keadventure.com; 32 Lake Rd, Keswick, Cumbria CA12 5DQ, UK) Organises mountain-biking tours and guided ascents of Tavan Bogd Uul.
Mongolei Reisen GmbH (☎ 030-4405 7646; www.mongoliajourneys.com; Chausseestrasse 84, 10115, Berlin, Germany)
Steppes East (☎ 01285-651 010; www.steppeseast.co.uk; 51 Castle St, Cirencester, GL7 1QD, UK)

office (in Beijing ☎ 010-6515 0093 ext 35; Beijing Tourism Bldg, 28 Jianguomenwai) opposite the Gloria Plaza Hotel.

With CITS it is possible to book up to two months in advance for trains originating in Beijing if you send a deposit of Y100; and you can collect your ticket from one week to one day before departure. There is a Y150 cancellation fee.

CITS only sells tickets from Beijing to Moscow or Ulaanbaatar – no stopovers are allowed. Tickets to Ulaanbaatar cost Y605/845/1031 in hard sleeper/soft sleeper/ deluxe.

You can also buy train tickets privately; they will be more expensive than at CITS, but you may be able to arrange a stopover and arrange visas while you are there.

In Beijing, **Monkey Business Shrine** (☎ 010-6591 6519; fax 6591 6517; www.monkeyshrine.com) can put together all kinds of stopovers and homestay programs. The company has a lot of experience in booking international trains for independent travellers. In Hong Kong, the company goes under the name **Moonsky Star Ltd** (☎ 2723 1376; fax 2723 6653).

Note that in April 2004 the Russian embassy in Beijing stopped selling tourist visas to nonresidents, which may require having your passport sent to Shanghai or Hong Kong.

From Russia

In Moscow, you can buy tickets at the building on ulitsa Krasnoprudnaya 1, next door to the Yaroslavl train station, from where the trains to Ulaanbaatar and Beijing leave.

Infinity Travel (☎ 095-234 6555; fax 234 6556; www .infinity.ru) in Moscow is affiliated with the Travellers Guesthouse and is one of the better private sellers.

The only reliable agency in Ulan Ude is **Buryat-Intour** (☎ 3012-216 954; fax 219 267; buryatia@ rex.burnet.ru; 12 Ranzhurov Sta, Ulan Ude 670000).

In Irkutsk, you can try **Irkutsk-Baikal Intourist** (☎ 3952-290 161; Hotel Intourist, 14 bulvar Gagarina 44) or the completely different **Irkutsk Baikal Travel Inc** (☎ 3952-381 938; fax 3952-381 935; www .irkutsk-baikal.com; PO box 106, Irkutsk 664000).

From Other Countries

Several agencies in Western countries can arrange tickets on the international trains, but their prices will be considerably higher than if you bought them from the point of departure. They often only make the effort if you also buy an organised tour from them.

Overseas branches of CITS or China Travel Service (CTS) can often book train and plane tickets from Beijing to Ulaanbaatar. Also try:

Australia

Gateway Travel (☎ 02-9745 3333; fax 02-9745 3237; www.russian-gateway.com.au)
Sundowners (☎ 03-9672 5300; fax 03-9672 5311; www.sundowners.com.au)

Canada

Exotik Tours (☎ 514-284 3324; fax 514-843 5493; exotiktours@exotiktours.com)

Germany

Lernidee Reisen (☎ 030-786 5056; fax 030-786 5596)
Travel Service Asia (☎ 07351-373 210; fax 07351-373 211; www.travel-service-asia.de in German)

UK

China Travel Service (☎ 020-7836 9911; fax 020-7836 3121; cts@ctsuk.com)
China Travel Service & Information Centre (☎ 020-7388 8838; fax 020-7388 8828)
Intourist (☎ 020-7538 8600; fax 020-7538 5967; www.intourist.com)
Regent Holidays (☎ 0117-921 1711; fax 0117-925 4866; www.regent-holidays.co.uk)
The Russia Experience Ltd (☎ 0208-566 8846; fax 0208-566 8843; www.trans-siberian.co.uk)

USA

White Nights International Tourism (☎ /fax 916-979-9381; www.wnights.com; 610 La Sierra Dr, Sacramento, CA 95864)

GETTING AROUND

Travelling around the countryside independently is the best way to see the country and meet the people, but there are several matters you need to be aware of. Annual outbreaks of forest fires, the plague, foot and mouth disease, and even cholera may affect your travel plans if there are quarantine restrictions.

Generally, shortages of petrol and spare parts are now uncommon, except in remote regions. Accidents are not uncommon. Try to avoid travelling at night when unseen potholes, drunk drivers and wildlife can wreak havoc. Driving in the dark is also a great way to get completely lost.

Lastly, if you think Ulaanbaatar is undeveloped and lacking in facilities, think again about travelling in the countryside.

AIR

Mongolia, a vast, sparsely populated country with very little infrastructure, relies heavily on air transport. There are 81 airports and airstrips, of which only 31 can be used permanently; only eight of these are paved.

Almost all of the destinations are served directly from Ulaanbaatar, so it is impossible to fly, say, between Dalanzadgad and Altai without returning to Ulaanbaatar and catching another flight.

Longer flights to the west stop to refuel, often at Tosontsengel or Mörön, so you can sometimes catch a trip to Khovd and Khövsgöl. It can be hard to get a confirmed seat if you try to pick up a flight on the second leg; if the flight happens to be full, you won't get on it.

In summer, extra flights go to Dalanzadgad and the Juulchin-Gobi ger camp.

Airlines in Mongolia

Mongolian Airlines (MIAT; 011-379 935; www.miat .com) is running on empty. Its domestic fleet was recently retired due to age and the cash-strapped government has been reluctant to buy or lease new planes, knowing full well that the domestic market is virtually unprofitable. If the government goes ahead with the upgrade of the fleet the flight information detailed in this book should hold up.

MIAT has had a poor safety record (five accidents since 1990, four of which were fatal), but since their ancient planes no longer operate, the matter is academic. Recent restructuring and new safety guidelines have resulted in dramatic improvements for international routes and a quasi-corporate culture, which should be reflected if a domestic service continues.

Aero Mongolia (☎ 011-330 373; www.aeromongolia .mn) MIAT's lone competitor, may be able to pick up some of MIAT's slack. At the time of writing, Aero Mongolia was flying to Bayankhongor, Choibalsan, Khovd, Mörön and Ulaangom.

DOMESTIC DEPARTURE TAX

This is paid when you buy your air ticket and it varies from T500 to T1000, depending on the airport.

Blue Sky Aviation (☎ 011-312 085; fax 322 857; www .bsamongolia.com) has a nine-seat Cessna that can be chartered for any part of the country.

Checking In

Go to all airports at least two hours before departure on the assumption that you will still have to struggle to get a seat on the flight, even if you have a ticket. In Ulaanbaatar, this is often less of a problem. (All flights from Ulaanbaatar depart between 8am and 10am.) Even if you have a ticket, flight number and an allocated seat number, don't assume the plane won't be overbooked. There are usually no assigned seats so you'll have to do some scrambling once on board. Try to make certain your luggage has gone on the plane. If possible, you'll save time and the worry of losing your bag by carrying your pack on as hand luggage.

Costs

The foreigner price is often several times more than what Mongolians pay for tickets. Anyone can buy a ticket on your behalf, but you will always have to pay in US dollars (or a credit card in Ulaanbaatar). Tickets range from US$46 (to Mandalgov) to US$185 for a four-hour, 1380km flight to the far west – pretty reasonable, considering the distances. Children aged between five and 16 years pay half; under fives fly free.

Local volunteer workers from the Peace Corps and VSO can buy a flight pass from MIAT for about US$55, which entitles them to air tickets at local prices. If you've come on a student visa you can get 25% to 50% off the cost of the ticket.

One real hassle is that the baggage limit on internal MIAT flights is 10kg and MIAT will charge you for every extra gram when you check in. The cost for excess baggage is around T1500 per kilo, depending on the distance of the flight. To avoid this carry some heavy stuff in your small, cabin luggage (which isn't weighed) or share the load among friends.

TRANSPORT

Reservations & Tickets

A domestic ticket reservation isn't worth diddly-squat until you have a ticket in your hand. In the countryside, buy your ticket as soon as you arrive – normally at the airport or, sometimes, at the town bank.

You can buy a return ticket in Ulaanbaatar but there is no computerised reservation system connecting the various airports around the country so you will have to reconfirm your reservation at the airport as soon as you arrive at your destination. Even if you have done this, you need to get to the airport early in the morning of your flight in order to get a boarding pass.

If you wish to fly in one direction and return by road in the other (for example to Mörön), it's best to fly from Ulaanbaatar, where you are more likely to get a ticket and a seat, and then return overland – otherwise you may wait days or more for a flight and ticket in Mörön.

Seats can be difficult to get in summer, especially in the July tourist peak and in late August as students return to college.

BICYCLE

Now that Mongolia is opening up to the outside world, bicycles occasionally appear on the streets of Ulaanbaatar and even in the countryside, but these are generally ridden by 'eccentric' expats. Most Mongolians don't see the point in bicycles: countryside towns are small enough to walk around; horses or motorbikes are the best form of transport between towns anyway; and buses run regularly around Ulaanbaatar.

Given the rough roads, a mountain bike is the logical choice, but there are a few pointers to keep in mind: maps are inadequate and there are few road signs, taking a bike on a public van or truck (it is better on a train) is fraught with problems, airlines have luggage restrictions, dogs will scare the living daylights out of you, the notoriously fickle weather should be taken seriously, villagers will take a lot of interest in you and your bike, and Mongolians are terrible at estimating distance – they usually grossly overestimate.

If you bring your own bike into the country by train you may have to put it in the luggage car and pay customs duty on it in Ulaanbaatar. On the plus side, once you get there nomads are often more than happy to swap a ride on your bike for a ride on their horse. You should bring all your spare parts and tools, although some bits and pieces can be found at the Naran Tuul Market in UB. A GPS is also a good idea; we've listed coordinates for many locations in this book and in the table on p265.

Hire & Purchase

Graham Taylor at Karakorum Expeditions (see p70) runs some mountain-bike tours in Mongolia and is a source of information on cycling around Mongolia. He can rent a bike for US$25 per day.

You can buy new Chinese mountain bikes at the Naran Tuul Market in UB, but these won't last long on Mongolian roads. Used bikes brought into the country by foreigners also end up at the Naran Tuul market, although some of these are stolen.

BOAT

Although there are 397km of navigable waterways in Mongolia, rivers aren't used for transporting people or cargo. The only two boats we have heard of in the country are the *Sükhbaatar*, which very occasionally travels around Khövsgöl Nuur, and a customs boat that patrols the Selenge Gol on the border of Russia and Mongolia. Both can be chartered by foreigners for lots of money.

BUS

Most long-distance bus routes have been replaced by private minivans and jeeps. The only bus worth seeking out is the decent Ulaanbaatar–Erdenet service, which uses modern Korean-made buses. Other buses to Kharkhorin, Arvaikheer, Öndörkhaan and elsewhere will be USSR-era rust buckets.

CAMEL & YAK

Intractable yaks and confrontational camels are recognised forms of transport in Mongolia. Camels, which can carry around 250kg, carry about one-third of all cargo around the Gobi Desert. Yaks are also a useful and environmentally friendly way of hauling heavy cargo.

At Ongiin Khiid you can arrange a multiple-day camel trek. A few travel agencies include a ride on a camel or yak in their program. Otherwise, you can always ask at a ger.

CAR & MOTORCYCLE

Travelling around Mongolia with your own car or motorcycle – without a driver –is not recommended.What looks like main roads on the map are often little more than tyre tracks in the dirt, sand or mud. All maps are inadequate, and there is hardly a signpost in the whole country. In Mongolia, roads connect nomads, most of whom by their nature keep moving so even the roads are semi-nomadic, shifting like restless rivers. Remote tracks quickly turn into eight-lane dirt highways devoid of any traffic making navigation tricky – some drivers follow the telephone lines when there are any, or else ask for directions at gers along the way. Towns with food and water are few and far between, and very few people in the countryside will speak anything but Mongolian or, if you are lucky, Russian.

If all this hasn't put you off, keep in mind that foreigners have been jailed for being involved in traffic accidents, even if they were not at fault. We've heard horror stories of Mongolians purposely causing accidents with foreigners simply to make them pay for damages (police tend to side with the home team). Contact your embassy immediately if you get in trouble. Another way to avoid jail is to claim an injury, in which case you'll be brought to a hospital.

To assist you find your way around, see the GPS coordinates table (p265) of many towns and villages, and some sights. The coordinates for a number of other sights are included in the regional chapters.

There is nowhere official in Mongolia to rent a car or motorcycle. If you want to buy one, you will have to ask around, or check out the 'car market' (Tsaiz zakh) in the northeastern part of Ulaanbaatar.

One traveller bought a new Ij Planeta – the Russian-made motorcycle you see all over the countryside – for the tögrög equivalent of US$900. A new Russian jeep costs around US$5000. In markets the sign 'zarna' (зарна) on a jeep means 'for sale'.

Travellers can use an international driving license to drive any vehicle in Mongolia; expat residents need to apply for a local licence. If you buy a vehicle, inquire about registration at the local police station.

Two types of Russian fuel are available: '93' is the best and the type used by Japanese jeeps, but only generally available in Ulaan-baatar; all Russian-made vehicles use '76', which is all that is available in the countryside. Petrol stations are marked by the initials 'ШТС', which is Russian for station.

HITCHING

Hitching is never entirely safe in any country in the world and we don't normally recommend it. People who choose to hitch will be safer if they travel in pairs and let someone know where they are planning to go.

Mongolia is different, however. Because the country is so vast, public transport so limited and the people so poor, hitching (usually on trucks) is a recognised – and, often, the only – form of transport in the countryside. Hitching is seldom free and often no different from just waiting for public transport to turn up. It is *always* slow – after stopping at gers to drink, fixing flat tyres, breaking down, running out of petrol and getting stuck in mud and rivers, a truck can take 48 hours to cover 200km.

Hitching is not generally dangerous personally, but it is still hazardous and often extremely uncomfortable. Don't expect much traffic in remote rural areas; you might see one or two vehicles a day on many roads, and sometimes nobody at all for several days. Along the road, just wave at the driver of any vehicle. In the towns, ask at the market, where trucks invariably hang around, or at the bus/truck/jeep station. The best place to wait is the petrol station on the outskirts of town, where most vehicles stop before any journey. Hitching out of Ulaanbaatar can be difficult because you must find the right truck or vehicle at the right time.

If you rely on hitching entirely, though, you will just travel from one dreary aimag town to another. You still need to hire a jeep to see, for example, the Gobi Desert, the mountains in Khentii or some of the lakes in the far west.

Truck drivers will normally expect some negotiable payment, which won't be much cheaper than a long-distance bus or shared jeep; figure on around T1000 per hour travelled. Rather than cash, drivers may prefer vodka or cigarettes, or anything of practical use to them.

Bring a water- and dust-proof bag to put your backpack in. The most important thing, though, to bring is an extremely large amount of patience and time, and a high

TRANSPORT

threshold for discomfort. Carry camping gear for the inevitable breakdowns, or suffer along with your travel mates. Bring all your own food and water, though the truck may stop at *guanz* (canteen) en route.

HORSE

Horses have provided reliable transport for Mongolians for the past few thousand years. If it worked for the Mongol hordes, it can work for you. In recent decades though,

many herders have acquired motorcycles, but most still use horses as their primary mode of transport. Mongolians rarely walk anywhere.

It's impossible to see everything by horse unless you have a lot of time, but it is the best way to travel around some areas (see p234 for some ideas). Most importantly, riding a horse helps you meet locals on a level footing and experience the country as Mongolians have done for centuries.

BLAZING SADDLES – TRAVELLING LIKE A LOCAL

A surprisingly large number of intrepid travellers arrive in Mongolia each summer with plans to travel across the country on horseback and why not? The following advice stems from the experience of one such intrepid neo-Chinggis, who survived to tell the tale.

How to obtain your horses is usually the first obstacle. Horses range in price from US$60 to many thousands of dollars for a racehorse. A tourist can expect to pay US$100 to $150, though you may well be charged more. Price is not really the issue, though; it's getting a good horse that is the challenge.

'Buyer Beware' is the rule of thumb. Herders are very protective of their best horses and these are usually not for sale for love or money. Taking a trusted local with you to assist selection and negotiate the sale is an excellent idea.

Mongolian horses come in two varieties – 'quiet' and 'terrible'. A *nomkhon moir* (quiet horse) is ideal, but these are often prized by herders for use by women and children. Geldings *(moir)* are preferable to mares *(gou)* and stallions *(asarak)*. Depending on the size of the group and duration of the trip, pack horses will also likely be required (figure on one pack horse for every two to three riders). Generally, it's best to select horses that can do both riding and pack duties.

The saddle is possibly the single most important item of equipment, and a comfortable saddle will make or break the trip. Definitely consider bringing a Western-style saddle from home (either a stock or pony saddle). Otherwise, Russian military saddles are available at Naran Tuul market. Only a masochist on a short horse-trip should consider using a Mongolian wooden saddle. For supplies, try Shonkhor Saddles, just east of the Mobicom building in Ulaanbaatar. Horse tack such as bridles, reins, hobbles, tethers etc are best bought locally, but it's worth bringing stirrup leathers from home. Other foreign items of tack make good presents for local herders, as do horse magazines.

Taking along a guide is an important consideration and is generally highly recommended. A wrangler will generally look after the horses, help load packs, navigate and deal with tricky local conditions. Just as important, a guide will offer insights into the Mongolians' close relationship with horses and will help you learn local techniques. Local horse guides normally charge between US$5 and US$15 per day.

In general, it is unnecessary to be 100% stocked with food for the journey. Shops along the way stock basic foodstuffs, and the hospitality of local herders will likely have you eating more dairy products than you ever thought possible. However, be considerate to local hospitality by not depending upon it.

A couple of simple rules apply to horse travel in the Mongolian countryside. Wherever there is water there will be herders and gers, and vice versa. A track of some sort will exist along every navigable feature in the country and if there is a trail, it will be going somewhere. Finally look after your horses and yourself and meet lots of local people!

Graham Taylor

Graham completed a 2000km horse trek through central Mongolia in 1997. You can read the story published in the *Australian Geographic* at www.mongoliadreaming.com.

If you are a serious rider, horses are everywhere; with some luck, guidance and experience, you should be able to find a horse suited to your needs. Mongolians swap horses readily, so there's no need to be stuck with a horse you don't like, or which doesn't like you. The only exception is in April and May, when all animals are weak after the long winter and before fresh spring plants have made their way through the melting snows. The best time for riding is in the summer (June to September), though it is usually wetter then.

You can rent a horse and guide in most tourist areas for between US$5 and US$20 per day (the latter at ger camps). Most foreign (see p257) and local travel agencies also organise horse-riding trips.

One thing to bear in mind is that when mounting a horse (or camel), do so only from the left. The animals have been trained to accept human approach from the left, and may rear if approached the wrong way. The Mongolians use the phrase '*chu!*' to make their horses go. Somewhat telling about the obstinate nature of Mongolian horses is that there is no word for 'stop'. If you are considering a multiday horse trip, remember that horses attract all kinds of flies. Also, if you're not used to riding a horse, you're likely to get mighty stiff and sore.

A few foreigners cherish the idea of buying a horse and taking off around Mongolia. It's a fine adventure (if you can get a visa long enough) but there are several pitfalls to be aware of. For some handy advice, see the boxed text p262.

Some final advice; watch and learn – Mongolians almost invented horsemanship. Also be prepared for at least one spill.

LOCAL TRANSPORT
Bus, Minibus & Trolley-bus
In Ulaanbaatar, regular and very crowded trolley-buses, buses and minibuses ply the main roads for around T200 a ride. Cities such as Darkhan and Erdenet have minibuses that shuttle from one end of town to the other, but you are unlikely to need them because most facilities are located centrally.

Taxi
Only in Ulaanbaatar and a couple of the bigger cities is there taxi service, though in UB any vehicle on the street is a potential taxi – just flag down the driver and agree on a price. The current rate is a standard T250 per km, but this will certainly increase.

MINIVAN & JEEP
Both minivans and jeeps are used for long- and short-distance travel in the countryside. They can be shared among strangers, which is good for a group of people headed from one aimag centre to another (or usually to/from Ulaanbaatar). Alternatively, they can be hired privately. In most cases, the grey, 11-seat Furgon minivans are used for longer cross-country trips that see a lot of traffic. Jeeps, khaki-coloured or green, are found in more remote areas such as *sum* (district) centres. They are nicknamed *jaran yös* (shortened to *jaris*), which means 'sixty-nine' – the number of the original model. The large and comfortable Toyota Landcruiser-style jeeps are owned by wealthy Mongolians and never used for share purposes (though some travel agencies might have them for hire, but expect to pay at least 30% more than for a good Russian jeep).

On the terrible Mongolian roads, these jeeps and minivans are an important form of transport, and are mandatory when visiting more remote attractions. They can typically only travel between 30km/h and 50km/h. The Gobi region generally has the best roads and here you can average 60km/h.

Shared Minivan & Jeep
Share jeeps and minivans are the most common form of public transport in Mongolia. Private vehicles go from Ulaanbaatar to all aimag capitals, major cities and tourist destinations. Less frequent and reliable services operate between most aimag capitals, but very few minivans go to the *sums*.

If you rely solely on share vehicles to get around, you'll see surprisingly little of Mongolia. Most vehicles drive between uninteresting cities with little of interest on the way. You'll still need to hire a car from the aimag or *sum* centres to see anything, and it's usually easier to organise this from Ulaanbaatar.

Another problem with share vehicles is that they are privately operated and won't leave until they are packed tighter than a sardine tin. In the countryside, most just park at the local market and wait for passengers to turn up, which means that if the

TRANSPORT

van isn't already mostly full you'll be waiting around all day for the seats to fill up, if they ever do.

The process can be agonising. Even after the 11-seat van has 20 or so passengers the driver will vanish for an hour or two for lunch; or to find more cargo, spare parts and petrol.

You could arrange to have the driver pick you up at your hotel when he is ready to go, which gives you all day to agonise over whether or not he forgot to pick you up. The waiting time from Ulaanbaatar isn't as bad, but you could still count on two hours or more.

For a long-distance trip bring all your own food and drink; stops will be few and far between, and often at a *guanz*, which usually has poor food. You can expect at least one breakdown and it would be a good idea to bring a sleeping bag and warm clothes just in case you have to spend the night somewhere. Long-distance travel of over 10 hours is fiendishly uncomfortable. Most people who take a long-distance minivan to Mörön or Dalanzadgad end up flying back.

Minivan fares are reasonable, costing the equivalent of US$12 to get to Dalanzadgad (21 hours) from Ulaanbaatar or US$15 to Mörön (25 hours). If there aren't enough passengers you could offer to pay for the empty seats, which is better than sitting around all day.

In the countryside, the post office operates postal vans, which accept passengers. They have fixed departure times, normally running once a week between an aimag capital and a *sum* capital. The local post office should have a list of departure times and fares.

Hiring a Minivan or Jeep

Easily the best way to see the countryside of Mongolia independently is to hire your own minivan or jeep, which will come with a driver and, for a little extra, a guide. If you share the costs with others it doesn't work out to be too expensive and with enough time, camping equipment, water and food, and a reliable jeep and a driver, you will have the time of your life.

You can save money by using public transport to major regional gateways – that is Mörön for Khövsgöl Nuur, Khovd for

the west, Dalanzadgad for the south Gobi and Choibalsan for the far east. Then, from these places, you will be able to rent a jeep fairly easily, though drivers outside Ulaanbaatar will have little experience of dealing with tourists. You probably won't find a local English-speaking guide, so bring one from Ulaanbaatar.

Don't expect to rent a jeep outside of an aimag capital. Most villages will have a jeep, but it may not be available or running.

In Ulaanbaatar, the best place to start looking for a driver and a guide is at the various guesthouses. These guesthouses will take a commission, but you'll get a driver and/or guide who understands the needs of a tourist. More importantly they know the tourist routes and can locate hard-to-find attractions such as caves, deer stones and ruined monasteries. Finding a driver from the jeep stand or market, and negotiating on your own, will be cheaper, but they will probably be in a hurry to get back home, which won't work well if you want to take it slow and see the sights.

On a long-distance trip, a hire rate that includes petrol is more convenient but you run the risk of your driver changing the itinerary to avoid places where petrol is expensive. A rate without petrol should be around 25% lower than that with petrol. Russian jeeps do around 5km to the litre; petrol was around T500 per litre at the time of research.

Avoid offers of 'all-inclusive' charges by 'the day' as you will almost certainly pay more than if you pay per kilometre (though this does deal with issues such as driver's accommodation costs and rest days). You can pay from T400 to T500 per km for more reliable jeeps and drivers from travel agents in Ulaanbaatar, or ger camps in the countryside. This charge may include a stove, tent and sleeping bag. At the market or bus station you may find a jeep for the taxi rate of T300 per km.

It is vital that you and the driver agree to the terms and conditions – and the odometer or speedometer reading – before you start. Ask about all possible 'extras' such as waiting time, food and accommodation. There are several private bridges and tolls around the countryside (each costing around T500), which is normally paid by you. If you arrange for a jeep to pick you up,

GPS COORDINATES TABLE

The table shows latitude and longitude coordinates for various locations in Mongolia, in degrees and decimal minutes. To convert to degrees, minutes, seconds (DMS) format, multiply the number after the decimal point (disregarding the decimal point) by 0.06. The result is your seconds, which can be rounded to the nearest whole number. The minutes is the number between the degree symbol and the decimal point. For example: 43°52.598' in degrees, decimal minutes is equal to 43°52'36" DMS.

CENTRAL MONGOLIA	Latitude (N)	Longitude (E)
Arvaikheer	46°15.941	102°46.724
Bat-Ölzii	46°49.028	102°13.989
Battsengel	47°48.157	101°59.040
Bayan-Öndör	46°30.218	104°5.486
Bayan Önjuul	46°52.859	105°56.571
Bayangol	45°48.505	103°26.811
Bayantsagaan	46°45.806	107°8.709
Bogd	44°39.971	102°8.777
Burenbayan Ulaan	45°10.276	101°25.989
Chuluut	47°32.830	100°13.166
Delgerkhan	46°37.097	104°33.051
Eej Khad (Mother Rock)	47°18.699	106°58.583
Erdenemandal	48°31.445	101°22.265
Erdenesant	47°19.071	104°28.937
Guchin Us	45°27.866	102°23.726
Gunjiin Süm	48°11.010	107°33.377
Ikh Tamir	47°35.221	101°12.413
Jargalant	48°43.716	100°45.12
Khandgait	48°7.066	106°54.296
Khangai	47°51.553	99°26.126
Kharkhorin	47°11.981	102°50.527
Khashant	47°27.034	103°9.708
Khotont	47°22.196	102°28.746
Khujirt	46°54.225	102°46.545
Manzushir Khiid	47°45.520	106°59.675
Möngönmorit	48°12.192	108°27.291
Naiman Nuur	46°21.232	101°50.705
Ögii Nuur (Lake)	47°47.344	102°45.828
Ögii Nuur	47°40.319	102°33.051
Ölziit	48°5.573	102°32.640
Ondor Ulaan	48°2.700	100°30.446
Orkhon Khürkhree	46°47.234	101°57.694
Övgön Khiid	47°25.561	103°41.686
Stele of Tonyukuk	47°41.661	107°28.586
Tariat	48°9.574	99°52.982
Terelj	47°59.193	107°27.834
Tögrög	45°32.482	102°59.657
Tövkhön Khiid	47°6.711	102°16.005
Tsakhir	49°6.426	99°8.574
Tsenkher	47°26.909	101°45.648
Tsetseguun Uul	47°48.506	107°0.165
Tsetserleg City	47°28.561	101°27.289
Tsetserleg Soum	48°53.095	101°14.305
Ulaanbaatar	47°55.056	106°55.007
Uyanga	46°27.431	102°16.731
Zaamar	48°11.843	104°46.59
Züünbayan-Ulaan	46°31.176	102°34.971
Zuunmod	47°42.357	106°56.861

EASTERN MONGOLIA	Latitude (N)	Longitude (E)
Asgat	46°21.724	113°34.536
Baldan Baraivan Khiid	48°11.910	109°25.840
Baruun-Urt	46°40.884	113°16.825
Batnorov	47°56.952	111°30.103
Batshireet	48°41.887	110°0.011
Bayan Tumen	48°3.076	114°22.252
Bayan Uul	49°7.550	112°42.809
Bayandun	49°15.276	113°21.565
Binder	48°36.967	110°36.400
Chinggis Statue	47°6.157	109°9.356
Choibalsan	48°4.147	114°31.404
Dadal	49°1.291	111°37.598
Dashbalbar	49°32.794	114°24.720
Delgerkhaan	47°10.735	109°11.423
Erdenetsagaan	45°54.165	115°22.149
Erdeentsav	49°52.163	115°43.406
Galshar	46°13.324	110°50.606
Khalkhgol	47°59.565	118°5.760
Khalzan	46°10.019	112°57.119
Kherlen Bar Khot	48°3.287	113°21.865
Khökh Nuur (Blue Lake)	48°1.150	108°56.450
Matad	46°57.007	115°16.008
Mönkh Khaan	46°58.163	112°3.418
Norovlin	48°41.449	111°59.596
Öglöchiin Kherem	48°24.443	110°11.812
Ömnödelger	47°53.469	109°49.166
Ondörkhaan	47°19.416	110°39.775
Ongon	45°21.509	113°8.297

	Latitude	Longitude
Shilin Bogd	45°28.350	114°35.349
Sükhbaatar	46°46.285	113°52.646
Sümber	47°38.174	118°36.421
Tsagaan Ovoo	48°33.864	113°14.380
Tsenkhermandal	47°44.673	109°3.909
Uul Bayan	46°30.036	112°20.769

NORTHERN MONGOLIA	Latitude (N)	Longitude (E)
Altanbulag	50°19.225	106°29.392
Amarbayasgalant Khiid	49°28.648	105°5.122
Arbulag	49°54.949	99°26.537
Baruunburen	49°9.753	104°48.686
Bayangol	48°55.472	106°5.486
Borsog	50°59.677	100°42.983
Bugat	49°2.874	103°40.389
Bulgan City	48°48.722	103°32.213
Chandman-Öndör	50°28.436	100°56.378
Chuluut and Ider	49°10.415	100°40.335
Darkhan	49°29.232	105°56.48
Dashchoinkhorlon Khiid	48°47.821	103°30.687
Dashinchinlen	47°51.179	104°2.281
Dulaankhaan	49°55.103	106°11.302
Erdenebulgan	50°6.880	101°35.589
Erdenet	49°1.855	104°3.316
Five Rivers	49°15.475	100°40.385
Gurvanbulag	47°44.499	103°30.103
Jiglegiin Am	51°0.406	100°16.003
Khangal	49°18.810	104°22.629
Khankh	51°30.070	100°41.382
Khar Bukh Balgas	47°53.198	103°53.513
Khatgal	50°26.101	100°9.599
Khishig-Öndör	48°17.678	103°27.086
Khötöl	49°5.486	105°34.903
Khutag-Öndör	49°22.990	102°41.417
Mogod	48°16.372	102°59.520
Mörön	49°38.143	100°9.321
Orkhon	49°8.621	105°24.891
Orkhontuul	48°49.202	104°49.920
Renchinlkhumbe	51°6.504	99°40.234
Saikhan	48°39.448	102°37.851
Selenge	49°26.647	103°58.963
Shine Ider	48°57.213	99°32.297
Sükhbaatar	50°14.196	106°11.911
Teshig	49°57.649	102°35.657
Toilogt	50°39.266	100°14.961
Tosontsengel	49°28.650	100°53.074
Tsagaan Uur	50°32.391	101°31.806
Tsagaannuur (Khövsgöl)	51°21.778	99°21.082
Tsagaannuur (Selenge)	50°5.835	105°25.989
Tsetserleg	49°31.959	97°46.011
Ulaan Uul	50°40.668	99°13.920
Uran Uul	48°59.855	102°44.003
Züünkharaa	48°51.466	106°27.154

THE GOBI	Latitude (N)	Longitude (E)
Altai City	46°22.388	96°15.164
Altai Soum	44°37.010	94°55.131
Altanshiree	45°32.046	110°27.017
Baatsagaan	45°33.266	99°26.188
Baga Gazriin Chuluu	46°13.827	106°4.192
Bayan Dalai	43°27.898	103°30.763
Bayan-Ovoo	42°58.607	106°6.994
Bayan-Uul	46°59.129	95°11.863
Bayanbulag	46°48.223	98°6.180
Bayangovi	44°44.017	100°23.476
Bayankhongor	46°11.637	100°43.115
Bayanlig	44°32.555	100°49.809
Bayanzag	44°8.311	103°43.667
Biger	45°42.583	97°10.354
Bömbogor	46°12.279	99°37.234
Böön Tsagaan Nuur	45°37.114	99°18.567
Bugat	45°33.440	94°20.571
Bulgan	44°5.312	103°32.297
Buutsagaan	46°10.411	98°41.637
Choir	45°47.994	109°18.462
Dalanzadgad	43°34.355	104°25.673
Delger	46°21.074	97°22.011
Delgerekh	45°48.157	111°12.823
Erdenedalai	46°0.418	104°56.996

	Latitude	Longitude
Erdentsogt	46°25.080	100°49.234
Galuut	46°42.061	100°7.131
Govi-Ugtal	46°1.916	107°30.377
Gurj Lamiin Khiid	43°29.030	103°50.930
Gurvantes	43°13.759	101°3.360
Jargalant	47°1.480	99°30.103
Khamaryn Khiid	44°36.038	110°16.650
Khanbogd	43°12.540	107°11.862
Khatanbulag	43°8.882	109°8.709
Khökhmorit	47°21.248	94°30.446
Khövsgöl	43°36.314	109°39.017
Khüreemaral	46°24.523	98°17.037
Mandakh	44°24.122	108°13.851
Mandal-Ovoo	44°39.100	104°2.880
Mandalgov	45°46.042	106°16.38
Manlai	44°4.441	106°51.703
Nomgon	42°50.160	105°8.983
Ondorshil	45°13.585	108°15.223
Ongiin Khiid	45°20.367	104°0.306
Orog Nuur	45°2.692	100°36.314
Saikhan-Ovoo	45°27.459	103°54.110
Sainshand	44°53.576	110°8.351
Sevrei	43°35.617	102°9.737
Shinejist	44°32.917	99°17.349
Süm Khökh Burd	46°40.937	105°45.590
Taishiir	46°42.671	96°29.623
Takhi Research Station	45°32.197	93°39.055
Tsagaan Agui	44°42.604	101°10.187
Tseel	45°33.266	95°51.223
Tsogt	45°20.813	96°37.166
Tsogt-Ovoo	44°24.906	105°19.406
Tsogttsetsii	43°43.541	105°35.040
Ulaanbadrakh	43°52.598	110°24.686
Yoliin Am	43°29.332	104°4.000
Zag	46°56.168	99°9.806
Zamyn-Üüd	43°42.967	111°54.651

WESTERN MONGOLIA	Latitude (N)	Longitude (E)
Altai	45°49.115	92°15.497
Altantsögts	49°2.700	100°26.057
Batuunturuun	49°38.578	94°23.177
Bulgan (Bayan-Ölgii)	46°55.559	91°4.594
Bulgan (Khovd)	46°5.486	91°32.571
Chandmani	43°39.100	92°48.411
Darvi	46°56.181	93°37.158
Deluun	47°51.553	90°44.160
Dörgon	48°19.768	92°37.303
Erdeneburen	48°30.131	91°26.811
Erdenkhairkhan	48°7.228	95°44.229
Khökh Nuur	47°37.207	97°20.546
Khovd (Uvs)	49°16.720	90°54.720
Khovd City	48°0.430	91°38.474
Mankhan	47°24.557	92°12.617
Most	46°41.626	92°48.000
Naranbulag	49°23.164	92°34.286
Nogoonuur	49°36.923	90°13.577
Ölgii (Uvs)	49°1.306	92°0.411
Ölgii City	48°58.070	89°58.028
Öndörkhangai	49°15.849	94°51.154
Otgon	47°12.488	97°36.391
Sagsai	48°54.688	89°39.429
Telmen	48°38.197	97°9.900
Tes	49°39.013	95°49.029
Tolbo	48°24.557	90°16.457
Tolbo Nuur	48°35.320	90°4.536
Tosontsengel	48°45.286	98°5.992
Tsagaanchuluut	47°6.531	96°39.497
Tsagaankhairkhan	49°24.209	94°13.440
Tsagaannuur	49°31.437	89°46.697
Tsengel	48°57.213	89°9.257
Tsenkheriin Agui	47°20.828	91°57.225
Tüdevtei	48°59.390	96°32.229
Ulaangom	49°58.764	92°4.028
Ulaankhus	49°2.525	89°26.929
Uliastai	47°44.591	96°50.582
Urgamal	48°30.653	94°16.046
Üüreg Nuur	50°5.236	91°4.587
Zavkhan (Uvs)	48°49.463	93°6.103
Zavkhanmandal	48°19.071	95°6.789

TRANSPORT

ROAD DISTANCES (km)

	Altai (Gov-Altai aimag)	Arvaikheer	Baruun-Urt	Bayankhongor	Bulgan	Choibalsan	Dalanzadgad	Darkhan	Khovd	Mandalgov	Mörön (Khövsgöl aimag)	Ölgii	Öndörkhaan	Sainshand	Sükhbaatar	Tsetserleg	Ulaanbaatar	Ulaangom	Uliastai
Altai (Gov-Altai aimag)	---																		
Arvaikheer	571	---																	
Baruun-Urt	1561	990	---																
Bayankhongor	371	200	1190	---															
Bulgan	874	373	878	503	---														
Choibalsan	1656	1085	191	1285	973	---													
Dalanzadgad	948	377	856	577	725	1074	---												
Darkhan	1122	596	779	751	248	874	772	---											
Khovd	424	995	1985	795	1180	2080	1372	1519	---										
Mandalgov	879	308	613	508	578	741	293	479	1303	---									
Mörön (Khövsgöl aimag)	583	679	1231	627	718	1326	1056	601	853	913	---								
Ölgii	635	1206	2196	1006	1344	2291	1583	1582	211	1314	991	---							
Öndörkhaan	1332	761	229	961	649	324	710	550	1756	417	1002	1967	---						
Sainshand	1234	663	340	863	781	531	516	682	1658	355	1134	1869	302	---					
Sükhbaatar	1214	688	871	830	340	966	864	92	1612	571	693	1823	642	774	---				
Tsetserleg	502	266	1013	218	289	1108	643	537	438	500	413	1220	784	855	629	---			
Ulaanbaatar	1001	430	560	630	326	655	553	219	1425	260	671	1636	331	463	311	430	---		
Ulaangom	662	1188	1896	988	1033	991	1585	1281	238	1383	680	311	1667	1738	1373	883	1336	---	
Uliastai	218	659	1544	497	807	1639	1074	989	465	967	388	676	1315	1355	1147	531	984	529	---

or drop you off, agree on a reduced price for the empty vehicle travelling one way.

Three can sit in the back seat of a Russian jeep, but it may be uncomfortable on longer trips. Five or six people can ride in a minivan. If you also take a guide, rather than just a driver, you can therefore take a maximum of three passengers in a jeep, though two would be more comfortable. There is usually ample room at the back of the jeep and minivan for backpacks, tents, water and so on.

DRIVERS

There are several other factors you should consider when embarking on a jeep or minivan tour of Mongolia. Before the trip explain your itinerary in detail to the driver and make sure that he has a map and agrees to the route. If you are going to be camping, ensure that the driver and guide have the correct equipment.

Your driver should supply a large petrol drum, as well as a jerry can, as a backup in case there are fuel shortages in the countryside. You'll also need at least one large

water drum, and preferably two, if you are headed to the Gobi. (These are available in the Ulaanbaatar's Naran Tuul Market for less than US$10.) Make sure the drum is watertight, otherwise your bags will get soaked. A wide-mouthed drum is also very useful for storing food, as boxes will rapidly disintegrate. A gunny sack is useful for vegetables and firewood (or dried dung). Resealable bags are useful for opened bags of sugar, pasta etc. Your backpacks will get filthy so it's a good idea to put them in a water- and dust-proof bag.

Drivers from tourist agencies will assume that you will feed them along the way. On a longer trip it's easiest for everyone to cook, eat and wash up together. If you don't want to do this you will have to agree to a fee for the driver's food or buy him the food yourself. Drivers will often not take enough food even if they have agreed to bring their own. You can almost write it off as an added expense, but this shouldn't cost more than T2500 per day.

An experienced driver will have his own Soviet-built petrol stove, though it's a good idea to bring your own stove as a backup, and to boil water for tea while the other stove is cooking dinner. If you are cooking for a group you'll need a big cooking pot and a ladle. A cloth is useful for chopping and peeling vegetables. Bring a couple of rolls of toilet paper for cleaning and mopping up. Everyone should bring their own penknife, cutlery, bowl and torch. Drivers normally bring their own dried meat, which can be added to soups and stews.

Packaged foods, canned goods, fruit and vegetables, chocolate, and camping needs such as washing liquid and candles are all available in Ulaanbaatar, so a group shop is ideal. Many travellers organise a kitty to pay for petrol and food costs on the road. If you are travelling with strangers it's a good idea to keep everyone happy by rotating seats so that everyone (including the guide) has a go in the front seat.

To avoid confusion and frustration explain to your driver the arrangements with cooking, cleaning up, water purification and the difference between communal and private food. Don't push the driver or guide too hard; allow them (and the vehicle) to stop and rest. However, regular and lengthy stops for a chat and a smoke can add time to the journey.

You have the right to decide which, if any, passengers you pick up along the way and whether or not to charge them. However, it's not a good idea to hang around the market and ask for local passengers. The drivers of private shared vehicles are territorial and will give your driver trouble if you're stealing their customers.

Lastly, if you are on a long trip, you'll find morale boosted by a trip to a bathhouse (hot water!) in an aimag capital. Another morale booster is the occasional meal in a decent *guanz*. If you are camping a lot then add in at least one night in a decent hotel to clean up and sort out your stuff.

GUIDES

No-one in the countryside speaks anything other than Mongolian and Russian, so a guide-cum-translator is very handy, and almost mandatory. A guide will explain local traditions, help with any hassles with the police, find accommodation, negotiate jeeps, explain captions in museums and act as linguistic and cultural interpreter.

Many Mongolians in Ulaanbaatar – from students up to professors – try to earn some money as guides during summer holidays. The most popular foreign language (besides Russian) is English, though some speak German, Japanese, Spanish and French, but standards of fluency may not be high.

Finding a guide is not easy. In Ulaanbaatar, ask at travel agencies (where guides will be more expensive), talk to a knowledgeable local, find some students at the universities or nearby cafés and hotels, or check out the classified ads in the English-language newspapers. In the countryside, there is nothing to do but ask, and ask, and ask – try the hotels and schools. Guides are easier to find between 15 June and 1 August, when schools and universities are on summer break.

For getting around Ulaanbaatar, a non-professional guide or a student will cost a negotiable US$5 to US$10 per day, although guides are only useful here if you have to deal with a bureaucracy. To take one around the countryside from the capital you will have to include expenses for travel, food and accommodation. In an aimag capital, a guide (if you can find one) costs about US$5 per day, plus any expenses. For a professional guide who is knowledgeable in a specific interest, such as bird-watching, and fluent in your language, the bidding starts at US$20 per day.

If you are camping you will need to ensure your guide (and driver) has the proper equipment (including basics such as water bottles and eating utensils) and warm clothes; don't leave it up to them or shrug it off if they have substandard equipment.

HAZARDS

Flat tyres are a time-honoured tradition. Insist that your driver bring a spare and a tyre-patch kit consisting of rubber patches, glue, extra tyre valves and a valve tool. Be sure the driver has a tyre pump, hydraulic jack and tyre irons. If the driver doesn't have a useable spare tyre, at least tell him to bring a spare inner tube.

The quickest distance between two points is a straight line, and the only thing that could (but not always) put off a Mongolian jeep diver from taking a shortcut is a huge mountain range or raging river. If renting a jeep by the kilometre, you will welcome a

TRANSPORT

TRANSPORT

shortcut, especially to shorten an uncomfortable trip. If you have an experienced driver, allow him to take shortcuts when he feels it is worthwhile, but don't insist on any – he is the expert. The downside of shortcuts is the possibility of breaking down on more isolated roads.

Serious mechanical breakdowns are a definite possibility. To be safe, it's necessary to bring tools and whatever spare parts are available. Should your vehicle break down irreparably in a rural area, you'll be faced with the task of trying to get back to civilisation either on foot (not recommended), by hitching, or by whatever means is available. The safest solution is to travel with a small group using two jeeps.

A warning: Russian jeeps easily overheat. There is no easy solution, but it helps to travel during the early morning or late afternoon hours when temperatures are relatively low.

Most of Mongolia is grassland, desert and mountains. You might think that mountain driving would pose the worst problems, but forests cause the most trouble of all. This is because the ground, even on a slope, is often a springy alpine bog, holding huge amounts of water in the decaying grasses, which are instantly compacted under tyres, reducing a wildflower meadow to slush. Drivers in Mongolia enjoy a high status, and Mongolians are loath to dig if you become bogged – it's just not in their nomadic blood. This has been known to infuriate visitors, who expect a flurry of activity as soon as a vehicle becomes bogged. Mongolians are more inclined to sit on their haunches, have a smoke and then send word to the nearest farm or town for a tractor to come and tow the vehicle out. Just be patient.

TAXI
Mongolia claims to have about 49,250km of highway – of which only 1724km is actually paved. Taxis are only useful along these paved roads, eg from Ulaanbaatar to Zuunmod, Terelj, Darkhan and possibly Kharkhorin. But just as you wouldn't try to drive a tank across Manhattan, it is pointless to take a Hyundai-style taxi across the unpaved steppes. The general appalling quality of roads around the countryside means that most travel is by jeep or Furgon minivan.

TRAIN
The 1810km of railway line is primarily made up of the Trans-Mongolian Railway, connecting China with Russia. (Both the domestic and international trains use this same line.) In addition, there are two spur lines: to the copper-mining centre of Erdenet (from Darkhan) and the coal-mining city of Baganuur (from Ulaanbaatar). Another train runs weekly from Choibalsan, the capital of Dornod aimag, to the Russian border.

From Ulaanbaatar, daily express trains travel north to Darkhan, and onto Sükhbaatar or Erdenet. To the south, there are daily direct trains from Ulaanbaatar to Zamyn-

---

TAKING A GPS

When you are travelling around the featureless plains of eastern Mongolia, the deserts of the Gobi or a tangle of confusing valleys in the west, a Global Positioning System (GPS) can be very useful in determining where exactly you are, as long as you have a reliable map on which to pinpoint your coordinates. We have given GPS coordinates for many hard-to-find places in this book, plus coordinates for *sum* and aimag centres (to an accuracy of up to 1km from the town centre). Many places are listed in the table in boxed text on p265.

A GPS won't help you every time, as you'll still need to know which road to take, even if you know the rough direction. Gobi and steppe areas are particularly tricky – except for the main routes there probably won't be any one road between places. Every few kilometres the track you're on will veer off in the wrong direction, requiring constant corrections and zigzagging.

It is always a good idea to ask about road conditions at gers along the way. Often a good-looking road will become impassable, running into a river, swamp or wall of mountains; herders can offer good info on the best route to take. If all else fails, you can always rely on the Mongolian GPS (Ger Positioning System), which requires following the vague sweep of the ger owner's hand over the horizon, until you reach the next ger.

Üüd, via Choir and Sainshand. There are also trains terminating at Choir twice a week. You can't use the Trans-Mongolian Railway for domestic transport.

When travelling in hard-seat class (see following), you will almost certainly have to fight to get a seat. If you're not travelling alone, one of you can scramble on board and find seats and the other can bring the luggage on board. Young boys and girls usually travel around the train selling bread and fizzy drinks. Otherwise, there is nothing to eat or drink on local trains.

Classes

There are only two classes on domestic passenger trains: hard seat and soft seat. In hard-seat class, the seats are actually padded bunks but there are no assigned bunks nor any limit to the amount of tickets sold, so the carriages are always crowded and dirty. If you get the hard-seat carriage but decide that you can't stand the mass of human bodies, walk to the soft-seat carriages and ask to upgrade – spare soft-seats tickets are often available.

Soft seats are only a little bit softer, but the conditions are much better: the price difference (usually at least double the price of the hard seat) is prohibitive for most Mongolians. The soft-seat carriages are divided into compartments with four beds in each. You are given an assigned bed, and will be able to sleep, assuming of course that your compartment mates aren't rip-roaring drunk and noisy. If you travel at night, clean sheets are provided for about T500, which is a wise investment since some of the quilts smell like mutton. Compared with hard-seat class, it's the lap of luxury, and worth paying extra.

If you're travelling from Ulaanbaatar, it is important to book a soft seat well in advance – it can be done up to 10 days before departure. There may be a small booking fee. In general, booking ahead is a good idea for any class, though there will always be hard-seat tickets available.

TRANSPORT

Health

CONTENTS

Mongolia's dry, cold climate and sparse human habitation means there are few of the infectious diseases that plague tropical countries in Asia. The rough-and-tumble landscape and lifestyle, however, presents challenges of its own. Injuries sustained from falling off a horse are common in the summer season. In winter, the biggest threats are the flu and pneumonia, which spread like wildfire in November. Mongolian food may be bland, but it's safe to eat.

The biggest risk may be the hospitals. The number of doctors is chronically low and the standard of medical training is patchy at best, and often very poor. If you do become seriously ill in Mongolia, your local embassy can provide details of Western doctors. Emergencies require evacuation to Seoul or Beijing. If in the countryside, make a beeline for Ulaanbaatar to have your ailment diagnosed.

The following advice is a general guide only; be sure to seek the advice of a doctor trained in travel medicine.

BEFORE YOU GO

Prevention is the key to staying healthy while abroad. A little planning before departure, particularly for pre-existing illnesses, will save trouble later. See your dentist before going on a long trip, carry a spare pair of contact lenses and glasses, and take your optical prescription with you. Bring medications in their original, clearly labelled, containers. A signed and dated letter from your physician describing your medical conditions and medications, including generic names, is also a good idea. If carrying syringes or needles, be sure to have a physician's letter documenting their medical necessity.

Western medicine can be in short supply in Ulaanbaatar. Most medicine comes from China and Russia and the labels won't be in English, so bring whatever you think you might need from home. Take extra supplies of prescribed medicine and divide it into separate pieces of luggage; that way, if one piece goes astray, you'll still have a back-up supply.

INSURANCE

If your health insurance does not cover you for medical expenses abroad, consider supplemental insurance. (Check the Lonely Planet website at www.lonelyplanet.com/subwwway for more information.)

While you may prefer a policy that pays hospital bills on the spot, rather than paying first and sending in documents later, in Mongolia the only place that might accept this is the SOS clinic (see p55).

Declare any existing medical conditions to the insurance company; if your problem is pre-existing the company will not cover you if it is not declared. You may require extra cover for adventurous activities – make sure you are covered for a fall if you plan on riding a horse or a motorbike. If you are uninsured, emergency evacuation is expensive, with bills over US$100,000 not uncommon.

RECOMMENDED VACCINATIONS

The World Health Organization (WHO) recommends that all travellers be covered for diphtheria, tetanus, measles, mumps, rubella and polio, regardless of their destination. As most vaccines don't produce immunity until at least two weeks after they're given, visit a physician at least six weeks before departure. Specialised travel-medicine clinics are your best source of information; they stock vaccines and will be able to give specific recommendations for you and your trip. This is especially important for pregnant women and children. Ask your doctor for an International Certificate of Vaccination (otherwise known as the yellow booklet), which will list all of the vaccinations you have received.

INTERNET RESOURCES

There is a wealth of travel health advice on the Internet. For further information, **Lonely Planet** (www.lonelyplanet.com) is a good place to start. The **WHO** (www.who.int/ith/) publishes a superb book called *International Travel & Health*, which is revised annually and is available online at no cost. Another website of general interest is **MD Travel Health** (www.mdtravelhealth.com), which provides complete travel health recommendations for every country and is updated daily.

FURTHER READING

Lonely Planet's *Healthy Travel – Asia & India* is a handy pocket size and packed with useful information including pre-trip planning, emergency first aid, immunisation and disease information, and what to do if you get sick on the road. Other recommended references include *Traveller's Health* by Dr Richard Dawood and *Travelling Well* by Dr Deborah Mills – check out the website (www.travellingwell.com.au). Lonely Planet's *Travel with Children* is useful for families.

IN TRANSIT

DEEP VEIN THROMBOSIS (DVT)

Blood clots may form in the legs during plane flights, chiefly because of prolonged immobility. The longer the flight, the greater the risk. The chief symptom of DVT is swelling or pain of the foot, ankle, or calf,

RECOMMENDED VACCINATIONS

The World Health Organization recommends the following vaccinations for travel to Mongolia:

Adult diphtheria and tetanus Single booster recommended if none in the previous 10 years. Side effects include sore arm and fever.

Hepatitis A Provides almost 100% protection for up to a year; a booster after 12 months provides at least another 20 years' protection. Mild side effects such as headache and sore arm occur with some people.

Hepatitis B Now considered routine for most travellers, it provides lifetime protection for 95% of people. Immunisation is given as three doses over six months, though a rapid schedule is also available, as is a combined vaccination for Hepatitis A. Side effects are mild and uncommon, usually headache and sore arm.

Measles, mumps and rubella Two doses of MMR are recommended unless you have had the diseases. Occasionally a rash and flu-like illness can develop a week after receiving the vaccine. Many young adults need a booster.

Typhoid Recommended unless your trip is less than a week. The vaccine offers around 70% protection, lasts for two to three years and comes as a single dose. Tablets are also available, although the injection is usually recommended as it has fewer side effects. A sore arm and fever may occur.

Varicella If you haven't had chickenpox discuss this vaccination with your doctor.

The following are recommended for long-term travellers (more than one month) or those at special risk:

Influenza A single jab lasts one year and is recommended for those over 65 years of age or with underlying medical conditions such as heart or lung disease.

Japanese B encephalitis Involves a series of three injections with a booster after two years. Recommended if spending more than one month in rural areas in the summer months.

Pneumonia A single injection with a booster after five years is recommended for all travellers over 65 years of age or with underlying medical conditions that compromise immunity such as heart or lung disease, cancer or HIV.

Rabies Three injections are required. A booster after one year will then provide 10 years protection. Side effects are rare – occasionally headache and sore arm.

Tuberculosis A complex issue. High-risk adult long-term travellers are usually recommended to have a TB skin test before and after travel, rather than a vaccination. Only one vaccine is given in a lifetime. Children under five spending more than three months in China/Mongolia should be vaccinated.

usually but not always on just one side. When a blood clot travels to the lungs, it may cause chest pain and breathing difficulties. Travellers with any of these symptoms should immediately seek medical attention.

To prevent the development of DVT on long flights you should walk regularly about the cabin, contract the leg muscles while sitting, drink plenty of fluids and avoid alcohol and tobacco.

JET LAG & MOTION SICKNESS

To avoid jet lag (common when crossing more than five time zones) try to drink plenty of nonalchoholic fluids and eat light meals. Upon arrival, get exposure to natural sunlight and readjust your schedule (for meals, sleep etc) as soon as possible.

Antihistamines such as dimenhydrinate (Dramamine) and meclizine (Antivert, Bonine) are usually the first choice for treating motion sickness. A herbal alternative is ginger.

IN MONGOLIA

AVAILABILITY & COST OF HEALTH CARE

Health care is readily available in Ulaanbaatar, but choose your hospital and doctor carefully. Ordinary Mongolians won't know the best place to go, but a reputable travel agency or top-end hotel might. The best advice will come from your embassy. Consultations cost around US$5, although SOS Medica, a reliable clinic in Ulaanbaatar with Western doctors, charges 20 times that amount. Most basic drugs are available without a prescription. See p55 for more details. Health services in the countryside are abysmal or nonexistent. Taking very small children to the countryside is therefore risky. Female travellers will need to take pads and tampons with them on a trip as these won't be available outside the main cities.

MEDICAL KIT CHECK LIST

Following is a list of items you should consider including in your medical kit – consult your pharmacist for brands available in your country.

- Antibacterial cream, eg Muciprocin
- Antibiotics – for travel well off-the-beaten track; see your doctor, as they must be prescribed, and carry the prescription with you
- Antifungal cream or powder, eg Clotrimazole – for fungal skin infections and thrush
- Antinausea medication (eg Prochlorperazine)
- Antiseptic (such as povidone-iodine) – for cuts and grazes
- Aspirin or paracetamol (acetaminophen in the USA) – for pain or fever
- Bandages, Band-Aids (plasters) and other wound dressings
- Calamine lotion, sting-relief spray or aloe vera – to ease irritation from sunburn and insect bites or stings
- Cold and flu tablets, throat lozenges and nasal decongestant
- Insect repellent (DEET-based)
- Loperamide or diphenoxylate – 'blockers' for diarrhoea
- Multivitamins – consider for long trips, when dietary vitamin intake may be inadequate
- Rehydration mixture (eg Gastrolyte) – to prevent dehydration, which may occur during bouts of diarrhoea; particularly important when travelling with children
- Scissors, tweezers and a thermometer – note that mercury thermometers are prohibited by airlines
- Sunscreen, lip balm and eye drops
- Water purification tablets or iodine (iodine is not to be used by pregnant women or people with a thyroid problem)

INFECTIOUS DISEASES
Brucellosis
The UN Food & Agricultural Organization (FAO) reports that Mongolia is a high-risk area for brucellosis. This is a disease of cattle yaks, camels and sheep but it can also affect humans. The most likely way for humans to contract this disease is by drinking unboiled milk or eating home-made cheese. Another way is for humans with open cuts on their hands to handle freshly killed meat.

In humans, brucellosis causes severe headaches, joint and muscle pains, fever and fatigue. There may be diarrhoea and, later, constipation. The onset of the symptoms can occur from five days to several months after exposure, with the average time being two weeks.

Most patients recover in two or three weeks, but people can get chronic brucellosis, which recurs sporadically for months or years and can cause long-term health problems. Fatalities are rare but possible.

Brucellosis is a serious disease which requires blood tests to make the diagnosis. If you think you may have contracted the disease, seek medical attention, preferably outside Mongolia.

Bubonic Plague
This disease (which wiped out one-third of Europe during the Middle Ages) makes an appearance in remote parts of Mongolia in late summer (from August to October), when the ban on hunting marmots stops and their meat is eaten.

The disease (also known as the Black Plague) is normally carried by marmots, squirrels and rats and can be transmitted to humans by bites from fleas that make their home on the infected animals. It can also be passed from human to human by coughing. The symptoms are fever and enlarged lymph nodes. The untreated disease has a 60% death rate, but if you get to a doctor it can be quickly treated. The best drug is the antibiotic streptomycin, which must be injected intramuscularly, but it is not available in Mongolia. Tetracycline is another drug that may be used.

During an outbreak, travel to affected areas is prohibited, which can greatly affect overland travel. All trains, buses and cars travelling into Ulaanbaatar from infected areas are also thoroughly checked when an outbreak of the plague has been reported, and vehicles are sprayed with disinfectant.

Hepatitis
This is a general term for inflation of the liver. It is a common disease worldwide. The symptoms are similar in all forms of the illness, and include fever, chills, headache, fatigue, aches and pains and feelings of weakness, followed by loss of appetite, nausea, vomiting, abdominal pain, dark urine, light coloured faeces, jaundiced (yellow) skin and yellowing of the whites of the eyes. People who have hepatitis should avoid alcohol for some time after the illness, as the liver needs time to recover.

Hepatitis A is transmitted by contaminated food and drinking water. You should seek medical advice, but there is not much you can do apart from resting, drinking lots of fluids, eating lightly and avoiding fatty foods. Hepatitis E is transmitted in the same way as hepatitis A; it can be particularly serious in pregnant women.

There are almost 300 million chronic carriers of hepatitis B in the world and the disease is endemic in Mongolia. It is spread through contact with infected blood, blood products or body fluids. The symptoms of hepatitis B may be more severe than type A and the disease can lead to long-term problems such as chronic liver damage, liver cancer or long-term carrier state. Hepatitis C and D are spread in the same way as hepatitis B and can also lead to long-term complications.

There are vaccines against hepatitis A and B, but there are currently no vaccines against the other types of hepatitis.

Rabies
In the Mongolian countryside, family dogs are often vicious and can be rabid; it is their saliva that is infectious. Any bite, scratch or even a lick from an animal should be cleaned immediately and thoroughly. Scrub with soap and running water, and then apply alcohol or iodine solution. Medical help should be sought promptly to receive a course of injections to prevent the onset of the symptoms and death. The incubation period for rabies depends on where you're bitten. If on the head, face or neck it's as little as 10 days, whereas on the legs it's 60 days.

HEALTH

HEALTH

STDs

Sexually transmitted diseases most common in Mongolia include herpes warts, syphilis, gonorrhoea and chlamydia. People carrying these diseases often have no signs of infection. Condoms will prevent gonorrhoea and chlamydia but not warts or herpes. If after any sexual encounter you develop any rash, lumps, discharge or pain when passing urine seek immediate medical attention. If you have been sexually active during your travels, have an STD check upon your return.

Tuberculosis (TB)

TB is a bacterial infection usually transmitted from person to person by coughing but which may be transmitted through consumption of unpasteurised milk. Milk that has been boiled is safe to drink, and the souring of milk to make yogurt or cheese also kills the bacilli. Travellers are usually not at great risk as close household contact with an infected person is usually required before the disease is passed on. You may need to have a TB test before you travel as this can help diagnose the disease later if you become ill.

TRAVELLER'S DIARRHOEA

To prevent diarrhoea, avoid tap water unless it has been boiled, filtered or chemically disinfected (with iodine tablets) and steer clear of ice. Only eat fresh fruits or vegetables if cooked or peeled; be wary of dairy

---

DRINKING WATER

- Bottled water is generally safe – check that the seal is intact at purchase.
- Be wary of drinking tap water and have ice in drinks only if you are certain it is OK.
- Boiling water is the most efficient method of purifying it.
- The best chemical purifier is iodine. It should not be used by pregnant women or those with thyroid problems.
- Water filters should filter out viruses. Ensure your filter has a chemical barrier such as iodine and a small pore size; eg less than four microns.

---

products that might contain unpasteurised milk. Eat food that is hot all through and avoid buffet-style meals.

If you develop diarrhoea, be sure to drink plenty of non-alcoholic fluids, preferably an oral rehydration solution (eg Dioralyte). A few loose stools don't require treatment, but if you start having more than four or five stools a day, you should start taking an antibiotic (usually a quinolone drug) and an antidiarrhoeal agent (such as Loperamide). If diarrhoea is bloody, persists for more than 72 hours or is accompanied by fever, shaking, chills or severe abdominal pain you should seek medical attention.

Giardiasis is a parasite that is relatively common in travellers. Symptoms include nausea, bloating, excess gas, fatigue and intermittent diarrhoea. 'Eggy' burps are often attributed solely to giardiasis, but may not be specific to giardiasis. The parasite will eventually go away if left untreated, but this can take months. The treatment of choice is tinidazole; metronidazole is a second option.

ENVIRONMENTAL HAZARDS
Altitude Sickness

Except in rare cases, only mountaineers will experience altitude sickness in Mongolia. Mild symptoms include headache, lethargy, dizziness, difficulty sleeping and loss of appetite. Treat mild symptoms by resting at the same altitude until recovery – usually a day or two. Paracetomol or aspirin can be taken for headaches. If symptoms persist or become worse, however, immediate descent is necessary; even 500m can help.

Heatstroke

This serious, occasionally fatal, condition can occur if the body's heat-regulating mechanism breaks down and the body temperature rises to dangerous levels. Long, continuous exposure to high temperatures and insufficient fluids can leave you vulnerable to heatstroke.

The symptoms are feeling unwell, not sweating very much (or at all) and a high body temperature. Where sweating has ceased, the skin becomes flushed and red. Victims can become confused, aggressive or delirious. Get victims out of the sun, remove their clothing and cover them with a wet sheet or towel and fan continually. Give fluids if they are conscious.

Hypothermia

In a country where temperatures can plummet to -40°C, cold is something you should take seriously. If you are trekking at high altitudes or simply taking a long bus trip across the country, particularly at night, be especially prepared. Even in the lowlands, sudden winds from the north can send the temperature plummeting.

Hypothermia occurs when the body loses heat faster than it can produce it and the core temperature of the body falls. It is surprisingly easy to progress from being very cold to dangerously cold due to a combination of wind, wet clothing, fatigue and hunger, even if the air temperature is above freezing. It is best to dress in layers; silk, wool and some of the new artificial fibres are all good insulting materials. A hat is important, as a lot of heat is lost through the head. A strong, waterproof outer layer (and a 'space' blanket for emergencies if trekking) is essential. Carry basic supplies, including food containing simple sugars to generate heat quickly and fluid to drink.

Bites and stings

Bee and wasp stings are usually painful rather dangerous. However, in people who are allergic to them severe breathing difficulties may occur and victims may require urgent medical care. Calamine lotion or sting relief spray will give relief and ice packs will reduce the pain and swelling.

Mongolia has four species of poisonous snakes: the Halys viper *(agkistrodon halys)*, common European viper or adder *(vipera berus)*, Orsini's viper *(vipera ursine)* and the small *taphrometaphon lineolatum*. To minimise your chances of being bitten always wear boots, socks and long trousers when snakes may be present. Don't put your hands into holes and crevices, and be careful when collecting firewood.

Bedbugs live in various places, but particularly in dirty mattresses and bedding, evidenced by spots of blood on bedclothes or on the wall. Bedbugs leave itchy bites in neat rows. Calamine lotion or a sting-relief spray may help. All lice cause itching and discomfort. They make themselves at home in your hair, your clothing, or in your pubic hair. You catch lice through direct contact with infected people or by sharing combs, clothing and the like. Powder or shampoo treatment will kill the lice and infected clothing should then be washed in very hot, soapy water and left in the sun to dry.

TRADITIONAL MEDICINE

Traditional medicine has made a comeback in Mongolia, after suppression during communism. Medicine often involves the use of native herbs, ground-up rock or bone, and even the swallowing of prayers written on tiny pieces of paper. Lamas are often employed to read prayers for the sick. Traditional medicine here is based on both Chinese and Tibetan practices. In Ulaanbaatar, there are traditional-medicine clinics at the Bakula Rinpoche Süm and Otochmaaramba Khiid (see p65).

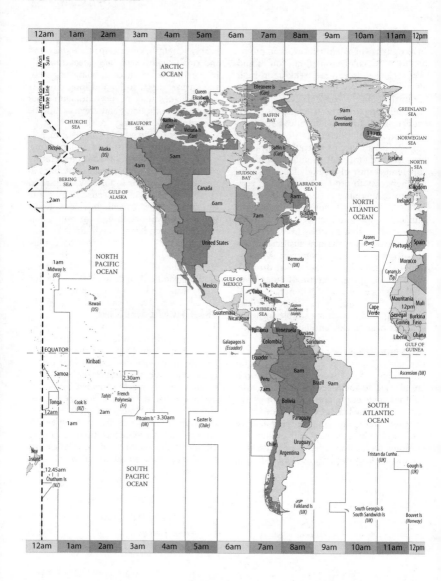

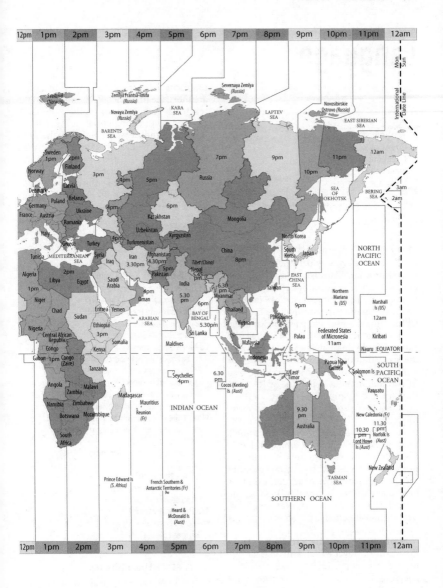

Language

CONTENTS

Mongolian is a member of the Ural-Altaic family of languages, which includes Finnish, Hungarian, Turkish, Kazakh, Usbek and Korean. The traditional Mongolian script looks like Arabic turned 45 degrees, and is still used by the Mongolians living in China (Inner Mongolia, parts of Xinjiang, Qinhai, Liaoning and Jilin). In 1944 the Russian Cyrillic alphabet was adopted, with the two additional characters, ө and ү. It remains in use today in Mongolia and also in two autonomous republics of Russia – Buryatia and Kalmykia.

Mongolian also has a Romanised form, though the 35 Cyrillic characters give a better representation of Mongolian sounds than the 26 of the Roman alphabet. Partly a result of Russian influence, different Romanisation schemes have been used, and this has caused widespread confusion. A loose standard was adopted in 1987, so the capital city previously written as 'Ulan Bator' (transliterated Russian spelling), is now Ulaanbaatar.

Mongolian pronunciation is not easy. In the words of travel writer Tim Severin, the Mongolian language is '...like two cats coughing and spitting at each other until one finally throws up'. One particular word, which conveys agreement (rather like nodding one's head) is little more than a sharp, guttural intake of breath, as if you were having difficulty breathing.

It's important to give double vowels a lengthened pronunciation, as getting it wrong can affect meaning. Syllables marked in italics in the following words and phrases represent word stress. If all vowels in a word are short, the first will take the stress and the rest will become 'neutral' (as the 'a' in 'ago'). In words with a long vowel, stress falls on that vowel and any short vowels in the word will become neutral. If there's more than one long vowel the stress will generally fall on the second-last syllable.

If you'd like a more comprehensive guide to the language, pick up a copy of Lonely Planet's *Mongolian Phrasebook*.

ACCOMMODATION

Can you recommend a good hotel?
ta *sain* zo·chid *buu*·dal zaaj ög·nö *üü*
Та сайн зочид буудал зааж өгнө үү?

Can you show me on the map?
ta gaz·*ryn* zu·rag deer zaaj ög·nö *üü*
Та газрын зураг дээр зааж өгнө үү?

Do you have any rooms available?
ta·*naid* sul ö·*röö* bai·na *uu*
Танайд сул өрөө байна уу?

I'd like a single room.
bi neg khü·*nii* ö·*röö* av·*maar* bai·na
Би нэг хүний өрөө авмаар байна.

I'd like a double room.
bi kho·yor khü·*nii* ö·*röö* av·*maar* bai·na
Би хоёр хүний өрөө авмаар байна.

What's the price per night/week?
ene ö·*röö* kho·nogt/do·*loo* kho·nogt *ya*·mar ün·*tei* ve
Энэ өрөө хоногт/долоо хоногт ямар үнэтэй вэ?

Can I see the room?
bi e·ne ö·*röög* ü·zej *bo*·lokh *uu*
Би энэ өрөөг үзэж болох уу?

Are there any others?
öör ö·*röö* bai·na *uu*
Өөр өрөө байна уу?

SIX ESSENTIAL PHRASES

Cynics say that the six most widely heard phrases in Mongolia are *medehgui* (don't know), *baikhgui* (don't have), *chadakhui*, (can't do) *magadgui* (maybe), *margaash* (tomorrow) and *za*, which roughly translates to, well, 'za'. *Za* is a catch-all phrase, said at the conclusion of a statement, meaning something akin to 'well ...', 'so then ...' or 'ok', and is a fiendishly addictive word.

LANGUAGE

MONGOLIAN CYRILLIC ALPHABET

А а	a	as the 'u' in 'but'
Г г	g	as in 'get'
Ё ё	yo	as in 'yonder'
И и	i	as in 'tin'
Л л	l	as in 'lamp'
О о	o	as in 'hot'
Р р	r	as in 'rub'
У у	u	as in 'rude'
Х х	kh	as the 'ch' in Scottish **loch**
Ш ш	sh	as in 'shoe'
Ы ы	y	as the 'i' in 'ill'
Ю ю	yu	as the 'yo' in 'yoyo'
	yü	long, as the word 'you'
Б б	b	as in 'but'
Д д	d	as in 'dog'
Ж ж	j	as in 'jewel'
Й й	i	as in 'tin'
М м	m	as in 'mat'
Ө ө	ö	long, as the 'u' in 'fur'
С с	s	as in 'sun'
Ү ү	ü	long, as the 'o' in 'who'
Ц ц	ts	as in 'cats'
Щ щ	shch	as the 'shch' in 'fresh chips'
Ь ь		* 'soft sign' (see below)
Я я	ya	as in 'yard'
В в	v	as in 'van'
Е е	ye	as in 'yes'
	yö	as the 'yea' in 'yearn'
З з	z	as the 'ds' in 'suds'
К к	k	as in 'kit'
Н н	n	as in 'neat'
П п	p	as in 'pat'
Т т	t	as in 'tin'
Ф ф	f	as in 'five'
Ч ч	ch	as in 'chat'
Ъ ъ		* 'hard sign' (see below)
Э э	e	as in 'den'

* The letters ь and ъ never occur alone, but simply affect the pronunciation of the previous letter – ь makes the preceding sound soft (the consonant before it is pronounced as if there's a very short 'y' after it), while ъ makes the previous sound hard (it prevents it being pronounced as if there's a 'y' after it).

CONVERSATION & ESSENTIALS

Hello.
sain bai·na *uu*   Сайн байна уу?
(literally: How are you?)
Fine. How are you?
sain ta sain bai·na *uu*   Сайн. Та сайн байна уу?

What's new?
so·nin sai·khan   Сонин сайхан
yu bai·na   юу байна?
Nothing really.
tai·van sai·khan   Тайван сайхан.
(literally: It's peaceful.)
Goodbye.
ba·yar·tai   Баяртай.

Yes.	tiim	Тийм.
No.	ü·güi	Үгүй.
Thanks.	ba·yar·la·laa	Баярлалаа.
Excuse me.	uuch·laa·rai	Уучлаарай.

I'm sorry, what did you say?
uuch·laa·rai ta yu gej khel·sen *be*
Уучлаарай, та юу гэж хэлсэн, бэ?
What's your name?
ta·*ny* ne·riig khen ge·deg *ve*
Таны нэрийг хэн гэдэг вэ?
My name is ...
mi·*nii* ne·riig ... ge·deg
Миний нэрийг ... гэдэг.
What country are you from?
ta a·li ul·*saas* ir·sen *be*
Та аль улсаас ирсэн бэ?
I'm from ...
bi ... ul·saas *ir*·sen
Би ... улсаас ирсэн.
How old are you?
ta *khe*·den nas·*tai ve*
Та хэдэн настай вэ?
I'm ... years old.
bi ... nas·*tai*
Би ... настай.
Are you married?
ta ger *bül*·tei *yü*
Та гэр бүлтэй юү?
No, I'm not.
ü·*güi* bi ger *bul*·güi
Үгүй, би гэр бүлгүй.
Yes, I'm married.
tiim bi ger *bül*·tei
Тийм, би гэр бүлтэй.
Do you have any children?
ta *khüü*·hed·tei *yü*
Та хүүхэдтэй юү?
Can I take photographs?
zu·rag avch bo·lokh *uu*
Зураг авч болох уу?
May I take your photograph?
bi ta·*ny* zur·*giig* avch bo·lokh *uu*
Би таны зургийг авч болох уу?

The Herder's Domain

We'd like to see inside a herder's ger. (felt tent)
bid malch·*ny* gert orj ü·zekh ge·sen yum
Бид малчны гэрт орж үзэх гэсэн юм.

How long will it take to get there?
tend *khü*·re·khed khir *u*·dakh *ve*
Тэнд хүрэхэд хир удах вэ?

Can we walk there?
bid *yav*·gan yavj *bo*·lokh *uu*
Бид явган явж болох уу?

Please hold the dogs!
nok·*hoi* kho·ri·o
Нохой хогио!

We'd like to drink some *airag*.
bid *ai*·rag uukh ge·sen yum
Бид айраг уух гэсэн юм.

If you're visiting a family, especially in the country, having agreed that everybody's fine, you should proceed to asking about family members and livestock and only then to more general matters:

How's your family?
ta·*nai* ger bü·*liin*·hen sain *uu*
Танай гэр бүлийнхэн сайн уу?

I hope your animals are fattening up nicely?
mal *sü*·reg *tar*·gan tav·*tai* yü
Мал сүрэг тарган тавтai юу?

Are you very busy?
ta a·jil ikh·tei bai·na *uu*
Та ажил ихтэй байна уу?

I'm very busy.
bi tun *zav*·güi bai·na
Би тун завгүй байна.

cooking pot	to·*goo*	тогоо
cowdung box	a·rag	араг
door	khaal·ga	хаалга
felt material	es·*gii*	эсгий
felt roof cover	es·*gii dee*·ver	эсгий дээвэр
ger	ger	гэр
***airag* bag**	khö·*khüür*	хөхүүр
smoke-hole	örkh	өрх
cover in a ger		
stove	zuukh	зуух
support post	*ba*·ga·na	багана
wooden frame	too·*no*	тооно
for flue in a ger		
wooden lattice	kha·na	хана
of a ger		

camel	te·*mee*	тэмээ
chicken	ta·khia	тахиа
cow	ü·*nee*	үнээ

donkey	il·jig	илжиг
enclosure	*ma*·lyn kha·*shaa*	малын хашаа
goat	ya·*maa*	ямаа
herding	mal aj ak·*hui*	мал аж ахуй
(literally: cattle breeding)		
horse	*mo*·ri	морь
pig	ga·*khai*	гахай
reindeer	tsaa bu·ga	цаа буга
sheep	kho·ni	хонь
summer camp	zus·lan	зуслан
yak	sar·lag	сарлаг

DIRECTIONS

How can I get to ...?
... *ruu* bi yaj o·chikh *ve*
... руу би яаж очих вэ?

Is it far?
khir khol *ve*
Хир хол вэ?

Do you have a (town) map?
ta·*naid* (kho·*tyn*) zu·rag bai·na *uu*
Танайд (хотын) зураг байна уу?

What ... is this?

e·ne *ya*·mar ... *ve*	Энэ ямар ... вэ?
square	
tal·*bai*	талбай
street	
gu·damj	гудамж
suburb	
düü·reg	дүүрэг
municipality	
kho·*tyn* za·khir·*gaa*	хотын захиргаа

north	khoid/*u*·mard	хойд/умард
south	urd/*öm*·nö	урд/өмнө
east	züün/*dor*·no	зүүн/дорно
west	ba·*ruun*/	баруун/
	ör·nöd	өрнөд

behind/after	khoi·no/ard	хойно/ард
in front/before	*öm*·nö/urd	өмнө/урд
to the left	*züün* tiish	зүүн тийш
to the right	ba·*ruun* tiish	баруун тийш
straight ahead	chi·*gee*·ree	чигээрээ
	u·rag·shaa	урагшаа

EMERGENCIES

Help!	tus·*laa*·rai	Туслаарай!
Stop!	zogs	Зогс!

Call ...!
... duu·*daa*·rai ... дуудаарай!

an ambulance
tür·gen *tus*·lamj түргэн тусламж

a doctor
emch эмч

the police
tsag·*daa* цагдаа

I'm ill.
mi·*nii* bi·ye öv·döj bai·na
Миний бие өвдөж байна.

Could you please take me to hospital?
na·*maig* em·ne·legt *khür*·gej ög·nö *üü*
Намайг эмнэлэгт хүргэж өгнө үү?

Could you help me please?
ta *na*·dad tsus·la·na *uu*
Та надад туслана уу?

I've lost my way.
bi töör·chikh·*löö*
Би төөрчихлөө.

I wish to contact my embassy.
bi *el*·chin sai·diin *yaam*·tai·gaa khol·boo
ba·ri·*maar* bai·na
Би элчин сайдын яамтайгаа холбоо
баримаар байна.

Where's the toilet?
bi·ye za·sakh ga·zar khaa·na *bai*·dag *ve*
Бие засах газар хаана байдаг вэ?

LANGUAGE DIFFICULTIES
Do you speak English?
ta an·*gliar* yair·dag *uu*
Та англиар ярьдаг уу?

Could you speak more slowly?
ta a·rai *aa*·juu·khan *ya*·ri·na *uu*
Та арай аажуухан ярина уу?

Please point to the phrase in the book.
ta e·ne khel·le·*giig* no·mon *deer zaaj* ög·nö *uu*
Та энэ хэллэгийг номон дээр зааж өгнө уу?

I understand.
bi *oil*·go·*loo*
Би ойлголоо.

I don't understand.
bi *oil*·gokh·güi bai·na
Би ойлгохгүй байна.

NUMBERS

0	teg	тэг
1	neg	нэг
2	*kho*·yor	хоёр
3	*gu*·rav	гурав
4	*dö*·röv	дөрөв
5	tav	тав
6	zur·*gaa*	зургаа
7	do·*loo*	долоо
8	naim	найм
9	yös	ес
10	*ar*·av	арав
11	*ar*·van neg	арван нэг
12	*ar*·van *kho*·yor	арван хоёр
13	*ar*·van *gu*·rav	арван гурав
14	*ar*·van *dö*·röv	арван дөрөв
15	*ar*·van tav	арван тав
16	*ar*·van zur·*gaa*	арван зургаа
17	*ar*·van do·*loo*	арван долоо
18	*ar*·van naim	арван найм
19	*ar*·van yös	арван ес
20	kho·ri	хорь
21	*kho*·rin neg	хорин нэг
22	*kho*·rin *kho*·yor	хорин хоёр
30	guch	гуч
40	döch	дөч
50	taiv	тавч
60	jar	жар
70	dal	дал
80	naya	ная
90	yör	ер
100	zuu	зуу
101	zuun neg	зуун нэг
1000	myang·ga	мянга
one million	sa·ya	сая

SHOPPING & SERVICES
Where's the nearest ...?
oir·khon ... khaa·na bai·dag *ve*
Ойрхон ... хаана байнаг вэ?

bank
bank   банк
department store
ikh del-*güür*   их дэлгүүр
hotel
zo-chid *buu*-dal   зочид буудал
market
zakh   зах
post office
shuu-dan   шуудан
public bathhouse
nii-tiin kha-*luun*   нийтийн халуун
us-ny *ga*-zar   усны газар

When will it open?
khe-*zee* on-*goikh ve*
Хэзээ онгойх вэ?
When will it close?
khe-*zee* khaakh *ve*
Хэзээ хаах вэ?
I'd like to change some money.
bi *möng*-go so-likh *ge*-sen yum
Би мөнгө солих гэсэн юм.
I'd like to change some travellers cheques.
bi chek so-likh ge-sen yum
Би чек солих гэсэн юм.
What's the exchange rate?
so-likh khansh hed bai-na *ve*
Солих ханш хэд байна вэ?

TRANSPORT
Where's the ... ?
... *khaa*-na bai-dag *ve*
... хаана байдаг вэ?
   train station
   galt te-re-ge-*nii* buud-al   галт тэрэгний буудал
   bus station/stop
   av-*to*-bus-ny *buu*-dal   автобусны буудал
   trolley-bus stop
   trol-*lei*-bus-ny *buu*-dal   троллейбусны буудал
   ticket office
   ta-sal-bag tu-*gee*-güür   тасалбаг түгээгүүр

How much is it to go to ...?
... hu-re-hed ya-mar ü-ne-*tei ve*
... хүрэхэд ямар үнэтэй вэ?
Can I walk there?
tii-shee *yav*-gan o-chij *bo*-lokh *uu*
Тийшээ явган очиж болох уу?

What times does ... leave/arrive?
... *khe*-den tsagt *yav*-dag/*ir*-deg *ve*
... хэдэн цагт явдаг/ирдэг вэ?
   the bus
   av-*to*-bus   автобус
   the trolley-bus
   trol-*lei*-bus   троллейбус
   the train
   galt *te*-reg   галт тэрэг
   the plane
   ni-seh *on*-gots   нисэх онгоц

Does this bus go to ...?
e-ne av-*to*-bus ... ruu *yav*-dag *uu*
Энэ автобус ... руу явдаг уу?
Which bus goes to ...?
... ruu *ya*-mar av-*to*-bus *yav*-dag *ve*
... руу ямар автобус явдаг вэ?
Can you tell me when we get to ...?
bid khe-*zee* ... khu-re-*hiig* helj ög-nö *uu*
Бид хэзээ ... хүрэхийг хэлж өгнө үү?
I want to get off!
bi *buu*-maar bai-na
Би буумаар байна!
Is this seat taken?
e-ne *suu*-dal khün-*tei yüü*
Энэ суудал хүнтэй юу?
What's this station called?
e-ne ya-mar ner-tei *buu*-dal *ve*
Энэ ямар нэртэй буудал вэ?
What's the next station?
da-*raa*-giin *buu*-dal *ya*-mar ner-tei *buu*-dal *ve*
Дараагийн буудал ямар нэртэй буудал вэ?

Glossary

See p49 in the Food & Drink chapter for some useful words and phrases dealing with food and dining. See the Language chapter (p278) for other useful words and phrases.

agui – cave or grotto
aimag – a province/state within Mongolia
am – mouth, but often used as a term for canyon
aral – island
arkhi – the common word to describe home-made vodka
ashkhana – restaurant (Kazakh)

baatar – hero
babal – stone figures believed to be Turkic grave markers; known as *khunn chuluu* (man stones) in Mongolian
bag – village, a subdivision of a *sum*
baga – little
baruun – west
bayan – rich
Bodhisattva – Tibetan-Buddhist term; applies to a being that has voluntarily chosen not to take the step to nirvana in order to save the souls of those on earth
Bogd Gegeen – hereditary line of reincarnated Buddhist leaders of Mongolia, which started with Zanabazar; the third holiest leader in the Tibetan Buddhist hierarchy
Bogd Khaan (Holy King) – title given to the Eighth Bogd Gegeen (1869–1924)
bökh – wrestling
bulag – natural spring
Buriat – ethnic minority living along the northern frontier, mostly in Khentii and Dornod and also in Russia

chuluu – rock; rock formation

davaa – mountain pass
deer stones – upright grave markers from the Bronze and Iron ages on which are carved stylised images of deer; known as *bugan chuluu*
del/deel – the all-purpose, traditional coat or dress worn by men and women
delger – richness, plenty
delgüür – a shop
dombra – two-stringed lute (Kazakh)
dorje – thunderbolt symbol, used in Tibetan Buddhist ritual
dorno – east
dov – hill
dund – middle

els – sand; sand dunes
erdene – precious

Furgon – Russian-made 11-seater minivan

Gegeen – saint; saintlike person
ger – traditional circular felt yurt
gol – river
guanz – canteen or cheap restaurant
gudamj – street

hard seat – the common word to describe the standard of the 2nd-class train carriage

ikh – big
ikh delguur – department store
Inner Mongolia – separate province within China
irbis – snow leopard

Jebtzun Damba – also known as Bogd Gegeen, a hereditary line of reincarnated spiritual leaders of Mongolia; the first was Zanabazar and the eighth was the Bogd Khaan

Kazakh – an ethnic group of people from Central Asia, mostly living in western Mongolia; people from Kazakhstan
khaan – king or chief
khagan – khaan; generally used for leaders during the Turkic (pre-Mongol) period
khaganate – Turkic (pre-Mongol) empire
khagas – half size
Khalkh – the major ethnic group living in Mongolia
khad – rock
khar – black
khashaa – fenced-in ger, often found in suburbs
kherem – wall
khiid – a Buddhist monastery
khödöö – countryside
khoid – north
khöndii – valley
khot – city
khulan – wild ass
khunn chuluu – man stones or *babal*; believed to be Turkic grave markers
khüree – originally used to describe a 'camp', it is now also in usage as 'monastery'
khuriltai – nomadic congress during the Mongol era
khürkhree – waterfall
khutukhtu – reincarnated lama, or living god
kino – cinema

lama – Tibetan Buddhist monk or priest
Lamaism – an outdated term, and now properly known as Vajramana, or Tibetan Buddhism

Living Buddha – common term for reincarnations of Buddhas; Buddhist spiritual leader in Mongolia
loovuuz – fox-fur hat

malchin – herder
maral – Asiatic red deer
mod – tree
morin khuur – horse-head fiddle
mörön – another word for river, usually a wide river
MPRP – Mongolian People's Revolutionary Party

naadam – a game; the Naadam Festival
nairamdal – friendship
nuruu – mountain range
nuur – lake

ömnö – south
ordon – palace
örgön chölöö – avenue
Outer Mongolia – northern Mongolia during Manchurian rule (the term is not currently used to describe Mongolia)
ovoo – a shamanistic collection of stones, wood or other offerings to the gods, usually found in high places

rashaan – mineral springs

shaykhana – tea house (Kazakh)
soft seat – the common word to describe the standard of the 1st-class train carriage
soyombo – the national symbol
stupa – a Buddhist religious monument composed of a solid hemisphere topped by a spire, containing relics of the Buddha; also known as a pagoda, or *suvrag* in Mongolian
sum – a district; the administrative unit below an *aimag*
süm – a Buddhist temple

takhi – the Mongolian wild horse; also known as Przewalski's horse
tal – steppe
talbai – square
thangka – scroll painting; a rectangular Tibetan Buddhist painting on cloth, often seen in monasteries
tögrög – the unit of currency in Mongolia
töv – central
Tsagaan sar – 'white moon' or 'white month'; a festival to celebrate the start of the lunar year
tsainii gazar – tea shop
tsam – lama dances; performed by monks wearing masks during religious ceremonies
tsas – snow
tsuivan gazar – noodle stall
tuuts – kiosk selling imported foodstuffs

ulaan – red
urtyn-duu – traditional singing style
us – water
uul – mountain
uurga – traditional wooden lasso used by nomads

yavakh – depart
yurt – the Russian word for ger, derived from the Turkish

zakh – a market
zochid budal – hotel
zud – a particularly bad winter involving snow and ice, and a huge loss of livestock
zun – summer
zuu – one hundred
züü – needle
zuun – century
züün – east

Behind the Scenes

THIS BOOK

This 4th edition of *Mongolia* was updated by Michael Kohn. Bradley Mayhew updated the 3rd edition, and Paul Greenway updated the 2nd. Graham Taylor wrote the boxed text 'Blazing Saddles – Travelling like a Local', which appears in the Transport chapter.

THANKS FROM THE AUTHOR

Michael Kohn Foremost, thanks to LP Melbourne staffers Rebecca Chau, Michael Day, Evan Jones and Hunor Csutoros for seeing this book through. Thanks also to fellow author Bradley Mayhew for his exceptional work on the last edition.

A great debt of gratitude is owed to Guido Verboom for his help all over Mongolia, particularly in Dornogov and various monasteries, and his camaraderie in UB. Cheers to Toroo at Khongor Guest House for logistics and translation help. Drivers Ochiro and Dorj, and mechanic Tserempil, got me around the countryside with nary a hitch.

Also in UB, thanks to: Peter Marsh, Sylvia Hay, Peter Zahler, Kirk Olson, Lee and Tsegi Cashell, Christo Gavilla Gomez, Chris Miller, P Puje, Silas Everett, Zaya at UNDP, Graham Taylor, Pierre Yves and Jargal at ICES. Special thanks to B Indra and the *Mongol Messenger* staff. Thanks to Dr Michael Frank for his assistance on the GPS coordinates.

I won't soon forget the epic session of karaoke with Ulaanbaatar's VSO crew, or the always entertaining 'Quiz Nights' at Dave's Place. Political debate and cultural musings were always more enjoyable in the company of Tjalling Halbertsma, Ule Herold and Nadine Kreisberger.

Cheers to Jon Phillips (Uliastai), Nazgul, Atai and Josh Gambrel (Ölgii), Christy (Dalanzadgad), Kent Maiden (Khövsgöl), Sarah Napper (Arkhangai), my western aimag travel mates Gary and Gregory, many *malchin* who invited me into their homes, and in Darvi *sum*, the petrol station attendant who refused to give the next driver petrol unless they gave me a ride (after a 12 hour wait!).

Back home thanks for patience and support from friends and family, most of all to Baigalmaa, for help with the Cyrillic, and for waiting, *bayarlalaa*.

CREDITS

This edition of *Mongolia* was commissioned by Rebecca Chau in Lonely Planet's Melbourne office and she assessed the manuscript. Korina Miller wrote the author brief and Kusnandar prepared the map brief. Coordinating production in the Melbourne office were Evan Jones (editorial), Hunor Csutoros (cartography) and David Kemp (layout). Overseeing production were Fabrice Rocher (project manager), Melanie Dankel (managing editor) and Corinne Waddell (managing cartographer).

Assisting Evan with the editing were Charlotte Orr, Peter Cruttenden, Simon Williamson, Katrina Webb, Helen Christinis, Vicki Beale, Barbara Delissen, Michael Ruff, Jacqui Saunders and Laura Gibb. David was assisted by Laura Jane. David also prepared the colour images for this book and did the artwork for the cover, which was designed by Julie Rovis. Wayne Murphy did the back cover map. Ryan Evans and Glenn Beanland helped with the images. Hunor prepared the colour map. Quentin Frayne coordinated the Language chapter with help from

Jodie Matire. Layout checks were done by Adriana Mammarella, Kate McDonald and Jennifer Garrett. Thanks go to Piotr Czajkowski for his advice on GPS units, Lachlan Ross for his help on the GIS maps and to Nick Stebbing, David Burnett and Rebecca Lalor for their technical assistance.

THANKS from Lonely Planet

Many thanks to the following travellers who used the last edition and wrote to us with helpful hints, useful advice and interesting anecdotes.

A Pia Adams, Hartig Alexander, Kurt Allenspach, Andre & Jane Ancomas, Edward Archibald, Ariel Atari, David Atkinson, Bob Audretsch, Rosemary Austin, Millo Avissar **B** Yilmaz & Astrid Baris, Joan Beckett, Mike Beishuizen, George H Bell, Rob Bertholee, Fabrizio Bervina, Aart Biewenga, Steve Bittner, Larry Blakeslee, Anthony Bolos, Paul Brand, Gavan Breen, Tally Briggs, David Bright, Thit Bundgaard **C** Julia Cartwright, Erica Champ, David Cimasoni, Jemetha Clark, Adam Clarke, Dean Clarke, Simon Clift, Aurelia Cloarec, Ross Cohen, Vince Colyer, Sim Combes, Robert Cosgrove, Mike & Sonoko Cowie, Jacques Crespy **D** Max D'Ambrumenit, Urana Dashtseren, Alexandra David, Henk de Jong, Paula Dearling, Andrea Dekkers, Chris Dekkers, Leonard den Hollander, Andy Diamond, Ingeborg Dijkstal, Jan Docherty, Fiona Doody, Otgonnasan Dorjzav, Ian Douglas, Gordon Dowsley **E** Susan Eggleton **F** Anita Fahrni, Erik Fantasia, Yuriy Fedkiw, Neil Fisher, Patty Fong, David Forbes, Jaime Forsyth, Penelope French-Mullen **G** Andy Ganner, Catriona Gardiner, Monique Gijsbrechts, Beat Goldstein, Jay Greenberg, Pen Greenwood **H** Adrian Haas, Tom Hall, Roy F Halvorsen, Paul Hannon, M R Hansen, Tom Harriman, Alexander Hartig, Rina Hirai, Christine Hoddie, Jacqueline C Hodge, Jenny Hogg, Carl Hopkins, Kim Horwood, Mergen T Hotala, Lynn M Hutchinson, **J** Chris Jackson, Jessica Jacobson, Yael Jacoby, Petr Jahoda, Batdulam Jambadoo, Aude Jamin, Marie Javins, Kara Jenkinson **K** Jennifer Kavanagh, Harrie Kerssies, Alexis Kienlen, C Kim, Jan King, Lucie Kinkorova, Geertje Koeman, Erik Kramer, Oleg Kronstadtov **L** Robert C La Mont, Benaifer Lakdawalla, Karen Lancaster, Benedicte Le Roy, Oded Leib, Barbara Lestak, Cathy Lim, Chris Little, Philip Livingstone, Johanna Lofvenius, N Logan, Barny Lucas, Graziella Lunetta, Jarno Lyytinen **M** Kent Madin, Karine Maerevoet, Kerrick Mainrender, Richard Mallett, Melissa Malouf, Thomas Malvica, David Salto Maquedano, Charles Masson, Simon & Georgie McCarthy, Edward McConnaughey, Joseph McGowan, John Milne, Togooch Munkhtur **N** Tim Newton, Uri Niv **O** David O'Connor, Simon O'Connor, Viktoria Olausson, Dax Oliver, Maryann O'Malloy, Taco Otten **P** Richard L Partridge, Ian Paterson, Christina Paul, Marcin Pawlowski, Bryan Pearson, Liron Porat, Toni Pudding **Q** Philippe Quix **R** Onno Raadsen, Karthig Rajakulendran, Jurrian Reurings, Burt Richmond, Joerg D Riedmiller, Karen Robbins, Viviane Rochon, Laurent Rossier, Jay Ruchamkin **S** James St Clair, Jennifer Sandblom, Dervla Sara, Byron Schmuland, Susanne Schultz, Barbel Schwitzgebel, Monika Sibila, Annabelle Singer, Gregory Walter Sitton, Herbert Smit, Katrina South, Mark Stebler, E Steel, Rachael Stewart, Matthew Strama, Chris Sutor, Jim Suttie **T** Wal Taylor, Aniek ter Riet, Ben W Tettlebaum, David Thomas, Peter Thorpe, Allan Tighe, Matt Tillett, Gerard Tobin, Theofilos Tsoris, John Twigg **U** Maria Valeria Urbani, Undraa Uugii **V** Leander Van Delden, Simon van den Boom, Angeline van Hout, Luuk van Luyk, Filip Vandamme, Jack & Sabine Vanhouwe, Eddy Veraghtert, **W** Mark C Ward, Jean-Louis Warnholz, Richard A Weaver, Sharon Weiner, Mario Weiss, Lily West, Vanessa Wong, C Wrentmore, Bob Wright, Jennie Wright **Y** Artour Yatchenko, Val Yerger **Z** Maria Jose Zamora, Samira Zingaro

ACKNOWLEDGMENTS

Thanks to the following for the use of its content: Globe on back cover © Mountain High Maps 1993 Digital Wisdom, Inc.

SEND US YOUR FEEDBACK

We love to hear from travellers – your comments keep us on our toes and help make our books better. Our well-travelled team reads every word on what you loved or loathed about this book. Although we cannot reply individually to postal submissions, we always guarantee that your feedback goes straight to the appropriate authors, in time for the next edition. Each person who sends us information is thanked in the next edition – and the most useful submissions are rewarded with a free book.

To send us your updates – and find out about Lonely Planet events, newsletters and travel news – visit our award-winning website: **www.lonelyplanet.com/feedback**

Note: We may edit, reproduce and incorporate your comments in Lonely Planet products such as guidebooks, websites and digital products, so let us know if you don't want your comments reproduced or your name acknowledged. For a copy of our privacy policy visit www.lonelyplanet.com/privacy.

Moscow.

Godzilla. 1740R. pn.
tel. +74956994223.
near Pushkin square.
Tsvetnoi Bulvar metro station
(smns)

Index

INDEX

INDEX

...

INDEX

monasteries & temples *continued*
  Buyandelgerüülekh Khiid 116
  Dambadarjaa Khiid 65
  Danrig Danjaalin Khiid 163
  Danzandarjaa Khiid 140
  Dashchoilon Khiid 65
  Dashchoinkhorlon Khiid 135
  Dashgimpeliin Khiid 176
  Dashichoinkhorlon Khiid 93
  Dashpeljeelen Khiid 196-7
  Dechinchoinkhorlin Khiid 181
  Dechinravjaalin Khiid 218
  Demchigiin Khiid 183
  Erdene Zuu Khiid 109-11, 7, 120-1
  Erdenemandal Khiid 167
  Gandan Muntsaglan Khiid 106
  Gandan Shadurviin Khiid 133
  Gandantegchinlen (Gandan) Khiid
    63-4, 8, 120-1
  Gesar Süm 65
  Gimpil Darjaalan Khiid 178
  Günjiin Süm 99
  Gurj Lamiin Khiid 191
  Ikh Khuree Zurhain Datsan 65
  Khamaryn Khiid 183
  Kharaagiin Khiid 127
  Khutagt Khiid 178
  Lamrim Süm 65
  Lamyn Gegeenii Gon Gandan
    Dedlin Khiid 193
  Maaniin Khiid 186
  Manba Datsan 65
  Mandal Khiid 194
  Manzushir Khiid 94-5
  Migjid Janraisig Süm 64, 120-1
  Monastery-Museum of Choijin
    Lama 64-5
  Ongiin Khiid 178
  Otochmaaramba Khiid 65
  Övgön Khiid 113
  Ovoon Khiid 169
  Pethub Stangey Choskhor Ling
    Khiid 65
  Shadavdarjaliin Khiid 154
  Shankh Khiid 109
  Süm Khökh Burd 177
  Tögs Buyant Javkhlant Khiid 223-4
  Tövkhön Khiid 108-9
  Türeemel Amarjuulagai Khiid 212
  Winter Palace of the Bogd Khaan 63
  Zayain Gegeenii Süm 115

Monastery-Museum of Choijin Lama
    64-5
money 239, 242-3
  ATMs 242
  costs 10, 240
  credit cards 242
  exchange rates, *see inside front
    cover*
Mongol Altai Nuruu 202
Mongol Daguur Strictly Protected
    Area 161
Mongol Els 114
Mongol empire 18-21, 31, *see
    also* Khaan, Chinggis
Mongolian Artists' Exhibition Hall 66
Mongolian National Artists Union 66
Mongolian National Modern Art
    Gallery 65-6
Mongolian People's Revolutionary
    Party 23, 24-5, 27, 132
Mönkh Khairkhan Uul 208, 216
monument to Bilge Khagan 118
morin khuur 80, 180-1
Mörön 138-41, **140**
Mother Rock 98
motorcycle travel
  to/from China 252
  to/from Russia 254
  within Mongolia 261
mountain biking 102, 145, 235, 260
  tours 70, 257
mountain climbing 102, 209-10,
    216, 235
  tours 257
mountains
  Altan-Ölgii Uul 100
  Baga Gazrin Uul 177
  Batkhaan Uul 114
  Bayanzürkh Uul 102
  Bogdkhan Uul 41, 94-8
  Bulgan Uul 116
  Burkhan Buuddai Uul 196
  Chingeltei Uul 102
  Dayan Uul 225
  Eej Khairkhan Uul 198
  Four Holy Peaks 95
  Ikh Bogd Uul 194
  Ikh Uul 144
  Jargalant Khairkhan Uul 215
  Khalzan Uul 184
  Kharkhiraa Uul 221
  Khogno Khan Uul 113-14
  Khorgo Uul 119
  Khuren Tovon Uul 196
  Khuren Uul 144

Lkhachinvandad Uul 171
Mönkh Khairkhan Uul 208, 216
Otgon Tenger Uul 225
Rashany Ikh Uul 209
Sairyn Uul 208
Shavart Uul 97
Shiliin Bogd Uul 170
Songino Khairkhan Uul 98
Sutai Uul 196
Tavan Bogd Uul 209-10
Togoo Uul 138
Tsambagarav Uul 215
Tsartai Ekh Uul 144
Tsast Uul 207-8
Tsetseegün Uul 95-7
Türgen Uul 221
Ugtam Uul 165
Uran Dösh Uul 144
Uran Uul 138
Yargaitin Ekh Uul 215
MPRP 23, 24-5, 27, 132
Museum of Arkhangai Aimag 115-16
Museum of Danzan Ravjaa 181
Museum of Natural History 60-1
Museum of Orkhon Aimag 133
museums & galleries
  Aimag Museum (Altai) 197
  Aimag Museum (Arvaikheer) 106
  Aimag Museum (Bayankhongor) 193
  Aimag Museum (Bulgan City) 135
  Aimag Museum (Erdenet) 133
  Aimag Museum (Mandalgov) 175-6
  Aimag Museum (Ölgii) 204
  Aimag Museum (Öndörkhaan) 154
  Aimag Museum (Sainshand) 180-1
  Aimag Museum (Tsetserleg) 115-16
  Aimag Museum (Ulaangom) 218
  Aimag Museum & Gallery
    (Choibalsan) 162
  Baruun-Urt Museum 166-7
  Central Province Museum 93
  Centre for Arts & Antiques 62
  Chandman-Öndör 147
  Ethnography Museum (Bulgan
    City) 135
  Ethnography Museum
    (Öndörkhaan) 154
  Ethnography Museum (Zuunmod) 93
  Fine Art Gallery 65-6
  History Museum, Uliastai 223
  Hunting Museum 62
  International Intellectual Museum
    62-3
  Jukov Museum, GK (Choibalsan) 162
  Jukov Museum, GK (Ulaanbaatar) 62

MAP LEGEND
ROUTES

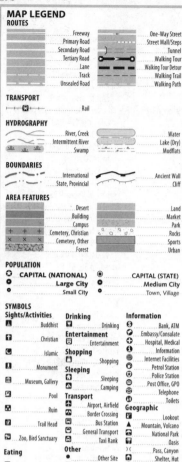

Freeway
Primary Road
Secondary Road
Tertiary Road
Lane
Track
Unsealed Road

One-Way Street
Street Mall/Steps
Tunnel
Walking Tour
Walking Tour Detour
Walking Trail
Walking Path

TRANSPORT
Rail

HYDROGRAPHY
River, Creek
Intermittent River
Swamp

Water
Lake (Dry)
Mudflats

BOUNDARIES
International
State, Provincial

Ancient Wall
Cliff

AREA FEATURES
Desert
Building
Campus
Cemetery, Christian
Cemetery, Other
Forest

Land
Market
Park
Rocks
Sports
Urban

POPULATION
○ **CAPITAL (NATIONAL)**
● **Large City**
● Small City

◉ **CAPITAL (STATE)**
● **Medium City**
○ Town, Village

SYMBOLS

Sights/Activities
Buddhist
Christian
Islamic
Monument
Museum, Gallery
Pool
Ruin
Trail Head
Zoo, Bird Sanctuary

Eating
Eating

Drinking
Drinking

Entertainment
Entertainment

Shopping
Shopping

Sleeping
Sleeping
Camping

Transport
Airport, Airfield
Border Crossing
Bus Station
General Transport
Taxi Rank

Other
● Other Site
P Parking Area

Information
Bank, ATM
Embassy/Consulate
Hospital, Medical
Information
Internet Facilities
Petrol Station
Police Station
Post Office, GPO
Telephone
Toilets

Geographic
Lookout
▲ Mountain, Volcano
National Park
Oasis
Pass, Canyon
Shelter, Hut
Waterfall

LONELY PLANET OFFICES

Australia
Head Office
Locked Bag 1, Footscray, Victoria 3011
☎ 03-8379 8000, fax 03-8379 8111
talk2us@lonelyplanet.com.au

USA
150 Linden St, Oakland, CA 94607
☎ 510-893 8555, toll free 800 275 8555
fax 510-893 8572, info@lonelyplanet.com

UK
72-82 Rosebery Ave,
Clerkenwell, London EC1R 4RW
☎ 020-7841 9000, fax 020-7841 9001
go@lonelyplanet.co.uk

Published by Lonely Planet Publications Pty Ltd
ABN 36 005 607 983

© Lonely Planet 2005

© photographers as indicated 2005

Cover photographs: Archer at the Naadam Festival, Ulaanbaatar, Michel Setboun/Getty Images (front); Wild horses in the Gobi, Justin Jeffrey/Lonely Planet Images (back). Many of the images in this guide are available for licensing from Lonely Planet Images: www .lonelyplanetimages.com.

Printed through Colorcraft Ltd, Hong Kong.
Printed in China